Then and Now

Then and Now
Egypt's Story

Hussein Shabka

Washington, DC

Copyright © 2017 by Hussein Shabka
New Academia Publishing, 2018

All rights reserved. No part of this book may be reproduced or transmitted in any form or by any means, electronic or mechanical, including photocopying, recording, or by any information storage and retrieval system.

Printed in the United States of America

Library of Congress Control Number: 2017958874
ISBN 978-0-9981477-5-8 paperback (alk. paper)

New Academia Publishing, 4401-A Connecticut Ave. NW, #236,
Washington, DC 20008
info@newacademia.com - www.newacademia.com

To Margaret
for her immeasurable help and support

An unraveling of the threads, the Egyptian weft, of our sons and our grandchildren's heritage. May they keep it close to their hearts.

Of Egypt however I shall make my report at length because, it has wonders more in number than any other land, and works too it has to show as much as any land, which are beyond expression great.

Herodotus circa 484 – 425/413 BCE

it [Egypt] is a wasteland

President Hosni Mubarak 1928–

Why do the senators sit there without legislating?
Because the barbarians are coming today.
    What laws can the senators make now?
    Once the barbarians are here, they'll do the legislating.

Alexandrian poet Constantine P. Cavafy 1863–1933

Contents

Note on Transliteration	xi
Acknowledgements	xii
Foreword	xiii
Timeline	xix
Chapter 1. Religion and the Rhythm of Life in Pharaonic Egypt	1
Chapter 2. Loss of Independence	9
The Last Pharaoh; The Break with the Past	
Chapter 3. The Point of No Return: Arabs at the Gates	25
The Conquest; Setting the Tone; The Institutionalization of Misrule; Instability; The Mamluks and the Ottomans	
Chapter 4. The Socio-Cultural Legacy of Subjugation	79
From Gleaming Marble to Devastation and Wretchedness; Coercion as the Only Foundation of Rule; Dual Calendars; Changing Demographics; Religious Conversion by Taxation; Women and Their Role in Society; The Law as a Basis of Social Organization; Work, Temporal Orientation, and Interpersonal Relationships	
Chapter 5. The First Glimpse of Modernity	103
Re-establishing Contact with Europe; The Promise of Change: Mohammed Ali; The Liberal Period	
Chapter 6. Abolishing the Monarchy	141
The Coup d'état; Initial Public Sentiment; The Warning Signs; The Clash of Values	
Chapter 7. A Squandered Opportunity	161
The Slide Towards Autocracy; The People's Voice: Down with Liberty; On the Road to Disaster; The Resignation; Nasser's Enduring Imprint; The Price of Personal Glory	

Chapter 8. Egypt's New Direction   225
The New Political Elite

Chapter 9. Realism and Reform   237
Sadat's Inheritance; New Style Different Priorities; Dislodging the Old Guard; The War Front; The Preparations; The Crossing; The Peace; The Countdown to Tragedy; The Fatal Mistake; The Tragic End; Sadat's Legacy

Chapter 10. Kleptocracy   285
Come the Revolution; Mubarak's Legacy

Chapter 11. Plus Ça Change   311
The Ignominious End

Chapter 12. The Legacy of Seven Decades of Military Rule   317
Cultural Decline; In Pursuit Of Shangri La; Essence of the Imported Ideology; The Triumphant Return; Gagging The Opposition; Society Transformed; Religion and the Lure of Celebrity; The Second Bedouin Invasion

Afterword   361

Appendix: Gamal Abdel Nasser   365
Upper Egyptian Roots; Early Life; Teenage Influences; College Experience; Political Education; Governing Style; Means of Political Control; Eloquence, Charisma, and Consequences; Final Note

Notes   394

Glossary Terms   516

Select Bibliography   519

Index   531

Note on Transliteration

Ease of use was the foremost consideration in transliteration and Arabic terms and names are generally spelt as they would be pronounced in Egypt except in cases where a certain spelling of a term is either widely used, or when a writer chose to spell his/her name in a certain way. The Arabic letter *ain* was denoted by a reversed apostrophe (') and the *hamza* was denoted by an apostrophe ('). The variations in the spelling of some terms such as *elfagr*, which is spelt Elfagr at times and el-Fagr at others, are due to variations in different sources.

Acknowledgements

I am indebted to many friends and colleagues who, over the years, provided a plethora of ideas and viewpoints that stimulated and clarified my thoughts. Specific thanks to Natasha Reatig for publishing advice and suggestions, Roy Townsend, American literature specialist, who assiduously critiqued the book and whose wide reading and areas of interest made his insights invaluable, and to sociologists Abdel-Hamid Abdel-Latif and Helen Rizzo for interrupting their vacations to read and offer valuable comments on the manuscript, my sons, Nabil and Omar, for suffering through and discussing early versions of this work, and my wife, Margaret, English literature and language specialist, who throughout the process unstintingly gave of her time as editor and critic. Her contribution has been invaluable.

Foreword

Sitting in a café in Cairo watching the world go by, I can't help but wonder about the long term significance of what I see. Am I seeing the past through the proverbial rose-colored glasses: is there really less color, less laughter, fewer smiles, and less gaiety on the streets? Many men and women are so drably dressed that they appear to have gone out of their way to prove the inaccuracy of the view that some anthropologists subscribe to which asserts that self-adornment is a universal value that can be found in all cultures. Many young women, often holding their boyfriends' hands, are, however, dressed in form-hugging jeans or skirts and skin-tight tops. Yet their hair is demurely covered by the now popular *hegab*, a seeming contradiction: clothing that leaves little to the imagination, but hair, as modesty supposedly requires, covered. It's the fashion of the day. More bizarre sights can be seen: a *hegabi* in a restaurant enjoying a beer, or stores displaying the latest *hegab* and *niqab* fashion next-door to shops with their windows full of saucy bedroom attire for women.

How and why are these seemingly contradictory attitudes so commonplace on the streets? Is this the Egyptian nature at work, playing lip service to the powers that be while molding things to their liking by following fashion in a way that is acceptable? I remember the more conservative *baladi women* wearing the traditional Egyptian burka made of widely-spaced netting that covered nothing, and the black sheet (*melaya laff*) that they wrapped around themselves under the arms then over one shoulder, often so tightly that what was designed for modesty became a sexy attire. Is my memory playing tricks on me? I doubt it, but some facts are indisputable. The triangle-shaped bright-colored scarfs with their dangling sparkling sequins, called *mandeel abu ooya*, has been replaced with a variety of unappealing drab-colored garments. Everyone seems to have forgotten that *hegabs* and *niqabs* are a relatively recent imported fashion that dates back to around the late 1970s. Prior to that one could have scoured the streets of Cairo or Alexandria or any town and not seen a single *hegabi*, never mind *neqabi*, or a single store selling such clothing. This change in fashion is, of course, reflective of a much deeper conservative trend in Egyptian society. So the question arises: Where did this all begin? How was a nation of jovial, fun-loving people transformed into what they have become today?

Researching and writing this book has been an intense journey for me. Beginning as an attempt to understand why so many societies are moving forward and solving their problems while Egypt seems to be not only standing still but going back, it took me back not only through the times of my own recollections but also through those of my forbears.

When Nasser came to power in 1952, I was a boy enjoying riding his bicycle around the tree-lined streets of Zamalek, Cairo, past the graceful villas and the many embassies with the comings and goings of foreign diplomatic functions; stopping at a friend's house to invite him along; and returning "hellos" from neighbors out for a stroll. Life was good for me, a boy from a middle-class family. From my perspective it was not so good for the farm workers and their families I saw on my visits to my grandfather's farm, but neither was it quite as dire as some people maintain. Life on the farms followed a soothing, almost mesmerizing, rhythm that paralleled the flooding and ebbing of the Nile waters. Crops grew with a minimum of human effort in the silt-rich soil, families worked the fields together, and food was plentiful. Strolling along one of the many irrigation canals there, I would hear the laughter of the workers in the fields, return the cheerful greetings of men, women and children alike, and be lulled by the undulating gait of the peasant girls and women performing what was to me the amazing feat of balancing pots or huge bundles on their heads. That slow, melodic, swaying gait was as timeless and flowing as the Nile and the twinkle of mischief in their eyes was like droplets from the river's flowing waters caught in a beam of sunlight. They went about their daily tasks shoulders relaxed, teasing each other—and me when I was around, eyes bright with a *joie de vivre* that seemed to say "live and let live," no matter the situation. Urban Egyptians largely shared that "live and let live" approach, and perhaps the most commonly used word was *ma'lish*, never mind, to almost any problem.

As a young boy I had no inkling of the future implications of the coup, of Nasser's era, or of his foreign adventures or nationalization plans. But then again I don't think any Egyptian did.

More than a decade into Nasser's rule, I returned to Cairo, after studying in England, with my English wife and two sons. By this time the full impact of Nasser's misguided policies and squandering of national resources was becoming clear. Daily life was fraught with problems. Limitations on imports and a breakdown in the domestic means of production and the agricultural sector resulted in periodic shortages of consumer goods as well as basic staples. Meat was rationed and increasingly beyond the means of more and more Egyptians; sugar and oil were rationed; people lined up to buy chicken—when it was available. Cornflakes were a luxury sold on the black market. The country was falling apart. The grand architecture of Zamalek and downtown Cairo had begun to look more like neglected ruins. The city had become permanently grimy, the government corrupt. The atmosphere grew more and more apprehensive and repressive. I found myself drawing a blank when I tried to remember why I had brought my wife and children here to live, so in the early 1970s we left.

After living abroad for over three decades, I returned to find superficial 'improvements.' The shops were full of every variety of consumer goods. Fast food chains such as McDonalds and KFC offered an alternative to traditional street food to those who could afford their prices. Everyone in the country seemed to have a mobile phone, and the rates of motor vehicle ownership soared, but the traces of problems and signs of decay were easily observed. The city is pretty much permanently at a standstill with undirected traffic. It's not uncommon to see a live electrical wire springing out from the wall of a nineteenth-century French design building, now in noticeable disrepair and sometimes causing great hazard when the occasional piece of masonry dislodges itself and falls to the pavement. More telling still and profoundly disturbing is the change in Egyptians themselves. As an Egyptian I know that the live-and-let-live attitude is deeply embedded in the psyche of every Egyptian, yet it is rapidly disappearing, just as the constant stream of jokes that used to circulate throughout the population and that always served as a safety valve is drying up. The word *ma'lish*, however, is not in danger of disappearing since now it is used to avoid addressing the very real problems in a society in which corruption and mismanagement are endemic and have become entrenched and institutionalized.

On my visits to Egypt during those thirty years away, I was pretty much like any other visitor. My goal was limited: to touch base with my family and the bigger picture was on the periphery of my attention. The bigger picture is not on the agenda of other visitors either; they come to Egypt to see the sites and that is what they have paid for. This is a blessing for Egypt since a significant percentage of its GNP derives from tourism. There is a telling irony in this though. What the visitor does not know is that many of those who depend on the tourist dollars for their bread and butter have learned to scorn, even despise, the very heritage that helps keep Egypt financially afloat; that some of the forbears of modern Egyptians went to great lengths over the centuries to try and wipe out the record of that ancient heritage that now supports them.

When the majority of societies excavate and proudly display their society's artifacts, why then do so many Egyptians scorn their ancient heritage? Why does an admittedly small minority view that heritage as heathen symbols that should be destroyed? Why did a rich country like Egypt stop building monuments and grand public buildings after the end of the pharaonic era?

The visitors also do not know, of course, that less than forty years ago all three of the pyramids there on the Giza Plateau could be seen from the beginning of the Pyramid Road. No buildings or pollution haze blocked the view, the land along either side of the road was agricultural, and it was not uncommon to drive that road and have it almost to oneself from the beginning to the end. And a moonlit evening visit to the pyramids with a group of friends was a unique and magical experience.

Visitors are not alone in not knowing these facts. The majority of Egyptians today were born after the 1952 coup, and they do not know either. They have no idea why they think the way they think, why they live the way they live. Nor do they appear curious enough to ask why. For the most part they seem to live reactively, not proactively, and appear to make little or no attempt to develop themselves as independent thinkers.

And the question remains: Why?

Curiously, many Egyptians seem to recognize these traits and seem to be self-critical, but in a most peculiar way: without the slightest intention of remedying the traits or making the criticism constructive. Instead they offer various glib reasons for this state of affairs: We are lazy; it's the system; it's too powerful to do anything about; we just can't organize ourselves to do anything; we need a just leader, etc., etc.

And the question remains: Why?

Both frustration and curiosity led me to the instinctive destination of most educators: the library, where I read anything that might provide the answers I sought, from politicians' and intellectuals' memoirs to ninth century historians. Initially I was ready to place all the responsibility on the shoulders of Nasser and his fellow 1952 coup conspirators. As I dug deeper, however, I began to find connections and causes that went further and further back in time. Initially I had no intention of addressing the worn out and seemingly unanswerable question of how the descendants of any sophisticated ancient civilization end up losing the traits of their forbears that created that ancient civilization. Yet I began to discover cause and effect connections that are traceable to Egypt's ancient civilization. So in this book, I have set out to map the series of events that reflected and influenced social and cultural values and practices in Egypt through the centuries.

Egypt is unique given the length of the occupation it endured and the degree to which its identity was diluted. A civilized society may survive the onslaught of an invasion of a less advanced social group that would eventually be absorbed into the social fabric and become part of the conquered society, but in Egypt's case the scale of migration of the Bedouins who brought their preliterate culture and social values with them from the Arabian Peninsula reversed this process and the indigenous population and native culture was overwhelmed by its conquerors.

Writing this book was an attempt to understand the present by peeling off the layers of the onion and finding clues to the hidden reasons for what is at the core of an Egyptian's worldview and self-view. For Egyptians like me, the exploration can be a journey of self-revelation. For the general reader interested in the world around them and in societies that today impact their own, the journey can be illuminating.

The journey has been a roller-coaster ride of pride and despair: pride in the magnificent ancient past that as an Egyptian I can lay claim to; pride in the ability of my forbears to survive, although not unscathed, their tumultuous history; despair at our inability to withstand the seemingly relentless onslaught of negative influences still invading our borders; and despair at having no satisfying answer to: What next?

What next? It was at the core of the questions that prompted me to take this journey, and it is the question to which I found no answer. What the journey did give me, however, is the backstory that I and my fellow Egyptians share and that provides answers to why we are where we are now, today. It sheds light on but does not attempt to justify the real face of Egypt today, the paradox of wealth coupled with mismanagement that Napoleon recognized.

It is the face that is hidden from the eyes of visitors marveling at the pyramids, gazing in awe on the temple of Karnak or the tombs of our distant ancestors. While visitors cannot fail to see the surface squalor, the real face of Egypt is as surely hidden from view as the facial features of those women who now wear the full facial veil, the *niqab*, in Egypt's public places. Hopefully this account will contribute to lifting that veil.

Timeline

Circa 3100 BCE	Namer unites Upper and Lower Egypt and becomes the first Pharaoh of Kemet, the black land (a reference to the color of Egypt's fertile soil).
2755-2255 BCE	The Old Kingdom of Egypt is characterized by advances in science and engineering building of the first pyramids.
Circa 1674 BCE	Weak pharaohs fail to repel an invasion by Semitic herders from Asia, the Hyksos, who occupy the Delta and rule it for about 105 years.
Circa 1550 BCE	Ahmos, succeeds in the struggle for liberation begun by his ancestors Seqnenre-Taa and Kamose expels the Hyksos and reunites the country. He founds the New Kingdom (Eighteenth Dynasty), restores neglected and ruined temples, and ushers in an era of security, stability, and prosperity.
331 BCE	Alexander the Great invades Egypt, founds the city of Alexandria.
51 BCE	Cleopatra VII becomes joint ruler of Egypt with her ten-year-old brother, Ptolemy XIII.
37 BCE	Cleopatra marries Marcus Antonius
31 BCE	Octavius, later known as Augustus Caesar, defeats Antonius and Cleopatra in the naval battle of Actium.
30 BCE-395 CE	Egypt is annexed by Rome after the suicides of Antonius and Cleopatra.
Circa 50 CE	St. Mark brings Christianity to Egypt and founds the Coptic Church.
64 CE	Emperor Nero begins to persecution Christians in the Roman Empire

395 CE	The Roman Empire divided into two empires after the death of emperor Theodosius. The Western half is ruled from Rome and the Eastern half, from Nicomedia then from Constantinople.
395-641 CE	Egypt ruled by Byzantium (the eastern half of the Roman Empire).
451 CE	Monophysitism, which the Coptic Church of Alexandria adheres to, is declared a heresy by the Council of Chalcedon.
641	Egypt is conquered by Bedouin Arabs led by Amr ibn el-Aas and becomes a province of the Islamic empire.
641-661	Egypt is ruled from Mecca then from Kufa during the reign of the Guided Caliphs.
661-750	The Umayyad caliphate. Egypt is ruled from Damascus.
750-935	The Abbasid Caliphate. Egypt is ruled from Baghdad.
870	Ahmad ibn Tulun, a Mamluk, seizes power in Egypt and becomes semi independent from Baghdad.
969-1171	The Fatimids invade Egypt; establish a new caliphate and el-Azhar University.
1171	The Ayyoubids led by Kurdish leader Salah al-Din el-Ayyoubi (Saladin) invade Egypt and defeat the Fatimids.
1249	The Seventh Crusade under Louis IX of France lands in Egypt and takes the town of Damietta.
1249	Sultan el-Salih Ayyoub, accompanied by his wife Shagaret el-Dorr, leads an army to confront Louis IX but succumbs to tuberculosis, dies of before the decisive battle and is succeeded by his son irresponsible Turanshah.
1250	Shagaret el-Dorr takes control of the critical situation. Turanshah is killed by the army commanders who repel the French taking Louis prisoner, and the jubilant army commanders,

	and later, the people proclaim Shagaret el-Dorr the first Mamluk ruler and the only Muslim queen to rule in her own right.
1517	The Ottoman sultan, Selim I, captures Cairo and ends formal Mamluk rule of Egypt but they remain more or less the de facto rulers of the country.
1798	Napoleon Bonaparte arrives in Egypt ending centuries of isolation from Europe and promises reform.
1801	France's loss in the Abu Kir naval battle and continuing skirmishes with the British-Ottoman alliance make the French presence in Egypt untenable and they leave and instability and public disorder ensue.
1801	Mohammed Ali, a junior commander of an Albanian contingent serving with the Ottomans arrives in Egypt, falls in love with the country, and impresses the *ulama* with his ideas.
1805	The Ottomans accede to the Egyptians demand and appoint Mohammed Ali to the post of viceroy of Egypt.
1811	The Mamluk massacre. Dozens are killed as they attempt to leave the Cairo Citadel after attending a dinner invitation with Mohammed Ali. The Mamluk era comes to an end with this event and Mohammed Ali becomes absolute master of Egypt and embarks of an ambitious program of modernization and reform.
1840	Treaty of London obligates Egypt to dismantle its arms industry and remove import tariffs designed to protect emergent local industry.
1854	Ferdinand de Lesseps is granted the concession to construct a canal from the Mediterranean to the Red Sea.
1866	Mohammed Ali's son, Khedive Ismail embarks on an extensive program of modernization and inaugurates Egypt's first parliament.

1869	The Suez Canal opens.
1882	Britain occupies Egypt.
1914	The British government changes the status of Egypt from a Turkish province to a British protectorate.
1919	When Britain imprisons the leaders of the independence movement the country erupts in Revolution. All social classes, including upper class women take to the streets carrying signs showing the cross and crescent as their emblem to show the Muslim-Christian unity. Riots and civil unrest continue for months.
1922	Britain grants Egypt limited independent with continued a British military presence in the Suez Canal area.
1923	Promulgation of the constitution.
1936	King Fuad dies and is succeeded by his son Farouk.
1952	Junior army officers led by Gamal Abdel Nasser take power after a military coup.
1953	Constitutional monarchy abolished and Egypt becomes a republic.
1956	Britain, France, and Israel attack Egypt after Nasser nationalizes the Suez Canal but the UN, with strong support from the US, condemns the attack. Britain, France comply immediately and withdraw their forces from the Canal area and Israel turns over control Sinai to UN. Peacekeepers and withdraws its forces in 1957.
1967	Nasser orders the withdrawal of UN. Peacekeepers from Sinai and Israel attacks Egypt, Syria, and Jordan, taking Sinai Peninsula, the Gaza Strip, the West Bank, the Golan Heights, and Jerusalem.
1970	Nasser, dies on September 28 and is succeeded by his vice-president Anwar el-Sadat.
1973	Egypt's army storms the Bar-Lev line on the eastern shore of the Suez Canal and begins the liberation of Sinai.

1977	Anwar el-Sadat travels to Jerusalem to propose a peace plan to the Israelis.
1978	Anwar el-Sadat and Menachem Begin sign an Egyptian-Israeli peace treaty mediated by President Jimmy Carter.
1981	A religious extremist assassinates Anwar el-Sadat and vice-president Hosni Mubarak succeeds him.
2011	Mubarak is ousted by a popular revolt led by Egypt's young men and women.
2012	Muslim Brothers' candidate Mohammed Morsi narrowly wins presidential election.
June 30, 2013	Mass demonstrations demand Morsi's resignation and accuse the Muslim Brothers of hijacking the revolution and attempting to monopolize power and impose shari'a.
July 3, 2013	General Abdel-Fatah el-Sisi, the armed forces commander announces the ouster of Morsi and nominates Adli Mansour, the head of the constitutional court as interim president.
May 2014	Presidential elections are held and General el-Sisi is elected president.

1

Religion and the Rhythm of Life in Pharaonic Egypt

The constant interaction between a people and their physical environment plays a major role in shaping the way of life, culture, and social values of society and is particularly evident in Egypt. There the concentration of population along the narrow strip of fertile land that constitutes the Nile valley and that is bordered by an arid and unforgiving desert was a major factor in shaping ancient society. These particular features of the physical environment made the setting up of permanent settlements possible, facilitated communications and transportation between the different settlements, and provided an incentive for the eventual establishment of centralized government. It also impacted all other aspects of the pharaonic culture and social values, and after thousands of years defined Egyptians at their core. The Nile was the pivotal axis around which life in Egypt revolved and its centrality in the culture and lives of Egyptians is evidenced by the fact that before being admitted to the abode of the gods, a deceased pharaoh had to attest in his negative confession that "I have never stopped [the flow of] water."[1]

Order, stability, and continuity were of paramount importance to the ancient Egyptians,[2] who believed that the goddess Maat created the world out of confusion and disarray and that the proper observances of religious rituals honoring the gods were the only means of maintaining order.[3] Disarray, disorder, and chaos were ever-living threats and perpetual dangers that the Egyptians were reminded of by the empty wastelands that surrounded their fertile valley.[4] Egypt was an agrarian society that owed its very existence to the Nile and to its annual inundation, which regenerated and fertilized the soil. This is what gave rise to the need for a central authority with the resources needed to keep accurate records of the levels of the Nile waters and to ensure that the maintenance and dredging of the irrigation canals were carried out in a timely manner and in accordance with the crop growing cycles.

It is this absolute necessity of regularity and predictability that may well have resulted in the Egyptians' traditional conservatism and fear of disorder and chaos.[5] Chaos was an ever-present threat that the Egyptians sought to protect themselves from by developing the first system of centralized authority in recorded history. At the head of this authority and the bureaucracy that served it stood the pharaoh who was an absolute ruler responsible for all aspects of life. As a semi divine being, the pharaoh was the people's only means of communicating with the gods. He controlled all of nature's forces and interpreted and implemented the gods' wishes, thus ensuring the provision of society's livelihood and maintenance of the order and stability Maat had created. As the pharaoh's legitimacy and authority stemmed from the belief that he was a living god and the preserver of Maat,[6] his absence would have been seen as an inconceivable transgression against the goddess of order.[7]

Dating back to the Old kingdom circa 2700 BCE, and perhaps even to the pre-dynastic period about a thousand years earlier, the social structure of Egypt revolved around the pharaoh. Through him (rarely, although occasionally, her), the main social institutions: economy, religion, government, and education, were closely linked. As both god and ruler, he was the mediator between the world of humans and the world of the ever-living gods, which he joined upon his death.[8] He was the provider of economic and political security as well as spiritual wellbeing.[9] The vital importance and centrality of the pharaoh in Egypt's culture cannot be overstated.

In his worldly role, the pharaoh stood at the top of the social structure and presided over every aspect of life in society and every sphere of daily existence.[10] His actions and policies made the growing of crops possible. He ordered and financed the building and maintenance of the irrigation canals that watered the fields. This task was crucial to the economy because the annual flood that brought silt and rejuvenated the fertile soil also weakened the levies and dykes and clogged the irrigation canals. He employed workers and scribes to measure and record the Nile flood levels. When the flood level was high and provided an abundance of crops, the pharaoh ordered the building and stocking of warehouses to ensure against possible future shortages. During the lull in farming when the land was inundated during the annual flood of the Nile, both peasants and craftsmen were employed in public works projects: maintaining waterways and irrigation canals, building temples, pyramids, and other structures that, while dedicated to the afterlife, were viewed as inseparable parts of this life.[11] In addition to economic security, the pharaoh provided physical security and safety through maintaining law and order and by defending his people against marauding nomads and the invaders who inhabited the world of chaos beyond Egypt's borders.

In this sense, the pharaoh played the role of a competent administrator as well as a benevolent father figure. Public works projects such as dredging irrigation canals were not necessary merely to ensure agricultural security but also kept people busy, productive and earning a living. The ancient monuments were huge public works projects that created a skilled economy and that additionally provided national coherence and pride. Fortunately for the ancients, a pyramid or monument was what a pharaoh required, not a horde of cash and mansions around the world.

Properly trained priests were necessary to perform religious rituals, and properly trained scribes were necessary to keep records. The pharaoh provided both training facilities and employment opportunities for both professions. Through endowing the temples and performing the appropriate rituals, he also ensured that the gods were pleased and that the Nile would, therefore, flood on time every year and bring with it the silt that fertilized the land and enabled Egypt to maintain its prosperity. The pharaoh both represented and controlled - to use Emile Durkheim's terminology - the sacred as well as the profane domains.[12] He personified the link between the supernatural that his subjects did not understand and the familiar routine of their daily lives. Sometimes he interceded with the gods on their behalf as he did after an extended period of drought when the Nile failed to rise to its usual flood levels in seven consecutive years causing crop failures, food shortages, and widespread suffering.[13] According to the myth preserved by a Ptolemaic inscription, the pharaoh, who might have been the Third

Dynasty King Djoser, travelled to the Island of Elephantine in Upper Egypt, which housed the floodgates.[14] There, he secured an audience with Khnum, the Nile god who lived there and controlled these floodgates of the Nile. Khnum told the Pharaoh that he had been less generous with his floodwaters because he was unhappy with the fact that his temples had not been properly maintained and attended.[15] The Pharaoh promised to remedy the situation, and in turn, Khnum promised to open the gates.[16] Upon the Pharaoh's return, he levied new taxes and the temples were spruced up and staffed.[17] The following year the river rose again as it had done before the drought and all was well again in Egypt.[18]

The pharaoh, therefore, was at the very core of religion and religious rituals and practices, and every aspect of the ancient Egyptian culture revolved around religion. The government, economy, law, language, literature, and worldview, were all tightly knit through religion and the pharaoh. Religion fueled, energized, and stimulated science and engineering achievements, and this interdependency between the different components of the social culture provided the basis for the wide-ranging social consensus that was the key to its durability and intransience for thousands of years.

The rhythm of life established over the millennia of pharaonic rule was disrupted at times by the numerous invaders tempted by the prosperity in the Nile valley. These less refined marauders were the nomadic Semites who, according to Egyptian mythology, inhabited the red lands,[19] the vast and desolate deserts that seemed to stretch endlessly beyond the fertile valley. They were less advanced than the Egyptians in every way, and their unceasing raids on what must have seemed to them paradise on earth were a perpetual threat that the country's rulers had to tackle. Strong pharaohs kept the raiders at bay during their reigns and often followed them beyond the borders of Egypt in the hope of discouraging future raids and maintaining peace and prosperity in the land. That ever-present threat and the manner in which the pharaohs dealt with it is shown in a relief from the First Dynasty at Abydos which depicts the gaunt figure of a Bedouin chief about to meet a violent end at the hands of his Egyptian vanquisher.[20] The term *amu* that appears to have been used to describe the Asian desert nomads is mentioned repeatedly in Egyptian records, and this relief is one of the earliest references to Bedouins.[21] The army's expeditions beyond the country's borders were generally intended to punish raiders and discourage future raids rather than to take control of foreign territory, and Egypt has had roughly the same borders for 6,000 years.

When a weak pharaoh who was unable to protect his subjects from pillagers and foreign incursions sat on the throne, there was unrest and social disorder, but the impact of the invaders was generally short-lived, and society enjoyed relatively long periods of order and stability. The two notable exceptions were the Persian invasion of 525 BCE and the Hyksos, who, at a time of political turmoil and social disintegration that had left the country in the hands of several weak regional rulers, managed to take over Lower Egypt after the conquest of Memphis in 1674 BCE. The Hyksos ruled the country until Ahmos, who founded the Eighteenth Dynasty and ushered in the era of the New Kingdom, finally expelled them in 1550 BCE and might have taken some of them as slaves and put them to work as builders. While there is some debate as to the origins of these people, they are known to have been nomadic sheepherders, possibly from central Asia, the Arabian Peninsula,[22] or Palestine. What is also not in doubt is that they were Semitic tribes who left no monuments or works of art that suggest an urban cultural tradition or a civilization. The Egyptians referred to them as the Hyksos, which can be translated either as shepherd kings or as captive shepherds. One of the most notable consequences of this period of subjugation to the nomadic herders was to make the Egyptians less inward looking,[23] but despite the Hyksos' long stay in Egypt, their impact on culture seems to have been relatively minor except in the field of military techniques, such as the use of the horse-drawn chariot and composite bow. The later Persian rule lasted almost a century, with independence regained after several revolts and challenges by several princes from Lower Egypt.

Thus, there were both successes and failures in the endless struggle to protect the coveted bounty of the Nile and repel aggressors. However, the impact of the marauders on religion and social culture remained relatively minor and short lived.[24] Although these foreign invaders posed a perpetual threat to Egypt from the beginning of history, the fertile Nile valley provided Egyptians with food and security, and a surplus that allowed them to develop a rich and sophisticated civilization that was usually able to defend itself and keep those invaders at bay. People expected and anticipated set backs such as droughts, foreign invaders and weak pharaohs, but were confident that through proper planning their effects could be minimized and in time balance would be restored.

By ancient standards, life for the majority of the Egyptians was very good and held the promise of more joy than suffering. The ancient Egyptians were open to all of life's pleasures, were spontaneous, and enthusiastically embraced all of the delights of life with a *joi de vivre*.[25] Socializing, parties, fashion, music, humor and wine were all part of an Egyptian's life. The ancient Egyptians' satisfaction with their life is also evidenced by their view of the afterlife. The afterlife that they conceived of was no more than a reproduction of life in Egypt except that it was on a grander scale. The crops were plentiful and never failed, the fish in the Nile were abundant, and the people were perpetually young, healthy, and well dressed.[26] For the Egyptians, the afterlife was simply eternal life in Egypt. They had no wish to leave *home* even after they died. That attachment to the soil still survives among contemporary Egyptians. The Egyptians' patriotism has always tended to be expressed in simple love of the soil rather than jingoism or sloganeering.

Measured against some contemporary standards, pharaonic Egypt may certainly not have been a paradise. However, for the nomads of that age who were not lucky enough to be living in the Nile valley, *paradise* was precisely the term that they used to describe Egypt.[27] Members of the primitive cultures that existed in the harsh and punishing physical environment of the red lands were not as fortunate as the ancient Egyptians. Hunger, poverty, utter deprivation, wretchedness, and constant threats to personal security were all that the nomads had to look forward to from the day they were born to the day they died. In such an environment, life may not be as precious as in a less hostile environment, and for them leaving home was a very attractive proposition. Attachment to the barren soil was minimal to nonexistent, and the willingness to abandon *home* was reflected in the value system,[28] in which dying for a "righteous" cause provided both an escape from suffering and an entrance to paradise. The best that members of such cultures could hope for was that the afterlife would be somewhere *other than home*. Unlike that of the Egyptians, the desert nomads' view of the afterlife was the exact opposite of what *home* was like. The nomads' conception of paradise in the afterlife was almost an exact replica of life in the Nile Valley. Unsurprisingly, the hungry, as the Egyptian proverb goes, dream of the bread market.

2

Loss of Independence

Life in Egypt continued in much the same manner until the arrival of Alexander the Great. Alexander's conquest of Egypt in 332 BCE[1] was clearly different in that, unlike some of the earlier invaders, he represented an advanced civilization, not a primitive nomadic mob. More importantly, under Alexander's rule, the all-important link between the world of the mortals and the world of the gods was maintained.

Alexander had always sought confirmation of his belief, derived from his mother, in his own godliness as the son of Zeus, and the myth relating the path he took to get that confirmation was nothing if not spectacularly dramatic. According to legend, Alexander sought the answer from the Oracle of Delphi who advised him to take his query the famed Oracle of Siwa.[2] Upon conquering Egypt, Alexander set off for the oasis of Siwa in Egypt's western desert. Today this is an eight-hour car journey through brutal desert; then it was an almost impossible twelve-day horse ride from the Mediterranean coast[3] in blistering heat with no food or fresh water en route. Legend has it that the Greek force led by Alexander was lost and out of water, until a blackbird appeared. Taking the bird as an omen, Alexander followed its flight path and reached Siwa. Once there he lost no time and immediately climbed up to the temple of the Oracle where he was informed in fluent Greek that indeed he was the son of Amon, the chief deity of Egypt.

It is not hard to imagine the speed with which the story of the young handsome god's heroic journey spread among Egypt's population and the impact of that story. Nor is it hard to imagine the impact on Alexander himself, after a nearly fatal desert trek, of miraculously reaching the lush green of Siwa and, finally, finding his holy grail.⁴

Certainly, the tone of the relationship between the Egyptian population and their new conqueror was set. Alexander accepted Egyptian religious beliefs and followed the traditional protocols that the pharaohs had observed for centuries. He secured the support of the priesthood and the acceptance of the general population by demonstrating through his deeds and actions that he was indeed the living god and the lawful ruler of Egypt. In the temple of Ptah in the city of Memphis, he made appropriate offerings to the god Apis,⁵ and he visited other temples, making offerings and sacrifices to Zeus-Amon and to the god Cyrene. He built a temple to the chief god, Amon, and issued instructions for the proper maintenance and provisions of the temple complexes.⁶ He traveled to Luxor where he visited the sprawling Karnak temple and ordered repairs to the temple of Thotmes II to be carried out,⁷ and he had himself depicted on the walls adorned with the appropriate Egyptian royal symbols and regalia.⁸ He then ordered plans for a new city to be built on the Mediterranean coast and approved those plans for the city of Alexandria before setting off to conquer India, where he died at the age of thirty-two.

Upon Alexander's death, one of his ablest generals, who had been appointed *satrap* (governor) of Egypt, brought Alexander's body back to Alexandria to be buried in the city. He ruled from Alexandria, which replaced Memphis as the capital of Egypt in 320 BCE and developed into a large city of trade, learning, and luxury. The general, Ptolemy I, continued the pharaonic king-god tradition,⁹ took the Egyptian name Meryamon Setepenre (Beloved of Amon, Chosen of Ra), and established the Ptolemaic dynasty, which ruled Egypt for more than three centuries and was the last dynasty that ruled using the title of Pharaoh.

The Last Pharaoh

One of the major accomplishments of the Ptolemaic dynasty was the successful blending of the Hellenic and Pharaonic cultures and the preservation of the internal harmony and interdependence of the components of the social structure in Egypt. By the time Cleopatra was born,[10] Alexandria had become what Diodorus of Sicily described in the first century BCE as "the first city of the civilized world."[11] It had grown into one of the largest, if not the largest metropolis in the world, and was the world's scientific and intellectual capital. Destined to be the last pharaoh, Cleopatra VII (69-30 BCE), the sixteenth ruler of the Ptolemaic dynasty, was only seventeen when she ascended the Egyptian throne and reigned as Queen Philopator and Pharaoh from 51 to 30 BCE. As a child, this remarkable and astute woman had witnessed a steady decline of Ptolemaic power, which coincided, with the rise of the Roman Empire's power. She witnessed the defeat of her guardian, Pompey, by Julius Caesar in a duel, and saw vast regions fall into the grip of the Roman Empire. The Ptolemies, who earlier had had the foresight to ally themselves with the Romans and conclude a pact that endured for two centuries, were steadily losing ground to that newly emerging superpower that was eventually declared guardian of the Ptolemaic Dynasty. Cleopatra's father, Ptolemy XII, who was not one of the more memorable pharaohs, had squandered much of Egypt's wealth and influence, and had found himself having to pay tribute to the Romans to keep them at bay.

Nevertheless, Alexandria was still a great seat of learning and unequalled in its beauty, wealth, luxury, and grandeur.[12] The city contained thousands of private luxurious stately residences and magnificent public buildings. The steps leading down to the royal port were marble, the waterfront was long and lined with magnificent buildings which housed schools, public buildings and halls, and the library with its vast collection of literary and scientific books and manuscripts which numbered in the hundreds of thousands.[13] The city was also home to the Temple of Serapis that the Roman historian Ammianus Marcellinus described in superlative terms:

> Its splendour is such that mere words can only do it an injustice but its great halls of columns and its wealth of lifelike statues and other works of art make it, next to the Capitol, which is the symbol of the eternity of immemorial Rome, the most magnificent building in the whole world. It contained two priceless libraries.[14]

Cleopatra had become co-regent of Egypt at the age of seventeen following the death of her father, and ruled jointly with her ten-year-old brother Ptolemy XIII. She proved to be an able administrator who brought peace and prosperity to a country that her father had left bankrupt[15] and plagued by civil war and destabilizing palace intrigue. She regained Egypt's position as second only to Rome in wealth and power.[16] She was an intelligent political strategist who spoke several foreign languages, had learned to read hieroglyphs,[17] and was well aware of the absolute necessity of handling Rome delicately if she was to keep her throne and maintain the independence of Egypt. She seems to have been cognizant of the fact that Rome was beginning to have designs on Egypt and becoming increasingly tempted by its wealth and lucrative trade routes.[18] When Julius Caesar came to visit Alexandria in 47 BCE, Cleopatra, in the midst of a power struggle with her brother's allies in the royal court who, led by Theodotus, were plotting to overthrow her, was in Thebaid where she had managed to flee with some of her supporters. According to legend she devised a bold and imaginative plan to smuggle herself into the royal palace, rolled up in a rug, to meet with Caesar and managed to charm him and convince him that it was in his interest to form an alliance with her.

The divinity of the ruler and its significance was certainly something that the politically astute Cleopatra fully appreciated. The Ptolemies had continued the Egyptian tradition of god kings, and ancient texts referred to Cleopatra III as "Isis Great Mother of the Gods."[19] The father of Cleopatra VII had been depicted as a god on coins and referred to as both king and god in records and proclamations.[20] Ever since she was a child, Cleopatra had been depicted on temple walls as a goddess and daughter of Isis,[21] and she never doubted her divinity.[22] As a shrewd stateswoman, Cleopatra later capitalized on her exalted status as a living god while maneuvering to maintain Egypt's independence. She invited Caesar to accompany her on an extended two-month trip down the Nile to visit temples and receive homage from the priesthood. She obviously hoped to impress him with the fact that while he may be the ruler of an empire, she was a goddess. When the couple married later both Egypt and Cleopatra's throne now seemed secure. Coins were struck depicting her as Aphrodite-Isis carrying her and Caesar's son who was depicted as Horus-Eros.²³ The birth of Caesarion was also recorded on the walls of temples in Thebes, where she was depicted as the mother of Ra the sun god.²⁴ Her position as the living goddess and ruler of Egypt was secure and unchallenged.²⁵

It must have seemed like a perfect state of affairs with advantages for everyone. Cleopatra kept her kingdom. Caesar sired a god. And Rome benefited from the knowledge of the Alexandria court scholars and from its close contact with an advanced civilization such as Egypt's. Rome's adoption of the Julian calendar, for example, on which our calendar today is based, dates to this period and was implemented under the supervision of one of Cleopatra's court scholars.²⁶

The situation changed drastically when Caesar was assassinated on the Ides of March in 44 BCE and the empire was split between Mark Anthony, who took the eastern Mediterranean and Octavian, who took Italy and the western territories. Cleopatra, still the astute stateswoman intent on preserving her throne allied herself with Mark Antony, whom she had met earlier. She hoped that her new alliance would enable her to keep Octavian at bay and to continue to preserve Egypt's independence.

Plutarch's account of Cleopatra's response when Mark Anthony's summoned her to meet with him at Cilicia illustrates her shrewdness and awareness of the importance of maintaining control of when and how to make an appearance.

> She received several letters, both from Antony and from his friends, to summon her, but she took no account of these orders; and at last, as if in mockery of them, she came sailing up the river Cydnus, in a barge with gilded stern and outspread sails of purple, while oars of silver beat time to the music of flutes and fifes and harps. She herself lay all along, under a canopy of cloth of gold, dressed as Venus in a picture, and beautiful young boys, like painted Cupids, stood on each side to fan her. Her maids were dressed like Sea Nymphs and Graces, some steering at the rudder, some working at the ropes. The perfumes diffused themselves from the vessel to the shore, which was covered with multitudes, part following the galley up the river on either bank,

> part running out of the city to see the sight. The marketplace was quite emptied, and Antony at last was left alone sitting upon the tribunal; while the word went through all the multitude, that Venus was come to feast with Bacchus, for the common good of Asia. On her arrival, Antony sent to invite her to supper. She thought it fitter he should come to her; so, willing to show his good-humor and courtesy, he complied, and went. He found the preparations to receive him magnificent beyond expression, but nothing so admirable as the great number of lights; for on a sudden there was let down altogether so great a number of branches with lights in them so ingeniously disposed, some in squares, and some in circles, that the whole thing was a spectacle that has seldom been equaled for beauty.[27]

Although Cleopatra's efforts paid off and the alliance with Mark Anthony was secured, her plans suffered a fatal blow when their combined fleets were defeated in the battle of Actium in Greece on September 2, 31 BCE and they fled to Egypt. Octavian pursued the couple there a few months later, and when Antony's troops deserted him near the present day neighborhood of Camp Caesar in Alexandria, all was lost. Both Antony and Cleopatra chose to commit suicide rather than be captured by Octavian, and Egypt lost its independence and became a Roman province administered as a personal possession of Octavian.

The Break with the Past

Cleopatra's defeat signaled the beginning of a phase that culminated in the loss of a culture and way of life that had endured for millennia. Rome's exploitation of Egypt's wealth and resources was thoughtless, callous, and not only led to economic ruin and social decay,[28] but began a process that was to continue for many centuries to come. As a mere province of an empire, Egypt was no longer in charge of its destiny, and its interests became secondary to the interests of that empire. Its wealth was now exported to Rome instead of being invested in local projects,[29] and its trade routes through the Red Sea were controlled by and run for the benefit of the occupying power. Under the Ptolemies, however incompetent some of them had been, Egypt's wealth had remained in the country.[30] Furthermore, as Egyptian monarchs, the Ptolemies had no reason to export Egypt's wealth anywhere, and their own self-interest required them to ensure the good health of the economy and the wellbeing of their subjects who were, after all, their only source of income.[31] The Romans on the other hand were only interested in what they could extract from the country regardless of the long-term consequences on its economy. Egypt was, after all, only one of the many provinces that belonged to the vast empire.[32] The country was, however, an important source of revenue for the Romans, and vast amounts of goods and resources were taken out over a short period of time.[33] "It is estimated that under Augustus well over one million tons of Egyptian grain may have arrived in Rome each year."[34] Grain, papyrus, glass, crafted artifacts, minerals, ores, porphyry and granite, were among Egypt's exports to Rome. The appearance of Egyptian-style architecture and sculpture, the building of public libraries,[35] and the worship of Isis and Serapis, were examples of the cultural influences that were also exported to Rome from Egypt.

Although Egypt had lost control of its destiny and resources and had become a province of a large Empire, the Romans did, however, respect the prevailing religious practices and adopted some of them. As the official head of state, the Roman emperor became the pharaoh whose authority and divinity was decreed by Egyptian religious, political, and social conventions,[36] and he was depicted on temples as the divine ruler in accordance with traditional practices.[37] He assumed pharaonic titles and had his own name inscribed as pharaoh on the cartouches of several temples. This was a necessity mandated by Egyptian religious, political, and cultural practices in which the pharaoh, as the symbol of order and stability, played a central role even if he was as far away as the Roman emperor was.[38] The Romans completed or added to some of the temples that were still under construction, and maintained good relations with the powerful priesthood. They blended their own pantheon of gods with that of the Egyptians often simply by giving Latin names to the Egyptian gods,[39] and attempted to gain legitimacy by linking themselves to the Ptolemies and the pharaonic line.[40] However, the Romans never became Egyptianized in the way that the Ptolemies had. The emperor was away in Rome and absentee rule left a serious void in Egyptian religious and cultural life. As mortals, the emperors' representatives in Egypt were not qualified to perform the rituals and ceremonial roles that formed an essential part of divine kingship. The emperor, Caesar, who lived in far away Rome could not provide Egyptians with the sense of harmony, security, oneness with nature, and connection to the world of the gods that their pharaonic god-king had provided.

It was only a matter of time before the Egyptians would begin to realize that they were ruled *in absentia* from Rome by a *man* not a living god. Most Roman emperors never visited Egypt, and those that did, came on rare occasions. The country was governed by a prefect who was appointed by Rome, granted vast powers, and presided over every aspect of life in Egypt. In that respect, his power in society was similar to that of the pharaoh, but his domain did not extend to the realm of the gods. He was a representative of Caesar, not of Amon or Horus. The fact that he curried favor with the priesthood, helped to maintain the temples, and financed religious projects may have initially ensured peace in society and guaranteed the cooperation of the population. Nevertheless, the core of the social structure, the living god, was no longer present, which meant that a substantial vacuum existed. Egypt was now in some ways similar to a boat that had lost its rudder and was floating without direction. The waters were relatively calm for a while, but it was inevitable that problems would arise sooner or later.

The death of the last Pharaoh, Cleopatra, and the Roman occupation of Egypt had severed the link between the world of humans and the world of the gods for the first time in Egypt's long history. From that point onwards, the Egyptians had to fend for themselves. They no longer had a god-king to insure their security and prosperity and intercede with the other gods on their behalf. Their pharaoh, who had provided security and stability and protected Egypt for millennia from the nomadic marauders and plunderers, was no more. The core of the Egyptian social structure was thus destroyed along with the harmony, stability, and continuity that had always been of paramount importance to the Egyptians and the fundamental essence of a society that had remained essentially the same over the millennia. Stripped of its core and the god-king who held that core together, the Egyptian social structure was no longer viable. It was only a matter of time before the impact of the loss would permeate all levels of society and inevitably lead to significant and wide-ranging social change. This was compounded by several revolts and years of social upheaval and unrest as the economy began to decline due to Rome's shortsighted exploitation of Egypt's resources and oppressive taxation to finance the growing needs of the Roman Empire.

The serious void left in people's daily lives due to the absence of the pharaoh was felt most acutely during this period of social unrest and upheaval because only the pharaoh was qualified to guarantee the orderly functioning of the universe. When St. Mark[41] the Apostle arrived in Egypt in the first century CE offering a way to fill this vacuum, people were ready to listen, and the new theology, Christianity, began gradually to take hold.

The striking similarities between some of the new theology's myths and the indigenous Egyptian myths must have made the imported creed appear far less alien and more plausible than it might have otherwise. The trinity of the gods Isis, Osiris, and Horus, the miraculous conception of Isis, the miraculous birth of Horus, and the death and resurrection of Osiris, seemed to lie at the core of the new religious myths and must have provided a comforting familiarity to many Egyptians that helped the new theology to spread. The similarities may or may not have been accidental but in any case the advent of the new theology that preached victory for the violent pastoralist over the peaceful farmer was a harbinger of the ultimate doom of the indigenous Egyptian religion, social system, and ancient civilization.

Rome was alarmed at this new development and began a vigorous persecution campaign against all adherents to the new religion. Septimius Severus issued a decree in 202 CE dissolving the Christian School of Alexandria and forbidding conversions to Christianity. Emperor Diocletian,[42] whose reign extended from 284 to 305 CE, ordered all churches demolished and all sacred books burned. He executed large numbers of Christians, including the Coptic Patriarch St. Peter I, who was later, dubbed the Seal of the Martyrs because he was the last to lose his life during this Roman campaign. The relentless persecution by the Romans certainly did nothing to endear them to the suffering Egyptian Christians, who wholeheartedly reinvented themselves when their new religious leaders adopted the year 284 CE, the year that Diocletian took power and began his purge, as the beginning of the Coptic calendar.[43] The persecution merely served to further erode the Roman Emperors' standing in Egypt, and allegiance to Rome had all but disappeared by the time Rome accepted Christianity as the official religion.[44]

The introduction of the new faith was a significant development and represented a radical paradigm shift. It advocated a fundamental change in the traditional social values and socio-religious structure in Egypt. As a monotheistic patriarchal religion, it allowed absolutely no possibility of tolerance for, let alone accommodation with, the ancient gods and goddesses. They were all relics of what was now considered a heathen past whose traces needed to be eradicated. That unfavorable view of what is sometimes described as Egypt's Golden Age is subscribed to by the followers of Islam who referred to the ancient era as "the age of ignorance." Saint Mark's new faith also cast the pharaoh in a negative role. Instead of being the living god, the benevolent fertilizer of the land and protector against the pillaging nomadic raiders, or Sand Dwellers, as the Egyptians sometimes referred to them,[45] the new theology cast him in the role of the evil enslaver of the virtuous believers. The ease with which the new faith took hold in Egypt despite what one contemporary writer terms its definite anti-Egyptian slant[46] is a clear indication of the extent of serious social conflict, confusion, and turmoil that enveloped Egyptian society during this period. In effect, the Egyptian Christians now came to view themselves through the eyes of the primitive nomadic marauders who had menaced and plundered their villages and fertile valley for millennia. No longer were they the possessors of a powerful and superior culture and an advanced civilization that their pharaoh protected against the foreign nomads intent on murder, pillage, destruction, and robbing them, the peaceful peasants who worked the land, of the fruits of their labor. The self-image the new theology now imposed on them was one of evildoers who had harassed the pious nomadic believers, those self-same marauding bands of Asian tribesmen.

Several of the myths, legends, parables, and fables of the newly imported theology are stories of what one Egyptian writer described as the age-old struggle between the peaceful farmers, symbolized by Cain, who was given the land and devoted himself to caring for it, and the pillaging nomadic herders symbolized by Abel, who was given the livestock. The parables and myths are related from the point of view of the herder whose offerings are accepted by their deity while the offerings of the farmer are rejected for no apparent reason.[47] The chronicle ends with the errant farmer being overtaken by his feelings of anger and envious jealousy and murdering the virtuous herder. His punishment was banishment, and in exile, he built the first city and named it after his son Enoch. These chronicles are replete with accounts of the wrath of the deity towards the pharaoh and/or the farmers, i.e. the Egyptians, for no apparently logical reason.

There is nothing surprising about this seemingly unnecessarily hostile and illogical stance. It is certainly understandable that the herders' beliefs and myths would cast them in a positive role, the role of the righteous, while assigning the role of the corrupt or evildoer to the other. Feeling good about oneself is inarguably one of the functions of folklore and popular legends in society. What is atypical and noteworthy is acceptance of a folkloric tradition that is self-negating and that casts one in the role of the sinful transgressor who deserves to be punished, vanquished, and hated. What is also surprising and unexpected is the acceptance of the absurd claim that the farmer is jealous of the herder when he knows from personal experience that it was the destitute poverty stricken herders who had always been envious and jealous of his prosperity and who had always attacked and pillaged his villages.

It is true that no culture is devoid of contradictions or beliefs that seem to fly in the face of logic or readily available evidence, but scorning and hating one's ancestors to that extent is certainly not a widespread phenomenon. Nor is it usual for a people to systematically and zealously deface and destroy their ancestors' monuments and temples as the Egyptian Christians did with their pharaonic heritage once they switched their allegiance to the newly imported Asian deity. These practices were, in effect, a manifestation of the accuracy of the maxim that history is written by the victors, and lends support to one author's hypothesis that the middle of the first millennium marks the herder's victory over the farmers.[48]

The most logical explanation for such a radical shift in socio-religious doctrines and convictions is the serious state of anomie that Egyptians were experiencing during this period. Their traditional gods and goddesses seemed to have abandoned them, and they no longer had a pharaoh who could communicate with the gods, plead their case, and discover the reasons for the gods' displeasure with them, the reasons for their abandonment, and the means of remedying the situation. What was the Roman relentless exploitation and persecution, if not evidence of their hopelessness? In sum, they now doubted their worldview and doubted themselves. The days of stability, security and harmony were now over and chaos prevailed: a situation Egyptians did not want and were desperate to be rid off.

Events outside Egypt also played an important role in this radical shift, both influencing the direction and hastening the pace of social change. By the time the Roman Empire split and Egypt became part of its Eastern territory, the Byzantine, Christianity had already been declared the official religion of the Empire and social turmoil took another direction. In Rome, Emperor Theodosius the Great ordered that pantheism be stamped out. In Egypt, Theophilus, who had been appointed Patriarch of Alexandria in 391 CE, was one of the more ardent representatives of the new orientation and encouraged Christian mobs to erase all traces of classical culture. Freed from fear of their own persecution, the Christians, now well established in Egypt, in turn pursued those they termed the infidels and their symbols with zeal, and it became increasingly difficult to be a pantheist and be left alone.

Monuments classified as wonders of the ancient world that had weathered the ravages of time for millennia were now viewed as idolatrous relics constructed by a heathen people and were certainly no match for the type of fervor and vehemence in which monotheists can excel. Images were chiseled out of the walls of ancient tombs, the insides of temples were scraped to erase pantheist symbols and writings, and statues were destroyed. Famous Alexandrian landmarks such as Serapis and the Serapeum were not spared. Alexandria, while still the prosperous center of gracious living, science and learning that it had been during Cleopatra's reign, was now in turmoil, and adherents to the old religions were mercilessly hunted down by the new converts regardless of who they happened to be.

The new Christian deity to which the Egyptians turned to fill the spiritual and social vacuum proved to be less forgiving and less easy going than the old pharaonic deities. Serious social upheaval, confusion, and turbulence accompanied the loss of the core of Egypt's social structure and its repudiation of its native identity in favor of the newly imported Asian religion. Perhaps nothing serves as a more potent symbol of Egypt's tragic break with its classical past than the appalling fate of one of its most illustrious citizens. The famed mathematician, astronomer, and head of the Platonic school, Hypatia (370-415 CE) earned the enmity of the Archbishop of Alexandria for tenaciously clinging to classical learning, science, culture, and religion, now viewed as heathen by the Church. In 415 CE,[49] a band of enraged Christian monks "full of passionate intensity," to borrow Yeats' phrase, ambushed Hypatia on her way home from the library, pulled her from her carriage, and subjected her to a torturous death by peeling her skin with oyster shells, cutting up her body piece by piece, and finally burning her.[50] St. Cyril, the See of Alexandria from 412 to 444 CE and a power hungry, ruthless, and intolerant man who endeavored to force the city's Jewish population out of Alexandria and to contain or stamp out the school of philosophy, had a hand in aiding and abetting her murder.[51] In addition to her learning and intelligence, Hypatia's beauty may well have been a motivating factor that inflamed the passions of St. Cyril and his monks and, threatened by a woman who possessed such qualities, they may well have perpetrated the first crime in Egypt motivated purely by misogyny: another import of the new theology.

The believers, who were no less ruthless to dissenters within their own flock than they were to non-believers, eventually brought an unanticipated catastrophe upon themselves. Their leaders became locked in the debate that evolved out of the ecumenical councils of Ephesus and Chalcedon. The focus revolved around the dual nature of Jesus Christ, the hypostatic union of the human, and the divine. One faction, the Monophysites, maintained that Christ, much like a pharaoh, had a single nature, which fused the human and the divine components. The Orthodox or Chalcedonian position, maintained that the human and divine natures of Christ were separate. This created a schism between Alexandria and Constantinople (capital of the Eastern Roman Empire, also known as the Byzantine Empire). As political power rested with Constantinople, once the Alexandrians' position was declared heretical, the Egyptian Christians were pursued with the same zeal that they had shown earlier toward those who did not share their recently imported Asian beliefs. Rather than bringing a return to stability through its rites and structure, Christianity now compounded Egypt's socio-cultural dislocation resulting from the final wrenching from its pharaonic roots, and the Coptic orientation worked, not as an instrument of cohesion between the people and their rulers, but as a powerfully alienating force from the despotic Byzantines. The wide gulf between the rulers and the ruled and the social turmoil created by the Eastern Romans' persecution of Egypt's Christians were to be the crucial factors that were to lead to the eventual displacement of Christianity as the religion of the majority in Egypt and usher in a new religious orientation for Egypt.

The turbulence, unrest, and relentless persecution of the Egyptian Christians were undoubtedly decisive in furthering the cause of the adherents to an Asian-rooted Semitic theology whose forces had been gathering momentum in the deserts of the Arabian Peninsula. The adherents to that new faith would soon carry out a raid on Egypt that was destined to be very different from all the previous raids that most pharaohs had repelled on an almost routine basis. And not so routine. Reliefs on the temple of Ramses III at Medinet Habu[52] provide one example of a strong pharaoh's success at repelling a threat that could have been more serious than the usual raids by the "sand dwellers." They also record his success in repelling an attempted invasion of "the Sea Peoples" who had wreaked havoc on the civilizations of the eastern Mediterranean and are thought to have been a major cause of the demise of the Mycenaeans and Minoans and the start of a century long dark age. A strong pharaoh, however, had saved Egypt from a similar fate.

Now there was no longer a powerful pharaoh to protect Egypt from the marauding nomads who had coveted its wealth from the beginning of its history. No longer was there an almighty pharaoh supported by the nurturing and caring ancient gods and goddesses. No longer was there the social cohesion created by a god-king. Now that the country was weakened and its people demoralized and alienated from their rulers, the next incursion would prove to be by far the most successful of all the nomadic raids and would administer the *coup de grâce* to Egyptian civilization.

3

The Point of No Return: Arabs at the Gates

The Byzantine rulers of Egypt had inadvertently paved the way for their own defeat by a small and ill equipped rag tag army of invaders. The assailants were members of the nomadic tribes who inhabited one of the most desolate, impoverished and least hospitable regions on the planet,[1] the Arabian Peninsula. Many, perhaps the majority, of contemporary writers, social scientists, religious leaders, and the general public in the Arab and Islamic societies view Bedouin life of the Arabian Peninsula through rose-colored glasses, and romanticize its real or imagined virtues. Life was simple, daily needs were few and easily satisfied, and elders were respected. Men were brave and honorable, women were upright and virtuous, and loyalty to the family and tribe was unshakable. Social equality prevailed, and generosity and hospitality to guests were the norm. Tribal leaders were learned, wise, and just. In short, it was an idyllic state of affairs. Anything that might mar that rosy view is promptly set aside by attributing it to the social values, practices, and conditions that prevailed during the Age of *gaheliyya* (ignorance), the pre-Islamic era. Any trait or characteristic that might reflect negatively on nomadic society is briskly consigned to that period and summarily dismissed.

This romanticized view of the Bedouin is reminiscent of the concept of the noble savage that captured the imagination of European travelers such as Wilfred Thesiger, Harry St. John Philby, T.E. Lawrence, and Richard Burton.[2] The concept, which may be traced back as far as ancient Greece and the works of Homer, is basically an idealized view of an individual who is pure and good and has not been corrupted by civilization. Such views belong in the genre of fiction and most certainly do not describe the few thousand nomads who constituted the next and more devastating raid on Egypt.

An objective examination of living conditions in the Arabian Peninsula produces a very different picture of the Arabian noble savage and provides some indication of the level of social, political, and economic development during that era. The area was a vast unforgiving desert inhabited by nomadic vagrant hordes that were plagued by interminable internecine wars. Hunger, extreme poverty, ever-present threats to the individual's life and meager personal possessions, destitution, and absence of the most basic needs were what characterized Bedouin life before the conquests. The Arabs had never found it necessary to develop a calendar that recorded the passage of years and had no currency of their own because it was rarely needed in such an impoverished economy where reliance on the use of Persian or Byzantine currency was more than adequate for their limited needs.[3]

The Nagdis and Hegazis in the Eastern Arabian Peninsula lived a simple life in "houses of hair,"[4] roamed the desert in search of suitable grazing lands for their small herds, and writing was unknown until almost the time of the Prophet Mohammed.[5] Science and philosophy were unheard of.[6] Ahmad ibn Jabir el-Baladhuri (d. 892 CE) recounts in his *Kitab futuh el-buldan* that at the advent of Islam, Quraish, the most powerful and prosperous tribe in the Arab Peninsula had only seventeen persons who could read and write, and goes on to list their names.[7] For other large tribes such as el-Aws wal Khrzag, Baladhuri's list of literate persons is less than a dozen.[8] Crafts were almost nonexistent, and the words for arms, manufacturer, and carpenter were borrowed from Aramaic.[9] The word *moshaf*, (which means the Koran in current usage) and those for window, bracelet, and ironmonger were borrowed from Ethiopia, and the idols that they worshipped were represented by unsculptured stones.[10] The Arab environment was so poor that when Bedouin plunderers returned home with the gold looted in foreign raids some of them swapped this metal that they had never seen or heard of before for silver, a metal with which they were familiar.[11] One Arab who returned home with a noblewoman as part of his share of the loot sold her for one thousand dirhams because, as the anecdote relates, he thought that that was the largest number in existence.[12]

The harsh desert environment of the Arabian Peninsula had, of course, a major influence on the lifestyle, social organization, culture, social values, and practices of those who lived in it. Food was scarce, and social groupings were forced to move regularly in search of grazing areas for their small herds. Hunger and famine were a fact of daily life. The Bedouins' main source of nourishment was dates and camel milk. Their regular diet contained no other solid foods but was supplemented on occasion with camel meat.[13] Scorpions, beetles, and "'*ilhiz*, that is, camel hair ground with stones, mixed with blood, and then cooked,"[14] were part of their normal diet. Bedouin attire was just as basic as their diet and usually consisted of a long robe worn with a wrap held by a rope to cover the head, and bare feet.[15]

The impoverished environment was, as could be expected, reflected in the Arabic language. The *gaheliyya* literature has far fewer terms to describe feelings of joyfulness, merriment, or pleasure than terms for unhappiness, distress, misfortune, or gloom.[16] There are over four hundred terms describing privation or unhappiness[17] but a dearth of terms describing the prosperity or material comforts that are a normal part of life in more advanced societies.[18]

The inhospitable physical environment precluded the establishment of urban centers of any consequence. Small settlements such as Mecca and Medina were no more than tiny, poverty-stricken settlements that lacked the resources to sustain the evolution of a central authority or a stable society. Consequently, social development beyond a simple tribal structure was impossible. Literacy, pursuit of knowledge and learning, the arts, music, health care, housing beyond the simplest of structures, the security that only a central government can provide, were all luxuries beyond imagination. Raids by other tribes were constant, and each tribe faced a dilemma. The only safety lay in numbers. The more numerous the tribe was the more able it was to defend its meager resources against raids by other tribes. At the same time, the larger numbers exacerbated the problem of finding enough to eat and was probably one of the factors that spawned development of the social practice referred to as *wa'd el-banat*. This practice, of burying newly born baby girls alive in the sand and leaving them to die, was widespread in the Peninsula before Islam prohibited it, and was probably functional for that type of social grouping. It served to reduce the number of mouths to feed, while at the same time allowing for a natural increase in the number of boys who would grow into fighting men who would help to protect the tribe in its never-ending wars with other tribes and participate in resource grabbing raids. The only problem was that the shortage of women became yet another cause of inter-tribal raids, as women became a scarce resource, just like food and came to be viewed as legitimate prey. Furthermore, the custom of allowing powerful men in the tribe to take several wives not only contributed to the vicious circle but also intensified the problem by creating personal conflicts and resentments within the tribe.

The birth of Islam proved to be a momentous event that would eventually improve every aspect of life in the Arabian Peninsula and endow the indigent Bedouins with unimaginable wealth, an endless supply of slaves and concubines, and the opportunity, once the conquests began, to escape their barren environment and migrate to the more hospitable lands of Persia (Iran), Egypt and the Fertile Crescent. Furthermore, they were destined to arrive at their new homes not as poor supplicants, but as conquering rulers who demanded subservience and deference from the native populations. Within a few decades of the start of the era of foreign conquests, the Bedouins, who had been fighting and killing each other for a bag of grain or a handful of dates, were composing poems about the *ghelman*,[19] offering opinions,[20] and consulting books about the relative merits of concubines from different parts of the empire and different ethnic groups.[21] As the raids enriched and empowered the Bedouins, captured foreign women became so plentiful that "a beautiful concubine was worth [only] five dinars."[22]

In the early decades of Islam, before the launch of the extensive foreign conquests, poverty and famine continued to be the main characteristics of life in the Peninsula, since improvements in living conditions brought about by the new religion were limited, gradual, and confined to the modification and refinement of some the more repellent social practices. New social values were introduced, some old practices such as *wa'd el-banat* were prohibited, inter-tribal raids among those that submitted to Islam were discouraged, and energy was directed toward building a more stable society. However, cultural and social practices that evolve over a period of many centuries cannot be radically altered within the span of a few short years. When the Prophet died in 632 CE, several of the tribes reverted to their earlier ways and refused to pay the *zakat* (annual tithe) to the new leader. There was also widespread tribal rebellion. Abu Bakr el-Seddik, a member of Quraish, the Prophet's tribe, and one of the more powerful ones, had been selected as his successor (caliph).[23] He found it necessary to wage a war on these rebellious tribes to preserve the new faith, re-impose his authority, and force a return to the fold. He began to send some of the troublesome tribesmen to raid their wealthier neighbors in Persia and outposts of the Byzantine Empire in Mesopotamia, Syria, and Palestine, and he punished the *murtadda* (apostate tribes) by refusing to allow them to take part in these raids and to share in the rich spoils the raiders brought back. These raids do not appear to have been aimed at gaining new territory, but at minimizing inter-tribal raids, which the new religion prohibited, by channeling the tribesmen's energies and penchant for war and pillage towards the countries that abutted the Arabian Peninsula.[24] Some of these raids were successful, and the fighters returned with spoils of war that were far richer than anything they ever got when they attacked each other.[25]

After Abu Bakr's death, his successor to the caliphate in 634 CE, Omar ibn el-Khattab, had the foresight to expand that policy to keep the troublesome tribesmen distracted from internal conflicts. The first act of the new leader was to include the *murtadda*,[26] who thus far had been denied the opportunity to participate in the lucrative raids on neighboring communities. Victories and notable successes such as the defeat of the powerful Byzantine army at the Yarmuk River, which extended the caliph's[27] rule to include Syria and brought him even richer spoils of war, helped to sustain the Bedouin interest in foreign conquests. In spite of the booty brought back from these foreign raids, poverty continued to prevail, however, in the Peninsula. The first caliph was not financially compensated for his work due lack of funding,[28] and the second caliph's wardrobe consisted of a single well-worn shirt and a patched up cloak.[29]

It was inevitable that Egypt would come into someone's sights sooner rather than later. Bedouin raids into Egypt had been taking place for millennia and Bedouin lore was replete with references to Egypt's wealth. One of the major Egyptian historians, Taqi el-Din Ahmad ibn Ali ibn Abdel Qadir ibn Mohammed el-Obaydy el-Maqrizi (1364–1441/1442), cites several of these references. Abu Basra el-Ghafary, one of the Prophet's companions, described Egypt as having "all the earth's treasures,"[30] and Abu Said Abdel Rahman bin Younes believed that Egypt had such well-organized rivers, dams, and bridges that "water runs under its houses and courtyards," and they, Egyptians, could stop it and use it as they liked.[31] Abu Zaham stated that "paradise runs on both sides of the Nile from Rosetta to Aswan."[32] The Arabs even believed that Adam, who fell from the Garden of Eden and, therefore, knew what he was talking about, described Egypt as paradise, and that Noah prayed that God would send the descendants of his favorite son Ham to live in Egypt, "which is the best place to live the world."[33] Maqrizi also reports a common belief among people that when foreigners come to Egypt and drink from the Nile, they forget their homelands,[34] and repeats el-Mas'udi's claim that, according to the *shari'a*, paradise was actually the source of the Nile.[35] The tenth century Egyptian historian, Omar bin Mohammed bin Yousef Al Kindi went as far as listing all the Koranic verses where Egypt is mentioned.[36] He summarizes the Arabs' view of Egypt, its wealth and its beauty[37] and describes "learned people" as having claimed that, "All people in the world find it necessary to go to Egypt to find sustenance, and its people do not look for sustenance anywhere else and never travel anywhere else because of the wealth of their country."[38] The number of times Egypt is mentioned in every one of the monotheistic holy books suggests a Semitic/Bedouin/nomadic preoccupation bordering on obsession with the country of the Nile valley. For example, Egypt or Egyptians are referred to 715 times in the Bible.[39]

With the growing prospect of lucrative foreign raids on offer, the various tribal chiefs and commanders of the Bedouin raiding parties were quickly losing interest in raiding one another and lined up behind their leaders, each vying for a piece of the action. One of the shrewdest of these commanders was Amr ibn el-Aas (died 664).[40] He had embraced Islam after it had become established among the tribes and had been exposed to urban life styles during his travels with trading caravans. Amr had also visited Egypt,[41] become aware of the country's wealth,[42] and was quoted as saying that the governorship of Egypt was equal to accession to the caliphate.[43] Amr had witnessed the successes of the other commanders, and being more ambitious than they were, he set his sights on a far bigger prize.

The Conquest[44]

The Caliph, Omar ibn el-Khattab, who was a pious man and is idealized until today for eschewing wealth and earthly rewards[45] was not overly enthusiastic about the idea of sending an army to Egypt. However, Amr, who was both cunning and persistent, finally won him to his side and set out in 639 CE to conquer Egypt with an army of four thousand Bedouins. For the ruler of an independent Egypt, this would have been little more than a minor irritant, no different from the other nomadic raids that had been repelled on an almost routine basis over the centuries. Even as a province of the Byzantine Empire, it should, under normal circumstances, have been relatively easy for the barefooted, poorly fed and badly equipped marauders to be repulsed. But conditions in Egypt at that time were anything but normal.

The Roman ruler, Emperor Heraclius, was detested by his Egyptian Christian subjects, whom he considered heretics and duly persecuted. The Empire's position in Egypt had also been weakened as a result of the decade long struggle to expel the Persians who had invaded Egypt in 616 CE and were finally expelled in 626 CE. The regional representatives of Constantinople had become despotic and corrupt, and the army commanders were incompetent. Cyrus, Bishop of Phasis, who was appointed as the Emperor's representative and Patriarch of the Byzantine Church in Egypt in 639 CE, was not Coptic and detested the Egyptian Christians for their tenacious clinging to their belief in the oneness of Christ. Patriarch Benjamin, the Monophysite Patriarch of the Coptic Christians, was a fugitive from Cyrus and the Romans and hiding in Upper Egypt. By this time, the Coptic Church had been the core of the social structure in society for almost six centuries, and the continuing persecution and the absence of its head had left society in a state of unrest and without effective leadership. Relentlessly persecuted and killed for a decade by Cyrus even while Alexandria was under siege by the Arabs, the Copts were in no position to fight off the invaders.[46]

Adding to the lack of cohesion in the country, the Byzantines had divided the country into three administrative regions, each of which was administered by an appointed *pagarch* (prefect or governor). The prefect was in charge of public security, public works, and the collection and remittance of imperial dues. All three prefects were corrupt, unpopular, and had a stake in maintaining the state of unrest in the country. Constantinople had been too weak to do much about the fact that they had been keeping the imperial dues for themselves for years, and the three prefects were to play an active role in delivering Egypt to the new invaders.

The Arabs, advancing from the eastern borders, engaged the Romans in several battles in the delta and in Upper Egypt before setting their sights on two key locations: the well-fortified fortress of Babylon[47] near present day Roda Island in Cairo, and the city of Alexandria. The prefect of Lower Egypt, Ammen Menus, cared little for the Egyptians, and the fact that he was kept in his position by Amr after the conquest is in itself an indication of his priorities. The prefect of Middle Egypt also readily offered his services to the invaders. George, the prefect of Upper Egypt, who is sometimes referred to by Arab historians as the Mukaukas,[48] actively assisted Amr's army in bringing about the betrayal and surrender of Babylon[49] after an ineffective siege by the Arabs whose feeble bows and arrows had been unable to penetrate its walls and well fortified defenses. Encouraged by their success in capturing the Fort of Babylon, the Arabs now proceeded to Alexandria. The city was very well fortified and could have easily withstood the onslaught of Amr ibn el-Aas's army of brave and desperate, but primitively equipped Bedouins. The city's wall was solid enough to withstand anything that the invaders could throw at it, and there had never been an occasion in history when an attacker had succeeded in taking the city by breaching its walls without the help of someone or some group within the city itself.[50]

Once more, it was treachery rather than military power that delivered the city. Despite the fact that the siege was ineffective, Cyrus, the Christian Malachite Patriarch of Alexandria, arranged the surrender of the city without the knowledge of its inhabitants.

When Amr's army camped outside the city, the Alexandrians were expecting the army to repel them, and were enraged to discover that surrender had been signed. On discovering that the Arabs were not rushing in to take the city by force but calmly marching in to take possession of it in accordance with their agreement with the treacherous leaders,[51] the city's inhabitants were shocked and infuriated. They were incensed at both Cyrus and the Roman officers who attempted to justify the surrender by claiming that it was impossible to fend off the attackers. The furious crowd ran to Cyrus' residence intent on making him pay with his life for his treachery.[52] Cyrus, however, managed to convince the crowd that the document he had signed guaranteed their life and property, and that it was God's Will that the Arabs should take Egypt.[53] That assurance proved to be meaningless and Egypt was irrevocably set on a course that would lead to the persecution and impoverishment of the native Egyptians and would affect another radical shift in orientation, culture, and social values, and virtually every aspect of Egyptian life up the present time.

When he entered Alexandria to inspect his prize, the normally smooth-tongued Amr was almost dumbfounded as he led his ragtag army of emaciated nomads along the glistening rows of white marble pillars and the city's opulent mansions.[54] Alexandria was a magnificent city and unlike anything that the wretchedly poor Bedouins had ever seen before. The fifteenth century historian Galal el-Din el-Suyuti recounts that the city, which was unlike any other city in the world, contained so much marble in its streets, columns, and pavements that the monks, he speculated, wore black garments to counter the glare of all that marble.[55]

Amr ibn el-Aas, the destitute Bedouin for whom simply staving off hunger for a day was an achievement and sleeping in a tent made of camel hair was the norm, found in this city riches, splendor, and luxury far beyond anything he could have imagined. It contained thousands of palaces and public baths, plentiful water, beautiful gardens with marble fountains, trees bearing fruits that he had never heard of, wide avenues, and impressive public buildings. The normally vocative and facile Amr was at a loss for words when he wrote informing the caliph in jubilant terms of the city that he conquered. "I cannot describe what is in it,"[56] he declared. He wrote of 4,000 public baths, "400 entertainment places for kings," and twelve thousand green grocers.[57]

Tellingly, there was no mention of books, works of art, schools, philosophers, or institutions of science and learning. Amr's description was a portent of things to come and a clear indication of the fate that now awaited Egypt in the hands of its new unrefined rulers. What impressed Amr was the wealth, not the civilization that created it. The ability to see a connection between learning and wealth was, as consequent developments in Egypt's history were soon to prove, a concept that was, understandably, beyond the comprehension of the mostly illiterate and untutored new masters.

The attitudes of the victors, as reflected in their own words, were a harbinger of things to come. Plunder and women were all that the conquerors saw. Amr's statement that "Egypt, its land is gold, its women are loose, and it is for the victor,"[58] and Ka'b bin Mane's (652 CE) statement that "he who wants to see what paradise is like should look to Egypt"[59] provide an indication of how the Bedouins saw Egypt and what they hoped to gain by ruling it. The indigent Semitic Asian nomads who had tried for thousands of years to capture Egypt's riches had finally succeeded in grabbing their prize. Amr was now the master of Egypt. Control of its wealth gave him an opportunity to maintain a semblance of control over the unruly and rebellious tribes that had accompanied him, and bringing them under the control of a central authority became possible for the first time since the beginning of history. The Arabs, as Amr once warned the Egyptians as he pointed to a banquet of Egyptian delicacies, would give their lives first rather than give all that up.[60]

Egypt was now set on a course that would lead it directly to its present culture, values, and social conditions. The far-reaching cultural change is aptly exemplified by the fact that the country of the fabled Library of Alexandria was now destined not to give birth to a single historian who would record its history and decay for almost two centuries. Abdel Rahman ibn Abdel Hakam (803-870/871) was the "first Egyptian historian after the Arab conquest to write about Egypt."[61] Being illiterate, the new masters of Egypt had no use for books or intellectual pursuits. They, as ibn Khaldun astutely observed centuries later, scorned scholars, and scholarship.[62]

Suspicion of scholarship and books is such an integral part of the Bedouin culture that, contrary to appearances, such as the building of ostentatious university campuses, it is still alive and well in the twenty-first century.[63]

Egypt's fate was now sealed and every aspect of life in Egypt was destined for eventual change. The native tongue, religion, the position of women in society, social values and cultural practices, relations with the outside world, the social structure, even the calendar system were all thoroughly transformed. The new wave of Bedouin immigrants into Egypt, who were eventually to overwhelm its population, society, and culture, radically change the course of its history and shape its future, would be the nomads of the Arabian Peninsula rather than the urban dwellers of the old empires of Greece and Rome.

The relocation of the capital from Alexandria to el-Fustat (the tent) located at the site of present day Cairo[64] by the Arabs is a noteworthy indicator of the eventual social change that was to transform society. It both symbolized and signaled the change of orientation for society from looking outward to the civilizations of the Mediterranean world from the fabled city of Alexander, to looking east from el-Fustat (the tent) towards the empty wastes of the Arabian Peninsula across the Red Sea. The caliph in Medina, whose instinctive Bedouin fear of the sea had been reinforced by an incident in Mesopotamia when thousands of tribesmen on one of their raiding missions had fallen off a bridge and drowned in the Euphrates river, ordered Amr to establish his capital wherever he wanted. His only stipulation was that there would be no water separating the site from Medina. The name selected for the new capital, el-Fustat, also symbolized the new orientation. The tent, not the house of culture and learning, now became the seat of power that both inspired and set the course for the future direction of society. The new mosque that Amr ordered built in el-Fustat may have given the Egyptians a glimpse of their future and of the new path that their society was now set to follow. The crudity, lack of architectural distinctiveness, austerity, and stark bleakness of that bare one-room structure was a sharp contrast to the opulence of Alexandria where the moonlight reflected from the white marble made the city so bright that a tailor could see to thread his needle without a lamp.[65]

Setting the Tone

Arab historians have always shied away from using terms such as conquest, colonialism, or occupation in connection with these events and have instead opted for the more benign sounding term *fath*, which means opening. Even today, the use of the term occupation is not readily accepted. The *fath* of Egypt in 641 is invariably depicted today in the rosiest of terms and described as an act of altruism by the pious believers who risked life and limb to come and rescue the Egyptians from tyrannical Roman rule and to bring them their new religion. The more accurate and objective view, however, would recognize that the invaders, just like earlier invaders, were simply wretchedly poor human beings in pursuit of nothing more complex than simple pillage and plunder. In fact, many of the invaders were neither pious nor even believers. Many were members of the *murtadda* tribes who had rejected Islam after the death of the Prophet. The astute caliph, tired of their constant warfare and raids to capture their neighbors' meager resources, simply rid himself of them by enticing them to join Amr and share in the rich plunder that awaited them in Egypt.

Proselytizing was clearly not on their agenda since, unlike the Roman Emperors, the new masters of Egypt promised to allow the Egyptians to practice their Christianity as they saw fit. While it is unlikely that Amr would have ever heard of the ecumenical councils of Ephesus and Chalcedon, or the concept of the hypostatic union of the human and the divine, he did learn that a problem existed between the two Christian Churches but was uninterested in taking sides in the dispute and cautious in his treatment of the native population. He met with a delegation of Coptic monks and sent word to Patriarch Benjamin, the Patriarch of the Coptic Christians who had been hiding from the Romans in Upper Egypt, inviting him to return and take his rightful position as leader of his flock. When the two men met, Amr was deeply impressed by the eloquence and dignified manner of Benjamin, acknowledged his full authority over the Egyptian Church, and took heed of many of his suggestions regarding the administration of the country.[66]

Although the church had been seriously weakened by the relentless persecution of the Romans, it had survived. Religion had always been central to the life of Egyptians, and the loss of the pharaoh centuries earlier had left the Patriarch as the only figure of authority readily accepted by the people. His return from exile, and the promise that they would be left free to run their lives as they saw fit, seemed to provide an opportunity to rebuild the socio-religious structure, and perhaps even to regain the harmony and balance that had been lost centuries earlier. At first, it seemed likely, therefore, that the impact of the new invaders on the society, culture, social structure, and institutions would be minimal.

The caliph, who was eager for the Bedouins to maintain their fighting abilities without the distractions of business and industry, decreed that they were to be prohibited from owning land and farms. The only exceptions that he made were one or two gifts of large estates to his friends. Once Amr secured control of the country, he therefore compiled a list of those who were termed *Ahl el-diwan*.[67] They were the Bedouin tribesmen who chose to remain in Egypt after the conquest rather than return to Arabia with their share of the spoils and captured slaves and concubines. The list later included the Arab tribes who migrated to Egypt after the conquest. Amr granted each of those listed a monthly living allowance. He also appointed men to go around daily to find out if there were any new babies born or visitors hosted or concubines bought by the Arabs so that they may be added to the list and taken into consideration when calculating the amount of regular disbursement. With increased migration from the Arabian Peninsula and the population growth among the original migrants, the number of *Ahl el-diwan* that the Egyptians were forced to support through the taxes levied on them grew quickly from the original sixteen thousand during the tenure of Amr ibn el-Aas to forty thousand during the caliphate of Mu'awiya[68] (661-680 CE), with a corresponding increase in the tax burden on Egyptians. The Egyptians continued to support the leisured Bedouins living among them in this manner until the Abbasid Caliph, el-Mo'tasem (833-842 CE), ordered the practice stopped in *AH* 218 (833/834 CE).[69]

The Arabs, partly as a result their economic independence, formed a separate community,[70] and their impact on civil society was minimal in the early years. As they were initially prohibited from owning farms, they lived mostly in el-Fustat, Alexandria, or

Giza, and only occupied themselves with tribal politics, intrigue, and customary matters of conflict and warfare. They kept themselves detached from the native Egyptians, and therefore had no influence worthy of mention apropos the spread of Islam or the Arabic language among the native Egyptian population.[71]

As the victors, the Arabs did not view the vanquished Egyptians as their peers and spurned any social contact with the male population of the country. They were content with the massive revenue that they collected and preferred to spend their time composing and reciting poetry,[72] and feuding with each other. Thus before too long after the conquest the literate among them were, as previously mentioned, consulting books about the merits of the different concubines brought from the newly conquered lands. Their separate community played no active part in any aspect of the mainstream culture. Furthermore, the fact that they did not build themselves a second mosque is evidence of their lack of personal investment in the country. Amr's one-room mosque, a mud brick enclosure with a dirt floor and palm leaf roof, remained, according to Maqrizi, the only mosque in Egypt until another army led by Abdullah bin Ali arrived from Iraq in AH 133 (750/751 CE), camped in an area north of el-Fustat and built themselves a second unremarkable structure there more than a century after Amr built the first one.[73] Some historians argue that the second mosque was built at an even later date. Sayyida Ismail Kashef maintains that Amr's mosque remained the only mosque in Egypt until el-Fadl ibn Saleh el-Abbasi built a second one in AH 169 (785/786 CE), one and a half centuries after the conquest.[74]

This may seem surprising at first glance. After all, the cost of building materials would have been next to nothing, especially in view of the massive revenue that the Arabs extracted from the Egyptians. Labor would also have cost the Arabs nothing. Forced labor was not uncommon in the seventh century, and as ibn Khaldun observed, the Arabs routinely forced craftsmen to work without pay, as they saw no value in such work.[75] They had in fact not hesitated to use forced labor to build the *Amir el-Momneen Canal* to speed up the transport of Egypt's wealth to the Arabian Peninsula. Yet they failed to build mosques in which they could observe one of the five pillars of their religion. The only logical explanation for such an omission is that building mosques was not high on their list of priorities. The reason for this could be that the Arabs' commitment to religion was weak, as Philip Hitti maintains, quoting a verse from the Quran to support his contention.[76] One other possible explanation is that, as Bedouins, they failed to develop an attachment to the land and continued over several generations to view their stay in Egypt as a transitory sojourn.

Whatever the reason, more than another century was to pass before a third mosque was built in Egypt. This time, almost two and a half centuries after the invasion, a more substantial structure was built by ibn Tulun in AH 259 (872/873 CE)[77] after he was appointed to the post of Egypt's *wali* (governor) by the caliph who sat in Baghdad. The fact that ibn Tulun, unlike his predecessors, was ambitious and aspired to found a ruling dynasty would tend to support the transience argument suggested above. Another indication of the separateness of the Arab and Egyptian communities is the strength of the Arabs' identification with their tribes as evidenced by the gravestones discovered in el-Fustat and Aswan that record the names of the deceased followed by the names of their tribes. This practice continued throughout the first two centuries following the invasion.[78]

Where the governing of the country was concerned, Amr, as later events were to demonstrate, was, relatively speaking, one of the more just and enlightened men who ruled Egypt after the Arab invasion. He was shrewd enough to realize that administering a complex society such as Egypt required different technical skills and abilities from those needed to lead an illiterate and poverty stricken nomadic tribe. He made no major changes in the sociopolitical structure, and in fact kept in place most of the personnel, both Roman and Egyptian, who had been running the country before the invasion. The civil service administration of Egypt was quite complex, highly organized, and sophisticated, and the Arabs for whom the term government simply meant a tribal chief, had neither a system of their own to replace it with, nor the knowledge and technical cadre to run it themselves. Amr, as Alfred J. Butler has pointed out, appointed Egyptians rather than Arabs to fill vacant positions left by Roman subjects who refused to serve the new conquerors and left the country, and Egyptians ran the government administration.[79] The illiteracy of the Arab invaders, which was in sharp contrast to the vanquished Egyptians, quite possibly gave rise to the popular contemporary stereotype that Copts make better accountants than Muslims.

The steps that Amr took to improve the squalid appearance of his army are also evidence of his shrewdness. He decreed that in addition to the poll tax, the Egyptians were to clothe his men. They were required to give each of his warrior's one-dinar (4.25 grams of gold[80]), one *gebba* (a type of robe that could be worn over the flowing dress that the Arabs usually wore), one *bornos* (another type of robe traditionally worn by Egyptian monks), one *emma* (turban), and two pairs of shoes per annum.[81] In return for complying with these orders, Amr, as historian Ahmad ibn Jabir el-Baladhuri (d. 892) relates, promised that the Egyptians' property would be safe, they would not be taken as slaves, and their women and children would not be taken and sold into slavery.[82] Ibn Abdel Hakam also mentions this extra tax and points out that in addition to the poll tax, the Egyptians had to provide food, grain, oil, honey, vinegar, and clothing to Amr's soldiers.[83] Obviously, the contrast between the Egyptian and Roman refined clothing and the grubby rags worn by the Arabs was not lost on Amr. He must have understood the psychological impact of that discrepancy on the Egyptians and its implications for the victors in maintaining their authority. Amr was also astute enough to have kept himself well informed of gossip within the caliph's entourage and may well have heard and understood the implications of Patriarch Sophronius's observation upon meeting the caliph, who had arrived on his camel to settle the capitulation of Jerusalem to the victorious Bedouins. The Patriarch, shocked by "his uncouth mien, his course fare, and his shabby raiment,"[84] said in an aside to his attendants in Greek, "Truly this is that abomination of desolation spoken of by Daniel the Prophet."[85] With the Arabs now dressed in their new attire, the conquered Egyptians doubtless soon stopped looking down their noses at their new masters.

Amr's motives for the policies that he followed have been studied extensively. Contemporary Arab historians invariably view Amr, his motives for the invasion, and virtually all his subsequent actions through rose-colored glasses. They present a romanticized view of a pious, noble, self-denying man who was merely carrying out God's plan in spreading Islam, and have put him on a pedestal and raised him to the status of a quasi-holy man.[86] That veneration may well be deserved, but delving into the man's motives beyond an attempt to put them in the context of their consequences on Egyptian culture and society is not relevant to the current analysis.

Whatever the man's personal motives were, logical analysis suggests that these policies were most likely influenced by two major factors. The first is the unceasing demands from the caliph back in Medina for gold, food, clothing, and anything else that could be extracted from the conquered Egyptians. These demands were, as correspondence between the two men clearly illustrates, incessant, and contained unambiguous threats. After all, the caliph was the man who had appointed Amr in the first place, and the one who had the power to replace him. When the caliph wrote in one of his communiqués to Amr, "I have the means to compel you to render me what I demand,"[87] Amr would certainly have known that this was not an idle threat. The second is that Amr had the farsightedness to grasp the fact that the only guaranteed means of meeting these demands was to allow the Egyptians to run their own country so that they could produce the wealth that he needed to seize from them and send to Medina if he was to keep his job. His correspondence with the caliph back home shows clearly that he readily complied with his orders. In one communication, the caliph ordered Amr to send him gold and "everything that you find in Egypt of food, clothing, onions, lentils, and vinegar."[88] Amr replied that he had sent him a caravan that stretches from Egypt to Medina.[89] As for the caliph's demand for gold, the amount sent to him in the first year of occupation alone was worth 12 million dinars, according to Maqrizi,[90] which works out to be fifty-one tons of gold.[91]

At the same time, Amr was astute enough to realize that excessive avarice could kill the goose that laid the golden egg. His policy, therefore, was essentially to let the Egyptians do what the Arabs did not have the talents and skills to do: namely, to run a complex society, their own, as they saw fit. He could then force them to hand over the wealth that they produced so that he could send it back to the caliph. Another example of Amr's pragmatism was his attitude regarding conversions to Islam. He was well aware of the caliph's decree that no poll tax should be collected from Muslims and shrewdly preserved his source of revenue by not forcing the Egyptians to convert to Islam, since that would only have served to lower his revenues. He had the farsightedness to realize that allowing the Egyptians some degree of autonomy and treating them relatively fairly was the most guaranteed means of achieving his aims.

To achieve these objectives, he followed a policy of consulting with the Patriarch of the Coptic Church regularly, and prudently followed his advice in most instances. At the same time, he had to placate the caliph. When the caliph learned about an ancient canal that had once connected the Nile to the Red Sea, and ordered Amr to find it and dredge it to provide a faster means of transportation than desert caravans for the food that was being sent from Egypt, Amr at first demurred. He realized that excessive avarice in the pursuit of the *omran* (affluence, prosperity, or inhabitedness) of Medina could result in the ruination of Egypt and tried, without success, to dissuade the caliph by using the argument that if the Bedouins of Arabia are too well fed on the bounty of Egypt they may not be as willing to go on foreign raids.[92] The argument certainly did have merit. However, the caliph, as the highly regarded Iranian historian Abu Ga'far Mohammed ibn Garir el-Tabari (838-923) reports, was not swayed and ordered Amr to dig the canal and "make haste, [and] may the prosperity of Medina come from the ruination of Egypt."[93] Left with no other option, Amr duly complied and dredged the canal using forced labor. Once the canal was dug, there was never another famine in the Arabian Peninsula until that route was neglected and abandoned after the death of Osman,[94] the third of the Guided Caliphs and the last to reside in the Arabian Peninsula.

Clearly, the two men, Amr and the caliph, held different views regarding Egypt. However, this difference did not stem from the altruism of one and the avarice of the other. It was merely a difference regarding the means not the ends. It was not a difference over what to do, but over how to do it. Amr was just as interested in Egypt's wealth as the caliph was and no less susceptible to the temptations of wealth and comfort than the other tribal chiefs who participated in foreign conquests. By the time he died, Amr had amassed fabulous wealth: seventy sacks of gold according to Maqrizi,[95] or two *ardab* (396 pounds) according to other estimates, in addition to other property, all of which his son viewed as the wages of sin, relinquishing all claims to it.[96] Although Stanley Lane-Poole suggests that the ten tons of gold coins that Amr is also reported to have left when he died was an exaggerated estimate,[97] contemporary Islamic scholars, and historians find the estimate to be wholly plausible.[98] In fact, the estates left by other members of Amr's tribe, who did not have the good fortune to govern bountiful Egypt, suggest that the figure of ten tons is not an excessive estimate.

Other tribal chiefs who participated in the foreign raids also amassed fabulous wealth from their plunder of the conquered territories. For example, el-Zubair ibn el-Awwam, one of the tribal chiefs who had accompanied Amr to Egypt, left a vast estate. Originally, he had demanded to "share out Egypt" with Amr, who refused and instead gave him, with the caliph's approval, "something that satisfied him."[99] There were no clues as to what that "something that satisfied him" was. However, when el-Awwam died he left a fabulous estate of gold coins; thousands of slaves and concubines; horses and camels; houses in Medina; houses and farms in Basra and Koufa in Iraq, as well as in el-Fustat and Alexandria.[100] El-Mas'udi (896-956) also reports in his *Murug el-dahab wa ma'adin el-gawaher* (Meadows of Gold) that less influential Bedouin notables such as Ya'la bin Munya left half a million dinars and properties worth 300,000 dinars.[101] El-Talha bin Abdullah el-Teemy had one farm in Iraq that brought him a daily income of one thousand dinars and even built a brick house with expensive wooden doors in Medina.[102] Zaid bin Thabet left so much gold and silver that they had to use axes to break it up,[103] presumably to divide it up between his heirs. The high estimates of the wealth Amr accumulated in around ten years of access to Egypt's wealth, then, are wholly believable.

Like most of the other non-Egyptians who ruled the country during the succeeding centuries, Amr was also captivated by the thought of finding buried Egyptian treasures and announced that any Egyptian found with concealed treasure would be put to death unless it was handed over to him. Ibn Abdel Hakam's well-known anecdote, to which Butler refers,[104] speaks to this preoccupation Amr had in the story of a man named Peter from Upper Egypt who was put to the sword after denying the rumor that he had hidden treasure, which Amr subsequently discovered under a cistern in

Peter's house.[105]

Amr's communications with the caliph, however, leave no doubt as to his awareness that excessive avarice would inevitably lead to a loss of income. When, on one occasion, the caliph writes, "I did not send you to Egypt to sate your lusts and those of your people, but because I hoped you would by good administration increase our revenue,"[106] he attempted to explain the situation to his boss. His reply was that it is "better to be merciful to them [the Egyptians] than to oppress them, or to force them to provide the money by selling their necessities."[107] The significance of these anecdotes, then, is that Amr clearly sought to and did extract as much of Egypt's wealth as he could, but he was astute enough to realize that making the Egyptians destitute was not the best means of achieving his goals.

There are numerous examples that illustrate the congruence of goals between Amr and the caliph. When the governor of the besieged town of Ekhna sought a meeting with Amr to inquire about the exact amount of poll tax that he demanded of the town's people if they surrendered to the Arab invaders, Amr refused to specify the amount. Instead, he pointed to a church and informed the governor that filling the church from floor to ceiling would not define the amount of the tax. The town and its people, Amr said, were "our [the Arab's] treasury and if our needs increase we shall increase your taxes and if they decrease we will lighten your load."[108] Not surprisingly, the town refused to surrender and was defeated in battle. The killing of all men, women and children in the town of Bahnasa after it fell to Amr[109] and the enslavement of Egyptian women and children from other towns, who were transported to the Arabian Peninsula to be distributed among the Bedouins as their share of the war spoils, are but a few of the examples that demonstrate the congruence of goals between the two men and that the welfare of the Egyptians was not uppermost in Amr's mind but was merely a means to an end.

Nevertheless, it is important not to lose sight of the fact that in the seventh century few people considered the acts described above to be too unusual. Viewed in the context of the years of persecution by Emperor Heraclius and his appointed Christian Patriarch Cyrus, this treatment is likely to have had less of an impact on the conquered society than a twenty-first century observer might assume.[110] What is of relevance to this analysis is the fact that the Arab impact on Egyptian society, culture, values, and social structure in the early years after the invasion was, as a result of Amr's pragmatism, minimal. He tried not to tamper too much with the administrative structure. He sought and heeded the Coptic Patriarch's advice not to demand any taxes before the farmers had the opportunity to harvest their crops, not to impose new taxes after the vintage, not to appoint tyrannical officials and tax collectors, and to insure the proper maintenance of irrigation canals.[111] Amr's statement, in reply to one of the caliph's incessant demands that more taxes should be levied on the Egyptians, that "the Egyptians were more desirous of enriching their land before Islam,"[112] i.e. before their country was occupied by the Arabs, suggests an intuitiveness that enabled him to make realistic judgments regarding how far he could go in raising taxes. Consequently, while the conquest itself signaled the onset of a far-reaching process that eventually brought about a drastic reorientation of Egypt's culture and society, Amr's relatively long tenure[113] from 641/642 to 646 CE, and then again from 658 to 664 CE[114] was less detrimental to the society and social structure than that of most of those who followed him.

The Egyptians certainly fared better under the rule of Amr than under other Arab *walis*. During Amr's tenure, Egypt had, as mentioned above, two separate communities. The Patriarch, who by all accounts was tireless and dedicated to his flock, played a central role within the Egyptian community, and the internal unity and cohesiveness that had characterized the system of norms, beliefs, and social practices within the community before the onslaught of outside forces took a small step on the road to recovery. The Egyptians went about the business of running their country and rebuilding their social structure, while the Arabs were content with composing oral poetry and living off the allowance provided to *Ahl el-diwan*. It has even been argued that the Arabs were prohibited from writing down the holy book or the collection of religious traditions due to the belief that: "Those who went astray before [them] had done so through literacy."[115] This partiality to illiteracy and mistrust of the written word served to limit the Arabs' impact on Egypt's culture during the early years of the occupation.

The pace of social change accelerated, however, after the removal of Amr from his position in Egypt. The caliph had never been happy with Amr's resistance to demands to extract more out of the Egyptians and when he was assassinated on November 7, 644, the new caliph decided to make his stepbrother, Abdullah ibn Sa'd, responsible for all of Egypt's revenues and limit Amr's authority to commanding the army.[116] Amr declined the position and chose to step down in favor of ibn Sa'd. Significantly, his reply to the caliph's offer, conveyed to us by Maqrizi, was that "I would then be like the one holding the cow by its horns while another milks it."[117] That statement provides yet again a very clear illustration of how the new rulers of Egypt viewed the country, but at least Amr had the farsightedness to realize that excessive avarice could be counterproductive. When his successor managed to squeeze an extra two million dinars per annum out of the Egyptians in taxes and thus collected fourteen million instead of the twelve million that Amr had collected, Osman, the new caliph, berated Amr by saying "The milch-camel gives more milk than in your time."[118] Amr's reply was "Yes, and the reason is that you are starving her young."[119] That exchange of opinion provides unambiguous clues as to what Amr wanted, how he went about getting it, and the consequences of the policy change on Egyptian society and culture after Amr was replaced.

The appointment of Amr's successor, Abdullah ibn Sa'd, as the *wali* (representative of the caliph)[120] of Egypt in 646 CE set the tone for the rule of Egypt in the following centuries. Ibn Sa'd, who "loved money and collected treasure for himself in Egypt,"[121] quickly earned the caliph's approval when he managed to extract the additional amount of two million dinars referred to above, even as, early in his tenure, Egypt suffered a serious famine.[122] During his tenure, ibn Sa'd was either not far sighted enough to realize that he was killing the goose that laid the golden egg, or he simply did not concern himself with the long-term consequences on his actions. Either way, Egypt was now headed in a direction that proved the astuteness of ibn Khaldun's observation, made centuries later that "places that succumb to the Arabs are quickly ruined."[123]

Amr was the first wali, and during the following centuries, Egypt was ruled by a series of individuals whose sole concern during their tenure was to squeeze as much as they possibly could out of the Egyptians in as short a period as possible. Sayyida Ismail Kashef, an Islamic scholar who generally portrays the Arab conquest of Egypt in positive terms concedes that the Arabs' main concern was the tax that they collected from the Egyptians.[124] The tax revenue, she goes on to add, went mostly to the caliph, his local representative, and the tax collector, without Egypt itself benefiting from it in any way.[125]

The traditional Coptic taxation system is said to have divided the revenues into four quarters: one for the king and his court, one for the troops that protected the country, one for land maintenance, and one to be saved and buried in the village for possible future need.[126] This division suggests a measure of both pragmatism and fairness. The Arab invaders' taxation system, however, exhibited neither a measure of pragmatism nor fairness. Crude, unabashed pillage and the view of the Egyptians as nothing more than a cow or camel to be milked[127] was the prevailing sentiment among its rulers from the seventh century onwards. Amr ibn el-Aas had likened governing Egypt to milking a cow, and the third caliph likened it to milking a camel. The Umayyad Caliph, Seliman ibn Abdel Malek (715-717 CE), expressed a similar attitude in a communication to Osama bin Zaid, his appointed tax collector in Egypt. A tenth century Egyptian historian reports that the caliph instructed his man in Egypt to "Milk the milk-giver till it runs out and milk the blood till it dries up."[128]

Egypt's rapid descent into economic ruin began as early as five years after the Arab invasion when Egypt suffered the famine under the governorship of Abdullah ibn Sa'd, who had, as mentioned earlier, earned the caliph's approval when he raised the taxes on the Egyptians to send more gold to Medina.[129] The level of taxation was so great that less than four decades after the Arab invasion, and starting with the rule of the Umayyad dynasty, Abdel Aziz ibn Marawan, in AH 65 (684 CE) noted that the *fellahin* (peasants) began to leave their land due to their inability to pay the enormous sums demanded of them. Whole villages were abandoned because of the high taxation,[130] as evidenced in an eighth-century papyrus ordering the *fellahin* not to leave the land,[131] without a permit.[132] The eighth-century *wali*, Qorra ibn Sharik, was even more determined to stop the peasants escaping from their villages and ordered every peasant to have the name of his village tattooed on his arm so that he could be punished and forced to return if caught away from that village.[133] In spite of these measures, the peasants, who had traditionally felt a very strong emotional bond to their land, continued to abandon their villages in large numbers, and the structure of land ownership began to change in favor of the Arabs who owned large areas of Egypt by the start of the eighth century.[134]

The Arabs' taxation policy, therefore, not only impoverished Egyptians but also robbed many of them of their land. The fact that it resulted in reducing the number of farmers from whom taxes could be collected, thus reducing the income of both the *wali* and the caliph, appears to have escaped the Arabs.

Everything it seems was either taxed or simply appropriated by Egypt's new masters. The Egyptians were required to both feed and clothe Amr's tribesmen from day one. Wheat was also taken as tax in kind for the Arab soldiers and their families.[135] Even wine did not escape the avarice of the invaders. As Muslims, the new rulers were prohibited by their faith from drinking alcoholic beverages, yet there is an eighth Century papyri demanding two jars of wine for the soldiers. To be sure, the document does not specifically state that these soldiers were Arabs, and the second caliph had indeed mandated that wine should not be taken but left to be sold by Egyptians, and then tax collected on the proceeds of the sale amount.[136] However, the fact remains that, as Egyptians were not allowed to join the army, the destination of the wine leaves room for speculation.

The already high tax burden and the peasants' resulting abandonment of their land were not, apparently, reason enough for the above-mentioned *wali* to delay or cancel another tax increase. Not surprisingly this latest tax increase led to revolts in several villages in 706 CE (AH 87).[137] There were several other tax revolts in Upper Egypt during Caliph Hesham ibn Abdel Malek's reign (724-743), and during the reign of Marawan ibn Mohammed (744-750).[138] These tax increases stemmed from simple shortsighted avarice on the part of both the rulers and their tax collectors. Incredibly, in the early eighth century, according to Stanley Lane-Poole, "the district officials reported the extraordinary intelligence that their treasuries were so full that they could hold no more."[139] The outcome of the many tax rebellions the abused Egyptian peasants staged almost never varied: large numbers of the protesting peasants were killed by the foreign rulers and their women and children sold into slavery.

The shortsighted policies, not surprisingly, eventually resulted in lower tax revenue. The revenue collected by the Umayyads fell to less than three million dinars due to corruption, ruination of much of the land, and constant unrest.[140] Periodic famines were another by-product of these policies, becoming a fact of everyday life in the previously fertile valley. The heavy tax burden imposed on Egyptians increased further after the fall of the Umayyad dynasty, which ruled from Damascus. The Abbasids (750-1258), who ruled from Baghdad, were probably worse than the Umayyads where extortionate taxation of the Egyptians was concerned.[141]

The rulers never had to suffer the hardships that their charges were subjected to. In good times, they enjoyed enormous wealth. When Egypt prospered during the reign of the more enlightened ibn Tulun, for example, he prospered too. Upon his death, he left a fabulous estate composed of ten million dinars, in addition to a hundred sailing vessels and thousands of horses and other animal stock.[142] The opulence of the marriage of his granddaughter to the caliph in Baghdad reflects this wealth. "The accounts given of the lady's wedding preparations boggle the mind and read like a tale out of the Arabian nights, for her father had palaces erected along the entire route, so that his daughter should sleep every night in a palace until she had arrived in Baghdad."[143] The dowry offered by her father, Khumarawaih, was "precious stones the like of which no caliph had ever possessed."[144] Ostentatious wealth was the norm for the rulers and their families. The estates left by the daughters of el-Mu'izz (953-975), one of the more benevolent Fatimid caliphs, are another example. One daughter left more than two million dinars and 12,000 dresses, and another left five sacks of emeralds and 30,000 pieces of Sicilian embroidery in addition to other valuables.[145]

The courtiers and hangers on that gathered around caliphs fared just as well as the caliphs' families. The Fatimid Caliph, el-Aziz (975-996), for example, paid his *wezir* (minister or high official), ibn Killis, an annual salary of 100,000 dinars.[146] The *wezir*, who employed a personal guard force of 4,000 and kept 800 concubines, left a fabulous estate of jewelry, property, and animal stock when he died in 991.[147] The enormity of such wealth[148] becomes even more apparent if we consider the income of the people who actually produced these fortunes. During the eighth century, a labor supervisor's wages were four dinars per annum and a field guard was given 6.5 *ardab*[149] of wheat per annum. The cost of wheat at that time was one dinar per three *ardab*.[150]

From the day that the triumphant Bedouins took possession of Egypt, they were intent on robbing the dead as well as taxing the living. The incident mentioned earlier of Amr's confiscation of the treasure of Peter, the Upper Egyptian who was put to the sword for not giving up his treasure, illustrates the victors' quest for buried treasure. History is replete with instances of wanton destruction of the pharaonic heritage of Egypt in search of such buried treasure. Many of Egypt's rulers, just like many of the European "Egyptologists" of later centuries, seem to have been obsessed with robbing the dead Egyptians' graves.

In the twelfth century, what historian Maqrizi referred to as "an ignorant foreigner," gave the Ayyoubid Sultan, el-Aziz Osman Salah el-Din bin Yousef, to believe that there was gold under a small pyramid, so he ordered masons and most of the army to dig it up for him.[151] They spent months trying to destroy the pyramid without success, and finally had no option but to abandon the task.[152] Impressed with the solidity of the structure, the sultan then asked the master mason if he could put back one of the stones as it had been if he gave him one thousand dinars. The mason's reply was that he could not do it even for several times that amount of money.[153] The incident is significant in that it reflects another devastating effect on Egyptian society of the Arab invasion: a dire loss of artisan skills, skills that had been finely honed throughout the thousands of years of pharaonic rule. In this instance, the Egyptian builders' skills had deteriorated to the extent that not only were they unable to destroy what their distant forbearers built centuries earlier, but they also could not even match their ancestors' construction know-how in replacing a single stone. It is safe to assume that a similar deterioration in all the artisan crafts took place after the conquest.

Perhaps the reason for el-Aziz Osman's failure to find treasure is the fact that previous pillagers and treasure hunters had already found the least concealed tombs and removed their contents. One of el-Aziz Osman's predecessors for example, Sultan Salah el-Din Yousef bin Ayyoub, is reported by Maqrizi to have destroyed many pyramids[154] during his search for buried treasure. A few centuries earlier, the Abbasid Caliph, el-Ma'moun (813-833), after ruthlessly putting down the Bashmurite tax rebellion, had also spent several months in Egypt conducting a more extensive archeological dig before going home to Baghdad with his looted treasure. El-Ma'moun managed to open the big pyramid of Giza and, according to Maqrizi, found mummies, jewels, a worthless sword, and an egg-sized ruby, all of which he took.[155] He continued excavating in the area and found statues and mummies.[156] Apparently, el-Ma'moun was also impressed with the structure, ordered a man to climb the big pyramid, and discovered that the top of it was big enough to seat eight camels.[157] The standard of measurement utilized provides an interesting contrast between the technology of the Egyptian builders prior to the subjugation of their country and that of the Arab plunderers centuries later. Maqrizi goes on to report that there had been eighteen pyramids facing el-Fustat, eight of them in Giza, and that el-Ma'moun found much gold in some of them.[158]

Another notable treasure hunter, according to both el-Mas'udi[159] and Maqrizi[160] was the Umayyad caliph, el-Walid bin Abdel Malek bin Marawan (705-715). The Romans, who had been aware of the possible use of the Alexandria lighthouse as a lookout for approaching hostile navies intent on attacking the city, sent a spy to inform the gullible ruler that Alexander the Great had buried an immense treasure under the lighthouse. True to form, the man who ruled Egypt and was ostensibly in charge of protecting it wasted no time in removing the mirror and starting to pull down the structure. After he destroyed half of it, the Alexandrians began to protest, the spy fled, and Marawan, realizing that he had been duped, simply left the structure in ruin.[161]

The plundering of Egypt's wealth by its foreign rulers: robbing the country of its heritage, exploiting the other more readily available source of wealth through taxing the living, continued unabated. Few rulers even bothered with the pretense that the tax revenue was earmarked for national projects rather than self-profit. Inexplicably, the belief of the Arab conquerors that Egypt was paradise does not appear to have given them pause. In effect, they were destroying paradise and either could not see the cause and effect relationship of their actions or instant gratification outweighed their reverence for their own myths about the country.

With every aspect of life deteriorating, Egyptian culture was now on a downward spiral. In the cause and effect equation, the Arab conquerors prospered, and the Egyptians were reduced to abject poverty. The poverty, however, in and of itself, would not necessarily have created long term damage to the people. It was the social and cultural impact of the conquest that had more serious and enduring ramifications and spawned some of the changes that have continued to plague Egyptian society today.

The Institutionalization of Misrule

The breach between the rulers and the ruled, which began when Cleopatra lost her bid to maintain the independence of Egypt, deepened steadily after 641 CE, and a new form of despotic government that served the goal of facilitating for the rulers the plunder of Egypt's wealth eventually became the norm. Bedouin Arab governorship of Egypt lasted a little over two centuries and ended in 868 C.E. when Ahmad ibn Tulun, a Mamluk, who was appointed to Egypt's governorship by the Abbasids, became the first non-Arab to govern the country since the invasion. By then the propensity for plunder and tyranny had succeeded in cultivating a culture of despotism that had begun to take root and to be accepted as a normal cultural practice. This tradition of misrule can be seen to continue to play a negative role in Egyptian society today, having become institutionalized and regarded as the natural order of things.

This is not to suggest that before the loss of independence, the pharaohs had been proponents of democracy, or adherents to egalitarian principles. The legitimacy of their rule, however, was never in question by the native Egyptians. Unlike the Romans or the Bedouins who replaced them, the pharaohs were believed to be the living gods who protected the people from the nomadic pillagers and marauders as well as from local thugs and lawbreakers. The pharaohs did not seize the nation's women and children and ship them elsewhere to be sold as slaves or distributed among desert nomads as war spoils. They interceded with the gods to bring about the annual Nile inundation and to guarantee the continued prosperity of Egypt. They did not transfer Egypt's wealth to faraway foreign rulers in foreign countries, but used it to maintain the infrastructure of society, to build and maintain the monuments that glorified and pleased the gods who made Egypt strong and its people secure and prosperous, thus allowing its civilization to grow and flourish. During the flood season, when the land was inundated and the peasants had no work and no crops to tend, the pharaoh employed them in what would today be called public works projects that benefitted society as well as providing employment. The pharaohs maintained order and stability and thus civilization.

Like the Byzantine rulers they ousted, the new Bedouin rulers did not enjoy such legitimacy. Their religion, language, and culture were constant reminders of their separateness. They had neither interest in the vanquished population's welfare, nor the ability to understand the need to maintain the infrastructure of society. The Bedouins were not a privileged ruling elite class who inspired awe, reverence, or respect through its learning, sophistication, or refinement. This new ruling class was not descended from an aristocracy composed of a small number of individuals who were respected and looked up to due to their elevated status that was legitimized by either age-old traditions or a value system that gave them legitimacy. On the contrary, these were people that John, Bishop of Nikiu (in the Egyptian Delta), referred to as "impious barbarians" in his Seventh century chronicle of the Arab invasion.[162] They were the tribesmen who had entered the conquered fort of Babylon upon its surrender by the Roman Patriarch barefooted and in their threadbare garb, causing the Egyptians to exclaim, "Alas! Why did we not know that the Arabs were in such an evil plight? For we would have continued to struggle and not delivered the city."[163] Even the dietary habits of the new masters dismayed the vanquished Egyptians. The banquet of camel meat boiled in salt the Arabs arranged to celebrate their victory in Babylon was not, to the invited Egyptians, the gourmet feast the tribesmen considered it to be, and having no appetite for such morsels, they walked away from the table,[164] a response they probably later regretted.

Brute force rather than legitimate authority became the foundation upon which the government that was imposed upon Egypt rested. The reaction of Amr ibn el-Aas, on the occasion of the banquet mentioned above, illustrates the point in no uncertain terms, and was perhaps the first indication of what was to come. After realizing that the Egyptians, who had walked away in disgust from the Bedouin style feast on offer, had been scornful of the ratty threadbare attire of his barefooted army, Amr took steps to clarify who the new masters of Egypt were. On the day following the first banquet, according to both Tabari (838-923),[165] and ibn el-Athir (1160-1233),[166] Amr held a second banquet and invited the same guests who had been unimpressed with his Bedouin cuisine. This time, however, he ordered his men fitted with clothes and shoes acquired from the Egyptians to attend a sumptuous banquet of Egyptian delicacies that he had had prepared by Egyptian cooks. On the third day he again invited the Egyptians, this time to a demonstration of his men's fighting abilities. At the end of this show of strength, he told the Egyptians that he wanted them to see what the Arabs ate and what they wore in their own country as compared to what they ate and what they wore in Egypt. The Arabs, he then proceeded to warn the Egyptians, would give their lives, rather than go back to wearing rags, going barefoot, and eating boiled camel meat as they did on the first day. He advised them to accept the fact that the Arabs had beaten them and that the Egyptians had now become the source of the Arabs' "livelihood."[167]

The new rulers of Egypt were, for the most part, untroubled by the Egyptians' view of them as no more than an unrefined, poverty stricken, armed group to whom protection money had to be paid on pain of suffering or death. They had no interest in establishing any kind of legitimacy to their rule. Certainly, the spectacle of the victorious Bedouins' interminable inter- and intra-tribal struggles and feuds over the governorship of Egypt and the wealth that was being extracted from the country is unlikely to have established their legitimacy as a ruling class or endeared them to the Egyptian population.

Instability

Predictably, the importation of the tribal social structure into a peasant-based society such as Egypt was a major source of volatility. The prosperity of an agrarian economy depends in large measure on peace and stability, which are functional prerequisites for that type of society. Nomadic society on the other hand exists in a different physical environment, which nurtures a more combative and conflict prone culture. Unrest, chronic instability, disorder, and personal insecurity had always been central elements of the nomadic existence in the Arabian Peninsula. The history of the Bedouins of the Arabian Peninsula is nothing more than a record of the inter-tribal raids[168] referred to as *ayyam al'-Arab*.[169] Conflicts were a permanent feature of these tribes. One of the better-known conflicts, *Harb el-Basus,* a war between banu Bakr and banu Taghlib, two Christian tribes in the northeastern part of the Arabian Peninsula,[170] is an example of the continuous state of war that was characteristic of nomadic life. The two tribes raided one another incessantly for a period of forty years, each exhorted, encouraged, and enthused by its poets to keep up the carnage. The cause of these raids was that a member of the banu Taghlib tribe had injured a camel that belonged to a member of the banu Bakr tribe named Basus.[171] Such examples provide an inkling of the tribal feuds that the Bedouin migrants would have brought with them to Egypt.

During the first decade or so of Arab rule Egypt enjoyed relative stability because the Arabs during that period were, as one Egyptian historian has observed, "busy opening countries."[172] Once that phase was over, however, with the stakes now higher, these perennial social problems not only continued unabated but intensified as the Arabs returned to the ways of the *gaheliyya* and fought relentlessly over the booty acquired from the subjugated regions. Inevitably, these social problems impacted the conquered provinces of the Empire. Quraish, one of the most powerful tribes in the Arabian Peninsula, had monopolized power over the conquered territories once foreign conquests provided its leaders with the financial resources that allowed them to cement the newly established central authority and dominate the other tribes. Various branches within the tribe itself, however, continued to fight each other relentlessly over control of the caliphate[173] and the power, wealth and privilege that it brought. Even after the establishment of central authority, force continued to be the generally accepted means of obtaining wealth and power since the Bedouins could not conceive of a system in which the rights and obligations of the ruler co-existed with the rights and obligations of the ruled. The continuing instability that this state of affairs gave rise to prompted ibn Khaldun centuries later to observe that, those living under Arab rule "live in a state of anarchy, without law [and that] anarchy destroys mankind and ruins civilization."[174] Chaos, as noted above, is inimical to the Egyptians' need for stability and their seemingly ingrained fundamental belief that it is this stability that allows civilization to flourish.

With Arab warlords constantly fighting one another[175] for a bigger share of the plunder, the perpetual state of war among the Arab tribes that settled in Egypt following the Arab conquest became a permanent source of instability, disorder, lawlessness, mayhem, and unrest in the country. On July 17, 656 Mohamed ibn Abu Bakr, son of the first caliph, led six hundred men to Medina, killed Osman, the third caliph, and secured the governorship of Egypt for himself. Amr ibn el-Aas, who had allied himself with Mu'awiya (head of another Quraish clan)[176] on the condition that he would be granted the governorship of Egypt in return for his support, attacked ibn Abu Bakr in Egypt with a force of four thousand men, beheaded him then stuffed his body into the belly of a dead donkey before burning it, thus starting another round of tribal clashes.[177]

The sources of turmoil and political instability in Egypt were both internal and external. The Arabs continued their incessant wars with one another both at home in the Arabian Peninsula and in Egypt where some of them settled.[178] The situation was exacerbated by the fact that once the Bedouins, whose ties to the land were weaker than peasant communities, had the opportunity to leave their inhospitable home environment and migrate to one of the newly conquered territories in Egypt, Syria, Iraq, and Palestine, they began to leave in large numbers. Most of the important tribes left el-Hegaz,[179] (the western region of the Arabian Peninsula) and some of them settled in Egypt. This turned Egypt, after the murder of the fourth caliph, into one of the power centers that those vying for the position of caliph tried to win to their side, whether sitting in Koufa (Iraq), or later in Damascus and Baghdad.[180] These feuds and tribal rivalries, whether they originated among the Bedouin who settled in Egypt or one of the other conquered territories, became a major source of conflict and unrest in the country.

Newly appointed governors often brought their tribes with them to Egypt in numbers ranging from a few thousand to tens of thousands,[181] and before long the early decree forbidding the Arabs from owning land in Egypt went by the wayside. The governors began to buy the loyalty of their fellow tribesmen by granting them land and estates throughout the country. These imported tribes had longstanding allegiances and feuds with tribes either already in Egypt or in other parts of the empire, and constituted additional elements of unrest. Periodic tribal warfare resulted also from the forcible movement of tribes around the country by governors attempting to subdue them whenever they became troublesome.[182] While the indigenous Egyptian population did not take part in this constant warfare,[183] their resistance to the encroachment on their land added to the social unrest.[184]

The tribal feuds resulted in constant changes of *walis*, further intensifying the atmosphere of impermanence, instability, and lack of continuity in the country. The seemingly never-ending procession of newly appointed *walis*, arriving in Egypt poor and then leaving a few years or a few months later with camel caravans laden with the wealth that they had accumulated during their short tenure, could not have enhanced the legitimacy of the rulers in the eyes of the conquered Egyptians. Egypt saw thirty-two separate administrations during the first century of Arab rule between 641 CE and 750 CE,[185] a period covering the tenure of *el-Kholafa' el-Rashedeen* (the Guided Caliphs) who sat in Medina, then in Koufa, and extending through the Umayyads, who ruled from Damascus. During this one hundred and nine year period the average tenure of the *wali* was, therefore, 3.4 years. The three longest governing *walis* were Abdullah ibn Sa'd (646-656), Moslema ibn Mekhled (667-672 CE), and Abdel Aziz ibn Marawan (685-705 CE). If these three administrations are discounted, the average tenure of the *wali* becomes 2.2 years.

When the Abbasid[186] clan of the Quraish tribe managed to defeat the Umayyad clan and gain control of the caliphate following a revolt in 747 CE,[187] they recognized a potential danger that their predecessors had not identified. That danger was the possibility of an ambitious *wali* of one the conquered territories being tempted to seek independence from their rule in Baghdad, which would have resulted in the loss of a source of revenue. To guard against such an outcome, they now instituted a policy of constantly changing their appointees in these territories.[188] Consequently, during the one hundred and eighteen year period from 750 CE to 868 CE Egypt had seventy-nine *walis*, making the average tenure of each *wali* during that period a mere 1.49 years.[189]

With such a short tenure, it is understandable that whoever was given the governorship of Egypt was interested primarily in keeping the caliph happy. He knew that he could, and in all likelihood would, be replaced suddenly and quite possibly on a whim. In fact, one folktale has it that one of the caliphs once replaced a judge in the city of Qom in Persia simply because the name Qom is also a word meaning: you have been replaced, and the caliph found it amusing to put the word twice in a short rhyme. In another incident, when the Caliph, Haroun el-Rashid, was informed by courtiers in Baghdad that the *wali* of Egypt was plotting against him, he retorted, "'By Allah, I will depose him. And in his place I will set the meanest creature of my court,' and promptly appointed a man who happened to be passing by."[190]

The establishment of an independent caliphate in Egypt by the invading Fatimids (969-1171) did not diminish political instability. The constant replacement of walis was exchanged for violent palace intrigues, which had disastrous consequences for the Egyptian public, and the rulers' attitudes towards the country continued to be feelings of possession rather than of belonging. Perhaps that disconnect is what made it possible for one ruler to burn his capital city rather than allow it to be possessed by another. For example, when the Crusaders invaded Egypt during the reign of Shawar bin Magid el-Sa'di (1162 -1169) whose fifteen predecessors to the post had all but one been murdered,[191] he set fire to el-Fustat rather than risk it falling to the invading army. The inhabitants were forced to flee the city, which continued to burn for more than fifty days.[192]

The interests of Egypt and the welfare of its people were clearly not uppermost in the minds of those who governed the country after the loss of Egyptian independence. The *wali* was not expected to concern himself with anything other than pleasing the caliph and his courtiers. Obviously, the most reliable means of maintaining his position was keeping the caliph well supplied with gold, precious gifts, and whatever else he was able to extract from the Egyptians regardless of the long-term local social, economic, or political consequences for the country. The uncertainty of the *wali's* tenure also underscored the urgent need to amass as much personal wealth as possible before the inevitable loss of position and his return home.[193] Moreover, if Abdullah bin Amr's statement that when Iblis (Satan) landed on earth, he had chicks in Egypt[194] reflected the sentiment prevailing among the Arabs, the negative implications for the Egyptians are obvious. The *wali*, most probably sharing this negative view of the people he was sent to govern, would in all likelihood have been quite unconcerned about the welfare of those he ruled. No one—let alone a true believer—is likely to have wasted any time or energy thinking about the physical or economic security of the offspring of Satan. Abdullah bin Amr's reference to Egyptians as the offspring of Satan is also interesting in that it reflects an emotional dichotomy in the Arab conquerors' approach to Egypt. On the one hand, as previously described, Egypt was referred to as paradise. At the same time, the inhabitants of that paradise were seen as the spawn of Satan, an attitude one can assume that was arose from envy of those who possessed paradise, an envy that eventually transformed the paradise into a land of dire poverty.[195]

The basic outlines of the relationship between the Egyptians and their rulers that was fated to last for centuries was now firmly set: tax collection was their main connection. A just ruler, as far as the Egyptians were concerned, was simply someone who did not tax them too exorbitantly and who did not appoint local officials who oppressed them and appropriated too much of what remained after the *wali* had taken his cut. This is not to suggest that local administrators had much authority beyond tax collection. Arab rule of Egypt was highly centralized[196] and all matters were directly under the *wali's* control, thus leaving local administrators with virtually no authority over local matters.[197] The *wali* was an absolute ruler, answerable only to the caliph who appointed him. Some *walis* were allowed more freedom of action than others, but none dared counter the caliph's edicts, and all were subject to his vagaries and caprices. Since revenue was a caliph's major concern, *walis* expected their petitions related to this issue to be granted. However, when ibn Sharik, one of the more avaricious, cruel and unpleasant characters who governed Egypt from 709 to 714 CE, wrote to the caliph asking for permission to annul the poll-tax exemption granted to individuals who converted to Islam, the caliph was persuaded by his courtiers to deny the request.[198] Ibn Sharik, most likely incredulous at the response, wrote again to point out that another *wali*, el-Haggag ibn Yousef, had been following that policy in Iraq, and that conversions to Islam in Egypt had resulted in reducing the funds granted to public officials in the form of salaries by twenty thousand dinars.[199] Inexplicably the caliph remained unconvinced and sent a message that stated, "I have bidden my messenger to give you twenty blows on the head."[200] Unsurprisingly, the sole determinants of the *wali's* actions and policies were his own and the caliph's moods, whims and passing fancies.

The root cause of misuse of authority was not merely due to the caliph making unfortunate choices of *walis*. The problem was systemic and linked to the historical development of the office of the caliphate. The caliphate is not a religious designation, but a political leadership position.[201] The term does, however, imply that the occupier of the office is God's representative on earth. The concept is somewhat similar to the Japanese concept of the Mandate of Heaven in that it allows for the possibility of deposing the ruler in certain circumstances. In practice, however, it was more analogous to the concept of the European Divine Right of Kings that viewed the right to rule as God given and irrevocable. Nevertheless, the religious cover never deterred plots and intrigues against a sitting caliph or protected him from those intent on murdering him when it suited their purpose.

Ibn Khaldun astutely asserts that the establishment of a central authority among the tribes of the Arabian Peninsula would not have been possible without the fusion of political and religious authority. Only the advent of Islam and the concentration of religious and political authority in the hands of the Prophet made central rule possible for the first time in the history of the Bedouins of the

Arabian Peninsula. After the passing of the Prophet, his successor must have been cognizant of the need to legitimize his position as the new leader. He did not, therefore, take a title such as ruler, king, sultan, or any title that connotes worldly authority. Instead, he took the title of caliph, which means successor or deputy. The implication of course was that he was the successor to the Prophet and, therefore, had a legitimate right to govern. Even the title *Amir el-Momneen* (Prince of the Believers), a title often used by the second caliph, implied religious authority. The legitimacy of the régime in Arab and Muslim eyes rested, therefore, on the implied notion that the caliphate was the manifestation of God's rule.[202] The first explicit claim to a heavenly mandate did not occur until the Abbasid era under the second Abbasid caliph, Abu Ga'far el-Mansour, who ruled from 754 to 775. He is credited with establishing the *hakimiyya* (rule in the name of God) principle by stating in a speech that he was God's sultan.[203] Although the Abbasid Caliphate (750-935) was founded by Abul Abbas Abdulla bin Mohammed, it was his brother, Mansour, who strengthened the state and is considered by many historians as the true founder of that dynasty.

The notion that the office of the caliphate has the explicit approval and blessings of religious doctrine gives it a powerful claim to legitimacy. Scholars as different as ibn Khaldun in the fourteenth century and Patricia Crone and Michael Hinds in the twentieth century came to the same conclusion about the caliphate. Namely, that the Arab Bedouins would have been very unlikely to accept central authority had that authority not been viewed as an intrinsic part of religious doctrine. Their radical change of fortune from starvation, indigence, wretchedness, or what Crone and Hinds termed "their immemorial life of 'sand and lice' for incredible wealth and power" would have been viewed as solid proof that the heavens were smiling down upon them.[204] And although the Arabs did revert to their *gaheliyya* practice of resisting central authority as soon as the first phase of the conquests ended, the office of the caliphate remained an influential basis of legitimacy for the person who occupied it.

Overt and unconcealed force remained the main foundation of rule in Egypt for about two centuries. The Arabs never found it necessary to pursue a path that might have created a semblance of legitimacy to their governance of Egypt until the majority of the population had become Muslim by about the middle of the ninth century.[205] For the native Egyptians, inherently conservative as many in peasant societies tend to be, and long accustomed to central authority, the office of caliph implied a stability that gave it a strong appeal. The belief that the world had been created out of disorder and disarray, and that only the gods could guarantee against return to the original state of anarchy and disarray, had always been at the core of traditional religious doctrine for millennia.[206] The threat of chaos that emerged periodically from the harsh deserts that bordered the Nile Valley[207] was an ever-present reminder of danger posed by disorder.

That fear of instability played very well into the hands of the country's foreign rulers. The Egyptians, perhaps even more than most peasant societies, craved order and continuity and feared sudden or unfamiliar changes.[208] Consequently, the notion that the caliph had the right to rule them simply because he was the caliph eventually took root and became generally accepted amongst Egyptians. The notion has even survived in some circles in contemporary society. Accepting the caliphate's legitimacy, however, did not necessarily imply loving or identifying with the person who occupied the office or with those individuals that he appointed to rule Egypt in his name. Rather, Egyptians sought stability and imagined that they had found it in the caliphate.

In time, the caliph's linkage to the Prophet weakened, and after the death of the fourth of the Guided Caliphs, Ali, the official fusion of religious and worldly authority became diluted.[209] The Umayyads, another clan of the Quraish tribe, who succeeded Ali, abandoned their home in the Arabian Peninsula, and ruled from the more pleasant environment of Damascus, did not enjoy the same religious authority. They were too far removed from the era of the prophecy to claim the same type of legitimacy that the Prophet's companions claimed and adopted. However, with the sanction of the religious establishment, they adopted the title *Caliphat Allah* (God's Successor) as their title,[210] and the religious inference conveyed by their chosen title served to provide a seemingly sacred and indisputable justification for their actions and policies and, therefore, cover for any injustice that they committed. The system did not provide for any effective oversight of the caliph's actions and policies. He was merely expected to be just and not oppress the people, and to obey divine law and uphold the tenets of religion. In many cases, he did none of that. The fact that he was an absolute ruler who controlled both the army and the state revenue meant that he could use both the carrot and the stick to insure the compliance as well as the cooperation of the notables, the rebellious tribesmen, the general population in the conquered territories, as well as the *ulama* (learned men of religion).

The income of the state came from taxes levied on the peoples of the conquered territories, and there were no other groups that had access to independent sources of income. Consequently, there were no centers of independent power that may have served as checks on the caliph's actions. The notables, the tribal chiefs, as well as the *ulama* were completely dependent on the caliph for their income and/or privileges.[211] In theory, the *ulama* were the only guarantee provided by this system that the ruler's actions would be just and in accordance with the tenets of religion. That principle had caveats added to it by some *ulama*. Abu Hamed el-Ghazali (1058-1111), for example, maintained that obedience should not preclude speaking out against injustice.[212] That caveat, however, was discarded by later scholars who began to stress the absolute necessity of obedience to the ruler regardless of any injustice.[213] Other *ulama*, such as Ali el-Mawardi (991-1031), also stressed the need to obey the ruler on the basis that the caliphate is a mandate by God, not based on man-made law.[214] Badr el-Din ibn Jama (1241-1333) went even further by claiming that the ruler is God's shadow on earth.[215]

Not surprisingly, the religious cover that obscured the different roles of government and religion, and the absence of checks and balances, led to despotic rule even in situations where actions were in clear violation of both tribal traditions and the tenets of religion. For example, when the caliph Abdel Malek was on his deathbed he called for his son to advise him on the procedures of succession. Instead of reminding the son of the tribal tradition of communal selection of leaders, the son was advised to call the tribal elders together and ask them for their homage and pledge of allegiance by the leaders, which is the traditional Bedouin method of selecting a ruler (*bay'a*). Anyone who did not acquiesce with the selection and make the pledge of allegiance, the father advised, should have his neck severed.[216] The Umayyad caliph Omar ibn Abdel Aziz (717-720 CE), who sat in Damascus, once decreed that the living relatives of deceased Egyptian taxpayers had to pay the poll tax that had been levied on them before they died.[217] The caliph had based his decree on the ruling, offered by Arrak bin Malek, that since the Egyptians were akin to slaves to the Arabs they should be able to tax them as they saw fit.[218] If that was the view of ibn Abdel Aziz, who is generally viewed by Arab historians as a paragon of virtue and the exemplar of just rulers, then the majority of less exalted rulers must have concurred with that position. In fact, Maqrizi, who related the incident, goes on to list several authorities that concurred with the view that the Egyptians were the slaves of the Arabs because the country was taken by force. Both the Muslim *ulama* and the Christian theologians have generally been only too happy to provide appropriate *fatwas* or religious rulings to justify any action taken by the caliph. Examples are not difficult to find. When the Umayyad caliph Yazid ibn Abdel Malek asked theologians (the *ulama*) whether God would make the caliphs account for their deeds on judgment day, forty of them assured him that God does not view caliphs like everybody else and exempts them from having to answer for their actions.[219] When the Ottoman Sultan, Mohammed III (1595-1603), expressed concern that a member of his family *could* be tempted to plot against him, or lead a palace coup to replace him, the accommodating *ulama* duly issued an expedient *fatwa*. They declared that religious doctrine does not prohibit the sultan from executing the suspects because he would be serving the nation by averting a *fitna* (sedition, tumult, or turbulence).[220] The sultan proceeded to kill nineteen of his brothers and two of his own sons who *may* or *may not* have been *thinking* of plotting to replace him.[221]

The Christian church leaders' position was no different from their Muslim counterparts. When the Abbasid Caliph, el-Ma'moun, travelled from Baghdad in 832 CE to put down one of the many tax rebellions in Egypt, he took with him Patriarch Dionysius of Antioch. Upon their arrival in Egypt, Patriarch Abba Joseph of Alexandria went to meet with the caliph and the Patriarch and both church leaders attempted, unsuccessfully, to convince the Christian rebels that disobeying the caliph is a sin against God. Patriarch Abba Joseph had already written to the rebelling Bashmurite villages in the

Nile Delta warning them of the dire consequences of insurgency, quoting passages from the Holy Book, and advising them of Paul's decree that disobedience of the sultan amounts to disobedience of God and merits condemnation.[222] The cause of the revolt had been the incessant demand for payment of exorbitant taxes despite the poverty of the taxpayers. The villagers were so destitute that, as Severus ibn el-Muqaffa' (d. 987), one of the most reliable historians of the Egyptian Church reports, a multitude of men, women and children died of starvation, and still others were forced to sell their own children to raise the funds mandated by tax collectors.[223] Others were "tied to the mills and beaten, so that they should work the mills like cattle."[224]

The caliph ruthlessly suppressed the rebellion, killing the men, then burning their houses, laying waste to their churches and selling their women and children as slaves.[225] Maqrizi confirms the account of what took place and reports that the caliph did indeed order the killing of the Egyptian villagers and the taking of their women and children to be sold as slaves.[226] When Dionysius timidly brought up the subject of the tyranny of the tax collectors, the caliph not only warned him not to discuss the subject, but also advised him to leave Egypt immediately because these tax collectors were supporters of his (the caliph's) brother, who would put Dionysius to the sword as soon as he was made aware of his criticism of the tax collectors.[227]

Examples of despotism and the whimsical actions of the caliphs as well as their appointed *walis* are not difficult to find. The Umayyad Caliph Abdel Malek ibn Marawan prohibited people from even speaking in his presence and decreed that if anyone advised him to fear God (*taqwa*),[228] he would order him to be beheaded. Warning his subjects of the dire consequences of disobeying him, el-Haggag bin Yousef el-Thaqafi once announced that if he ordered someone to exit the mosque from one door and the person exited from another, he would sever his neck.[229] El-Walid bin Abdel Malek was giving the Friday religious sermon out in the open on a hot day, and it gradually became too hot for his audience to remain sitting in the sun while he continued his seemingly interminable monologue. When a member of the congregation attempted to draw his attention to the situation, he ordered his guards to sever his neck immediately.[230]

One of the most eccentric rulers was the Fatimid Caliph el-Hakem bi Amr ellah (985 - 1021), who once decreed that Egyptians were prohibited, on pain of death, from eating *mulukhiyya*, a soup dish still popular in Egypt today.[231] At another time, he decreed that everyone should sleep during the day and work at night only.[232] He also decreed that women were not to go out of their houses and that any shoemakers who made women's shoes were to be executed. In addition, he prohibited singing; dancing, and taking pleasure boat rides on the Nile.[233] The eccentric blue-eyed caliph's next act was to announce to the population that he was divine, a claim that was supported by the newly established Druze sect.[234] Shortly after that, he went out for a ride on his donkey one evening in the nearby Muqattam Hills and was never heard from again.

In theory, the system provided for some checks on the caliph's actions, whose duties were, as Afaf Al-Sayyid Marsot points out, to rule justly and in accordance with the tenants of Islam and the *Sunni* tradition.[235] The *ulama*, who enjoyed moral authority stemming from their knowledge of the Book of God and religious tradition, were supposed to perform the supervisory role in the system by insuring that the caliph's actions were consistent with religious doctrine. However, as the examples cited earlier show, the imbalance of power between the two parties did not contribute to the facilitation of the *ulama's* task. The system, as the following example further illustrates, was far from perfect. The Fatimids, whose North African caliphate had made several unsuccessful attempts to invade Egypt from the west, finally succeeded in taking the country in 969. When their Caliph, el-Mu'izz, who maintained that he descended from the Prophet, arrived in Egypt to claim his prize, the *ulama* met him to enquire about his descent before they could accept him as one of the small group of *Ashraf* (descendants of the Prophet). El-Mu'izz's answer to the query was to draw his sword and tell them that that was his genealogy, then to scatter gold coins on the floor and tell them that that was his lineage. The delegation made no further enquiries of man.[236]

To be sure, el-Mu'izz turned out to have qualities that were in very short supply among those who had ruled Egypt since the Arab invasion. He was an educated and compassionate ruler[237] whose policies toward peasants were fair and just.[238] Nevertheless, his response to the *ulama* provides a clear illustration of the complexity of the *ulama's* task and the ease with which they could be intimidated or co-opted, especially by the more tyrannical rulers, of whom there were many. In many cases, the rulers were basically tribal chiefs or warlords with a limited understanding of the role of government as a social institution, which did not extend beyond grasping its utility as a tool of personal wealth and personal aggrandizement. They had a very short-term view of their tenure in office and no vision for the country that they ruled. As there were no written laws clearly spelling out their rights and obligations, beyond their obligation to abide by God's laws as interpreted by the *ulama*, they were more or less free to follow their whims.

The centuries following the Arab invasion witnessed the continued Bedouinization of Egyptian society's culture; the reinforcement, albeit in varying degrees, of despotic rule and oppression; and extended periods of instability and unrest. Instability continued when the caliphate changed hands and went from the Umayyads who sat in Damascus to another branch of the Quraish[239] tribe—the Abbasids—who were descended from the Hashemite branch[240] and sat in Baghdad. In addition to their employment of the revolving door policy for the appointment of governors to the conquered lands, the caliphs increasingly began to favor Iranians and Turks for appointments to prominent positions in the court. These non-Arabs were neither supported by a powerful tribe nor able to claim religious legitimacy on the basis of belonging to the Prophet's tribe, Quraish. The Abbasids believed that these two factors served to reduce the likelihood of insurgence. As an additional precaution, the caliphs began to use Mamluks[241] as personal guards, and before long they and the local *walis* had also begun to rely on them to staff their armies.

Mamluk is an Arabic term that means the owned one. The Mamluks, therefore, were—at least technically—slaves, but slaves with a difference. Brought as children from countries as far as away as Armenia, Bosnia, Georgia, Greece, Russia, Sudan, and Western Europe, they were trained as soldiers,[242] and instead of occupying the lowest ranks on the social scale and being forced into the least desirable occupations in society, they were an elite group that formed a separate aristocracy. They lived apart from the rest of the population and rarely intermarried with the natives. Their children were usually employed in clerical and administrative positions and were not allowed to join the army, which was always staffed by newly imported Mamluks.[243] They were granted special privileges, treated as favored courtiers enjoying both power and privilege, and granted titles such as prince and bey. They rode around on thoroughbred horses, dressed in the most luxurious attire, and were extremely loyal to their overlords. Those who belonged to the same overlord felt a very strong bond to one another.[244] As their influence increased, they became yet another element in the continuing unrest, with the various princes fighting one another as well as the rebellious Arab chieftains.

As a direct outcome of this policy, the year 868 CE witnessed the start of a new trend in the rule of Egypt. Instead of selecting an Arab to be the *wali* of Egypt, as had been the norm since the invasion, the Abbasids, in keeping with their new strategy, appointed Ahmad ibn Tulun, the son of a Turkish Mamluk from Mongolia whose name means the perfect or complete Bedouin.[245] However, ibn Tulun turned out to be not only ambitious but also shrewd, and he soon accomplished what the caliphs in Baghdad had always feared—almost autonomous rule. He arrived in Egypt poor, in dire straits, and looked down upon by everyone.[246] In contrast, the local tax collector was living in utter luxury and employed a hundred bodyguards, all attired in luxurious outfits, accompanying his every move.[247] Despite his poverty, ibn Tulun was astute enough to refuse a gift of 10,000 dinars (worth over one and a half million US dollars today)[248] offered him by the collector, and quickly preceded to build himself a power base.[249] He canceled some of the taxes levied on the Egyptians,[250] repaired the country's neglected infrastructure, such as the Nilometer and the Alexandria lighthouse, and gained popular support for maintaining security and law and order throughout the country. Egypt enjoyed a period of relative stability and prosperity. Eventually ibn Tulun built a new capital, el-Qatae', and established a nominally independent state that he intended his descendants to rule.

Ibn Tulun's successors, however, lacked his leadership abilities, and in 905 CE, the Abbasids sent an army led by Mohammed ibn Seliman el-Kateb that defeated the then *wali*, Shayban ibn Ahmad ibn Tulun. Afterwards, they burnt el-Qatae', looted el-Fustat, raped the women, and committed what one historian termed "skin curdling atrocities."[251] They went on a rampage "severing necks, cutting hands and feet, tearing backs with whips, and crucifying people on palm trees."[252] The era of nominal independence and relative stability was thus ended. Kateb governed Egypt for only four months before setting off for home with his army. By the time he arrived in el-Sham (Greater Syria), an emissary from the caliph reached him with instructions to hand over all the gold, horses, and valuable fabrics that had been looted from Egypt.[253] Naturally, this had the worst impact on the victorious commander and members of his entourage.[254] One of his commanders, an officer of the defeated Tulunid army named ibn el-Khalig, was elected by a number of troops and other officers to command a new army that set off to re-re-conquer Egypt and re-establish the semi-independent state, starting yet another cycle of unrest that did not end with his defeat seven months later.[255]

Following the end of the Tulunid dynasty, the Abbasid caliphate resumed its policy of constantly changing the *walis* in Egypt. The official count was seventeen different administrations during the period between 905 and 934 CE, with the average tenure of each administration being 1.7 years.[256] This figure is, however, inaccurate since the number of people who actually governed the country during this period was greater, but historians have excluded several names from the list of *walis* for various reasons. For example, the first ruler, el-Kateb, is excluded on the basis that he was the leader of the re-conquering army and was not a formally appointed *wali*. The same applies to ibn el-Khalig, referred to above, who ruled for seven months and twenty days,[257] and was seeking to re-institute the Tulunid rule rather than represent the caliph. Another *wali*, Aba Qaboos, is excluded because his tenure only lasted three days.[258]

This pattern of pernicious government, long periods of unrest, instability, fighting among the various factions, and concomitant suffering inflicted upon the Egyptians continued during the succeeding centuries. The change of the governorship of Egypt from the Arabs to their agents and retainers did nothing to ease the instability or the tax burden on the indigenous population, and the Egyptians were constantly rebelling against the extortionist taxation system. Periodic tax protests of varying intensity and seriousness became a permanent feature of the Egyptian social scene during the succeeding centuries, with actual tax rebellions occurring every few years.[259] The much abused and exploited peasants sometimes resorted to physically attacking or even murdering those who arrived at their villages to collect the tax.[260] There were even instances where the villagers resorted to the desperate measure of destroying their crops, and fleeing their villages rather than giving them up to the tax collectors.[261]

Semi independence was achieved again when another ambitious *wali* who had been appointed in 935 CE managed to follow in the steps of ibn Tulun and to found the nominally independent Ikhshidi dynasty only to be defeated in 969 CE by the Maghrebis who attacked Egypt from the west. Earlier invasions by the Maghrebis had been repulsed, but Egypt had been weakened by a major famine in 967 and a major epidemic that took the lives of hundreds of thousands.[262] These latest invaders belonged to the *Shi'a* branch of Islam and believed themselves to be the true and legitimate heirs of the Prophet. They established the independent Fatimid Caliphate in Egypt and the country enjoyed relative stability until their inevitable eventual decline and defeat at the hands of the Ayyoubids, who attacked from the east. Subjecting the country to a period of large scale murder, pillage and looting, which extended to burning the extensive Fatimid library, they ruled Egypt from 1169 to 1250 as a nominally independent province.[263]

The Mamluks and the Ottomans

The Ayyoubids, who were *Sunni* Kurds, introduced a new element that was to play a decisive role in the history of Egypt until the nineteenth century. Instead of using Mamluks as personal guards as the Abbasids did, they began to rely on them increasingly as their fighting force and imported large numbers of them during the twelfth and thirteenth centuries.[264]

As the demand for Mamluks increased, slave traders in both the east and Italy competed to supply them. Turks, Circassians, Mongols, Sicilians, Greeks, Spaniards, and Germans were among the Mamluks brought to Egypt.[265] Some came from as far as the

Baltics.²⁶⁶ Knowledge of the wealth of Egypt and of the opportunities for riches and high position that awaited a talented and skilled Mamluk served to encourage some parents in these faraway countries to sell their children and guaranteed an ample supply of Mamluks.²⁶⁷ The increase in numbers and influence of the Mamluks finally culminated in their killing of Toran Shah, the last Ayyoubid ruler, and the ushering in of a new chapter in the history of the much suffering population.

The first ruler of the Mamluk era in Egypt proved to be a new and unique phenomenon that has not reoccurred until the present time. On June 6, 1249 CE, Louis IX, the king of France, led a crusade that landed at Damietta in Northern Egypt and took the town. The ruler, el-Malek el-Saleh Ayyoub mobilized his army, rushed to confront the invaders, and engaged the French in several minor but inconclusive skirmishes.²⁶⁸ Accompanying Ayyoub was his closest confidant and advisor, his wife, Shagret el-Dorr (the tree of pearls).²⁶⁹ She was a beautiful and intelligent Armenian who had been a concubine he had fallen in love with and married. As his son, Toran Shah, was an impulsive and unreliable playboy, Shagret el-Dorr became Ayyoub's intimate companion and counselor in all matters of state. When Ayyoub succumbed to tuberculosis and died on November 23, Shagret el-Dorr understood the catastrophic implications of such news on the army's morale on the eve of a major battle, and decided to conceal her husband's death.²⁷⁰ She sent a trusted messenger to summon his heir, Toran Shah, from Syria, while she assumed command of the Egyptian army. Shagret el-Dorr told the commanders that her husband was sick, wanted to rest, and ordered food brought daily into their tent as usual.²⁷¹ Mamluk officers loyal to Shagret el-Dorr guarded the royal tent and the army commanders were ordered to report to it daily, ostensibly to brief their commander-in-chief on the situation and to receive his written orders.²⁷² As one of Shagret el-Dorr's trusted eunuchs was able to forge the sultan's signature, she was able to maintain the charade, direct the course of the war, and keep the situation under control until the arrival of Toran Shah. Her courage and resourcefulness saved the day, and the French were temporarily repelled on February 11, 1250.²⁷³

When Toran Shah finally arrived at the scene at the end of February 1250 with a group of his Syrian cronies, Shagret el-Dorr announced the death of el-Malek el-Saleh and proclaimed his son as his successor. He immediately proceeded to quarrel with Shagret el-Dorr, to alienate the senior army commanders by appointing his incompetent friends to high positions, and to spend all his time drinking with his pals. Nevertheless, the army commanders maintained discipline and the French were finally routed on April 5 and Louis IX taken prisoner. However, the new Sultan's irresponsible behavior had only served to reinforce the army commanders' loyalty to Shagret el-Dorr, and having eliminated the invasion threat, the Mamluks turned their attention to the foolish young man. They killed him on May 2, 1250, thus ending the Ayyoubid dynasty that had ruled Egypt since Salah el-Din el-Ayyouby.[274]

The Mamluks then proclaimed Shagret el-Dorr as the new ruler of Egypt and returned to Cairo where the people were exhilarated with the victory over the French and endorsed their choice. Shagaret el-Dorr took the business of running the country seriously and pursued policies that increased her popularity. She is also credited with having started the tradition of *el-Mahmal*, a tradition of manufacturing and sending to Mecca a rich cloth embroidered in gold with religious verses to cover the Ka'ba.[275] This custom continued until the Wahabis, viewing it as an expression of vanity and indulgence, prohibited it in the nineteenth century[276] but was resumed after their defeat by Mohammed Ali.

An astute woman, Shagaret el-Dorr recognized the prevailing misogynist tendencies she had to contend with and chose el-Mo'tasema el-Salehia, Queen of the Muslims, after the Arab Caliph el-Mo'tasem in Baghdad, as her official title[277] in the hope of appeasing him. The strategy did not work and Mo'tasem, a man not known for either astuteness or statesmanship but who nevertheless commanded a great deal of religious prestige as the caliph, did not approve of the Egyptians' choice. He sent a message stating that if they cannot find a man in Egypt to rule over them, he would send them one.[278] A compromise was reached whereby Shagret el-Dorr married the victorious army's commander-in-chief, Prince Aybak, who was proclaimed sultan and ruled under the name el-Malek el-Mu'izz, thus ending a unique episode in the history of the Islamic Empire. To this day Shagaret el-Dorr remains the only Muslim queen to have ruled in her own right and to have had currency struck and prayers in mosques said in her name as well as that of the Abbasid caliph.

The Mamluk rule of Egypt, which began so promisingly with Shagaret el-Dorr, quickly developed the same traits as earlier eras. Periodic instability, famines, constant clashes between the various Mamluk factions and concomitant terrorizing of the population, despotism, and excessive taxation, were the major characteristics of the Mamluk period. Each Mamluk believed that he had just as much right to rule as any other Mamluk. Any news of the death or illness of the sultan, or of a defeat suffered by his army somewhere, usually triggered a cycle of unrest, rape, and pillage.[279] The inescapable result of the absence of an accepted means of succession and transfer of political authority was that violence eventually became the only means of power transfer, and during the time the Mamluks ruled Egypt, murdering the sultan was the generally accepted method of taking the reins of power.[280] In addition, the Arab tribes that had migrated to Egypt following the invasion had not abandoned their antipathy towards central authority, and continued their age-old tradition of periodic rebellion against the rulers in Cairo and pillage of Egyptian villages in the rest of the country. By the middle ages, numerous tribes had come to Egypt and spread to various parts of the country, and they were a constant source of both agitation and subversion for the rulers and of robbery and plunder for the rest of the population.[281] Historical accounts of these tribes' lives in Egypt during the Mamluk era are nothing more than lists of their murderous rampages throughout the country.[282] Whenever contemporary historians analyze this period, they do so under the heading "corruption caused by the Arabs."[283]

The Arab tribal chiefs nursed a deep grievance against the Mamluks. They believed that they, simply by virtue of being Arabs, had more right to rule the country that their ancestors conquered.[284] There were constant rebellions by the tribes at the start of every new sultan's reign or whenever the sultan was weak. In 1250, for example, one tribe rebelled, and its chief declared himself king of Upper Egypt. He proceeded to attack Lower Egypt in 1253 but was defeated by Sultan Aybak.[285] In 1290 there were two rebellions; in 1300 they rebelled again and were defeated a year later.[286] After their defeat in 1301 and throughout the fourteenth and fifteen centuries, the Arabs tended to limit their activities to the relatively safe pursuits of pillaging and robbing unarmed villages of their crops and animal herds.[287] When the Arab tribes rebelled once again in 1661, their leader was caught and hanged.[288] After that, there were no other major rebellions by the Arabs.

Though sometimes singled out for a negative assessment by contemporary historians, perhaps because they were not ethnic Arabs, the Mamluks were not as different from many of the other rulers who preceded them as some historical analyses might imply. The Mamluk era was undoubtedly characterized by the instability, injustice, despotism, economic ruination, and famine that had characterized earlier eras. In the words of one historian, "the plagues and famines that inflicted Egypt during the reign of the Mamluks are too many to examine."[289] Nevertheless, it would be incorrect to conclude, as is fashionable for many contemporary historians to do, that the Mamluks' negative qualities were unique among Egypt's rulers. They were simply following a long tradition of despotism and misrule that the Egyptians had been subjected to in one form or another since they lost their independence following the death of Cleopatra.

The Mamluk rule ended with the appearance of the next crude and untutored invaders, the Ottomans, who defeated them and captured Cairo on January 31, 1517. They began their reign in Egypt with the by now familiar cycle of rape, pillage, destruction and terrorization of the Cairenes, while some of the Mamluk princes fled to Upper Egypt and continued to resist the new invaders.[290] The Ottoman capture of Cairo on that January day was, according to Mohammed ibn Ahmad ibn Iyas (1448-1522), "a great catastrophe, the like of which had never been heard of,"[291] and over ten thousand people were killed in four days and their bodies either left in the streets or thrown in the Nile.[292]

The Ottoman rule of Egypt ushered in yet another dark episode in Egypt's history. Sultan Selim I, commander of the victorious army, was not content with robbing Egypt's gold and valuable objects but took its people too. He remained almost eight months in Egypt during which time he attempted to strip the country bare of all material and human resources of any value and take them home with him. According to ibn Iyas, the Ottomans took valuable books from schools and systematically press-ganged, and shipped to Turkey many scholars, merchants, and craftsmen.[293] In April/May 1517, they transported both Muslim and Christian stone workers, builders, engineers, marble cutters and polishers, carpenters, ironsmiths, and tile layers.[294] On June 11, 1517, to the dismay of the local population, the invaders even took the Chief Justice and other administrators and sent them to Istanbul,[295] and on 26 June 1517, they transported another 1800 craftsmen.[296] The Egyptian economy was devastated and over fifty crafts died overnight.[297]

In addition to plundering Egypt's human resources, the Ottomans also took almost everything else that was transportable. They stripped the marble[298] and the ornate columns[299] from the Cairo Citadel to ship to Istanbul, and the troops even took doors off their hinges and stripped carved wood from ceilings to take with them.[300] When Sultan Selim I eventually left, his caravan consisted of one hundred camels laden with gold and looted valuables in addition to a multitude of life stock, horses, mules, camels, and his viziers and troops left similarly laden.[301] The Ottoman invasion created considerable and widespread suffering throughout Egypt.[302] In addition, the villages of the Sharqiyya province, which borders the desert, suffered further as the Arabs there took advantage of the turmoil caused by the Ottoman conquest and began to loot and pillage the villages.[303] The Egyptians, ibn Iyas maintained, "had not seen worse suffering since Amr ibn el-Aas opened Egypt."[304]

Social instability was further exacerbated by the Ottomans' inability to eradicate the influence of the Mamluk princes who were renowned fighters. Eventually they were forced to share power with them, thus weakening the central authority. All the major decisions were made either by the Mamluk princes or with their prior approval. The Ottoman appointed *wali* was effectively no more than one of several centers of political power in the country. He governed at the Mamluks' pleasure and was only allowed to retain his position for as long as he was accepted by them.[305] Once he fell out of favor with the *beys* (Mamluk Princes), they simply sent him a messenger telling him to pack up and leave or risk losing his life.[306]

Political instability during the Ottoman era is evidenced by the fact that one hundred and forty three pashas (*walis*) were appointed to govern Egypt during the two hundred and eighty one year period between their conquest of Egypt in 1517 and the arrival of the French in 1798, making the average tenure of each one a mere 1.96 years.[307] However, even that figure is distorted since a small number of governors were able to retain their positions for several years. Seliman Pasha[308] and Dawood Pasha,[309] for example, ruled for ten years (from June/July 1525) and eleven years (from June 1538), respectively. But a few months tenure (as little as two and a half months in one case) was the norm for the majority of governors.[310] The Turkish occupation was a dark period of ignorance, isolation, stagnation, and instability during which Egypt, as one writer put it, "exited history."[311]

Hence, there was not a great deal to distinguish Ottoman rule from the Mamluks' apart from the addition of the Ottomans as another element of instability and despotism in society. The country remained isolated from the rest of the world, and its people were abused and exploited. The tradition of misrule that began when Egypt fell victim to foreign invaders continued unabated except for short periods when a just or enlightened ruler happened to take charge of the country. Otherwise, each ruler's single concern was extracting as much tax revenue as possible from the long-suffering people then taking his loot home when he was deposed and forced to leave the country.

Egypt's foreign/Arab rulers, throughout the long period of their occupation of the country, never made any pretense that the taxes they collected were intended for the common benefit of society or for the maintenance of services to the population. Over a thousand years after the Arab conquest a delegation of sheikhs (learned men) led a large number of people in June/July 1795 to the house of Ibrahim bey (one of the senior Mamluk princes) to complain about excessive taxes levied on a village by el-Alfi bey, another senior Mamluk prince. He refused to see them himself and sent his *dafterdar* (treasurer) to listen to their petition. Upon learning their demands, he informed them that taxes could not be reduced because "if we do that our living conditions will be restricted, and we'll not be able to meet our expenses."[312] When soldiers looted a Cairo neighborhood and Sheikh el-Dardeer, a religious scholar, appealed on their behalf to Ibrahim bey, he dismissed the complaint stating: "We're all looters, me, you, and Murad bey."[313]

The legacy of misrule in Egypt became so pervasive and entrenched that even today some of the weaker members of society do not feel that same confidence that their distant ancestor felt in the ability to obtain justice. An empirical study conducted by Sayyid 'Uways,[314] and published in 1988 examined the phenomenon of sending letters to dead holy men in contemporary society. The letters are usually deposited at the mosques where these holy men are buried. In carrying out a content analysis of these letters, the researcher found that they generally consist of pleas for help on a wide variety of issues. One of these letters was from a peasant living in Bani Swaif in Upper Egypt. When he analyzed its content, the researcher was surprised to find it very similar to the 4000-year-old papyrus scroll known as *The Tale of the Eloquent Peasant*. The papyrus was a letter that had been sent by a peasant to the Chief Clerk of the pharaoh's court complaining about an influential person in the Royal Court who had unlawfully taken some of his possessions, and the complainant was seeking redress of this injustice.[315] The contrast of the ancient Egyptian seeking justice through his government, and his modern descendant seeking justice from a dead holy man exemplifies the difference between the legitimacy, roles and concerns of the ancient and modern rulers of Egypt and the legacy of centuries of misrule. The modern peasant had evidently learned after centuries of despotism that an appeal to the deity rather than the system of justice was his only hope of righting a wrong. He was unknowingly following the advice of the eighth century Abbasid Caliph Abu Ga'far el-Mansour who once made a speech advising people to pray to God to inspire him to be kind to them.[316]

In effect, those who ruled Egypt after it lost its independence were, more often than not, little more than neighborhood thugs who terrorized the population and demanded "protection" money. They were foreign rulers who neither identified nor shared a great deal with the Egyptians. One old Egyptian proverb, that encapsulates the tragic history of Egypt, sums up the Egyptian people's feelings, and expresses the disconnection from their rulers in the simplest of terms, states: *bilad Misr khairha lighairha* (the land of Egypt, its wealth is for others).[317]

4

The Socio-Cultural Legacy of Subjugation

The culture, social structure, and values of ancient Egypt evolved over the millennia in response to the challenges and opportunities offered by the physical features of its environment. Central authority, the pharaoh's role, religious rituals, the calendar, social values, the role of women were all influenced to one degree or another by the country's physical features. Stability and continuity were core values and the social structure with the pharaoh as its central axis was designed to harmonize the relationship between the social and ecological forces. This balance was upset once Egypt lost its independence and became part of the Roman Empire. The introduction of Christianity and the establishment of the Coptic Church offered the hope of a return to stability based on the gradual construction of a new social order. That hope was thwarted by the systematic persecution of the Copts by the Romans, which weakened the country and enabled a relatively small group of poorly armed Bedouins from the Arabian Peninsula to occupy it with relative ease in 641 CE. The conquest gave the inhabitants of the Peninsula an opportunity to leave their impoverished home and whole tribes began to move to Egypt and initiate a demographic transition that altered the face of society. The culture was completely transformed and the waves of Bedouin migrants eventually brought about a change in language, religion, social structure, and values, as well as centuries of recurring invasions, instability, misrule, and socio-economic decay. The social contact that legitimized pharaonic rule was replaced by flagrant coercion and use of naked force to extract the wealth of Egypt and export it to faraway places rather invest it in homegrown projects. Instability and despotism became the most visible historical thread that linked Egypt's rulers from that time onwards.

The previously mentioned Murad bey, his fellow eighteenth century looters, self-identified or not, and all the other looters that had come before them from 641 CE onwards, had done much more, however, than plunder Egypt's treasure and ruin its once thriving economy. It was as if they had gutted it, ripped out its heart, and replaced it with an incompatible transplant with all the ensuing complications of such a mismatch. The effect was profound and devastating, and the general apathy, mistrust, and cynicism of modern day Egyptians towards government and those who hold the reins of government can be linked directly to the Egyptian experience ever since the seventh century. Where the ruler sat, in the Arabian Peninsula, in Damascus, Kufa, or in Istanbul, had become irrelevant, since all the rulers shared the same goal of extracting Egypt's wealth and taking it home with them. What is of utmost relevance, however, is that the immigrant Bedouin tribes had in time swamped the country and changed its very social fabric and value system.

Over a millennia of exploitative control of Egypt's resources and of Egyptians themselves had created individual anomie in a now Bedouinized society. That anomie and Bedouinization of society can be seen to have had a number of sources: the corrupt and dysfunctional system of government that was imposed on the country, the economic decline under this system, and the incompatible alien social and cultural values that this system imported into the country.

From Gleaming Marble to Devastation and Wretchedness

The diametrically opposite first impressions of two of Egypt's conquerors, whose arrival in Egypt was separated by more than a millennium, serve as a stark indicator of what befell Egypt during that period of rule by primitive, crude and avaricious invaders. In 641 CE, Amr ibn el-Aas, who had a reputation as a loquacious and persuasive talker, was almost struck dumb by the splendor, size, prosperity, and spectacular opulence that he found when his impoverished Bedouin army took Alexandria. He was awed by the colonnaded streets, the four thousand public baths, the "400 entertainment places for kings,"[1] and the twelve thousand green grocers.² But the city that one historian described as containing so much marble and alabaster that it was lit at night without lanterns,³ and that awnings of green silk were hung over the streets to relieve the dazzling glare of the marble and alabaster, this city no longer existed.

When Napoleon arrived in Alexandria in 1798 all he found were a few begrimed, destitute, and poverty-stricken shacks.⁴ He must have been as tongue-tied as Amr ibn el-Aas by what that fabled metropolis had turned into. The country that Maqrizi quoted Amr ibn el-Aas's son Abdullah as likening to paradise⁵ had changed a great deal. By the time of Napoleon's arrival in Egypt, extortionate taxation, plunder, accumulation of personal wealth by any means possible, and the search for buried pharaonic treasures, threads that connected the majority of its rulers from the seventh century onwards, had taken their toll. A millennium of extracting Egypt's wealth and exporting it to faraway destinations had left the country's infrastructure in ruins and the majority of the indigenous population living in squalor, so that what Bonaparte found was a "scene of devastation and misery."⁶

An unprecedented decline in the population of Egypt is also indicative of the personal and economic woes that the Egyptians suffered. This was the direct result of mismanagement and increasingly shortsighted avaricious and despotic rule after Amr was replaced as the representative of the caliph in Egypt. The figures indicate that despite the steady stream of Arab tribes arriving in the country over the centuries, there was an extraordinary drop in the population. The size of the population, which was thirty million in 641 CE, if we accept the highest estimate,⁷ or fifteen million if we accept the lowest, had dropped to just less than two and a half million in 1800.⁸ Famine, desertification, and land abandonment by the rural population, who were often reduced to indigence and destitution, were a direct result of the short-sighted avarice, despotism, and desire for immediate gain by the caliph's representatives

Coercion as the Only Foundation of Rule

Legitimate government in Egypt after the death of its last pharaoh became a distant memory as control of the country's destiny, resources, and people fell into the hands of one foreign ruler after another. In 641 CE, the wide chasm that developed between the ruler and the ruled begun with a Byzantine overlord deepened further. The next overlords were the early Arab *walis*, followed by Turks, Kurds, or Mamluks from a variety of backgrounds, and then the British, all of whom regarded the Egyptians as lesser beings. The Arabs viewed Egypt's disenfranchised population as a different and inferior caste. The first Umayyad caliph, Mu'awiya ibn Abi Sufyan (661-680), maintained, according to Maqrizi, that "three types of people [are] to be found in Egypt: a third are people, a third are pseudo-people, a third are non-people. The third that are people are the Arabs, the third that are pseudo-people are the *mawali* (subject peoples including Egyptians who converted to Islam), and the third that are non-people are the Copts [Egyptians]."[9] The disconnect between the rulers and the ruled resulted from the behavior of the rulers, which was a clear reflection of their attitude towards Egypt and its people and of the rulers' own limited world-view and socio-cultural paucity. The rulers of post 641 Egypt were no longer viewed as the preservers of the order and stability created by the goddess Maat, and Egyptians, as the eighteenth century historian, el-Gabarti, has pointed out, grew to "hate rulers of all shapes."[10] More recently, Abbas el-Aqqad has asserted that Egyptians feel suspicion and animosity toward governments.[11] Anne Rivlin, although less critical of the Turko/Mamluk era than many Egyptian researchers, has echoed the same sentiment. "Virtually the only link between the Egyptian people and their rulers," Rivlin states, "was through the system of taxation."[12] Afaf Al-Sayyid Marsot is even more explicit in the preface to her *A Short History of Modern Egypt*. "The major theme of this book" Marsot states "is the alienation of the population of Egypt from their rulers."[13] Gamal Hamdan maintains that "oppression, force, hatred, and despotism" have always characterized the relationship between the Egyptians and their rulers"[14] who act as if the country is their private property, and are "usually its biggest enemy."[15]

"Ruling gangs" rather than "ruling elites" would, Gamal Hamdan maintained, be a more accurate description of Egypt's rulers, who relied solely on the use of naked force to maintain their position.[16] He points to the fact that the primary function of the army in

Egypt was to protect the ruler and wage war, and that an attitude of paternalism has always characterized the country's rulers.[17]

Perhaps the word paternalism is overly generous since it implies a degree of love and care, albeit authoritarian, that seems to have been rather noticeably lacking. What was in abundance was the use of force to achieve the ruler's avaricious goals that could have left no doubt in the minds of the indigenous population that their welfare was not uppermost in their rulers' minds and was simply off their rulers' radar screens. Force of arms, then, rather than the rule of law or a popularly recognized social contract, formed the basis of their relationship. More often than not, the use of force against the population was ordered from the faraway capital of a foreign empire.

By about the middle of the ninth century the majority of the population of Egypt was Muslim,[18] but in spite of the religious veneer of legitimacy provided by the office of the caliphate, naked force continued through the centuries to be the main guarantor of submission to the rulers' bidding. Positive characteristics in the rulers seem to have been in short supply. In listing the various rulers' virtues, the historian ibn Iyas (1448-1522) does not find a great deal to say about some of them other than "it may be said that he was good natured, controlled his temper, and considering his passions was not overly violent,"[19] or, that the ruler "understood poetry."[20] By way of contrast, tyranny was taken for granted to the extent that el-Gabarti began his review of the events of the year AH 1209 (1794/1795 CE) by stating: "In AH 1209 no external events took place other than the princes' continued oppression and injustices."[21] Such statements tend to lend support to the claim made here that the gap that opened between the people and their ruler after the death of the last pharaoh was never bridged and continued to widen over the centuries.

Dual Calendars

Language was another daily reminder of the foreignness of the rulers. Many of Egypt's rulers did not speak the language of those they ruled. According to Maqrizi, Caliph el-Ma'moun (813-833), referred to earlier in connection with the Bashmurite rebellion, only spoke Arabic, and could not communicate with his Egyptian subjects without the use of translators who accompanied him everywhere.[22] The immigrant Bedouin tribes spoke Arabic, which did not become the language of the majority for at least two centuries, and Coptic was the native tongue used in Upper Egypt until the seventeenth century.[23] By the time Arabic had become the national language spoken by the majority of Egyptians[24] many of the Mamluk and Turkish rulers did not speak it.

Even the lunar calendar that was imposed on the country after the conquest became a constant reminder of the chasm with the foreign rulers. For an agrarian society that owes its existence to a single lifeline, the Nile, a calendar that is in tune with the local seasons, crops, and Nile inundation is central to its survival.[25] One of the most important tasks of the government was to design and implement appropriate policies for the organization and administration of the land and water resources,[26] and the Egyptians had developed an accurate calendar that met these needs. Every aspect of Egyptian life was organized around the Coptic, i.e. Egyptian calendar: from preparing the seeds, to the planting and gathering of each crop, to tax collection, to the foods that were consumed at different times of the year, to the local feasts, celebrations, and days of rest.[27] Even the dates of *mouleds* (the local holy men or saints' birthdays) in Egypt were set according to the Coptic calendar based on the agricultural cycle.[28]

In their very different physical, social, and political environment, Bedouins, on the other hand, never saw the need to develop a calendar. A simple reckoning of the months according to the phases of the moon suited their lifestyle. *Moharram*, for example, a term that means prohibited, denoted the month during which raiding and pillaging, which was the Bedouin men's major occupation, was prohibited.[29] *Safar* denoted the month when the villages and settlements were usually empty because the tribes went out to raid one another, and *Sha'ban* was yet another warring month.[30] *Ramadan* is called thus because the weather happened to have been hot at that time of year when the month was named, suggesting that the Bedouins did not appear to have realized that a lunar year is approximately eleven days shorter than the seasonal heat and cold cycle, and *Zulqe'dah* was another month when they rested from their warfare.[31]

The Arabs' need for a calendar only arose when vast amounts of gold, valuable objects, foodstuffs, and manufactured goods looted from the peoples of the conquered territories began to fill the empty deserts of the Arabian Peninsula. That need came to light when one of the second Guided Caliph's agents wrote to him asking whether a communication that he had received applied to the current year's month of *Sha'ban* or the next one.[32] Recognizing the seriousness of the new problem, the caliph gathered his companions and informed them that they had a great deal of money now and did not know how to divide it up in an accurate manner.[33] They were all perplexed and unable to make any suggestions. Advice was then sought from el-Hormozan, King of Ahwaz, who had been taken prisoner and sent to Medina after Fares (present day Iran) was invaded.[34] Iran had an old and advanced civilization before the Bedouins invaded it, and seeking the advice of Hormozan was the logical course of action. He informed the group that they (the Iranians) used a system that they call the *'mah rouz'*, which means in Farsi the calculation of days and months and which began with the first year of the reign of each of their kings, and he went on to explain how that system worked.[35] They Arabized the Farsi term for calendar but were unable to agree on a date for the start of their calendar.[36] Finally, they decided to select the date of the *higra* (the Prophet's migration from Mecca to Medina) because it was the only date of which they were certain.[37]

The development of a calendar solved the caliph's problems but complicated life for the Egyptians. The Arabs discarded the Egyptian solar calendar and based their tax collection on their newly developed lunar calendar.[38] The imposition of a calendar that met the requirements of those who collected the taxes rather than the needs of those who grew the crops, which formed the tax base, forced the people to use two different calendars and served as a daily reminder of the indigenous population's separateness from their rulers. What the Egyptians needed in a calendar was one that marked when to plough the land, when to sow the seeds, and when to reap their crops, not when to go to raid and pillage their neighbors and when to take a rest from warfare. The appropriateness of the Coptic calendar to the local environmental conditions, and the significant role it played in people's day-to-day pursuits is demonstrated even today in the fact that it continues to be the point of reference when contemporary Egyptians discuss topics such as crops, vegetables and fruits in season, or the weather.

Another indicator of the them and us attitude that characterized the relationship between the rulers and the ruled was communal celebrations. Annual or seasonal social events, such as festivals that most communities celebrate, play an important role in society by reaffirming what sociologists refer to as the collective consciousness. They reflect shared values and function as a means of affirming community solidarity and reasserting the group's collective identity. Outsiders who witness these events are unlikely to experience the events in the same manner as the in-group members. They are often unable to make the same emotional investment, or feel the often-poignant emotional attachment that might allow them to derive the same pleasure, joy, or sense of contentment those members of the group experience by taking part in these festivities. For non-members, the different aspects or facets of these events are more likely to evoke feelings of indifference, or give rise to negative attitudes that may be spawned by a sense of exclusion or separateness from spectacles of collective pleasure. The reaction of the interlopers to the traditional Egyptian New Year celebration is a case in point. This had always been an important annual community event that the Egyptians usually celebrated by relaxing the social etiquette that they adhered to for the rest of the year. They sang, danced, drank, and playfully splashed water on each other. The Arabs, the Ottomans, and the Mamluks, on the other hand, were outsiders and viewed the merry-making, as Maqrizi has related, as lacking in *haya'* (shame, shyness, bashfulness, timidity, or modesty) and in *heshmah*, (prudery, seemliness, decency, or reservation).[39] What was in plentiful supply, however, in the opinion of the Arabs was *fogoor*[40] (libertinism); and *'ohoor* (salaciousness, or licentiousness).[41] It would seem that the harsh nature of Bedouin life made the gaiety and joviality, which are a normal part of life in peasant societies, appear totally alien to the Arabs. Not surprisingly, the Arabized Mamluks, demonstrating their alienation from the population they ruled, prohibited Egyptians from holding their annual New Year celebrations.[42] Once again, Egyptian's natural inclination to enjoy and celebrate life was being stifled by the Arabs' view of life as hardship.

Changing Demographics

The native Egyptians, despite the constant waves of Arab migration, remained a majority in their country for almost two centuries following the Arab invasion; however, what was to prove pivotal in the direction taken later by Egyptian society, and which started the process of edging the society gradually towards the adoption of Bedouin culture and social values, was demographic change. Not surprisingly, when word spread in the Arabian Peninsula that those who went to Egypt would never again worry about earning their daily sustenance and could expect to be supported by the hardworking Egyptian peasants and to live in what was to them utter luxury with no obligation to do anything in return, this became a major incentive for Arabs to move to Egypt. In the beginning, the change was most evident in the urban areas where the Bedouin newcomers settled in larger numbers, but eventually the process enveloped the whole country. The seeds of demographic change in rural Egypt were, however, planted at a very early stage after the invasion when the caliph granted an estate of one thousand feddans[43] that was said to be the best estate in Egypt to his friend, ibn Sandar,[44] in violation of his own decree.[45] The decree, which was prompted by the fear that, as landowners, the Arabs would become soft and cease to be a fighting force, was completely forgotten in time, and more Arabs were given arable land. In addition, other decrees, issued after the caliph's death, that exempted Arabs from the burden of taxes or, later, taxed them at a lower rate than Egyptians,[46] facilitated their acquisition of farming land and, therefore, encouraged migration to rural areas in pursuit of wealth from farming. The rate of migration increased steadily over time, and whole tribes hoisted their tents on the backs of their camels and journeyed to Egypt. During the Umayyad reign alone, twelve tribes immigrated to Egypt.[47] It was inevitable that the steady waves of immigrants from the Arabian Peninsula would gradually overwhelm the native population and result in a radical transformation of the character and identity of society.

In addition to this mass immigration, two other factors likely tipped the population balance in favor of the invaders. The first was that conversion of Egyptians to the religion of the new conquerors was an irreversible decision as the penalty for a change of heart and a return to the convert's original religion was execution. The second was that, as Christians, the Egyptians were monogamous, whereas the Arabs were polygamous. Consequently, the birth rate among the Arabs[48] was much higher than among the Egyptians. In addition, the Arabs were permitted by tradition to have as many concubines as they could buy, which also boosted their birthrate, of course. The success of their incursions into the territories of both the Byzantine and the Persian Empires had supplied the Bedouins with both an ample supply of female captives to trade in, as well as the financial means to acquire them. The extent of their immense new-found wealth and their willingness to expend vast amounts on such purchases is attested to by the fact that during the reign of Osman ibn Affan (644-656),[49] "concubines were sold for their weight"[50] in gold. There are other indications that slaves and concubines were in great demand. For example, when Amr was unable to induce the caliph to come and live in the house that he had had built for him in el-Fustat, it was turned into a slave market in compliance with the caliph's decree that the house should be used as a market for the Muslims.[51]

Religious Conversion by Taxation

Along with these demographic changes, some Egyptians began gradually to convert to Islam. A number of them may well have been sincere in their adoption of the new faith. Nevertheless, the increasing burden of taxation and the hope of escaping the poll tax would, in all likelihood, have provided an additional incentive for the switch of allegiance. Another incentive for the adoption of the new faith and of Bedouin social values is the practice observed as long ago as the fourteenth century by ibn Khaldun whereby "[t]he vanquished always want to imitate the victor in his distinctive marks, his dress, his occupation, and all his other conditions and customs."[52]

Twentieth century researchers such as Kashef echo the same sentiment when they contend that the privileged status of the Bedouins vis-à-vis the Egyptians would have acted as a powerful force for promoting Bedouin values and culture over their native counterparts, and some of the conversions to the new faith stemmed from the desire of the people to be like their rulers.[53] The effort of some Egyptians to construct fictitious Arab descent credentials for themselves provides support for this viewpoint. A recorded episode, in which an Egyptian family had, to the chagrin of the Bedouin Arab immigrants, managed to bribe a judge to falsify an Arab lineage for them,[54] could not have been an isolated incident. The reaction of the Arab immigrants to that incident is also indicative of both the social separation of the two communities (Arab and Egyptian), and the relative rank of each one. The Arabs, who never allowed their daughters to marry Egyptians, reacted by composing poems that disparaged the judge and taunted him by suggesting that if he really believed that that family was Arab and not Egyptian then he should offer one of his daughters to one of them in marriage.[55] The intensity of the Arab's opposition to allowing their women to marry Egyptians is accurately reflected in the Arab maxim "better the crocodile should eat her than the peasant [i.e. Egyptian] should marry her" [ya'kolha el-temsah wala yakhoha el-fallah].

Another critical factor that played a significant role in the spreading of Arab/Bedouin social values was the identification of the social norms and values of nomadic life with religion, i.e. Islam. From the birth of Islam, the Bedouins had failed to distinguish between the tenets of Islam and the customs, traditions, and social norms and values of nomadic life. With the integration of Egypt into the Islamic Empire, this failure served to obfuscate in the minds of Egyptians whatever differences existed between these elements. Any Bedouin custom, tradition, or practice came to be viewed as Islamic rather than simply Bedouin. This lack of distinction was, then, a significant factor in the process of Bedouinizing Egyptian social values, a process that became far reaching because of the powerful attachment Egyptians had always had to religion, an attachment that led Herodotus to describe them as "religious excessively beyond all other men."[56] Ironically the religion to which they now attached themselves was imported by an illiterate people whose *gaheliyya* roots were in a tradition of oral poetry and oratory rather than in theological scholarship or philosophical studies.[57] Furthermore, this religion, according to Philip Hitti, "[sat] very lightly indeed on his [the Bedouin's] heart."[58] Hitti further claims that, "in the judgment of the Koran (9: 98), 'the desert Arabians are most confirmed in unbelief and hypocrisy.' Up to our day they never pay much more than lip homage to the prophet."[59] Hitti's assertion is supported by the fact that it took the Arabs one and a half centuries after their conquest of Egypt to build themselves a second mosque to pray in.[60]

That Egyptians have always tended to be conservative when it came to their religious beliefs served, then, both to promote as well as to preserve Bedouin social values and practices that were imported to their country, which they now imagined to be part of Islam and which began to supplant their native Egyptian counterparts. Once the Bedouins of the Arabian Peninsula began to arrive in Egypt in large numbers, it was inevitable that they would impact indigenous social values and practices. It is this impact on the Egyptian social value system that has probably been the most detrimental, enduring, and far-reaching legacy of the Arab invasion. Certain elements of the imported values seemed to have permeated every aspect of social life like an all-enveloping miasma that has continued to have a negative impact on society until today.[61]

Women and Their Role in Society

As Bedouin patriarchal social values began to replace indigenous matriarchal values and love of mother, monogamy, temperance, and coexistence were replaced by obedience of father, polygamy, and revenge, the attitude towards women and their position in society was one of the first areas to be impacted. The Bedouin value system had always put a premium on boys who would be an asset in tribal wars. The Bedouins were, therefore, disappointed by the birth of girls and resorted to the practice of burying newly born baby girls in the desert (*wa'd el-banat*,) referred to earlier, to cope with the unwelcome event. Bedouin society was a patriarchal one in which women had few rights. They were secluded and generally not allowed to participate in what were termed men's affairs, since they were considered less intelligent and incapable of thinking rationally or controlling their emotions. The freedom of women to come and go as they please was severely curtailed, and veiling, which was partly intended to protect women from being kidnapped by other tribes, was the norm. These traditions tend to continue to be the norm in Bedouin societies until today.

Peasant societies where wives work on the fields alongside their husbands, sons and daughters, are usually far less restrictive towards their women than nomadic societies. In comparing the rights of ancient Egyptian and Bedouin women, a modern legal scholar[62] maintains that the latter, in contrast to their Egyptian counterparts, suffered discrimination in twenty nine areas ranging from the laws regulating marriage, divorce, custody of children, and inheritance and wills, to women being given away as part of blood money payments.[63] Other areas of inequality between the sexes that are listed in the study include better care of male than female babies, socialization of females to be subservient to males, forced marriage, marriage of young girls to old men, blaming the female for infertility and for giving birth to females, and honor killings.[64]

When they arrived in Egypt, the Arabs, not surprisingly, were shocked to find that Egyptians did not share their misogynism. Egyptian men and women dealt with one another on an equal basis, and it was normal, for example, for a husband and wife to discuss a joint purchase that they were contemplating. The fact that the historians, ibn Abdel Hakam,[65] and Maqrizi,[66] both found it necessary to refer to this practice and explain the reasons for it would suggest that the Arabs must have been puzzled by the novel phenomenon and tried to account for its prevalence among the vanquished Egyptians. The "learned" amongst them sought to explain the Egyptians' odd behavior. Since, as a preliterate society, the Arabs relied on oral history to convey and comprehend past events, the knowledge of these very few "learned men" was limited to familiarity with some of the stories in the holy books, and they were acquainted with the story of Moses and his parting of the Red Sea. They reasoned that all free Egyptians must have drowned in the sea while in pursuit of Moses and that would have left the children, women and slaves as the only people alive in the country. Consequently, the Arabs reasoned, women had no choice but to marry their slaves and that is why the men treated them as equals and with respect. For that reason, according to ibn Abdel Hakam, writing two centuries after the Arab invasion "until today Egyptian men would not buy or sell without saying I will check with my wife."[67]

Egypt, then, had a different tradition in gender relationships from Bedouin tribal society. Women in pharaonic Egypt had extensive social and legal rights. Under the law, they had the same rights as men regarding property purchase, ownership, and inheritance. Ancient Egypt was, on the whole, a monogamous society, but surprisingly casual about the relations between the two sexes.[68] Women married whomever they wished, Egyptian or not.[69] Consequently, there were no restrictions on marriage to slaves.[70] Marriage was regarded as a completely private undertaking, and society left them to make arrangements as they saw fit.[71] Virginity and premarital relations were not matters of great concern to the majority of people.[72] In terms of financial arrangements, there were no funds or financial resources demanded of either party as part of the marriage arrangements.[73] All resources accumulated by the married couple were owned jointly.[74] In terms of descent and inheritance, both parents were equally acknowledged and honored.[75] It was only after the conquest by Alexander that Egyptian women began to lose some ground when the less egalitarian Greek and Roman laws began to be implemented, and women found themselves being deprived of some of their indigenous ancient rights.[76] Nevertheless, women in Egypt continued to be free and active members of society and participated freely in all communal activities.

For some time after the Arab conquest, the practical considerations of an agrarian economy acted as mitigating factors in the process of importing the restrictive Arab attitudes towards women. As a farming community, Egypt needed the labor of both sexes working alongside each other in the fields, and complete segregation of women was an impractical proposition. However, the gradual Bedouinization of Egyptian social values eventually led to a severe deterioration in the position of women in society and to the incorporation of a certain degree of misogyny into the Egyptian social value system. In time, women became mere sexual objects, lesser human beings than men, in need of being kept in check, in part, ostensibly, to protect them from themselves. In theory, women were allowed to own property, but in practice, male relatives controlled this property. The ideal that society began to aspire to became the Bedouin ideal reflected in the veil, often a complete cover from head to toe with only small slits for the eyes; in women's seclusion in the house in a female only environment; and in their monitoring by their male guardians, even if these males happened to be children. The see-through dresses and topless outfits worn by women in ancient social gatherings depicted on pharaonic monuments were now considered indecent vestiges of a heathen past by the descendants of these fun-loving women. Scenes such as that of the three musicians depicted in Nebamen's (1550-1307 BCE) tomb in Thebes[77] are no longer viewed by the black clad women in contemporary Egyptian society, who symbolize the Bedouin ideal of womanhood, as illustrations of the *joie de vivre* in ancient Egypt, but of their distant pharaonic grandmothers' lasciviousness and lack of modesty and propriety. The Bedouin view of women and their place in society is now so embedded in contemporary Egyptian culture that some historians are either unwilling or incapable of comprehending that their use of the term harem (meaning the prohibited ones) in a book about the role of queens in ancient Egypt[78] would have been anathema to those queens about whom the author writes. Since it was not unusual for pharaonic society to depict a queen in a see-through dress, the use of the term harem conjures the wrong images in the readers' minds and misrepresents the society that the author purports to describe.

What is surprising, however, is that the indigenous Egyptian culture does continue to display itself in some aspects of contemporary daily life and has not been completely taken over by Bedouin culture. For example, it is quite common in Cairo to see young women dressed in form-hugging jeans or skirts and skin-tight tops yet also wearing the *hegab* (head cover) and often holding their boyfriends' hands. Such behavior might appear to exhibit contradictory social values but it is probably no more than instinctive or unconscious attempts to reconcile the normal urge to look one's best while keeping critics at bay by adhering to prevailing standards of modesty.

Perhaps more significantly, festivities (weddings for instance) have remained, for the most part, unsegregated and are enjoyed by both sexes participating together. Men and women, for the most part, still listen to music, dance, laugh, talk, and enjoy themselves in mixed company.

The Law as a Basis of Social Organization

The attitude towards the law was another area that the Arabs impacted. As a preliterate society, the nomads of the Arabian Peninsula had no need for complex institutions, and the Bedouin system of government consists of a tribal chief who governs without the need for multileveled institutions or written laws spelling out specific rights and obligations of the ruler and the ruled beyond unquestioning obedience and strict adherence to tribal mores. This may have been perfectly adequate and socially functional in an environment such as the poverty-stricken wastes of the Arabian Peninsula where the lack of resources acted as an effective check on the tribal chief's actions. However, when the tribal chief acquires the resources to mete out punishments and rewards, despotism, capriciousness, and randomness of action on the part of the ruler tend to proliferate.

The lack of concern with laws was, as ibn Khaldun stressed, deeply embedded in the Bedouin traditions and social values that viewed looting, for example, as an acceptable, even desirable activity. The Arabs' interest in the law was limited to its possible use as nothing more than a means of taxing people in the conquered territories and not as a means of maintaining order, discouraging criminal acts, or protecting property.[79] The inevitable result of the Arab conquest and penetration of all levels of Egyptian society was that the law came to be seen as simply the whims and wishes of the ruler at a particular moment in time, and not as a generally accepted set of norms to which everyone in society was expected to adhere. Fear of the ruler became the motivator for compliance, and in many instances, violation of the law lost its social stigma if the perpetrator could get away with it.

It is ironic that in Arabic dictionaries the term pharaonic, as Hamdan points out, is a less than favorable adjective with negative connotations and implications of despotism,[80] even though the pharaonic era enjoyed a codified legal system upheld by the pharaoh, and which those who later ruled Egypt never managed to replicate.[81] The term pharaoh actually has a more benign, perhaps even paternal meaning and refers to the "Great House" where his subjects lived and were protected.[82] While not a paragon of virtue by any means, the pharaoh generally abided by the law despite, or perhaps because of, his status as semi-divine. This was in sharp contrast to the rule by caprice exemplified and personified by rulers such el-Hakem bi Amr Ellah (The One Who Reigns by the Order of God). He, according to Maqrizi, prohibited singing, playing chess, and eating *gargeer* (a variety of roquette), *molukhiyya*, a type of soup that is still popular in Egypt today, and whimsically executed many people, one of whom was the chief justice.[83] Whatever shortcoming it may or may not have had, pharaonic rule was the antithesis of such practices. Thotmos III (1151-1182 BCE), in contrast to The One Who Reigns by the Order of God, decreed that his minister was prohibited from passing judgment in any case before checking the papyrus that specified the type of punishment that the law assigned to the specific violation,[84] and workers in the royal graves once felt safe enough to go on strike in support of their demands for better pay during his reign.[85] While it would be an error to portray their rule as akin to utopia, the law did protect the workers' rights,[86] and the pharaohs had a sophisticated system of laws that reflected their legitimacy. Examples of decrees and judgments dating back to the Old Kingdom exist and cover an extensive list of offenses, ranging from stealing a donkey to nonpayment of taxes and murder.[87] Diodorus Siculus, a first century Greek historian who spent several years in Egypt, wrote admiringly of the Egyptian justice system and the practice of requiring judges to be in possession of and to reference the eight scrolls upon which the laws were recorded before making any judgment.[88]

In contrast to the capriciousness and rule by whim that the Egyptians had to endure and came to accept in later centuries, the pharaonic system of justice was more equitable and contained checks and formal avenues for redress of grievances.[89] It gave any citizen, male or female, the right to petition an official and to place a civil action before the local court, a tribunal made up of respected citizens who convened as and when needed.[90] One example of such a petition is reviewed by Joyce Tyldesley. It is a request to review an unfair tax assessment that dates back to the Nineteenth Dynasty (1293 - 1185 BCE).[91] In contrast, when Egyptians rebelled against the exorbitant Arab taxation nearly two thousand years later, in 832 CE, the Arab Caliph, el-Ma'moun, responded by killing thousands of the protesting villagers and taking their women and children to be sold as slaves.[92] Another example of the role of laws in pharaonic society is the well-known *Tale of the Eloquent Peasant* from the Middle Kingdom (2040-1640 BCE),[93] referred to earlier, which is a patent demonstration of the dogged insistence of a weaker member of society to obtain justice and of the fact that he felt that it was possible for the legal system of his society to correct a wrong. Recourse to the law was lost under the foreign masters, and until today Egyptians have little faith that the legal system protects them or their property.

Work, Temporal Orientation, and Interpersonal Relationships

Another key social value the foreign rule of Egypt eventually impacted was the attitude towards work and the value of labor. The link between the production of food and the acquisition of daily necessities is very clear in an agrarian society. Irrigation canals must be maintained, land must be ploughed, seeds must be sown at certain times of the year, and the crops tended and nurtured regularly and then gathered. The value of work in the native culture is clearly reflected in the traditional chant repeated by work groups: "Work, work! Work is gold" [*hob, hob ya shughl al-nob*].[94] In a Bedouin environment, on the other hand, the tending of camels and goats does not require strenuous or sustained effort. Moreover, it was often designated as the occupation of women and children and seen as unmanly. To supplement their meager resources in the paucity of the desert environment, however, the men were motivated to devote much of their time to raiding other tribes. Looting and pillage were, therefore, the Bedouin men's main occupation, and they held work, in any form, in contempt. When they migrated to the newly occupied countries, the Bedouins brought their ways with them, eschewing all work in the crafts or in the fields,[95] and in traditional Bedouin folklore, they took pride in describing themselves as "people who do not farm and do not manufacture, but live off the booty that we win from the nonbelievers."[96] All work in the crafts or the fields was, therefore, considered beneath them and assigned to the *mawali* (subject peoples) who occupied an inferior status in the social structure, and the policy followed in all the conquered territories was to leave farming and practicing the various crafts and professions to them. They were viewed as a separate, inferior class whose labor the Bedouins felt entitled to simply by virtue of being Arabs,[97] and were sometimes referred to as the donkeys (el-'oloog)[98] The *mawali*, retained their inferior status even after converting to Islam.[99] Warfare and composing poetry were, as evidenced by the poetry itself, the Bedouin culture's most desirable occupations, and even a century after conquering Egypt, the Arabs had not produced any artistic, literary or scientific works of any kind and continued to scorn any Arab who showed any inclination to pursue the crafts of the *mawali* or their learning and scholarship.[100] The centrality of disparaging work in the Bedouin system of cultural values is clearly demonstrated in an incident recounted by Hafez Wahaba, the long-term Egyptian advisor to King Abdel Aziz Al-Saud. According to Wahaba, the king once insulted a member of another tribe in public by calling him "a son of a craftsman," which led the man's wife to demand a divorce, as it would shame the tribe for her to be married to him.[101]

Ibn Khaldun perceptively noted that the Arabs' reliance on plunder for their sustenance, and their scorn of labor and craftsmen had a corrosive effect on society[102] and eventually resulted in deterioration and decay. He went on to argue, and that that is why "civilization always collapsed in places the Arabs took over and conquered."[103]

There is much historical evidence to support ibn Khaldun's conclusions. The existence in Egypt of a parasitic class of Bedouins (*Ahl el-diwan*) who enjoyed income, high social rank, and privileges without contributing to the economy would have produced a shift in the attitude to labor and served as a powerful role model to be emulated, thus denigrating the value of work. This group, numbering in the thousands, must have served as a daily reminder to both the craftsmen and the peasants that there is no link between skill and labor, and income and status.

Among the other aspects of the Egyptian social value system that went through a Bedouinization process were the individual's temporal orientation and even interpersonal relationships. The brevity of the foreign *walis*' tenure in Egypt would not have been lost on the population, who could not have failed to notice, and be influenced by, the absence of long-term planning, or by the *walis'* purchasing of concubines, jewelry, and fine garments that they could enjoy and then take with them when they left Egypt to return home. *Walis* were rarely interested in using the riches they extracted from the Egyptians to finance lasting monuments, infrastructure projects, or even opulent residences that they planned to enjoy for the rest of their lives and then leave as a lasting legacy to their offspring.

After the Arab conquest the rulers were either foreigners who viewed their sojourn in the country as transitory, or Bedouins whose culture fostered the development of a short-term outlook because that was more functional for the desolate desert environment and the need for constant movement. In either case they did not build opulent palaces to live in, pyramids to keep their memory alive, or public buildings that served the population and might have become part of the national heritage in time. They were certainly more intent on immediate personal gratification than they were on the country's long-term prosperity. Extortionist taxation clearly was not motivated by concern for the welfare of the subject peoples, or for that matter for the country's future, since a *wali's* actions frequently resulted in an eventual loss in future tax revenue after his departure. This short-term outlook clearly set the tone for society, and the relationship of animosity and mutual suspicion thus fostered between the ruler and the ruled inexorably seeped into interpersonal relationships in society as a whole.

Another characteristic of Bedouin social values that seeped into Egyptian society was the Bedouin concept of authoritarianism. There is a sharp contrast between pharaonic and Bedouin authoritarianism. The former rested primarily on the ruler's semi-divine status and the very practical role that he played in creating and maintaining social order and economic stability. The latter rested on the veneration that a strong leader demanded by imposing his will by force. Nabil Hilal observed that Bedouins view the *inability to be unjust* as a flaw, an imperfection, and they actually took pride in being despotic and unjust. Such despotism is, as he demonstrates, deemed a lofty social value and is glorified in their poetry.[104] Acceptance of despotism as the norm is also implied by Maqrizi, who often seems to use the term *estabadda* (meaning: became a despot, or tyrannized) and *walla* (meaning: came to power, was given the authority) synonymously.[105] Government then was embodied in the person of the tribal chief rather than in a complex social institution that provided checks on the actions of those who represented it. Simply stated, the concept of the right to be despotic was a more extreme version of the belief in absolute power articulated in the statement: *"L'etat, c'est moi"* that is attributed to the French king Louis XIV (1638-1715). Alien as this view of government initially was to Egyptians, inevitably it became part of their social fabric. The passive acceptance, even expectation of, injustice, as expressed in the popular proverb: "A beating by the ruler is an honor,"[106] became a cultural norm as Egyptians gradually came to regard despotism as a perfectly normal state of affairs and incorporated authoritarianism into all levels of society.

The impact of Bedouin culture on Egyptians also includes influence on values in areas that are interconnected: learning and the arts. As an illiterate society, rote learning was the only means available to the Arabs to preserve their poetry. This, and the nomadic lifestyle and paucity of their environment, are obviously the main reasons that led to poetry and oration becoming their only means of artistic expression[107] and accounts for the Bedouins' penchant for exaggeration[108] and concern for form at the expense of content, which developed into salient social values and elevated the poet as seer, annalist, narrator, and recorder of past events of his tribe.[109] When Bedouin social values were imported to Egypt, ancient arts such as sculpture, painting, and music on string instruments became taboos and all but died out.

Societies generally tend to make a virtue of their weaknesses and Bedouin traditions glorified the illiteracy and poverty that characterized nomadic culture. This was reflected in the maxims and Bedouin folklore, which reaffirmed their pride in being people who were illiterate, and "d[id] not read or do arithmetic."[110] At the same time, however, they claimed to encourage learning and reasoning. This may sound laudable, but it also appears to be a contradiction. If, however, the Bedouin culture's penchant for valuing form over content is taken into consideration. If the narrow limits the culture set beyond which the individual was not supposed to venture in learning and reasoning is taken into account, the contradiction could be resolved and the claim turns out to be a great deal less liberal than it might appear on face value. In other words, the individual is encouraged to think, but told what to think, and warned at the same time that thinking is fraught with danger. At least one contemporary writer, Nabil Hilal, suggests that this tradition of scorning reason has deep roots in Bedouin folklore and is reflected in the old and accepted axiom: "Most of those in paradise are fools."[111] Etymological analysis provides further support for this viewpoint. Ibrahim el-Zaini, an Arabic language specialist,[112] points out that the term *'aql*, which means mind or brain, comes from the same root as the verb *'agala*, which means to tie. The implication, therefore, is that understanding and conceptualization are circumscribed.[113] This belief is what led an Arab poet once to sing the praises of ignorance in a verse, and a popular Egyptian television preacher, Sheikh Sha'rawi, to advise his listeners that using the mind could lead to demise through apostasy,[114] a capital offense. "God," the sheikh once told his audience, "has created the brain to tie things and comprehend them, not to think about them, because if one thought about them one would be venturing outside the assignment that God has mandated."[115] Even contemporary Arab laypersons sometimes declare that those who think too much become perturbed and confused.

The impact on society and the long-term consequences of these values were not lost on ibn Khaldun, who could equally well have been referring to Egypt's conquerors when he wrote about the loss of the Persian civilization's knowledge and scientific heritage after the Arab conquest. When the Arabs conquered that country they were at a loss as to what to do with the vast number of books they found there and the Bedouin chieftain who commanded the conquering army[116] wrote to the caliph asking for instructions. The caliph opined that if the books' contents contradicted religious tenets then people should be protected from them, and if the contents did not contradict Islam then there was no need for them. In either case, the safe course would be to either burn all the books or throw them into the river.[117]

Such social values and practices may be functional for a preliterate nomadic society that needs to travel light and has little use for books and art objects, but not for a sedentary society, and the

Bedouin tradition of taking pride in illiteracy did not completely survive transplantation into the Egyptian value system. However, a related characteristic did: the propensity to disparage learning beyond specified limits and to tread carefully around prohibited avenues of thought.

Despite the historical process described above, despite the vast waves of Bedouin migration and the long centuries of oppression and servitude, the Egyptians' conversion to Bedouin values does not seem to have been as complete or as irreversible as outside appearances may lead us to believe. Some spark of the indigenous age old values of veneration for learning, of shunning extremism, of gaiety and the love of life, of aversion to treating women as mere sexual objects who should be controlled and traded like pieces of property, and of celebrating the pleasures of life in mixed (i.e. male and female) company seem to have survived, somehow. This was demonstrated in the manner in which many Egyptians were not only willing, but also apparently eager, to embrace the less restrictive French social mores when Bonaparte's arrival in the country gave them the freedom to choose.

5

The First Glimpse of Modernity

While Egypt languished for centuries under the rule of foreign overlords who had plunged the country into poverty, backwardness, and isolation, and kept it there, Europe was on the cusp of a profound social change. The enlightenment brought about new ideas and new inventions that were beginning to radically transform Europe's economic, political, and social institutions. The introduction of coal-fueled, steam-powered machinery had been on the horizon since the middle of the eighteenth century and the promise of dramatic improvements in industrial production capacity and living standards was becoming a reality. It became evident that the new economy would create a demand for new markets and raw materials and major powers such as Britain and France entered into a fierce competition for control of communications and trade routes. Inevitably, Egypt's strategic location made it a desirable and coveted prize. Alarmed by the prospect of a British attempt to grab Egypt, which constituted a vital link in their communications route to India and the Far East, the French, decided to grab the country for themselves. Napoleon Bonaparte set sail for Alexandria in May 1798 in command of a fleet of 355 ships and 40,000 men, and it seemed that Egypt's disengagement from the civilized world was about to come to an end.

Re-establishing Contact with Europe

When the French landed in 1798 in that very same city that had awed Amr and his Bedouin compatriots when they took possession of it eleven centuries earlier, Alexandria had been transformed. The city that had left the smooth-tongued Amr speechless in 641 had far more in common in 1798 with the improvised squalid settlements that Amr had left behind in the Arabian Peninsula than the city he "opened" in the seventh century. The French, wrote Napoleon, found the legendary Alexandria to be nothing but a collection of dirty, destitute, and poverty-stricken huts that offered none of the services and amenities that one might expect to find in a city.[1] The sight that greeted the French commander upon landing in Alexandria is probably the most potent symbol of the utter destruction to which Egypt's uncivilized conquerors subjected the country and its people to during the preceding eleven centuries.

The Alexandrian palaces of gleaming white marble, the wide avenues, the famed house of learning, wealth, culture, and gracious living had long disappeared and instead Napoleon found the population to be living "in a state of utter barbarism."[2] As for the rest of the country, which had been described in such hyperbolic terms by Amr's son when he compared it to paradise, Napoleon found it in a sad state of misery, wretchedness, and deprivation.[3] Yet, to his surprise, the country was "richer than any country in the world in coin, rice, vegetables, and cattle."[4] That such a statement could still be made about Egypt after more than a thousand years of its wholesale plunder by the avaricious and untutored marauders, is testament to the country's still abundant but misused wealth and agricultural production and to its potential.

The arrival of the French gave Egyptians a fleeting glimpse of another culture, another system of social values, and another approach to government and political leadership, and dealt an almost fatal blow to the outdated Ottoman/Mamluk régime. While it would be naïve to suggest that Napoleon came to Egypt for any reason other than to serve the French national interest as he defined it, the French incursion was not merely a military campaign. Nor was it simply the latest of Egypt's many invasions. This was an event of monumental importance that promised to end the era of Egypt's tragic history and to usher in an age of renewed hope.

What distinguished the French invasion from both the earlier invasions of the primitive nomadic tribes and the later invasion of the more race conscious British, was that it had scientific and sociocultural goals in addition to its military objectives. The French neither packed Egypt's wealth onto long camel caravans and headed home with their loot nor did they take Egyptian women to be distributed among the French population as concubines. Napoleon's actions would have been utterly unfathomable to the Egyptians. He attempted to educate them about the principles of the French Revolution and promised reform and just government. He brought with him dozens of prominent scholars and scientists. Among them were artists, linguists, administrators, economists, mathematicians, physicians, engineers, botanists, zoologists, archeologists, and others. He brought a printing press with type for French and Arabic script, a vast array of scientific instruments, as well as a library of thousands of books on a variety of subjects. The extensive library included books on the arts, science, geography, history, poetry, theater, romance, politics, and morals.[5]

Less than two months after he arrived in Egypt, Napoleon established what is now the region's oldest functioning academy of arts and sciences: *L'Institut d'Egypte*. The Institute's mandate was to research every aspect of life in Egypt, and its findings were later published in a twenty-volume work entitled *Description de l'Égypte*. Bonaparte was intent on reforming and reorganizing every aspect of life in the country, from city planning, to public hygiene, to the legal system, to the educational system, to local administration, to name but a few of his areas of interest. He informed the Egyptians that he intended to govern Egypt according to the principles of the French Revolution, *Liberté, Egalité, Fraternité*. These concepts were novel and completely alien to the Bedouinized culture that characterized Egyptian society by then, and in which the people fully expected their rulers to be despotic and corrupt. A ruler who was only moderately corrupt and despotic was venerated as a just ruler and any individual or communal rights that existed were viewed as generous gifts from a benevolent ruler.

The most reliable historian of that era is Abdel Rahman el-Gabarti (1754-1822), and his account of the French occupation of Egypt leaves the reader with the impression that the freedoms granted by the French to the women were viewed by the Egyptians in general, and the women in particular, as a breath of fresh air. Surprisingly, the yearning for openness, at least in some women, must have remained dormant somewhere in their psyches despite over a millennium of socialization in the oppressive Bedouin values and of being forced to dress in the oppressive black garb that covered them from head to toe. The reaction of some of the Cairenes of both sexes to the less restrictive norms of social intercourse followed by the French men and women who arrived with Napoleon is reminiscent of someone who finally wakes up from a long nightmare and is eager to forget the horror of it.

El-Gabarti's eyewitness account of that period is both informative and insightful. A majority of women, el-Gabarti relates disapprovingly, eagerly threw off their veils and abandoned modesty and shyness (*heshma* and *haya'* were the terms that he used) in imitation of French women and went out to have fun.[6] "Many" of the daughters of the elite married French men,[7] many others walked the streets alone without male minders, and still others walked with friends and went on pleasure trips on the Nile both during the day and in the evenings. They sang, danced, and drank.[8] The ease with which some Egyptians embraced the liberties offered by the French,[9] "seems to have happened with amazing speed,"[10] suggesting that the spark of life had not been completely extinguished. The revolutionary step of discarding centuries of oppression with such apparent willingness and ease implies that the Bedouinization of Egyptian culture was not as deep rooted as one might have expected after a millennia of forced compliance with its tenets and the threat of possible loss of life and limb for even minor violations. The fact that the French, as one eyewitness, Nicola Turk (1763-1828), states were "amazingly attentive to the country's administration,"[11] must have intrigued the Egyptians.[12]

The majority of the population, Turk recounts, were attracted to the French,[13] who maintained peace and order; banished the thieves and the pillaging Arabs; were just, honest, and concerned with public welfare; and maintained discipline among their soldiers.[14] El-Gabarti was dumbfounded when Napoleon executed French soldiers who looted a house in Cairo. The Egyptians were hungry for a benevolent dictator who could bring stability and fairness to their lives, and he seemed to have arrived. Surprisingly, after being repressed for so long, the true Egyptian nature of *joie de vivre* and easygoing acceptance of different ways of life quickly re-emerged.

The events recorded by el-Gabarti were not merely accounts of individual behavior but a description of the behavior of a cross section of all of society's social strata.[15] He was, as Louis Awad rightly points out, reporting on a widespread social phenomenon not on individual cases of idiosyncratic behavior.[16] Awad goes on to point to the work of Turk who also reported that both the highest and the lowest social classes mixed freely with the French and that it was only the small middle class, whose businesses were negatively impacted by the presence of the French, that did not do so.[17] El-Gabarti himself used the term "most" to refer to those who participated in the "women's revolt" or the "harem's revolt" in 1800, which took place with the knowledge and approval of their men and guardians.[18] Awad asserts that the facts support his contention that what el-Gabarti described were neither individual acts nor acts confined to one social class. Upper class women attended public functions along with men,[19] and joined with their husbands in handling public transactions,[20] and in Rosetta, women staged their first public demonstration to demand the right to use the public baths.[21] Zainab el-Bakriyya, the daughter of *Naqeeb el-Ashraf* (doyen of the descendants of the Prophet), Sheikh Khalil el-Bakri, was among those who discarded her veil, consorted with the French, attended their functions, all with the full knowledge and approval of her father. The unfortunate girl paid for her brief taste of freedom with her life after the French left, when the returning Ottoman ruler executed her in July 1801[22] as punishment for associating and socializing with the French.[23] Even if the majority of Egyptians rejected both French rule and Ottoman subjugation, as some contemporary historians claim, most Egyptians, Awad asserts, either partly or fully accepted Western civilization.[24] The reaction of a substantial segment of Egyptian society to the French and their way of life was, as Awad notes, nothing less than a social movement and an expression of public opinion that was open and receptive to the modern civilization and modern social values that the French represented.[25]

It must have seemed to most Egyptians that the country was entering a new era and finally emerging from the backwardness and isolation that its insular, untutored, and despotic rulers had imposed upon it. Napoleon, it seemed, was going to be a very different type of ruler from the norm. However, the appearance of the British as a new player in the local power struggle denied Egypt the opportunity to test Bonaparte's sincerity.[26] Both the success of his invasion of Egypt and the prospect of French control of the route to their jewel in the crown, India, alarmed the British. The "white man's burden," from the British point of view, did not include the introduction of *Liberté, Egalité, Fraternité* to what they termed the subject races, and the British would, almost certainly, have viewed such ideas as real threats to their interests. Hence, they formed an alliance with the Ottomans, the Mamluks, and some of the thuggish elements among the foreign—mainly Turkish and Maghrebi—residents of Cairo, and conducted a successful campaign of instigating external military skirmishes and local riots and mayhem to harass the French and terrorize the local population. These events were later dubbed the Cairo rebellion.

Many contemporary Egyptian historians claim that the Cairo rebellion was a rejection of both the French occupation and French social and political values. A closer look at these events, however, reveals a very different picture. The Cairo rebellion, as Awad correctly points out, was planned, instigated, led, and carried out by Turks and Mamluks who were camping outside Cairo and who sneaked into the city with the help of their Maghrebi and other foreign agents.[27] They were mere thugs who began by robbing and killing Christians, but were soon robbing and killing Muslims too.[28] A notorious hooligan from the Maghreb[29] (present day Morocco, Algeria, and Tunisia) led a group of Maghrebis and Hegazis (present-day Saudi Arabia) to pillage and kill not only men, but also women and children,[30] in one instance mutilating a little girl to rob her of her jewelry.[31] There appears to have been little opportunity to escape the violence. Some of the terrorized people who fled the city in search of a safe haven in the countryside were foiled in their attempts by the Bedouin Arabs who roamed the deserts outside the Nile valley's towns and villages and robbed them of everything.[32] These acts did not endear the Arabs to el-Gabarti who denounced them in harsh language, calling them "these damned Arabs who are the ugliest of people and the greatest of worst affliction affecting the populace."[33]

El-Gabarti's eyewitness account is very specific and actually names some of these thugs who terrorized the Cairenes, such as el-Mahdawiyya the Maghrebi[34] and el-Gilani, another Maghrebi leader of an armed gang of Maghrebis and Hegazis.[35] Other gangs of Maghrebi thugs from the Fahhamin, Ghouriah, and Tulun neighborhoods,[36] as well as Turks from the Khan el-Khalili neighborhood[37] took part in riots and looting. El-Gabarti's frequent use of terms such as *"awbash"* (rabble) and *"hasharat"* (insects)[38] to describe some of the Maghribis, Hegazis and Turks who participated in these events leaves no doubt that he viewed them as thugs rather than as liberators trying to help the Egyptians free themselves from the French. His unequivocal condemnation of this violence and frequent use of terms such as *"nahb"* (pillage) and *"qatl"* (killing)[39] to describe the perpetrators and their actions clearly indicates that he viewed the events as criminal rather than as an altruistic national uprising. He is explicit in his denunciation of those he called "the rabble soldiers who claim to be Muslims" fighting a religious war when in fact they were killing and robbing to "satisfy their animal desires."[40]

Far from being a political rebellion carried out by native Cairenes, the so-called Cairo rebellion was, then, nothing more than a spree of murder and pillage carried out by mainly foreign criminals as well as elements of what el-Gabarti termed the rabble[41] throughout his narrative. The "rebellion" was instigated and financed by the Turks, the Mamluks, and the British. The Egyptians and their leaders of learned men, who were caught off guard by the events, were scrambling to save themselves and their families from the carnage. Although el-Gabarti's record of the events does mention prominent Egyptians such as Omar Makram and Ahmad el-Mahrouqi, he does not suggest that they played a leadership role in this rebellion, which was led by the Sublime Port and its helpers and agents who incited the rabble by accusing the Egyptian leadership of treason.[42] To be sure, el-Gabarti does state that some prominent Egyptians called upon the people to fight against the French[43] but he does not tell us whether they were sincere in their call or simply trying to save their own necks. What he does tell us is that one the Maghrebi thugs threatened to behead anyone who refused to join him in the fight against the French because he wanted the disturbance to continue so that he and his gang could continue to rob and pillage.[44] He goes on to add "that man caused the destruction of most houses in el-Azbakiyya [a Cairo neighborhood]" and that "he was one of the *balaa* [afflictions] that befell Egypt."[45] As for public sentiment, el-Gabarti states that when the Ottoman soldiers took control of one of Cairo's neighborhoods during the disturbances and proceeded to rob and pillage, "people wished for their [the Ottomans'] disappearance and the return of the French."[46] When the mayhem became widespread after the final departure of the French, "most people" el-Gabarti states, "especially the *fellahin* [peasants] wished for the return of the French *ahkam* [rule]."[47] Furthermore, public sentiment was not in favor of re-embracing the oppressive social mores of their returning Mamluk and Ottoman masters. It was foreigners, for the most part, not Egyptians who hounded and persecuted those who had consorted with the French. It was, for example, the Ottoman minister and his men who, in July 1801, executed the previously mentioned sixteen-year-old daughter of Sheikh Khalil el-Bakri as a punishment for her having associated and socialized with the French.[48]

In addition to instigating internal unrest, the British also cut off Bonaparte's supply line to France when their fleet, commanded by Rear-Admiral Horatio Nelson, trapped the French fleet off the north coast of Egypt and sank it during the battle of Abu Kir. Bonaparte's position in Egypt became precarious, and he returned to France on August 23, 1799 leaving General Jean-Baptiste Kléber in charge during his absence.[49] On June 18, 1800, a young man stabbed and killed Kléber in his home in Cairo. The guards gave chase and the murderer was caught hiding in the next-door garden. He turned out to be a Syrian thug from Aleppo who had been hired by the Ottomans to commit the murder. The French, according to el-Gabarti, realized that the people of Egypt were innocent of the deed, and conducted a lengthy investigation.[50] The murderer, Seliman el-Halabi, "a reckless tramp,"[51] was tried and executed, but the loss of one of Bonaparte's most experienced Generals dealt a serious blow to the French cause and was one of the factors that eventually resulted in the defeat of Bonaparte's venture and the departure of the French from Egypt in 1801. The victory of the unlikely alliance of the British, the Mamluks, the Ottomans, and the local criminal elements and thugs of various nationalities had successfully extinguished the Egyptians' nebulous glimmer of hope for a reprieve from ignorant and despotic rule.[52]

Egypt was back in the hands of the same unenlightened, tyrannical rulers who had governed it for so long. The population was subjected to yet another cycle of instability, looting, pillage, and rape as the British, the Ottomans, and the Mamluks vied with each other in their attempts to deliver the governorship of Egypt to an individual of their choosing. Chaos enveloped the whole country and "Arabs and highway robbers haunted all routes, south, north, east, and west,"[53] attacking peasants and villages, stealing livestock, and destroying crops.[54]

The Promise of Change: Mohammed Ali

A glimmer of hope appeared in the midst of the suffering and chaos. One of the Ottoman officers, who had arrived as part of the Albanian contingent of the Ottoman army, was a young, intelligent, ambitious, and determined man named Mohammed Ali. Despite being illiterate he was open minded and always willing to listen to fresh ideas,[55] and like Bonaparte whom he admired, Mohammed Ali quickly grasped the fact that Egypt had the potential to become a rich and powerful country. He fell in love with Egypt and once told a nineteenth century European traveler: "I love Egypt with the ardor of a lover, and if I had ten thousand lives, I would willingly sacrifice them all to possess her."[56] One clear example of Mohammed Ali's astuteness was that he established good rapport with several of the Mamluk princes as well as with the *ulama* (religious leaders), whose views carried a great deal of weight with the general public.[57] He met regularly with the latter, impressed them with his knack for talking in a judicious and levelheaded manner, and convinced them that a sound economy and affluence were not beyond reach under the stewardship of a good government.[58]

The Ottoman appointed *wali* (viceroy) failed to stem the unrest, pillage, and looting that had intensified after the departure of the French. When he lost control of a particularly violent contingent of several thousand Syrian soldiers he had brought over to reestablish order in the country, the *ulamas*, anxious to stop these soldiers' pillaging and raping, decided to take action.[59] They mobilized the population behind their cause and approached Mohammed Ali, telling him that the *wali* had to be deposed and sent home, and asking him to step in as viceroy of Egypt.[60] They assured him that their decision was unanimous and that they would not accept anyone else in the position.[61] Fearing a real rebellion this time, the Ottoman sultan had no choice but to ratify the people's choice of *wali*, and Egypt's fortunes appeared to brighten once more when a new era was ushered in on May 17, 1805.[62]

Like most of the other *walis* before him, Mohammed Ali was ruthless and despotic. However, he turned out to be a different type of ruler than Egypt was used to. According to Antoine Clot bey (1793-1868), the Frenchman whom he appointed in 1825 to develop a public health service and to found a medical school, and who knew him personally, Mohammed Ali was an illiterate man who began learning to read and write at the age of forty-five.[63] He was interested in books in spite of his illiteracy and had them read to him, and his readings included ibn Khaldun's work as well as books about Napoleon Bonaparte.[64] He was a brilliant and ambitious man who was determined to transform Egypt into a stable, prosperous, and independent state and to found a ruling dynasty. In spite of the fact that the Mamluks remained a power to be reckoned with, Mohammed Ali began to institute important reforms such as land reform and registration of land ownership as early as 1809.[65] He gradually consolidated his grip on the country and generally avoided open conflict with the Mamluks until they decisively defeated a British force that attempted to occupy Rosetta in 1807 while he was fighting rebels in Upper Egypt. Then a planned military campaign in the Arabian Peninsula made it necessary for him to secure his position before dispatching his army to dislodge an extremist religious sect (the Wahabis) that had taken control of the holy cities of Mecca and Medina.

Mohammed Ali decided to hold a lavish and opulent formal ceremony to invest his son, Toussoun, who was to command the expedition. Naturally, the elite of the elite of Egyptian society were invited to attend the ceremony and the sumptuous banquet that was to follow in the Cairo Citadel. The Mamluk princes, accompanied by their lieutenants and courtiers, arrived on their thoroughbred Arab stallions in their finest attire. The ceremony went well and the mounted Mamluk procession, preceded and followed by Mohammed Ali's honor guard, set off to leave the citadel via the narrow alleyway that led to the outside gate. As the leading honor guards passed through the gate it was suddenly slammed shut and the Mamluks were attacked from behind as well as from the towers above and all but one were slaughtered. Legend has it that one prince escaped what became known as the Mamluk massacre, but was quickly captured and killed. Historical estimates of the number killed vary, but Marsot's conservative estimate of twenty-four beys (princes) and several hundred of their lieutenants seems plausible.[66]

It was certainly ruthless, but it was effective. The Mamluk era can accurately be said to have ended on March 1, 1811, and the Albanian born Mohammed Ali began to carve his place in history as the father of modern Egypt. Instead of regarding Egypt as a cow to be milked so that the proceeds may be sent to some faraway destination to be used for the purchase of concubines and the maintenance of a lavish lifestyle, he saw it as a country with potential for greatness. The Turks and the Mamluks had kept the Egyptians poor, ignorant, and isolated from the rest of the world, and Mohammed Ali was determined to change all that and carry out a radical transformation of the country.

The most important step that the new viceroy took is that he, as Marsot put it "Egyptianized Egypt."[67] For the first time since the Bedouin Arabs conquered Egypt in 641 CE, Egyptians were allowed to join the Egyptian army. They had been prohibited from joining the army because their foreign rulers had always feared that that might lead to a revival of the national spirit.[68] Now, Mohammed Ali's eldest son and army commander, Ibrahim Pasha, who felt loyalty to Egypt rather than the Ottoman Empire, was determined to Egyptianize the army.[69] Mohammed Ali's French advisors had recommended drafting Egyptian peasants into the army just as Bonaparte had drafted French peasants into his army and succeeded in turning them into good soldiers.[70] Egyptians began to be appointed to positions of responsibility in the administration of their country for the first time after centuries of foreign subjugation and relegation to the position of the hired servants of their alien conquerors.[71]

Mohammed Ali's reforms touched every aspect of society. Farmers appointed by the Ottomans as their tax collectors were evicted, and some of their land was given to the newly created elite of native Egyptians who now replaced them and administered the villages.[72] Land reclamation and irrigation projects were embarked upon, and a scheme of tax exemptions for those who wished to cultivate the newly reclaimed land was put in place.[73] The existing irrigation canal system was dredged and improved, and the production of long-staple cotton was encouraged. New modern industries, such as arms, textiles, and silk were established, and import duties were levied to protect the new manufacturing industry.[74] Mohammed Ali founded the first printing press in Egypt, apart from the one that Bonaparte had brought over and which the French had taken back with them when they left. He published the first Egyptian newspaper, *el-Waqai' el-Misriyya*. He formed a consultative assembly. A modern educational system was put in place, and schools of engineering, medicine, midwifery, metallurgy, accounting, industrial arts, agriculture, veterinary medicine, and a military staff college were established.[75]

The newly available educational opportunities were open to anyone able and willing to take advantage of them, with the state covering all the students' expenses including room and board.[76] Students were sent abroad to acquire modern skills, and the first group, composed of forty-four students who were to study a variety of subjects such as administration, law, military arts, political science, military engineering, navigation, medicine, mineralogy, irrigation engineering, cannon manufacture, printing, and chemistry, left for France in July 1826.[77] By1849, 311 Egyptians had been sent to study in England, France, Italy, and Austria.[78] Not surprisingly, the Ottomans mocked Mohammed Ali, referring to him as Pasha el-Nasara (the Christians' Pasha) because of his policy of making skill and competence, rather than religion, his only criteria in appointment to high positions.[79]

Mohammed Ali was attempting a huge leap forward by transforming Egypt from a backward and stagnant subsistence economy to a modern industrial one. Building a modern army in which Egyptians served and introducing a modern system of education were radical policies that resulted in a significant modification to the social structure that was to impact the course of events in Egypt long after his incompetent descendants had squandered his legacy.

The First Glimpse of Modernity   115

In taking these steps, Mohammed Ali was creating the one social stratum that is capable of providing the impetuous for reform and modernization in society, namely the educated middle class.

Egypt was finally joining the modern world and the future looked bright. It was starting to redress the effects of centuries of misrule by corrupt, avaricious, and ignorant foreign rulers. It was breaking out of its subjugation, enforced isolation, stagnation, and backwardness and turning its face from the arid desert of the Arabian Peninsula to the Mediterranean and to Europe. Rifa'a el-Tahtawi (1801-1873) personified Mohammed Ali's vision of the new citizen of the new Egypt that he was fashioning out of the chaos and devastation to which Bonaparte had borne witness. Tahtawi was a brilliant young man who had been sent to Paris with the first group of students simply to be their *imam* (prayer leader and religious advisor), but instead turned into a true renaissance man. He became fluent in French, read everything he could lay his hands upon, and absorbed the ideas of modernity and the philosophies of the enlightenment. His extensive reading list included biographies, works in the humanities and social sciences, and books in the fields of the natural sciences among others.[80] On his return to Egypt, Tahtawi made a significant and lasting impact not only on the Egyptian educational system but also in the area of nurturing a new class of intellectuals in the country. He even proposed the revolutionary and almost heretical concept for his era that the ruler's exercise of his absolute power should be carried out within the limits of the law.[81]

In view of Egypt's tragic history during the previous millennium, it all seemed too good to last. And it was. Had the term been coined at the time, Britain would have described Mohammed Ali's vision for an Egypt that had a sound economy, a modern educational system, and a solid industrial base, as a program to manufacture weapons of mass destruction. All the major European powers had colonial ambitions, and an independent modern Egypt was inevitably viewed as a possible threat to European hegemony over the Mediterranean. The British had watched the growing power and influence of Mohammed Ali with increasing concern, and colluded this time around with their European and Ottoman allies to find a way to thwart him. On October 20, 1828, a force of British, French, and Russian naval squadrons destroyed the Egyptian fleet in the Greek port of Navarino signaling the beginning of the end of Egypt's budding industrial revolution and its power and influence. Mohammed Ali was eventually forced into signing the 1840 treaty of London, which mandated a drastic reduction in the size of the army to eighteen thousand men, the dismantling of all arms factories, and the removal of all the import duties that were designed to protect the infant industries and to nurture the industrial revolution started by Mohammed Ali. The treaty effectively ended Egypt's bid for independence and modernization, and the country once again became a province of the Ottoman Empire. It paved the way for Britain to replace the Ottomans as the country's occupiers a few decades later and to turn it into a mere cotton farm for the British textile mills.[82]

Mohammed Ali died in 1849 and his vision for Egypt died with him. None of his descendants, who ruled Egypt until the military coup of July 23, 1952, matched him in stature, intellect, vision, judgment, or personal qualities. Mohammed Ali's son, Ibrahim Pasha, who had been appointed viceroy in March 1848 during his father's terminal illness, seems to have had some promising qualities, but tragically, he died of tuberculosis before his father on November 10, 1848. Mohamed Ali's grandson, Abbas Pasha, was then appointed viceroy, and it was back to business as usual, a *déjà vu*.

Abbas was a throwback to the type of ruler Egypt had grown accustomed to ever since its first subjugation by illiterate conquerors. His father Toussoun would, by all accounts, have been a far better viceroy, but he had died young. Abbas was a man who had no vision and no plans for the country apart from undoing his grandfather's reforms, at which he succeeded in the five short years of his rule before he was assassinated. He closed the schools started by his grandfather,[83] and put an end to almost all public education in the country.[84] He reversed his grandfather's reforms in every single field, exiled Rifa'a el-Tahtawi to the Sudan, and saw no need for an army or navy. In a nutshell, he was content to be an Ottoman vassal,[85] and to continue to collude in the millennium old process of exporting Egypt's wealth to a far away capital rather than investing it in building the country's infrastructure.

After the death of Abbas, it was the turn of another of Mohammad Ali's sons, Said Pasha. He revived some of his father's development projects in the fields of agriculture, irrigation, and education, and would have been remembered as a reasonably enlightened ruler had he not done anything else. However, he was naïve enough to believe that he would gain world fame by signing the inconceivably one-sided Suez Canal concession that his friend Ferdinand de Lesseps had drawn up.[86] It obligated him, among other things, to borrow money to buy the company's shares and to provide corvée labor of twenty thousand persons per shift for three shifts a day to dig the canal, using their own tools because the company provided them with almost nothing.[87] One hundred thousand Egyptians eventually lost their lives toiling under these difficult conditions. The young man's gullibility and credulity seem beyond comprehension today. The rights that he signed away and the endless list of obligations to which he committed Egypt[88] and his successor were staggering.

That successor was Ismail Pasha (1863-1879), who was granted the title of Khedive by the Sublime Port in Turkey. An intelligent man with a compelling personality,[89] he was the only one of Mohammed Ali's descendants who seems to have had some of his grandfather's vision for Egypt. However, he was hampered by the onerous financial obligations inherited from his predecessor, which he tried, without success, to renegotiate. For example, the canal treaty obligated him to construct a freshwater canal to bring Nile water to the new cities along the Suez Canal, then to purchase the land at the newly inflated prices after its development, and to buy back the now available freshwater from the Canal company.[90] At the same time, Ismail's ability to finance his reforms was hampered by the fact that forcing tens of thousands of peasants to leave their fields to build the Canal inevitably resulted in a drop in agricultural production and a concomitant drop in government revenue. Adding to his problems, the price of cotton, Egypt's main export, collapsed after the end of the American civil war, and he ran into severe financial difficulties.

Ismail was also not as wary of the British or as suspicious of their motives and intentions as Mohammed Ali had been. He made the mistake of asking Britain, which together with France owned the largest part of Egypt's debt, to nominate two financial experts that he could employ in his finance department.[91] Britain, to Ismail's surprise, sent its paymaster general, Stephen Cave, with a mandate to look into Egypt's finances and report to London. France, which was competing with Britain for control of the country, proposed the establishment of a local bank that would operate under international oversight to handle the debt crisis.[92] Britain, on the other hand, was maneuvering to use the debt crisis to eliminate French influence in Egypt and vetoed that proposal. When the British Prime Minister made a public announcement in parliament that Ismail had informed the British representatives that he objected to the publication of Cave's findings, the announcement, predictably, set off a panic in the financial markets and a selloff of Egyptian securities.[93] Ismail was forced to sell his shares in the Suez Canal Company to pay off some of the debtors. Britain, which purchased Ismail's shares for a fraction of their original cost,[94] was then a step closer to ridding itself of both the ambitious Ismail and the French.

By 1876, Egypt was nearly bankrupt, and the *Caisse de la Dette Publique*, a four-member commission, was formed in an attempt to oversee Egypt's finances. The financial crunch was further exacerbated by Ismail's personal extravagance and the ambitious and comprehensive nature of his reforms. He had borrowed from European moneylenders at extortionate rates of interest to finance these reforms.[95] The commissioners of the *Caisse de la Dette Publique* were unable to find a satisfactory solution to the deteriorating financial situation. One of the four commissioners, Sir Evelyn Baring, whose family was one of Ismail's main debtors, lobbied the British government to oust Ismail.[96] The British government was receptive to the proposal, and once again, Egypt's hopes for development and reform were dashed when the Ottomans, who were the nominal masters of Egypt, yielded to British pressure and deposed Ismail, the architect of these plans, and appointed his spineless and insipid son, Tawfiq (1879-1892), in his place.

Some contemporary Egyptian historians criticize and unfairly dismiss Ismail as a mere despot and a spendthrift with grandiose and unrealistic ideas. The severest criticism usually comes from post 1952 historians who were either lacking in knowledge or too intimidated to deviate from the official party line of demonizing Mohammed Ali's dynasty and denying that any of his descendants ever did anything positive for the country. Whatever the man's faults were, to his credit, Ismail had a vision for the country that he ruled. Not content to simply tax the Egyptians to finance a lavish lifestyle, he had instead attempted to implement an enlightened and ambitious modernization program. Among his many achievements were: opposition to the slave trade, which was suppressed in 1877; the reestablishment and expansion of the education department abolished by Abbas; the building of a modern infrastructure, which included hospitals, irrigation canals, transportation and communication facilities such as telegraph lines, ports, roads, railways, and bridges;[97] the opening of the first school for girls in the country; and establishment of Egypt's first Consultative Assembly in 1866.[98] He moved his residence from the citadel high above Cairo to the newly built Abdin Palace in the center of the city, a city he transformed into a modern metropolis that boasted the first bridge to be built on the Nile from its source to the Mediterranean (Kasr el-Nil bridge), several scientific societies, and an Opera House.

The new Khedive, Tawfik, had none of his father's qualities, and it appeared at first that apart from reversing some of his predecessors' reforms, his reign was destined to be as unmemorable as Abbas's. However, the seeds planted by both his father and his grandfather had begun to bear fruit. Egypt now had a small, educated middle class that had aspirations for their society as well as for themselves. In 1881, a new law was proposed barring Egyptians from promotion to senior ranks in the army and reserving these ranks for the Turco-Ciracassian class. Ahmad Orabi, an officer from one of the better-off rural families, led a protest by army officers opposed to the new law. Orabi was supported by several educated pashas, intellectuals and other notables who had been demanding a broad constitutional reform.[99] Tawfik, who had neither inherited his father's nor his grandfather's forceful personalities, was frightened, did not know how to respond to Orabi, and sought the advice of the foreign consuls. Britain and France, alarmed at the possibility of a rebellion, issued a series of demands that included the exile of Orabi and his supporters, and sent units of their navies into Alexandria in a show of support for Tawfik.[100] This created an atmosphere of panic and hysteria in the city. Alexandria was finally beginning to emerge from the state of decay and rot into which centuries of ignorant and despotic rule had transformed it. It was fast developing as a cosmopolitan center of trade and commerce, and several thousand Europeans had taken up residence in the city. The threat of an imminent British or French invasion by the war ships visible off the coastline inflamed nationalist feelings, and many of the foreign residents feared for their lives and began to arm themselves. The situation was volatile and the spark that ignited the explosion was a fight that broke out between a drunken European and an Egyptian donkey-boy he had hired for a ride and then refused to pay for the service provided. The Egyptian boy was killed in the altercation and serious riots broke out. The situation quickly got out of control and 163 Egyptians and seventy-five Europeans were killed.[101] Tawfik panicked and requested the foreign fleets to shell the city then land troops to confront the rebellious Egyptian army. The French refused and sailed off, but the British complied. They bombarded the city on July 11, 1882 [102] and then landed an army that began the military occupation that was to last until 1954. The Khedive, a grudging, petty and intolerant man who was scared enough to have fled to the safety of a British ship during the disturbances, was reluctant to return to his capital where the prospect of seeing his officers wearing their swords in public unnerved him.[103]

Egypt now entered a new era in which the official ruler was sidelined and became irrelevant. The new ruler of Egypt was a new type of despot who went by the title of Her Britannic Majesty's Proconsul-general and Agent. Sir Evelyn Baring, who had returned home after his service on the *Caisse de la Dette Publique* and tried unsuccessfully to run for Parliament, was appointed to the post[104] in 1883 and remained in it for almost a quarter of a century until 1907. Sir Evelyn Baring had a great deal in common with the many tyrants who ruled Egypt before the arrival of Mohammed Ali. Like previous despots, Baring left Egypt far wealthier than he was when he first arrived almost a generation earlier. Like them, he was also intent on extracting as much of Egypt's wealth as possible and exporting it to a faraway capital, although he accomplished the task in less obvious ways. Like previous despots, he had no love for the country that he was sent to rule. He even denied that an Egyptian nation existed,[105] and felt that Egypt was an unremarkable and characterless country.[106] The Egyptians, Baring believed, were generally lesser human beings, and like most of the rulers imposed on the country by foreign empires, the one-time president of Britain's "Men's League for Opposing Woman Suffrage" was not known for his progressive sentiment.

Lord Cromer, as Sir Evelyn Baring later became, is a name that most Egyptians have come to loathe with a passion. He had far more in common with el-Alfi bey—the Mamluk prince who viewed Egypt as a cow that if well fed would give more milk—than with Napoleon, who tried to bring in modern ideas and methods and who attempted to preach the principles of the French revolution and the concept of citizenship to Egypt's *ulama*. The subject races, Cromer believed, were neither able to, nor did they deserve to rule themselves, and keeping them fed was all that was required to keep them quiet and compliant.[107] In communicating his views on the composition of the Egyptian government to Lord Salisbury in London, he stated that the notion that the Egyptians could rule themselves was almost as ridiculous as the notion that a "savage" Native American chief could be appointed to govern Canada.[108]

Nevertheless, Cromer was a comparatively benevolent despot who realized, much as Amr ibn el-Aas did centuries earlier, that relatively benign rule, an efficient administration, and non-extortionist taxation would be in his personal interest as well as Britain's. For example, while Cromer was undoubtedly cruel and despotic, to his credit he did not go as far as the textile factory owner who appointed an English supervisor to oversee the Egyptian workers and whose job it was to walk around with a long whip and flog the workers because they were believed to be slothful and unwilling to work.[109] He also differed from many of the rulers who preceded him in that he did not amass his wealth by simply taking it from the Egyptians under the guise of taxation as most of them did. He acquired his fortune in the same manner as the Turkish *wali*, Ahmad ibn Tulun, in the ninth century: by trading. Cromer traded, or perhaps more accurately speculated, in Egypt's main crop, cotton. He was an able administrator who ran the country reasonably efficiently, reformed its finances, returned it to solvency, and restructured the justice system.[110]

Cromer's most damaging, long lasting, and heinous deed, however, was assigning to his tennis partner, Douglas Dunlop, absolute control of every aspect of education in Egypt. Dunlop retained that control for almost a whole generation, during which time he deliberately stifled any attempt to nurture an intellectual elite in Egypt,[111] and fought successfully to thwart the efforts of the country's small number of educated individuals to establish a national university. Dunlop, labeled "the assassin of Egyptian education,"[112] by the onetime minister of education, Sa'd Zaghloul, was a Scottish missionary who, like his friend Cromer, had little fondness for the Egyptians. Despite his thirty years of residence in Egypt, he never found it necessary to learn Arabic and refused to hire any British teachers who spoke Arabic[113] because he felt that acquaintance with the language would give them an unrealistic view of Egyptians.[114]

The Egyptian educational system, which Khedive Ismail had been in the process of developing before the British occupied the country and took control of it, had been molded by the European influenced Rifa'a el-Tahtawi and Ali Mubarak, who had had different priorities from Dunlop's. Both Tahtawi and Mubarak, who played a major role in modernizing the school system, were products of Mohammed Ali's policy of creating and nurturing an educated class of professionals. He had sent them to study in France, where they were exposed to the French views of nationhood and the positive role that it could play in education. They viewed the concepts of nationhood, belonging, and active citizenship as important goals to be nurtured in schools.[115] Dunlop's educational philosophy, on the other hand, consisted of promoting the *kuttab*, the traditional system of village education in which peasant children were simply taught to memorize the Koran and nothing else. Dunlop saw that as a cost effective method of educating the Egyptian public. He severely limited access to primary education by raising the school fees and followed a policy of teaching very little more than reading, writing, and arithmetic to provide Cromer's administration with clerical workers.[116] Cromer, perhaps unwittingly echoing Karl Marx's dictum that religion is the opiate of the people, also felt that increasing the number of hours devoted to the study of religion would distract people from thinking about independence and keep them placid.[117] This is somewhat ironic in view of the fact that he worked so diligently to prove that there was no such thing as the Egyptian nation. Cromer's declared goals, quoted by his authorized biographer, the Marquess of Zetland, were to reform the country's financial situation and help its people to prosper, to save them from oriental despotism, and to guide them "towards the true civilization of the west" and prosperity guided by the "Christian moral code."[118] Evidently, there was no room for education among these lofty goals.

By his own standards, Cromer was certainly successful. He did lead Egypt to financial solvency, but he did it by eliminating all investments in the future. His economic legacy was the destruction of local industry due to the imposition of taxes on Egyptian manufactured products[119] and the transformation of the country into a monoculture.[120] He turned Egypt into a gigantic cotton farm[121] in which ignorant and uneducated workers toiled to produce the raw materials needed by the mills in faraway Lancashire. When he left in 1907 after almost a whole generation as the effective ruler of Egypt, only 1.5 percent of Egyptians were enrolled in primary education, a smaller percentage than the 1.7 percent under Ismail a generation earlier.[122] Cromer had lamented the position of women in Egypt, which he had viewed as an obstacle to his attempts at "civilizing" the Egyptians.[123] Yet, according to his own 1901 report, when he had been the country's virtual ruler for eighteen years, the number of Egyptian women who were literate was a mere 0.3 percent.[124] Furthermore, Egyptian roads became unsafe,[125] and the country settled into a period of financial solvency coupled with utter social and political stagnation.

It appeared that Egypt was destined to remain as Cromer's fiefdom for the rest of his life. He was satisfied with his position, and the British government was satisfied with his job performance. The arrangement was certainly financially rewarding for both parties, and the notion that *Liberté, Egalité, Fraternité*, might have informed British colonial policy was, as evidenced by their correspondence, considered to be a preposterous idea. Relief from Cromer's tyranny only came when the notorious Dinshway incident[126] turned public opinion in Britain against Cromer.[127] On a hot June day in 1906, a group of British officers accidentally killed the wife of a villager during a pigeon-hunting excursion into the countryside and a threshing barn caught fire, which might have been an unfortunate coincidence but the villagers believed that British gunfire had started it. The villagers, already unhappy at the destruction of their live-stock (pigeons were bred by the peasants' and formed part of their meager diet), were enraged and chased the culprits one of whom died of sunstroke before arriving back at the British camp. In a demonstration of British justice, to which Cromer claimed to have introduced Egyptians, a special court was swiftly convened in a nearby town, and gallows were set up outside the village before the court examined the case. Four young men were convicted and hanged in full view of their families while others received sentences ranging from life imprisonment to public flogging as the frightened villagers watched.[128] The liberal British press covered the incident in some detail, and there was a public outcry against the draconian response to what should have treated as an unfortunate but relatively minor incident. Both deaths were accidental, but an entire Egyptian village paid for the sunstroke that killed the British officer, and no British officers were brought to task for the shooting of the village woman.

When Cromer, claiming ill health,[129] finally retired in 1907 in the wake of Dinshway, Egypt began to take timid steps towards reversing some of his "reforms" despite the obvious difficulties caused by the continuing British occupation. December 21, 1908 saw the official opening of Egypt's first modern university. It was a public institution established with funds donated by a cross section of the population. Donations ranged from personal pieces of jewelry donated by members of the royal family, to land donated by Princess Fatima Ismail, to cash donated by the public.

The man on the throne, Tawfik's son Khedive Abbas Helmy II[130](1892-1914), was not the cowardly, servile, and compliant individual that his father was. He admired his grandfather Ismail, was scornful of Tawfik, whom he referred to as *"le défunt,"*[131] and had demonstrated his defiance when, as the new khedive, he had apparently dared to disobey Cromer's minions while Cromer was away on home leave.[132] When the Great War was declared in 1914 and Turkey took Germany's side, Britain decided to take that opportunity to sever Egypt's link with the Ottomans. The country now became a British protectorate; the independent-minded Abbas Helmy was deposed; and his uncle, Hussein Kamel, was installed in his place and given the title of sultan rather than khedive.[133] After Kamel's death in 1917, his son, Prince Kamal el-Din Hussein, had no interest in the throne, and Britain placed Khedive Ismail's son, Fuad (1917-1936), on the throne.

The cause of education took another small step forward when the British finally agreed to allow an American missionary group devoted to education in the Middle East to establish an institution of higher learning in Cairo. Charles R. Watson, a missionary and the founder and first president of the new institution, was an Arabic speaker who believed that the cause of modernization and self-rule in Egypt would be served by establishing an American liberal arts institution of higher learning.[134] He had tried for years to obtain approval for the project from successive British officials without success. Dunlop, as Watson knew, did not have a great deal of affection for the Egyptians,[135] and when Consul General Lord Kitchener was approached, his response was that the time was not right to be considering such a venture.[136] The reaction of the High Commissioner, Sir Reginald Wingate, to the Americans' requests was to appoint a committee to study the project in 1916, but was not convinced that such an institution of higher education was an appropriate venture.[137] The Americans, true to their ideals, did not give up, and the institution that eventually became the American University in Cairo finally opened its doors in 1919, coincidentally the same year a major revolt against the British occupation took place.

Led by members of the educated middle class,[138] calls for independence, which had been heard in one form or another since 1882 when the British first landed in Egypt, were now intensifying. The spark that ignited the 1919 revolution, however, was the British refusal to allow a delegation (*wafd*), headed by Sa'd Zaghloul, to travel to London to put the case for Egypt's independence before the British government. The idea of sending a *wafd* originated with Prince Omar Toussoun and enjoyed wide public support. The British overreacted by arresting the *wafd* members and deporting them to Malta, fully expecting that these harsh measures would quell calls for reform and for independence. Instead, massive strikes and demonstrations took place in all major cities. Every segment of the population became involved: government officials and employees, teachers, students, industrial workers, lawyers, and other professionals. Even veiled women took to the streets demanding independence and the return of their exiled leaders. The country was paralyzed. In response, the British resorted to force, and several European residents, British soldiers, and hundreds of Egyptians were killed. The British finally had to accept that nationalist fervor was making the country ungovernable and driving it towards chaos. The *wafd* leaders were eventually released, and Egypt was granted independence in 1922, but that independence was nominal and proscribed by very narrow limits.[139] Nevertheless, the timid steps that Egypt had taken toward democracy and constitutional monarchy more than half a century earlier with Khedive Ismail finally culminated in the promulgation of the 1923 constitution, and the liberal experiment began.

The Liberal Period

In spite of the suspension of the reforms that had been started by Mohammed Ali and Khedive Ismail, mainly as a result of British meddling in Egypt's affairs, the seed that was planted had continued to grow, albeit very slowly. By the turn of the twentieth century, a tiny educated middle class had begun to emerge. Attitudes towards modern education began to change, and its usefulness was more widely acknowledged. It began to be valued both for its own sake and as a means of social mobility. Many upper class families sent their sons to universities in Europe, and the number of graduates began to increase when the national university finally came into existence. The graduates of Cromer and Dunlop's educational system had been tutored only in the rudiments of language and mathematics with the aim of providing low-level functionaries for the administration. Nevertheless, this allowed them to read one or more of the dozens of newspapers and periodicals that proliferated during that period. They began to develop a consciousness of their reality as an occupied country and to be educated about civic affairs, the world that existed outside Egypt, and how different forms of government operated. They were exposed to the ideas of nationalist leaders such as Mustafa Kamel, and Sa'd Zaghloul, and to the writings of leading intellectual figures such as Mohammed Abdu, Gamal el-Din el-Afghani, Ahmad Qasem Amin, and Ahmad Lutfi el-Sayyid, who articulated the need for reform in Egypt and mobilized public support for it.[140] Although Kamel and his political party, *el-Hizb el-Watani*, as well as el-Sayyid and *Hizb el-Umma* party sought independence and reform, they represented two very different approaches to these issues. Kamel viewed Egyptian nationalism as independent of Arab nationalism and defined independence as ending the British occupation while preserving of Egypt's link with the Ottoman Caliphate.[141] His base of support came from the Turkish and Circassian elite,[142] the lower middle class, and the masses.[143] These groups were essentially traditionalists who opposed radical social reform and the calls for women's emancipation,[144] and felt that independence from Britain should precede any attempts at reform. El-Sayyid and the *Hizb el-Umma* on the other hand were composed of the upper middle class, large landowners, and the Western-oriented educated class.[145] They were non-traditionalists, lacked mass support,[146] defined nationalism in purely territorial terms without reference to religion, and felt that independence from Britain would be easier to achieve after political and socio-cultural reform was carried out.[147]

Lord Cromer had unwittingly created a venue for lively debate and discussion by allowing Egypt to have a free press. He may have thought that what the Egyptians thought and read was inconsequential and could do his administration no harm, or he may have considered a free press to be a safety valve that would allow any malcontents to vent off in a harmless manner. Whatever his reasons were, Egypt became a magnet for writers and journalists escaping the oppression of the Ottomans in other parts of the Arab world, especially Syria and Lebanon, and who established several newspapers and magazines that provided for vibrant intellectual debate.

The period between the two world wars in Egypt was characterized by intellectual and artistic dynamism, vibrancy, innovation, and exploration of new ideas, as well as political turbulence and turmoil. Many of the young men who yearned for independence from Britain were frustrated by the establishment politicians' inability, or in the view of some, unwillingness, to take serious steps to secure that goal. The 1919 revolution that had eventually resulted in gaining limited independence from Britain and the promulgation of the nation's first constitution in 1923 seemed to have run out of steam. The themes of independence, of national regeneration, and how to achieve these goals, reverberated in all corners of the society and especially among the younger generation. Tawfiq el-Hakim's novel *'Awdat el-roah* (Return of the Spirit) about a charismatic leader was published in 1933 and Mahmoud Mokhtar's famous statue *Nahdat Misr* (Egypt's Renaissance) was completed in 1928. Both typified the national frame of mind and the concerns of the educated classes during that period which the poet Hafez Ibrahim (1870-1932) articulated in his well-known poem "Egypt Talks about Herself."[148] The thoughts expressed in the poem also gained a much wider audience when it was put to music and sung by the popular singer Om Kalthoum. Even the Arabic language and its written form were debated. There were proposals to Egyptianize Arabic; to use colloquial to educate the masses and leave the *fosha* (classical Arabic) to the educated elite;[149] or to replace the Arabic script with Latin letters.[150] Louis Awad took the unprecedented step of using colloquial Egyptian Arabic to write a book about his student days in Cambridge.[151] There was a profusion of books, magazines, and newspapers representing every intellectual current and political ideology from the right wing fascist to the left wing communist. There was a burst of activity and experimentation in all areas of art and creativity and artists were breaking new ground in the fields of poetry and literature, music, song, novels, theater plays, and films. The younger generation of Egyptians searched for an identity,[152] and for solutions to their society's problems among these conflicting and competing ideas. The lively political and intellectual debates and controversies created a charged atmosphere in society. Agitation, protest marches, and violent demonstrations became regular events. There were also both failed and successful assassination attempts on politicians and public figures for a variety of reasons.

Independence, incomplete as it was, marked the start of what historians such as Marsot have come to refer to as the liberal experiment of 1922 to 1952. The 1923 constitution, the best that could be achieved under the circumstances was, however, imperfect and gave the king far too much power. King Fuad, an autocrat who did not want any limits placed on the exercise of his authority, was backed by the British, who remained the *de facto* rulers of the country[153] with no interest in nurturing democracy in Egypt. The imperfect constitution and the continued British control of the nominally independent Egypt are perhaps the two key factors that helped to pave the way to the next seminal event in Egypt's history, the military coup of 1952.

The liberal experiment was complicated by a combination of factors. Being an autocrat, King Fuad I constantly undermined the democratic process.[154] Although he was a reasonably enlightened monarch who sponsored the establishment of the Arabic Language Academy as well as several museums and many scientific societies, he was a man of small stature who lacked both his father's and his grandfather's vision and ambitious outlook for Egypt. The British, who in view of the terms of independence were the effective rulers of the country, ignored the democratic structure whenever they found it convenient to do so, and continued to pursue a high-handed policy that constituted a serious impediment to the development of a democratic culture. *El-Wafd*, the delegation that had been formed originally to negotiate with the British, had been transformed into a political party with the same name, but it lacked a formal mechanism for mass recruitment and membership.[155] Likewise, none of the other small political parties that were founded had a mass membership. Consequently, there was no mass participation in the democratic process. That remained the preserve of the small, educated class. Personal rivalries between politicians, pursuit of self-interest, differences in temperament and philosophy, all contributed to further reducing the effectiveness of political parties.[156] In addition, the elected governments seemed unable or unwilling to alleviate the hardships caused by the 1930s world economic depression, which caused the annual per capita income in Egypt to drop by one third.[157]

Liberalism, it seemed at the time, was not going to lead to real independence for Egypt, to eliminating the nepotism and corruption that permeated the upper ranks of its political system, or to solving its economic problems. Segments of the petty bourgeoisie such as low rank government employees and small business owners began to be attracted to some of the new social and political movements that had started to form in Egypt. A group of young lawyers who were fascinated by Europe's fascist régimes established *Misr el-Fatat* (Young Egypt), an organization modeled on Mussolini's party in Italy. Idealists formed several communist and socialist organizations, and a preparatory school teacher in the town of Ismailiyya formed the Muslim Brothers Society.

Each of these groups had a different conception of Egyptian nationalism[158] and was descended from a different intellectual lineage. They not only differed in the political programs that they advocated but also in their view of what should form the core of the Egyptian national identity: Islam, territoriality, or language.[159] The most eloquent proponents for the cause of independence during the first decades of the twentieth century were Mustafa Kamel and Ahmad Lutfi el-Sayyid. The former advocated some type of limited political link with the fellow Muslim Turks and felt that supporting the Ottoman caliph against British designs in the region strengthened Egypt's struggle for independence and did not detract from the concept of Egyptian nationhood in which Muslims and Copts formed one *umma* (nation).[160] Ahmad Lutfi el-Sayyid on the other hand advocated a purely territorial, secular identity, arguing that religion could lead to divisiveness, and rejected the notion of any political link with the Ottomans.[161] The Arabic language centered identity was the least deeply felt link among Egyptians before WWI,[162] after which it made some gains in popularity. The strongest felt link after WWI was the territorial secular identity, whose proponents' tended to deemphasize religion as a source of identity and hold negative attitudes towards the Arabs.[163]

The most prominent Egyptian intellectuals of that period, such as Ahmed Lutfi el-Sayyid, Tawfiq el Hakim,[164] Mohammed Hussein Heikal,[165] Salama Musa, Taha Hussein, held very negative views of the Arabs and saw Egyptians as having little in common with them and nothing to gain by association with them. The Arabs were viewed in the context of the age-old conflict between the hardworking peasant and the uncouth, marauding Bedouin bent on terrorizing him and robbing him of the fruits of his labor, and the term Arab was associated in their minds with "savagery and backwardness."[166]

The attitude towards Arabs even extended to those who were not viewed as Bedouins, such as the Syrians, albeit for different reasons. They were resented for their collaboration with the British occupiers and their lack of allegiance to Egypt. For example, Abdullah el-Nadim (1844-1896), in his call for national unity, excluded the Syrians "whom he attacked with particular violence as foreigners (*dukhala'*) [intruders], exorbitant money-lenders, and tools of the foreign conqueror."[167] Mustafa Kamel shared el-Nadim's view of the Syrians as *dukhala'*.[168] El-Sayyid also balked at the idea of the annexation of Syria by Egypt that some Syrian dignitaries proposed to him.[169] The Syrians felt that bringing together Egypt's wealth and Syria's men would benefit both countries, but el-Sayyid's reply to the Syrian delegation that proposed the scheme to him was that Egypt had nothing to gain by such an association.[170] He advised them that the Syrians who chose to make Egypt their permanent home should instead declare their allegiance to Egypt by taking its citizenship.[171] El-Sayyid's reply stemmed from the resentment that some early twentieth-century intellectuals felt towards the Syrians who lived and prospered in Egypt but collaborated with the British and felt no allegiance to the country.[172] Some of Egypt's politicians, such as Sa'd Zaghloul, the leader of the 1919 revolution, shared these opinions, and had no interest at all in associating Egypt with the Arabs. Zaghloul's well-known phrase: "zero plus zero equals zero," was directed at Abdel Rahman Azzam when he attempted to win him to the cause of Arab unity.[173]

The intellectual climate in Egypt was, however, beginning to change by the late thirties and early forties as a result of two factors. The first was the growing influence of a new and increasing educated class that one researcher dubbed "the new *effendiyya*,"[174] who divided the world into east and west and placed Egypt in the east.[175] This new group differed from the more Western-oriented pre 1930s intellectuals in that they came from a lower social stratum,[176] and most of them were educated in Egypt and had not had the opportunity to travel to Europe, which might have broadened their horizons. It was this group that, by the 1940s, began to dominate public debate and determine the course of intellectual discourse in Egypt.[177]

The upper middle class Western-oriented elite began to be marginalized, and their focus on Egypt's pharaonic heritage was condemned by Islamists who viewed it as foreign inspired.[178] The Islamists called for modifying the school curriculum to deemphasize this ancient heritage, with the result that the periods prior to the Arab invasion of 641 came to be "simply ignored" in the school curriculum.[179] The considerable number of Arab immigrant writers and journalists in the Egyptian media strengthened and promoted this attempt to erase the Egyptian identity and replace it with an Arab one.[180] These immigrant journalists were mainly from Syria/Lebanon where support for Arab nationalism "had become the dominant ideology."[181] One indicator of this dominance was that the Syrians and Lebanese had constituted almost half (180 of the 387) of those who sent telegrams of support to the June 1913 First Arab Congress held in Paris[182] which the Egyptians were not allowed to participate in or to address,[183] presumably because they were not considered Arabs. By the early twenties, however, the Syrians had had a change of heart and were attempting to convince the Egyptians that they were fellow Arabs after all. Yet curiously, these immigrants, as el-Sayyid noted, were reluctant to take Egyptian citizenship.[184]

Evidently, a number of Arab intellectuals had begun to have second thoughts about Egypt's Arab credentials. Perhaps the line in Hafez Ibrahim's poem "Egypt Talks about Herself" where Egypt states "if the Lord determines that I should perish you will not see the East raise its head" struck a cord and they began to realize that an association with Egypt could be beneficial. Abu Khaldun Sati el-Hosary, an Iraqi writer, clearly recognized that an association with Egypt could be useful for the Arabs, as the title of his 1936 essay, "*dawr Misr fil nahda el-qawmiyya el-Arabiyya*"[185] (Egypt's Role in the National Arab Renaissance), indicates. He lamented Egyptian disinterest in Arabism and expressed the hope that the new intellectual trend of placing Egypt in the east (as opposed to the west or the Mediterranean) would eventually lead to the spread of Arabism in Egypt.[186] Correspondence between the prominent Syrian/Lebanese intellectuals Shakib Arslan and Rashid Rida also shows clearly that they saw benefits in associating themselves with Egypt. Rida wrote to Arslan in 1921 urging him to berate the Egyptians for their aloofness from the Arabs and inform them of the Arab countries' wish to subordinate themselves to the Egyptian state if they are granted self-determination in the future.[187] The Syrian attitude was a classic demonstration of the love-hate relationship that the Arabs seem to have always felt towards Egypt. On the one hand, they yearned to associate themselves with it and to go to Egypt because they coveted its wealth and were drawn to a society that had a heritage that was far more sophisticated than their own. On the other, they had a visceral hatred for it because of that very wealth they coveted and the ancient culture and civilization, which they lacked. They used the term pharaonic in a derogatory sense and labeled as arrogant Egyptians who took pride in their heritage. At the same time, however, they sought to associate themselves with the very culture and civilization the pharaonic era produced by claiming that the pharaohs were actually Arabs.[188]

Although Egyptian writers such as Salama Mousa, Hussein Fawzi, Ismail Ahmed, Amir Boqtor, and Amin el-Kholi continued to champion the Mediterranean Western orientation during the 1930s,[189] it was becoming clear that they were swimming against a powerful prevailing tide. The new *effendiyya* class referred to above was more open to both the Arab and the Islamist orientations. The contrast between the two orientations is exemplified in Taha Hussein and Hassan el-Banna. Taha Hussein included the Arabs when he wrote about the cruel treatment of Egyptians at the hands of foreign invaders, for which he was vilified.[190] Hassan el-Banna, on the other hand, claimed that, "Arab rule in Egypt had been 'a spiritual, enlightening, cultural imperialism'."[191] The turbulence produced by competing nationalist and political ideologies was contained to a certain extent by the firm, authoritarian, and severe King Fuad. However, it was becoming increasingly clear that the *effendiyyas'* orientation was in the ascendance. While King Fuad's autocracy was effective in maintaining stability in the short term, that same trait had a very negative influence on the way he raised Farouk, his only son and heir to the throne, and proved eventually to be one of the major factors that contributed to political instability during his, Farouk's, reign.

When Fuad died and Farouk ascended to the throne of Egypt on April 28, 1936, he enjoyed enormous popularity. All segments of society viewed the enthronement of the handsome young man as a portent of a new age of reform and progress. At best, that was a remote possibility, given the new monarch's personal characteristics and lack of any meaningful training for the position that he occupied as head of state. Born February 11, 1920, Farouk had been, according to the published diary of a one-time palace nanny,[192] a very lonely child[193] who ate all his meals on his own and had to sit in the palace garden for an hour every day to learn patience. His father kept him isolated in the palace and never allowed him to have friends of his own age. His one friend, whose photograph he kept next to his bed, was his nanny's nephew, Jan, whom he turned into a make-believe friend.[194] Adel Sabet, whose mother was a cousin of Farouk's mother, Queen Nazli, wrote that Farouk was even isolated from the royal family and was not allowed to see or play with their children.[195] His education was conducted by private tutors at the palace and consisted of learning languages and little else. In October 1935, Farouk was sent to continue his education at a minor military college in England, Woolich Military Academy, where he was allowed to sit in on some classes while private tutors helped him to prepare for the entrance examination. Even though, according to his Oxford educated Egyptian tutor, Ahmad Hassanein, Farouk wasted all his time sleeping, or shopping in London,[196] it is possible that in time some of the gaps in his education might have been filled. However, fate intervened, and King Fuad's sudden death six months after Farouk's arrival in England brought his education to an abrupt end, and he was summoned back to Egypt to take his father's place on the throne.

By the time Farouk ascended to the throne of Egypt on April 28, 1936, his childhood experiences had turned him into a weak-willed individual who lacked the wherewithal to become an effective monarch. Either his palace tutors had been incompetent and unable to teach him what his future role as king would entail, or he lacked the ability to comprehend that role, or perhaps he simply did not care. Whatever the case, he was never able to grasp the fact that a king's public and private actions are scrutinized by his subjects and could have serious negative consequences. Socially inept, he seems to have been comfortable only in the company of his servants and hired domestic help, who became his closest advisors. These included Antonio Pulli, an Italian electrician, Mohammed Hassan, his Egyptian valet, Mohammed Helmi, an Egyptian car mechanic, and Karim Thabet.[197] Thabet, whom he appointed to the post of press advisor against the prime minister's advice, was a Lebanese individual of dubious reputation who had been accused of corruption[198] and authored a book[199] of embarrassing sycophancy in which he presented the king as a legend and as the icon of perfection in everything imaginable.[200] The Swiss palace barber and Italian dog trainer were also close confidants of Farouk.[201] Even his Italian manicurist authored political reports for him.[202] His second wife, Queen Nariman tried unsuccessfully to convince Farouk to fire Thabet and the other servants.[203] It gradually became widely known that these unqualified and corrupt courtiers controlled access to the king, and issued instructions in his name to public officials, but the king appeared unaware of or unwilling to question their actions or their blatantly corrupt practices and influence peddling. Some of those who came in contact with Farouk did attempt to advise him to rid himself of these people, but he never took heed of the advice. The Captain of his yacht, el-Mahrousa,[204] Admiral Galal Alluba, whom Farouk apparently trusted and requested be the one to take him on his last journey on the royal yacht,[205] when he was deposed in 1952, was one of those who attempted to make him aware of the harm that his staff were doing to his reputation and urged him, unsuccessfully, to replace them.[206] He relates several incidents when he, Alluba, refused inappropriate requests from the courtiers, such as a request to promote a male nurse on the yacht's crew[207] or to avoid payment of import customs by including a shipment of goods among the king's personal belongings as they were being loaded onto the yacht.[208] In both cases, Pulli, who was making the request, complained to the king, who rebuked Alluba but was forced to back down when Alluba explained his reasons for the refusal and Farouk was unable to present a counter argument.[209] Others also advised the king against his partiality for and dependence on servants, but to no avail.

One plausible explanation that might throw some light on Farouk's partiality to the servants was his persistent feelings of inadequacy. Admiral Alluba, who first met the king in 1946 when he was appointed to the crew of the royal yachts, spent months with him sailing around the Mediterranean and frequently chatted with him in private. Admiral Alluba suggests in his memoirs that Farouk felt inadequate when he compared himself to his politically savvy father, Fuad, and his brilliant great grandfather Mohammed Ali.[210] These feelings of inadequacy probably stemmed from his lack of education and were intensified by his humiliation at the hands of the British ambassador in 1942; his popular and strong willed first wife, Queen Farida, and the public's disapproval of his divorce from her on November 19, 1948. All these factors would have contributed to making the company of servants even more appealing. It would be reasonable to assume that Farouk's preference for such company also resulted in part from his wish to avoid disputes, even if they were minor ones, with those who might have the strength of character and disinterest needed to counter him, such as the one with Alluba mentioned above. His sense of inadequacy may also explain his apparent need to be seen in public with beautiful women, a need that perhaps outweighed the negative press he received when, for example, he sailed to Famagusta in Cyprus to take part in judging a beauty pageant in which the Egyptian actress Camellia was participating.[211]

The start of the Second World War in 1939 was another factor that further complicated the situation in Egypt and added to the problems engendered by an incompetent monarch. All of the country's resources had been mobilized to contribute to Britain's war effort, and Egyptians suffered high prices and food shortages as a result. The country was overrun by allied troops, whose needs were met regardless of the cost to the population, and whose crude and arrogant behavior did not endear them to the Egyptian public. The irony was not lost on Egyptians that the war against Nazi Germany was touted as a war against dictatorship and for democracy, even though Britain was, at the same time, denying Egypt independence and subverting its democratic institutions. It is ironical that while democracy gained ascendancy in Europe throughout the nineteenth and twentieth centuries, the British systematically denied it to what was sometimes referred to by some as the subject races.

The myriad of competing ideologies on the Egyptian political scene made the British suspicious of the loyalty of many of Egypt's politicians, and when the government resigned on February 2, 1942, the British demanded that the king invite the anti-fascist leader of the Wafd party, Mustafa el-Nahhas Pasha, to form a new government. The king was not keen on the idea and would have preferred a coalition government headed by Nahhas. It was unfortunate for all parties concerned that the British ambassador in Cairo at the time, Sir Miles Lampson, happened to be a man whose arrogance and high-handedness belonged in the nineteenth century era of gunboat diplomacy rather than the mid-twentieth century epoch of rising aspirations for freedom.

Two days after the government's resignation on February 4, 1942, Lampson presented the king with the non-negotiable demand that he invite Nahhas to form a government before 6:00 P.M. that day. The ultimatum implied that there would a high price to pay if the demand was not complied with.[212] When the king did not meet the deadline, units of the British army surrounded the royal palace in Abdin, and Lampson swaggered in, accompanied by several officers, and demanded the king's abdication. The boy, as Lampson liked to refer to the king, caved in at once, and invited Nahhas to form the new government.[213] Ironically, had Lampson been even more arrogant than he was, and insisted upon abdication, he would, in all likelihood, have done the country a great favor and changed the course of history.

Lampson's arrogance and lack of foresight inflicted significant long-term damage not only on the king, the monarchy, and the main political institutions of Egypt's fragile democracy, but also on British interests in the region. His idiotic actions demonstrated to the Egyptian masses that the monarch, the parliament, and the country's biggest political party could be brushed aside easily and rendered irrelevant and incapable of pursuing national interests. The previously popular Wafd Party now lost its legitimacy in the eyes of the electorate, who witnessed its leader's willingness to form an alliance with the British for purely political gain. The king's humiliation at the hands of the occupying power fueled a surge in anti-British feelings. Unrest, agitation, violence, and demands for independence continued during the post war period. Strikes became regular occurrences and some groups began calling for a guerrilla war against the British forces based in the Suez Canal Zone. The establishment of the State of Israel in May 1948 was another event that added to the turmoil in Egypt. Both the king and the Muslim Brothers called for Egypt to go to war with the new state to protect the Palestinians. The Muslim Brothers, who were tacitly supported and funded by the British as a counter weight to the independence movement, declared it to be their religious duty, and the king was still smarting from his humiliation at the hands of Lampson and looking for a role for himself. The prime minister, now Mahmoud Fahmi el-Nuqrashy Pasha, and his minister of war met with the king and warned him that the country was unprepared for an armed conflict, and the king appeared to heed their warning. The very next day, however, the two men were surprised by the king's call in the media for Egypt to go to war on behalf of the Palestinians. The inevitable result of this rash decision was a defeat by Israel. Public opinion was inflamed, the king's popularity sank to a new low, and a new element of disquietude was added to the explosive situation in the country. Yet another serious development was the military training that some members of the Muslim Brothers Society received during the Palestine war. El-Nuqrashy Pasha recognized that this could have serious ramifications and ordered the Society dissolved. His fears proved justified when he was murdered three weeks later by a member of the group.[214]

The king's irresponsible conduct was progressively eroding his standing and authority. In addition to the fiasco of the Palestine war, his divorce from the much-loved Queen Farida, his personal conduct in the Cairo nightclubs, and the involvement of his corrupt courtiers in shady business deals[215] put him on a very slippery slope. There were indications that the democratic institutions, flawed as they were, would, in all likelihood sooner rather than later, force reform upon the incompetent, uneducated, and politically inexperienced monarch. One such attempt at affecting court reform was made on October 18, 1950 when sixteen prominent intellectuals and politicians, including a former prime minister, wrote advising the king that there was a general belief in the country that servants ruled Egypt and urged him to rid himself of them. Their warning of the dire consequences of his irresponsibility could not have been more explicit. They warned him of the widespread knowledge and disapproval of his conduct and fear that it could lead to the spread of destructive ideologies, political unrest, and even rebellion.[216] Although this attempt was unsuccessful, it is unlikely that these leaders, and perhaps members of his own family, would have allowed this state of affairs to continue indefinitely.[217] A military coup was one possibility that many politicians hoped to forestall by intensifying their calls for reform and persuading the king to heed the ominous signals, of which there were certainly many. The king had lost the enormous popularity and good will that he had enjoyed when he first ascended to the throne. His graceless personal life, inappropriate public and private behavior, and scandals in the corrupt royal court were widely known and discussed in all quarters. The public no longer looked up to him, and his family must have been both worried and embarrassed by his inability to curb some of his excesses. He must have been aware of the stream of negative newspaper and magazine articles exposing cases of corruption that appeared regularly in the Egyptian media, yet he alienated all political forces and made no attempts to build alliances. He apparently had no love for the British and saw no need to court them or to try to exploit their considerable influence in the country. He made no serious effort to cultivate any of the political groups or to try to repair his image among public figures and opinion makers. He knew of his lack of popularity among certain segments of his army,[218] yet made no serious attempts to regain the army's loyalty. His only allies seemed to have been his domestic help and a few opportunists and sycophants.

After almost three quarters of a century of British promises of independence, it became clear to most people that force was the only means of encouraging them to leave. Several secret groups organized armed resistance, and attacks on British military personnel and property in the Suez Canal Zone became daily occurrences. Events began to accelerate, and either an explosion or a major political change became inevitable. Successive governments seemed unable to cope with society's problems, and political parties and informal groups and societies of every shade competed for public support in the volatile and unpredictable political environment. In addition to the Muslim Brothers and the pseudo fascist *Misr el-Fatat* Societies, there were several leftist organizations, some of which were led by members of Egypt's cosmopolitan community. These included: *Iskra* (a Russian word that means spark), *el-fagr el-gadid* (The New Dawn), *el-haraka el-dimuqratiyya lil taharrur el-watani* (The Democratic Movement for National Liberation) (HAEDITU or DMNL), and The Egyptian Communist Party (ECP).[219]

Finally, British forces provided the spark that ignited the explosion when they demolished several peasant homes to clear a road that led to a water supply for their army base in the Suez Canal Zone. This imprudent and ill-considered act provided further fodder to the already strong anti-British sentiment in the country, and attacks on British military bases intensified. On January 25, 1952 the British commanders' idiotic response was to escalate the situation by laying siege to a police station in the Canal town of Ismailiyya that was believed to be helping the guerrillas, and demanding that the policemen surrender their rifles. The policemen refused the ultimatum and the British troops assaulted the station. By the time the Egyptian policemen ran out of ammunition and surrendered, forty of them had been killed, and seventy were wounded. The spectacle of lightly armed policemen standing up to the might of the British army provided further stimulus to the growing nationalist sentiment and anti-British feelings and led to riots in Cairo where British businesses were burned and the downtown area was set on fire.[220] *Misr el-Fatat, Shabab Mohammed,* and the Muslim Brothers were among several political groups that were implicated in the riots.[221] The Shepeard's Hotel, a famous Cairo landmark that was a favorite British haunt, was among the first casualties of the fires. Dozens were killed, hundreds were injured, the country was plunged into chaos, and fear gripped the rest of the Cairo population. The burning and destruction began to spread to other shops and establishments before the government was able to regain control of the streets and put the fires out.[222]

The king responded to the crisis by dismissing the government, and the four successive administrations that followed each other within a few months seemed powerless to control the competing political groupings or to return the country to normality. A major social upheaval was inevitable. The king's ineptitude, weak character, and lack of preparation to rule effectively; his corrupt and incompetent governments; and the British inability to understand that nineteenth-century policies and methods could not be relied upon to solve twentieth-century problems, all contributed to the looming chaos and to making the country ungovernable. Rumors of a planned military coup were rampant.

6

Abolishing the Monarchy

The only certainty in 1952 appeared to be that a significant change on the political scene was imminent. The nature and desired shape of the expected change, however, was up for debate, and that debate created considerable turmoil. Some sense of Egyptianness seems to have survived into the early 1950s in spite of the foreign rulers' attempts at stifling it throughout the centuries of occupation. The persistent spark that was rekindled during the French period received further nourishment during the tenures of Mohamed Ali and Ismail, and a small educated class that was exposed to European values began to emerge. European interest in, knowledge of, and admiration for ancient cultures, in particular Egypt's, must have influenced this new educated class by providing them with knowledge of their ancient heritage that had not been available in Egypt, and by nurturing a sense of pride in that heritage. The Egyptian sense of identity was, however, about to be challenged yet again, and the effects of the centuries of misrule were about to prove crucial in determining the nature of the eventual resolution of the continuing turmoil in the country.

The blunders and abuses of both King Farouk and the British occupation authorities had intensified the struggle for reform of the political system and for independence from Britain. The conclusion of that chapter in Egypt's history, however, was not destined to bring about a happy ending. Instead, it ushered in a new era of misrule, one that was rooted in the cultural Bedouinization process that had taken place in Egypt in the previous centuries and that would threaten to extinguish the few remaining weak flickers of indigenous Egyptian identity that tenaciously persisted in the population. Egypt was to eventually disappear from the map and be replaced by the "Southern Province" of the United Arab Republic.

The Coup D'état

The situation created by the Cairo fire in January 1952 was clearly untenable. Rumors of secret plans, plots, and conspiracies contemplated by one or more of the many active political groups were widespread, and everyone was anticipating that *something* was about to happen. Thus, on the morning of July 23, 1952, when Egypt awoke to the news that a group of army officers calling themselves the Free Officers (FO) had taken charge of the country under the apparent leadership of General Mohammed Naguib, no one was surprised. Few realized, however, that the claim was exaggerated and that the situation was far from settled. Certainly no one, perhaps not even the real leader of the FO, Colonel Gamal Abdel Nasser, anticipated that the outcome of their actions would be the demise of the fragile democracy that had been going through protracted foetal development and the systematic dismantling and destruction of the major social and political institutions that formed the core of the nascent democratic system. Equally significant is that this date, although not realized at the time, signaled a radical shift in the system of social values and the start of a deep cultural stagnation and decline that has continued until today. The lively, even frantic, intellectual debates; the fierce competition between conflicting ideologies and opposing viewpoints; the vibrant literary scene; and the flourishing theater, cinema, music, and artistic productions and creations that were all hallmarks of the first half of the twentieth century were all about to come to a complete halt. The first act of this drama, however, gave no indication of the tragedy that was to follow; it was in fact a tragic comedy of errors.

When the FO, a disparate and disorganized group, went into action on the night of July 22, 1952, fate was smiling upon them, in spite of the significant blunders they made. Their plan called for the first move to be made by Colonel Youssef Seddik, an idealist left leaning officer whose assignment was to occupy the army's General Command Headquarters at midnight.[1] Zero hour had apparently been changed to 1:00 AM, yet no one informed Colonel

Seddik. He set out from his base camp at midnight,[2] promptly got lost in the streets of the Cairo suburb of Heliopolis, and was unable to find the support unit that was supposed to join his small force of sixty lightly armed infantrymen carrying one hundred bullets each.[3] Some reports suggest that those in the support unit were also unfamiliar with the area and had also lost their way.

Perhaps unperturbed, or perhaps in need of something to steady his nerves, Seddik apparently then left his small force in a side street and went to the nearby Palmyra Bar, had a couple of brandies, and came back to find that his troops had arrested two civilians who had been lurking around the unit in a suspicious manner. The civilians turned out to be Colonel Gamal Abdel Nasser, the group's actual leader,[4] and his fellow conspirator Major Abdel Hakim Amer, apparently on their way to inform him that they were postponing the coup because the authorities had discovered their plans.[5] Seddik, insisting that it was too late to stop because he had already arrested a senior officer who had turned up unexpectedly at the base camp,[6] proceeded to the General Command Headquarters.

The seven guards at the entrance challenged the attackers and exchanged shots with them for two or three minutes until the five to ten bullets that each of the guards had been issued ran out. Seddik then entered the building and, when a guard attempted to stop him as he was proceeding to the upper floors, shot him in the leg.[7] He went on to find General Hussein Farid, the Chief of Staff, who was meeting with other high-ranking officers, and promptly arrested all of them.[8] Taking over the General Command Headquarters was a major stroke of good fortune for the FO. With no other command center that could countermand them,[9] the group began to issue orders from command headquarters that appeared lawful and gave the impression to other army units that the junta was in full control of all the armed forces. This spectacle, of a small group of individuals, acting more like Keystone cops than a well-organized and well-coordinated movement, managing to take control of the country, said much about the impotence of Farouk's régime at the time. That impotence was further demonstrated when troops surrounded the king in Ras el-Tin palace in Alexandria on July 26. A few shots were fired by the Royal Guard, wounding two of the attackers. The attackers returned fire, and a few minutes later an officer walked out of the palace carrying a white flag and surrendered.[10]

The group that took control of the country with such incredible ease on July 23, 1952 consisted of less than a hundred junior officers, a number Naguib refers to when he recounts the events of the "coup" (his term) in his memoirs.[11] Only fifty or so of them[12] actually took an active part in the coup, and none of the Free Officers were Copts.[13] The Free Officers were a disparate group of idealists, opportunists, adventurers, nationalists, sycophants, and hangers on. They came from diverse political backgrounds, ranging from membership in or sympathies with: the secret pro-monarchy *el-haras el-hadidi* (the Iron Guard); the right wing Muslim Brothers Society (MB); the fascist leaning *Misr el-Fatat* (Young Egypt Society); and the Marxist, *el-Haraka el-dimuqratiyya lil taharrur el-watani* (HADETU), to no political party affiliations or strong sympathies with any of the other activist groups that proliferated in Egypt during the thirties and forties. An analysis of FO members conducted by Anouar Abdel Malek found that twenty of the twenty-three leading officers of the group had their social roots in the petit bourgeoisie class with ties to Islamic nationalism or fascist supporting organizations.[14] Most of them were opposed to rational liberalism and the democracy that was represented in 1952 by the Wafd Party and the Marxists.[15] With little in common other than their youth, junior army ranks, lack of education and experience beyond their limited military training, and the goal of changing the régime by force, this small group of about ninety officers was only one of the many groups that had been constantly forming and dispersing in the years following the end of WW II. Independence from Britain and reform of the inept political system and the corrupt royal court were in one way or another at the core of each of these groups' aims, and all evidence suggests that the original group was, for the most part, sincere in its pursuit of these goals. The FO, as one of its members admits, were certainly neither the most progressive, nor the most revolutionary of these groups, but they were the best organized.[16]

The most credible threat to the success of a contemplated military takeover in Egypt had been the possibility of British intervention. Their seventy-year occupation of the country had provided them with an intimate knowledge of the society, its politicians, and the political currents within it. They were well acquainted with all the active political forces and could assess their relative strengths and weaknesses, as well as the strategies and incentives most likely to motivate them and/or win their support. The more than seventy thousand British troops based in the Suez Canal Zone constituted a clear and present reminder of their ability to back their words with action if the need ever arose. Unlike the politically untutored King Farouk, Colonel Nasser understood this very well and took steps early on to neutralize that threat. His knowledge of prevailing political currents allowed him to do so with relative ease. The Americans at that time were secretly competing with the British for influence in Egypt,[17] and were intent on driving them out of the Middle East.[18] Nasser's knowledge of current affairs, if somewhat superficial, is probably what prompted him to instruct Abdel Menem Amin and Ali Sabry, two upper middle class officers in his secret organization, to open a covert communication channel with the Americans.[19] The two officers met several times with US embassy personnel before the coup in an attempt to win their support.[20] Nasser probably did not know it at the time, but fate it seemed was smiling upon him because Jefferson Caffery, the American Ambassador to Egypt in 1952, was descended from Irish stock and seemed to dislike the British, which would have made him well disposed towards those who were striving to expel them from Egypt.[21] In addition to that fortunate coincidence, both the US President and his Secretary of State had misgivings about Britain's approach to world affairs and saw it as outdated and a vestige of its empire building past.[22] The Americans, according to Khalid Mohi el-Din, were receptive to the conspirators' approach and assured Ali Sabry that they would pressure Britain not to intervene if a coup took place so long as it was not a communist coup.[23] Nasser's response was prompt. He instructed Khalid Mohi el-Din in March 1952 to stop using the term Anglo-American imperialism in the fliers that they were secretly distributing around the country and to use the term British imperialism instead.[24] Since the British were well aware of the extent of the régime's corruption and had come to the conclusion that the king was unlikely to initiate or support any serious attempts at reform, they went along with the American non-intervention strategy. They felt that a military coup might prove to be a positive development[25] and, therefore, made no attempt to protect the régime or to prevent the power seizure by the Free Officers, thus allowing the takeover to proceed relatively smoothly and to succeed.

The warning the king received on October 18, 1950 had proved to be prophetic, but when the FO moved against the régime of King Farouk that night they could not possibly have foreseen how quickly the régime would collapse or how easily they would take absolute power in the country. By this time, though, it seems the king had become fatalistic. He was fond of declaring that before too long there would be only five kings left in the world, one in England, and four in a pack of cards.[26] This defeatist attitude presaged disaster, and Farouk, as his queen, Nariman, asserted, presented Egypt to the junta "on a silver platter."[27] To be sure, the régime was corrupt, but the king, whose tragic circumstances had sealed his fate since the day he was born, was not the monster depicted by the group and their supporters. He was simply a hapless character struggling with a sense of his own inadequacy, with neither the personal traits to govern the country nor the will to put up even a semblance of resistance to the few dozen junior officers who rebelled against him.

The army had, in fact, few Free Officers, and support for the coup was limited to only a few army units. Corroboration for this appraisal of the situation on the morning of July 23 comes from sources as varied as Ahmad Hamroush, a member of the FO,[28] and Yasin Serag el-Din, a pre 1952 politician who maintained that the Royal Guard, the entire navy, and half the air force were loyal to the king.[29] The Navy's loyalty to the king was demonstrated in no uncertain terms when its Commander accepted Admiral Alluba's authority as the most senior officer present at the palace on the morning of the coup, and ordered the destroyer Ibrahim to patrol the coast of Alexandria. The Commander of the destroyer was fiercely loyal to the monarchy and kept repeating that he owed loyalty to none other than the king.[30] He requested Admiral Alluba's permission to strafe the Mustafa Pasha Barracks where the rebels had set up their headquarters, but Alluba refused to give him permission.[31]

The reaction of the king, in Alexandria for his annual summer vacation, to the threat to his throne can only be described as pathetic. When Farouk was informed that an attempted coup was taking place, his response was to summon his close advisors: the electrician, the dog trainer, the barber, the driver, the valet, two adjutants, an officer of the Royal Guard, and his pilot and order them to defend the palace.[32] The whole government was in Alexandria, the summer capital. The Commander-in-Chief of the army, who had not been among the senior officers detained in their Cairo headquarters by the junta, was also in Alexandria and available to advise the king. Yet he chose to look to the servants for help in coping with the most serious threat that he had faced in his life. Clearly, none of these individuals were in a position to provide him with useful advice, a sound assessment of the situation, or an intelligent analysis of his strengths and weaknesses, and as he should have expected, they lost no time in denouncing him and running for cover after his fall.

General Abdel Mohsen Kamel Mortagi was a junior officer in the Royal Guard stationed at Ras el-Tin Palace on the morning of the coup when the small army unit led by one of the FO attempted to enter the palace grounds. He recounted in an interview that the palace guards fired on the small army unit attacking the palace, forcing them to retreat,[33] and maintains that the coup would have failed had the king not been a coward[34] and not ordered the palace guard to surrender.[35] He too claimed that not all the army supported the coup, that the air force's loyalties were split fifty-fifty, and that the navy was completely loyal to the king.[36] The fact that none of the senior officers in Alexandria were detained by the FO[37] is indicative of the limited number of troops at the coup's disposal in Alexandria and adds weight to the claim that the king could have put down the rebellion with relative ease if he had had any leadership qualities. The accuracy of Mortagi's and others' assessment of the situation is also supported by the fact that it was only when the king showed his weakness by caving in so quickly and agreeing to their demands that the FO decided to go beyond their original plan. That plan had been to present the king with a demand to fire his corrupt court officials, to appoint Naguib as Commander-in-Chief, and to invite Ali Maher, a politician unaffiliated with any political parties, to form a new government.[38] Up until that point, the conspirators had had no plans beyond presenting the king with these three demands, then tailoring their actions to his response after an anticipated period of negotiations.[39] What must have been their stunned shock at the ease of their success is palpable in the first question that officers, meeting at the General Command after having taken it over, asked: "What do we do now?"[40]

The king appears to have panicked even before the success of the coup was certain or any demands were made. According to Admiral Alluba, Farouk telephoned him at home in the early hours of July 23 and ordered him to get the royal yacht ready to sail at once because a coup had taken place in Cairo.[41] Alluba carried out the order, went to report to him in Montaza Palace on July 24, and urged him not to flee but to order the Northern Army Command to blockade the road from Cairo to prevent the rebels from entering the city of Alexandria.[42] Farouk, anxious and apparently determined to flee, claimed that he did not wish to see the army units fighting each other and that no one knew how far the rebels would go in their demands, but compromised by moving immediately to Ras el-Tin palace, where the yacht was moored, instead of fleeing.[43] That same night the king, before receiving any further demands, summoned Alluba at 3.00 A.M. on July 25 and ordered him to prepare to sail before dawn.[44] He was apparently frightened and talked about the fate of France's king and queen after the revolution.[45] Alluba calmed him down again and urged him to accede to only one of the rebels' demands, firing the corrupt courtiers.[46] The frightened king ignored the advice and accepted all the demands immediately.

In view of the king's prompt acceptance of their initial demands merely hours after the coup, the officers met throughout that night to consider their next move. It was only then that they decided to depose the king and to keep their decision secret from the newly appointed Prime Minister.[47] Clearly, the revolution's goals were put together rather hastily. Salah Salem, one of the coup's leaders, admitted in an interview that he had not even read the much-vaunted proclamation, issued immediately after the king's ouster, listing the six goals of the revolution, and never knew anything about them until after the coup's success.[48] These goals were the elimination of imperialism and its Egyptian collaborators; the elimination of feudalism; the elimination of monopoly and control of government by capital; instituting social justice; building a strong army; and building a healthy democratic life.[49] Evidently eliminating the revolution's enemies, as Louis Awad observed years later, preceded its social and economic goals in the eyes of the plotters.[50]

Eventually, on July 26, Ali Maher, the new Prime Minister, was informed of the officers' decision and asked to obtain the king's signature on a document proclaiming his abdication in favor of his six-month old son, Prince Ahmad Fuad, and a commitment to leave the country before 6:00 P.M. of that same day.[51] Farouk immediately caved in, signed the document, took his family, and boarded the Royal Yacht el-Mahrousa, which was moored in the private harbor of the Ras el-Tin palace. A few minutes later General Naguib, the nominal coup leader, arrived at the yacht by launch accompanied by four officers.[52] While the junior members of the group did not find it necessary to observe accepted norms of etiquette and protocol,[53] Naguib, a respected and correct military man, saluted the king and expressed his regret at the necessity of having to do what they were doing. He was determined to honor the Free Officers' pledge that the king would leave with full honors including a twenty-one-gun salute.[54] This was perhaps a testament to the Egyptians' veneration of authority, to their non-violent nature, to the conspirators' caution, or to a combination of all three factors. In any case, a few minutes later, the officers returned to the palace grounds, and el-Mahrousa set sail for Italy at 6:30 P.M. The fact that it was the American rather than the British ambassador that the king requested to meet with as he prepared to go into exile[55] is indicative of the palace's adverse relationship with the British as well as testament to the king's utter lack of understanding of the political currents in the country that he ruled.

Although the king, as Alluba recounted, wept as they lost sight of the coast of Egypt, he regained his composure later that same evening, summoned Alluba and talked about how sad he was to have left Pulli (the Italian electrician) behind in Egypt.[56] He went on to instruct him to write a list of items that he wanted to have sent to him in Italy. The list included his clothes, including some that were still at the tailor's, as well as his favorite Mercedes. Alluba knew full well that no such requests would be granted and did not bother writing anything down,[57] but the incident suggests that even at that moment, the king, amazingly, did not appear to comprehend the enormity of what had befallen him. In Italy, he lived an unremarkable life in exile until his sudden death thirteen years later, while Egypt, as a result of this accidental revolution, entered a new era that some describe as tumultuous and eventful, and others as catastrophic and calamitous.

Initial Public Sentiment

The liberal establishment and the leftist parties all supported constitutional democracy, as did a sizeable segment of the public[58] at this point. The old political parties and the liberal elite of the ancien régime were, however, incapable of comprehending the new breed of young officers who now occupied the seats of power in the country and did not know how to handle them.[59] They were the product of a different social, educational, and experiential milieu, and were motivated by different values. In the run up to July 23, indications that something serious was bound to happen had been percolating for months, and yet none of the old establishment's prominent figures managed to grasp the new realities and regain their balance after being jolted by the coup. They continued to bicker with each other and were unable to present a united front to oppose the dismantling of the democratic system that they all believed in, and none of them even made a semblance of challenging the measures that were clearly intended to marginalize them and render them and their parties irrelevant.[60] The minority parties had no popular following and more or less melted away as their leaders began to run for cover. The Wafd party had a sizable popular following and might have been able to challenge the drift toward dictatorship. Despite its mass following, however, the Wafd was reluctant to oppose the anti democratic moves because it feared losing its popular base to the new junta.[61] That in itself was evidence of their lack of comprehension of the new breed of men who replaced them in power.

Behind-the scenes chaos following the ouster of the king reflected the far from expected outcome and the FO's lack of preparedness or aptitude to run the government. Plainly put, they were flying by the seats of their pants. On the surface, though, the transition seemed to be going smoothly. The coup,[62] despite the fact that it started as a mere military action carried out by a very small number of junior officers and was not the mass movement it was later depicted as being, gained very wide popular support after the fact—a revolution in reverse, one might say. The majority of intellectuals, regardless of their political views—liberal, leftist, independent, or Islamist—made statements of public support for the coup. Many writers, journalists, and public opinion makers also declared their support as soon as it took place. This is not to suggest that everyone who declared support for the coup understood its hastily put together goals or was motivated by altruistic or nationalistic impulses. Some may well have been opportunists who hoped that a régime change could be utilized for personal benefits even if they did not fully understand the young officers' end goals. Others may have understood, or thought that they understood, the officers' objectives but, faced with the uncertainty that seemed to lie ahead, thought it prudent to declare their support as a means of self-protection.[63] It is perhaps ironic that the only exceptions to the gushing support were the Egyptian Communist Party (ECP) and the leftist Workers Vanguard Movement (WVM). Both groups understood the full implications of what had just happened and the ECP referred to the events of that July 23 as a fascist military coup, while the WVM termed it a military dictatorship.[64] These two prophetic and lone voices of courage, reason, and rational assessment represented a small minority of Egypt's intellectuals and were easily ignored by everyone and drowned out by the outpouring of messages of support for the coup.

The vast majority of the Egyptian public viewed the ousted régime as corrupt and incompetent, and the coup leaders seemed to inspire hope for a change for the better. Their youth and perceived dynamism seemed to promise new solutions to the old problems that were plaguing society, and they inspired optimism. At the same time, the fatherly figure of the older, more experienced, better educated, and principled Naguib, provided reassurance that there would be a steadying influence that would act as a balance to any possible impetuousness or rashness by the junior officers that might lead to unforeseen disasters. Naguib spoke English, French, Italian, German, and had knowledge of Hebrew, Turkish, and Swahili.[65] His education included two graduate diplomas in law in addition to his having registered in a Ph.D. program.[66] He came across to the Egyptian public as a modest, self-deprecating man who readily acknowledged that his experience as an officer was not the type of experience political leadership required.[67] He made a point of assuring the population that any change would be gradual, that stability would be maintained, and that he viewed the goal of the coup as reform rather than radical change. He understood, as he stated later in his memoirs, the dangers of both xenophobia[68] and theocracy, which he believed to have no basis in the religion, and he believed in the parliamentary form of government.[69] He went to great lengths to assure every segment of the population that their rights would be protected and that their voices would be heard.

Naguib's fatherly demeanor and amicable personality made him extremely popular. He became the new régime's public face, and the newly formed Revolutionary Command Council (RCC), originally composed of the nine main conspirators from among the FO and expanded to fourteen with the addition of five other officers on August 15, 1952, became the junta's decision-making body.[70] The RCC members were largely unknown, and they tended to remain in the shadows. This was seen by the public as evidence of their altruism and lack of interest in personal gains, which projected a positive image and served to generate massive public support for the coup during its early days.[71] The general mood, therefore, was optimistic. The country appeared to be set on the right course, and most segments of the population felt confident that the new régime would right all wrongs.

The Warning Signs

Cracks in this image soon began to appear; however, only a very small minority took note of some of the early indications that the military men who had grabbed power in the country may not have been the altruistic and idealistic reformers that they claimed to be. One of the first cracks was the "thievery" by officers that Naguib himself, in his memoirs, noted began from day one after the coup.[72] Evidence of the Free Officers corruption, though plentiful, is mostly anecdotal. The majority of people either did not see this evidence, were too scared to speak up if they did, or simply chose to ignore it and give the new junta the benefit of the doubt. Although Naguib himself noticed, he apparently ignored what he may have discounted as minor indiscretions by a few bad apples.

Examples of the officers' behavior are not hard to find and include plunder of the royal palaces and of the property and personal belongings of members of the ancien régime who had been declared corrupt and placed under sequestration.[73] Many of the people who witnessed the events of 1952 have personal anecdotes of abusive or less than ethical conduct by those who billed themselves as the idealistic saviors of Egypt. For example, neighbors of Prince Omar Toussoun, in the exclusive Cairo neighborhood of Zamalek, witnessed his house being stripped of its contents by the Free Officers over a period of several evenings. They watched in fear from their darkened windows as army officers, detailed to inventory the house's contents following the coup, threw boxes, small pieces of furniture, and rolled up rugs over the garden wall into the street, then loaded them up into army jeeps and drove away.[74] A valuable dinner service from that same house was later sold in a major auction house in Europe. When a member of the family that owned it attempted to prevent the sale, he was informed that the Egyptian army officer offering the item for sale had presented official documents issued by the Egyptian government showing him to be the legal owner of the set.

Other royal residences were stripped bare of jewelry, antiques, and even clothes in many cases.[75] A leading journalist, 'Adel Hammouda, alleges in his book *el-Malek Ahmad Fuad el-Thani* (King Ahmed Fuad II) that King Farouk's valuable stamp collection; Queen Farida's tiara, encrusted with the Star of the East diamond that weighed 286 carats; and 1056 other precious stones disappeared after the coup.[76] He also reports having seen some antiques that were stolen from royal palaces in the Paris residence of King Farouk's son, Ahmad Fuad II, who had purchased them when they were offered for sale in Europe,[77] presumably by the very same individuals who grabbed power in Egypt to eliminate corruption. Another anecdote is provided by one of the FO who asserted that Salah Salem, a fellow Free Officer, helped the king's sister, Princess Fayza, to leave the country with her jewelry and later had trouble proving his ownership of the diamond ring that he received for his trouble when he tried to it sell in Geneva. However, the military government stepped in and "helped him."[78] This help would presumably have come in the shape of an official document similar to the ones provided to other officers seeking to sell other valuable objects in Europe. Another obvious example of large-scale pillage is the fact that the international auction that was arranged by the junta with much fanfare in 1953 and conducted by Sotheby's of London to sell rare stamps, 164 platinum and 261 gold pieces of jewelry, eight thousand rare gold coins, and various art works only netted the paltry sum of 700,000 pounds.[79] That would suggest that the king was either far poorer than the military junta claimed, or that someone had taken off with his stash! There is a small, admittedly inconclusive, perhaps even trifling, but nevertheless poignant reminder of the pillage by the officers, Free or otherwise, in Abdin Palace today. A few rooms at the back of the palace, which was the king's main residence in Cairo, are now designated as a museum and are open to the public. Even the most gullible visitor to these rooms can easily see that the whole collection consists of items that are quite worthless, difficult to sell on the open market, or no more valuable than many similar items found in antique or second hand shops in Cairo.

There were whispers at that time of pillaging and that a Major Magdy Hassanein, one of the Free Officers in charge of inventorying the royal palaces, had "freed" many of the royal jewels. He was asked decades later to explain the whereabouts of these jewels. Hassanein's answer was that there were indeed many jewels arranged in boxes in an underground tunnel in the Qobba Palace and that apparently indicated to him that the king had been getting ready to smuggle them out of the country.[80] However, he denied that any of the officers stole anything or became rich after the coup.[81] When the interviewer countered by telling him that he was reputed to be one of the richest men in Egypt and that it was reported in the media during the sixties that he donated 60,000 pounds to the army, Hassanein's reply[82] was both odd and disingenuous. His said that when he left the *Moderiet el-Tahrir* project[83] his monthly pension was only 23.23 pounds, and he had to give up his apartment because he could no longer afford the rent. He goes on to state that he then proceeded to give a Chinese diplomat a 4,000 pound bribe to arrange a deal to supply the government with 80,000 pounds worth of sugar from China, which earned him 20,000 pounds in profit. After that, he went to Russia, imported twenty-two tons of coal, and paid another bribe to someone in a large coal company to buy it from him.[84] Clearly, years of being above the law had either led Hassanein to believe that he had to answer to no one for his unlawful and corrupt actions, or that he was too dim-witted to think of a less incriminating story.

Far more serious for the country than the pillage of what was essentially part of the country's national heritage was the tendency to regard the law as mere form and to ignore or bend it whenever it was convenient to do so. President Naguib recounts an incident when Gamal Abdel Nasser, the then Minister of Interior, sought his signature on a list of persons he wanted to arrest. When Naguib objected to the inclusion of the former Prime Minister and leader of the Wafd party, el-Nahhas Pasha, his name was removed from the list and Naguib signed the order only to discover later that his signature had been forged on another document authorizing the arrest of el-Nahhas. He recounts another incident when he refused to sign a presidential decree stripping six persons of their citizenship only to find the decree published in the state's official record (*el-Waqai' el-Misriyya*).[85]

The king's abdication had presented the new rulers with a serious dilemma, and bending legalities took on a more sinister aspect. The new king was a minor and someone had to assume the task of performing his constitutional duties until he came of age. Paragraph fifty-one of the 1923 constitution stipulated the setting up of a Regency Council that would be confirmed and sworn in by a joint meeting of the Upper and Lower Houses of Parliament. The junta neither wanted to recall the parliament that they had dissolved, nor hold elections to form a new one. At the same time, they were afraid of public reaction if they were seen to be violating the constitution only days after taking power and pledging to uphold it. They asked the State Council, the highest court in the land and the one designated to adjudicate constitutional issues, to examine the matter and render an opinion.

The State Council met to discuss the constitutional position on the appointment of Regency Council on July 31, 1952,[86] and rendered an opinion that provided the officers with the legal cover that they required. The Council determined that it would not be a violation of the constitution to amend the Royal Decree of April 13, 1922 by adding a paragraph to it. The added paragraph stated that in the event of the king's abdication in favor of an underage crown prince, the Cabinet was empowered to select a temporary Regency Council composed of three persons who could be sworn in before the Cabinet and assume the king's authority until a permanent Regency Council could be appointed.[87] Waheed Ra'fat was the only member of the State Council who argued for adherence to the constitution and a recall of Parliament.[88] He and one other member resigned their positions on the Council shortly after that.[89] A Regency Council composed of Prince Mohammed Abdel Menem, a senior member of the royal family, Bahi el-Din Barakat Pasha, a respected public figure, and Rashad Mehanna, an army officer and member of the Shabab Mohammed Society,[90] was set up.[91] The Council exercised no effective power or influence and seems to have been viewed by the coup leaders as no more than a harmless necessary formality that provided a cloak of legitimacy and the appearance that all political forces were represented during a transitional period. Abdel Menem and Barakat would have provided a sense of security for all the democratic elements and Mehanna for the anti democracy elements and the army. Rashad Mehanna, however, did not see his role as merely ceremonial and began to meet with public officials and journalists. As a result, he was fired on October 13, 1952.[92] Barakat resigned shortly after that[93] and the Council was effectively, although not formally, disbanded.

One of the sad ironies, and an indication of the fragility of Egypt's institutions, is that some of the best legal minds in the country were the ones who taught the mainly uneducated new rulers how to ignore the constitution and how to tailor laws to suite their purposes. Khalid Mohi el-Din, one of only two of the fourteen members of the Revolutionary Command Council (RCC)[94] who were university graduates (the other was Mohammed Naguib), acknowledges this in his memoirs. He states that some of the top legal scholars in the country validated the officers' violations of democracy and the constitution by assuring them that a revolution makes its own legal precedents.[95] These scholars included Sayyid Sabry, a professor of law, Abdel Razzaq el-Sanhouri, head of the State Council, Seliman Hafez, his deputy, and attorney Fathi Radwan.[96]

Beyond theft, disregard for the constitution, and the growing power of the RCC, there were other danger signals that were overlooked. The trial proceedings as well as ruthlessness shown to the striking workers of the Kafr el-Dawwar textile factory a mere month after the coup should have been another red flag. In August 1952, ten thousand workers of the Misr Spinning and Weaving Company went on strike to back up their demands for better terms of employment and were brutally suppressed, with eleven laborers as well as three policemen killed.[97] The junta identified the young strike leaders and set up a military court to try them. The prosecutor asked for the death sentence for twenty-nine of the strikers, and two young men who were barely out of their teens were actually executed. The trial was a sham. The proceedings had already started when Colonel Abdel Menem Amin, a member of the tribunal, apparently noticed that there were no lawyers present to defend the young men on trial for their lives. He was able to remedy the situation immediately when he discovered that one of the journalists covering the trial had graduated from the faculty of law and asked him to defend the accused.[98] The significance of these proceedings was that they were an indication of the military junta's conception of what constituted justice and of how other individuals who might oppose the new rulers in the future could expect to be treated. The court was a precursor of the kangaroo courts that were to become the hallmark of the new régime. The communists were the only group that understood the significance of the trial. Ismail Sabry Abdullah, one of the founders of the Egyptian Communist Party, noted that they, the ECP founders, thought all along that the widespread public support would enable the junta to solidify its position but did not know what policy the FO would pursue. After the workers' execution, the ECP concluded that the Free Officers were fascist demagogues.[99] One possible explanation for both the lack of public outrage at the death sentences as well as Naguib's ratification of them is that communism was widely viewed as a major threat in the fifties, and the young strikers had been branded as dangerous communist agitators bent on destroying society. This may also explain why the future implications of trying civilians before a military court went unnoticed by the majority in the country.

Arrests became a regular occurrence. The many arrests, ranging from military officers who were pro-democracy, to other individuals whose only crime was having been prominent sometime in the past, to others who had no idea why they had been arrested, could also have provided an inkling of the intentions of the junta. The only political group that escaped the wave of arrests altogether was the Muslim Brothers.[100] Against this background of increasing arrests, Fathi Radwan, the first minister of the newly established propaganda arm of the RCC, the Ministry of Culture, and National Guidance, would not even offer an answer to a very general question about what policy Egypt was going to follow.[101] He simply stated that the time to answer that question had not come yet.[102] Such a reply did not seem, once again, to be a cause of general concern or to raise any alarm bells. Given the fragility of the democratic institutions,[103] the social mood of discontent that corruption and the king's callousness and scandalous behavior had nurtured, and some of the intellectual currents at the time, the ominous signals went unheeded. Only the more astute observers might have suspected either lack of direction at best, as indicated in the Minister's reply, or budding autocratic tendencies at worst, as demonstrated in the Free Officers' conduct.

The Clash of Values

The RCC and the remainder of the FO who had participated in the ouster of the king were a diverse group, but despite that diversity, two main political wings, reflecting different social and personal values can be identified. The first was represented by the thirty-two cavalry officers who constituted about one third of the less than one hundred original conspirators.[104] Many of these officers came from Western-oriented upper middle class backgrounds and tended to be liberals who viewed parliamentary democracy as the most desirable form of government. What they sought was reform. The king had already been exiled and once basic reforms such as ousting incompetent and corrupt politicians and passing the Land Reform Law had been carried out, this group believed that the next step should be for the army to return to its barracks, hand over the reins of government to a freely elected civilian government, and return the country to a parliamentary democracy that would continue the reform process.

Most officers of the second group, but certainly not all, came from the ranks of the lower middle classes, "the new *effendiyya*."[105] Ahmad Hamroush, an FO turned journalist, interviewed all those who participated in the coup and found that none of the fathers of members of this group had a civil title (Bey or Pasha) nor were they laborers or peasants.[106] They all belonged to the petit bourgeoisie,[107] and their social values echoed the socially conservative, authoritarian, and xenophobic tendencies[108] that were the hallmarks of that socio-economic stratum and the Arab Bedouin culture. None of the active participants on the evening of July 23 for example, had a father who owned more than fifty feddans (51.9 acres) in 1952.[109] None, with the exception of Naguib, came from military families, and a few of them had had trouble paying the eighty-pound annual tuition fee of the Military College and had gone into debt to pay it.[110] Very few had traveled outside Egypt or spoke a foreign language. Their most distinguishable characteristic was, to use P. J. Vatikiotis's description, their *baladi*[111] background.[112]

Most members of this group were reluctant to relinquish the power they had gained, either because they had quickly developed a taste for it and for the privileges that went along with it, or they were, to give them the benefit of doubt, sincere in their belief that a return to democracy was not in the best interest of the country. The differences between the two groups were too fundamental to paper over indefinitely. While some rumors of differences of opinion within the RCC did reach the public, the general mood remained optimistic at first; however, a clash between the two groups was inevitable, and it would not be long in coming.

7

A Squandered Opportunity

The significance of the 1952 military coup, though no one noted it at the time, was that it signaled the passing of the mantle of leadership from one social class socialized in one set of values to another that was socialized to a very different set of social values. Some social scientists characterize the process that took place in Egypt after 1952 as a militarization of society. There was certainly no doubt that the army had come to play a much bigger role in all aspects of life in the country. However, what the term militarization does not convey clearly is the extent and depth of social change that the military men brought about that is not related to their military affiliation but to their socio-economic backgrounds. The lack of an established military tradition in Egypt meant that the military was the secondary rather than the primary source of identity for these military men and that the main influence that shaped these officers' social values and worldviews remained the socialization process that they had experienced in the particular socio-cultural environments that they came from. Vatikiotis correctly points out that "[a]fter 1936, there was a 'proletarianisation' of the officer corps with the influx of mainly children of lower-class Muslim families, the same class of families from which were also recruited the followers of the Ikhwan [Muslim Brothers] and Young Egypt."[1] It seems most likely, therefore, that the village and the urban lower-class Muslim subculture remained a strong, if not the strongest, contributor to the officers' social values and personal identities. The change in society wrought by the new military elite was, therefore, a deep and complex process of peasantization and proletarianization rather than a militarization. As the political elite in any society has a disproportionate influence on the system of social values, the new elite's values were bound to eventually penetrate the social structure and remake society in the image of this new elite, and the most evident of these new values during the first two or three years following the coup were the preference for dictatorship over democracy, the suspicion of intellectuals, lack of interest in aesthetics, and disparagement of expertise.

The Slide Towards Autocracy

Egypt was now rid of the incompetent government, the inane and uneducated king, and the flawed democratic parliamentary system with its ineffectual political parties. Its destiny was about to fall into the hands of another uneducated man whose unhappy childhood, lower middle class authoritarian origins, shallow world view, and dreams of self-aggrandizement would eventually undo the small gains brought about by over a century of slow progress, negatively impact the value system, and take the country to the edge of bankruptcy and ruin.

Soon after the coup, one name other than Naguib's began to come to the forefront: Gamal Abdel Nasser, the FO's real leader, organizer, and main conspirator, who, in the two years before he became president, was pulling all the strings behind the scenes like a master puppeteer of a diverse cast of characters. One of the main differences between Nasser and the other FO was his intense yearning for power.[2] He expressed this yearning clearly during a meeting that took place in December 1952, less than five months after the coup. The FO were still allied with the Muslim Brothers at that time, and the meeting took place in the house of one of their prominent members, Abdel Kader Helmi, with four other MB, five RCC members, and one other army officer in attendance.[3] One of the remarks that Nasser addressed to Farid Abdel Khaleq, one of the MB leaders present during that meeting, is illuminating. He told Abdel Khaleq that he was consumed by the thought of acquiring such total control of the country within a couple of years that he would be able to move it or stop it at will by simply pushing a button.[4] Those who did not know Nasser well might have viewed such a statement by the unrefined thirty-four-year-old army colonel as a preposterous pipe dream. However, those who knew the single-minded scheming man would have taken that statement more seriously.

Nasser's social background and personal attitudes and values placed him firmly in the petit bourgeoisie group of the RCC, the anti-democracy faction. He held a deep personal antipathy towards the socio-economic elite and once asserted to fellow officer, Fathy el-Deeb, that wealthy people can never be patriotic.[5] That antipathy was also reflected in his apparent inability to accept that patriotism rather than personal gain might have motivated a member of that class to join the FO.[6] He felt no affinity with the cavalry officers, and did not share their social values and belief in parliamentary democracy, but was astute enough not to campaign openly for either of the two competing groups within the RCC. His policy was to keep his opinions to himself during the council's meetings and appear to bend with the wind, while keeping his cards close to his chest.

Naguib and most RCC members either publicly supported the call for democracy, or were reluctant to come out openly in support of dictatorship. Nasser, therefore, also professed support for democracy, while at the same time maneuvering the players behind the scenes and manipulating them to his will. He cunningly stage-managed the RCC's meetings[7] and dictated most of its important decisions from day one, while at the same time claiming to have no designs on the leading position in government. He astutely gave each of his colleagues the impression that he was, or at least that he could be, on that colleague's side whenever a difference of opinion regarding an issue under discussion arose. At the same time, he separately lobbied the RCC members, who were often divided by their own problems or personal interests, and usually managed to secure the majority opinion that he wanted.[8] Once a decision that suited him was taken, he openly supported it by claiming that he was only yielding to the democratic majority. When, for example, along with the differences of opinion already developing within the RCC, resentment arose among some members over Nasser's increasing grip on its decision-making process, Nasser adroitly managed the situation. Salah Salem, one of the RCC members, proposed reducing the council membership to five and sending the other four members back to their army units.[9] Nasser, on the other hand, opposed the proposal, claiming that he wanted a democratic style of collective leadership and resigned when his proposal for expanding the RCC's membership was not accepted immediately. The clever strategy worked and the council voted for the expansion.[10] A cunning and effective maneuver that served to dilute the power of troublesome members such as Salah Salem within the council and to make it easier for Nasser to isolate the troublemakers.

Again, when Seliman Hafez, the legal advisor to the RCC, and all the council members except for Naguib, Khalid Mohi el-Din, and Yousef Seddik argued against the recalling of parliament and against holding new elections and returning the country to democracy, Nasser, according to Seddik, supported the stance for democracy *in the beginning*.[11] He only abandoned this position when he found acceptance from the RCC members for the idea of taking power for themselves.[12] While publicly espousing support for democracy, Nasser at the same time privately implied his opposition to the democratic trio when he confided his true position to Abdel Latif Boghdadi, another RCC member. He told Boghdadi that he was unhappy with Naguib's insistence on following "normal legal channels."[13]

His ostensible support for democracy and opposition to what he referred to at the time as dictatorial tendencies within the RCC was, therefore, not genuine and most likely stemmed from his belief that the democratic forces, represented by the Wafd party with its wide popular support, were too powerful for him to be seen as opposing them. That obstacle, however, was soon to be overcome. The Wafd had put credence in the officers' promises to reinstitute parliamentary democracy and hold elections, and when the crunch came, its leadership proved to be no match for Nasser's machinations. Once Nasser realized that the party was not as powerful as it appeared and that establishing military rule in the country was possible,[14] he began to lobby his colleagues in the RCC against a return to parliamentary rule[15] and for the eventual exclusion of the old parties from the political process.

The first blow to the political parties was the General Command's announcement on July 31, 1952 that political parties, government departments, and all public organizations were to be "purified."[16] All the political parties were now required to reapply for registration and the new law, drafted by the officers' competent but gullible and compliant legal advisors, gave the Ministry of the Interior control over their registration and organization. Some members of the liberal establishment's intellectuals were not blind to the looming threats to democracy. Journalist, Ahmad Abul Fath, for example, grasped the significance of the call for purification immediately and published articles in which he urged the army to steer clear of politics, and the political parties to avoid antagonizing the new régime.[17] Jurist, Waheed Ra'fat also understood the serious implications of the new powers granted the minister of interior over party registration, and writer, Mohammed Mandour warned of the threat that abolishing political parties or putting restrictions on their formation posed to the democratic process.[18] The leftists, on the other hand, sought to take advantage of the new law by seeking to form a new party, and the Islamists, who had no interest in political parties, ignored the issue altogether.[19] The MB, which did not believe in democracy, was collaborating with the officers and believed that they would be part of the emerging autocratic régime. As for the party leaders, they continued their petty squabbles with each other, and the opportunists within each party attempted power grabs and precipitated internal battles.[20] None had the combination of street savvy and public stature to offer a credible alternative to the officers. This allowed the military junta to mount repeated assaults against both parliamentary rule and the parties while they were paralyzed and unable to respond.

First, the constitution was abrogated on December 10, 1952. Then all political parties were dissolved in January 1953 and their funds confiscated.[21] Finally the Temporary Constitution, promulgated on February 10, 1953, merged the legislative and executive functions of government and assigned both powers to the RCC and the Cabinet jointly.[22] Parliamentary rule was now successfully eliminated and the political parties rendered irrelevant. The use of the term temporary to describe the new constitution probably helped to blur the significance of this step at the time. Four months later the Regency Council became officially redundant when the monarchy was abolished on June 18, 1953.

In addition to eliminating the political parties, in particular the Wafd, another of Nasser's strategies for consolidating his power was sidelining Naguib within the RCC. The tactic that he followed was to meet often with RCC members both individually and as a group to ensure a united front when they met formally with Naguib present. While Naguib may well have been aware of the tactics behind the RCC's united front[23] when they met, his naiveté and democratic sentiments always led him to accede to the majority vote[24] and to ignore the many indications that Nasser was slowly increasing his political influence and grip on the various arms of government.[25] Thus, although opposed to abolishing the monarchy on the grounds that the king was only two years old and the Regency Council would not interfere in the governing of Egypt,[26] when the RCC voted to abolish it,[27] Naguib played into Nasser's hands and chose, as was his practice, to go along with the majority vote.[28] Naguib's selection as the first president on June 18, 1953 did not reflect his standing in the RCC. He was, it would seem, simply a pawn, but his popularity made him the only acceptable candidate for the position at the time.

The flurry of meaningless reforms in the early days after the coup, such as the abolition of civil titles, reduction of the number of government cars,[29] and the unrealistic announcements about forthcoming desert reclamation projects and other ambitious plans kept the public enthralled. At the same time, all the actors in the unfurling drama appear to have been playing the role assigned to them by the skilled director, Nasser, who had systematically eliminated all other potential opposition from the early days of the coup.

Troublesome FO and other prominent figures that continued their demands for a return to parliamentary government were dealt with relatively smoothly. Sarwat Okasha, for example, had been appointed, against his wishes, to the post of military attaché in Switzerland and left Egypt in September 1953.[30] Khalid Mohi el-Din was sent to Europe in 1954, ostensibly as a member of a trade mission, but with the understanding that he would not return.[31] Yousef Seddik, like Khalid Mohi el-Din, was a member of HADETU. He supported democracy and resigned in protest against censorship, the execution of the two striking Kafr el-Dawwar workers, and the large-scale arrests of army officers, politicians, and leftists, and was exiled to Europe.[32] When he returned to Egypt against Nasser's wishes, he was arrested along with his wife in 1954[33] and each of them received a five-year jail sentence.[34] Their servant was arrested along with the couple.³⁵ Ahmad Hamroush, another FO, was arrested on January 15, 1953 and released after fifty days, which led him to avoid any political activity after that, as he was aware of being under constant surveillance.³⁶ FO Abdel Menem Amin was appointed as Ambassador to Holland and told to either accept the post or be arrested and charged with plotting a coup.³⁷ Rashad Mehanna, who sympathized with the Muslim Brothers and was a member of the Regency Council, was put under house arrest in October 1952,³⁸ then taken into custody on January 7, 1953, tried before a military court at 3:00 AM, and sentenced to death. He was fortunate. The sentence was commuted to life imprisonment, and he was released a couple of years later.³⁹ A large number of cavalry and artillery officers were also arrested, retired, or transferred to remote locations during 1953 and 1954. One infantry officer, Colonel Hosni el-Damanhoury, made history by becoming the first officer in the Egyptian army to be sentenced to death for a charge other than treason. His trial lasted ten to fifteen minutes.⁴⁰ His sentence was commuted to life with hard labor a few months later.⁴¹

Troublesome public figures were also dealt with in a similar fashion, and all left-leaning intellectuals were neutralized soon after the coup. For example, Ahmad Fuad, the judge who had composed the six goals of the revolution at Nasser's request,⁴² was summoned by Nasser and warned that he was keeping bad company, so he cut all ties with the left leaning HADETU.⁴³ Abdel Aziz el-Shal, a physician, was arrested in January 1953, told that he would not need a lawyer to represent him in the upcoming court case because it was going to be a "family trial;" he was sentenced to ten years in jail, but released after two.⁴⁴ Fathi Khalil, a journalist, was arrested in 1953 and released in September 1955.⁴⁵ Zaki Morad, a lawyer, was arrested November 27, 1953, sentenced to five years, but kept in jail until 1964.⁴⁶ Thousands of others were rounded up and received varying prison terms.

While such purges and critical changes were being implemented, the new power elite successfully continued to distract and entertain the public with months of a stream of street dancing, parades, public exhibitions, and show trials that Ahmad Abul Fath describes in some detail.⁴⁷ Army officers accompanied by famous singers and dancers toured the country to collect donations for the poor during the newly launched Winter Aid Week. There was the Army Entertainment Week, the Chicken Week, and the Tree Week when trees were planted (but died shortly afterwards because no funds had been allocated to tend them).[48] There was the announcement that ministers would no longer be supplied with government cars to take them to their offices, and the newspapers published photographs of ministers traveling on crowded buses. There were photographs of ministers eating cheap *ful* and *ta'miyya* sandwiches,[49] and a stream of announcements about fantastic, unrealistic, and illusory plans published by journalists who did not dare question anything they received from any officer who wanted it published.[50] The string of gimmicks and theatrics that kept the masses entertained also distracted the intellectuals and kept them off balance. All failed, therefore, to react when Nasser announced on January 23, 1953, the formation of the Liberation Rally, now the only political party allowed in the country.[51] The public continued to ignore the signs when they appeared, and initially there was no public reaction when people finally woke up to discover that the officers controlled all ministries and public and private clubs.[52]

Everything had gone relatively smoothly for the FO from the first day after the coup and as the months went by, Naguib proved to be an extremely fortuitous choice as the junta's public face. Nasser, however, was jealous of his popularity and eager to take the spotlight for himself, but he prudently bided his time and avoided a public break with him. The masses saw Naguib as their only protection against an ominous military dictatorship,[53] loved him for his simplicity, and believed that he was not responsible for the new repressive measures that the junta was beginning to put into place.[54] His actions reflected his politics, and his swearing in ceremony as the first president of Egypt included speeches by the Sheikh of the Azhar, the Patriarch of the Coptic Church, and a representative of Egypt's Chief Rabbi, who was ill and unable to attend.[55] He toured the country, meeting with every segment of the population and attending services in Jewish, Coptic, Greek Orthodox, Armenian Orthodox, Catholic, Maronite, and Protestant places of worship.[56] The public saw Naguib as a scrupulously ethical man who practiced what he preached. He once issued an order preventing his youngest brother Mahmoud, who was an instructor in the Faculty of Veterinary Medicine at Cairo University, from accepting a scholarship to go to graduate school in Britain because of his concern that it might appear that the award was granted because of his, Naguib's, position as President. The terms of the scholarship were in fact in full accordance with both the university and ministry of education's regulations, and the court ruled in favor of the brother when he contested the presidential decision in a court of law.[57]

The way Nasser chose to deal with Naguib was to leave him to tour the country, make speeches, and cement public support for the new régime, while he himself worked behind the scenes to gain control of the army command structure, the ministries of interior and national guidance, the Liberation Rally, the media, and the labor unions.[58] Within a few months after the coup, he seems to have felt secure enough to begin to move cautiously towards his goal of replacing Naguib in the top post. He surrounded Naguib with spies who reported his every move. He began to minimize the president's public exposure by instructing the censors to limit publication of his public statements and by preventing his speeches from being aired on the radio.[59] The Liberation Rally, as its assistant secretary general recalled, began a propaganda campaign to bolster Nasser's public image.[60] At the same time, Nasser used the military intelligence to spread anti-Naguib rumors and enlisted the help of opportunists and sycophants in the media, such as journalists Mustafa Amin, Mohammed el-Tabei, Galal el-Din el-Hamamsi and Mohammad Hassanein Heikal, to plant stories that were intended to mock or embarrass Naguib.[61] One prominent journalist, for example, reporting on Naguib's visit to a poultry farm wrote that the chickens began to shake with pleasure at seeing the president.[62] In contrast, the same journalist's account of Nasser's visit to a mosque appeared to accord him a superhuman status and reported: "He stood there like all other human beings."[63] In his own public speeches, as RCC member Hassan Ibrahim has pointed out, Nasser warned against dictatorship[64] but this appears to have been little more than a cynical attempt to imply that Naguib was the dictator.[65]

His plan, however, had a temporary setback when he misjudged the situation and decided to speed things up by openly provoking Naguib. The inevitable clash with Naguib and the supporters of democracy took place thirteen months after the formation of the Liberation Rally during the last week of February 1954 when Naguib, the chairman of the RCC, learned that the Council was holding a meeting without him despite his presence in the building at the time. When his secretary, sent to inquire about the reasons for the exclusion, was insulted and thrown out, Naguib immediately resigned the presidency and went home.[66] But Nasser had overplayed his hand, had underestimated Naguib's public support, and had failed to take the pulse of the people accurately.

The new military elite was becoming unpopular. As members of the RCC started to carve out spheres of influence for themselves, they sent *mandoubs* (delegates) to spy on,[67] harass, and intimidate staff in ministries, public and private organizations, and even a movie studio.[68] The public, as a result, had started to sour toward the officers some of whom were beginning to be viewed as plunderers, who imposed repressive measures, and who swaggered around in their uniforms and wearing their side-arms[69] intimidating both government functionaries and the public. Naguib's resignation finally galvanized them, and large street demonstrations in support of Naguib were held on February 25, 26, and 27.[70] The masses obviously saw Nasser's scheming behind the ouster of Naguib and chanted: "To jail Gamal. No revolution without Naguib."[71] Students and professors also held similar demonstrations at Cairo University. The cavalry officers, together with the artillery officers, held a protest meeting in the cavalry officers' mess on February 26,[72] and the majority of officers in Alexandria declared their support for Naguib.[73] A United National Front that represented all political currents was formed at the universities and the Front demanded an end to marshal law, release of all political prisoners, formation of a coalition government to conduct elections, and dissolution of the RCC.[74] The university faculty, represented by the board of directors of their association, supported these demands. No one had any illusions about the threat facing the country, and many of the fliers being distributed ended with the slogan: "Down with military dictatorship."[75] The RCC met in haste to consider these developments and develop a response.

The situation was serious, and it appeared that the young adventurers who had attempted to take power in the country and set up a military dictatorship had failed in their attempt and were about to be sent to jail, as the masses were demanding. The dozen or so officers who constituted the RCC certainly had no illusions about their standing with either the masses or the various political forces in the country. They knew that they represented no one but themselves, and that their council had no popular base of support. Nasser privately acknowledged this to el-Boghdadi during the crisis,[76] and another RCC member, Kamal el-Din Hussein, publicly admitted to this several years later.[77]

By three o'clock on the afternoon of February, 27 the RCC members, who had been meeting in almost continuous session to discuss the crisis, were tired and voted to adjourn for four hours to go home and take a short rest. Nasser, who apparently needed no rest, informed them that he was going to stay behind in their headquarters to continue to monitor the situation and make decisions on their behalf. Shortly afterwards Salah Salem returned to the building and informed Nasser that the streets were full of angry demonstrators. He was shaken, agitated, and kept insisting that they have no choice but to return Naguib to his position as president. Nasser did not object, and Salem ordered Cairo radio to make the announcement. The other RCC members were still at home when they heard the news on the radio at 6 P.M.[78]

While others panicked, Nasser appears to have been the only one involved who managed to stay calm and to continue to manipulate, strategize, bend with the wind, and do whatever was necessary to contain the dangerous situation. All the other RCC members, claims Ahmad Abul Fath, who knew them personally and who witnessed these events, behaved with cowardice.[79] El-Boghdadi was afraid to leave his home and cried on the phone, and Zakaria Mohi el-Din, despite being the Minister of Interior went and hid in his village.[80] Salah Salem was utterly shaken when he encountered the hostile demonstrations on his way home. When Captain Mahmoud Hegazi of the cavalry telephoned Amer at one point demanding the release of all imprisoned officers and threatening to blast the RCC building where the council was meeting,[81] Amer also fell apart and threatened to commit suicide.[82]

The panic was not limited to the RCC members. A group of second line officers that had begun to attach themselves to one or more members of the RCC became hysterical at the news of Naguib's return to power.[83] They attempted a physical attack on the pro-democracy RCC member, Khalid Mohi el-Din, surrounded the cavalry barracks with artillery, and sent planes in flyovers over the barracks.[84] Two young captains took it upon themselves to go to Naguib's home and arrest him.[85] Nasser, on the other hand went calmly into the lions' den. At 3:00 A.M. he met with pro-democracy and, therefore, hostile artillery officers who had been holding a sit-in in their mess and attempted to calm them down. He informed them that the RCC has voted to dissolve itself and that its members would return to their army units. He also informed them that Khalid Mohi el-Din would form a six months transition government that would arrange for elections to be held and a permanent constitution to be prepared.[86]

Although the unrest and public demands for democracy continued unabated, Nasser neither panicked nor gave up the fight. He met with his colleagues on March 5 and informed them that they needed to release the pressure accumulating on them by the forces of democracy, calm the situation, and buy themselves some time. They voted to end the censorship of the media, lift martial law, release political prisoners, repeal the prohibition on political parties, and take steps to return the country to parliamentary rule.[87] The decree proved to be a masterstroke by Nasser who, as later developments would confirm, was calmly and astutely playing for time, and had not the slightest intention of acceding to the demands for democracy.

The protestors were placated and appeared to have won, and a joke circulating at the time reflected both disaffection with the coup and the belief that the rule of the military junta was over: An army officer begins to harass a woman traveling on a train with her husband. Her husband slaps the officer's face and another passenger sitting at the back of the train rushes forward and slaps the officer. When other passengers express surprise at such daring, the man replies, "Well the revolution is over isn't it?"[88] Many public figures also shared the public's relief at what was perceived as the end of military rule. For example, the prominent jurist, Waheed Ra'fat, and the leading intellectual, Louis Awad, were naïve enough to believe that the officers would return to the barracks.[89] The public sense of throwing off a yoke also resulted in the large incongruous coalition that had supported Naguib and democracy and that included the Wafd Party, the Muslim Brothers,[90] the communists, other leftists and the cavalry officers losing its raison d'être and crumbling.[91]

Ehsan Abdel Qoddous, a seasoned journalist who knew Nasser before the coup and seems to have understood him better than others, did not however share the sense of optimism.[92] He insisted that Nasser would never retire from politics. He also understood that the public debate was not about the return to parliamentary government but about the fate of the coup leaders if they lost their grip on power.[93] That, of course, was before Nasser jailed him for three months and he came out of detention demoralized and subdued,[94] never spoke so freely again and tended to confine his writing to novels and fiction. The accuracy of Abdel Qoddous's assessment of the situation was confirmed beyond doubt decades later when former RCC member Hussein el-Shafei admitted that his fear of going to jail was what led him to oppose dissolving the RCC and returning to democratic rule.[95]

The People's Voice: Down with liberty

Nasser, who with hindsight can be said to have been scheming to set himself up as an absolute ruler all along, was taken aback by the strength of the democratic sentiment in the country. He was worried and frustrated by the failure of his bid to oust Naguib, but he was far from being defeated. While claiming to support fully the decision to return to democracy, the excellent strategist and schemer was, in reality, planning his next step. Unlike the rash Salah Salem who once said he would have no problem executing a million people to ensure the success of the revolution,[96] Nasser kept his own council and told people only what they needed to know or what he wanted them to know. He appealed to the self-interest of his colleagues without seeming to do so, and played on their fears in a subtle manner while appearing to confide in them. He reminded them during the crisis, as Abdel Latif Boghdadi recalls in his memoirs, that the revolution had been supported by neither the masses nor the army.[97] He reminded them that those who carried out that revolution were only ninety officers whose number had shrunk by then to no more than fifty (the others having been disposed of in various ways). To Baghdadi's response that the implication of what he had just said was that they should impose themselves on the country by force, Nasser's firm and unhesitating reply was in the affirmative.[98] That might have seemed like a bold statement from a man whose brief foray into the limelight appeared about to end with the RCC's dissolution; however, subsequent events showed clearly that it was not as unrealistic as it might have seemed.

Nasser's bag of tricks was far from empty, and what happened next was an early sign of what became an ability to manipulate the Egyptian masses and toy with their emotions. On March 19, six bombs exploded in various public places around Cairo, including the railway station, the university, and a coffee shop,[99] thus providing Nasser with the excuse for his next move. He stressed the gravity of the situation in an RCC meeting and emphasized the need for firm action before the country was plunged into chaos. He, along with Salah Salem, proposed "purifying" the Journalists and the Lawyers Syndicate (professional associations); confiscating *el-Misri*, a pro-democracy daily newspaper, and putting its owner on trial; expelling the students who participated in the pro-democracy demonstrations; and retiring eight of the professors who had supported them.[100] Naguib objected to the draconian measures and insisted on dealing with the situation through the normal legal channels.[101] Nasser overcame these objections by playing the chaos and breakdown of law and order card. He appealed to Naguib's military and conservative instincts by asserting that the explosions were a direct result of the government's indecisiveness and that unless firm measures were taken, anarchy and disarray would ensue. The proposals were passed, and on March 25, the RCC voted, with Khalid Mohi el-Din, whom Nasser later exiled, providing the only dissenting vote, to annul its March 5 decree that abolished censorship, repealed the prohibition on political parties, and mandated a return to parliamentary rule.[102]

Everything now quickly fell into place, and the next episode in the unfolding drama was played out on the streets of Cairo over three consecutive days and served to reinforce the impact of the bombings. On March 27, 28, and 29, large demonstrations chanting: "Down with liberty" and "Down with democracy, down with the educated,"[103] brought life in the downtown area to a standstill and were broadcast live on Cairo Radio. The demonstrations were ostensibly a spontaneous show of support by the public for the RCC and an affirmation of the masses' opposition to everything associated with the ancien régime. They were, as their chants indicated, opposed to the old political parties and to what they termed the reactionaries who were demanding a return of parliamentary democracy and civil liberties. They were also critical of professional organizations such as the lawyers' syndicate, which had met and issued a call to the military to return to their barracks and hold parliamentary elections, and the journalists' syndicate, which had a meeting of its own scheduled for that day. The demonstrations were well planned. The sequence of events began with the daily newspaper *Akhbar el-Yom*, which was owned by the Amin brothers, publishing a news item falsely implying that the State Council was going to meet to denounce the revolution.[104] Several of the organizations under Nasser's control such as the Liberation Rally and the military police immediately went into action and set in motion their preplanned transportation strike and mass demonstrations.

Abdel Razzaq el-Sanhouri, the accomplished jurist and head of the State Council, who had made a pact with the devil in 1952 when he taught the uneducated officers that inconvenient laws need not be respected, now learned the hard way the consequences of his earlier legal rulings. The security force guarding the offices of the State Council was withdrawn, and the mob rushed in, attacked, and physically injured him.[105] They beat up other Council members and forced them to sign a declaration in support of the RCC.[106] El-Sanhouri, whose expertise in formulating and justifying the new régime's decisions had been very useful in the early days of the coup,[107] had outlived his usefulness to the junta. He had initially believed that the changes taking place in Egypt were positive changes that would result in reform[108] but was now gradually returning to his original position of support for liberalism, democracy, and parliamentary government.[109] He was beginning to realize his mistake in supporting Nasser and had begun to urge Naguib to return to parliamentary government.[110] El-Sanhouri accused Nasser, during the investigation that followed, of orchestrating the attack despite knowing full well that the State Council's meeting was a routine matter and that the only item on their agenda was the appointment of a replacement clerk for the court of administrative law.[111] It was, however, far too late for his views to matter, or for him to influence the course of political events in any way. The well respected but naïve jurist had been outwitted and rendered irrelevant.

The governor of Cairo's announcement to the press that "the law is on vacation,"[112] was still a few years into the future, but the signs pointing in that direction were already beginning to proliferate. Sayyid Qotb, one of the major theoreticians of the extremist Islamic movement and Nasser's friend and advisor, was writing: "Down with the law, down with the routine."[113] The assault on the highest law edifice in Egypt and on the head of the State Council convinced Naguib, as he later recounted in his memoirs, that the use of naked force had replaced the law as the foundation of society.[114] Others, such as FO Ahmad Hamroush, also concluded that the attack signaled the end of the sanctity of the law and the ushering in of the era of force and violence.[115] Nasser's comments to el-Boghdadi about the events after the fact provide another indicator of the new direction that Egypt was taking. He told him that the peasants' and workers' consciousness was a new major element that had been introduced to Egyptian politics, and that the working class was the one segment of society that would determine the country's policy from then on and not the students as had been the case in the past.[116] The comment is illuminating in that it reveals his mistrust of the educated and provides a glimpse into the deeply ingrained social values that were to affect the whole society in subsequent years. The crisis must have also shown Nasser how easy it would be for him to manipulate the feelings of the peasants and workers and use them to achieve his goals.

This display of violence, from the six bombings on March 19 and the public demonstrations and attacks on the State Council eight days later, illustrates the lengths that Nasser was prepared to go to in order to maintain his grip on power. Nasser confided to Boghdadi sometime later that the six bombs had been planted at his instigation to cause confusion, create a sense of insecurity, and to make people feel that they needed someone to protect them.[117] He also admitted that he had paid el-Sawi Ahmad el-Sawi, Head of the Cairo Transport Workers Syndicate (Union), four thousand pounds to arrange the anti-democracy demonstrations[118] in which members of the military police, dressed in civilian clothes, had also taken part.[119] Hussein Arafa, Director of the Military Criminal Investigations Office was another officer who played a central part in that drama. He recounted in an interview that Ahmad Anwar, the Commander of the Military Police, summoned him to inform him that a newspaper had reported that the State Council had scheduled a meeting and ordered him to prevent it from taking place, by force if necessary.[120] As part of the ruse, Arafa went to the offices of the State Council dressed in civilian clothes, thus camouflaging his identity, to demand a cancellation of the meeting. When el-Sanhouri refused to see him, Arafa sent a police messenger to the two army officers who oversaw Nasser's newly organized *Hai'at el-Tahrir* (Liberation Rally) to apprise them of the situation. Shortly afterwards, demonstrators chanting: "Death to the traitors" arrived at the locked gates of the Council building, which Arafa then opened for them.[121] He followed the demonstrators to the Council's meeting chambers as the mob began to attack the council members, and pretended to have come to protect el-Sanhouri and his colleagues. He added to the dramatic ambience by firing two bullets at the ceiling, ostensibly to disperse the mob, and then presided over the Council members' signing of a declaration of support for the RCC. He left the chamber only after this was done to hand it to Salah Salem, who had arrived to take the document and rush it to the radio station with orders for it to be broadcast immediately.[122] The attack on the State Council had an immediate and chilling effect on other groups calling for democracy. No one showed up to attend the meeting that the Journalists' Syndicate had scheduled for that afternoon,[123] and the pro-democracy Executive Council of the Syndicate was dissolved by the RCC on April 15, 1954.[124]

Nasser assumed the premiership on April 17, 1954,[125] and was now well on his way to winning complete control of the country. The RCC, according to former member Kamal el-Din Hussein, was rarely convened after that.[126] But Nasser was not quite there yet. Pockets of opposition among professionals and intellectuals remained. Naguib was still the president and enjoyed public support, and Nasser still had the MB to contend with. He worked on all fronts simultaneously.

All other opposition had been neutralized with relative ease. Political parties had been easily sidelined; jurists had begun tailoring laws according to the military junta's specifications, empowering the junta to do whatever they wished with the political system and the democratic institutions;[127] and labor leaders were fearful after the Kafr el-Dawwar executions. The new intelligence organizations had begun to extend their tentacles into every area of life,[128] and the other groups that posed a potential challenge: the educated class of professors, students, journalists, writers, lawyers, and other professionals who continued to resist the drift away from parliamentary rule and to demand a return to civilian rule, were also silenced. A minority of this group had either belonged to or sympathized with one of the left leaning political groups such as *el-Fagr el-Gadid*, HADETU, or the ECP. The crackdown on professionals effectively neutralized all these groups. The ECP, which had denounced the July 23 event as a fascist military coup,[129] had no mass following and its leaders were in jail. HADETU had cooperated with the FO[130] conspiracy and supported the coup until it became clear that the RCC was drifting away from constitutional government, and the group had begun to call for a return to civilian rule. They were dealt with in a variety of ways. Sa'd Kamel, a journalist, was arrested along with his wife in June 1954 and each was sentenced to five years in jail.[131] Universities had been the biggest force of protest against dictatorship, and Nasser dealt with them in several ways. Fifty professors were fired;[132] others were transferred to posts in rural areas. Some students and faculty members were jailed,[133] and the system was changed to ensure that the students would be occupied with exams throughout the academic term and that stricter penalties would be applied for absenteeism.

Intellectuals soon realized that the military régime brooked no criticism and that there were no laws or democratic institutions to protect them. Almost all fell silent. Intellectuals, as Mustafa Abdel Ghani points out, fell into three categories. The first was composed of those who supported the régime, which included many Islamists and Communists after their release from jail. The second was those who coexisted with it, such as Taha Hussein and Tawfiq el Hakim, who publicly declared their support for Nasser even as they criticized him in private, and Hussein Fawzi who also criticized him in private but expressed no support in public. The third was those who simply kept silent, such as Ahmad Lutfi el-Sayyid, who declined Nasser's offer to become Prime Minister on the pretext that Egypt needed new blood, and never again wrote on any political topics.[134]

While systematically eliminating this opposition, Nasser also worked on two other fronts: ridding himself of Naguib and the MB. Limiting Naguib's official presidential functions effectively quarantined and sidelined him on the official level to the point that when the British Minister Anthony Nutting asked to make a courtesy visit to him at the end of the Canal Zone evacuation negotiations, he was told that Naguib was indisposed.[135] Dealing with him on the popular level, however, was not so straightforward. Naguib, powerless to prevent the large-scale arrests, resorted to visiting people in jail, which irritated Nasser who was already resentful of his popularity.[136] A further irritation was that wherever Nasser went the crowds' chants were still for Naguib, so he began to attack him openly when he met with army officers and journalists and tried, for example, to convince journalist Ahmad Abul Fath that Naguib was a dictator and worth no more than a single bullet.[137] Clearly, eroding Naguib's position even as a figurehead president was not enough. Nasser may also have realized that the convenient bullet he seems to have fanaticized about for his *bête noir* had the potential to backfire and recreate the chaos of February and worse. The alternative was to turn his attention to drawing Naguib's popularity with the masses to himself with a measure that was sure to gain popular support. According to Khalid Mohi el-Din, the masses were already happy with the slogan: "Raise your head brother,"[138] that Nasser coined, and in October 1954, he was able to take credit for another popular development.

He had been busy making secret concessions to the British to reach an agreement for the evacuation of their Suez Canal bases. There is some evidence, albeit circumstantial, that Nasser might have been willing, from the first day after the military coup, to treat the national interests of Egypt in a cavalier fashion if they conflicted with his goal of monopolizing power. Many sources agree that the evacuation treaty with Britain, which was a major factor in solidifying his position in the power struggle with Naguib, came at a high price. At best, Nasser's accomplishment was the outcome of his being insufficiently attuned to Egypt's national interests, and at worst, of his having knowingly compromised these interests. Tawfiq el Hakim, for example, points out that several former politicians, including the respected Mustafa el-Nahhas Pasha, informed him in private that the terms of the agreement were the same ones that that had been offered by Britain thirty years earlier and had been rejected by all political parties.[139] What is not in doubt is that the bargain with Britain could never have been struck without Nasser accepting a thinly camouflaged British presence in the Canal Zone and making concessions over Sudan,[140] which had been united with Egypt since the eighteenth century. The British terms treated the two countries as separate entities and stipulated that Sudan should at this point decide whether or not to remain in the union. This had the potential of jeopardizing the security of the Nile water for Egypt. The agreement, initialed on July 27, 1954 and finally signed on October 19, 1954, was opposed, therefore, by every political faction in the country,[141] including the Muslim Brothers who were still allied with Nasser. Even Nasser's fellow Free Officers were not happy with the terms of the agreement, and only voted to ratify it by a thin margin after an exhaustive effort by Nasser to pressure them and secure their approval.[142] Salah Nasr, Nasser's intelligence chief, also claims that Salah Salem's mission to Sudan was secretly sabotaged by Nasser. The RCC had sent Salem to meet with the Sudan's political leaders and urge them to remain united with Egypt, but Nasser never intended the mission to succeed and worked behind the scenes to foil it. Nasser's goal, according to Salah Nasr, was to use the failure to get rid of his fellow RCC member because of his constant criticism of Nasser's attempts to monopolize power.[143] The failure of Salem's mission must also have had the added benefit of helping Nasser to convince the RCC to accept the terms of the agreement. The notable speed with which an agreement was reached within days of the start of negotiations once Nasser became the Prime Minister and took over as head of the negotiating team also convinced Naguib later that Nasser had been in secret contact with the British negotiators all along.[144] Riad Sami (Naguib's Press Secretary) and Khalid Mohi el-Din have also suggested that there was something underhand in these negotiations.¹⁴⁵ The British evacuation did, however, achieve Nasser's purpose of improving his popularity with the masses, thus taking him another step closer towards deposing Naguib.

He still had the Muslim Brothers to deal with,¹⁴⁶ but it was simply a matter of time before the Machiavellian Nasser would finally rid himself of this remnant of the disparate coalition of individuals and groups who helped him to take power.¹⁴⁷ His strategy this time produced a bonus; in addition to eliminating the MB, it raised his popularity to new heights. His biggest threat all along had been the Muslim Brothers, but Nasser had wisely avoided a confrontation with this powerful group and had kept dangling before them the possibility of sharing power. The MB had good reason to expect to play a major role in the new régime because of their close ties with the FO. Several prominent figures in the military junta were either members of the group or sympathized with it, and the MB had been informed of the intended coup shortly before the event and had pledged their full support. Nasser, once a member of the group, had accompanied Free Officer Kamal el-Din Hussein, also an MB, on a visit to Hussein Ashmawi and Saleh Abu Raqiq, both members of the MB Guidance Office, and informed them of the date that had been selected for the coup and asked for their cooperation. The MB leadership had been receptive to the request and had helped to maintain public order on the morning of July 23, 1952 by guarding public buildings and places of worship.¹⁴⁸ The junta's good will towards the MB was demonstrated by the October 11, 1952 pardoning and release of the murderers of a judge who had sentenced several MB members convicted of planting a bomb in the Khediwiyya School before the coup. The school bombers were also pardoned and released.¹⁴⁹ Immediately after the coup's success the junta also reopened the investigation into the assassination of the MB's founder Hassan el-Banna three years earlier.¹⁵⁰ Furthermore, when the junta issued a ban on all political parties, the MB was the only political group that was exempted from the ban and offered two ministerial posts in the Naguib Cabinet. Perhaps significantly, the MB members that were actually selected for these posts were not, however, those recommended by their Supreme Guide.¹⁵¹

Nasser, ever attuned to the intrigues of all the groups that he dealt with, must have known of the existence of two rival factions within the MB. He began to cultivate Abdel Rahman el-Sanadi who headed their Secret Apparatus,[152] the military wing in charge of terrorist activities, and whose views on several issues were at variance with the views of Hassan el-Hodeiby, the Supreme Guide.[153] The aim was to deepen the rift within the group and destroy it from the inside.[154] Ma'moun el-Hodeiby, the son of the MB Supreme Guide, confirmed in an interview that serious differences existed between el-Sanadi and his father, whom el-Sanadi once threatened with a gun in an attempt to force him to resign his position as the group's leader. He claimed that the incident, which he witnessed, was instigated by Nasser after he (Nasser) had a heated argument with the father.[155]

By 1954, it was beginning to dawn on the MB that Nasser had no intention of sharing power with them. Nasser's position was growing more secure, and when the MB led a violent demonstration at Cairo University on January 12, the RCC responded two days later with a decree disbanding the group. The pretext for the ban was transparently flimsy.[156] It was claimed that the Supreme Guide had supported the coup only after the king's departure, had opposed the agrarian reform law, had tried to act as the junta's guardian, did not support the Liberation Rally Organization, and had organized a new Secret Apparatus. A clash was inevitable and seemed imminent, but Nasser still bided his time.

He was certainly aware of the MB's secret military apparatus and of its ability to mobilize the masses and put large numbers of people on the streets. He was also obsessed with the thought that the MBs might entice some police and army personnel to join their cause despite continuous periodic expulsion campaigns within the ranks of both organizations.[157] Because of these risks, Nasser preferred not to provoke them or force them into an open confrontation,[158] and in a demonstration of his exceptional aptitude for manipulation and playing both sides of the field, Nasser made a public visit to the grave of the MB founder on the anniversary of his death only one month after the ban. He was accompanied by Ahmad Hassan el-Baqoury, a Cabinet minister who had been expelled earlier from the group for disobeying the leader's orders not to accept the post. At the grave, Nasser made a speech that included a testament to God that he was working to achieve the goals of the MB.[159]

By the time the MB attempted to assassinate him while he was making a speech in Alexandria on October 26, 1954, a week after the Suez Agreement was signed, he was ready for the confrontation. The assassination attempt failed, and his popularity soared as people began to warm up to him for the first time since he burst onto the scene in 1952. There was sympathy for him as the intended victim of violence, and admiration for his courage at remaining in his place amid the turmoil caused by the shots that were fired at him. The rumor, spread mainly by the MB, that it was all part of a theatrical play directed by Nasser,[160] was never proven. However, Nasser's stage-managing of the bombings in March of that year, of the street demonstrations that followed, and of the attack on the State Council was not known at the time either and, therefore, leaves a question mark over whether the assassination attempt was real or not.[161] In either case, the group was vilified as a terrorist organization and tens of thousands of its activists were rounded up and jailed.[162] Others went underground or fled the country, and the threat, in spite of the group's attempt to resurface a few years later, was effectively eliminated. Moreover, Nasser's mass popularity was solidified.

Nasser also appears to have been shrewd enough to use to his advantage the concept of *el-mostabedd el-'adel* (the just dictator)[163] which had been floating around the intellectual terrain in Egypt since Mohammed Abdu discussed it following the failure of Orabi's revolt in 1882.[164] Tawfiq el Hakim asserted in the introduction to his 1938 book, *Shagaret el-hokm*[165] that ideal rule comes from ideal individuals not ideal systems. Ehsan Abdel Qoddous, the prominent journalist and owner of *Rose Al Youssef* magazine, once published an article entitled "Egypt needs a dictator, could it be Ali Maher?"[166] Fikry Abaza,[167] another prominent writer, also wrote in the weekly magazine, *el-Mosawwar*, of the desirability of a just dictator.[168]

This is hardly surprising in view of the fact that autocracy is deeply rooted in nomadic tribal mores. The Arab Bedouin culture, according to some, is an egalitarian one where the tribal leader's decisions are made collectively in consultation with the tribe's elders and notables. *Shura* (consultation) is a term that is much bandied about and offered as evidence of the existence of an indigenous democratic system if people could only be persuaded to turn the clock back and return to seventh century practices. That era is viewed as a golden age and a paradise lost. That, however, is a highly selective, unrealistic, and romanticized view of the past. Certainly, a degree of consultation did exist in the distant Bedouin past. However, it owed its existence mainly to the ruler's abject poverty and absolute dearth of resources, which prevented him from either forcing or enticing others to comply with his decisions. There is no better evidence of this than the fact that once the large-scale pillage of the rich neighboring societies began to provide the Bedouin Arab rulers with the resources, *shura* was relegated to the realm of poetry. Poets were paid by a newly enriched and empowered ruler (especially the Umayyads)[169] to sing his praises and perpetuate the belief in the now mythical *shura* in return for a sliver of the previously undreamed of wealth. The designation *el-saffah* (the slaughterer) that is given to Abul Abbas Abdulla bin Mohammed, the founder of the Abbasid Caliphate (750-935), certainly does not call to mind the term *shura*. This imported cultural heritage may have played a critical role in facilitating the drift towards autocracy in 1950s Egypt since the democratic impulses in society may not have been as strong or as clearly defined as the demonstrations by the students might have suggested. Most likely, the public was evenly split on the issue with support for democracy being most widespread among the educated classes and the already vilified and marginalized Western-oriented elite of the ancien régime. Even the family of the lone voice against the RCC's anti democratic measures, Khalid Mohi el-Din, disapproved of his stance in support of the restoration of democracy, and he stated in a recent interview that they too believed in just dictators.[170]

Mohi el-Din's belief that autocracy had popular appeal appears to have been supported by the public debate in the press that took place in 1953 between two prominent journalists, Mustafa Amin, and Mohammed el-Tabei, about the virtues of dictatorship. Mohammed Hassanein Heikal,[171] the editor of the magazine *Akher Sa'a*, decided to settle the argument by holding a competition among his readers. The magazine offered its readers a prize of one hundred pounds for the best answer to the question of whether they supported the one party system or the multi party system. The competition ran for two weeks from September 9 to 23, 1953. The results, published on October 7, 1953 showed that more than fifty thousand entries had been received with 62 percent of the votes opting for dictatorship.[172] The era of winning 99.999 percent of the vote was still a few years into the future, and what the Egyptian public did not know, until it was revealed nearly three decades later, was that the competition was staged at the instigation of Nasser. He had met with both Mustafa Amin and Mohammed el-Tabei and suggested that Amin should write in defense of the multi party system and that el-Tabei should launch an attack on him and defend the one party system. The agreed upon script was then turned into a referendum on which of the two systems would be more suitable for Egypt.[173] Amin has confirmed this version of events in an interview and even added that he was surprised that all documents connected with the competition were taken from the offices of *Akher Sa'a* to the office of Gamal Abdel Nasser in the RCC.[174] It appears that it was the RCC and not the magazine that counted the votes.[175] While this obviously makes the results of the competition suspect, given the influence of the cultural heritage, the apparent rigging of those results may not have been necessary and is indicative of Nasser tendency to go overboard to achieve his goals. It also illustrates his astuteness in grasping the power of the media as a tool to manipulate public opinion and magnify to his own ends an idea already in circulation. What is even more significant is that the incident provides a clear indication that Nasser, never sincere in his pronouncements about democracy, had been planning to take sole control of Egypt all along.

With the monarchy consigned to the annals of history, the MB effectively eliminated, the pro-democracy opposition powerless, and the masses now placated, Nasser was now ready to dispose of Naguib. The first president of Egypt was arrested on November 14, 1954[176] in his office in Abdin palace and imprisoned in a small rest house confiscated from the wife of a former prime minister. The house, as his (Naguib's) press secretary reports, was stripped bare of all furniture, curtains, even tablecloths, and other amenities that might have made it habitable,[177] and Naguib was reduced to hanging his clothes on a rope strung across the room.[178] The journalist Helmi Sallam, a Nasser supporter, admitted that Naguib was subjected to psychological torture by being kept in isolation and denied access to newspapers, books, or the radio.[179] His only companions were the cats that he fed and slept with in order to protect him from the mice that turned his every night into agony.[180] His family, according to nephew Mohammed Ali Abdullah, was not allowed to visit him, and the soldiers assigned to guard him marched back and forth on the roof above his bedroom at night and fired their weapons in the air outside his window in a war of nerves against him.[181] Adel Hammouda's book: *el-Wathaiq el-khassah bil ra'is Naguib* (President Naguib's Private Documents) provides a glimpse of the daily psychological torture and harassment to which Naguib's jailers subjected him. The book contains copies of several letters of complaint sent by Naguib throughout his period of incarceration. Captain Hussein Sorour, the officer in charge of his guards, was the subject of many of these complaints. In addition to psychological torture, Sorour apparently also resorted to the type of harassment reflective of a petty and vindictive mind. He dug up Naguib's flowerbed, put barbed wire around it, planted vegetables for his own home use in their place, and used the military detail assigned to buy Naguib's food to run his own errands, thus making Naguib wait for his food deliveries.[182] Sometimes, he would not allow in the nurse who came to give Naguib his injections when he was sick; at other times, he stopped milk deliveries.[183] Whether the original petty, vindictive mind that devised these strategies was Sorour's or someone else's is a matter for speculation. What is all but certain is that it would have been out of character for Nasser not have made it his business to keep himself apprised of every insignificant detail of Naguib's life in detention.

Hammouda's examination of Naguib's documents also sheds light on the financial degradation to which Naguib was subjected. In another demonstration of petty vindictiveness, the man who had acted with honor and dignity throughout his career and left office with a balance of 899.061 pounds in his bank account was forced to support himself and his family during his confinement on his small army pension of 183.866 pounds per month.[184] He was reduced to having to borrow from his brother, and Hammouda found among his documents a letter dated November 28, 1956 to Ahmad Anwar, Commander of the Military Police, requesting him to deliver two letters, one to his son and one to his brother with a check for twenty pounds enclosed in part payment of a loan.[185] When his youngest son needed a medical operation, Naguib had to resort to making an application to the ministry of finance on August 28, 1957 for an advance on his pension, which reduced it by twenty pounds per month.[186] In spite of his straitened circumstances, he still donated ten pounds to the war veterans association.[187] Naguib was destined to live in loneliness, poverty, and misery for sixteen years until President Sadat released him after Nasser's death in September 1970 and ordered his pension raised by one hundred pounds per month.[188] It is worth noting that none of the Free Officers, who had courted him until they took control of Egypt, and whose actions on July 23, 1952 had paid them handsome dividends, pleaded his case with Nasser or attempted to temper his petty vindictiveness. Nasser never outgrew this pettiness and his spitefulness, which increased over time,[189] and went as far as being directed towards a child on one occasion because he had quarreled with the child's father. He had noticed the boy attending a children's party at his house, and ordered him dragged out crying and thrown out of the party.[190]

It could perhaps be argued that November 14, 1954, more than July 23, 1952, marked the end of one era and the beginning of another in Egypt's story. Sarwat Okasha, one of the FO who was in the cavalry, accurately describes the transformation that took place in 1954 as the defeat of one social class by another. He argues in his memoirs that the events that culminated in the deposing and arrest of President Naguib on November 14, 1954 signaled the defeat of the upper middle class, which was demanding a return to democracy, free elections, and parliamentary government.[191] The victors, Okasha maintained, were members of the lower middle class who believed in "just dictators," and to which most of the revolution's men belonged.[192] They were what one researcher termed "the new *effendiyya*."[193] Okasha asserted in an interview with the British Broadcasting Corporation (BBC) that he "would never, never" have joined the conspiracy if he had had any inkling of what it would eventually lead to.[194] Vatikiotis also maintains that society was transformed by these new elite who were responsible for the destruction of "some of the finer foundations of Egyptian society."[195]

Nasser's deft handling of the 1954 crisis put him well on the way to achieving his political goals, and once he dismantled the ancien régime's democratic structure, he began to consolidate his grip on power and his control of all society's institutions. His steely determination, his ability to remain focused on his goals, to adapt quickly to changing situations, and to take advantage of his opponents' perceived weaknesses is illustrated by the manner in which he planned his moves and dealt with the possible threats to his power grab when the time came.

Nasser had prudently continued to court the Americans after the coup's success. He met with them openly and dined with Caffery and four other US embassy personnel at Abdel Menem Amin's house only a few days after the coup. Naguib, Zakaria Mohi el-Din, Abdel Hakim Amer, Abdel Latif el-Boghdadi, and Mohammed Riad were also present.[196] During that meeting, the Americans offered the CIA's assistance in combating communist influence in Egypt but Naguib declined the offer.[197] Naguib's naïveté could not have escaped Nasser's notice. The Americans, according to Riad, also advised against cooperation with the Wafd on the basis that the democratic Wafdists would be more likely to yield to public opinion and spawn an environment that would facilitate the spread of communism.[198] The implication of that advice was far too obvious to have gone unnoticed by Nasser. The Americans obviously feared democracy and could be counted on to support a military dictatorship as long as it catered to their concerns about communism. Their views at the time appear to have echoed the views of that segment of the Egyptian people who longed for a just dictator. The Americans felt that only a dictator could maintain peace and that democracy would not be suited to Egypt's particular circumstances.[199] This must have been music to Nasser's ears. It suited him and fit in perfectly with his own personal goals.

Satisfying the Americans' requirements certainly did not pose any hardship for Nasser. He was definitely not a communist, and none of the RCC members, including the leftist leaning Khalid Mohi el-Din and Yousef Seddik, felt any attachments to the ECP, which had already denounced them as fascist demagogues.[200] The RCC, with Nasser's dexterous guidance, was careful to maintain American support and considered their wishes when making senior personnel appointments.[201] When the junta granted a pardon to all those who had been convicted of a political crime during the period between August 16, 1936 and July 23, 1952, and released all political detainees on October 16, 1952, the decree specifically excluded the jailed communists. The justification offered by the new régime for that exclusion was that communists did not qualify as political prisoners because communism is not a crime directed against the political system, but against economic and social systems.[202] This feeble and unconvincing distinction illustrates Nasser's ability to select the right legal experts, and from his point of view that meant the ones who were prepared to tinker with legal minutiae and to tailor laws that suited his purposes. In return for this apparent readiness of the junta to join them in their struggle against communism, the Americans, proving to have been as naïve as Naguib, cooperated with the new régime, and provided Nasser with wide-ranging assistance in the field of intelligence.[203] That assistance proved to be of vital importance to Nasser later as he began to build the vast network of security apparatus that he relied upon to consolidate and maintain his grip on power until his death in 1970[204]

He gradually and effectively eliminated all threats and established several intelligence organizations that were charged with spying on the population as well as each other and recruited tens of thousands of Egyptians who were turned into spies that served his régime.[205] The army became a security rather than a defense organization and Nasser began to run the country as a private fiefdom, or as a powerful Bedouin chief ran his tribe. He appeared to view social and political institutions and processes as either part of the décor or as mere personal sources of information or tools of control. His socio-political system was, therefore, relatively simple. He, like many of those who succeed to power through coups tend to, continued to view the world around him in terms of machinations, plots, and schemes.[206] He passionately believed in secrecy and viewed most events around him as stemming from deception or duplicity. [207] He viewed himself as primarily a conspirator,[208] had a natural inclination to listen to rumors, and was predisposed to giving credence to gossip and hearsay.[209] He assembled several small cliques of trusted opportunists (towards the end of his life he referred to them as "gangs"), and used them as the centerboard of his governing structure. These cliques ran the country and reported directly to Nasser, the ultimate authority. The legislative, executive, and judicial branches of government thus became subsumed in the person of Nasser and vulnerable to his caprices. The media was censored, the press nationalized and tightly controlled, and the whole country was viewed as little more than an extension of the original secret group over which Nasser could maintain sole control and direct all political activity.[210] He personally appointed the heads and members of all public organizations and company presidents.[211] He often checked and/or selected the main newspapers headlines before publication,[212] and regularly sent notes to the editors instructing them on what to publish and who to attack.[213]

Nasser's personal charisma and ability to manipulate the masses and keep them enthralled and awestruck by his rousing rhetoric and dazzling slogans also played a major role in maintaining his position as the absolute master of Egypt.[214] He was a talented speaker who often resorted to using informal, conversational, and idiomatic language, which resonated with the masses and created a feeling of familiarity and closeness with them, thus making them feel that he was one of them.[215] His gifted demagoguery successfully counterbalanced the atmosphere of fear in the country and enthralled and, some would say, almost hypnotized the nation with an unending string of 'victories' that soothed and reassured the public. These were usually presented in well-choreographed settings to a carefully selected audience of mostly uneducated workers and peasants. Mohammed Hassanein Heikal,[216] who became a close friend and confidant to Nasser, played an important role in contributing to his ascent to power and to the support of his régime. Heikal was undoubtedly a knowledgeable and superb strategic thinker whose logical analysis of news and events must have been useful to Nasser. He was very well-read, and his work as a reporter and a journalist had immersed him in the political scene and acquainted him with many politicians and activists. He had an exceptional ability for retention and recall of the minutest details and for relating and linking facts and events in a manner that helped to make sense of them. In addition he was a prolific and talented writer who exhibited an exceptional command of the Arabic language.

As Nasser tightened his grip on the levers of power in the country, his régime began to resemble that of the foreign *walis* and Mamluk sultans of earlier eras.[217] The most obvious common feature was that the country was ruled in both cases by men whose only training had been in the military field. The difference, however, was that the Mamluks were very well trained and formed a formidable fighting force that protected the people and successfully repelled foreign invaders on several occasions. Nasser's Mamluks, on the other hand, were poorly trained, badly led, and powerless to protect the people or repel foreign invaders. There is little debate about their deplorable performance against Israel's series of minor raids and major attacks on Egyptian soil over the years, which, in several instances, were the inevitable outcome of Nasser's brinkmanship and his vitriolic, bombastic, and fiery speeches. However, like each Mamluk prince who had a sphere of power and influence that he jealously guarded against encroachment from other princes, Nasser's officers also carved themselves spheres of influence in the country and vied with each other to preserve them.[218]

The Egyptians, who, as Herodotus observed long ago,[219] cannot live long without a king, found a king in Nasser, and society began to be gradually reshaped in Nasser's image. After 1956 xenophobia became widespread.[220] Foreign schools[221] were closed and the thriving Egyptian Jewish community as well as foreigners of all nationalities, encouraged by Nasser and troubled by the xenophobic tide that began to permeate society, began to leave Egypt.[222] The impact on education, the economy, culture, and society in general was nothing less than disastrous, but this either escaped Nasser's notice or he considered the price worth paying. Fear and suspicion permeated every level in the country and competence and expertise became devalued.[223] Unqualified and inexperienced officers replaced competent bureaucrats[224] and professional personnel in every branch of government and every sector of the economy.[225] Many publicly owned manufacturing and commercial organizations began to incur large losses as the officers who ran them were accumulating wealth. "Ignorance," as the prominent journalist Ibrahim Se'da asserts: "spread everywhere."[226] *El-ra'is* (the boss) as Nasser was referred to, clearly planned to remain in his position until he died, and the longer that his reign lasted, the more entrenched the social values that his reign promoted became and the more unlikely that Egypt might return to parliamentary rule in the near future appeared.

On the Road to Disaster

As Nasser began to feel more certain of his grip on power, he drifted from one ill-considered venture to another. He nationalized the Suez Canal in 1956, which led to an invasion by Britain and France who occupied the Canal Zone and by Israel, which occupied Sinai. When President Eisenhower saved the régime by insisting on the withdrawal of the invading forces from Egypt, Nasser claimed it as a personal victory and began to believe that he defeated three armies. He rushed into an ill-considered union with Syria in 1958 only to see it collapse three years later. He sent the army to support the 1962 rebellion against the Imam of Yemen where it became mired for years in a costly and unwinnable tribal conflict.

On the eve of Nasser's most disastrous gamble Egypt was in terrible shape. The national gold reserves had disappeared, the financial reserves had been squandered, and foreign debt to finance Nasser's adventures abroad, as well as the bloated bureaucracy and badly planned industrialization programs, had soared. The infrastructure was rotting away due to lack of maintenance and bad management by incompetent military officers, and the public began to experience shortages of food and basic commodities and rising inflation. The rural population lived in fear of the Committee to Liquidate Feudalism, formed in 1966 to ferret out 'feudalists', interrogate them, confiscate their properties and jail them. The army, led by loyal but incompetent opportunists was in no better shape. It suffered shortages of critical equipment, and training exercises were almost never carried out lest they "tire" the officers after their service in Yemen.[227]

In April 1967 the Syrians claimed that Israel was massing troops on their common border and called on Nasser for help. The news, according to some historians, was fabricated by the Soviets to force Egypt's involvement in a tense situation that was developing along Syria and Israel's common borders because of Syrian provocations. They feared that an Israeli military retaliation might topple the weak Ba'thist régime that was allied to them. Senior army officers were sent to Syria to assess the situation and returned with the news that it was a ruse, but their report was not enough to bring Nasser back from the edge of the precipice.

Despite the failing economy and the lack of preparedness of the military, Nasser chose to believe the Syrian claims and declared that he stood by them. He ordered the massing of troops in Sinai, demanded the withdrawal of the UN force that had been placed on the Egyptian-Israeli border after Israel's attack in 1956, then announced a blockade of the Tiran Straits to Israeli shipping and provoked Israel further by making fiery speeches and issuing threats.

Everything that happened from the moment that the UN force was requested to leave Sinai until the end of the crisis was handled with the same incompetence that the military rulers of Egypt had displayed since they took power in the country in 1952. A mobilization plan had been prepared in 1965 but it was never practiced,[228] and the army was unfamiliar with the new positions that it was sent to occupy because the terms of Nasser's 1956 'victory' had barred Egypt from stationing troops within a ten-kilometer zone along the border.[229] Personal friction that had developed between Nasser and his army commander and old friend Amer led to changing the plans for massing troops four times.[230] The forces were sent into Sinai with no clear objectives. Conflicting orders, a confused command structure, and complete disorganization resulted in units running around in circles.[231] One of the armored divisions, for example, dubbed the *hairan* (confused) division was moved around over one hundred kilometers in a few days, which meant that it lost its technical readiness to fight before even one shot was fired.[232] The reservists who were called up and sent to Sinai arrived at their posts wearing their civilian clothes and without weapons or equipment, and no one was aware of any plans to supply them.[233] Whole divisions spent days moving from one position to anther in Sinai for no discernable purpose, and their commanding officers had to pretend to their troops that they knew what they were doing.[234] General Mortagi was appointed Commander of the Front, but was not party to the planning, and had no authority to act without permission from the higher command in Cairo.[235] The senior officers at the front were often not informed of orders that came directly from Cairo to specific units in Sinai,[236] thus making the whole situation more vague and ambiguous to field commanders such as Lieutenant General Salah Mohsen.[237]

The Israeli response was not long in coming. At 8:45 on the morning of June 5, 1967, while Amer was in the air on his way to Beer Tamada in Sinai to meet with twenty-eight high-ranking officers and field commanders who had left their posts throughout Sinai to go and wait there for him,[238] Israel attacked. An early warning from radars stationed in Jordan that waves of Israeli planes had taken off at 7:00 A.M. and appeared to be heading for Egypt was received but not deciphered because the code had been changed earlier, and no one was given the new code.[239] There was a rare Israeli blunder when their land forces attacked the front position at Um Basis at 7:30 (before their agreed upon zero hour), but the commanders failed to grasp the significance of an event that would have given a ninety-minute warning of the air attack.[240] Syria, which precipitated the descent to disaster, acted "cautiously" and refused to intercept Israel's planes as they returned with empty tanks after their raids on Egypt.[241] A few days later, they withdrew their forces from their strong positions on the Golan Heights and repositioned them around Damascus "to protect the revolution."[242] The Ba'thist régime was in such disarray that they announced the fall of the city of Qonaitra before Israeli forces approached it.[243]

The moment the attack began Amer panicked. He sent for the Soviet Ambassador within one hour of the assault and asked him to try to arrange a ceasefire.[244] Then, he began to issue conflicting orders to his senior commanders. At 11:30 on June 6, for example, he ordered General Mortagi to move the fourth armored division to the second defensive position, then telephoned that same division at 3:30 and ordered it to relieve el-Kosayyema, which was under siege, then he ordered General Fawzi to prepare a withdrawal plan in twenty minutes.[245] When Fawzi returned with the plan, Amer told him that he had already issued a verbal order for the whole army to withdraw to west of the Canal at 4:30, but neither Fawzi nor anyone else present had any clue to the identity of the officer to whom the order was given.[246] Chaos reigned. General Mortagi, Commander of the Front, only learnt of the order by chance hours later at 3 A.M. on June 7[247] when the Commander of the Military Police visited him at the front and told him.[248] General Ali was puzzled when ordered to withdraw at a time when there was no military pressure on his forces.[249] In fact, he did not even see any Israeli land forces until three days after the June 5 attack.[250] Despite losses to the air force, the situation on June 5, General Mortagi asserts, would have been nowhere near desperate had the army been allowed to fight.[251] In fact, the troops did fight when they were given the opportunity. A mere thirty commandos who remained in a small pocket east of the Canal in Ras el-'ish,[252] successfully repelled repeated Israeli attacks on their position, destroying several tanks and forcing the attackers to withdraw, and the position remained the only point on the east bank of the Canal in Egyptian hands until 1973.

On the morning of June 6, the losses were only one fifth of the forces and General Mortagi recommended regrouping and fighting, but Amer disagreed and adamantly insisted on withdrawal.[253] The disorderly withdrawal without a fight or air cover led to a humiliating defeat: 90 percent of the equipment that was lost to the air bombardment happened as they withdrew,[254] and the Egyptians, essentially, were left with no army to defend them. Israel occupied the whole Peninsula, and its actions since its establishment by the United Nations in 1948 left no doubt as to its expansionist plans and to the fact that once it occupied any part of its neighbors' land, big or small, it had no intention of giving it up. Even France, Israel's main ally at the time: main supplier of arms, know-how, equipment, and materiel to manufacture its nuclear weapons, and ally in the 1956 attack on Egypt, saw the possible threat to Egypt's territorial integrity. After Israel's attack, France announced:

> Indeed, we watched the emergence of a State of Israel that was warlike and set on expansion. And then the action she was taking to double her population through immigration gave us to think that the territory she had acquired would not suffice her for long and that she would be led to expand it whenever an opportunity arose.[255]

Losing a major part of Egypt's soil (one third of the area of the Nile Valley) was, therefore, a distinct possibility. Amazingly, in spite of that dire situation, what seems to have been uppermost in the mind of the President of Egypt, the leader whose inane policies and irresponsible provocations precipitated this catastrophe, was how to protect himself. He left the front undefended and ordered the few tanks that had escaped destruction by Israel's well-planned attack to move to Cairo to protect him while he contemplated his next move.[256]

The Resignation

Only four days after the catastrophe, Nasser finalized plans for another of his masterful *coup de theatres*: a speech broadcast to the nation. The affair would be a classic Nasserite event complete with the requisite massive crowds and appropriate choreographed chants and slogans, with the dramatic accompaniment of a complete blackout in Cairo and the sound of anti-aircraft fire filling the air. No one who witnessed the spectacle of the ninth and tenth of June 1967 could deny that the show was a truly magnificent production.

In the immediate aftermath of the 1976 debacle Nasser played the role of the sincere and contrite leader who owned up to his mistakes and was now thinking only of what was best for his wounded nation. He informed his army chief, Amer, that the two of them must resign because they had both "deceived the people."[257] He added that he was planning to make a speech to take responsibility for the disaster and to announce that they were both resigning in favor of an interim president. Amer, according to Shams Badran, accepted the argument, went along with the plan, and nominated him, Badran, for the interim presidency, and Nasser agreed.[258] Mohammed Hassanein Heikal wrote the resignation speech. It was yet another example of his superb command of the language: his artful word choice, his talented coining of appropriate phrases and slogans, and his manipulation of Arabic speakers' fascination with their language and their willingness to suspend reason and be hypnotized by beautifully strung together words and passionate prose. He brought the speech over to Nasser's house on the morning of June 9,[259] and they discussed its content and deliberated over which was the most effective word to use when announcing the sad news to an anxious nation.

Semantics and linguistic subtleties were not problems the Egyptian public was grappling with on that unhappy June day. No one had any doubts about to how to describe what happened, or about the most accurate word to characterize the events of the previous few days. No one had any doubt that ignominious *hazima* (defeat), and an unprecedented *nakba* or *karitha* (both words mean catastrophe) were the most accurate terms to describe what their *ra'is* (boss or president) had inflicted upon them. Foreign radio broadcasts and their own returning defeated, disheveled, dispirited troops who were in a state of shock had already told them that much. The Bedouin in Nasser, on the other hand, knew instinctively that words are important and that while his army was defeated, the right choice of words could make *him* victorious. After all, it happened once before in 1956. His Bedouin heart appreciated the allure of language to nomads. He knew that form is far more likely to sway his audience than content, and he sat alongside Heikal and discussed the most appropriate words to use in his speech when describing the momentous events of the previous few days. Heikal explained to Nasser that he had considered and rejected several words. Apparently, *hazima*, *nakba*, and *karitha* were all deemed inappropriate. Even the relatively mild term *sadma* (shock), was considered, and rejected. Heikal, true to form, had finally found the best term. *Naksa* (setback), with its more benign meaning, and this was the word that was finally settled upon.[260]

It seems reasonable to assume that the leader of a defeated nation whose aggressive enemy had attacked and easily destroyed its army, occupied a substantial part of its territory and may well have been poised at that very moment to continue its advance towards its capital, which lay defenseless a mere one hundred kilometers away from the invading army, might have found better use for his time than semantic discourse and play directing. Moreover, the fact that Nasser could spare the time for word selection (he was with Heikal for ten hours)[261] at such a critical moment is revealing. It provides evidence that he never intended to resign and that the whole exercise was a ruse to forestall the possibility that the shock might induce what el-Hakim termed a return of consciousness to the Egyptian people. It also bolsters the claim that staying in power whatever the cost to the long-suffering population was uppermost in Nasser's mind.

When Nasser finally made his speech on June 9, 1967,[262] he knew that he was speaking to a population that was traumatized. They had been stunned by Israel's blitzkrieg, by the speed of their army's collapse, by the magnitude of the defeat, and by the apparent ease with which Israel vanquished the officers who had pranced so confidently and arrogantly around their streets since 1952. They were shocked by the loss of the Soviet equipment that had cost them so dearly and that was supposed to be almost invincible. Only two days earlier the Nasser controlled news media had been telling them that Israel made a grave mistake and dug its own grave by attacking Egypt. The speech had utilized all the strategies that had worked so well in the past. Now, on June 9, aware of the public trauma, Nasser spoke in a grave and a serious tone, addressing his listeners as "brothers," rather than the usual "citizens." He utilized the "confidentiality technique"[263] which had served him well in the past and, speaking as if he was having a personal chat with a close friend, he began by saying:

> We have become accustomed to sitting together to discuss things, both at moments of triumph and of tribulations, in the sweet and the bitter hours, and to speak frankly of facts, in the belief that this is the only way we can find the right path however difficult circumstances may be.[264]

Nasser then went on to tell them that "we" have suffered a "setback." He deftly turned the responsibility for the debacle into a collective responsibility and implicated his blameless listeners as partners in the responsibility by the use of the plural pronoun. He skillfully shifted responsibility for the calamity to Amer and Badran,[265] and reached into his bag of tricks and produced many of the old tried and tested ploys. He blamed the imperialists who were plotting against both Egypt and him personally. He told his listeners that the army was well trained, well equipped, and fought bravely against insurmountable odds. He blew his own trumpet while appearing to show humility by telling his listeners that he "always used to tell [them] that it is the nation that lives on, and that the individual, whatever his role and however great his contribution to the causes of his country, is only a reflection of the nation's will."[266] He cleverly went on to remind them of *his* great contributions to the causes of his homeland by listing the many achievements of what he termed "the revolution's generation." He went through the usual list: independence, nationalization of the Suez Canal, industrialization, the High Dam, desert reclamation, electrification, and oil discoveries. He did not add, although his audience knew already, that the Suez Canal had ceased to be a source of revenue when the Israelis occupied its east bank or that the oil discoveries that he took credit for were in the area that Israel now occupied. He implied that he had already been busy at work on their behalf and that there were "international guarantees" that the "traces of the aggression would be removed." To an English language speaker, the phrase might seem more appropriate when referring to swatting a fly rather than the eviction of Israeli's efficient and formidable army from its well-fortified positions. In Arabic, however, all of this sounded more reasonable, more palatable, and more plausible than it might sound in English. He went on to say that he accepted full responsibility for "the setback" and that he had decided to resign and nominate his Vice-President Zakaria Mohi el-Din as interim president.

The speech was a masterpiece of rhetoric and a classic example of Nasser's ability to utilize the ingrained Bedouin fascination with words and the force of his own charismatic personality to mesmerize millions of listeners. The speech was also the first act of a superb performance, a splendid *coup de theatre* that Nasser had an unmatched ability to stage.

Hassan Ibrahim, one of the original FO, listened to the speech at his home in the Heliopolis neighborhood of Cairo with two other friends, Dr. Rashwan Fahmi, and former RCC member Abdel el-Latif el-Boghdadi.[267] As the speech ended, the three friends were surprised to hear loud chants in the street. Ibrahim sent his driver out to find out what was happening, and the man came back to report that trucks were bringing hundreds of young men and depositing them in the courtyard of the Heliopolis Secondary School two hundred meters from the house. As soon as the young men got off the trucks they ran chanting toward Manshiet el-Bakry (the nearby neighborhood where Nasser lived).[268] The three friends went out and saw the Arab Socialist Union's buses and trucks continuing to bring in people despite the blackout and the sounds of anti-aircraft artillery fire filling the air. It was only when they drove towards Nasser's house and saw the large crowds there that it began to dawn on them that it had all been pre-arranged. They went home feeling depressed at the thought that while young men were dying in Sinai at that very moment, Nasser was busy arranging this theatrical spectacle.[269] Salah Nasr, Nasser's once feared intelligence chief concurs with the view that the show was all part of a "theater play."[270] He also confirmed that one of the Arab Socialist Union's groups, brought over from Bani Swaif in Upper Egypt, arrived at the Cairo railway station one hour before the speech started and had to wait there before moving on to Nasser's house to take up their assigned positions.[271] Yet another group, one of the Cairo groups, arrived outside the house before the speech ended.[272] All these facts point to the demonstrations having been preplanned and part of the "theater play." The partial script of a taped telephone conversation between Nasser and Heikal that had taken place the previous day and is quoted in Nasr's memoirs appears to support yet again Nasr's contention that the event was staged.[273]

The demonstrations intensified the next day and brought life in Cairo to a complete standstill. The demonstrators demanded a parliamentary resolution rejecting Nasser's resignation, and their chants called on the Parliament's Speaker, Anwar el-Sadat, to take note of their wishes as they chanted: "*saggel saggel ya Sadat ehna khtarna Gamal bizzat*" (take note Sadat that we have specifically selected Gamal). The chanting was impassioned, was anti Zakaria Mohi el-Din, and called on Nasser to rescind his resignation. In a classic Nasser maneuver, at the last moment he had apparently substituted Zakaria Mohi el-Din's name for Badran's as the proposed interim president without having notified Mohi el-Din of his decision to resign or having forewarned him of his intention to nominate him as his replacement.[274] Mohi el-Din, an intelligent man whom Nasser had long ago nicknamed the *asfarawi* (the cunning one),[275] rejected the nomination, and the Cabinet met and convinced Nasser that a radio statement to that effect should be made. Mohi el-Din taped a statement announcing his rejection of the nomination, and it was rushed to the radio station. At the last minute, and again without telling anyone, Nasser ordered the radio station not to broadcast Mohi el-Din's statement. Mohi el-Din, who was sharp and had been around Nasser long enough to be familiar with his methods, understood immediately that his name was being used in a cynical ploy to alarm the public and force them into Nasser's corner, and he never forgave Nasser for what he did.[276] The rubber stamp parliament met that morning and unanimously called on Nasser to rescind his resignation,

On cue, Nasser promptly "acquiesced" to the will of the people, rescinded his resignation, and secured his hold on power. And once again, the people had been duped. The whole affair was a charade to which Nasser more or less admitted a few months later when he compared it to his earlier 1954 resignation and declared to Emmanuel d'Astier that he "calculated" and "maneuvered" in both instances.[277]

Former RCC member Kamal el-Din Hussein, who had been out of favor for several years when the 1967 attack took place, felt that the dire situation obligated him to rise above his differences with Nasser and attempt a rapprochement.[278] He went to see him on June 19 and 21 and suggested that carrying out reforms such as doing away with the hated intelligence organizations would strengthen the internal front and enhance the country's ability to resist any further Israeli incursions. He also suggested that since there was not a single artillery piece left intact in the Canal area, the army units that were helping to fight the ousted Imam in Yemen should be recalled immediately. Nasser had no interest in any of that and asked nothing more of Hussein than to organize the popular resistance.[279] Hussein left in disgust with the impression that all Nasser cared about was securing his position.[280] Organizing the popular resistance was clearly intended to be no more than a show to be staged for the public's benefit.

Even a national catastrophe of the magnitude that was inflicted upon Egypt in 1967 could not persuade Nasser to contemplate any basic changes in the way he ruled the country, let alone countenance his own retirement. When the June catastrophe could no longer be glossed over, Nasser's demagoguery, possibly combined with his staged demonstrations, had kept the masses in check, but demands for change had been growing. In his speech on July 23, 1967, he had no longer been able to ignore those demands, but he had addressed them on his terms. After going through the usual list of "the revolution's achievements," and the imperialist plots, he then attempted the deflect blame by laying responsibility for the defeat on the senior army commanders and by claiming to have warned them to expect an Israeli attack on June 5.[281] He then acknowledged the public's demand for change and for putting an end to the privileges that some undeserving individuals acquired and declared, "I am with the people in this."[282] Evidently he had lost none of his arrogance or his belief that he could continue to manipulate the masses with words since he claimed that Israel's occupation of Sinai was only secondary to its (and the imperialist plotters') main goal which was to end the (Egypt's) revolution, thus implying that all was well as long as *he* remained in power.[283]

This time, however, the effect of the speech was short-lived. People representing the whole spectrum of the political arena, from the extreme right to the extreme left, had finally, to use el-Hakim's terminology, begun to regain consciousness, and the large crowds that began to demonstrate starting early 1968 chanted *la Sidky walal Ghoul Abdel Nasser el-mas'ool*[284] (Not Sidky, not el-Ghoul, Abdel Nasser is the one who is responsible).[285] Their chants: "Heikal, Heikal, you servant, you forger of dreams,"[286] appeared to reflect, finally, a recognition of Heikal's central role in inducing their state of unconsciousness by feeding them a steady diet of meaningless but hypnotic slogans and empty rhetoric. Their chants: "Who made you chief? Gamal, you are asleep; wake up, Gamal. Use your army against Dayan [Israel's Minister of Defense], not against us,"[287] expressed their long pent up frustration at the repression and fear that they had been subjected to for so many years. The masses' use of the pronoun 'your' rather than 'our' in reference to the Egyptian army was a damning confirmation of the régime's lack of legitimacy. The violent 1968 anti-government demonstrations by workers and students were the first such spontaneous expression of public sentiment since the 1952 coup,[288] and both the Muslim Brothers and communists were involved in the massive November demonstrations that took place throughout the country.[289]

Nasser could no longer avoid facing the fact that people wanted a change, but he seemed incapable of comprehending or unwilling to accept that his system did not work. He resorted to the use of his tried and tested, dual-pronged weapon of repression and new rhetoric to cope with the crisis. He tried several people who were accused of the usual charges of espionage, plotting assassinations and attempting to change the régime.[290] He blamed all problems on his newfound enemy: "the centers of power," which was the new term that Heikal had selected in response to the new crisis, and all blame was laid at their door.[291] At the same time, he denied any personal responsibility for the violent suppression of the demonstrators by blaming the police and accusing unnamed reactionaries for instigating the violence.[292] He reshuffled the Cabinet, appointed civilians to it, including twenty-four new ministers,[293] and announced his "March 30 Program" which promised an open society[294] and was touted as a "mandate for change."[295]

On the media front, the propaganda machine went into full swing with Heikal leading the chorus. He absolved Nasser of any responsibility for the crisis and placed it on the shoulders of subordinates to whom Nasser had entrusted many affairs of the state due to his ill health.[296] Nasser, Heikal claimed, never wanted power and was only opposed to the king, not to the political parties and parliament in 1952. Heikal, as always, simply ignored the countless examples that pointed to the lack of truth in his statement. It was certainly no secret that Nasser had outlawed all the political parties after the coup with the exception of the Muslim Brothers,[297] who opposed parliamentary rule and supported a dictatorial form of government. He obviously saw no reason to abandon the strategy that he had used so successfully throughout his career.

In October 1968, Heikal, full of righteous indignation, called for the elimination of the centers of power. He wrote a series of articles in *Al Ahram* on 13, 14, 15, and 17 October 1968, and another on 8 November 1968 entitled *el-Ma'na el-haqiqi likul ma takashshaf ba'd el-naksa* (The Real Meaning of All That Came to Light after the Setback). His articles called for an open society and criticized the minister of justice and the state minister for state security over the arrest of a statistician for releasing data on national nutrition.[298] He blamed the centers of power for ignoring Egypt's pharaonic past and for their exacerbation of the national identity crisis, and wrote of the officers' lack of political experience.[299] Some of these leaders, the propaganda machine now claimed, had a penchant for secrecy, were incompetent, were interested in little more than personal gains, were not up to the responsibilities they were entrusted with, and tended to operate in the dark.[300] They denigrated intellectuals yet attempted to join their ranks by obtaining doctoral degrees through unethical means.[301] Criticism of the régime, albeit mild criticism, began to be tolerated, and Ahmad Abdel Mo'ti Hegazi wrote criticizing the role of the school curriculum which ignored Egypt's pharaonic history in blurring the Egyptian national identity.[302] Other journalists criticized the media for its lengthy reporting on unimportant issues such as soccer while ignoring important ones such the economic state of the nation.[303] Heikal suddenly became a champion of free speech and led a campaign for a freer press.[304] Reform, it appeared, was at hand and seven million registered voters cast their vote on May 2, 1968 on Nasser's program for change. The turnout was reported as 98 percent, and the "Charter" was approved by a 99.98 percent of the voters, with only 798 voters in the country casting a negative ballot.[305]

A realist would, however, have remembered previous 99.99 percent results, and viewed the latest numbers as evidence that Nasser did not intend to make any real changes. He saw no need for a change in anything other than rhetoric. The gang that he had once complained to Sadat about was, after all, his gang. It did not come to power by accident. It was at the core of the régime that Nasser foisted upon the country and was its main constituent component. This was the way Nasser designed the system, and no one knew this better than he did. He informed Okasha in a private exchange that he knew that the commander of the Navy "was the uncrowned king of Alexandria," that that the country was "composed of feudal fiefdoms: the army fiefdoms, the Socialist Union's fiefdoms, the National Assembly's fiefdoms, the government's fiefdoms," and that he (Nasser) was the only one who could control all these fiefdoms.[306] In reality, this was the only type of government that Nasser could live with, and the only change that he was in the process of fashioning was a change in rhetoric. This is evident in the fact that the principle of opting for trust and ignoring expertise not only continued to be the main basis for selection to Cabinet appointments, and that the public was well aware of this. While Nasser espoused sympathy with the demands of the 1968 demonstrators, and Heikal called for the elimination of the centers of power, ministerial appointments told another story. The choice of a regional university's president (Asuit) for the position of minister of higher education did not come as a surprise to anyone. The appointee was "the youngest, least experienced, least competent," of all of Egypt' university presidents[307] but he was the only one among them who had not only tried, but also succeeded in, containing the student demonstrations at his institution. The message was clear, and after that all other university presidents began to devote more time and energy to stopping student demonstrations and this became an integral part of their job.[308] Heikal's articles about free society were no more than a cynical attempt to absorb public anger, and he kept up the charade while Nasser devoted his energies to tightening his grip on power and consolidating his secret Vanguard Organization.[309]

His complaints during the above-mentioned private conversation with Okasha were about the individuals, not about the system that produced them or the basis for their selection to their top posts. He was obviously determined to deny the fact that the problem was systemic. His trusted friend and right hand man, Amer, had had a slew of responsibilities at one time or another. He was Nasser's resident representative in Syria during the period of unity with Egypt. He supervised the oil industry, the tourist sector, agricultural reform, the liquidation of feudalism, and several other assorted organizations, and Nasser had never expressed any reservations. Now, however, he justified giving Amer so many responsibilities by telling Okasha that he only gave him all these responsibilities to "satisfy his wishes."[310] He also said that he was aware that Shams Badran, whom he had appointed minister of war, was neither competent nor intelligent, and lacked expertise, and that Amer left the Armed Forces to Badran "to play with it as he pleased."[311] He stated that he told Amer that the senior army officers were a "mere decoration," and that junior officers were left to "play with the armed forces as they wished."[312] He went on to claim that he had been aware all along of Amer's lack of qualifications to command the armed forces and had tried for ten years to get rid of him by [rather strangely it seems] appointing him minister of defense, but Amer had refused the appointment.[313] Interestingly, Nasser never explained to Okasha why he provoked Israel with his brinkmanship and fiery rhetoric that led to their attack when he was aware that the armed forces were in such a bad shape.

Instead, he went on to reveal to Okasha his plan for reforming the system. He confided to him that he changed his views about the superiority of the one party system. The multiparty system, he now believed, was the best insurance against the "dictatorship of cliques." This change of heart, he added, was the reason that he intended to ask Abdel Latif el-Boghdadi and Kamal el-Din Hussein to form an opposition party![314] Such a cosmetic change indicated, as did the entire conversation with Okasha, that he was either incapable of grasping or unconcerned about the immensity of the catastrophes that his régime brought upon the country and the absolute lack of logic in his argument. Clearly, the prospects for change as long as Nasser was alive were nil.

Retaining power seems to have continued to be a major, perhaps the major preoccupation of Nasser until he died. Abdel Meguid Farid, his close aide for eleven years, apparently found him very engrossed in thought one day and asked him what was on his mind.[315] What was on his mind did not turn out to be the dire situation in the country after the catastrophe that had taken place the previous month. It turned out that what worried him, as he stated to Farid, was that while he knew that the Americans wanted to get rid of him, he was beginning to doubt the extent of Soviet support for him personally.[316] Another significant clue to Nasser's priorities was that he appeared to Farid to have been more saddened by Amer's attempt to turn the army against him in an effort to hold onto his own position as Commander-in-Chief than he was by the disastrous defeat.[317] Obviously, his inordinate obsession with power outweighed any feelings of remorse for the unprecedented damage he inflicted upon his country. The war, according to Nasser's own, probably understated, pronouncements, cost 19,500 casualties,[318] and billions in material damage. Yet in a speech that reflects an amazingly warped sense of values, he saw nothing reprehensible in declaring: "if Israel accepts the 242 [UN] resolution, then we will not have lost anything."[319]

In spite of Nasser's initial success in containing the situation, the public began to stir during the following months and to show signs of "regaining consciousness," to use el-Hakim's term. Some voices began to call for change but Nasser continued to run the country in the much same way as he had all along and appeared to have learned very little from his humiliating defeat. The vast intelligence apparatus and his rhetoric continued to be his main supports, and only the slogans changed. It was only his death in 1970 that made it possible to begin to repair some of the immense damage that his reign of almost two decades wrought on society.

Nasser's Enduring Imprint

There is little doubt that what Nasser accomplished was a truly impressive feat. The statistical probability that a boy born to a *sa'idi* (Upper Egyptian) family near the bottom of the socio-economic scale would grow up to become the absolute ruler of Egypt was infinitesimally small. Yet this admittedly remarkable man led an incongruent group of no more than three or four dozen active participants who had no education, no unifying ideology, no special skills or abilities, and no articulated vision for Egypt's future, to take control of the country in the face of potentially powerful opposition. Clearly, Nasser was no a run-of-the-mill individual. Dictators never are. And like all dictators, Nasser left an imprint on Egypt, but in his case the shape of that imprint has proved, perhaps, more difficult to erase that many others. While Nasser's personality for its own sake is not the focus here, his personal character traits and idiosyncrasies are clearly pertinent to understanding both the confluence of these with the main political influences on him and the consequent social and the continuing political developments that took place in Egypt between the years 1954 and 1970.

Tawfiq el Hakim rightly claims in his *'Awdat el-wa'i* (The Return of Consciousness), that Nasser subsumed Egypt in his person,[320] and reduced it to a mere reflection or manifestation of his own moods, feelings, sentiments, and emotions at any given moment in time. P. J. Vatikiotis, the author of what is probably the best-documented and most insightful analysis of Nasser and his régime concurs with el-Hakim's assessment of the importance of understanding Nasser's character, not to be judgmental,[321] but to have a handle on what took place in Egypt during his era.[322] Like el-Hakim, Vatikiotis sees Nasser's imprint on Egypt during his time in power as so pervasive and all encompassing that investigating the period is tantamount to investigating Nasser's personality.[323] This is hardly surprising. Other absolute rulers have affected their societies and the course of events during their time in office in a similar manner. Even in democratic societies the personality of strong leaders such as Winston Churchill, whose actions and policies were constrained by long established social institutions and an enduring democratic tradition, had a significant impact on the course of events in their societies. Few, however, have left such a deep imprint as Nasser did.

Although Nasser was born in Alexandria, he was as culturally removed from that cosmopolitan city as his Bedouin ancestors who conquered it in the seventh century had been. His attitudes, social values, and view of himself made him more of an Arab than an Egyptian. He shared his distant ancestors' negative views of both the Egyptians and their pharaonic heritage and their conception of the term pharaoh as a derogatory term. Their xenophobic tendencies, disdain for education and expertise, exaggerated sense of personal dignity,[324] and social conservatism were reflected in many of Nasser's policies. His somewhat restrictive attitudes towards women were, however, extremely mild by Bedouin standards, and his régime exhibited a decidedly secular outlook. The *hegab* and *niqab* fads were still a few years into the future and Nasser's female family members dressed normally.

One of the most enduring consequences of Nasser's policies was the impact on education. The deterioration of the educational system was a gradual process that was set in motion with the lowering of standards that began with the appointment of an army officer, Kamal el-Din Hussein, to the post of minister education on August 31, 1954, a position he kept until July 15, 1961.[325] With his focus on personal loyalty above all else, Nasser appointed a man whose education beyond high school was limited to a few months training in the military college, and who viewed educational reform as merely the increase in numbers of student. As an RCC member, he was also not accountable to anyone but Nasser.[326] The combination of these two factors began the downward spiral that has continued until today. The number of students per classroom increased, green areas in schools decreased as new classrooms were built on the grounds, some schools began to operate two shifts to accommodate the increase in numbers, and parents began to resort to private lessons to compensate for the deteriorating quality of education.[327] Out of class activities, such as sport, music, theater, and anything that was not connected to memorization from a book, were considered a waste of time by Egypt's new decision makers and gradually phased out and replaced by what was termed national subjects, which were little more than slogans to be memorized. To be sure, rote memorization was not invented by the revolution. It was a negative feature of Egyptian schooling that pre-coup educators had always been concerned about but were unable to combat effectively because of the central place that it occupied in the Arab culture. It was, however, a legacy of Bedouin social values that penalize individuality, discourage independent thinking, nurture neophobia, and stress blind obedience. What the new policies did was simply reinforce these traits and create the perfect environment in which they flourished and became even more firmly rooted in the culture. Teachers were turned into parrots singing the praises of the glorious revolution and the endless sins of the deposed royal family. The impact of this practice on the students' attitudes and sense of identity in later years was negative and long lasting. A whole generation grew up with little knowledge of their nation's history. Some of those who believed the simplistic propaganda that they were fed at school developed into adults who sought one-dimensional explanations for the most complicated problems in society. This vulnerability led them eventually to become easy prey for the demagogues who divide the world around them into black and white, believer and infidel, empty slogans, simplistic solutions to all problems, and an opportunity to die a martyr and go to paradise. The wide powers enjoyed by Kamal el-Din Hussein set a new trend that did not end with his departure from the ministry because department heads were granted dictatorial power to hire and fire as they pleased regardless of the qualifications of the new appointees.[328] The next minister of education, el-Sayyid Youssef, was an employee of the ministry who was related by marriage to Nasser. He was more of a bureaucrat than an educator and his tenure was characterized by "frightful stagnation."[329] Youssef, who enjoyed the same dictatorial powers as Hussein, remained in his post until June 18, 1967,[330] and every stage of the state educational system from kindergarten to graduate school continued to decline despite several attempts at reform.

Most private schools in Egypt, but not all, fared no better than the state schools. The private foreign community schools appeared for a while likely to escape the downward spiral. There were two hundred and eighty-one of these schools in Egypt in 1952.[331] They were initially established to meet the needs of the foreign community such as the British, French, Italian, German, and Greek residents, but their popularity among the general population gave them an important role in the field of education, and by 1949, about sixty-seven percent of their student body was Egyptian.[332] The schools followed their own syllabi, although several of them established sections that followed the ministry of education syllabus,[333] and the standards were generally high. It was only a matter of time, however, before xenophobia led to law 201/1953 that abolished foreign language teaching at the elementary school level. Such xenophobia appears to have persisted in some segments of society till today and leads to some patently illogical statements at times. For example, one researcher[334] derides the preference of multi-national corporations today for filling their staff vacancies with graduates of what are referred to as language schools, and claims that the practice is discriminatory despite admitting that these graduates are hired because of their foreign language skills.[335] Other "experts" suggest that, contrary to all research in this area, learning a foreign language before the end of the primary stage (age six to twelve) "deforms the children's minds."[336]

The 1956 invasion of Egypt by Britain, France, and Israel led to a more concerted effort to eradicate Western influence from the country, and most of the foreign schools were impacted in one way or another by the ensuing Egyptianization policy.[337] Some schools were taken over, and their faculties were either deported or left the country voluntarily and were replaced by often less qualified Egyptian teachers. In some cases, such as The English School in Heliopolis, which was taken over, re-staffed by Egyptians, and renamed, the negative impact on the academic standards, as a former student, social scientist Leila Ahmad, recounted in her memoirs, was almost instantaneous.[338] In other cases, such as the school dubbed Egypt's Eton,[339] the descent into mediocrity was more gradual and took years rather than months. The school had originally opened its Alexandria campus in 1902 and had quickly become an elite multi-ethnic, multi-religious, and multi-cultural institution with students from a variety of backgrounds. The student body included the future King Hussein of Jordan, the future King Simon of Bulgaria, Crown Prince Zog of Albania, Prince Abdullah of Iraq, various members of the Libyan, Saudi, and Kuwaiti ruling families, in addition to Edward Said, and actor Omar Sharif.[340] After 1956, both the Alexandria and Cairo campuses were taken over and the British General Certificate of Education (GCE) syllabus was replaced by an Egyptian syllabus and examinations. Law 160/1958 decreed that heads of all private schools had to be Egyptian citizens, and that the Ministry of Education's syllabi in Arabic, history, geography, civics and religion had to be followed.[341] The students at this school, as an old graduate recounted, witnessed the changes in their curriculum first hand when government bureaucrats arrived at the school armed with red pens and scissors and expunged objectionable material such as a part of *L'Avare* (a play by Molière) and chapters of history books.[342] Out of class activities deteriorated also after the takeover when parts of the playgrounds were expropriated or built upon,[343] and the theater and gym of the school's Cairo campus were closed down and the swimming pool became a garbage dump.[344]

Even today, more than half a century after the coup, successive ministers have been unable to stem the decay. Media reports illustrate the extent of the system's deterioration. Government officials have admitted that 25 percent of the students in primary and preparatory schools in the town of Kafr el-Dawwar cannot even write their own names.[345] The minister of education also recently admitted that almost all high school students and many university students have to take private tuition[346] because of the deteriorating standards of instruction in the public institutions. The ministerial Cabinet's information center publicly admitted that the Egyptian family spends about 20 percent of its income on private tuition[347] under this system of "free education." Cheating in examinations is so blatant that in one recent incident, teachers were too frightened to prevent parents taking the final exams in place of their children.[348] In another incident, a large number of parents gathered outside a boys' school in the town of Kafr el-Sheikh, where the final exams for the Preparatory School Certificate were being held, and started pelting the proctors with stones in an effort to intimidate them and force them to allow their children to cheat.[349]

At the university level, the standards began to drop with the phenomenal increase in admissions and the introduction of subjects such as Arab Society which consisted of little more than slogans and in which students were rarely failed despite their low standards.[350] The purges of qualified faculty members who were not considered loyal to the military junta after having one of various political labels attached to them (reactionary, leftist, rightist, religious extremist, etc.), despite the sudden expansion of admissions, led to a shortage of teaching faculty. The shortage was partly met by hiring less qualified but loyal faculty members and by speeding up the process of granting graduate degrees, which began the downward spiral on that level. Social Science researchers began to limit their research to traditionally safe topics such as prostitution, theft, and drug abuse, and either steered away from studying what were considered sensitive topics such as sex, terrorism, religious extremism,[351] and anything remotely connected to politics. The principle that loyalty was the only route to advancement[352] virtually guaranteed mediocrity. Some of the better-qualified faculty members either became demoralized and nonproductive, or simply gave up trying to maintain standards and began to swim with the tide to protect their livelihood. The lucky few who succeeded in obtaining exit visas left the country. Egyptian universities, once the Arab World's leading institutions of higher education, began to compete with other Arab universities for the prize in mediocrity and lack of relevance to the modern age.

Between 1952 and 1970, the number of university students more than quadrupled.[353] According to official figures, the number of university students in 2006/2007 was 2.3 million,[354] and the total number of university faculty members for the same year was 44,684,[355] which translates into a ratio of 51.5 students per faculty member. That ratio increases to 63.4 if the 36,288 *mo'eedin* (instructors working on their masters or doctoral degrees) are excluded. Even these figures are inflated since they include the faculty members on loan to other Arab universities and because certain faculties such as law have a much higher enrollment than other faculties.

In 2007 the student body at Cairo University, according to its vice-president, stood at one hundred and eighty thousand.[356] The faculty of commerce had 376 students per professor (fifty thousand students to 133 professors). The Faculty of law had 450 students per professor (twenty seven thousand students to sixty professors).[357] No real education can take place under such circumstances, and the unavoidable outcome is that the value of such university degrees becomes questionable. Tens of thousands of graduates who barely understand the rudiments of their purported specializations flood a job market that requires skills they have not acquired. Ministers of Education appear to have no problem admitting to the media that the whole educational system is in a dire state yet they are either unable or unwilling to reverse the downward spiral.[358]

The major cause of this downward spiral was clearly the new elites' lack of appreciation for education, competence, or expertise.[359] Their devaluation of technical competence, knowledge, and expertise filtered down and influenced society's culture and system of social values. The new social value that took root and became an integral part of the Egyptian value system was that acquiring expertise was not the best means of self-advancement. The specter of unqualified people of trust occupying the positions of power and prestige in the new Egypt served as living examples of the validity of the new precept. The public knew and the post 1952 régime implicitly acknowledged that the standards of education at all levels went into a free-fall after the military coup.

The military coup of July 1952 left a negative impact on almost every aspect of society. Its leader's confused sense of national identity, despite the fact that it had been centuries since his ancestors immigrated to Egypt, exacerbated the dilution of the national identity that two thousand years of foreign rule bequeathed Egypt. Nasser formally robbed the Egyptians of their identity by deleting the word Egypt (*Misr*) from the map. Egyptians were no longer Egyptians, citizens of Egypt, but Arabs, citizens of the United Arab Republic. Some of the converts to Nasser's point of view continue to preach these same confused notions of selfhood. One such example is a professor from a provincial university[360] who believes that it would be a dangerous for an Egyptian to identify with his native homeland. He makes this preposterous claim in a book published fifteen years after Nasser's death in which he states, "One of the most dangerous consequences of the French campaign" of 1798 was that it revived in Egyptians their sense of independence that existed before the Islamic *fath*.[361]

Although it is highly unlikely that Nasser would have known the origin of the term *Misr*, ironically the change of the country's name was a case of ancient history repeating itself. *Misr*, the term that he tried to erase was actually the name that his nomadic ancestors had forced upon the country. The country was referred to as Misreen in Aramaic, and Misrayem in Hebrew, which means the border. The Ancient Egyptians, before being subjugated by foreign forces, called their country Kemet or Kemi, which means the black land in reference to its fertile soil.[362]

Nasser's promotion of Arab rather than Egyptian selfhood effectively aborted the hesitant march towards regaining the distinctive native Egyptian identity. One of the manifestations of this problem of a blurred and fuzzy identity is the way in which some Egyptians seek an identity in religion, others in lamenting the days of the Ottoman occupation, and others in deriving pride from their non-Egyptian origins such those who join the Ashraf[363] Syndicate.[364]

A serious problem bequeathed to Egypt by the 1952 coup was then the negative impact it left on the national identity. That fragmented sense of national identity reflects the tragic history of the country's centuries of subjugation and abuse, and is reflected in Nasser's public utterances that suggest he identified himself as an Arab rather than an Egyptian. In a speech in Damascus on March 9, 1958, for example, he made this identification clear when he declared his allegiance to Arabism rather than Egyptianism.[365] His repeated comments to Ahmad Abul Fath that there is not a single man in Egypt[366] and that the best way to handle Egyptians is to frighten and intimidate them because they would rebel if treated well,[367] are surprisingly similar to his Bedouin ancestors' negative statements about Egyptians centuries earlier.[368]

Also like his Arab ancestors, Nasser appears to have considered the term pharaoh as derogatory, and he went to lengths to disassociate himself from Egypt's ancient past, declaring in another speech in Egypt on July 22, 1959, for example, that "pharaonism" (stressing Egypt's pharaonic identity) is an imperialist conspiracy.[369] His scorn for the pharaonic heritage provides another striking parallel with his Bedouin ancestors and their disdain for the true value of the ancient world's monuments and achievements. Numerous anecdotes illustrate this scorn. On one occasion, the Egyptologist, Kamal el-Mallakh was showing Nasser the newly discovered Sun Boats that he, el-Mallakh, had discovered[370] and which were considered one of the most important discoveries in decades. With journalists present, Nasser derided the find, saying he did not come to see this "nonsense" but to raise el-Mallakh's spirits.[371] On another occasion, when he was upset with the Germans, he poured scorn both on them and on the Kalabsha Temple, an important pharaonic monument that the Germans, at their own expense, had disassembled and moved before it was submerged by the waters collecting in the lake forming behind the High Dam. In addition to the rescue of a temple of significant historical value, this was also considered a major technological feat. Nasser evidently had a different perspective and referred to the rescued temple as "the few rocks that they [the Germans] disassembled and put together again," and scornfully declared that the Germans can take "them away; we do not want them."[372] Again reflecting his forbears' cultural values, he also had no time for the arts in general, except for his love of and capacity for oratory, which was valued by Bedouins.

The rather sorrowful sight, decades after Nasser's death, of a sportsman raising the Saudi flag during the opening ceremony of the 2016 Rio de Janeiro Olympics in spite of the fact that he was not a Saudi but an Egyptian member of the Egyptian delegation,[373] is a clear expression of the depth of the blurred national identity affliction bestowed upon the country by what was originally referred to as "the blessed movement."

Nasser's success in less than two decades of rule in reversing the small gains in mitigating that serious identity problem was a testament to both his total hold on society and the arduousness of the process of modernization and value change. Nasser's legacy was pervasive and not limited to the reorientation of the national identity, the change in the values system and the transformation of social institutions. It encompassed every aspect of life in Egypt including the urban environment and the country's ecology.[374]

One of the stated goals of the 1952 coup was building a healthy democratic life. The legacy it bequeathed to Egypt, however, was the destruction of Egypt's fragile democratic institutions and the revival and reinforcement of the culture and system of social values that Egypt's preliterate Bedouin conquerors introduced to the country centuries earlier. It is a value system that sanctifies the concept of *ghazw* (raid), and imbues the term with sacred connotations. Religious extremists used the term with pride, decades after Nasser's death, to describe virtually all of their exploits. The murder of an individual who does not share their worldview, robbing an "infidel's" shop or a "usurious" bank, and planting a bomb were all acts that were referred to by the perpetrators as *ghazwas* (raids). Prior to 1952, it had taken the much-maligned Western-educated members of the ancien régime more than a century to take a few tenuous steps towards modernizing a society that had stagnated for centuries. The process of discarding some of the social values that were at the root of the country's sluggishness, inertia, and inability to join the modern world had been difficult and painstaking, and the distance that had been covered on the path to modernism had been miniscule. Public awareness of the need to keep moving in that direction had been spreading, however, notwithstanding the modest gains that had been made. 1952 saw an end to that progress, however slow.

The coup's impact on Egypt was so pervasive that it extended to Egypt's physical environment. The Aswan High Dam was one of Nasser's proudest achievements. Although Nasser did not allow any discussion of its actual economic benefits or of the ecological damage that it might cause, the dam's dubious benefits were well known to both local and foreign scientists. Silt carried by the annual floodwaters that fertilized the land was lost and resulted in soil erosion. The loss to the Mediterranean[375] of the most fertile land in Egypt as a direct consequence of soil erosion was, however, almost completely ignored.

The serious coastal erosion[376] caused by the Dam also led to the disruption of the food chain to the fish in the Eastern Mediterranean and the demise of the sardine fishing industry, which employed tens of thousands of fishermen. It resulted in an increased reliance on expensive chemical fertilizers,[377] and estimates of the amount of water lost to evaporation from the lake behind the Dam ranges from eight to fifteen milliard cubic meters and to seepage at nine milliard cubic meters.[378] One of the leading authorities on managing the Nile waters warned that the loss of silt would destroy the brick industry, which used the silt as its raw material, and would increase the water velocity in the river, which would erode the riverbed and pose a threat to all structures downstream. His words went unheeded.[379] The rising sea level caused by global warming is accelerating the rate of erosion and a recent report warns that, depending on the level of that rise, Egypt could lose between twelve and thirty-five percent of its most fertile land.[380] The argument about the actual economic benefit accruing to the country is now moot, but only the most diehard apologists for the military rulers continue to deny the immense negative impact that the High Dam has had on Egypt's ecology.

Also glossed over in the construction of the Dam were the social and financial costs of relocating the thousands of Nubians whose villages were flooded.[381] Even today, more than half a century later, some of the displaced Nubians are still waiting to be resettled and threatening to take their case to the European human rights organizations and ask for their help in pressuring the government to build them the new villages that were promised.[382]

The coup also left its imprint on Egypt's cities. The capital that the military junta captured in 1952 "was considered one of the most beautiful cities in the world."[383] The center of "Paris on the Nile," as Cairo was sometimes referred to, was dotted with beautiful Art Nouveau, Baroque, Art Deco buildings,[384] and French Neo-Renaissance architecture. A soon as the military took control of the country they confiscated scores of villas and other buildings and either handed them over to favored allies and supporters or turned them into schools[385] and government offices, and the urban face of Egypt began to change. Many of these buildings were graceful villas that were architectural treasures. Some were designed by world-renowned architects,[386] and others contained valuable wall and ceiling frescos. As art appreciation was not one the new elite's values, much of this architectural heritage was destroyed. Frescos were either painted over or left to deteriorate and rot, and shops or other unsightly makeshift structures replaced their beautifully landscaped gardens.

Helwan, one of Egypt's oldest cities around thirty kilometers outside Cairo, was developed by Khedive Ismail as a health resort because of its sulfur spring and became a fashionable winter resort from the thirties.[387] Now the "dream," as one journalist has termed it, "has turned into a nightmare," and Helwan has become one the most polluted cities in the world.[388] The cement particles in Helwan's air are now fourteen times the internationally permitted level, and twenty nine percent of its schoolchildren suffer from chest diseases.[389]

Egypt's cities began a steady process[390] of decay and uglification[391] in 1952 that is difficult to reverse, and the ongoing effort, which began after Nasser's death, to rebuild and modernize the neglected infrastructure has been and still is a costly and challenging task. Most of the deterioration in the urban environment can be attributed either directly or indirectly to the spreading values of the new middle class. For example, rent control, which deprived landlords of both the financial means and incentive to maintain their buildings[392] stemmed from hostility to the old elite and the view that landlords were exploiting the tenants. This attitude has resulted in the currently untenable situation where the monthly rent for some apartments is less than the price of one pack of cigarettes, yet many of the tenants simply do not have the financial means to pay a reasonable rent. Another factor that contributed to the degradation of downtown Cairo was the mass exodus of nationals of several European countries who were either expelled or encouraged to leave the country starting in 1956. This was a direct result of one of Nasser's core social values, xenophobia, and the 1956 attack by Israel, Britain, and France, which provided him with an excellent pretext for eradicating all foreign presence in Egypt.[393] Their businesses and residences were taken over almost overnight by rural migrants who did not share their view of the neighborhoods and the streets as extensions of the private spaces that they felt a responsibility to maintain.[394]

The Price of Personal Glory

Obviously, Nasser's did not set out to bankrupt and ruin Egypt, but he could not possibly have been unaware of the country's problems

A Squandered Opportunity 219

as he set out in pursuit of personal glory. Yet he was either incapable of comprehending the seriousness of these problems, or viewed them as a price worth paying for that personal glory. "Overpopulation, illiteracy, unemployment, malnutrition, and undernourishment were some of the problems that faced Nasser's Egypt,"[395] with overpopulation central to all the other problems either directly or indirectly. The régime Nasser ousted in 1952 had certainly been aware of the need to confront the population problem. One month before the coup, the newspapers reported that the prime minister met with the minister of social affairs to discuss the problem of the high birth rate.[396] One indication of how seriously they viewed the problem was that one of the options they discussed was outlawing polygamy, which would have been a drastic measure.[397] After the coup, Naguib also recognized the problem of overpopulation and the need for birth control.[398] Amin Huwaidy, who occupied several high positions during Nasser's era (e.g. chief of the *mokhabarat*, minister of defense and of national guidance), reported in his memoirs that Nasser took the issue of birth control rather lightly. Hafez Badawi, whom he appointed as minister of social affairs and a member of the committee on family planning, was constantly mocked by Nasser who wondered aloud how Badawi, who had twelve children, could convince others to plan their families when he himself had such a large flock.[399] Some observers at the time suspected that Nasser, himself a father of five, felt that a bigger population gave Egypt much greater weight in Arab, Middle Eastern, and international affairs. Some of his public statements seem to substantiate this suspicion.[400]

The pursuit of personal glory appears to have always taken precedence over national interests with Nasser. For example, Egypt and France enjoyed good relations until Nasser decided to meddle in Algeria. Nasser's friend and longtime aide, Heikal, admits that France only participated in the 1956 attack against Egypt because of Nasser's support for the Algerians who were involved in a bitter fight with France for their independence.[401] Nasser's intelligence chief has proudly admitted that one of his assignments was to arm and finance the Algerian war of independence and that in addition to arms Nasser ordered him once to send twenty thousand tons of sugar to Algeria at a time when there was a sugar shortage in

Egypt.[402] Financial support of Algeria continued even after it won its independence. For example, several factories that had been purchased and were en route to Egypt, such as a textile factory that was to be located in Shebeen el-Koam, were ordered diverted to Algeria to demonstrate to the Algerian masses that their "revolution" was giving the people something tangible.[403] There were funds for Algeria in Egypt's national budget,[404] in spite of Egypt's mounting burden of foreign debts and the acute shortages of food and consumer goods in the country. However, neither Nasser nor his minions had to stand in line for hours in the hope of getting a bag of sugar or other basic food ingredients as the rest of the population was often forced to do.

Nasserists might argue that he simply viewed the national interests differently from many others, that he may have been sincere in his belief that he was serving those interests by seeking a power monopoly, or that perhaps the motivation behind some of these actions was nothing more sinister than bad judgment. They might argue that squandering national resources on foreign adventures and on supporting liberation movements in the Third World raised Egypt's stature and influence on the world stage. None of these reasons, however, begins to justify Nasser's cavalier attitude towards Egypt's national interests or the wanton squandering of its human, financial, and political resources in pursuit of personal glory. His obsession with power was always a major motivator for his actions, remaining an end in itself and not a means to an end, and his actions provide ample confirmation of the view that he put personal aggrandizement before solving Egypt's problems. His devotees, however, are never at a loss when asked about Nasser's achievements. The usual list has been memorized well. Breaking the arms monopoly; abolishing feudalism; nationalizing the Suez Canal; securing constitutional and social gains for workers and peasants; abolishing capitalism, exploitation, and partisanship; resisting colonialism; strengthening the army; providing justice for the peasants and workers; industrializing the country; and unifying the Arab nation from the ocean to the Gulf.[405] A mere cursory examination of this long list exposes it as either mere empty slogans or cover-ups for failed policies and disastrous undertakings.

Those who view the Nasser era through rose-colored glasses maintain that the revolution achieved the six goals that it announced when the junta seized power in 1952.[406] These goals were: 1) to eliminate imperialism and its Egyptian collaborators; 2) to eliminate feudalism; 3) to eliminate monopoly and control of government by capital; 4) to establish social justice; 5) to build a strong army; 6) to build a healthy democratic life.[407] The first three of these items would be more appropriately termed a list of enemies rather than a political platform. Viewed in that context the revolution could be said to have succeeded in achieving its first three goals. They were relatively easy to achieve and required little more than secret concessions to Britain that led to the evacuation of their forces, large-scale arrests of a wide assortment of individuals, and confiscation of properties. As for the other three goals, no neutral observer could present a plausible case for claiming success in achieving them. Even the most biased observer could not deny the repeated failure of the Egyptian army to protect Egypt against Israel's repeated incursions, or that repression and terror rather than popular participation in decision-making were the mainstays of the Nasser régime. His policy of tolerating corruption and of devaluing expertise and relying on trust as the only criterion for public appointments led to the institutionalization of these traits which have taken root in the culture and turned into major impediments to reform in contemporary society.[408]

A favorite ploy of the régime, the 99 plus percent plebiscites, rather than reflecting the will of the people reflected the opposite. Certainly, some people both in Egypt and abroad may have viewed these results from the beginning with a degree of skepticism. Some may have doubted the assertions of Nasser's de facto spokesperson, Heikal, that the results did indeed reflect the will of the people and that only a few hundred people in a population of about thirty million voted against Nasser.[409] Jokes, the usually reliable barometer of Egyptian public sentiment provide an inkling of how the rest of the population came to view these figures in the fullness of time. As soon as the results of one such poll were published, the following joke, recounted by a veteran journalist, was whispered around the country.[410] Nasser's spies told him that some people were mocking him by making jokes about his régime and that made him very angry. He ordered his intelligence chief to compile a list of the best jokes, the ones that make people laugh the loudest, then track down and arrest the man who composed them. The man was duly found and brought over so that Nasser could personally interrogate him. Nasser asked him if he admitted to being the person who made up the joke about extracting teeth through the nose; the man replied that he was. Nasser then asked him if he admitted to being the person who made up the joke about the dog that escaped to Libya. The man replied that he composed that joke too. Nasser went through all the jokes and his anger was rising as the man admitted his responsibility for each one of them. Finally, Nasser could not contain his fury and yelled at the man asking him how he dared to make jokes about the man who was elected by a 99.9 percent of the people. The man replied that he could not take credit for composing that joke.[411] In spite of the jokes, the results served as useful fig leafs that provided the appearance of legitimacy to a régime that lacked it. This trend continued after Nasser's death, and the results over the past fifty years have been consistently impressive.

It was inevitable that Nasser's pedestrian understanding of complex issues would eventually prove to be his greatest failure.[412] He had a simplistic view of the world and was never able to comprehend that he might have been able to achieve the greatness that he coveted so much by making his country great instead of simply telling the masses that it was great. Mohammed Ali the Great, whose achievements Nasser tried to erase from Egypt's history books, earned this sobriquet by making Egypt a great regional power, not by making speeches. Rather than insulting the Ottomans who were the regional superpower of his age by telling them to "drink from the Mediterranean or the Red Sea" as Nasser did to the United States,[413] Mohammed Ali earned their respect by modernizing the country, and building an army that rivaled theirs. Nasser never viewed him as a 'real' Egyptian because he was born in Macedonia, but Mohammed Ali loved Egypt and put its name on the map. Nasser, who was born in Egypt and whose Bedouin ancestors had lived in Egypt for generations, claimed that he cared for Egypt but erased that word from the map and from the official name of the country.

When the long process, begun with Mohammed Ali, of slowly shedding the culture of underdevelopment and inching towards modernity came to an abrupt halt as the street smart Nasser wrested control of the country from King Farouk, the last, and one of the least intelligent and most incompetent of Mohammed Ali's descendants, providence was not smiling upon Egypt. However, it was certainly smiling upon Nasser, who appeared at a time when the Egyptians were wishing for a just dictator. They thought they found one in Nasser. Unfortunately, the dictator they got was one who had a limited vision, had a pedestrian worldview, tolerated corruption so that he could blackmail his minions with their misdeeds, and was obsessed with power and the quest for personal glory. Worse, he was inflicted with an acute case of the Egyptian malaise, a fractured sense of identity. He did not stop at dismantling the country's budding, fragile, and imperfect democratic system, but went on to subvert all social institutions and rule Egypt in the manner of a tribal chief whose will preceded all legislative, judicial, and executive institutions. He hankered after his Bedouin ancestors and identified with them, and like his Arab forbearers who resented the Mamluks, he believed that being an ethnic Arab gave him more right to rule Egypt than Ali's descendants who were not. It was a recipe for disaster, and Nasser delivered it.

No objective observer can deny that the health of Egyptian society is not as good as it could be, or that the military régime which ruled Egypt for more than half a century is directly responsible for the sad current state of affairs. The area of disagreement is likely to be about the extent of current physical, urban, and cultural degradation that exists and the reasons for that. The "revolution" even failed to achieve the relatively simple task of eradicating illiteracy, and the "General Authority for Illiteracy" which claimed to have reduced illiteracy by a meager one percent was finally dissolved by presidential decree and the task was transferred to local authorities.[414] There is a wide-ranging acknowledgment among Egyptian intellectuals[415] that every aspect of culture in Egypt entered a period of decline[416] as a direct consequence of the military junta's rule and the repression of intellectuals and of the freedom of thought and speech.[417]

Both Mohammed Ali and Gamal Abdel Nasser left their imprints on Egypt. The former was dubbed the father of modern Egypt, and the latter lost Sinai, bankrupted the country, but built the High Dam. The Dam and the lake that was formed behind it are probably the biggest offenses against Egypt's ecology. The lake submerged several Nubian villages, ancient buildings, and important sites. One landmark that now lies under the lake is the fortress built for the defense of Egypt by Snefru, the first Pharaoh of the Fourth Dynasty, and the father of Khufu, builder of the Great Pyramid who counted "Smiter of the Barbarians" among his titles. That coincidence provides a potent symbol of Egypt's age-old struggle against the foreign conveyors of ruin and destruction. It is perhaps appropriate that the lake was named Lake Nasser.

8

Egypt's New Direction

None of the few dozen junior officers who participated in the grab for power on July 1952 could have had the slightest idea of the scale of the socio-cultural consequences of their venture. The military coup of July 1952, however, brought about a radical reorientation of Egyptian society that impacted almost every aspect of life. Passing the mantle of leadership from the ancien régime to the military junta could easily have gone down in the history books as merely a change in Egypt's government and a reform of its political system. Nasser was the one variable that transformed a run-of-the-mill military coup into a major event that halted the process of inching, albeit painfully, towards regaining Egypt's distinct national identity, a more stable democracy, and a system of social values that is more in tune with the modern world. Single individuals who change the course of history in their societies do not materialize out of a vacuum. They are more likely to be the product of ideas and social forces that are dormant in society and are waiting for an actor who has the credentials and personal characteristics to represent and implement them and for the right socio-political conditions that would facilitate their emergence. The conditions in Egypt were ripe for a change in 1952 and Nasser possessed the appropriate combination of personal characteristics that allowed him to become the change agent. The change he brought about, however, was the reintroduction and reaffirmation of pre-modern social values, and an exacerbation of the national identity problem that two thousand years of foreign rule bequeathed to Egypt, bringing about the country's economic ruin and establishing a system of dictatorship that returned the population to a political impotence that still prevails today.

The New Political Elite

The social transformation of Egypt began within days of the coup's success. Egypt, as noted earlier, lacked the military tradition, common in parts of Europe, of an officer class socialized in values and rites exclusive to the military. The military tradition of spit and polish that reflected the special meaning the uniform carried and instilled in those who wore it in Britain or France, for example, a personal pride in its correctness, had not taken root in Egypt yet. Senior officers rather than tradition embodied that pride and enforced military discipline. After the coup, when many senior officers were cashiered, military pride and discipline collapsed. Some of the junior officers wearing the military uniform in July 1952 could have been more accurately described as peasants wearing uniforms rather than as professional soldiers. Nevertheless, with the military now in power, that uniform conferred higher status than it had before the coup and implied power and authority. These officers donned their uniforms as they began haunting government offices and civilian establishments in search of opportunities for a share of the wealth, power and influence that some of the coup leaders began to acquire almost from their first day in power. The result was that Egypt's cities, especially Cairo, witnessed a sudden increase in the numbers of the new masters strutting around in their uniform. However, with the collapse of military discipline, many dispensed with the cumbersome military cap that they obviously found superfluous. Soon civilians followed suit and began to imitate the new masters who were already acquiring visible status symbols that indicated their newly elevated positions in society, such as expensive cars and sumptuous apartments and villas that they confiscated under various pretexts from their legal owners. They discarded the *tarboush* (fez), which was traditionally worn by white-collar workers, the educated, and the social elite and was a relic inherited from the masters of another age, the Ottomans.[1] While initially, the social elite may have discarded the fez to avoid identification with the ancien régime, before long the practice became widespread as a form of identification with the new military régime.

Abandonment of the fez in itself was an inconsequential act, but its significance lay in the fact that it was a visible indicator of the population's awareness of the demise of one master and its readiness to begin modeling itself on the new one. What was not as visible was the slow and steady shift in social values that began to take place and gradually took root and influenced attitudes and interpersonal relationships across society.

Predictably, Nasser, the master of all the new masters, had the most significant impact, both direct and indirect, on the direction and substance of the social change that began to take place. Those who shared his values were the individuals more likely to be selected by him for positions of wealth, power, and authority. Though few in number at first, they provided visible evidence of the efficacy of adopting the new masters' social values, perspectives and worldviews, thus becoming the new role models. The ideal that the new generation would look up to and seek to emulate was no longer the European-educated, Western-oriented elites who were being vilified as vestiges of a corrupt and detestable bygone era. Instead, they were *ahl el-theqa* the "people of trust," those who formed the centers of power that Nasser created, and upon which he depended to maintain his own grip on power even though he later came to refer to them as "gangs." These role models who occupied positions for which they were unqualified and enjoyed wealth and prestige provide some insight into the values that became associated with success in the new revolutionary Egypt and eventually became the prevailing social values of mainstream society.[2]

The first segment of society to become consciously aware of the emerging trend and, therefore, to be directly impacted by the devaluation of education, competence, and expertise, was the military. Although the dismissal of officers who belonged to what was termed 'the feudalist and reactionary classes' immediately after the coup,[3] was probably viewed as a one-time purge and not recognized as the start of a new trend, it in fact was. The first clear indication that the traditions of the ancien régime were now passé, and that the junta was setting new standards was on January 12, 1953, when five hundred officers were cashiered out of the army and several of them arrested and taken to jail in their uniforms.[4] Kamal Hassan Ali (army officer, intelligence chief 1975 to 1979, war minister and deputy prime minister 1981 to 1984 and prime minister 1984 to 1985) recounted in his memoirs that he began to realize soon after the coup that trust rather than expertise was the route to plum assignments. He also noted that some junior officers were granted Soviet commissar-like authority within the army. The people of trust, it became apparent to him, formed a new privileged class within the army.[5] The practice of relying on trust rather than expertise as a criterion for selection to positions of huge responsibility was established soon after the military coup's success.[6] The very first presidential decree ordered the promotion of Abdel Hakim Amer from the rank of Major to the rank of General,[7] and appointed him Commander-in-Chief of the Armed Forces.[8] Incompetent but loyal individuals, such as Shams Badran (Minister of War in 1967),[9] were also handed control of the armed forces.

The elevation of people of trust was not limited to promotions within the military or assignments to leading government positions. The policy also extended into all walks of life. Junior officers were appointed to run everything from banks to manufacturing plants to department stores.[10] Before too long, the officers were running every sector of the national economy.[11] By the mid sixties, most Cabinet ministers, provincial governors, heads of boards of directors of trading companies, under secretaries in ministries, all of Egypt's ambassadors in Europe,[12] and 73 percent of its ambassadors worldwide were army officers.[13] Many, but by no means all, of these new appointees were colorless, undistinguished, and unexceptional individuals. Hussein el-Shafei, for example, whom Nasser trusted despite referring to him as useless, was someone whose shallowness, limited worldview, and meager intellectual resources typified those who replaced the old pre 1952 elite in Egypt. El-Shafei was nicknamed *ragol el-sa'a* (man of the hour/clock) behind his back.[14] In Arabic that meant that he neither gained nor lost, that he was irrelevant and contributed nothing. Hassan el-Tohami, also one Egypt's new elite occupying the highest positions in the political hierarchy, was given to conversing with individuals who were only visible to him. The caliber of Nasser's men was demonstrated par excellence in the choice of political advisor of the three most powerful men in the régime. In the critical period after their patron's death, the Minister of the Interior and Deputy Prime minister, the Commander of the Armed Forces, and the Minister of State for Information consulted a dead sheikh in a séance.[15]

One of the phrases often used by the media during the Nasser era was the revolution's generation. It was used to refer to those who were too young to have been corrupted by the values of the ancien régime and who would be socialized in the new values. Taking a closer look at some of the individuals who rose to the top in the so-called revolutionary era and would, presumably, have been considered suitable role models for the new generation provides a clear portrait of the social values that the revolution nurtured, valued, rewarded, and helped to spread in society.

Sami Sharaf, who was described by Gamal Hammad[16] as the second most powerful man in the country,[17] is a good example. He had come to Nasser's attention only weeks after the coup when there was widespread discontent among artillery officers who were demanding that membership on the board of directors of the officers club and in the RCC should be through elections. Forty-five of the protesting officers were arrested on January 15, 1953, partly because of Sharaf spying on them and informing Nasser of their activities. Nasser, in turn, obviously recognized in Sharaf a quality that he valued and rewarded him with an appointment to Zakaria Mohi el-Din's staff then transferred him to his own staff.[18]

Sarwat Okasha, one of the original FOs recounts in his memoirs how he first met Sharaf. He was having dinner with Nasser during the summer of 1955 when a junior officer whom he did not recognize came in to give Nasser some papers. When Okasha enquired about the man's identity, Nasser told him that his name was Sami Sharaf and that he was not one of the Free Officers, and he proceeded to praise him profusely. He stated that he chose him as his secretary because he carries out his orders without any doubt or hesitation, and that he trusted the man completely. When Okasha asked how he could be certain of the man's loyalty, Nasser stated that Sharaf had informed against his own brother, Ezz el-Din Sharaf. The brother's crime, for which he was arrested and imprisoned, was criticizing the revolution. Nasser went on to add that Sharaf had taken an oath before him to slit the throat of one of his children if Nasser ordered him to do so. Okasha almost choked and could not refrain from saying that no one in a normal state of mind could ever take such an oath.[19]

Sharaf's[20] values and personal characteristics appear to have been widespread among Egypt's new elite,[21] and one of the values propagated by these role models, however high the position they occupied in the new régime, was that behaving like a street ruffian was an acceptable practice. The following incident, for example, was related by an eyewitness and became widely known among the public. One of Egypt's ambassadors to a European country[22] apparently upset about a conversation rumored to have taken place between the embassy's counselor and Nasser's aide, wanted to question the counselor about it, but the man refused to answer any questions. The Ambassador, a leading member of the Egyptian diplomatic corps, called the press, cultural, and military attachés into his office where they witnessed him insulting the counselor in the foulest language.[23] Then, under the pretense of shielding the counselor, the military attaché pinned him down, and the Ambassador proceeded to beat him so severely that the man suffered a concussion.[24] While the press attaché stood by frozen and watching in terror, the narrator (the cultural attaché) tried in vain to plead with the Ambassador and to separate him from his victim. Finally, the counselor was taken home and kept there under guard until he managed to escape and leave the country.[25]

Such stories about the behavior of the new elite spread quickly among the Egyptian population, but nothing perhaps speaks more forcefully of the caliber of these elite than their own words. Their published recollections, either in the form of memoirs or interviews granted to journalists and researchers, are among the most revealing sources of information about the level of mediocrity of people who occupied positions of power and authority after the military coup, and who ran the country for Nasser and were often entrusted with making life and death decisions. What is perhaps most telling in these recollections is the consistent lack of awareness of how self-damning their own words are, the consistent lack of self-reflection, the revelation of ineptitude and narrow and uninformed worldview.

Sami Sharaf's memoirs, coauthored with journalist Abdulla Imam, are a prime example of such self-revelatory recollections. They give the reader some insight into a man who worked closely with Nasser for fifteen years, who was privy to every meeting and every political decision, who controlled access to him, and who chose which documents would be brought to Nasser's attention and which would not.[26] Sharaf helped to rule Egypt, became a role model for its youth, and was obviously proud enough of his achievements to want them published, but the memoirs reveal a man whose character, ability, and general caliber are stunning in their poverty.

Sharaf had years to plan his memoirs, even to fabricate them, and he had help in writing them, but all that he produced is a litany of contradictions; implausible explanations and stories; vacuous, self-serving anecdotes; simplistic platitudes; and feeble attempts to try and show that he was still relevant. His cloak and dagger references in insignificant anecdotes to Mr. B doing this or Colonel D saying that would be comical if they did not in fact reveal the depth of dysfunction in the members of Nasser's administration. Evidently, fifty years on he still wished to give the impression of being privy to state secrets of such significance that they still could not to be divulged. Sharaf's contradictions are particularly telling. Within a few paragraphs he claims both that Nasser's private safe contained nothing but recordings of Om Kalthoum songs and family letters and, forgetting his earlier assertion, that the safe was where the much whispered about secret funds were kept.[27] He also denies being the keeper of these secret and undocumented funds, yet all but admits it a few pages later when writing about his trial for plotting against Sadat. When questioned about these funds during the trial, he confirms existence by warning the judge to steer clear of this subject since both he and another judge on the bench next to him had received monies from that fund.[28] It may be worth noting that this comment also reveals the kind of arrogance that unfettered power nurtured in men such as Sharaf.

Other comments he makes are singular in their lack of perspicuity. To the claim that publicly owned companies made large losses and failed because army officers rather than suitably qualified managers ran them, his answer is that military men are capable of managing factories.[29] His elaboration of this point is worthy of note:

> Looking at it scientifically, trustworthy persons in my opinion can execute general policy without deviating from the political line but experts will give you technical expertise

each in their area of competence based on theories that often conflict with practical applications and may not achieve political goals.[30]

His explanation of the reasons for Nasser's selection of Sadat as vice-president is equally disingenuous: Sadat, he claims, needed to serve for one year in that senior post so that he could qualify for a pension.[31] His explanation clearly fails to take into account a number of factors; for example, the astuteness Sadat demonstrated in keeping on Nasser's good side and that Ahmad Abul Fath recognized,[32] or the possibility, even probability, that the reader is well aware that the régime had never allowed rules and regulations to get in its way. The explanation also ignores the fact that money certainly was not the issue since all that was needed was a word from Nasser and Sadat would have received a wad of cash out of his secret accounts, as did many others. His explanation implies that the judgment of his idol, Nasser, was impaired if he made such an important appointment on such flimsy grounds. A further claim that Sharaf makes stretches the reader's credulity to the limit: that he was so poor at the time of his arrest for plotting against Sadat that his wife had to sell their furniture to meet household expenses, and that they had to move out of their villa and borrow money from relatives to buy an apartment.[33] What comes out of the book with crystal clarity is that its author had neither the education nor the intellectual aptitude that should have been prerequisites for appointment to his position of power. Instead, Sharaf's main qualifications appear to have been in the area of sycophancy, plots, intrigues, and secret machinations.

Abdulla Imam's book length interview with Hussein el-Shafei, who was Nasser's onetime vice-president and one of the original FOs, provides another unwitting example of the shallowness, limited worldview, and meager intellectual resources of those who replaced the old pre 1952 elite in Egypt. Imam asked el-Shafei to explain to his readers the reasons behind Nasser's decision to risk a war with Britain and France by nationalizing the Suez Canal in 1956 when Egypt would have regained control of the Canal in a routine and peaceful process with the expiration of the Canal's concession only a few years later. El-Shafei's convoluted answer was:

When people gauge events they do not take into consideration that things are within the realm of higher authorities, it is possible that the July revolution or Nasser are the instruments of God and used to prevent famine by building the High dam to be merciful to us. People sometime philosophize and do not take into consideration that these are dispositions that are of a higher authority than ours, God has determined and will do as he wishes. But if we talk of such things people think that we are flying within what is not tangible, meaning that we are not thinking about what this material age requires us to consider.[34]

His answers to other questions were even more nonsensical. When asked to speculate, based on his long years of experience in high office, on what the outcome would have been if the 1956 battle (when Britain, France, and Israel attacked Egypt) had lasted longer than it did, the best response he could think of was: "You make strange assumptions, and every situation has certain evaluations and calculations."[35] His responses clearly demonstrate that regardless of the degree of complexity of an issue or question, he had nothing to say. When asked why the army remained in power after the 1952 military coup instead of returning to their barracks and holding parliamentary elections? His answer was: "To protect the revolution."[36] Even more telling was a question on the significance of the army's 1967 humiliating defeat by Israel. It [the defeat] was, he responded, "a necessary surgical operation to return the army to its barracks."[37] Such was the depth of analysis years later of a man who helped to determine the country's fate. It would seem that in the intervening years he had had no cause for reflection, saw no need to enroll expert help to prepare for the interviews, or even to protect his image, saw in fact nothing amiss with the responses he gave.[38]

Plots, in el-Shafei's view, were the simple explanations for many events. For instance, he maintained that Sadat lured him to the Fayed Airbase on the morning of June 5, 1967 before the Israeli attack so that he would be killed by an Israeli air raid.[39] He failed, however, to offer any evidence or explanation of how Sadat came to learn of the exact timing of Israel's surprise attack. Egypt's unsuccessful unity with Syria in 1962 was a "very, very cleverly planned plot" by Sadat, the USA, Britain, and Israel that was "designed to fail and to undermine Nasser," and to benefit "imperialism and its agents."[40] Nasser's ill-advised and disastrous intervention in the civil war in Yemen was both "the biggest victory for Egypt," and at the same times a plot by the agents of imperialism[41] who also schemed to give Egypt's presidency to Sadat so that he could save Israel.[42] The fact that vast amounts of oil have not been discovered in Egypt was also a plot by the imperialist companies.[43]

Ali Sabry, who counted the premiership among his numerous positions of power and who once confided in Hussein el-Shafei that in fact he was the man who had the real power in Egypt,[44] was still in 1987 trying to impress his readers with slogans to illustrate the coup's, and by implication his, achievements. These achievements, in Sabry's opinion, were supporting liberation movements in the Third World, breaking the armaments monopoly, liberating the economy, Egyptianizing the economy, industrialization, Afro-Asian solidarity, building the High Dam, and agricultural reform.[45] A more objective interviewer might have asked Sabry about the type of industries that were built, why they were built, where they were built, what they produced, and the economic and social consequences of all these decisions. He might also have asked about the economic and environmental cost of the High Dam, and the socio-economic impact of the revolution's achievements in the area of land reform. The passage of time should have helped Sabry to put all these issues into a proper perspective and to realize that without Nasser's charisma behind them, these slogans did not have the same power to move people, but he seemed unable to grasp something so obvious. A sampling of his other views reveals similar shallowness to that of his cohorts. For example, he shares el-Shafei's belief that Sadat succession to the presidency was the result of a wide-ranging plot to save Israel.[46] He also shares Sami Sharaf's belief that army officers are suitably qualified to run any commercial enterprises successfully because running a business requires making political not economic decisions.[47]

Another example of Egypt's new elite who occupied the highest positions in the political hierarchy was Hassan el-Tohami. He was one of the original FO and later worked in the intelligence field and on the presidential staff in various capacities. According to Sami Sharaf and Sha'rawi Gom'a, el-Tohami had a habit of suddenly jumping up and uttering a greeting to no one in particular. When his colleagues asked him whom he was greeting, he would reply that the Prophet Mohammed had been passing by and greeted him so he returned the greeting. At other times, it would be one of the caliphs who happened to have been passing by and greeted him.[48] When Nasser died, el-Tohami apparently made a facemask of wax or plaster of Paris of the President's head and took a cutting of his hair, but no one had the slightest idea what the man planned to do with these items.[49] Amin Huwaidy a onetime chief of the *mokhabarat*, minister of defense, and minister of national guidance recounts the same anecdote of a colleague greeting passing individuals who were only visible to him, but does not mention Tohami's name. He merely attributes the episodes to one of the Cabinet ministers, and goes on to reassure his readers that Nasser did not seem to be taken in.[50] Huwaidy also goes on to add that when the Cabinet discussed the Israeli occupation of Sinai and discussed their options for liberating it, that same minister would smile and urge them not to waste so much effort on discussing the topic because he was certain that God would send them birds (that had supernatural abilities) to destroy the occupiers.[51] After offering this advice to his colleagues, the serious discussion would continue while the man who had just offered his advice to his colleagues would sit smiling serenely.[52]

Members of Nasser's rubberstamp parliament were of the same caliber as all his other appointees. On the morning of June 10, 1967, the whole population was still in shock at the magnitude of their army's defeat, Israeli troops were dug in a mere one hundred kilometers from Cairo, on the east bank of the Suez Canal, and the permanent loss of the whole of the Sinai Peninsula appeared to be a real possibility. Nevertheless, Nasser chose that day to conclude the theatrical production that he had conducted the preceding evening when he announced his resignation. The Parliament met that morning and called on Nasser to rescind his resignation. On cue, Nasser announced that he would acquiesce to 'the people's will' and withdrew his resignation of the previous evening. Upon receiving the news, the Member of Parliament who represented Bani

Swaif (in Upper Egypt) could not contain his pleasure at Nasser's announcement and danced on the floor of the parliament in full view of the media, and the television cameras.[53] The loss of Sinai, the loss of thousands of innocent lives, the fact that at that very moment there were soldiers, very possibly from that member's own constituency, literally dying of thirst in Sinai while at the same time attempting to dodge the enemy's bullets were apparently not consequential enough to lessen the man's elation.

9

Realism and Reform

Yousef el-Seba'i, an officer turned novelist and journalist, purporting to speak in the name of Egyptians, once claimed that they wanted Nasser to remain in power for the fifty years that he might expect to live. According to el-Seba'i, Nasser's professed goal of liberating the Arabs and Africans and guaranteeing freedom for Egyptians "for hundreds or thousands of years" was worth a half century of military dictatorship.[1] In the event, Nasser lived for only eighteen years after the coup, and it is difficult to imagine what further damage would have resulted from another thirty-two years of his policies. He died around 6:15 P.M. on September 28, 1970,[2] and was succeeded by his Vice-President Anwar el-Sadat. A brief comparison of the state of affairs in the society that Nasser bequeathed to Sadat with the state of affairs in Egypt on the morning of that fateful day in July 1952 would provide a succinct summary of the revolution's much touted "achievements" in eighteen years.

In 1952, Egypt was not rich, but it was solvent. Its currency was pegged to the Sterling at 0.975 Egyptian Pounds to the British Pound. It had no external debts.[3] It had a reasonably efficient road and rail network and an adequate educational system.[4] It was a parliamentary democracy, albeit a flawed one. Save for the dormant conflict with Israel, which could well have been resolved peacefully, Egypt was at peace with its Arab neighbors, Europe, America, and the rest of the world. The country was by no means free from corruption, but the level of corruption was checked, to a degree, by a free press, by that imperfect, but nevertheless functioning, democracy, and by the limited scope of the public sector. The king was ineffectual and incompetent but his powers were not absolute and his actions were partially restrained by the parliament, the press, and the public. The country was occupied by a foreign power, but was in the process of negotiating for removal of the foreign troops, and the only major impediment to a successful conclusion was the two parties' disagreement about the future position of Sudan, which had been united with Egypt since the nineteenth century. There was no threat to the integrity of the country's borders.

Sadat's Inheritance

Upon taking office in 1970, the new president, Sadat, summoned Hassan Abbas Zaki, the Minister of Finance and Economy, and asked for a briefing about the state of the economy.[5] Zaki informed him that the country was almost bankrupt and was very nearly at the stage when the government would not be able to pay the salaries of the army at the war front.[6] Nasser's legacy included shortages of food and basic consumer goods[7] that had become a normal part of life. The gold currency reserve, five hundred million gold sovereigns, which were kept in the Central Bank, had disappeared and its whereabouts are still a mystery.[8] Much of the country's industrial production was at a standstill, the factories being idle due to shortages in spare parts.[9] Even when in operation, they produced substandard products that the public was forced to accept for lack of choice. Nasser's tightly controlled media had praised the industrialization program on a daily basis, but its claims that everything "from needles to rockets" was being manufactured in Egypt were false.[10] The military factories according to the media were producing missiles, but the only products of these factories that the public ever saw were home appliances.[11] The millions employed in the public sector and in the army contributed little to the economy and had become a serious drain on the country's resources.

Sadat inherited a country in shambles. Every component of the infrastructure: roads, sewage systems, transport, telephones, and education was in a virtual state of collapse and the inept officers who ran these systems were either oblivious to the problems or incapable of solving them. In the area of public transportation, for example, the very profitable Cairo Transport Company had been nationalized, and its owner had left the country in 1960. By 1967, the company was making huge losses, and Cairenes had to endure endless waits for buses that sometimes never arrived and had literally to hang on to the doors and bumpers of the dilapidated overcrowded buses when they did. Nasser, desperate to demonstrate to the public a modicum of ability to solve one of the many problems that plagued society, had turned for help to a member of the social class that he had spent years heaping insults upon. Abdel Latif Abu Regaila. The self-exiled former owner of the company answered Nasser's call and returned to Egypt to bring the company he once owned back to life.[12] He quickly discovered, however, that bad management had ruined the company beyond the point of salvage and had no option but to give Nasser the bad news and return to his new home in Italy.[13]

By 1970, nothing had improved. The roads and sidewalks were crumbling. Trees lining the streets of Cairo's neighborhoods were no longer tended on a regular basis, as they had been before officers were put in charge of the city's management, and falling branches that on occasion injured pedestrians and damaged cars no longer surprised anyone. The sewage system overflowed on a regular basis, and anyone living in Cairo during the sixties remembers the way that the officers in charge handled the problem. Cylindrical cement walls up to a meter high that jutted up in the middle of some streets were built around manholes to prevent the overflow from spilling onto the once elegant streets. A seven-year wait for a new telephone and spending an hour or longer connecting a local call was the norm. *Mabeygamma'sh* (does not combine) was the new term coined by the suffering public to describe the problem.

Public education had gone from bad to worse. While free education from kindergarten through graduate school was claimed as one of the proudest achievements of the revolution, many educators were aware that the whole system of education was in decay.[14] A phenomenal increase in student numbers, had inevitably led to a drop in standards in keeping with the various impediments facing teachers in the classroom. What the revolution could rightly take credit for was the increase in the number of students per classroom because of the almost doubling of enrollment in secondary schools and the trebling in primary and preparatory schools between 1952 and 1970.[15] It seems that ignoring the high birth rate went hand in hand with a lack of planning for the increase in the number of children to be educated. In addition to the overcrowding that forced some schools to operate in shifts, the revolution could also take credit for the elimination of green areas in schools; the initiation of the private tuition trend;[16] and the introduction of new subjects like *el-tarbiya el-wataniyya* (National Education), the syllabus of which consisted of political speeches, media reports and other propaganda messages.[17] It could also take credit for making loyalty to the régime rather than competence and expertise the basis for appointing university faculty. Standards in graduate study programs were also lowered to speed up the production of the large number of doctorate holders needed to replace those who were labeled disloyal and dismissed and to accommodate the increasing numbers of newly admitted students.

In the governmental sphere, the imperfect but evolving democracy was swept away after the coup when Nasser became the sole master of Egypt, and his whims and caprices replaced the legislative, judicial, and executive branches of government. Virtually all major, and many minor, decisions were made by presidential decrees, and the judicial system only functioned at Nasser's pleasure.[18] Some of the military men who occupied almost all senior positions in government and the public sector did not even bother with the pretense that the law mattered, and Sa'd Zayed, the junior officer appointed Governor of Cairo, saw nothing amiss in once announcing to the press that the law was "on vacation."[19] Malevolence and the use of force, as Sadat noted, became prevalent in the country.[20] Yet Nasser's supporters were adamant that Nasser was not a dictator and the country was a democracy. The system of government that operated in Egypt was explained succinctly by one of Nasser's less intelligent minions when he said that Nasser listened to people's points of view, which is what he understands democracy to be.[21] Nasser's proponent, Heikal, was better able to play with words and described his system of government as "democracy through consensus" which was moving towards "democracy through participation."[22]

Nasser had run Egypt like a private fiefdom, and Egypt's foreign policy had become hostage to his moods and whims. He had wasted its wealth and resources on several foreign adventures and on supporting "liberation movements" around the world, and his interference in the Arab countries' affairs had become a source of constant friction.[23] Nasser had severed diplomatic relations with the United States and several Western European and Arab countries[24] for a variety of reasons. Egypt had running feuds with several countries around the world and the number of its friends had dwindled as Nasser had continued to add to the list of what he termed reactionary régimes or agents of imperialism. Even Nasser's main supporters, the Soviets, were not "cooperating," he told Sadat after his last visit to Moscow shortly before his death in 1970.[25]

Corruption had become widespread[26] and Nasser had tolerated it[27] because it kept his underlings happy, beholden to him, and vulnerable to blackmail. A sequestration order was more often than not a license to steal for those assigned to carry it out.[28] Corruption had become rife in the administration of sequestrated properties and in the various organizations that were part of the public sector where the annual losses was at times astronomical—a topic no one dared to discuss in public.[29] More than a hundred officers had been tried at different times for coup attempts, but not a single one had ever been tried for abuse of authority or corruption,[30] and bribery had become such a normal part of everyday life that public officials had begun to demand it openly. The extensive and complex web of official codes and bureaucratic bylaws had created an incentive to circumvent them in one way or another, and the emergence of an army of corrupt fixers and facilitators who knew how to get around these rules had been inevitable.[31] Army officers stationed in Yemen earned vast profits on the black market by transporting tons of foreign goods on military ships and planes and avoiding the payment of customs duties.[32] A sum of one hundred million pounds intended for financing efforts to defend the régime against its enemies if the need ever arose, was widely rumored to have been hidden away abroad.[33]

The British bases in the Suez Canal Zone were long gone, but the treaty that led to their departure was the same imperfect one that successive governments of what the revolutionary press termed the feudalist era had rejected thirty years earlier. Instead, Israeli forces were dug in on the east bank of the Canal, and Egypt, for the first time in its five thousand years of recorded history as a centralized political entity, was in danger of permanently losing part of its territory. The seriousness of Nasser's blunders and the desperate situation they had created for Egypt had forced him to attenuate his obsession with dignity and not only give up the defense of Egypt's skies to Soviet pilots and military personnel,[34] but to go as far as asking the Soviets to appoint someone to take over complete control of Egypt's air defense.[35] He also put aside his fiery rhetoric about independence, positive neutrality, and opposition to foreign military pacts, and offered to sign a pact with the Soviet Union two months before his death, an offer they had declined.[36]

What Anwar el-Sadat inherited was a society that was in ruins and where the most efficient institutions were the extensive sordid assortment of intelligence services.

New Style Different Priorities

Nasser's choice of Sadat had not been due to his trust in him or to his confidence in Sadat's abilities. Nasser was a suspicious person who trusted no one. Some dictators were enlightened enough to understand the need to provide for a smooth succession after their departure. General Francisco Franco of Spain, for example, planned carefully for succession and decreed that the monarchy should be restored upon his death (d. 1975) and that Prince Juan Carlos would then become head of state. Nasser seems to have never given any serious thought to succession. The most likely reason for Sadat's selection as vice president was that he, Sadat, simply outsmarted *el-ra'is*. Nasser began within a year or so after the success of the military coup to believe that he was the most intelligent and capable of all the co-conspirators, and began to belittle his colleagues and give them derogatory nicknames. Sadat's was "Colonel Right."[37] Sadat, however, did not allow that to perturb him and was smart enough to keep on Nasser's good side.[38] Sadat's detractors, such as Nasser's former minister of foreign affairs, Mahmoud Riad, claim that Nasser refrained from appointing Sadat to a major post because he had no confidence in his abilities.[39] Sadat, who proved to have been the wiliest of the Free Officers, cultivated Nasser's impression of him as vacuous and harmless, never sought a Cabinet post,[40] and appeared perfectly contented with unglamorous positions such as editor of *el-Gomhuriyya* newspaper when it was established in 1953, Minister of State in 1954, Secretary of the Islamic Conference when it was formed in 1955, and Speaker of the rubberstamp parliament. He made sure that he kept out of the power struggle within the RCC[41] and the rivalry between Nasser and Amer that was beginning to come to the surface by the early sixties.[42] His views on politics and foreign policy, as demonstrated by his actions once he succeeded Nasser, were in total opposition to Nasser's views, but he kept on his good side by never giving the slightest hint of that. After the 1967 debacle, Nasser began to realize that the monster that he created, the centers of power or gangs, could turn on him if it suited their purposes. Amer's death that year, following his failed attempt at using the army to keep his position, had eliminated the most powerful center of power, but there were others. Heikal, for example, had long ago ceased to be a journalist.

According to Sadat, Heikal believed that he had become co-ruler of Egypt,[43] and strengthened his position by making alliances with other smaller centers of power. Sadat, on the other hand, had reacted to the 1967 debacle astutely by offering his resignation as Speaker of the Parliament, calling on other leaders to do the same, and had met with Nasser to inform him that he did this to give him maximum freedom of action after the defeat.[44] In the spring of 1970, Nasser confided in Sadat that he had decided to expose the power centers by appointing Heikal and Sami Sharaf to ministerial posts.[45] By that time there was no one left to rely on but Sadat, who had never been associated with any power centers and had never complained at being excluded from Nasser's secret Vanguard Organization or at being appointed to a string of unremarkable positions. Consequently, it is understandable that Sadat became Nasser's closest confidant during the last seven months of his life.

Sadat's personality, however, differed from Nasser's in very significant aspects. He was more interested in concrete achievements than slogans and sought to repair the damage inflicted upon the country by Nasser's policies. He lacked Nasser's obsession with plotting and intrigue as well as his exceptional aptitude for them. He was not afflicted with the same blurred identity disorder that Nasser suffered from. He had no illusions of grandeur, and no aspirations to be the leader of all Arabs or the liberator of the Third

World. He saw himself as an Egyptian, the President of Egypt, and his main responsibility, evidenced by the personal risks that he took, as the pursuit of Egypt's interests rather than personal glory. One of the most prominent aspects of Sadat's character was his strong emotional connection with the land. He never lost his attachment to Mit Abul Koam, the village where his family came from, and preferred his home there to any other place. Musa Sabry, the prominent journalist who was granted access to the presidential archives, and with whom Sadat taped many hours of conversations, states that he once told him that the scent of the soil made him feel that he was a part of it.[46] Culturally, Sadat was an Egyptian peasant who felt a powerful attachment to his land, rather than a rootless Bedouin Arab who scorned tilling it and the people who earned their livelihood by tilling it. He was the most politically active, and the most politically experienced of the original coup leaders. His experiences before the coup were also very different from Nasser's experiences. He had been jailed twice, once on suspicion of attempting to make contact with the German forces that were advancing towards Alexandria during the Second World War, and once because of his involvement in plots to assassinate two politicians in the forties. He used his period of confinement to broaden his education, learn German, and improve his proficiency in English. On one occasion, he escaped from jail with six of his fellow inmates, and in an early demonstration of his penchant for resorting to dramatic acts to get his point across, went to the king's official residence, Abdin Palace, with one of the other escapees, and signed the visitor's book, adding a complaint about their treatment in jail and declaring their intention to return there at once. They then took a cab back to jail, knocked on the door, and were readmitted. On a second occasion, he escaped from jail and spent months as a fugitive working in a variety of laboring jobs.[47] Sadat's colorful political history was public knowledge, yet he did not attempt to build up his image as the hero who had been destined to lead Egypt from the day he was born as Nasser did. He was also realistic enough to recognize that he did not have Nasser's charisma and that his legitimacy would have to be based on institutions, and not on personal appeal. Institutional building, therefore, became one of the favorite themes in his speeches. He may well have never heard of Max

Weber but what he was aiming for was an administration based on what Weber termed rational-legal authority.[48]

The accounts of Nasser's and Sadat's admission to the military college also provide some insight into the differences in personality between the second and third presidents of Egypt, the type of public image that each of them tried to promote, and their impact on their policies. Sadat, who graduated from the military college in February 1938,[49] (Nasser graduated in July of the same year) tells an entertaining story of his meeting with Ibrahim Khairy Pasha to seek his support for his application to the military college that contrasts sharply with Nasser's account of his meeting with Khairy for the same purpose. Nasser's version, which is accepted by some of his biographers, such as the French journalist Lacouture, despite its patent implausibility is that he "demanded" [50] a meeting with Ibrahim Khairy Pasha who "was utterly charmed by him" and admitted him to the college.[51] The British statesman Anthony Nutting, who met Nasser on several occasions, also states that Khairy Pasha had been delighted with Nasser, who had come knocking on his door uninvited. Khairy, according to Nutting's version, was impressed with Nasser's personal qualities despite his humble social background.[52] He judged him to be an earnest and devoted man who would make an outstanding officer.[53] The version of that meeting, advanced by Nasser's daughter, Hoda, on his official web site, is unexpectedly brief for a publication that is intended to preserve his myth. It is confined to a single sentence, which simply states that he managed to secure a meeting with Khairy who "admired his frankness, patriotism, and determination to become an officer and approved his admission."[54]

Sadat's account of his meeting with Khairy sounds far more plausible to anyone who knows something about the pre 1952 social class system in Egypt, and is worth quoting in full from the English language version of his memoirs. He, like Nasser, knew that he needed to plead his case for college admission to Ibrahim Khairy Pasha, but there was no way that someone from his modest social class could "demand an audience" with him, as Lacouture suggested Nasser did. His recollection was that he had been at a loss as to how to meet the Pasha.

Khayri was typical of the cream of the aristocracy at the time. He had given lessons in "horsemanship," on King Fuad's orders, to the young King Farouk, and so was the king's tutor; he was Under-Secretary to the War Minister; and his wife belonged to the royal family. Ibrahim Pasha was, in a word, a very prominent social figure indeed. How could we hope to approach him when we could hardly reach a minister's secretary?

It eventually dawned on my father that he had a friend — a warrant officer who had served with him in the Sudan — who happened to be working for Khayri. It was this friend who arranged for us, I don't know how, to see the pasha. One morning my father took me to the pasha's palace in al-Qubbah Gardens, an aristocratic district of Cairo at the time.

We entered the smart house and stood in the hallway. That was the arrangement: the pasha had to pass by us on his way out, would notice our presence, and ask us what we wanted. The pasha did in fact come down a few minutes later, whereupon the warrant officer whispered a few words to him. The pasha looked at my father and said very haughtily: "Oh, yes. You're the senior clerk of the Health Department, and that's your son who ... I see ... all right, all right!" Then he shot toward the door with my father following and mumbled something I could not distinguish; nor could my father, I believe.

It was an experience that has remained with me all my life. I don't think I shall ever forget it. It was the first time I had ever visited a pasha's house or seen a member of that class.[55]

The more plausible version of Nasser's admittance to the Military College is provided by Attorney Mahmoud Abdel Latif, who first met Nasser in 1927 when Nasser was sent to live with him in his apartment and attend primary school in Cairo.[56] According to Abdel Latif, Nasser sought his help when he faced the same dilemma as Sadat after he graduated from high school and wanted to join the military college. Abdel Latif was able to secure a meeting with an influential person, Abdel Meguid Ibrahim Pasha, whose family originated from the same village as Abdel Latif's family, and he introduced Nasser to him. Abdel Meguid Ibrahim took Nasser in his car, putting him in the front seat with the driver, went to see Khairy, and pleaded his case.[57]

Both Nasser and Sadat's applications were accepted because of their meetings with their sponsors and Sadat returned the favor years later after the coup when Khairy sought his help in connection with problems that he and his children were having with the sequestration department regarding their confiscated property.[58] In contrast, Nasser, once in power made sure that he got even with Abdel Meguid Ibrahim for not having treated him with the deference that he felt was owed to him when he sought and received his help in joining the military college years earlier. Nasser sought Ibrahim after the coup and told him that he had never forgotten the time when he sat him at the front seat of the car next to the driver,[59] and made him pay for the imagined insult. The dejected man died in the late fifties.[60]

The dire consequences of that hatred for the social elite, the exaggerated and unhealthy obsession with dignity, and the damage done to the country as a result of Nasser's enduring bitterness at countless imagined insults were part of the legacy that Nasser bequeathed to the new president.

This legacy was similar in many ways to that which Mohammed Ali Pasha inherited when he became Egypt's *wali* in the nineteenth century: an economy on the verge of collapse because of misrule and a body politic where control was in the hands of the Mamluk princes in the case of Ali, and the centers of power, in the case of Sadat. Sadat's task was even more daunting in some respects than Mohammed Ail Pasha's. He had to conduct his reforms while Egypt was in a state of war. The Israeli's were well dug in less than a hundred kilometers from Cairo behind the line that they boasted of as the strongest defensive line in the history of military combat. The Egyptians watched helplessly as the Israelis ignored international law and exploited Sinai's oil and natural resources at an alarmingly rapid pace. Israel even boasted that it was leasing a giant oil-drilling platform to drill for more oil in the Gulf of Suez.[61] Egypt's few oil wells and the income from the Suez Canal which might have staved off economic collapse were now lost. The incompetent army leadership was no match for the well-run Israeli army and incapable of evicting it from Sinai. Over a million people had been evacuated from the cities of Port Said, Ismailiyya, and Suez, which were under constant bombardment by Israeli artillery across the Canal from them, and they turned into an added economic burden.[62] Industrial production was down and some factories stood idle for lack of spare parts that could not be imported due to a shortage of funds.[63] The national savings rate was low, since the public was reluctant to place any funds in banks lest their savings were confiscated, and the industrialization program had to rely on foreign loans to finance it.[64] Yet Nasser had chosen to buy expensive modern technology and waste scarce capital on the military and on capital-intensive industries,[65] in a society that suffered high unemployment and overpopulation. He wasted tens of millions of pounds on setting up an aircraft industry that never got off the ground [66] when a manufacturing plant that produced mopeds would have been far more economically sound.

Everything in the country seemed to be disintegrating. Fear, hatred, the possible loss of livelihood, and the prospect of jail had been the hallmarks of the Nasser era,[67] and family members had spied on one another.[68] Nasser had turned people into wards of the state, reliant on it for everything from food to employment, housing, and education, since the state controlled every area of life,[69] yet incompetence, bad management of the economy, wars, foreign adventures, and corruption had left that state almost bankrupt. All intellectual activity and all voluntary organizations were state controlled,[70] and intellectuals had become little more than salaried government functionaries[71] whom Nasser used to keep the masses quiet and compliant.[72] All banks, heavy industry, insurance companies, transportation, mining companies, and all the major economic sectors had been nationalized.[73] Midsize companies had had to accept 51 percent government ownership and management.[74] Even department stores, wine makers, and hotels were nationalized.[75] Officers controlled all public organizations,[76] held most diplomatic postings,[77] and were the vast majority of members and heads of the boards of public companies, of ministers, deputy ministers, ministerial under secretaries, and of leaders in culture, the media, radio, and television.[78] The government was marginalized, and Nasser made all the major decisions. The minister of finance, for example had no control over the state's finances and no clue as to the purpose of the funds that he was sometimes instructed to hand over in sealed envelopes to the head of state or one of his minions.[79] The ministry of foreign affairs became superfluous as foreign policy became nothing more than a reflection of Nasser's moods,[80] and Egypt's relations with many countries were either severed or strained. The centers of power were well entrenched and likely to stand in fierce opposition to any attempt at reform.

Faced with this situation, Sadat worked quietly on all fronts at the same time. On October 20, 1970, he appointed Mahmoud Fawzi as the first civilian Prime Minister since the 1952 coup.[81] He was aware that he derived his legitimacy from being Nasser's successor, so he astutely continued to court his disciples and parrot his slogans. He paid lip service to his policies in public as he tried to repair the damage that was caused by nearly two decades of rule by whim and impetuous caprice through making radical changes in both domestic and foreign policy. The public, as evident from popular humor, was aware of this strategy. The joke repeated around Cairo's cafés at that time provided the most accurate and succinct description of his policies. The joke was that Sadat was being chauffeured in the presidential limousine by the driver that he had inherited from Nasser when they came to a T-junction. The driver turned to Sadat and asked him whether to turn right or left. Sadat countered by asking him which direction Nasser usually took at that junction. The driver said that he always turned left, so Sadat told the driver to give a left turn signal, and turn right.[82]

Dislodging the Old Guard

Although Sadat's first steps towards reform were tenuous and cautious, the new policies alienated or alarmed four groups of people. The first group was the old guard of senior leaders within the vast state bureaucracy[83], the military, legislative, economic, and political institutions. They owed their positions of power and privilege to Nasser, and the most senior among them viewed themselves as his legitimate heirs and Sadat as a lightweight and a traitor to the cause. They included a vice president, Ali Sabry, several key ministers such as the Defense Minister, the Interior Minister, the Minister for Presidential Affairs, the Minister of Information, leaders of the Arab Socialist Union (ASU), the Speaker of the National Assembly, and the intelligence chief. They had expected to be able to control Sadat[84] and obviously shared Nasser's view of him as ineffective.

The second group consisted of the multitude of incompetent and corrupt senior government and public sector bureaucrats who had enjoyed relatively high incomes, power, and authority under Nasser. They were people of trust rather than expertise, and they understood the implications of Sadat's passing references to the value of expertise and had good reason to be concerned about the consequences of reform.[85] As it turned out, most of them had nothing to fear since Sadat had no option but to rely on them to run the bloated bureaucracy, despite their unceasing efforts to thwart his efforts at reform.

The third group the reforms alienated was those who had grown accustomed to relying on the state, rather than personal initiative, in every aspect of life. With education from kindergarten to graduate school free, a resulting astronomical increase in university enrolment and the number of graduates, and purges of university professors, there was an equally steep decline in standards, which appears to have been of little concern to the usually incompetent people of trust who had been placed in leadership positions in the universities. This had a ripple effect as new generations of schoolteachers, in many cases barely literate with little to offer their students, emerged from the system. Of course, the ripple effect extended beyond the educational system into all areas of employment. New job creation was virtually non-existent, and new job seekers increased at the same speed as the birthrate. However, contrary to the laws of supply and demand, competition in the workplace ceased in a system that did not demand excellence and that guaranteed every university graduate work. All that a university graduate had to do was submit an application to the Manpower Office. After a year or two, the government placed the applicant in either a civil service position or a public sector job. In either case, little or no work was required, and at times as much as half the employees of these organizations would be absent from their posts[86] while new laws prevented slackers from being terminated. The system applied also in the professions. Regardless of their interest in or aptitude for their field of specialization, many graduates in the professions, especially medicine and engineering, had been channeled into these fields after achieving the highest scores in the *thanawiyya 'amma* (high school graduation examinations), more often than not due to an aptitude for memorization. The only exceptions to the norm within the system were graduates with personal or family contacts who filled the more prestigious jobs, regardless of their qualifications. While Sadat's new focus on expertise failed to reform a system that continues until today, it did, however, introduce an element of insecurity that alienated those with a stake in the status quo.

The fourth group of alienated people was the poorest segment of the population that had come to rely on the artificially low prices of food and other basic necessities. Fuel and basic commodities were subsidized and rents of state owned farmland, apartments, and shops were kept low. The rapidly increasing population meant, however, that the subsidies were taking an ever-increasing percentage of the state budget, which made the situation untenable, and Sadat began to consider possible reductions in these subsidies.

As soon as Sadat's independence became clear to the first group, they began a concerted campaign to undermine him and plotted to topple him barely six months after he took office. The newspapers, all government owned and staffed by compliant functionaries rather than professional journalists, were instructed to fill their pages with news items about the Arab Socialist Union (ASU) and its meaningless activities to counter any news on Sadat. When Sadat made a speech, the choreographed chants were about Nasser, whose pictures were carried by the planted audience, and Hassanein Heikal made sure that the influential *Al Ahram* newspaper that he controlled did not give prominent coverage to Sadat. Cabinet ministers appearing on the television or being interviewed on the radio invoked Nasser's name constantly, and his picture remained on display in all official buildings.[87] The group used their public rejection of Sadat's proposal to join with Libya and Syria in a vague, loose federation as an opportunity to display their strength. Members of the High Executive Committee of the ASU convened a meeting and voted against the terms of the proposal[88] despite the fact that the terms were identical to those that had been proposed by Nasser.[89] After the meeting, the minister of interior ordered policemen dressed in civilian clothes to surround the Cairo radio station and prevent Sadat from speaking to the nation if he decided to make an appeal for public support. Heikal, while not party to these machinations learnt of them, but did not inform the president.[90] Sadat was not intimidated and responded on May 2, 1971 by announcing that he had fired Ali Sabry from his position as vice president.[91] He was well aware of the risk that he was taking and expecting a major confrontation to ensue, he slept with a gun under his pillow, and his wife locked their bedroom door every night.[92]

Sadat's position received an unexpected boost from a young loyal intelligence officer. On May 11, 1971, the officer managed to bypass the eyes posted around Sadat by making contact with his (Sadat's) brother-in-law and accompanying him to meet with the president. The visit appeared to the spies as a family visit and did not arouse suspicion. They brought along tape recordings of telephone conversations between Gom'a (the Minister of Interior), Sharaf, and others in which they discussed a plan for ousting Sadat. Sadat sat listening to tapes until 4 A.M.,[93] then told the officer to return them to where they were kept and ordered the immediate arrest of the director of State Security Investigations.[94] The next day he kept his official engagements and visited an Air Force base with the war minister. Then on May 13, Sadat sent a message to the minister of interior telling him to either resign or be fired and appointed Mamdouh Salem to replace him.[95] The next day the other conspirators resigned en masse in the belief that the Arab Socialist Union (ASU), the only permitted political party, and the Vanguard Organization, both of which were under their control, would be able to organize mass anti Sadat demonstrations and bring about his ouster. In reality, the ASU was a mere empty shell. Nasser had designed it that way. Due to his suspicion of political organizations, it was little more than decor intended to look good and give the impression that a political institution existed. While membership was high, it grew out of either fear or expediency, much like membership in the Communist Party in the USSR, and the party had no popular base of support. It was riddled with spies belonging to the secret Vanguard Organization, which counted tens of thousands among its members, but was little more than an information gathering body and a means of handing out secret funds, well-paid high prestige positions, and assorted favors and fringe benefits to its leaders and hangers on. While the planned demonstrations did take place on May 14, 1971, they were small and ineffective, and the demonstrators were actually chased away by the public in one instance.[96] On May 15, all the plot's leaders were rounded up and placed under arrest, thus securing Sadat's position. Finally, after nearly two decades of unenlightened authoritarian leadership, Egypt had a leader more interested in solving Egypt's many problems than in personal grandeur, leading the Arab world, or obsessing over plots and conspiracies.

It is perhaps a befitting irony that it was Nasser's legacy and his policies throughout his term in office that led to the discovery and foiling of the plot by the Nasserists bent on preserving Nasserism. Since loyalty rather than expertise and competence were Nasser's criterion for selecting his men, it was not surprising that the plotters planned their coup with their characteristic incompetence. They taped Sadat's telephone conversations, but the culture of fear, suspicion, and mutual mistrust that Nasser promoted also led them to tape each other, and[97] these tapes were handed over to Sadat.

Neutralizing the threat to his administration allowed Sadat to continue with his reforms that eventually, (especially after 1974) touched every aspect of life in the country. He put an end to the *mokhbarat's* reign of terror, ordered an immediate end to telephone wiretapping, and appointed a committee to investigate the excesses of the security apparatus. He abolished press censorship, took steps to reform the economy and to encourage free enterprise, and terminated the practice of sequestration and property confiscation. He eliminated the exit visa system and granted everyone the freedom to travel. He returned the Egyptians' identity to them by consigning the United Arab Republic to the history books and designating the Arab Republic of Egypt as the country's official name.

By far the biggest and most pressing time bomb that Nasser bequeathed to Sadat was the Israeli occupation of Sinai, which constituted one third of the area of the Nile Valley. Egyptians, like all peasant societies, are deeply attached to their land, which they view in almost sacred terms. The prospect of the permanent loss of Sinai was a deeply felt wound on the Egyptian psyche as evidenced by the January 1972 university student strikes and demonstrations demanding the liberation of Sinai.[98] Yet there appeared to be no realistic hope of regaining it. Sadat had moved quickly to restore good relations with the rest of the world. He put an end to meddling in the internal affairs of the Arab countries,[99] and stopped the fiery rhetoric and Nasser's practice of clandestine shipments of arms and funds to any group around the world that called itself a revolution or a national liberation movement. This practice had become so ridiculous that it became a national joke. When the movie *Mutiny on the Bounty* (translated to Arabic as *Revolution on the Bounty*) was showing in Cairo, the Minister of Information, the joke went, issued a statement of support for the Revolution on the Bounty.[100]

Good relations with Western Europe and the United States were restored, but that newly found goodwill did not translate into pressure on Israel to abide by the United Nations Resolution 242 and withdraw from Egypt's soil. President Eisenhower who had saved Nasser by ensuring that Israel complied with UN resolutions to withdraw when it occupied Sinai after the 1956 attack was long gone and America had become Israel's main arms supplier and financier by that time.

The years of fiery, hostile, and irresponsible rhetoric by Nasser had convinced the Israelis, who had always coveted their neighbors' lands, that their only security was their army not a peace agreement. It quickly became apparent to Sadat that force was the only option open to him to regain the lost land. Yet, he knew that his army was no match for the well armed, well led, and efficiently run Israeli army which was well dug in behind the formidable Bar Lev defensive line about one hundred kilometers from Cairo. Moreover, he had failed to convince the Soviets, despite four separate visits to Moscow (March 1971, October, 1971, February 1972, and April, 1972) to sell him offensive weapons.[101] They had nothing to gain by a military attempt to liberate Sinai or by helping Sadat to strengthen his régime.

The War Front

Sadat was well aware that building an army that could storm the Bar Lev line was not an easy task.[102] Nasser had seen the army as simply one of several tools available to him for controlling civilian organizations.[103] The army's primary mission had been protecting Nasser and his régime rather than the country. He had viewed it as merely one component of the large organization used to hand out rewards and punishments and never allowed it to develop as a real professional military force.[104] Yet the fear of another military coup had been ever-present and had led him to ration the army's fuel supplies and to set a twenty-kilometer cordon around Egypt's cities which army units were not allowed to breach after 1967.[105]

The army had to be kept occupied and so had been allowed to busy itself with everything but the country's defense. Its officers had been given the responsibility to manage, supervise, or oversee commercial enterprises, flourmills, newspapers, mines, and the football federation.[106] Its commander-in-chief had either headed or was a member of a vast array of organizations ranging from the Fishery Organization to the Atomic Energy Organization, the Committee to Liquidate Feudalism, the National Football Federation, even the Sufi Organization.[107] It had repaired and maintained Cairo's dilapidated public transportation buses,[108] and had even been in charge of assigning vacant apartments[109] that had been appropriated from their owners and given to favorite minions. The officers had become traders, bribe-takers and, during the involvement in Yemen, smugglers.[110] The military factories that Nasser had claimed to be producing rockets had been used to manufacture profitable cooking ranges and bathroom heaters.[111]

Training had not been a priority. Mohammed Fawzi, the chief of staff in 1967, testified before The Committee to Record the History of the July 23 Revolution, chaired by Hosni Mubarak (Sadat's vice president at the time),[112] that some army units had not fired a single shot between 1965 and 1966, and had used only 11 percent of the fuel that had been allocated to them for training.[113] Mahmoud Sidky, who commanded the air force in 1967, testified that he had learned that Egypt was massing its troops in Sinai only from reading the daily papers and that when he had called Amer to express his surprise he had been told not to worry because it was all merely a show that had no concrete significance.[114] The caliber of the two men that Nasser had put in charge of Egypt's defense was such that one of them, Amer, the commander-in-chief of the armed forces, had collapsed in shock and had been unable to function as soon as he had learned of Israel's 1967 surprise attack. The other, Badran, the Defense Minister, had been incapable of comprehending the enormity of the event and had flippantly joked about it. Okasha relates in his memoirs that when he, together with Salah Nasr, the intelligence chief, went to the Armed Forces Command Center on June 8, 1967 to meet with Amer, they had been met there by Badran, who had shocked them by saying "It was such a bluff [Israel's surprise attack] that we were taken in by it."[115] Getting no reaction from them to what he obviously regarded as a witty remark, he had gone on to say, "Why are you both so upset? Are you at a funeral? Shall I order you unsweetened coffee? [Customarily offered to mourners at funerals]."[116] The defense of Egypt did not appear to have been taken terribly seriously by any of the officers who led its army. General Mohammed Fawzi, Amer's chief of staff in 1967 and Nasser's choice for commander-in-chief on June 11, 1967[117] following Amer's suicide, had even objected to using the term setback to refer to the 1967 decisive defeat of his armed forces on the basis that it exaggerated an event that had been no more than "a momentary loss in battle."[118]

Sadat had made it his business to understand the reasons for the devastating defeat as soon as it had happened and long before he became responsible for reversing it. Three years before taking office, when Nasser had been busy with his scheme to remain in power in the immediate aftermath of the 1967 war, Sadat had quietly tried to find out what caused such a disaster. For example, he went to the military hospital in the Cairo suburb of Ma'adi and spoke at length with several of the wounded officers being treated there. Kamal Hassan Ali, who had led a tank brigade, told him that the reason for the defeat had been neither bad equipment nor the troops' lack of will to fight, but the incompetent leadership.[119] Ali told Sadat that he had confidence in his troops and that Sinai could be regained if the army was led by "people of expertise" rather than "people of trust."[120] Ali was also interviewed by Nasser but Nasser's questions had been about the reasons Ali had not used smoke to hide his tanks from the attacking Israeli planes.[121]

Both the country and the army had witnessed profound changes in the aftermath of 1967. The public, to use Tawfiq el Hakim's words, regained consciousness, and people no longer accepted slogans as a substitute for concrete achievements. The army had begun to change immediately after the war when Abdel Hakim Amer and Shams Badran had been ousted and Nasser had appointed Mohammed Fawzi Commander-in-Chief on June 19, 1967 and Minister of Defense on February 24, 1968. In spite of being one of Nasser's people of trust, Fawzi had implemented some important changes. The army had shed some of its non-defense related responsibilities. Many administrative units, departments, and tasks had been either disbanded or assigned to other branches of government. These had included the criminal investigations unit; the customs guards; the fishery, bird, and supply monitoring; and drug enforcement units.[122] Numerous units that seemed designed to waste the armies' time had also been disbanded: for example the agricultural unit growing corn on fifty thousand feddans, the engineering unit responsible for building houses in the Cairo neighborhood of Abbasia, the Cairo public transportation unit, and the organization for airplane manufacturing.[123] University graduates, feared for what was referred to as security reasons, had been generally exempted from doing the compulsory military service and had constituted no more than 7 percent of those conscripted.[124] The lower ranks, then, had also in a sense consisted of Nasser's "people of trust" since they were for the most part the uneducated peasants who were the most easily swayed by Nasser's rhetoric. After Fawzi's appointment conscripted graduates in the military rose to 93 percent.[125]

Once Sadat secured his position in the country, he made it one of his priorities to rid the upper echelons of the army of "people of trust" and bring in "people of expertise" to plan for Sinai's liberation. He sidelined many of Amer's incompetent cronies, and several of the competent senior officers that Nasser had retired from the army were returned to service,[126] putting the army, for the most part, in the hands of professional soldiers. Nasser's people of trust were no longer in charge of military intelligence, and the people of expertise that Sadat put in their place were no longer in the business of spying on the troops[127] or swaggering around the country and terrorizing the civilian population. They were doing what they were supposed to do, gathering intelligence about their enemy's strengths, weaknesses, and capabilities so that the professional military planners did not have to operate in complete ignorance of their adversaries' strengths and weaknesses.

Sadat, however, was faced with a dilemma. In addition to the lack of offensive weaponry, his assessment of the situation was that America, Israel's financial backer and arms supplier, would never allow its defeat by Egypt. The US Secretary of State, Henry Kissinger later confirmed the accuracy of this assessment in the clearest of terms.[128] Sadat's strategy in coping with that difficult situation was in stark contrast to Nasser's usual impulsive responses. He did not view these actions and attitudes as slights upon his dignity or react emotionally. He did not hurl insults, or direct the media to begin a senseless campaign against the imperialists, the feudalists, or any of the bogeymen that Nasser always blamed for his failures. Instead, he continued his efforts to mend fences with all the players in the international arena and to explore quietly the possibility of avoiding a war to liberate Sinai from Israeli occupation.

The sharp contrast between Nasser and Sadat's attitudes to the loss of Sinai illustrates one of the differences in their social values. Sadat's attitude was rooted in the farming peasant culture whereas Nasser's attitude was rooted in the Bedouin herding culture. The loss of land to a peasant represents a loss of livelihood, and triggers a powerful incentive to use his wits and any resources available to him to regain it. The Bedouin, on the other hand, is more likely to be impelled to action by the perceived loss of face. Restoring his honor, but not necessarily his land, could suffice to heal his wounded pride and satisfy him. The former wants to regain the source of his livelihood, and the latter wants to gratify his emotions.

Sadat reasoned that if the Soviets refused to supply offensive weapons, and the Americans would not allow an Israeli defeat, he could at least demonstrate that Israel was not invincible and that he was determined to evict the occupiers from his land. The Israelis, as well as the majority of knowledgeable international military analysts, believed that the defensive position that Israel had built on the east side of the Suez Canal, the Bar Lev line, was impenetrable by any modern army, let alone the demoralized and shattered army that was bequeathed to Sadat. Sadat reasoned, therefore, that if liberating Sinai was too ambitious for his limited resources, perhaps he should lower his sights and limit his goals to taking the Bar Lev line in the expectation that this might get his message across.

That however was easier said than done. Even if the enormous obstacles of financing, of finding competent planners, of retraining a demoralized army, and of acquiring the equipment were overcome, massing a large army of tens of thousands of troops and their equipment at the Canal would be an invitation to disaster. The Israelis on its east bank would certainly see the buildup, the American spy satellites would promptly supply them with the minutest details of the troop positions, and Israel's superior air force and powerful artillery would devastate it in no time.

There is no doubt that the obstacles appeared insurmountable. Nevertheless, had Sadat taken heed of what was conventional wisdom among experienced military planners, both Egyptian and foreign, he would have accepted the view that he was a fool following a pipedream and attempting an impossible task. His chances of success if he attempted to take the Bar Lev line were zero at worst and almost zero at best. Not only were the Soviets, aided by the Nasserists in the Egyptian media, promoting the notion that liberating Sinai by force was impossible, but General Mohammed Ahmed Sadek, a Nasser era "man of trust" and Sadat's commander-in-chief was making the same point in his speeches to his troops.[129] Some of the army's senior commanders who were also "men of trust" felt the same way as their leader.

During the summer of 1972, Sadat ordered General Sadek to get the army ready for a crossing of the Canal by November 15, and Sadek's response was to assure him that the army would be ready by November 1, two weeks before the deadline given by the president.[130] Yet on October 24, 1972, during a stormy meeting of the Supreme Council for the Armed Forces, Sadat was surprised to discover that the senior military commanders not only knew nothing of his order, but also that they were afraid to go to war.[131] They maintained that the army was not ready to liberate Sinai by force.[132] A few days later, Sadat fired the Minister of Defense, the Assistant Minister of Defense, the Commander of the Navy,[133] and the Director of Military Intelligence.[134] The incompetent defeatist commanders attempted, unsuccessfully, to topple Sadat three weeks later.[135]

Sadat was also realistic about the possibility of receiving any meaningful assistance from the other Arab countries and knew that if he went to war, he would be on his own and the Arabs would act as spectators unless their public forced them to do something.[136] He was aware, for example, that the Syrian régime could not hope to remain in power once a war started if they stayed on the sidelines. What he did not know, however, was that Syria asked the Soviets shortly before the start of Egypt's attempt to liberate Sinai in October 1973 to propose a ceasefire within forty-eight hours of Egypt's firing the first shot.[137]

The apparent hopelessness of his goals, however, did not deter Sadat, and he would not rest until he liberated Sinai. By early January 1973, General Ahmed Ismail, whom Sadat had recalled from retirement and appointed Minister of Defense and Commander-in-Chief of the Armed Forces, reported to him that he had carried out his orders and completed a plan to take the Bar Lev line.[138]

The Preparations

The most pressing problem that Sadat had to address at that point was the low morale of both the troops and the public. Neither group had any confidence in the competence or sincerity of the individuals who occupied the upper echelons in the military or the political structure. After 1967, people had begun to mock and insult the army that had arrogantly swaggered around the country but failed to protect its borders, and Nasser had been forced to order the troops not to appear in public in their uniforms[139] and to resort to asking the public in one of his speeches to stop making jokes about the army.[140]

The Egyptian public's feelings about Nasser's army are clearly illustrated in an anecdote recounted by one of its officers in his memoirs. He was in uniform and driving past the faculty of engineering in Cairo when three students motioned him to stop.[141] At first, he thought that they were going to ask him for a lift, but when he stopped, it turned out that they were concerned for his safety. They appeared embarrassed as they advised him to take another route because the students would destroy his car if they saw him.[142] In another incident witnessed by this author a bus conductor on a crowded bus in Cairo a few months after the army withdrew from Sinai in 1967 asked one of the passengers, an army officer in uniform, to move back a little so that he could pass him. The words the conductor used were "please withdraw." Everyone on the bus understood the implied insult and burst out laughing. When the officer attempted to assault the conductor, the other passengers manhandled him and threw him off the bus. Knowledge of such incidents and of the strength of the public's feelings had been a new experience for Nasser and must have been a great source of anxiety. Desperate for a way to placate the public and to stem the growing opposition to his régime, which had brought about an unprecedented catastrophe, Nasser had begun what he termed a "war of attrition" against the Israeli lines across from the canal in September 1968.[143] The plan, at least to the layperson, appeared illogical and certain to lead to further loss of life, property, and critical facilities. The Egyptian army was stationed along the west bank of the Canal and in the cities of Port Said, Ismailiyya, and Suez, across from where the Israeli army was dug in on the east bank of the Canal at the western edge of the Sinai desert. The war of attrition consisted of using heavy artillery to pound the well-fortified Israeli positions and achieved little more than irritating the Israelis by forcing them to remain in their bunkers and creating ditches in the desert sand around them. The Israelis on the other hand had the three cities, their civilian populations, and their industrial facilities all within the range of their artillery.[144] The three cities in the Canal Zone were constantly bombarded causing substantial loss of civilian life, and forcing Nasser to empty the three cities and move all their residents out,[145] which created a new set of problems that the régime appeared powerless to address.

Israel also enjoyed complete air supremacy,[146] and responded to the war of attrition with an extensive and sustained campaign of attacks on both military and civilian targets throughout the country.[147] A strategically important oil refining plant and extensive storage facilities were bombed and burned for several days.[148] The feeble Egyptian air defenses were powerless to prevent the superior Israeli air force from flying freely around the country and taking its pick of targets ranging from river dams to electricity generating plants to schools.[149] Targets near Cairo, el-Tel el-Kabir, Inshas, Abu Za'bal, Helwan, and Bahr el-Baqar School, where thirty children were killed, were shelled as part of a psychological warfare operation.[150] The war of attrition cost between five and eight billion dollars in damage to the Canal cities and the country's economic infrastructure,[151] and delayed the rebuilding of the army and, therefore, the liberation of Sinai.[152]

Troops stationed in the Canal Zone had been exposed to an intensely demoralizing situation. As well as sharing the same feelings of despondency as the rest of the population, these troops were subjected to constant harassment and morale destroying tactics by the Israelis. They set up loudspeakers across the waterway and broadcast messages designed to spread rumors and to humiliate the Egyptians. Since the two armies were within hearing range of one another, the troops on both sides of the Canal were also able to hurl insults at each other. One of the Israeli troops' favorite demoralizing messages, according to an officer who was stationed at the Canal during that period, was for one of them to shout across to the Egyptians that he had spent the previous night having sex with one of their sisters.[153] The Israelis also set up a large sign in Arabic, English, and Hebrew, which stated: "1948 we took Palestine, 1956 we took Sharm el-Sheikh, 1967 we took Sinai, 1970, we will enter Cairo."[154] These tactics had the desired negative impact on the already demoralized Egyptian troops. They knew from experience that their commanders were corrupt and incompetent and did not take the business of war seriously. They were aware that almost everyone agreed that the Israeli line was impregnable, and they could see for themselves, as they looked across the Canal, that taking it by force and liberating Sinai would be well nigh impossible.

The line had been heavily bombarded during Nasser's war of attrition, and there had been regular announcements to the media that parts of it had been destroyed.[155] Some people may well have believed these claims. Even Nasser might have believed them. Although the intelligence chief, Amin Huwaidy, did send Nasser photographs showing that the bombardment inflicted no harm at all on the line, his trusted aide, Sami Sharaf, had apparently kept them from him because he thought that Nasser was too ill to see them.¹⁵⁶ The troops on the front line, however, could see for themselves that the Israeli line was intact.

Sadat had been convinced all along that if Egypt could cross the canal and retake just a few centimeters of its east bank, that act would change the international situation.¹⁵⁷ Liberating a few centimeters of Sinai by force became his goal. In June 1973, he gave the final orders to prepare for a coming battle.¹⁵⁸ Once the decision to storm the Bar Lev line was taken, the next objective to be tackled was how to maintain secrecy and preserve the element of surprise. This was a daunting task because keeping anything secret in Egypt has never been an easy undertaking, and public knowledge of any one of the thousands of small details that a large-scale military operation necessitates would compromise it. Full-scale mobilization and massing tens of thousands of troops and materiel on the western shores of the Suez Canal would not escape the ever-vigilant Israeli eyes across the waterway or the ubiquitous American spy satellites.

Sadat's strategy was to play a psychological cat and mouse game that made excellent use of preconceived notions. He ordered a mobilization of the civil defense forces in May 1973 and again in August. Israel responded both times by declaring a full mobilization.¹⁵⁹ The army began a tactic in January 1973, whereby it would call the reservists, keep them for a few days or a few weeks, and then discharge them.¹⁶⁰ By October 1, this had been done twenty-two times.¹⁶¹ On 4 October, twenty thousand reservists were discharged.¹⁶² Tanks were constantly moved to the front then withdrawn.¹⁶³ To the Israelis, used to the incompetence of Nasser's military commanders and his use of such tactics to deceive his population, it appeared like a normal state of affairs. The news media carried unceasing reports of military maneuvers,¹⁶⁴ which foreign military observers must have dismissed as no more than a public relations effort to mollify the restless local public. The army announced that it was conducting large-scale military exercises during the period between the first and seventh of October, but that was not accompanied by any special restrictions on the forces.¹⁶⁵ These measures made the exercises appear similar to the routine maneuvers carried out in January and August 1973, which had led Israel to carry out a costly mobilization and put their forces on high alert.¹⁶⁶ The ploy worked and the Israelis saw no need to mobilize this time.¹⁶⁷ The media also reported that the army was accepting applications from military personnel who wish to go on the '*umra* (visiting the holy sites in Saudi Arabia) during the approaching holy month of Ramadan.¹⁶⁸ The troops at the front were instructed not to wear their helmets.¹⁶⁹ On the morning of October 6, Israel's Minister of Defense, General Dayan, accompanied by senior officers, visited the front and observed the Egyptian troops relaxing on the shores of the Canal, playing soccer, and swimming.¹⁷⁰ Only two hours before storming the Bar Lev line, the troops sat in their under shirts sucking on sugarcane stalks by the side of the Canal in full view of the Israeli observation points.¹⁷¹

Everything appeared normal, and the Egyptian troops the Israelis observed across the Canal must have seemed no different from the badly trained and poorly led troops of 1967. A further reassuring factor for the Israelis must have been that the Egyptians no longer had the help of the Soviet military advisors that they had in 1967 because Sadat had expelled them a year earlier.¹⁷² In addition, they had good reasons to feel secure behind what was termed an impregnable defensive line.¹⁷³ The highly regarded General Dayan had boasted that Egypt would need the help of both the US and the Russian Corps of Engineers to cross the Canal and break through the Bar Lev line.¹⁷⁴ Their Prime Minister Menahem Begin had warned the Egyptians that if they tried to cross the Canal they would meet the same fate as their pharaoh had many centuries earlier.¹⁷⁵

The Bar Lev line¹⁷⁶ was composed of a series of defenses built along the whole length of the Suez Canal (193 kilometers) and stretched to a depth of thirty kilometers behind it.¹⁷⁷ There were thirty-six fortified positions with three hundred tank firing platforms facing the Canal.¹⁷⁸ The Israelis ripped out the railway line that stretched across Sinai from the Suez Canal to Gaza and the tens of thousands of steel railroad tracks and wooden ties were utilized in the building of this formidable defensive structure. Most of these strong points had one four-meter-wide entrance on their eastern side to allow entry of tanks and other vehicles.¹⁷⁹ Some were three floors, two of them underground, and the structures were covered by several layers of rock and reinforced concrete, topped with tons of sand.[180] These defenses formed a barrier that stood at a forty-five to sixty-five degree incline,[181] rose to a height of twenty-five meters in certain locations, and stretched to the edge of the water.[182] All the doors of these bunkers were made of steel, and each fortress contained machine guns and heat sensors that operated them automatically at the approach of enemy personnel.[183] Each point was designed and equipped to operate independently of all the others for several days without the need for any new supplies.[184] General Abdel Ghani el-Gamasy gave an example of what was found in one of these fortresses in his memoirs: twenty-six heavy and medium machinegun positions, twenty-four bunkers, four anti-tank positions, four anti-aircraft positions, three tank-firing platforms, six mortar positions, and fifteen circles of barbed wire with mines and booby traps strewn among them.[185] A system of pipes connected to storage tanks, each with a capacity of about two hundred tons,[186] was designed to pump highly inflammable liquid, commonly referred to as napalm, onto the surface of the Canal. Once ignited, the Canal would turn into a wall of fire with flames up to a meter high and temperatures of seven hundred degrees Celsius[187] (1292 degrees Fahrenheit) that would be well-nigh impossible to extinguish[188] and would instantly incinerate anyone attempting to cross it.[189] A second line of defense five to seven kilometers away from the Canal contained several fortified positions, command centers, bunkers, anti-aircraft missiles, long-range and self-propelled artillery, tank platforms, artillery combat sections, and bases for counterattacks.[190]

The Egyptian troops had no illusions about what they would be facing if they were ever ordered to liberate Sinai. What was easily visible to them from their positions on the west bank of the Canal was the wall of sand, twenty-five meters high in some places, that stretched along the whole length of the waterway along the east bank of the Canal, and they knew that that was only the tip of the iceberg. They knew that if any soldier, by some fluke, succeeded in getting to the east bank without being incinerated in the burning inferno on the surface of the water, he would have to carry his equipment and climb the slippery sand hill. This would have to be done while the soldier who survived the napalm was dodging the bullets and artillery shells that would rain down on him incessantly from the Israeli positions. If he (there were no women in the military) survived that too, then the lucky soldier would have to dodge the heat sensors that would automatically set off another barrage of guns and shower him with bullets. Only then would he be in a position to storm and attempt to take the fortified positions from the well-trained and well-armed, and well-led Israeli defenders before he ran out of the little amount of ammunition that he would have been able to carry with him. He would have to accomplish this task while the second line of Israeli defenses, secure behind a two hundred meter area covered with barbed wire and strewn with anti tank and personnel mines,[191] rained heavy artillery shells upon him. After such an unlikely feat, the lucky trooper would then need to proceed through the minefields and take the second line of defense with the few bullets, if any, that he had left. Such an unlikely scenario is normally found in books of fiction and on movie screens rather than real life situations.

The Crossing

On the night of October 5-6, Egyptian army engineers swam underwater and blocked up the pipes designed to deliver the inferno to the surface of the Suez Canal.[192] Sadat[193] took his place at the command center at 1:30 on the afternoon of October 6, 1973.[194] He had embarked, with his military commanders, on a mission that would certainly have seemed foolhardy to many and could well have been pointed to a day or two later by seasoned military experts around the world as an obvious example of the incompetence of these commanders. Only six months earlier Henry Kissinger had advised Sadat's National Security Advisor to accept Egypt's status as the defeated party, and that any attempt to change the military situation would bring about a defeat worse than 1967.[195] The odds at that moment were that on the seventh or eighth of October, at the latest, an array of military sages and retired generals would be hastily assembled to sit around tables in the studios of the various European and American television stations. They would be asked to explain the reasons for the impregnability of the Bar Lev line and to offer their expert analyses of the devastation that befell the bungling Egyptians. They would have tut-tutted sadly and explained to their lay viewers that Sadat and his inept commanders had brought another disaster upon themselves by failing to understand basic military rules, and that the attackers had attempted what would have been a very difficult undertaking for even the best-trained best-led, best equipped troops, let alone the demoralized, badly led, badly trained, and badly equipped Egyptians. Since the attack took place during the month of fasting when Muslims abstain from food and drink from sunrise to sunset, the experts and analysts might also have suggested that the troops were probably thirsty, hungry and tired too. Henry Kissinger told Sadat later that when he heard the news he had been surprised by the decision to storm the Bar Lev line and felt very saddened by the sorry fate that awaited Sadat. The Israelis told the world that the Egyptians would perish in the Canal sooner rather than later.[196] Everyone believed that the Egyptians would be dealt a devastatingly swift and decisive trouncing. This did not happen.

In spite of the daunting task that faced them, morale among the troops was extremely high. The Israeli campaign of psychological warfare had backfired, and instead of convincing them of the invincibility of their enemy and the hopelessness of regaining their land, it fired them up with the determination to expel the invaders from their soil or die trying. Brigade commanders such as Brigadier Adel Yousry received their orders at dawn, senior officers at 8:00 AM, and the troops at 12:00 noon.[197] The operation did not follow the military tradition of attacking at first or last light, but rather at 2:00 P.M.[198]

Two hundred Egyptian air force planes took off from various airports around the country and synchronized their arrival at the Canal at 2:00 P.M.[199] When the planes, almost hugging the ground to evade Israeli radar, crossed into occupied Sinai, the troops who looked up in the sky and saw them went wild with joy.[200] It was a sight they had not witnessed since the 1967-ceasefire agreement had prohibited Egyptian planes from approaching the Canal Zone, and the sight of their planes flying over them and crossing into their occupied Sinai galvanized them.[201] Earlier, when the unit leaders were given their final orders and handed Egyptian flags to raise over the positions that they were assigned to take in Sinai, they were overcome with emotion and wept.[202]

Then two thousand guns of various calibers opened fire along the whole length of the Canal, and kept up the barrage for fifty-three minutes at the rate of one hundred and seventy-five shells per second for the first minute, which prevented the Israeli tanks from climbing their pre-prepared platforms atop the sand barrier to take up their firing positions.[203] The engineers crossed a second time to check that the pipe system they blocked during the night was still inoperable.[204] It was, and the Israelis were unable to pump any of the napalm or start a single fire.[205] The infantry, using seven-hundred-and fifty vessels, began to cross under cover of the barrage.[206] Within minutes the number of troops on the east bank was eight thousand, rising to fourteen thousand within an hour then thirty-three thousand after five hours (at 17:30).[207] The leaders set a good example for their troops. *Saraya* (company) leaders were the first to cross, and were followed by *kata'b* (battalion) commanders within fifteen minutes, then *liwa'* (brigade) commanders thirty minutes later, and *firaq* (divisions) commanders within ninety minutes of the start of the operation.[208] Commanding from the front as these officers did was the reason for the unusually high rate of casualties among the officers.[209] The first Israeli position fell at 2:46 P.M., less than one hour after the first units crossed the Canal.[210]

However, the newly won positions were vulnerable without tank and artillery support, and the Israelis had boasted that it would take a nuclear bomb to open a gap in the high wall of sand that covered their fortified bunkers and create passages that would be wide enough to accommodate tanks and armored vehicles.[211] Instead of a nuclear bomb, the Egyptians directed 350 powerful water pumps[212] at the sand wall, which began to crumble, and the first gap was opened at 3:25 P.M.[213] A junior army officer, Baqi Zaki Yousef,[214] is credited with proposing this low-tech solution.[215] The pumps had been purchased earlier from Germany, and the Germans had been scornful of the gullible Egyptian bureaucrats who thought that they needed such expensive and powerful pumps ostensibly to put out fires.[216] The Soviets, as Sadat reminded their Prime Minister later, had refused to sell Egypt modern bridges that could be erected in half an hour, and the Egyptians made do with antiquated World War II bridges that required five hours to erect. [217] Nevertheless, twenty bridges, ten for personnel, and ten for heavy equipment, were constructed in record time facing the gaps created by the water hoses, and despite the constant need to move the bridges to new locations during the operation to minimize losses to Israeli air raids,[218] the army began its crossing.[219] By 7:30 P.M., less than six hours after the start of the operation, eighty thousand troops had crossed over a one hundred and seventy-kilometer front and were in control of the Bar Lev line.[220]

Sadat's army achieved what only six hours earlier would have been considered a pitiful pipedream and succeeded in convincing America that Egypt would not accept the loss of its land. The Americans quickly recovered from the surprise and began a huge airlift that delivered vast amounts of advanced weaponry, some of it still in the experimental stage, directly to the Israelis in Sinai, in addition to the American spy satellite photographs of Egyptian positions.[221] Two hundred and twenty-eight U.S. planes over a period of thirty-three days transported twenty-two and a half thousand tons of equipment to the beleaguered Israelis.[222] By October 10, the Syrians, who had managed to liberate parts of their occupied land on the Golan Heights while Israel was preoccupied with the Egyptians, lost it all again, when Israel made a counter attack.[223] The Egyptian commanders then made a serious mistake by deciding to relieve the pressure on the Syrians. On October 14, they continued their advance towards the mountain passes in Sinai and strayed beyond the range of their air defense missiles. They succeeded in saving Damascus but were forced to retreat to the Canal and failed to regain the passes that controlled the entrance to central Sinai.[224]

In Washington, Henry Kissinger summoned the Egyptian Ambassador, and demonstrating that he had not quite grasped the new situation yet, proposed a cease-fire and a withdrawal of Egypt's forces from their newly won positions, which Egypt refused in no uncertain terms.[225] The Americans, however, needed to give Israel at least one success prior to the cessation of hostilities because total defeat would have meant their (US) political defeat in the face of Soviet weapons.[226] One of their spy planes, flying at an altitude beyond the range of the Egyptian air defense missiles, identified on October 13 and 15 a weak spot in the Egyptian lines[227] and the Israeli commanders quickly exploited the weakness.[228] Ten days after the fall of the Bar Lev line, an Israeli force succeeded in penetrating the gap in the Egyptian defenses and moved seven tanks across to the Defresoir area on west side of the Canal. The area was under the command of General Sa'd Ma'moun, who had been taken to hospital on October 14 after suffering a heart attack, and his Chief of Staff, General Tayseer Fuad, had taken command in his absence.[229] General Fuad proved to have been an unfortunate choice, since his actions showed that he was not ready for the leadership position that was thrust upon him.[230] Not only did he fail to act immediately and destroy the small Israeli force,[231] but he also failed to inform the general command of the crossing until the morning of the sixteenth, claiming that it was of negligible importance.[232] When the Israeli tanks were engaged the next day, it turned out that they had managed to get thirty tanks across.[233] On October 16, General Fuad was returned to his position, and General Abdel Menem Khalil was appointed in his place.[234]

Sadat ordered the Chief of Staff, General Saad el-Shazly, to deal with the situation immediately. Unfortunately, el-Shazly was in competition with General Ismail, the Minister of Defense and Commander-in-Chief of the Armed Forces, and spent several critical hours gathering intelligence and setting up an unnecessary new command structure to rival Ismail's.[235] By October 19, the Israelis had managed to reinforce their position and General el-Shazly lost his nerve and recommended a complete retreat from Sinai.[236] The General may well have been influenced by the time that he served under Field Marshal Amer, whose expertise in military tactics seemed limited to ordering an immediate and complete withdrawal of all forces whenever he was informed of an attack. General Ismail on the other hand strongly disagreed and asked Sadat to join them in the command center to make the decision.[237] Sadat reviewed the situation, and both he and all the senior commanders saw no need to withdraw.[238] The forces were ordered to stay in place and Sadat immediately fired Shazly[239] and appointed General Abdel Ghani el-Gamasy in his place as Chief of Staff.[240]

The Defresoir crossing was daring and illustrated the professionalism of the Israeli military leadership and their ability to respond rapidly to changing situations. Although the operation had no military value because the Israeli force was trapped in a small area surrounded by an Egyptian armored division that could, as

Sadat informed Kissinger,[241] annihilate the trapped force, it was an excellent propaganda move and a useful morale boosting exercise for the Israelis.

Sadat recounts that by the evening of October 19, after fighting a proxy war with the United States America for ten days and with the Soviets poised to betray him, he decided to accept a cease-fire[242] because he was realistic enough to acknowledge that he could not match America's power and resources.[243] Both combatants accepted the U.N. proposed cease-fire on October 22. Although the Israelis, with the blessing of Henry Kissinger,[244] ignored the cease-fire for six days while attempting to advance to less vulnerable positions,[245] they finally complied after all their attempts to break out of the trap and enter the cities of Ismailiyya and Suez failed.[246] The cease-fire took hold after these Israeli units on the west bank of the Canal succeeded in cutting off the Cairo-Suez road, but they were still trapped in a narrow strip of land.[247] They had achieved a tactical success but their strategic position was untenable. They had six or seven brigades trapped in a small area of land that was surrounded by natural or manmade barriers, and needed five divisions on the east bank of the Canal to defend the entrance to the breach.[248] Israel's daily losses and long supply lines also forced it to maintain the highest level of mobilization.[249] Lacking the strategic depth needed for both operational defense and effective attack turned that force into a hostage rather than a threat.[250] However, Israel launched a successful mass media campaign, and the Egyptians who have never been able to match their skill in that field had no media campaign of their own.[251]

By the beginning of November, when Henry Kissinger arrived in Egypt for his first visit,[252] it had become clear that Sadat had achieved his purpose of getting America's attention. On Kissinger's December 11 visit, Sadat informed him that he had lost patience with the delaying tactics that he was being subjected to and had decided to close the gap and expel the trapped Israelis.[253] Kissinger replied that he had been briefed by the Pentagon on the military situation, and did not dispute Sadat's ability to make good on his warning. He, however, had a warning of his own to make. He informed Sadat in no uncertain terms that America would not allow this to happen and urged him to wait for the start of the negotiations that he was in the process of arranging.[254] Sadat's goal of convincing both the Americans and the Israelis that Egypt was serious about regaining its land was accomplished, and the long process that finally led to the peace agreement began.

For the first time in many, many years Egyptians had a real sense of national pride again over a real and tangible accomplishment. Without foreign assistance, without proper equipment and in complete secrecy (almost impossible in Egypt) and against all odds, Egypt had accomplished an amazing feat and done what everyone had said was impossible, and retaken its land.

The Peace

Once Sadat put his thorniest problem, the war to liberate Sinai, behind him, he quickened his pace of reform. A comprehensive program to free the economy was launched in 1974.[255] The Suez Canal was reopened on June 5, 1975, eight years to the day after Israel's attack. The one party system was abolished and several political parties were formed. Then Sadat surprised the world by taking the very courageous step of going to Israel to sue for peace on November 19, 1977, and a peace treaty was finally signed on March 26, 1979.

The Nasserists, who continued their efforts to undermine Sadat's efforts at reforms on every front and to criticize vehemently every step that he took, found new ammunition for their attacks in some of the negative outcomes of the reforms. To give Sadat his due, it must be remembered that he was attempting to right the wrongs of almost two decades of misrule. Although virtually each one of the steps taken towards reform was important and necessary, they, like any radical social change, had a negative aspect, gave rise to unintended outcomes, and created their own set of social problems. Nasser had been successful in destroying the entrepreneurial class and had vilified businessmen and capitalists throughout his rule. The new generation was socialized into a culture of dependence on authority and never sought or had the opportunity to acquire business skills. Their role models were the mostly incompetent military men who had occupied the leadership positions in virtually all large and midsize business organizations, from insurance and theater companies to department stores and food processing plants. These officers had prospered in spite of the fact that they had run most of these public enterprises into the ground and had consistently reported huge losses.

It was inevitable that once Sadat removed the restrictions on private business, the majority of the new businessmen who prospered in the newly freed economy would not be genuine entrepreneurs or innovators. The people who were best positioned to take advantage of the market economy were either the corrupt officials or those who managed to establish mutually beneficial relationships with them. These people had been nurtured in a society where expertise was suspect, excellence undervalued, and obsequiousness and opportunism well developed and highly rewarded. They had perfected the practice of trading in influence and the techniques of negotiating the corridors of power.

It was to be expected, therefore, that many of the new business ventures would be started by individuals who either had access to inside information, or possessed the necessary expertise to find their way around the maze of regulations created by the bloated bureaucracy. The new businessmen made their fortunes the only way they knew how, by knowing whom to bribe and being privy to useful information gained from their close proximity to one or more of the decision makers.

That is why many of the new ventures tended to be parasitic and sought merely to exploit existing regulations and to generate as much profit as possible in as short a period of time as possible. They brought no new ideas to the market and their contributions to sound and sustainable economic development were negligible. Activities such as securing local agencies and distributorships for foreign manufactured consumer goods or for fast food chains requires little talent or business acumen, creates a very limited number of low-paying jobs, and adds little to the overall health of the economy. Becoming rich by acting as middlemen who steer legitimate businessmen through the maze of bureaucratic regulations and help them to win large government contracts to carry out much needed infrastructure repairs only added inflationary pressures and created public dissatisfaction. Buying government owned land at giveaway prices in areas earmarked for urban development, then making a large profit by selling it at market value, only served to encourage speculation and further feed inflation.

A small but influential segment of this new breed of businessmen was composed of the religious extremists who had escaped Nasser's repression and taken refuge in Saudi Arabia and the mini states of the Gulf region. The governments of that region had welcomed these refugees with open arms for two reasons. The first was that they had long been vilified by Nasser who sought to topple them and were only too glad to find a way of paying him back. The second was that the refugees and their hosts shared extremist views and Bedouin social values and felt a kinship with each other. The hosts offered their guests a great deal of assistance in financing and setting up business ventures which prospered, and when Sadat allowed them back into Egypt they brought with them capital, useful contacts within the international extremist networks, and the skills honed by operating businesses in the corrupt tribal-based societies that hosted them during their exile from Egypt. Most of these newcomers to the business world did not have the necessary expertise to invent new products, to conceive new ideas or creative approaches to existing business, or to generate wealth in the overall economy in the same way that people such as Bill Gates, Steve Jobs, Michael Dell, or Richard Branson did. Nevertheless, the new freedom in the market allowed this new class of businessmen to amass vast personal fortunes almost overnight while the rest of the population watched on in frustration and increasing alienation.

The Countdown to Tragedy

The freedoms Sadat granted also created their own set of social and political problems and turned into a major headache for him. Nasser had never had a problem dealing with the media. Some newspaper, for example, had an annual "banish season" when staff members who had fallen out of favor for one reason or another were dealt with. During one such season, for example, a hundred and twenty journalists were fired, and no other organization in the country had dared to employ any of them.[256] Some troublesome journalists were simply transferred to one of the public sector organizations, such as shoe retail outlets or refrigeration and meat processing plants.[257]

Sadat, however, stopped these practices, but removing the restrictions on freedom of expression allowed an unprecedented torrent of publications representing all shades of opinion ranging from the extreme right to the extreme left. Everyone it seemed had something to say and much of it was negative. Sadat had unwittingly opened a floodgate that he was unable to control. Some of the criticisms directed at his policies was undoubtedly fair, objective, and warranted, but much of it either reflected frustration stemming from unfulfilled and unrealistic expectations of sudden affluence or bitterness at lost privileges or settling old scores. For example, when Sadat released the prominent journalist, Mustafa Amin, after nine years behind bars for a trumped up charge of spying, and his twin Ali was allowed to return from London where he had fled upon his brother's arrest by Nasser, their articles, not surprisingly, were very critical of the Nasser era.[258] Heikal, bitter at the loss of his exalted position and searching for a role, joined the chorus of Sadat's critics,[259] and through a student newspaper, whose editor was close to him, used the Amin brothers' articles as a means to attack the régime,[260] thus turning them into another problem for Sadat.

Other critics were simply in search of a role in the political arena. The New Wafd Party; Fathi Radwan, a former Nasser minister and *Misr el-Fatat* member; and Helmi Morad of the newly licensed Labor Party, for example, all yearned to play a political role even though they neither had any ideas to offer nor a popular base. They solved both problems by allying themselves with the religious extremists, who were well organized, well financed, and had both an urban and a rural popular base,[261] and their criticism of Sadat's policies became their *raison d'être*. Even the Vice-President, Hussein el-Shafei, apparently feeling left out, added to Sadat's headaches by violating government policy and mixing religion and politics in speeches and press interviews.[262]

Another disgruntled group consisted of the various self-styled leaders of assorted "liberation movements" who had lived in luxury on the generous allowances provided by Nasser and had jetted around the world feeling important, attending conferences, and issuing press statements condemning imperialism and the usual assortment of bogymen. Sadat was not as generous with the Egyptian state funds as his predecessor and they had to find new sponsors.

The only available alternative for these individuals was to join the opposition chorus and get on the payroll of detractors of Sadat and the peace treaty, such as Arab leaders like Saddam Hussein of Iraq. Prominent journalists, perhaps tempted by the financial rewards, also wrote for anti Sadat publications such as the London published Saudi financed newspaper *el-Sharq el-Awsat*.[263] The oil bonanza following the October 1973 war provided the Gulf Arabs with unprecedented riches. These oil-rich mini states of the Arabian Peninsula, fearing the wrath of Saddam Hussein, who vehemently opposed Egypt's peace treaty with Israel, threw fists full of dollars at journalists and bought their pens.

The disgruntled Marxists and Nasserists also provided a constant stream of criticism directed at the new policies and helped to create some apprehension and dissatisfaction among certain segments of society. The days when a verbal order from Nasser, or even his secretary, was all that was needed to fire a journalist[264] were gone. The feared intelligence apparatus had been dismantled, and criticizing the president no longer risked inviting what had been referred to as the dawn visitors. Sadat's reforms became a liability that threatened to destabilize his régime.

The consequence of Egypt's tumultuous history, which was personified in Nasser's distorted and blurred sense of identity was at the core of some of Sadat's problems. The governments and the populations of the Arab countries considered the high price in blood and treasure that Egypt had paid in fighting for the Arab cause to be the normal state of affairs. To them it was Egypt's obligation, as what they saw as the biggest Arab nation, to sacrifice the lives of its sons and impoverish itself defending them, while they busied themselves with their own interests or personal career and business pursuits. Sadat, who suffered no illusions of grandeur and had no dreams of being a leader of the Arab World, began to balk at the ludicrousness and injustice of that arrangement. When he put Egypt's interests first, regained the Sinai, and signed a peace treaty with Israel, he was therefore labeled as a traitor and vilified, and all the Arab countries, with the exception of Sudan and Oman, severed diplomatic relations with Egypt and boycotted it. Egypt's membership in the Arab League was suspended, and the Arab League's offices moved out of Cairo and relocated to Tunis. Much of the opposition to Sadat was motivated by the Arab leaders' fear of Saddam Hussein who was seeking a role as a pan Arab leader and openly threatening anyone who did not fall in line with his opposition to Egypt's peace treaty. Some Arab governments directed a media campaign at the Egyptian public in an effort to curry favor with their own populations, to erode Sadat's popular support at home, and tacitly to encourage attempts at his life. Others, such as Syrian, Iraqi, Libyan, Southern Yemeni, and Palestinian organizations made several attempts themselves at assassinating him. Fourteen different local and foreign Nasserist, communist, or religious organizations carried out thirty-eight separate attempts at murder or sabotage during his period in office.[265]

The Fatal Mistake

Sadat had pardoned or released the thousands of religious extremists who had languished in Nasser's jails for years. This period of incarceration had, for many of them, sharpened rather than blunted their extremist views. Sadat had, as previously mentioned, allowed many of their leaders, who had fled to Saudi Arabia and the mini states of the Persian/Arab Gulf, to return to Egypt, and they brought with them the vast fortunes that some of them had accumulated, the organizational experience they had gained, and the international contacts they had developed. As the Nasserist and socialist opposition began to mount, Sadat sought to combat it by giving the extremists the freedom of action that was denied them during the Nasser era. Perhaps Sadat was unaware that the Saudis, as WikiLeaks revealed decades later, were "a cash machine for terrorists."[266] Or perhaps he imagined that since religious extremists were the natural enemies of his enemies, they could make common cause. That was his fatal mistake. He failed to heed the lessons of history.

The British had made the same mistake in the twenties when they had sought to weaken the nationalist movement that was calling for their evacuation from Egypt. A common belief is that the establishment of the Muslim Brothers Society (MB) in Ismailiyya was no coincidence [267] as the presence of a British military base likely exerted a strong influence on the Suez Canal Company which provided financial backing for the MBs. This claim is bolstered by the fact that the group, founded by a primary school teacher with no financial resources, managed to open a considerable number of offices and spread throughout Egypt in record time. The only reason such a speedy expansion was possible, according to some reports, was the support that the group received from the company at the behest of the British, who later had cause to regret their support. Sadat too had cause later to regret his alliance with the religious extremists.

The elimination of the May 15 plotters had made Sadat's position more secure, but the Nasserists continued to be a serious impediment to the implementation of most of his reforms, and the extremists proved to be less helpful than he had hoped in dealing with them. They had other priorities and instead quickly turned into another problem that he had to be concerned about. The free market economy provided those who returned to Egypt with their petrodollars with good investment opportunities. The extent of the extremists' infiltration of the Egyptian economy has not been systematically surveyed, but media reports[268] suggest that they have been successful in building a solid business and financial base that is helping to increase their influence in society and to finance various organizations that espouse their goals and further their causes. They have, according to media reports been particularly successful in monopolizing some segments of consumer trade in rural towns and use their strong market position to finance their varied activities and win new converts to their causes.[269] The MB began to build a popular base by setting up free clinics and social services centers in poorer areas where such services where not available. They also used their financial power to gain access to the newly freed media either by buying some pens or establishing their own publications and television stations.

At the same time, the extremists were able cynically to use the very same freedoms that they benefited from to inflame the masses and solidify their popular base. The excesses, ostentatious consumerism, and corruption within the ranks of the newly emerging wealthy class were blamed on the new policies and presented to the public as evidence of the iniquity of the régime. In public, the legitimate religious and charitable organizations formed by the extremists were careful to distance themselves from political violence and terrorist activities. In reality, however, many of them were mere fronts for channeling funds from the Arabian Peninsula into the country to spread extremist and hate ideologies. Many of these groups turned into fertile grounds for nurturing, bringing together, and providing ideological indoctrination to a new generation of young men and women who began to form secret terrorist cells. As some of these cells began, with increasing frequency, to conduct violent attacks against Copts, against moderate Muslims who were viewed as traitors to the cause, and against the security services, Sadat began to recognize the threat that they posed to society. The attacks against Copts played into the hands of extremist elements in the Coptic community, and incidents of sectarian violence between the two groups began to occur with increasing frequency. Most of these incidents were minor and easily contained, but a few, such as the violent clash on June 17, 1981 in the impoverished Cairo neighborhood of el-Zawya el-Hamra, were more serious and shocked the public. Although the extremists on both sides were a minority,[270] both Pope Shenouda III and Sheikh Abdel Halim Mahmoud of the Azhar were rigid, confrontational and disliked each,[271] which made them part of the problem rather than part of the solution. Sadat began a crack down on the extremists on both sides. The head of the Coptic Church, Pope Shenouda III, was banished to a monastery, and *el-Gama'a el-Islamiyya*, an extremist group, was outlawed and its members arrested. But it was too late. The genie was out of the bottle. The freedoms granted by Sadat had allowed the well-financed, well-organized extremists to establish deep roots in society, and the policy of cooperating with the US and allowing extremists to join the mujahedin in Afghanistan where they received weapons training did not bode well for future stability.

Sadat's problems were exacerbated further by the prevailing economic conditions. On the local level, his reforms and the peace treaty, which had been popular, did not produce the overnight widespread prosperity that the public hoped for, and that played into the hands of his detractors. The foreign hate campaign found an echo on the local level with those whose Arab or Muslim identity took precedence over their Egyptian identity, Sadat's popularity among that segment of society began to drop, and a small fanatical group of individuals began to plan his murder.

The Tragic End

President Sadat was murdered by a religious extremist on October 6, 1981 as he watched his air force conduct a fly-by during a military parade. Tragically, it was his reforms that not only incensed his murderers and provided them with the incentive to kill him, but also created the conditions that allowed them the necessary freedom of action to carry out their crime.

Sadat's funeral accurately highlighted his tremendous achievements as well as his most serious mistake. Three former American presidents were among the over eighty heads of state or their representatives present.[272] Among the Arab countries, only the president of Sudan and a representative of the Sultan of Oman[273] had the courage to risk displeasing Saddam Hussein of Iraq by attending. His onetime vice-president, Hussein el-Shafei was the only member of the defunct Revolutionary Command Council who did not attend.[274] Instead of diminishing Sadat's stature, the Arab leaders' absence focused attention on their own irrelevance and Lilliputian stature. After all, apart from Saddam Hussein's name, which lives on in ill repute, it is doubtful that anyone can remember the names of the other absentees.

More telling was the curtailed processional route and the absence at the funeral of the Egyptian public. Millions had turned out to cheer Sadat during his visit to the town of Mansoura only days before the assassination but most people were prevented from participating in his funeral because of the obvious security considerations.[275] The state security organizations had no time to assess the risks: to ascertain the degree to which the extremists may have infiltrated the army or the security forces, to determine whether the assassination was part of a wide-ranging plot to topple the régime rather than an individual act. To protect the visiting dignitaries, attendance at the funeral was necessarily limited therefore to the small number of individuals issued with special passes,[276] and the funeral procession was restricted. Regrettably, this was the only prudent course of action and doing otherwise would have been irresponsible, but his fellow countrymen, to whom Sadat had attempted to return their usurped identity and had succeeded in returning their occupied land, were robbed of the opportunity to bid farewell to their courageous and visionary leader on his last journey: one whose motivations were at least clear and honest—the betterment of the country he loved and belonged to.

Sadat's Legacy

Sadat's most important achievement was ending the senseless constant state of war with Israel that was destroying and bankrupting the country. He drew a line between empathizing with the Palestinian cause and going to war with Israel on their behalf. Once Egypt regained the Israeli occupied Sinai Peninsula it had no reason not to normalize relations with Israel and to begin interacting with it as a neighbor with whom Egypt shares many common interests. That is an accomplishment of epic proportions, which will continue to pay dividends for the foreseeable future.

Some of Sadat's problems were his own making, but many were not. Only the most biased of observers would deny that Sadat succeeded in carrying out major reforms that touched every area of life and set the country on the path to rebuilding some of the social institutions that Nasser destroyed. Sadat's successes were tangible gains and not mere slogans to be chanted by the masses in public rallies. No objective observer could argue that restoring the usurped national identity by returning the word Egypt to the country's official name, putting an end to the *mokhbarat's* reign of terror, freeing the economy, abolishing the one party system, restoring the freedom to travel, regaining the Sinai, and making peace with Israel were not momentous achievements. Even the most cursory analysis would show that Sadat left the country in a vastly better shape than it was when took office.

This is not to suggest that Sadat was a saint or that he made no mistakes during his term in office. We can speculate that, with more time, Sadat could have taken the country forward in leaps rather than steps. Nevertheless, the fact remains that, as one of his more objective critics has pointed out,[277] he was a product of his social environment, and he never succeeded in rising above the authoritarian attitudes established while Egypt was under occupation and nurtured during the Nasser era.

If he saw that true democracy was the only route to solving

Egypt's problems, he was unable to establish that democracy. On one level, he appeared to view democracy as a desirable goal and the best long-term solution to many of Egypt's problems, yet he was the product of socialization in an authoritarian culture and had a visceral aversion to ceding too much power to the populace. If he recognized that a free economy could not be established through reliance on Nasser's "people of trust", who were products of the "revolution's generation" and socialized in values that did not equip them to function in a market economy, he could not get rid of them. For almost two decades, successful businessmen of the pre 1952 era had been publicly vilified as exploitive capitalists and expertise and free enterprise were disparaged, while privately those "people of trust" had accumulated wealth. Without a real reversal of what had become the status quo, his program to liberalize the economy led to a profusion of parasitic economic activity [278] and an explosion of consumption at the expense of production, and it was doomed. If he saw the patronage system Nasser had put in place as inefficient and corrupt, he was either unable or unwilling to change it. Top positions in the administration continued to be fringe benefits for retiring senior military officers. Again, these "people of trust" possessed neither the qualifications to fill the positions nor the inclination or ability to carry out the much-needed reforms. The tradition of appointing retired officers to plum civilian positions had become too well entrenched for Sadat to discontinue it without infuriating the serving officers who had become accustomed to being awarded these lucrative positions upon retirement and came to regard the practice almost as a birthright. A radical reform of the system in which sycophancy, corruption, and abuse of public office had been the only paths to financial and professional success could not have been carried out by the same individuals who benefited from it.

Despite his extensive political experience, his rational pursuit of Egypt's interests, and his freedom from the type of personality problems that plagued his predecessor, Sadat was, in the final analysis, one of the neo-Mamluks. In his defence, the havoc wreaked on Egypt's social structure, system of social values, and social institutions by what was originally referred to as the blessed movement of July 23, 1952 was perhaps too extensive to rectify in an eleven year presidency during which major political changes such as the liberation of Sinai, the rebuilding of international relations, and the establishment of peace, required significant attention. In spite of the admittedly serious shortcomings of Sadat's presidency, enlightened leadership could possibly have addressed them in a matter of years rather than decades. However, what was far more serious was his resorting to religion as a source of legitimacy, which subverted much of his reform program, facilitated the spread of religious extremism, and eventually proved to be his undoing. He lacked Nasser's charisma and ability to intoxicate the masses with meaningless rhetoric, and was faced with Nasser's "gangs" who, not surprisingly, fiercely resisted his reforms every step of the way and posed a serious threat to him. These factors were probably what led him to fall into the same trap that in recent years ensnared both the Americans and the Israelis and from which he could not extricate himself. His policy of strengthening religious extremists in the hope of using them to fight his enemies inevitably backfired, cost him his life, and enabled the extremists to penetrate Egyptian society so deeply that eradicating their influence in the near future seems very unlikely. They became, in effect, a fifth column, or the advanced troops that paved the way for the second Arab invasion of Egypt that could well alter the lives of Egyptians in the twenty-first century in a similarly profound manner to the first one in the seventh century.

10

Kleptocracy

Egypt's fourth president was the longest-serving leader since the nineteenth century, yet he is, in spite of the contradictions in his character, much easier to characterize than any of his three predecessors. He was a man of shallow intellectual abilities, with no vision for the country he ruled, and neither competence nor interest in the mechanics of governorship. But even his detractors do not question his seemingly instinctive love of the country and determination to preserve the integrity of its soil. Mubarak's interest in the presidency was limited to his enjoyment of its pomp and circumstance. He enjoyed its fringe benefits and passively accepted widespread corruption within his inner circle as the normal state of affairs.

It had appeared, after President Sadat was murdered and was succeeded by his vice-President, that Egypt was headed for a period of quietly building on the reforms started by Sadat. Sadat had finally brought Sinai back to Egypt and put an end to the constant senseless state of war with Israel, which bankrupted the country and provided the perfect excuse for ruthlessly stifling even the mildest of criticisms of the country's rulers or their domestic and foreign policies. Many Egyptians at that point imagined their country to be on the cusp of a less eventful era of quietly strengthening the economy and the social institutions, and directing the nations' resources towards creating a better life for its long-suffering population.

Sadat had been a seasoned politician and had chosen his vice-president carefully. Hosni Mubarak, born in a village in the Nile delta on May 4, 1928, had graduated from the Military College in

1949 and later trained in the Soviet Union before Sadat selected him to command the Air Force in 1972. He was a competent but not an imaginative commander who did everything by the book and neither questioned the tasks assigned to him nor questioned his superiors' orders. Sadat's choice of him as his vice-president in 1975 was almost certainly partly due to his military background, which gave him credibility with the powerful military establishment. Perhaps more importantly from Sadat's point of view, Mubarak was neither an independent thinker with a sharp mind nor an ambitious man who might have entertained thoughts of replacing him. He was reputed to have never read a single book after completing his military training, had no strong political views or ideologies, and would therefore have been unlikely to create friction on the Egyptian political scene. Mubarak knew that Sadat was continuing the Nasser tradition of giving retired Generals plum assignments, often as ambassadors, and the extent of his ambition, as he once stated, was to be appointed as Egypt's ambassador to Britain. He was, in many ways, the perfect yes man who would have been happy to do his boss's bidding without any fuss. Unfortunately fate intervened and the assassination suddenly put him in the position that he had never imagined for himself, was never prepared for, and had neither the education, experience or intellectual ability to perform.

Although Mubarak's coming to office took place under inauspicious circumstances, as the direct result of Sadat's murder, it nevertheless appeared that his time in office would be marked by gradual improvements as the reforms initiated by Sadat began to bear fruit. The peace treaty with Israel was holding and apart from the Arab boycott, Egypt had good relations with the rest of the world. Mubarak was a cautious man who was unlikely to initiate any radical changes and his tenure began well. He released all political prisoners. The Arab countries that had severed their relations with Egypt when it signed a peace treaty with Israel found the transition to be the perfect fig leaf to hide behind and a useful face-saving device to reestablish relations with Egypt despite the fact that Mubarak had announced that his administration would not renege on any treaty obligations. Mubarak had a certain degree of native cunning despite his limited intellectual resources but possessed no ideological pretensions, and was neither capable of nor interested in conceiving a national venture or enterprise that might have defined his presidency. Comfortable with the way things were and wary of change, what carried him to the presidential palace was his natural inclination to keep his head down and avoid doing anything that might rock the boat. He seemed to be more interested in the trappings of the presidency than in the decision-making process and was content to allow the vast bureaucracy to keep the country ticking over quietly while family and friends amassed large fortunes through corrupt practices. It appeared that his time in office would be relatively short and uneventful since he announced that he did not intend to run for more than two terms.

At the time, however, no one took into consideration Mrs. Mubarak. Suzanne, born February 28, 1941, came from an urban middle class family and was the daughter of a British trained Egyptian pediatrician and a Welsh nurse. She met her future husband at the home of her older brother Mounir, whom Mubarak had taught at the air academy and the couple were married a year later and had two sons, Alaa and Gamal. Unlike her husband, Suzanne was well educated. She began to prepare herself for a role in public life as her husband's career began its rapid rise and earned a Bachelor's degree in Political Science from the American University in Cairo and a Master's degree in Sociology from the same university in 1982. She was reputed to be more intelligent, determined, and ambitious than her husband. She was also rumored to have quickly developed a taste for the trappings of power and a determination to hang on to it as long as possible.

Suzanne became publicly active in the usual First Lady's areas of work: children, health, family, and women's issues. In private she began to act as more of a queen than a first lady and to exert an increasing influence within the inner circle, especially during the latter part of her husband's presidency, eventually deciding that she wanted her favorite son, Gamal, to inherit the presidency. As an untutored man who was reputed to have found it onerous to read more than one page at a time, his father was impressed with Gamal's academic achievements, and experience of working for a bank in London, and imagined him to be a brilliant economist. He appointed him to the general secretariat of his ruling party (NDP) in February 2000, and Gamal immediately brought in a number of his friends and associates to the party secretariat and the Cabinet.

Up until that time Egypt appeared to have no pressing economic or social problems. A good portion of the national debt was forgiven because of Egypt's participation in the first Gulf war. Remittances from Egyptians working abroad were on the increase. The infrastructure was gradually improving with new roads, sewage systems, and modern communication facilities replacing old antiquated systems. Political and cultural stagnation enfeebled the secular opposition and its activities were restricted. The state security apparatus kept a lid on extremist organization and the Muslim Brothers remained an illegal organization but were somewhat placated by being allowed to win parliamentary seats, dominate the boards of several professional associations, and establish a host of charitable organizations, commercial enterprises, and newspapers. In addition to these concessions, the régime also followed an ill-thought out and shortsighted policy of attempting to outdo the religious extremists by coopting parts of their agenda. It expanded the coverage of religious topics in the state owned media, and television channels aired programs that covered some of their favorite topics: for example, the relationship between humans and the jinn.[1] The extent to which the administration was prepared to go to appease the extremists was also clearly illustrated by an incident that economist and writer Galal Amin recounts. He was intrigued by a news item in one of the daily newspapers on the Minister of Education's order to expunge from a school textbook a poem entitled "By the Wall" and to exclude any questions "in any form" about the poem in the final examination in all schools in the country.[2] The imperativeness of the minister's phrasing led Amin to find the textbook, which was included in the syllabus for eleven to twelve year-old students (first year Primary), and read the offending poem, which was by a well-known contemporary Syrian poet.[3] The poem, about a child sitting in the sun next to a wall describing how a nine-year-old girl came, asked him his name, and invited him to play, after which they walked home together, was expunged because the Ministry of Education found it to be "in breach of the needs of education."[4] The poem does no more than express a simple innocent childhood sentiment and pleasure. In contrast, when Amin read the rest of the book to discover what the Ministry of Education deemed appropriate to "the needs of education," he found not a single reference to a human relationship either across the sexes or within the same sex.[5]

The régime also acquiesced in the extremists' use of intimidation and the threat of being accused of blasphemy against intellectuals,[6] and the label has led to serious consequences in some cases. Feminist Nawal el-Sa'dawi was subjected to threats and attempts to use the legal system to annul her marriage,[7] and deprive her of her citizenship.[8] The same strategy was used to intimidate Professor Nasr Hamed Abu Zeid, whose marriage was annulled[9] by the courts in 1995[10] because of the views expressed in his published academic research. Writer Farag Foda, an outspoken supporter of secularism, was murdered on June 8, 1992. There were attempts on the life of Nobel Laureate Naguib Mahfouz,[11] and former information minister Safwat el-Sherif.[12] Islamic scholar Sayyid el-Qemany moved his family to an undisclosed location and announced that he would stop writing after receiving death threats in July 2005.[13] He decided to resume writing only after the authorities provided him with round the clock protection following his receiving of the State Merit Award for Social Science in 2009.[14]

None of these policies contributed to solving Egypt's long-term problems and all served to merely keep a lid on a pot that was going to boil over eventually. The slide towards disaster began in earnest around the time that Gamal was given a political role. An increasing reliance on the security apparatus as the mainstay of the régime had already been underway following one failed attempt by religious extremists to assassinate Mubarak in Ethiopia in June 1995, followed by a second attempt in Port Said in 1999. Personal security became an overriding concern and Mubarak reinvigorated and vastly expanded the remnants of Nasser's security apparatus and relied on brutality, repression, and rigged elections to maintain his rule. He believed the opportunists that he surrounded himself with, who were telling him what a great president he was and what great things he did for the country, and soured towards what he viewed as an ungrateful people who repaid him by trying to murder him. This led him to limit his public appearances and become increasingly isolated from the people he ruled. The family, especially Gamal and his clique, took corruption to astronomical heights and oversaw an extensive kleptocracy whose tentacles extended to every corner of society of the. The régime also reinvigorated and accelerated the process that Nasser began of emasculating and virtually destroying Egypt's main social and political institutions.

Despite his obvious enjoyment of power and the trappings of power, Mubarak all along showed little interest in the small details of running a country. Mahmoud Sabra, a senior staff member of the Presidential Information Office who worked for Mubarak for eighteen years (1984-2002),[15] maintained[16] that the President demanded that the world press summary prepared daily for him be short and once threw a four page report back at his secretary telling him that he would not read a *kashkoul*, a term that vaguely describes a long mish mash document. This only confirms what had long been rumored about Mubarak's disinclination to read anything of any length, regardless of its importance. He had no programs that he was eager to implement and no wish to make any changes or risk rocking the boat. The vast bureaucracy ran the country and he was content to let the vast engine tick over while he enjoyed the trapping of power.

The First Lady, however, had no such problems. She headed a long list of organizations ranging from The Reading for All Project, to the Egyptian Red Crescent Society, the Heliopolis Development Society, the Suzanne Mubarak International Movement for Women and Peace, the Egyptian Society For Childhood and Development, the National History Museum for Children, and several others. All such activities were, as Awatef Abdel-Rahman, professor of Media Studies at Cairo University points out, more self-serving than useful.[17] It appears that she also found the time to play a major role in the selection and appointment of senior bureaucratic positions. None of these activities gave Mrs. Mubarak any semblance of popular support.

Unlike Sadat, Mubarak neither cared much for his family of origin, who apparently never visited him, nor for his place of birth, Kafr el-Meselha, in the province of Menoufiyya. He never did anything for the village, which did not endear him to its inhabitants who returned the favor by refusing to express any support for him during the January 2011 revolution.[18] Suzanne's family, on the other hand, made billions out of their relationship, and their influence peddling was more than brazen, but no one dared comment until after his ouster in 2011. For example, the semi-official newspaper, *Al Ahram*, reported that her brother, Mounir, began a business career after retiring from the Air Force in 1982, a few months after Mubarak became president, and landed a contract in March 1983 to provide land services at Cairo Airport for a fee of thirty-two thousand pounds a year. Egypt Air had up to that point provided these services, which earned it thirty-two million pounds a year.[19] Other deals were equally lucrative and many billions were made by both Mounir and other members of the family.

Gradually, as her husband began to spend more and more time in his villa in the resort of Sharm el-Sheikh, Suzanne's and Gamal's stamp on all major decisions became more apparent. The President was happy spending his time playing backgammon,[20] visiting the Gulf countries to socialize with Arab sheikhs, or hosting them in Sharm el-Sheikh. It seems inconceivable that he was unaware that these very same people were the main financiers of terrorism,[21] but he appears to have been unperturbed by that. This apparent lack of interest in the mechanics of governing intensified after his twelve-year-old-grandson, to whom he was very close, died suddenly in May 2009. He cancelled a trip to the United States and gradually began to spend more and more of his time away from Cairo. He spent as much as ten months of the year during his last few years in office in Sharm el-Sheikh and effectively became a president in absentia.

Once Suzanne decided, around 2000 according to rumors, that she wanted Gamal to succeed his father, virtually all decisions, senior government and ministerial appointments, policies initiated or plans made were directed towards serving that goal. Gradually, Gamal's friends came to occupy several leadership positions in the government bureaucracy, the public sector, and the governing National Democratic Party (NDP). Corruption rose to even higher levels. Vast parcels of government land were sold for giveaway prices and then resold for astronomical amounts.[22] Public companies were sold for a fraction of the value of the real estate plots that they stood upon and were often paid for by unsecured loans[23] from government owned banks that were rarely paid back, and a lucrative monopoly on the supply of construction steel was granted to Gamal's best friend. Gamal's arrogance and attitude of entitlement to authority made him very unpopular in most segments of society. Constitutional amendments had been tailored to make it almost impossible for anyone but Gamal to have the remotest chance of seriously competing for the presidency, and he began comporting himself as if he were a crown prince in a monarchical dynasty. With his father's lack of imagination he failed to devise and sponsor even a small plan or popular project that might have given him a modicum of public appeal. One feeble attempt at public service was the establishment of the Future Generation Foundation, which offered programs to prepare recent university graduates for careers in business and related fields, but was popularly viewed as nothing more than a public relations exercise.

It did not, for example, occur to him to try something as uncontroversial as sponsoring a plan to relieve a small portion of the misery suffered by Cairo's millions in the almost constant traffic gridlock. Instead the family added to this misery by blocking large sections of the city for extended periods whenever they travelled around the city in their motorcades. He might have championed the cause of solar energy, or small business loans to unemployed university graduates, or a myriad of other uncontroversial projects that might have earned him a modicum of popularity and given him a base of support among the masses. Arguably even more unwise than blissfully neglecting the masses, he also disregarded the military. He either failed to comprehend the central role that the military had played in the country since the 1952 coup or was too arrogant to make any serious attempts to court the powerful military establishment. Instead, he simply took his position for granted.

The country during the third decade of Mubarak's presidency appeared to be once again on a gradual downward trajectory marked by corruption, deterioration, and degradation in all fields of endeavor. Social and cultural stagnation, degradation of every aspect of life in society, decline of the middle classes coupled with a rapid increase in the numbers of those living in poverty, the spread of slum areas around Cairo, and the growth of a corrupt, parasitic, fabulously wealthy class became the hallmark of the Mubarak era. Religious extremists were pandered to and allowed to extend their influence and consolidate their bases among the masses, while all secular opposition movements were weak and easily crushed. Continuous decline and an undignified chaos appeared to be Egypt's inevitable fate. The end, when it came was as dramatic as it was sudden. One of the dozens of small protest demonstrations that had taken place on a regular bases for years turned into a mass movement and millions went out onto the streets and achieved what seemed like an impossible dream.

Come the Revolution

Until January 25, 2011 conversations regarding Egypt's future were bleak and dominated by the same statements heard for years: statements meant to scare Egyptians and the world into keeping Mubarak in power, to be followed by his son Gamal, to protect Egypt, the West and Israel from religious extremists. The theory that democracy could not work in Egypt was supported by those who believed that, with democratic elections, the rampant Wahabism resulting from the post 1970s Arab cultural invasion of the country would lead to an Islamist government à la Iran, with greater oppression and loss of freedom. This indeed was the official argument convincingly used to defend the status quo when questions were raised on the international level about Egypt's political system.

On January 25, 2011,[24] however, the unimaginable and unprecedented happened. To the surprise of everyone (anyone who says differently is being disingenuous), a "normal" protest on Police Day turned into a revolution as Egypt's young men and women shocked the nation by doing something that their parents had either been unwilling or unable to do. They used networking sites such as Facebook and Twitter to organize a mass revolution. In some ways the event was a version of something that they had organized numerous times before simply for fun and entertainment. What the young men and women did was organize a flash mob of sorts, or rather several flash mobs. They held demonstrations in a number of the country's cities and in several parts of the capital and demanded reform of the political system. The main event was to be in Tahrir Square in the center of Cairo where all the demonstrators in the other neighborhoods were to gather. This was not the first time that ordinary citizens went out on the streets to demonstrate against their corrupt autocratic leaders and demand redress of various grievance, but in the past the protestors' numbers were often smaller than the security forces dressed in intimidating riot gear that surrounded them. The protestors had been, for the most part, hemmed in by these security forces and left alone till they became tired and went home.[25] Arrest, intimidation, or coopting of the protest leaders usually followed. On this occasion this did not happen.

What is now referred to as the January 25 Revolution happened when it did for a number of reasons. Simply put, it was a confluence of events, a perfect storm. Some may argue that it was sparked by Mohamed Bouazizi setting himself on fire on December 17, 2011 in Tunisia, and no doubt the overthrow of the government in Tunisia resonated in many people's imaginations in Egypt and had struck a chord. Others may argue that the spark was the abduction of Khaled Said, a twenty-eight year old Alexandrian man, the previous June by members of the security apparatus who beat him to death and left his body on the street. Khaled's crime was that he used the Internet to expose some incidents of corrupt practices. The police later claimed that Khaled had been picked up for questioning and swallowed a bag that contained a drug of some sort and died in the ambulance as the police were rushing him to hospital. Khaled was not the first person to be tortured and murdered by the security police, but his death struck a chord among the young men and women who did nothing more criminal than innocently vent their frustration in cyberspace. It was a stark reminder to this new generation of internet savvy Egyptians that merely sitting at the keyboard and typing could lead any one of them to jail, torture and death.

One of those enraged by the senseless murder was Wael Ghoneim, a young Egyptian Google marketing executive based in the United Arab Emirates. He decided to fight back using the only weapon that he was trained to use, his keyboard, and twenty-first century technology. He, in cooperation with others, created the *"Kolina Khaled Said"* (we are all Khaled Said) page on Facebook.[26] It was only one of many pages created by young Egyptian men and women attempting to solicit support for political change in their country, but this page caught on. Tens of thousands of similarly enraged young Egyptians logged on and began to express their feelings and share their grievances and experiences. They were not activists but merely people who were concerned, worried, and angry. Their numbers swelled to half a million within months and they began to share personal stories of police harassment, intimidation, and corruption, and express their anger at the recent more brazen than usual rigged parliamentary elections as they began to organize flash mobs. Young men and women would gather in small groups at certain spots and begin to sing the national anthem, at other times a group would dress in black, gather at certain spots and simply stand in silence. One group attempted to fly a kite with an Egyptian flag attached to it before they were arrested. Different groups began to discuss how to turn their modest efforts into a mass movement for reform. Ghoneim scrupulously guarded his anonymity as the page's originator and administrator and successfully campaigned online to keep the movement focused on one goal, searching for a way to reform the political system in Egypt and prevent the future occurrence of such atrocities by the security forces. The movement remained independent and unaffiliated with any political parties or religious and ideological doctrines. It strove to foster a democratic climate among its members through remaining leaderless to keep the focus on the group itself rather than any individual.

Much of the support for the *Kolina Khaled Said* group came from the April 6 Youth Movement, a group founded by three young people in 2008 (Ahmed Maher, Esraa Abdel Fattah, and Asmaa Mahfouz) in support of striking textile workers in a small town north of Cairo that organized several demonstrations calling for reforms. The demonstrations had been small and both Maher and Abdel Fattah had been detained for a few days by the security forces. The third founder, Mahfouz, recorded an articulate and impassioned video and uploaded it to YouTube on January 18, 2011 calling for large demonstrations throughout Egypt as well as outside Egyptian embassies abroad.[27] The day selected for the event, dubbed the "Day of Anger," was Police Day, Tuesday January 25, 2011.

People had simply had enough. They wanted reform; they were tired of being ruled by corrupt dictators. The Mubaraks had gone too far in trying to foist their son, Gamal, onto them as their next president — a man who appeared to have total disregard for the country and its people. Gamal was viewed by many as even more corrupt than his brother, who was rumored to have taken a cut on every large business transaction in the country. For ten years Gamal had seemed to push cronyism and corruption beyond what people were willing to put up with by installing his friends in key positions and allowing them to privatize the economy through what can only be described as blatantly illegal deals: for example, selling nationally owned land to friends who then sold it with a mark up of ten thousand percent in certain cases. Most of the public only learned of the full extent of the unabashed corruption after Mubarak's fall but the existence of widespread corruption had become public knowledge years earlier.[28] The circle around Mubarak privatized the economy into their back pockets while a majority in the country went hungry or suffered the hopelessness of unemployment. Although the January 25 explosion took everyone by surprise, the pressure had been building up for a long time and intensified as corruption became more and more flagrant and Egyptians began to see Gamal as a real possibility in their future. Movements such as *Haraket Shabab 6 April* (the April 6 Movement) referred to above, and *el-Haraka el-Misriyya men agl el-taghyeer* (the Egyptian Movement for Change) which adopted the sobriquet *kefaya* (enough), founded in 2004 were the early indicators of a possible shift in the national psyche.

Considering the forgiving tendency of the Egyptians, had Mubarak merely introduced some modest reforms and addressed some of the major grievances, he would have been remembered as a hero, and Gamal may well have been "elected" president, especially if he had managed to endear himself to the military establishment. But the ineptitude, shortsightedness, and avariciousness of the Mubarak administration was staggering. The régime had become too greedy and too blatant in its corruption, utter lack of concern for the people's welfare and treasonous disregard for Egypt's national interests. Every aspect of society smoldered and rotted away while the ruling clique appeared oblivious, uncaring, and drunk with power.

The goals on January 25 may have seemed overly ambitious. They were, in all likelihood, more reflective of the organizers' hopes than their expectations. The régime, represented by the usually anonymous security sources informed the press that three thousand policemen and one thousand members of the secret police would be on the streets to maintain order and protect both the public and the demonstrators.²⁹ While there were always calls for people to attend protests in Egypt, most went unheeded and they were poorly attended due to both fear and feelings of hopelessness. The authorities certainly did not appear to be worried as they, no doubt, expected to outnumber the demonstrators, as was often the case. After all, Gamal Mubarak, the heir apparent to the presidency had been so dismissive of the various young protest groups that he arrogantly burst out laughing a few months earlier when a journalist asked him if he would be prepared to enter into a dialogue with the young dissenters on Facebook. He had scornfully asked the other journalists, who obsequiously and dutifully burst out laughing with him, to answer the question for him.³⁰

Although several small civic groups decided to take part, virtually all of the country's political parties announced that they, for a variety of reasons, would not be taking part in the planned demonstration. The Nasserist party, for example, announced that they would boycott the event because they do not know the real organizers, and the leftist Tagammo' Party stated that Police Day is "not a suitable day" for a demonstration.³¹ The best-organized political group in the country, the Muslim Brothers, had apparently not been impressed with the non-religious, non-partisan nature of the movement and announced that they would not take part. Many of the *Imams* (prayer leaders) in the mosques called on their worshippers to keep the peace, and avoid causing *fitna* (sedition), a highly charged term in a culture which is essentially patriarchal and authoritarian. The Pope of Alexandria, apparently concerned for the safely of his flock, also advised Christians not to take part.

As it turned out, these factors proved to be major contributors to the success of the event and insured that those who took part came as Egyptians rather than as representatives of a religious sect, political party, or ideology. These individual participants all left their religious and party affiliations behind and felt united by their common identity as Egyptians rallying behind their common national flag and chanting for *Misr* (Egypt) and *horiyya* (Freedom) rather than for a sect or political party. The only flag carried by the demonstrators was the Egyptian flag. Party flags and religious symbols and chants were noticeably absent from the event. A message regularly chanted and appearing on numerous banners was: Muslims Christians, we're all Egyptians. This unifying focus made the event unique and served to confirm the sincerity of these mainly young educated middle-class men and women who had the courage to face a brutal régime and demand freedom, justice, and dignity for everyone. It also served to counter the régime's tactic of creating a tension between these two religious groups of Egyptians that ran counter to traditional Egyptian easy going tolerance. Every protester remembered the bombing of the church in Alexandria on the previous New Year's Eve and the mounting evidence that this had been a plot by the régime. Perhaps more importantly, the chants were a firm rejection of the sentiment expressed in a public statement by the Supreme Guide of the Muslim Brothers: "to hell with Egypt," or "who cares about Egypt,"[32] or in Sayyid Qotb's declaration that the homeland is nothing but a handful of rotten soil.

It may well have been this uniqueness that caught the imagination of the country and inspired so many people from all political views to shed their fears and inhibitions and come out to join them, swelling in numbers in subsequent days to more than two million by some estimates. Instead of it being a demonstration carried out by the youth it became a demonstration by all the people. There were Muslims, Christians, leftists, liberals, rightists, religious extremists, men, women and children of all ages united around one goal: reform of their political system. No one, least of all the organizers, were prepared for the tens of thousands who came to take part. For decades the régime had attempted to nurture divisiveness and fear by playing on the political, ideological and sectarian differences that existed in the country, but something in the Egyptian psyche finally came to the surface on January 25, ignited their Egyptianness and reminded them that what unites them was far more than what divides them. A virtual revolutionary circle was created that stretched out from Cairo to Alexandria and around the country.

Their over-riding chant on Midan el-Tahrir where the main protest was taking place: *"selmiyya, selmiyya"* (peaceful, peaceful), and *"erhal"* (leave) reflected the traditional peaceful nature of the nation. They were not demanding the head of a despot who brutally oppressed them for three decades and relied on hundreds of thousands of security personnel to keep the régime in power. They simply wanted reform of the system and the Mubaraks out.

The authorities kept hands off at first and allowed the demonstrators to remain on the streets—no doubt hoping that the event would run its course and the people would be satisfied with the usual promises of coming reform—and then return to their homes, but instead of going home the demonstrators spent the night on the square. By the second day, when numerous groups began to make their way to the square to join the main event, the authorities decided that they had had enough and sent in the riot police to try and prevent these groups from reaching the Square by deploying their arsenal of water cannons, teargas, and rubber bullets. Members of the secret police, who are nothing more than licensed thugs, were also sent in to beat up and arrest the demonstrators. This turned the peaceful event into a violent street drama. There were casualties, but the demonstrators stood their ground and beat back the police and thugs. By late afternoon the Square belonged to the protesters. This surprised many and served to empower the protesters and make them more determined. It also encouraged more people to join in support of the revolution.

The politicians who ran the country still lived in an age that predated the mass communications revolutions and thought that they could keep the rest of the country in the dark by directing the state controlled television stations and press to downplay the event. The press wrote of small numbers of demonstrators on the streets and claimed, incorrectly, that tens of thousands were demonstrating in support of Mubarak.[33] The Ministry of the Interior made an announcement blaming the turmoil on the usual bogeymen, the Muslim Brothers. The state controlled television stations did not show what was taking place, but the public switched to the international news networks such as CNN, BBC, and Al Jazeera, all of whom were reporting live from the streets. The specter of police violence witnessed by the rest of the country on their television screens galvanized the rest of the population and many more showed up in the following days to add their voices to those who remained in Tahrir Square overnight.

The régime was becoming increasingly desperate by the minute. Mobile phone services and the Internet were shut down, causing a glitch in communication but not a complete breakdown. The voices were not to be silenced. The technically savvy used satellite links and international Internet access to continue to get the message out through calling, texting, tweeting, using Facebook, YouTube, cameras, and video. Landline telephones came back into vogue, and information was passed the old-fashioned way by word of mouth. And the voices grew as more Egyptians crossed the fear barrier that the young protesters had shown them was pregnable.

After six decades of enforced silence, Egyptians rediscovered themselves and their love of conversation and laughter. The sense of humor for which they had once been famous in all Arabic speaking countries and which had traditionally served as a buffer against hardship re-emerged as an avalanche of pithy jokes on the banners they carried and did the rounds in this new flurry of conversations.[34]

The out of touch politicians that ran the country could not comprehend this new development and each move by the régime to quell the demonstrations had the opposite effect and served to increase the national conversation and highlight the régime's weakness. Shutting down the Internet, for example, led the apathetic and apolitical, who probably did little more than surf the Internet, to become politicized at this invasion of their personal life. The repeated claims by the state controlled press and television that the number of people out on the streets was insignificant was belied by the international media such as BBC, CNN, and Al Jazeera, and the state media was ignored.

The police believed up to the morning of Friday, January 28 that their one and a half million strong terror machine would quell the demonstration and subdue the participants. A police Captain was reported as having advised his officers at 8:00 AM not to worry because "the demonstrators are a bunch of kids that we will collect in a couple of hours and you will be able to go home."[35] By 4:30 that terror machine was collapsing and the officers were told to shed their uniforms, run for cover, and leave dealing with the demonstrations to their *baltagiyya* (hired thugs). A nighttime curfew from six in the evening to seven in the morning proved to be unenforceable.

The régime's desperation turned into increased brutality in addition to criminal irresponsibility as the protesters grew. Ironically, the inability of the régime to comprehend the event made it appear as if it were seeking to energize the crowd and keep up the momentum whenever the protesters appeared to be losing steam. Rather than demoralizing the demonstrators, the withdrawal of the police force from the whole country, leading to mass breakouts from the prisons and releasing thousands of criminals[36] in order to create chaos, simply reenergized the demonstrators and strengthened their determination and their sense of solidarity.

The criminals and the *baltagiyya*, who had routinely been relied upon in the past to carry out assignments that varied from quelling demonstrations to terrorizing voters and helping to rig the elections, looted some shops and began to terrorize some neighborhoods. They also attacked the protesters in Tahrir Square. The army was deployed to control the demonstrators. They ignored the *baltagiyya* and the protestors welcomed the tanks in the knowledge that the army had a tradition of not shooting at civilians and the aging commander-in-chief implicitly conveyed that message by appearing in Tahrir Square ostensibly to survey the situation. Furthermore, the top ranks had their own agenda. Although they were an integral part of the régime they never accepted Gamal Mubarak as a president-in-waiting and must have seen the revolution as an easy way to sideline him.

To counter the threat from the escaped prisoners and the *baltagiyya*, citizens formed protective neighborhood watches. After the initial shock wore off and once these groups were organized to defend their homes and neighborhoods, the members settled into what often turned out to be a relatively pleasant routine. The aura of suspicion developed over sixty years of brutal dictatorship, of not being able to trust others who could well be on the payroll of the internal security apparatus, had resulted in an isolation contrary to the attributes of the Egyptian outgoing character. In this new situation, they got to know neighbors they had never met and the local community spirit that had been lost kicked in once more. Sitting in groups on the streets of their neighborhoods throughout the night, they chatted, played cards and backgammon, and protected each other. They chatted with protesters who divided their time between Tahrir Square and their neighborhoods. After the police fled young men took the responsibility of standing at major road intersections and directing the traffic. The chaos card the régime had played in an attempt to exploit the visceral Egyptian fear of chaos had backfired. The people felt empowered, and the crowds grew.

To attack and disperse the crowd, the régime let loose some of the *baltagiyya* on horse and camelback, brandishing whips, swords, and clubs, in a surrealistic scene reminiscent of the desert nomads' invasions of Egypt, intent on robbing, killing and pillaging, since the beginning of history. It was a clash between twenty-first century citizens demanding basic rights and a brutal régime that still inhabited earlier centuries. The protesters again beat them back and set up field hospitals for the injured. Wise to the régime, many of the injured refused to be taken to local hospitals, knowing full well the fate that awaited them once they became isolated from the group. Some lost their lives in the battles. An old woman caught on camera cried out: "Ya Hosni, we mourned with you at the death of your grandson. Why are you now killing our children?" The battle of Kasr el-Nil Bridge symbolized the struggle that was taking place. The thugs advanced and took part of the bridge; the protesters stood their ground and pushed back. This happened a number of times, then the protesters prevailed, and the thugs were completely removed. Fear, of the police, of thugs, that most people had lived with their entire lives, turned to disgust. And the crowds grew.

The atmosphere in Tahrir Square turned festive, with the constant singing of the national anthem, of folk songs and of traditional songs from the time of the fight for independence. Regardless of age, gender, religion or political affiliation, "Today we are all Egyptians," they chanted, "The army, the people are one." There were at least two weddings held on the square. The wedding "party" switched their chants briefly in honor of the occasion. Instead of *el-sha'b yoreed esqat el-nezam* (the people want to fell the régime) they chanted the bride and groom want to fell the régime. In Alexandria as well as Cairo Christians formed a protective barrier around Muslims as they knelt down to pray in the square. Good humor prevailed, even at the checkpoints set up around the square to prevent infiltration of the *baltagiyya*.

By now the revolution's young leaders were anticipating every dirty trick the régime could play and countering it. At the checkpoints they caught plain-clothed thugs with police identification cards and weapons, both of which they displayed to the international media. The régime restored mobile phone services and the Internet and at the same time proceeded to attack and arrest human rights activists and foreign and local journalists, to break reporters' cameras, and to revoke al Jazeera's license. Everyone's mobile phone became a source of coverage of events in Tahrir. The picture quality suffered, but the pictures got out and countered the continued attempts of the state controlled television stations to present images of calm and support for the régime. The taunting chants became: "One two, where is State Security?" Some protesters donned pans on their heads to thumb their noses at a régime that had sent thugs onto rooftops to shoot them, hurl Molotov cocktails among them, and send rocks down on their heads. That incendiary devices were hurled outside the Egyptian Museum, which houses priceless artifacts and records of the nation's heritage, was a gravely irresponsible act. That these irreplaceable relics were so poorly protected that looters were able to enter the museum simply by climbing a fire escape and breaking a glass window on the roof is another illustration of the régime's unforgivable negligence. The national heritage was of little concern to the self-important bureaucrat responsible for the museum, who appeared on state television to glibly claim, incorrectly as it later turned out, that an immediate audit had been carried out and nothing was missing. His reward for this and his neglect of the museum's security system was his appointment as minister of culture in the Cabinet newly appointed during Mubarak's last days in office.

The revolution's young leaders were, however, more responsible. As soon as word got out that the museum was under threat, they formed a human cordon around it. They were also well organized. In addition to the field hospitals, they had established supply lines of food, water, and blankets for those camping in Tahrir and organized the collection of trash. They arranged for shops and apartments around the square to open their bathrooms to them. They set up large television screens for the demonstrators to follow newscasts and charging stations for their mobile phones. As the crowds grew, they spread themselves out around the square, keeping up their chant of "peaceful, peaceful" and succeeding in preventing violence among the thousands gathered, even after Mubarak's speech when the resignation all had been expecting did not materialize and anger erupted. Mayhem could well have engulfed the country after the raised hope expressed loudly in the chant: "Freedom! May God make it happen! May it be tonight!" But the protesters vented their anger with an insult: each raising the sole of one of their shoes at Mubarak's image on the screen." The revolution's young organizers continued to contain the anger throughout the next day even around the Presidential Palace where protesters gathered for the first time and the potential for violence was very real.

The régime made one bad decision after another, and the course it chose to follow underscored how out of touch with the people it was. Had Mubarak made any significant concessions early and agreed to step down and change the constitution, people may well have gone home and the régime would have survived. Instead it promised grudgingly small concessions. After each speech some people were ready to throw in the towel and "give it a chance." The Egyptian tendency to avoid confrontation, to respect their leaders, to fear chaos and insecurity might have prevailed if Mubarak had been more astute. But this time something snapped. The tone and message of Mubarak's speeches, when he finally made an appearance on state television, and those of the newly appointed Vice-President and Prime Minister, were a mixture of paternalism, condescension, and threats. Mubarak referred to himself as everyone's father and the people as his children. Such an approach had been effective in the past. After all, the Egyptian culture is both authoritarian and patriarchal, but a father who has been killing his children loses the foundations of his authority. He attempted to play on the crowd's emotions by referring to his military career. The audience remembered the many others who fell defending their country. His expression of sympathy for those who were killed during the protests rang hollow when he referred to them as "your" rather than "our" martyrs. He promised to investigate the charges of vote rigging in the recent brazenly rigged parliamentary elections when the ruling party (NDP) won 420 of the 508 contested seats. And viewers remembered his mocking remarks at the People's Assembly when he was informed of the formation of a "parallel assembly" by the opposition, and he mockingly dismissed them with the remark: "Let them entertain themselves."[37] The newly appointed vice-president and prime minister fared no better. The vice-president told a hastily held meeting with the press that he would be asking the young protesters' parents to tell them to go home. When asked why Mubarak is refusing to leave, the prime minister gave a lecture on King Farouk's civilized style of departure following the 1952 coup forgetting that when the army demanded the king's departure he sailed out of the country on the same day. When the Air Force sent two fighter jets to fly over Tahrir Square in an attempt to intimidate the protestors, they mockingly said that Mubarak was taking one last look at Tahrir on his way out of the country.

As these events unfolded, the United States, Mubarak's long ally and supporter, was attempting to walk a tight rope between supporting Mubarak and avoiding the appearance of denying Egyptians the rights to free expression and democracy that they were demanding. Washington was torn between supporting their ally who maintained the stability of a pivotal country in a troubled region and supporting protestors who were demanding nothing more than the freedoms cherished by America. The United States, despite some initial hesitation, realized that stability based on repression is false stability that could not last forever and could lead to an explosion that might give rise to extremism and intolerance expressed support for the demonstrators aims. Most Western countries followed their lead and the only leaders to publicly urge the West to deny these rights to the Egyptians were the king of Saudi Arabia, the Crown Prince of Abu Dhabi, and the Prime-minister of Israel.[38]

Friday, February 4, dubbed "The Day of Departure" and the following "Sunday of Martyrs" came and went as Mubarak kept hanging on. On February 8 dubbed "The Day of Loving Egypt" some of the demonstrators took their protest to the parliament while hundreds of thousands remained in Tahrir. Workers strikes and protests were spreading beyond Egypt's main cities but Mubarak showed no sign of leaving. By February 11, the second "Day of Departure" the United States was becoming more forceful in suggesting that Mubarak acquiesce to his people's wishes.

In a last ditch, desperate attempt to spread chaos and fear, the régime pulled out its final card: the foreign spies in our midst conspiracy theory with staged attacks on foreigners. But the public did not buy it, and the rumors fizzled out. It was reported two weeks later that Gamal Mubarak had proposed releasing the wild animals from the Cairo Zoo on the demonstrators to spread fear among them and send them running home.[39] The report appears far too preposterous to be taken seriously, yet the feeble-mindedness that produced the "Camel Battle" incident and Gamal's reputed lack of vision led some people to view the report as credible.

Affronted at the dirty tricks the régime had repeatedly played and sensing its weakness, the protesters in for the long haul applied more pressure. The régime, seen as existing in a parallel reality, had failed to understand that a new generation was running this show. The small concessions and the dirty tricks insulted their intelligence, angered them, showed them their power, and underscored the régime's weakness.

When the vice-president finally announced Mubarak's resignation on Friday, February 11, Egypt erupted in celebration. An almost forgotten sense of pride and dignity was restored and engulfed the country. The chant became: "Raise your head, you're Egyptian." After the celebrations, protesters returned to the square with brooms, trash bags, paint, and flowers to clean up after themselves. In a city not known for its cleanliness, it was a sight to see. What a difference a sense of ownership makes. Egyptians had pride once more and were all working together.

Perhaps there is no greater testimony to the inherent peacefulness of Egyptians that accompanies that sense of pride and dignity than what did not happen when the police disappeared off the streets except for a few traffic officers. In Cairo, a city of eighteen million, there was an unprecedented increase in burglaries and muggings, but mayhem did not breakout (in spite of the thousands of released prisoners). To keep the muggings in perspective it may be useful to imagine what would happen in a large city such as Paris, Rome, New York, Los Angeles or London with no police for a few days and thousands of escaped convicts on the loose. What took place was unique and January 25, 2011 might have come to be viewed by future historians as a tipping point in the country's tragic history if it had turned out well. Sadly, it did not.

Mubarak's Legacy

Perhaps the most positive aspects of Mubarak's rule are that he was, despite his condoning of corruption a patriot who preserved the integrity of Egypt's borders and never ceded the sovereignty of an inch of Egyptian soil. He doggedly pursued Egypt's sovereign rights to Taba, which was no more than a few hundred meters of beachfront, for six years until an international arbitration panel ruled in Egypt's favor.[40] He scrupulously observed the peace treaty with Israel and attempted, though perhaps with limited success, to close the network of smuggling tunnels Hamas dug between Egypt and Gaza.[41] He slyly followed the true and tried traditional strategy of paying lip service but not acquiescing to Saudi Arabia's persistent perusal of a project to take over the Tiran and Sanafir islands in the Gulf of Aqaba and use them to build a causeway linking them with Sinai.[42]

Nevertheless, Mubarak was, in the final analysis, no different from the long line of despots who cared little for the people's welfare and who are remembered for their avarice rather than their national accomplishments. He was so insensitive to nuances that he did not comprehend the ethical implications of his proud statement to a journalist once that his son Gamal was so smart that he made a fortune trading in Egypt's national debt while working in a bank in London.[43] When a member of the Saudi royal family asked Mubarak once if he was grooming his son to take over the presidency of Egypt after him he replied that he would not do so because he did not want to bequeath to his son a *kharaba* (wasteland or ravaged and destroyed land).[44] Evidently he lacked the sagacity to connect his three decades of rule to that wasteland. Or to wonder why the land described by Herodotus as having "wonders more in number than any other land, and works too it has to show as much as any land, which are beyond expression great"[45] had turned into a wasteland.

His attempt at excusing widespread corruption by stating to a palace employee once "Egypt has been plundered since the time of the Pharaohs and will always continue to be plundered"[46] exposes his limited knowledge of history. The Pharaohs used tax revenue to build the country's infrastructure, part of which is still the only source of livelihood for millions of Egyptians who work in the tourist industry. The country's plunder only began when it fell victim to foreign occupation and the tax revenue began to be exported to the foreign occupier's capitals far away. The looted billions and the régime's apparent pillage of objects of historical value from the royal palaces, especially in the final days before Mubarak's ouster[47] were common events in the country's history. They illustrate the successful buttressing of Bedouin values that limit veneration of history and heritage to the oral heritage[48] and glorify looting as a desirable and honored occupation for men, a practice revived with the Free Officers' plundering of the nation's heritage from these same palaces after the 1952 military coup.

As Egypt's third dictator since the military coup of 1952, Mubarak inherited a constitution that gave him almost total power, a society whose civil institutions were either destroyed or emasculated by Nasser, and a system of repression that Sadat had not been able to completely dismantle before his murder. Lacking charisma, acumen and any vision for the country, he merely expanded the security apparatus, gave it a free hand, and relied on it as the sole mainstay of his rule while the vast bureaucracy continued to run the country, albeit inefficiently. He aided the cause of religious extremism by giving its proponents a great deal of space in the state media while using the extremists as the scarecrow to point to as the only alternative to his rule and claiming that terrorism was a major threat. The negative impact on society that stemmed from the kleptocracy that he presided over might have been easier to overcome if it had not lasted for three decades. But when fraud, theft of public funds, and lack of civil responsibility become the norm and the expected mode of behavior for a whole generation these traits become so embedded in the social fabric of society and of its social values that the task of eradicating them turns into a major challenge. Thus, cultural rot and social stasis could probably be said to have been Mubarak's most memorable legacy to the country he ruled.

Hosni Mubarak is sometimes referred to as the last Pharaoh, but it would be far more appropriate to refer to him as one of the many *walis*. The Pharaoh was always accepted as the legitimate ruler of the land, and while Mubarak's succession to power did give him legitimacy, he eventually lost it by rigging elections, tailoring the constitution to fit his plans, and relying on violence and brute force to maintain his power. Just like the *walis*, he appears have lost no sleep over threats to Egypt's national interests, and both his domestic and foreign policies revolved around what was good for Mubarak rather than what was good for Egypt. To be sure, these interests did coincide at times. Maintenance of the peace treaty with Israel and preserving good relations with the West, for example, are cases in point. Neglect, however, of Egypt's relations with the African countries where the Nile originates can only be termed treasonous. To state that Egypt is the gift of the Nile is now redundant because it has become so obvious. The country has no other source of water. Yet Mubarak preferred to spend his time socializing with Arab sheikhs than cultivating the leaders of important Nile source countries such as Uganda, Ethiopia, Tanzania, and Burundi. He stopped attending the summits held by the Organization of African Unity years ago. Mubarak's minister of irrigation missed an important meeting of the Nile Basin countries that was held in Addis Ababa to discus sharing out the Nile waters.[49] The result is that the source countries are going ahead with a treaty that might reduce Egypt's share of the Nile water by as much as a third.[50] This issue is so serious that Sadat declared over three decades ago that Egypt would go to war to protect the share allotted to her by international treaty. Little could be more serious than jeopardizing Egypt's only lifeline, a neglect shameful to Mubarak and displeasing to the gods in the eyes of a real Pharaoh.

11

Plus Ça Change

Mubarak's final act as president was as ill-considered and short-sighted as many of his previous acts. He simply handed over the reigns of power to the twenty-one senior officers who form the Supreme Council of the Armed Forces (SCAT). The council headed by seventy-five year old Field Marshal Mohamed Hussein Tantawi pledged commitment to Egypt's regional and international obligations and treaties and promised to oversee the transition to an elected civilian government within six months.

The members of SCAT, as could be expected, turned out to be politically inexperienced and ham-fisted, and proceeded to make a series of blunders that ranged from violently putting down the mostly young demonstrators, resulting in scores of deaths, to putting thousands of protestors on trial in closed military courts, to subjecting women activists to strip searches, virginity tests, threats of prostitution charges, and physical torture. The blunders resulted in SCAT being hoodwinked into inadvertently contributing to the implementation of the Muslim Brothers' agenda.

One of the fundamental goals of the revolution was amending the constitution. The old constitution gave the president almost total power over the executive and legislative branches of government and provided him with many avenues to subvert the judicial branch. It allowed him to remain in his position for life and was more or less designed to insure that no one but Gamal Mubarak could become a serious candidate in any future elections.

In an exhibition of either amateurishness or ineptitude the military council delegated the task to a committee of what was referred to as constitutional experts,[1] who either had ties to the defunct régime,² or the Muslim Brothers. In a strategy reminiscent of the deposed régime's, the state owned media described Tareq el-Beshri, the "constitutional expert," who headed the committee to propose the amendments, in superlative terms, referring to him as a "prominent judge and historian" and as not only the "godfather of the Egyptian judiciary" but also as "an inspiration to Egypt's movements for change and dissent."³ However, his justifications to the mass media for the proposed amendments convinced the layperson of neither his sincerity nor his expertise.

These proposed amendments brought to mind Mubarak's grudging concessions to the young men and women who went to Tahrir Square to demand reform. The piecemeal nature of the concessions showed that he was unwilling to substantially reform the system but was instead intent on offering as little as would be needed to convince the protestors to go home. The committee's constitutional experts appear to have followed the same strategy. They had no option but to propose certain significant amendments, such as limiting a president's term in office to two terms, but did not address the more urgent demand to limit the president's vast powers. Instead they proposed a requirement that appeared to either lack urgency or be designed to bar specific individuals from possible future nominations. They proposed that a presidential candidate should not only be native born Egyptian, but also that neither one of his/her parents or his/her spouse had at any time been dual nationals, thus disqualifying Wael Ghoneim, one of the instigators of the movement for change, along with many other promising potential candidates, from competing in future presidential elections. Other proposed amendments were more cosmetic than substantive, leaving the almost dictatorial powers of the presidency unchanged and giving a future president the opportunity, at least in theory, to orchestrate an effort to rescind the amendments and put the clock back.

Tareq el-Beshri's answers to questions from the media reflected his sympathies with the Muslim Brothers' program, and had little substance. Various talk show guests demonstrated a deeper understanding of jurisprudence than he did. Tahani el-Gebali, Egypt's first woman judge, was but one of several constitutional specialists who impressed the television viewers with her expertise but unfortunately did not impress the decision-makers. Her exclusion from the committee, most likely due to the fact that she was a female, was an example of the difficulty of changing entrenched social values and illustrated some of the attitudes that the young men and women who were trying to reshape society had to confront.

Parliamentary elections were held on January 2 - 4, 2012 and seventy percent of the seats in the People's Assembly went to the MBs and their allies.[4] Presidential elections were held on May 23-24, 2012 and Egyptians were asked to choose between thirteen candidates. With no clear winner, a second round run-off election between the two candidates who scored the highest number of votes was held on June 17 - 18, 2012 and the MB candidate, Mohamed Morsi, whose campaign was well financed by the mini states of the Persian/Arab Gulf, was declared winner on June 24, 2012. Neither the parliamentary nor the presidential elections were free of fraud and vote rigging but the blatant violations were kept to a minimum.

SCAT, whose interest was confined to preventing Gamal Mubarak from inheriting the presidency, had begun to realize that it had not been able to find a satisfactory formula for governing the country and was eager to hand the responsibility to an elected body. The United States, which was Egypt's main weapons supplier, had considerable influence on the senior members of the armed forces and imagined that handing power over to an MB candidate would lead to a settling down and the formation of a stable government. It was an unfortunate miscalculation.

President Morsi, who had not been the MB's first choice for candidate, is in many ways a sympathetic character. Events threw him into a role that he was neither interested in nor able perform in an adequate manner. He was naïve, inept, uninformed, and totally lost and overwhelmed by the office of the president. Nevertheless he, apparently in accordance with instructions from the MB Supreme Guide and the Guidance Office, embarked on a blatant, wide-ranging program to *"ikhwanize"* the state. He was determined to remake Egypt into the MB's image in arrogant defiance of most sectors of society. When the Supreme Constitutional Court ruled that the parliamentary elections were unconstitutional, and disbanded the Islamist-dominated parliament on June 14, 2012, Morsi issued a decree reinstating it. He issued a decree in late November that in effect granted him unlimited powers. When the Constitutional Court urged him to reverse his decree and the judges threatened a nationwide strike his supporters laid siege to its premises.[5]

He ordered lifting the ban against admitting MB members and radical Islamists to the military[6] and police academies, and the military intelligence was soon alarmed to discover that secret cells of radicals were being formed in the army.[7] And in what could only be described as a surprising exhibition of insensitivity and arrogance, Morsi not only freed one of the leaders of el-Gama'a el-Islamiyya, which carried out a horrifying attack on November 1997 on innocent visitors to Luxor's Temple of Queen Hatshepsut, killing more than sixty people, but also appointed another of that group's leaders, Adel As'ad el-Khayyat, as governor of Luxor. He presided over the official ceremony to commemorate the thirty-ninth anniversary of the 1973 October war and appeared to be deliberately slighting President Sadat, the country's commander-in-chief at the time, by inviting Tarek Al-Zomor, who had been convicted of taking part in Sadat's assassination, and by not inviting the military commanders who played a crucial role in that war.[8]

His choice of Prime Minister, Hesham Qandil was ill-considered, misguided, and widely unpopular. Qandil, whose only qualification for the post appeared to be his sympathies with some of the religious extremists' causes, was ineffectual, maladroit, and generally unfit for the position. Morsi's ties to Hamas and his seeming indifference to their involvement in the developing unrest in Sinai led to further erosion in his popularity. In August 2012, terrorists ambushed a group of Egyptian troops as they sat in their canteen to begin their evening meal after the day's fast during the Muslim month of Ramadan and murdered all sixteen soldiers.[9] The attackers were religious extremists believed to be linked to Hamas, and when the Prime Minister went to attend the murdered soldiers funeral angry mourners attacked him, pelting him with their shoes.

President Morsi appointed thousands of MB members or sympathizers to every level of the national and local government bureaucracies from provincial Governors all the way down to village administrators and neighborhood council members. Professional, labor, and academic organizations were also packed with MBs or their sympathizers.

Seemingly oblivious to the developing storm he was creating, he issued a decree on November 22, 2012 giving himself sweeping powers and his decisions immunity from judicial oversight, sparking immediate mass protests. More than 200,000 people packed Tahrir Square calling for Morsi to resign and hold new presidential elections. Similar demonstrations broke out in other parts of the country. When Morsi's supporters besieged the Supreme Constitutional Court in an attempt to intimidate it as it was set to rule on the legality of the Islamist-dominated task force that was formed to draft a new constitution, it canceled its session and declared an open-ended strike.

The Ignominious End

It became obvious to everyone but the MB, whose numbers do not exceed half a million or so by most estimates, that they could not impose their will on the rest of the population. While religion has, since ancient times, occupied a very important place in Egyptian society, religious extremists have always been a small minority and most of the population has been consistently easy going despite their religiosity. The demonstrations against Morsi's policies intensified, and the headquarters of the Muslim Brothers in Cairo was stormed and ransacked. The young men and women who had brought to an end the Mubarak era organized themselves once again, this time joined more quickly by an even bigger portion of the public than in 2011, and a popular movement calling itself *Tamarrod* (rebellion) began to collect signatures on a petition calling for new presidential elections. On April 26, 2013 they announced that they had collected twenty-two million signatures. When Morsi appeared to ignore the petition, demonstrations erupted on June 30, 2013. Millions went out on the streets calling for Morsi to step down, and the military, backed by the almost unanimous support of the population, finally decided to intervene and issued an ultimatum to the President to resolve the situation or the military would. When Morsi ignored the ultimatum, the military chiefs met with several religious leaders and prominent members of the opposition, then announced on July 3, 2013 that it had deposed Morsi and named Adly Mansour, Chief Justice of the Supreme Constitutional Court as interim president, until new presidential elections were held.

Morsi was detained and the military began a crackdown on the MB activity, arresting several hundred of its leaders and activists. Morsi's supporters retaliated by burning a number of churches, attacking several police stations across the country, and taking over the Rab'a el-'adawiyya mosque in a Cairo suburb where they set up a sprawling camp. Their numbers grew into thousands as they began to stockpile arms and their rhetoric became more belligerent. The new government made numerous unsuccessful attempts at negotiating with the protestors before it was decided to dismantle the camp by force, resulting in several hundred casualties among the protestors and about a dozen deaths among the police force clearing the camp.

The interim president Adly Mansour remained eleven months in power, and a presidential election was held on May 18, 2014. The candidates were the former General Abdel Fattah el-Sisi, head of the Egyptian Armed Forces, and Hamdeen Sabahi, an independent populist politician. General el-Sisi was elected with 97% of the vote.

12

The Legacy of Seven Decades of Military Rule

Contemporary Egypt bears little resemblance to the country that the Free Officers took control of in 1952. Nobody could have predicted the nature or the extent of the social change to come, largely due to the youthful adventure pursued by a few junior officers.[1] The population has quadrupled, and the rural and urban environments, along with the social, political, and economic landscapes, have all been radically transformed. The monarchy, the imperfect democracy, and the dominance of the liberal Western-oriented elite became history, with a concomitant radical shift in social values. None of the major social institutions: family, education, religion, government, economy, came through the tumultuous events of the last seven decades unscathed. Defenders of the 1952 venture, or what they term the revolution, claim most of the changes have been positive and that any problems remaining today are both manageable and a small price to pay for the benefits brought about by the military regime. Detractors of the coup see most of the changes as negative. They suggest that the increasing Bedouinization of the culture and social value system, the spread of extremism and intolerance, the debilitating stasis, and the seeming inability to solve the simplest of social problems or spawn a leadership that exhibits any measure of vision for the country, do not bode well for the future. What almost everyone seems to agree about, however, is that contemporary Egyptian society is not as healthy as it should be, and that it faces a number of serious challenges. A review of the state of Egypt today clearly suggests that the 1952 venture proved to be more of a step back in time than a step forward.

One of the most significant legacies that the coup/revolution bequeathed to Egypt was the social value system of the new middle class. Values, as Max Weber demonstrated in his classic study, *The Protestant Ethic and the Spirit of Capitalism*, shape every aspect of life in society. The demise of the old middle class and the rise of a new middle class with very different social values is, from that perspective, the most socially significant characteristic of the post 1952 era. Most senior and leadership positions within the bureaucracy became the exclusive preserve of the military, which constituted the core of the new middle class. As previously discussed, officers were put in charge of managing everything from the nation's cities to the nationalized industries, banks, department stores, the national circus, the opera house, and film production studios. They became the new elite who enjoyed power and prestige in society and eventually shaped the system of social values in their own image by serving as role models that were emulated by the rest of the population.

Passing the mantle of leadership from one social class to another is a normal historical process and has been a constant feature of settled societies. The consequences of the replacement of one elite class by another in Egypt were no different from the outcome of that process in other societies: namely, the adoption of the new elite's social values. Radical changes in nineteenth-century Europe and the impressive achievements of that era were, for example, a direct consequence of the entrepreneurial class's ascendancy to political and economic power. Other consequences, however, were not so impressive: for example, poorly planned cities filled with slums, disease, and pollution.

In the same way, crediting the 1952 coup plotters and those who were nurtured and prospered under their tutelage with achievements accomplished during their era is, therefore, reasonable. However, logic dictates that they are also responsible for negative developments and that contemporary Egyptian society is the direct product of more than seven decades of rule by the "people of trust," whose social values were discussed in earlier chapters.

Cultural Decline

One of the most significant and far reaching developments to take place in the Middle East in the twentieth century was the discovery of oil in the Arabian Peninsula. This discovery contributed to the decline of the cultural influence of the region's most socially and culturally developed countries and the emergence of the least socially and culturally developed as the leading determinants of culture and currents of intellectual pursuits in the Arabic speaking world. The surrender, more or less willingly, of the mantle of cultural leadership in the Arab World to the oil rich countries began in the 1970s, and was facilitated by the new middle class, which was more sympathetic to Bedouin social values and more accepting of the severe limits it put on behavior and expression than the group it displaced in 1952. These values were a major factor in precipitating the cultural decline that appears to have spread to every corner of society, from the language of daily discourse, where obscenities and abusive language appear to have become the norm,[2] to the large number of books published on sorcery, charlatanry, and quackery[3], with a concomitant decline in creativity. This trend is clearly reflected in the mediocrity of contemporary Egyptian cinema, theater, song, and literature.[4]

This decline is clearly connected to the restrictions placed on the freedom of thought and expression[5] by the post 1952 régime, which sought to control all cultural activities, put quantity before quality, stress appearance over content,[6] and turn thinkers and intellectuals into mere bureaucrats and government functionaries.[7] The ensuing impoverishment of the cultural landscape[8] contributed to making society more vulnerable to the 1970s Bedouin cultural invasion. The deep rootedness of Bedouin culture in Arab societies[9] and the view that not only are Bedouin values an ideal to aspire to[10] but also that Bedouinism is a value in itself[11] were key factors that facilitated the spread of Bedouin social values.

This imported culture views the very use of the term creativity as sinful and advocates controlling all thought in society. Deep-rooted hostility to innovation in the Bedouin system of social values is reflected in the double meaning of the Arabic word *bid'a*: novelty and heresy. Proponents of Bedouin values often market their wares as religious rather than cultural or political precepts. Providing, such a veneer of legitimacy serves to intimidate many of those who might have opposed them and steps up the pace of cultural decline.

By the 1980s, the Egyptian academic community was feeling

the impact of the imported values. When a professor of English Literature, for example, used terms such as "globalism" and phrases such as "the scientific and technological revolution"[12] in reference to an international conference on literature and civilization that she was organizing, she faced a charge of atheism,[13] and calls to "investigate that suspicious conference."[14] A "Creativity Seminar" that the College of Education introduced in 1990 was also viewed as atheistic because creativity (*ibda'*) is one of God's attributes; therefore, attributing it to humans is tantamount to apostasy. The seminar was cancelled. Efforts to limit freedom of thought were not, however, limited to the academic arena. In 2016, novelist Ahmed Nagi was sentenced to two years in prison because a character in his novel *Istikhdam al-Hayat (Using Life)* was considered offensive to public morals.[15] Poet Fatima Naoot was sentenced to three years in prison and a twenty thousand pound fine for criticizing the practice of inhumane slaughtering of sheep[16] during the celebration of the feast of sacrifice.[17] Researcher and television presenter Islam el-Behairy served a one-year prison sentence on charges of contempt of religion for questioning the authenticity of some old texts.[18]

The social, political, and economic environments that facilitated the importation, adoption, and proliferation of these cultural practices had been created and nurtured by the 1952 coup plotters and their heirs. Egypt's loss of independence centuries earlier and consequently its loss of a sense of identity may have been the root cause of many of its problems, but the re-importation of Bedouin social values that stress tribal rather than national identity reignited and exacerbated the millennium old problem. The Egyptians, as one writer[19] had the courage to state in a public seminar a few years ago, suffer alienation and loss of identity because neither the past nor the future belong to them. They speak a language that was imposed upon them by foreign conquerors, practice a religion imposed upon them by foreign conquerors, much of their culture and social traditions were imposed upon them by foreign conquerors. At the same time, they have been "standing at the gates of modernity for two centuries and lacking the ability to enter."[20]

Some individuals find it difficult to cope with this loss of identity and absence of a sense of belonging to Egypt or to the modern age.[21] They either escape from the world they are in by physically migrating to the oil states where they earn higher salaries but are treated "like wild dogs," or they take refuge in *salafiyya* (retrogression),[22] which is essentially an emotional and intellectual migration. The new make-believe world that they migrate to is a perfect one and better than the real one in every way.[23] They dress in what they imagine to be the fashion of the Middle Ages or earlier.[24] The escapees also parrot modes of speech from these earlier times and advocate the philosophies and standards of past eras.[25] They believe that what they are doing is living as distant virtuous ancestors once lived and try to recreate that mythical world and force the rest of society to share their illusion. What they are doing in essence is attempting to destroy a world that they cannot understand and join a mythical world. Sometimes that involves going on suicide missions.[26]

The military regime bears a major portion of the responsibility for this alienation and cultural decline. In 1952, just as the Egyptians were beginning to feel Egyptian and take a few tenuous steps towards modernity, the young military rulers began to promote an Arab identity. Ironically, Egyptians, heirs to a great civilization, were being encouraged and trained to identify with a people whose own history is devoid of achievements in virtually any field,[27] is in effect a history of brigandage and perpetual internecine tribal warfare, and who scorn them for not being Arabs. Many Egyptians working in the Arab/Persian Gulf witnessed Arabs, imagining it to be an insult, call Egyptians "pharaonic" during interpersonal altercations, and Bedouins and their Egyptian disciples appear offended by any link that Egyptians have to their ancient ancestors. That may well be the motivation behind the *fatwa* declaring it a sin to celebrate *Sham el-Nessim*, the spring holiday that Egyptians have observed for thousands of years,[28] or to observe the tradition of eating salted fish on that occasion.[29] There seems to be no other explanation for expending energy on convincing Egyptians to refrain from celebrating a traditional holiday or enjoying a traditional dish. A Google search produced 102,000 Arabic pages linking *Sham el-Nessim* and the Arabic word for prohibition,[30] and 104,000 pages linking the words *feseekh* (salted fish) and the Arabic word for prohibition,[31] as well as a slew of YouTube clips referencing the subject.[32] Clearly such an innocent celebration is too much of a reminder of Egypt's rich heritage and a cause of much consternation to Gulf Arabs.

In Pursuit Of Shangri La

As the Western-oriented middle class declined and Bedouin inspired values spread in Egypt the Arabian Peninsula experienced a change of fortune. One of the consequences of the 1973 war with Israel was a disruption of oil supplies, followed by dramatic price increases that resulted in an equally dramatic increase in the funds flowing to members of the Organization of Petroleum Exporting Countries (OPEC). By the end of the decade, the OPEC members' reserves had climbed to 300 billion dollars.[33] Saudi Arabia and the mini states of the Arab/Persian Gulf region, all OPEC members, used a portion of their newfound wealth to finance ambitious infrastructure, development, and building projects. As these countries lacked the skilled manpower to design, implement, and staff these projects, they turned for help to non-oil-rich Arab countries such as Egypt, Lebanon, Jordan, and Syria for their manpower needs. Professionals, craftsmen, skilled, and unskilled workers from these countries were recruited with offers of salaries that were undreamt of in their home countries. Workers, in some cases, were being offered as much as ten times what they were earning at home, and millions flocked to take advantage of the new opportunities.

These workers provided cheap labor for the Gulf states' growing economies, and their salaries cost a fraction of what similarly qualified Americans or Europeans would demand in salary and living arrangements. As native Arabic speakers, they were also able to staff positions where knowledge of the language, such as teaching in the newly built schools and universities, was a prerequisite. Another major advantage that accrued to the oil-rich countries from meeting their manpower needs by recruiting Arabs was that the recruits posed no threat to the pre-modern tribal social and political structure of the host countries. The Arab recruits were used to living in totalitarian societies where despotism was more or less the norm and where they had few rights, so the fact that their new employers stripped them of a few more rights was viewed as a fair exchange for the salaries on offer. After all, the new recruits had largely internalized the main tenets of the Arabian Peninsula's system of social values, imposed upon their native cultures when the triumphant Bedouin armies conquered their countries centuries earlier. They were, therefore, reasonably at ease with the terms being offered, made no special demands on their employers, and considered themselves lucky to have found these lucrative opportunities. The constant stream of media reports on the vulnerability of migrant workers[34] to the harsh medieval[35] punishments meted out for infractions and violations[36] were not a deterrent. Severe punishments such as beheading a Sudanese worker convicted of "sorcery,"[37] executing an Egyptian pharmacist for "using witchcraft to try to separate a married couple,"[38] or arresting a Lebanese man who happened to be on pilgrimage in Saudi Arabia and sentencing him to death for fortunetelling in a television show that he hosted in Lebanon are not unusual.[39]

Only a small minority of the millions of new Arab recruits balked at being treated in much the same way as fourteenth-century serfs and chose instead to forgo the new opportunities and return home to their meager salaries and less Kafkaesque social sanctions.[40] Fatalism, a characteristic of the Arab culture, led the majority of migrants, however, to view their newfound wealth as an unexpected heavenly blessing and a gift from Providence, bestowed through the generosity of their blessed employers. Good fortune rather than a good education or exceptional skills was responsible for their high incomes. After all, large numbers of their compatriots back home, some of whom were much better qualified and far more skilled than they were, earned a fraction of what they were earning. In addition, the fact that their employers' wealth was an accident of birth in an oil-rich country provided a daily reminder of the fickleness of Providence in the allocation of good fortune. Providence supplied the black gold as well the experts with the know-how to discover the oil fields, to extract or refine the oil, and to market it. The evidence before them tended to confirm the workers' fatalism and their strong belief in Providence over personal initiative in the allocation of worldly wealth and career opportunities. The employers shared this fatalism, believing the oil to be a gift from a divine entity that also sent all these workers, only one rank above that of slaves, to serve them and cater to their every wish.

The high salaries also predisposed the job seekers to view their employers as benefactors rather than employers, to feel beholden to them, to seek their approval, to ingratiate themselves with them, and to go to great lengths to please them. After all, in their minds, the migrants felt that their employers were paying them far more that they deserved. The inferiority of the worker was further reinforced by the knowledge that the *kafeel* (sponsor) system gave their employers the right to cancel their employees' residence permits and send them home to their meager salaries at a moment's notice, without being required to provide any reasons for the cancellation. The terms of employment under the *kafeel* system are relatively simple and more or less standard in all the host countries. Any local citizen, government, or business entity could arrange to bring foreign workers into the country by sponsoring them. The sponsor would then be allowed to obtain residence permits for these workers and would pledge to repatriate them at his or her expense at the end of their contracts. The workers were often required to surrender their passports to their sponsors and were allowed neither to leave the country nor to change jobs without their sponsors' permission.[41] "The workers' families were also subject to the same restrictions, thus leading some of these workers to resort to desperate measures at times. The power that employers enjoyed over their employees was clearly illustrated by a case that was reported in the media. An Egyptian professor teaching at a Saudi university was unable to convince her *kafeel*, the university, to grant her home leave.[42] The husband, however, apparently luckier than his wife, was granted permission to leave. Desperate to leave the kingdom *en famille*, the couple found a novel, if extreme, solution to their plight: the wife, along with the couple's two children, climbed into the trunk of the family car and the husband, taking the car with him, boarded a ship bound for Egypt where they arrived safely. The Egyptian customs authorities, startled but sympathetic to their plight when they discovered them, released them without charge,[43] and one can assume that the Saudi authorities now check the trunk of every car leaving the Kingdom.

Predictably, the almost unchecked authority that labor laws grant the *kafeel* over his employees leads to widespread and constantly recurring serious abuses, which continue unabated despite repeated reports of some of the worst instances by the Egyptian media.[44] A recent news item about a sponsor refusing to allow the hospital to release the body of an employee who died in a work related accident for burial by his family until they signed a declaration that the dead employee was owed no wages shows clearly that the power of the *kafeel* does not end at the employee's death.[45]

The terms *wafed* (foreign recruit) and *mowaten* (local Arab citizen) gradually acquired the connotations of lower and higher castes in the minds of both groups.[46] The obvious income and status differential and ensuing imitation of the locals by the foreign workers was another textbook illustration of ibn Khaldun's assertion, referenced earlier in the book, that the slave would always imitate his master in his attitudes, dress, and way of life.[47] Such social practices have been closely studied by social scientists. For example, behaviorism[48] in the tradition of Pavlov, Watson, and Skinner also provides a plausible explanation for the spread of the Arab Peninsula's Bedouin costumes and social values among the expatriate Arabs recruited to work in the region. As the natural outcome of "operant conditioning," the workers imitation of their employers earns the approval of those employers, thereby reinforcing the newly acquired practices. Over a number of years, these patterns of dress or behavior can become normal, even after returning home. As a schoolteacher explained to a journalist, she continued to wear the *niqab*,[49] even though she wanted to give it up on her return home from Saudi Arabia, because she simply could not bring herself to abandon it.[50]

Egyptians who went to work in Saudi Arabia and other Gulf states after the 1970s oil boom were not, however, the first to seek employment in that region. A relatively small number of mainly professional Egyptians had worked there during the nineteen-fifties and nineteen-sixties. There were, nonetheless, marked differences between the two groups that very clearly reflected the deep changes that took place in Egyptian society after the coup.

Most of expatriates of the fifties and sixties were professionals whose educational qualifications and social backgrounds placed them firmly in the middle stratum of Egyptian society, and their values and lifestyles reflected, therefore, the *old* middle class practices that were prevalent at that time. Their incomes prior to traveling were, for the most part, sufficient for them to enjoy a standard of living that was commensurate with their middle class status. What temporary migration for a few years offered this group was the opportunity to fund a few extra luxuries, to start a nest egg for future needs, or augment an existing one. Their status gave them a high degree of self-assurance and confidence in their social values, and their proficiency in their fields of specialization and their professional ethics served to reinforce these values. Many of them were acquainted with societies and cultures other than their own. Some were graduates of European educational institutions, and their personal experiences and years of residence in these societies had, in many cases, contributed to their development of a cross-cultural perspective. As a result, their stay in one of the oil-rich states did not usually lead to a discernable change in their life style or social practices after they returned home. The self-confidence and absence of doubt or uncertainty about their social practices is exemplified in the answer a female member of the *old* Egyptian middle class once gave to a *mowaten* who was a fellow professor in the university where they both taught. He was critical of her because she did not cover her hair and suggested that she should wear a *hegab*.[51] She firmly reminded him that she had been hired to come to his country "to teach, not to be taught."[52]

This self-confidence was unfortunately lacking in later groups of migrants. Many were uneducated and had little or no knowledge of societies other than their own. Those classified as educated could more accurately have been described as trained or skilled. They possessed certain skills, but their educational experiences were confined to training in their respective technical fields. Many of these workers fell into the age group sometimes referred to as the revolution's generation and were, therefore, the product of an educational system that had been in decline for a generation. Having been taught, as Tawfiq el Hakim, points out, that whatever happened before 1952 was of no importance, and that Egypt was only as old as the revolution,[53] they felt no confidence or pride in their national heritage. Their school texts were designed to cultivate an Arab rather than an Egyptian identity, which contributed to the dilution of their sense of national identity and cut them off from their historical roots. To compound the problem, they had spent their formative years in a school system that nurtured unquestioning obedience to authority and discouraged independent thinking.

A significant characteristic that also distinguished this group of migrants from the earlier one was that the majority were either from rural areas or from what Vatikiotis described as "the urban milieu of Egypt without genuine urbanites."[54] This group came from families that lived in cities but retained their village culture and attitudes, limited their social contacts to those who shared these attitudes, and eschewed any of the cross-cultural opportunities that an urban lifestyle offers. They tended to view any cosmopolitan attitudes or practices with suspicion and sought the emotional security that came through clinging to their traditional village values and attitudes. Even the few among them who had had the opportunity to experience foreign travel and had lived in societies other than their own while pursuing graduate education in Europe or the United States retained, in many cases, their traditional mind-set. This holds especially true for those whose wariness and suspicion of different customs and practices led then to isolate themselves in cultural ghettos thereby insulating themselves from the host societies' influence. Such "ghetto" mentality deprived this group and their families of the opportunity to develop the cross-cultural perspective that many members of the earlier generation of Egyptian travelers had acquired. Sadly, their experiences often left them with negative views of the foreign world to which they were exposed during their time away from home. Seeking the psychological comfort of the familiar was often a reaction to an inability to comprehend an unfamiliar way of life or find a comfortable spot in a different culture. Sayyid Qotb, one of the major theoreticians of the extremist Islamic movement, is a prime example of those whose cross-cultural experiences proved disquieting and probably played a significant role in influencing his quest for a religious identity.[55]

The migrants of the seventies and later decades, who shared the above-described social characteristics, were, therefore, less cosmopolitan and less self-assured than the earlier migrants. They were less able to put their experiences in the oil countries into a comparative or a cross-cultural context. That, in turn, combined with the lower and somewhat precarious status of the *wafed* vis-à-vis the *mowaten*, tended to make them more impressionable and more likely to be influenced by the culture, social practices, and social values of their host countries than the earlier group. Not only was the host culture not viewed as alien to them, but in many cases, it was also seen as the more authentic and purer manifestation of their own culture. They felt a need, possibly tinged by an element of fear, to acculturate and to assimilate in the host societies that the earlier group had never felt. Their limited critical faculties, possibly also affected by fear, and their tendency to view the world in stark contrasts of polar opposites: good and bad, black and white, obscured the difference between religious and cultural practices, and left them vulnerable to the influence of Bedouin socio-cultural attitudes and general assumptions about life.

Far more alarming, then, than permanently dressing in medieval garb is the adoption of medieval cultural attitudes and beliefs that is spreading like a cancer throughout Egypt and the rest of the Middle East as migrants return home and Saudi Arabia makes growing headway with its proselytizing campaign and its plans to build a bridge.

Essence of the Imported Ideology

The Wahabi sect is widespread in the Arabian Peninsula and is both a cause and an effect as far as contemporary Arab/Bedouin culture and social conditions are concerned. It has both molded and been molded by the Bedouin way of life. Wahabism is a retrogressive movement founded during the eighteenth century in the Arabian Peninsula by Mohammed ibn Abdel Wahab. Fiercely opposed to almost all aspects of modernity, Wahabism strives to use all available resources to return society to the seventh century, which its adherents believe to have been a golden age of simplicity and virtuous living,[56] while having a high degree of tolerance for the pursuit of profit and amassing of wealth. It is ultra xenophobic and isolationist, embodies the cultural values and practices of that harsh, arid desert environment, and constitutes the single most powerful influence on that region's mass culture. The harsh punishments meted out for the mildest of violations, such as criticizing religious members of the Committee for the Prevention of Vice and Propagation of Virtue, and advocating freedom of thought,[57] or practicing witchcraft,[58] have been relatively effective in maintaining these norms and insulating that region from outside influences. News reports claiming that the vigilant Committee apprehended a witch who attempted to escape by flying "like a bird" out of a fourth floor window,[59] would suggest that a considerable segment of the public find the Committee's work credible.

Isolation from outside influences, however, is not as easy a task as it used to be when the Arabian Peninsula shunned all foreign products, with the exception of guns and coffee, up until the early nineteen hundreds.[60] The King of Saudi Arabia took a major step forward in 1959 with the opening of the first school for girls in the country's history. That he found it necessary to bring out the army[61] was a reflection of the powerful forces at work opposing modernization. Fear of the modern world is clearly reflected in the constant stream of *fatwas* from the highest religious authorities in the Arabian Peninsula banning almost anything not part of Bedouin life in the seventh century and calling for the murder of those who disagree with them. Recent examples include the fatwa that playing Pokémon Go is a sin,[62] and the President of the Saudi Superior Council of Jurisprudence's call for the murder of owners of television stations that broadcast soap operas because they were deemed to be spreading "depravity and debauchery."[63] Soap operas, as well as all those responsible for putting them on the air, are enemies of God and his Prophet, according to the head of Saudi Arabia's most authoritative religious organization.[64] Mice, including Mickey Mouse, declared two prominent Saudi religious authorities, are agents/soldiers of Satan.[65] Three-dozen prominent Saudi religious leaders have recently demanded a total ban on the appearance of women in any magazines, newspapers, or television.[66] The Olympics, the same sheikh who is worried about mice declared, is a satanic event, and playing soccer is sinful,[67] while another declared that allowing schoolgirls to participate in any sports is sinful.[68] Yet another religious authority called for the execution of those who oppose segregation of the sexes.[69]

The seeming obliviousness to cultural trends outside that region is demonstrated in an example from Kuwait, which is often pointed to as a more "democratic" and more "progressive" society than other Gulf States where democracy and elections are denounced as sins against God.[70] Yet it was a female Kuwaiti "political and social activist" who dreamt up a grotesquely bizarre proposal to "find a way to circumvent" the international ban on slavery and enable Kuwaiti men to buy concubines; thereby, putting an end to prostitution in her country. Russian women prisoners taken by Chechen rebels could, the lady proposed, be bought and given to men who would pay for them through salary deductions.[71] She was not taken seriously at the time but only four years later Da'esh began kidnapping Yazidi females and using them as sex slaves.[72]

Although the view that *kol bed'a dhalala wa kol dhalala fil nar* (loosely translated as all novelty leads to hell) is widely adhered to, it would be misleading to conclude that social change in the Arabian peninsula is impossible. Change does take place, but much more slowly than in many other societies. The following examples illustrate the torpid pace of social evolution. The first radio transmission occurred on July 18, 1949.[73] In 1962 a relatively progressive King Faisal, flush with income from petroleum exports, decided, "after discussions with [President] Kennedy,"[74] to join the rest of the world in outlawing slavery, bought all slaves in the kingdom for one thousand pounds per head, and freed them all.[75] The king, despite violent opposition to the proposal, also introduced television transmission in 1965.[76] Faisal was assassinated by his nephew ten years later to avenge the killing of his brother Prince Khaled bin Musaid, who opposed the introduction of television and was killed leading an assault on the television station. Many Saudis, though not all, have finally accepted the notion that the earth is not flat or that the sun revolves around the earth.[77] Furthermore, the introduction of an immense variety of foreign consumer goods, made possible by the oil income and displayed and sold in immense, luxurious shopping centers, has been relatively smooth.

Another significant change in Gulf society was the establishment in Saudi Arabia of an appointed consultative council, which meets twice a week, thus leading the International Parliamentary Union to grant full membership to the kingdom in 2003.[78] Yet another indication of some attitude change was the Crown Prince's cancellation of a court ruling against a professor of linguistics at King Saud University for writing articles that the religious establishment deemed offensive.[79] The court had sentenced Dr. El-Mazini to four months in jail, two hundred lashes, and banned him from ever writing again, but the prince decided that the court was not authorized to consider cases related to publishing since such cases fall within the purview of the ministry of information.[80] A Kuwaiti court showed similar leniency when a professor of political science, Dr. Ahmad el-Baghdadi, was charged with denigrating the Islamic religion by writing that he would prefer the school to teach his son music rather than religion. He was found not guilty, but the appeals court reversed the decision and sentenced him to a one year suspended sentence on the condition that he did not return to "his criminal ways."[81]

Women also appear set to benefit, albeit slowly, from the new ideas.[82] In 2016 a new law that allows a married woman to obtain a copy of her own marriage certificate *'aqd el-nikah* (literally sexual intercourse contract) was passed.[83] And in 2010 the government provided legal assistance to a twelve-year-old child seeking to divorce her eighty-year-old husband.[84]

Furthermore, the Saudi Ministry of Culture and Information announced in 2006 that women would be allowed to enter public libraries, and that the Ministry was in the process of reorganizing the system so that certain periods could be set aside for women.[85] Saudi women are apparently making advances in other fields too. Dr. Faten Abdel-Rahman Khorshid, claimed the Saudi Gazette, "is responsible for one of the Kingdom's greatest national achievements in the field of science for her work which began with the urine of camels[86] and concluded in a potential cure for cancer."[87] The building of women only cities is another development that is intended to allow women the freedom to work while maintaining the customary segregation of the sexes.[88] However, neither the Royal family[89] nor the religious establishment[90] accepts women driving, so some women were still risking jail in their fight for the right to drive until that right was granted recently.[91]

Another significant step was taken recently with the announcement that a woman has been appointed as a deputy minister in Saudi Arabia. Performance of her duties will be somewhat affected by her having to abide by the legal requirement of gender segregation, which prohibits her from meeting her male staff face to face and necessitates closed circuit television conferencing. Nevertheless, she appears undaunted and stated to the Egyptian media that she was planning to tackle the "difficult mission" of unifying the school syllabi [not the classrooms] between boys and girls.[92] Such occurrences show that even the most closed societies do change eventually, but the slowest change tends to relate to core social values.

Inordinate concern with women and sex are major features of Bedouin culture and a great deal of time, energy, and resources are expended in the pursuit of sexual indulgence as well as the control of every single aspect of women's lives regardless of how trivial or insignificant it might be. Women are generally viewed as little more than instruments of sexual gratification and baby producers whose husbands could legally divorce them whenever the mood strikes them. A simple text message is all that is necessary if the husband so wishes.[93] However, husbands are also bound by very strict rules and are, in some extreme cases, prohibited from ever seeing their wives' faces.[94] Women in this culture never reach legal adulthood which is why it is perfectly legal for a father to keep his twenty-one year old daughter in what amounts to an improvised prison cell at home for four years for having kissed a boy when they were living in the UK.[95] A woman, simply by virtue of being a woman, must have a male guardian throughout her life, and there is nothing that she can do to earn the right to make decisions about her life or to protect her children. For example, when one woman's former husband married off the couple's eight-year-old child to a fifty-year old man for a dowry of eight thousand U.S. dollars, the mother petitioned a Saudi court for a divorce for her child. The court ruled that the woman did not have the right to submit the case on her daughter's behalf.[96]

The serious implications of this perpetual childhood are also evident in an article about Saudi women prisoners published on the site of an electronic magazine, which lists its mailing address as the more liberal Dubai.[97] The article, written by a female reporter, found that some women prisoners remain in jail for periods of up to ten years after the end of their sentence for the sole reason that their families refuse to "take delivery of them."[98] The reaction of all those who were interviewed for the article provides a rare glimpse into the world that Wahabis and their local cohorts are attempting to inflict upon Egypt.

Sara el-Shwai'ir, a social worker in the Riyadh women's prison, told the reporter that she disapproves of families who shirk their responsibility towards their women. Apparently, it was not the unfairness of the situation that upset the social worker but the concern that these woman might be taught how to commit other crimes if they remained in jail.[99] Dr. Mohammed Hassan el-Derai'i, a professor at Imam Mohammed bin Saud Islamic University, also disapproves of this situation. He told the reporter that it is a violation of religious principles for a woman's guardian to refuse to take charge of her because she might be tempted to commit suicide or sully her honor by looking for someone to give her a home.[100]

The reporter visited the jail and met with some prisoners to ask for their reactions to the problem. Warda, imprisoned after being convicted of committing "a moral crime" (she gave no other details) stated that when she completed her sentence four years earlier, her father refused to take delivery of her at the instigation of her mother, who believes that keeping her in jail will teach her good manners and respect for family traditions.[101] Hessa, a thirty-year-old prisoner claimed that her brother refused to "take delivery" of her because he disapproved of her conduct before she was jailed.[102] Thirty-nine year old Salwa, a divorced mother of four children who was jailed following a complaint by her former husband, has been waiting for nine months for her uncle to "take delivery" of her.[103] The uncle, she stated, was unhappy with her because "she did not take good care of her children." Asma' was put in jail by her brothers "to teach her good manners."[104] They disapproved of her female friends and "noticed" that she watched "immoral movies and looked at immoral photographs."[105] Although her twelve-year sentence has ended, the brothers are still refusing to take delivery of her, and she cannot understand why she has not been allowed to repent and to be forgiven by her family.[106]

The concern with women's conduct evident in the above examples is a patent manifestation of the severe, almost neurotic, obsession with women, which is a major tenet of the new culture being foisted upon the Egyptians from the Gulf.[107] A woman being viewed as more of a commodity than a human being, probably explains why the incident of a father forcibly preventing a lifeguard from rescuing his twenty-year-old daughter from drowning off a Dubai beach because it would sully his honor to have her touched by a man,[108] hardly raised any eyebrows when reported in the news.

A large number of the free or almost free books that are sent to Egypt in huge quantities every year revolve around women and controlling the smallest details of their existence, from what they should wear in and out of the house, to what they should eat, to how they should treat their friends and family, to how they should please their husbands, to how they should help him select a second, third or fourth wife.[109] The message that all these books preach, as a recent investigative media report discovered, is that "woman was created for man's pleasure and to serve him."[110] The reply of one of the new breed of Wahabi influenced preachers to a journalist who asked about the role of women in the *Salafi* (retrogressive) movement succinctly reflects this attitude. He stated, "Woman is nothing but a fragrant flower to caress and enjoy its scent."[111] Many of the books referred to above are replete with dire warnings about women, their schemes and intrigues, and the dangers that might ensue if they are allowed full participation in society.[112] This obsession is also exemplified in an article entitled "*50 Mokhlafa taqa' fiha el-nisaa,*" (fifty violations that women fall into) which appeared on the internet site of *el-Akhbar*, a major national Egyptian daily newspaper, as well as numerous other web sites and blogs.[113] The violations listed are wide-ranging and include: consulting fortune tellers; improper dress; using gold or silver cups, glasses or dinner plates; hanging pictures on the walls of the home; disobeying husbands; neglecting housework; revealing marital conversations and secrets.[114] They also include: going out while wearing a perfume because male non-relatives might be able to smell it; riding in a vehicle with an unrelated driver; mixing, joking, or shaking hands with male relatives; using a black hair dye instead of henna; and mourning a diseased person for more than three days (but a widow is allowed four months and ten days of mourning for the husband).[115]

The Bedouin culture and way of life may very well be suited to the Arabian Peninsula's tribal desert societies. That is for the local inhabitants to determine. Egypt's long history, however, provides ample evidence that imposing Bedouin culture on Egyptian society after the first Arab invasion had a major negative impact on Egyptian civilization, and contributed to its decline. The history, economy, and geographic location of Egypt make openness to the world beneficial in every way. Yet, by the time, the Egyptian migrant workers are ready to return home from their sojourn in the Gulf many of them have become part of the Arabian Peninsula's mass culture and have adopted many of its misogynist, xenophobic and insular values and cultural practices. The social change that adherents to the Bedouins' social values are attempting to force upon Egypt is, therefore, a descent into darkness. Whereas the Bedouins are inching forward, however slowly, from the seventh century towards the twenty-first century, they and their surrogates are determined to take Egypt back to the seventh century. What makes this campaign insidious rather than comical is its considerable success in initiating a trend that has begun to impact society in profound ways.

The Triumphant Return

The greatest impact of the repatriation of the migrant workers on Egypt's culture and social values began to be felt as major infrastructure projects in the Gulf were completed during the latter part of the nineteen eighties and large numbers of foreign workers began returning home. Estimates of the number of Egyptians who worked in the Gulf over the last three decades of the twentieth century vary, but the figure certainly runs into millions. The Minister of Manpower and Immigration estimates the total number of Egyptians working abroad in 2009 at between seven and eight million.[116] The sheer numbers of the returnees intensified their impact on the rest of society, influenced the direction of social change already been taking place in Egypt, and boosted its strength, becoming, therefore, a major factor in the spread of the new patterns of social practices.

The cultural practices of their Gulf hosts that these returnees acquired are what one sociologist has termed "alien" customs, social values, and religious sects.[117] Gradually, as another writer notes, Egyptian airports came to be the location where a social change in progress took a physical form and was brought to life. Male Egyptian schoolteachers, who departed for the oil countries walking hand in hand with their wives, both of them dressed in normal Western attire, returned wearing slippers and dressed in *gallabiyyas* (traditional Arab flowing dress) and *hegabs,* with each wife walking respectfully behind her husband.[118]

Some of these acquired practices would have stemmed from what behaviorists term operant conditioning, and others would have been viewed, either consciously or subconsciously, as status symbols. For example, when a popular Egyptian telepreacher who had spent a few years in Saudi Arabia abandoned the *kakoola*, which was the traditional Egyptian clerical attire worn with pride to indicate graduation from the thousand year old Azhar University, and appeared on his regularly scheduled television program wearing another traditional flowing dress, no one attached any significance to the switch. But the new attire was significant. It was neither the traditional collarless wide-sleeved Egyptian *gallabiyya* of the type worn in villages, nor the collared type found in urban areas. It was a Saudi Arabian *thobe*, which is recognizably different from the *gallabiyya.* The most likely explanation for the choice is that the new media star was, either consciously or subconsciously, advertising his newly felt higher status and his close link to what he perceived to be the new masters.

Regardless of the causes, the values and lifestyles normally associated with Bedouin and rentier societies, such as rigid separation of the sexes and the ostentatious public display of wealth, began to proliferate. *Hegabs* and *niqabs* began to make their appearance on Egyptian streets with increasing frequency as early as the late seventies. Parochialism, familism, tribalism, denigration of work, the absence of a link between effort and reward, and concern with the outer trappings of religion rather than its core principles and values were among the most obvious practices that began to be introduced into Egypt.[119]

At first, some of the imported Bedouin practices appeared relatively harmless. Their impact and inconvenience were limited to the individuals who adopted them, and the unusual customs might have seemed more laughable or amusing than threatening. Inserting the word 'bin'[120] between one's first and second names in imitation of the Gulf Arabs[121] may be viewed as somewhat ridiculous and worth commenting upon in the media by some, but the practice certainly does no harm to society. The new fad among some Egyptians of changing their pronunciation of certain words or speaking in unfamiliar accents that one writer has noted[122] certainly does no harm to society either. Wearing a *hegab* or a *niqab* and insisting on rigid separation of the sexes were viewed as nothing more than personal choices, which every individual had the right to make. Using a twig instead of a toothbrush and toothpaste to clean one's teeth, as was the custom among some seventh century Bedouins, might cause dental problems or gum diseases, but the damage is limited to the new adherent to the fad. Shortening the length of one's *gallabiyya* as proscribed by the newly converted Wahabis might not enhance the appearance or might seem unusual, but it does no harm. Insistence on the use of a specific term of greeting[123] instead of the usual good morning or good evening might prove to be slightly irritating to those who happen to be merely interested in observing social etiquette by making a passing salutation, but it does not go any further than that. Growing an untidy beard, as well as all the above-mentioned fads are all relatively innocuous individual preferences regardless of from where the customs were imported.

These minor practices, however, proved to be harbingers of a more serious trend that began to impact society in more profound ways. One example of these trends was the spread of the *niqab* among nurses and female physicians working in government hospitals.[124] The appearance of someone wearing black gloves and draped in black from head to toe is unlikely to be a source of comfort or solace for any hospital patient let alone a sick child, or a patient regaining consciousness after a surgical procedure. What is more alarming is that these medical practitioners apparently refuse to take their gloves off to disinfect their hands, as is the norm prior to entering operating theaters.[125] Even covering up from head to toe in a loose black outfit complete with black gloves and socks is apparently not enough for some Saudi religious leaders, one of whom declared recently that the small slits for the eyes in that type of dress are sinful, too revealing, and one eye, therefore, should be covered up.[126]

It is a truism to say that a great deal of effort and sensitivity is required to balance individual rights and society's interests. The ban on religious symbols in schools and public offices is viewed by some as an expression of the principal of separation of state and religion whereas others might see the ban as an infringement on personal freedom. Dress style has always been a means of expressing ones identity, be it religious, national, or otherwise, but it could also be viewed as a challenge or even an insult to those who do not share that identity. Attempts to regulate modes of dress are, therefore, problematic. The controversy[127] over France's ban on the burkini illustrates the complex nature of this issue. Since burkini wearers regard others as immodest or worse, bikini wearers might feel that the mere appearance of a burkini is intended as an insult to them. The dress issue in Egypt is further complicated by the fact that history has amply demonstrated that holders of extremist positions: religious, political, social, or otherwise, have never been easily placated, and making concessions to them inevitably leads to demands for further concessions. The mass media provides us with a constant stream of examples of such extreme demands, ranging from harassment of female university students who have chosen not to follow the new fashion and do not wear the *hegab* and demands that they be expelled,[128] to teachers cutting the hair of uncovered girls by force,[129] to harassment of schoolteachers by their principals for the same reason.[130] One example of the futility of attempting to placate the extremists was the fatwa[131] issued against a female university professor who already wears the *hegab* but expressed her belief that the *niqab* is not mandated by religion.[132]

Even relatively minor issues such as dress codes and calls for segregation of the sexes can lead to serious consequences if they are taken to extremes. Further examples from Saudi Arabia should serve as dire warnings that Egyptians would do well to heed. Fourteen girls died on March 11, 2002 in a fire at their school in Saudi Arabia. Panic, confusion, or the fire itself prevented them from grabbing their *abayas*[133] before trying to make a run for their lives. Representatives of the Committee for the Promotion of Virtue and the Prevention of Vice did not, however, view the fire as a good enough reason for the girls to appear in public without their black cloaks and forced them back into the building to be burned to death.[134]

In a more recent incident, a nineteen-year-old Saudi woman, sitting in a car with a man, was abducted and raped fourteen times by seven men who also raped her male companion.[135] The rapists were apprehended, tried, and sentenced to between ten months and five years in jail. The victims were also found guilty of violating the sex segregation laws by sitting in the car with a member of the opposite sex who was not a relative, and were sentenced to ninety lashes each for their offense.[136] When the woman appealed the verdict, her sentence was increased to six months in jail and two hundred lashes because the court felt that her lawyer tried to influence them by speaking to the media about the case.¹³⁷

Viewing the ideas brought back by the migrants as mere expressions of personal choices of attire or lifestyle, therefore, discounts their true significance and the serious threat that they pose to Egyptian society as they spread to other areas of life. The dress code could even affect national policy. A member of the National Assembly, believing dress standards should be imposed on foreign entertainers performing in Egypt, brought the issue to parliament, suggesting that two popular female Lebanese singers should be prohibited from entering the country because they "dress immodestly."¹³⁸

More serious, perhaps, is the potential impact on the national economy. Unlike Saudi Arabia, which does not need to advertise to attract the huge numbers of visitors to the holy sites that netted an estimated 18.6 billion dollars in 2014,¹³⁹ Egypt, earning a fraction of that amount, must advertise its attractions. Bedouin concerns over what women should or should not wear, therefore, needs to be approached rationally and not allowed to influence economic policies.

The controversy that arose over some Ministry of Tourism promotional television clips clearly demonstrates that need for rationality. The clips, showing a belly dancer in one scene and bikini clad women relaxing on the beach in another, to be aired on Arab television channels as an enticement to western expatriates resident there, as well as Arabs, to vacation in Egypt, offended many people, who saw the clips as damaging Egypt's reputation and called for the campaign to be cancelled.¹⁴⁰ The protestors who found these clips offensive apparently had alternative ideas for their replacement. One so-called "advertising expert" was quoted in the media as suggesting that the cause of tourism would be better served if Egypt followed Dubai's example of showcasing high-rise buildings in their tourist promotion clips.¹⁴¹ No one, apparently, asked the obvious and only germane question: how much of a desperately needed boom is tourism going to get when what is advertised as being on offer is multi-story buildings and a sunny beach populated by women shrouded in black from head to toe? Hampering efforts to support Egypt's tourist industry and, therefore, slowing down or even preventing economic recovery does not serve Egypt's national interests nor the welfare of a suffering population. Plainly put, it can be seen as a deliberate attempt to damage Egypt's national interests.

To make matters worse, the trend, started by the returning Gulf migrants and encouraged by the Saudi authorities' subtle marketing efforts, of making repeated visits to the holy places in Saudi Arabia rather than once in a lifetime, as was the custom prior to the 1970s, costs the Egyptian economy three to five billion dollars annually,[142] while its revenue from tourism dropped[143] to 500 million dollars in the first quarter of 2016.

Many areas of life in Egypt have already been significantly impacted by what one writer termed "the imported black culture"[144] which propagates "laughable myths."[145] For example, a number of students in the College of Fine Arts in Cairo failed to see the absurdity of their claim to journalists that what they were studying at the college is sinful because any representation of the human form such as sculpture and photography is a sin.[146] More alarming than the absurdity of this attitude is the possible psychological dichotomy that it perhaps indicates. Professors at the college are well aware of these attitudes,[147] which are shared by some of their colleagues. One professor at that same college has resigned citing the futility of teaching students who wear the *niqab* and believe that the study of art is a sin and of working under an administration that does not hold any art seminars, but holds instead numerous religious seminars.[148] The college in one instance went as far as asking the professor to dismiss his class and vacate the lecture hall so that it could be used to hold a religious seminar.[149] Egypt's Grand Mufti, Ali Gom'a, joined the new trend by decreeing that the display of statues is idolatrous and therefore sinful.[150] Shenouda III, the previous Pope of Alexandria, Patriarch of the Coptic Church, perhaps feeling left out of a national movement, joined the fray, issued a condemnation of idolatry, and likened sculptors to adulterers.[151] The belief that representing human form is a sin led one young woman to go to a museum that exhibited the works of Hassan Heshmat, a prominent sculptor, and smash four exhibits while screaming "this is sinful you infidels."[152] These incidents clearly illustrate that the possibility of future demands to close down the college and ban the study of art in Egypt is no longer as remote as it once was.

More alarming than the possibility of seeing Art Colleges closed in the future is the specter of the total erasure of not only Egyptian culture but also the destruction of its ancient symbols and monuments. Envisioning a time in the future when demands for the destruction of the Egyptian

Museum and the ancient Egyptian temples, especially since they often depict women whose dress code does not conform to the Bedouin ideal, is no longer as preposterous as it might have seemed only a few decades ago. Destruction of ancient sites for religious or political justifications cuts across cultures and historical periods, ranging from the early Christian defacement of pharaonic images on ancient monuments, to the Serb and Hindu destruction of mosques, to the Chinese destruction of monasteries and the dynamiting of the giant 1,700-year-old figures of Buddha at Bamiyan by religious zealots in Afghanistan.[153] The Saudi destruction of Biblical sites,[154] however, did not preclude replacing them with more profitable luxurious hotels and Disney-like commercial edifices and tourist attractions,[155] as Bedouin values do not proscribe amassing wealth or profit-making.[156]

Egypt is certainly, or at least one hopes, nowhere near that stage yet, and anxiety over the preservation of Egypt's might seem a little paranoid to some. However, if the Saudi king deemed it necessary to bulldoze the house of the Prophet's grandson as soon as it was identified, lest it became a site of pilgrimage, and if the remains of the Prophet's birthplace are in danger of destruction too,[157] how safe could Egypt's pharaonic heritage be as Saudi influence continues to increase in the country? A religious Internet site once asked its members whether they would "call for destroying the idols in Egypt including the pyramids and the sphinx."[158] Nearly a quarter of the respondents answered yes and another third said, "the issue is complicated."[159] These types of surveys may have no scientific validity, but the mere fact that anyone would even countenance the destruction of the pyramids and the sphinx illustrates the extent to which the extremists might go and is an ominous reminder of the fate of the giant Buddha at the hands of the Taliban. The more recent destruction of the ancient city of Palmyra in Syrian by *Da'esh*[160] clearly suggests that concern about the preservation of Egypt's heritage is not far-fetched.

Bedouin values, unfortunately, are also creeping into attitudes towards crime and punishment. The whip, as a means of enforcing compliance with the laws and conformity to Bedouin social norms, appears to have won some supporters among persons who might be in a position to influence legislation. One member of the National Assembly has proposed banning alcohol in Egypt and subjecting violators to forty lashes, and another member has proposed lashes for journalists who violate the press law.[161] Severing spinal cords as a punishment for a crime, as one Saudi judge decreed, has not been proposed by anyone yet;[162] however, public stoning and amputation of offenders' hands and feet were among the penalties proposed by other members of the Egyptian parliament.[163] Certainly, neither *Da'esh* nor Saudi Arabia hesitates to implement such punishments,[164] and even sports offences are not exempt from corporal punishment in Saudi Arabia where one soccer player was sentenced to twenty days in jail and twenty lashes for striking another player, and a second player to seven days in jail and ten lashes for the same offence.[165]

The position of women in Egyptian society has been among the first areas to be impacted by the spread of Bedouin values, and misogynist attitudes are beginning to take root and affect every area of life in Egypt. The impact might appear relatively minor in certain instances, such as the case of the Assistant Dean of a medical college who was offended by the sight of male and female students sitting next to each other in class and decided, in violation of official college policy, to seat them separately.[166] Perhaps it might also be considered inconsequential that writer and poet Mona Helmi, complaining in a recent essay of the constant insults heaped upon women in the press,[167] provoked a hysterical reaction to her announcement that she would use her mother's name as a middle name in her literary publications,[168] and claims by some men that she must be mentally disturbed to consider such an idea.[169] The fixation on women indicated in some of the issues brought up for debate in parliament by members who have been won over to the Bedouin cause might also be viewed as trifling or amusing. For example, the serious issue of female genital mutilation (FGM) was reduced to farce when one parliamentarian called for repealing the law criminalizing FGM. Apparently he believed that reducing women's sexual desire was necessary as men are too "sexually weak" to match their women's natural sexual appetites.[170]

Some parliamentarians have protested the founding of a School of Modern Dance. Others have proposed legislation to ban kissing in Egyptian movies, mixed-sex schools, beauty contests, the use of models in the College of Fine Arts, and the sale of Barbie Dolls because they are "sexually stimulating."[171] These parliamentarians did, however, demand that the Minister of Health speed up the process of manufacturing Viagra pills locally to enable men "to carry out their marital obligations."[172]

Seeing such conduct as having no negative affect on society is naïve. It is these same petty concerns that are at the core of the male judiciary's refusal to accept the possibility of a female judge joining the profession on the basis that women are incapable of logical thought and lack the ability to control their emotions. Major policy decisions that could have significant impact on daily life are already being influenced either directly or indirectly by this retrogressive trend.[173]

Gagging The Opposition

The imported practices are ominous portents rather than passing fads, but few critics are willing to risk expressing their views publicly or to warn against the looming danger.[174] The influence of the religious establishment in contemporary Arab societies is considerable, and researchers are generally wary of venturing beyond the limits proscribed for them. This wariness is amply justified by the proliferation of militant groups who have appointed themselves guardians of society and whose views are more extreme than those of the religious establishment. A significant factor in facilitating the spread of these imported practices is, therefore, intellectual terrorism as any discussion of Wahabi practices could be construed as a critique of religion and lead to dire consequences. With Bedouin values often confused with religion, suggesting that the practices and lifestyle of a preliterate, isolated group of people who fear the modern world might have been more appropriate to the eleventh than to the twenty-first century carries considerable personal risk. Exploring Wahabi practices from a sociological perspective is, therefore, fraught with dangers and has never been a popular area of research. Many Arab and Egyptian social scientists, perhaps as result of their tendency to steer away from controversy, especially if it is even vaguely associated with religion, have been content, therefore, to leave the analysis to the theologians and the self-appointed guardians of morals.

Merely questioning the social impact of these traditions could result in being denounced as an apostate.[175] The Enlightenment has been declared by no less an authority than the Saudi Director General of the Islamic Organization for Education, Culture and Sciences to be "unsuitable" for Arab and Islamic societies,[176] and advocating its values could also invite the apostasy charge[177] One writer, who had the courage to write a strong critique of the absence of democracy, giving his book the title *el-Istebdad* (despotism), still, however, found it necessary to qualify many of his statements with praise for some aspect of the imported culture or one of its heroes. He states, for example, that freedom of opinion and consultative rule were nonexistent throughout Muslim rule, but then goes on to add a disclaimer stressing that this does not include the reign of the Guided Caliphs,[178] and clarifying his statement further by adding, "Everything was handled in an ideal manner"[179] during the rule of the first two caliphs.[180]

Awareness of the dangers of discussing taboo subjects has led other writers to seek refuge in the Bedouin-rooted fondness for oration and the tendency to value form over content when attempting any critiques of society. They avoid using certain code words, limit their criticism to safe topics, such as the lack of support for science and education in society, or quote public figures or respected scientists rather than appear to be expressing their own views.[181] Those who attempt even the mildest criticisms pay for their courage. An Islamic researcher who merely questioned the credibility of some of the sources of some of the Prophet's quotes was sentenced to one year in jail for his transgression.[182] Judgments such as this explain the tendency to be circumspect when discussing topics that could be viewed as too close to the religious heritage, as evident in contemporary historical analysis. Objective, candid analysis of Egypt's history since 641 is, therefore, the exception rather than the rule, even in serious publications, which results in the loss of potentially valuable insights into the present.

Almost all writers are careful to distinguish between the Arabs and the slew of other conquerors that came to Egypt who are considered foreign. Arabs are never referred to as foreign, and their conquest is called *el-fath el-Araby* (the Arab opening). Even researchers such as Gamal Hamdan,[183] who have not shied away from documenting some of the many abuses suffered by Egyptians at the hands of their numerous unsavory rulers throughout the long centuries of despotic rule, have gone to great pains to find something positive to write about the Arab conquest. Hamdan, for example, acknowledges that Arab "settler migration," changed Egypt irrevocably.[184] He describes the social dislocation and instability created by the policy of constant forced relocation of warring immigrant tribes adopted by some of Egypt's Arab rulers.[185]

He supports his findings by citing older sources such as el-Gabarti (early nineteenth century) as well as more recent sources like el-Aqqad (mid twentieth century). Yet he describes the Arab Islamic Empire as a "liberating empire" and claims that the Arabs, unlike the Europeans, did not come to Egypt as colonialists.[186] In contrast, he is very critical of European migration to Egypt during the late ninetieth and early twentieth centuries and refers to it disparagingly as "settler colonialism."[187] Although the figures that Hamdan cites: 216,580 Europeans immigrants to 11,189,978 Egyptians or 2 percent of the population,[188] clearly indicate that that migration was demographically insignificant, he does not attempt to contrast that migration with the earlier, and by his own acknowledgement, more demographically significant Bedouin migration. Hamdan concedes that the European migrants "introduced most of the modern industries" that were established in Egypt during that period, yet he claims very few had any skills and that most of them were criminals or adventurers.[189] He fails, however, to take his analyses of the impact of the Arab conquest to their logical conclusions and avoids discussing the level of education of the Bedouin immigrants, almost all of whom were illiterate.

The Mamluk, and to a certain extent, the Ottoman eras are the only historical periods open to analysis without the need to tread carefully. Mamluk rulers, while Muslims, were neither ethnic Arabs nor caliphs and are, therefore outside the tabooed area and fair game for the critics. Some segments of Egyptian society, however, are passionately opposed[190] to labeling the Turkish conquest an occupation on the basis that the Ottoman Sultan, though self-appointed, was the Caliph. Studies detailing the abusive aspects of that era are relatively plentiful, however, even though critical or objective analyses of the Arabs or the caliphs, both taboo areas, tend to be circumspect. One author, for example,[191] avoids using the term Arab in his analysis and instead uses the less common term *'Erban*. Although this term is a derivative of the same root word and has the same meaning,[192] perhaps the author felt that it obfuscated the issue somewhat when he discussed the never-ending cycle of pillage and plunder of Egyptian villages by Arab tribes during the historical period that he was examining. It is possible that this strategy served to make his critical statements vague enough to allow the reader, and perhaps even himself, a certain measure of cognitive dissonance

The numerous satellite television stations established in recent decades to spread the message of intolerance and extremism also play an increasingly prominent role in threatening those who might express a different viewpoint, often more or less openly advocating terrorism. One of these stations denounced the publication of a book entitled *Love in the Prophet's Life* and gave the address of the publisher to viewers, in a thinly disguised incitement to violence towards those who were deemed to have insulted the Prophet.[193] The only positive outcome of this was that the Egyptian company that owned the satellite found the thinly disguised incitement to murder embarrassing and canceled the station's contract.[194]

Even researchers who are prepared to risk writing about what are euphemistically referred to as sensitive subjects such as despotism are circumspect and reluctant to give the impression that they are criticizing the culture or *turath* (heritage or traditions) lest what they say may be taken as a criticism of religion. An example of this reluctance is the UNDP's Arab Human Development Report 2004 that was written by researchers from several Arab countries. The report was deservedly praised for its candor in reporting about the lack of democracy and basic freedoms in the Arab World.[195] It is significant, however, that the authors who had the courage to risk the ire of their governments as a result of their bluntness did not even tiptoe around anything that could be remotely pointed to as criticism of culture lest it be taken as a criticism of religion. The report does not shy away from expressing disapproval of the many constraints that Israel puts on Christian churches yet does not make a single reference to that topic in the course of its analysis of the Arab countries.[196] The authors go even further in their efforts at self-protection by making it absolutely clear that they are criticizing governments and policies and not the *turath* by stating, "Undoubtedly, the real flaw behind the failure of democracy in several Arab countries is not cultural in origin."[197] In spite of the clarity of their disclaimer, the authors still find it necessary to stress the purity of their intentions and the lack of any wish on their part to be critical of the culture by quoting one of the revered Guided Caliphs,[198] despite the fact that he had never claimed to be a champion of democracy or universal human rights. The authors' caution becomes even more obvious when they take their clarification a step further by quoting religious verses in support of their claim that writing about the need to respect human rights is not inconsistent with religious teachings.[199]

The intimidation practices have turned almost all aspects of Bedouin Arab customs and traditions into sacred cows. Critically addressing any of these sacred cows invites an endless list of charges that include "apostasy, being a [foreign] agent, treason, degeneracy, ignorance, plotting and stupidity."[200] It has led to a situation in which, one writer claims, the dead control the living and the only individuals in society allowed to discuss these topics are the self-appointed, mostly uneducated, preachers,[201] and opportunists seeking financial gain or celebrity. For example, a group of lawyers calling themselves "Lawyers without Restrictions," attempted to obtain a court ruling compelling the government to confiscate all copies of the *1001 Nights* book and to jail the ministry of culture officials who authorized the publication of what they deemed to be a book offensive to public morals.[202]

All writers and researchers across the Arab world are subjected to the same pressures and face the same dilemmas. The Iraqi historian Sayyar Al-Jamil has called repeatedly for a de-sanctification of Arab history and for subjecting it to open and objective critical analysis.[203] Ibrahim Badran, a prominent Palestinian educator, asserts that there is an utter historic failure in solving the problem of the state in most Arab countries and that despotism is widespread.[204] He is critical of the seemingly unbreakable attachment to the past of Arab societies in the areas of culture, language, religion, values, morals, thought, ideology, politics, and literature. He argues that this strong attachment inhibits social change and adaptation to new conditions and changing circumstances,[205] and results from focusing only on aspects of the past perceived as positive, ignoring the negative ones, and then proceeding to mold the present and the future through the "positive" lens of the past.[206] In spite of such a critical assessment, Badran is either being cautious or is unable to practice what he preaches since he finds no contradiction in digging into the past to support his argument. For example, he cites as evidence of the democratic credentials of a seventh-century ruler his mere statement that his expectations of obedience from his subjects were contingent upon his adherence to God's tenets.[207]

Such commendable, even though cautious, attempts at presenting reasoned arguments for democracy and freedom of thought are unlikely to sway the public. The small circle of Egyptian intellectuals who, in spite of the obvious risks, have persistently ventured into the dangerous terrain of suggesting that much of Wahabism reflects Bedouin cultural practices rather than religious tenets have been singularly ineffectual in stemming the tide of Wahabism. Appeals to sentiment and emotions being generally more effective than appeals to reason and rationality, the thinking minority has failed, at least until now, to persuade the emotive majority to put these practices into their appropriate cultural context.

Society Transformed

The outward appearances of religious practices have become all-consuming issues and a constant point of reference for the vast majority of the Egyptian public. Preachers have become permanent fixtures in sports clubs, schools, universities, and private homes; and a new breed of them has become more famous than box-office stars.[208] They are the most visible part of an extensive media campaign aimed at steering the pubic away from the traditionally moderate Egyptian approach to religion and towards the more rigid Wahabi Bedouin interpretation now broadcast from all media outlets. These broadcasts also serve to spread values such as fatalism and non-rational attitudes, that support and perpetuate underdevelopment, to solving normal everyday problems: for example, consulting jinn (genies)[209] who, according to some Saudi telepreachers, are not too difficult to contact as some of them communicate through Whatsapp Messenger.[210]

Some national newspapers devote a section to faith questions readers have sent in that have been forwarded to self-appointed opinion leaders who are presented as religious scholars and intellectuals and are afforded the opportunity to provide direction to the public. The questions reflect a level of ignorance found in segments of most, if not all, societies, and reveal little more than the fact that these segments view the world through a distorted prism.

What is more significant than the shallow thinking of what appears to be substantial segments of the public, and arguably of greater significance for this study, however, are the answers.

The following samples, although not scientifically drawn, nevertheless provide an indication of the public's concerns and of the attitudes that appear to be gradually spreading from a subculture that was on the fringes of society but has now begun to influence an increasing percentage of the population.

The questions cover a wide range of topics, but some of the recurring concerns include: the Jinn's religious beliefs;[211] the times of year when getting married would be a sin;[212] consulting fortunetellers and whether that is allowed.[213] Other readers want to know if it is a sin for females to vote in elections,[214] or for a couple to keep their marriage a secret, or for a man to marry a woman against her will.[215] Almost all questions call for a simple yes or no answer and the inquirers are presumably satisfied with the brief answers.[216] Potentially complex questions do, however, receive more detailed responses. One reader wanted to know whether the dead are aware of what is happening in the world of the living. A one time director of public relations at Al Azhar University,[217] assured the reader that the dead are indeed aware of what is happening in the world and that they especially keep up with family news.[218] Living family members' good deeds please the deceased relatives and their deviation from the path of righteousness saddens the deceased. The sheikh went on to add that records of all such behavior are presented to God for review [by some unnamed entity] on Mondays and Thursdays, and then on Fridays to the deceased parents of the living, whose "faces flush with happiness when they hear of their offsprings' good deeds."[219]

Fringe publications that cater to the interests of specific subcultures, whose members take such issues seriously but which mainstream culture may find amusing, are not an unusual phenomenon. The above reviewed questions and answers do not reflect such a phenomenon. They were published in the most prestigious national daily newspaper in the country, and the preoccupations and attitudes they express appear to be well on the way to becoming the prevalent mainstream culture in Egypt. Devoting space to these answers in the government owned media implies either an official endorsement of them, incompetence, or an inability to understand the implications of the new fad for a society that has suffered in recent decades from religious extremism and terrorism. This does not bode well for the future, since realistic and workable solutions to pressing economic, social, and political problems were needed yesterday.

Religion and the Lure of Celebrity

Capitulation to the new trend is widespread and has entered the hallowed corridors of Al Azhar University. Al Azhar has occupied a prominent place in Egyptian society since it was established over a thousand years ago. Its graduates have traditionally been viewed as the final authority on religious matters and revered by the public. Although some brilliant Azhar graduates such as Taha Hussein and Rifa'a el-Tahtawi were forward-looking and made significant and lasting contributions to society, the majority of Azharites have tended to be traditionalists who fought many progressive or modernizing influences, defended the status quo, and allowed themselves to be used by the rulers to further their purposes. Nevertheless, the Azhar has always reflected the Egyptian moderate tradition rather than the extremist Wahabi view of the world. However, the institution has begun to lose its dominance over religious matters in recent decades. Two of the factors that have contributed to the decline are government incompetence and the substantial flow of funds from the Arab Peninsula.

The same policies that contributed to the decline in the quality and standards of other institutions of higher learning in Egypt have impacted the Azhar, and its graduates are no longer as learned as they once were. Media reports of low standards, academic plagiarism among its professors, accusations of unprofessional conduct, and court cases involving a host of other irregularities have not helped the institution's standing in society.[220] In spite of the decline in prestige, however, Azharites are often invited to the oil countries either to teach in their newly established universities, to give public lectures on religious occasions, or to participate in public seminars. The financial rewards of these activities are considerable, and since the invitees are well aware that preaching the more moderate Egyptian tradition is unlikely to earn them return invitations, they, consciously or subconsciously, tend to adopt the extremist views of their host societies.

The proliferating number of Gulf owned satellite television stations play the same role of co-opting the Azharites and enticing them away from their traditionally conservative but tolerant position. With thirty-five percent of the airtime on radio and television slotted for religion, as a former minister of information admitted,[221] lucrative appearances on these stations, regardless of whether the broadcasting studios are in Egypt or the Gulf, dangle the prospect of possible fame and fortune. Several of the new breed of telepreachers, many of whom are not Azharites, have amassed considerable fortunes after these stations catapulted them to stardom.

The unavoidable result of the stampede towards these enticing television studios and of the constant search by telepreachers for new angles that might make them standout in a field that is becoming increasingly crowded and competitive is the constant barrage of *fatwas* (religious ruling) covering every conceivable aspect of daily life even down to the most trivial. Many of these *fatwas* are illogical, simplistic, or bizarre.[222] Perhaps one of the most bizarre fatwas was the one offered by one of the most popular telepreachers in Egypt, Abu Ishaq el-Hawini, who proposed a novel solution for solving the problem of poverty: legalizing the looting and enslavement of "nonbelievers." If two or three *ghazwas* (raids) were to be conducted every year, according to the sheikh, then the raiders would come home with valuable booty as well as several slaves that they could put to work, sell for extra cash, or take as concubines.[223] Another bizarre fatwa by a telepreacher calls for cutting off the hands of all those who take part in movie production because they are stealing time from the public.[224] The threat to society here lies more in the apparent inability to comprehend the startlingly heinous nature of such statements than in the warped minds that produce them and paved the road to the birth of Da'ish.

It may well have been the inability to resist the temptation to be different that led the respected Grand Mufti of Egypt to opine that a woman who gives birth four years after her husband's death may not have indulged in sex with anyone else after the death of her husband. The Grand Mufti justifies his ruling on the basis that there are records of such incidents having taken place in the past.[225] He cautions, however, that if the latent pregnancy were to last one day above the allowable four years, the woman would definitely be considered an adulteress.[226] The most charitable interpretation of this is that the man believes that the deceased can do more than merely observe the behavior of the living.

The attempt to stand out in the crowded field may well have been behind another bizarre *fatwa* supposedly intended to help women whose work environment necessitates spending time alone in an office with a male colleague, which is considered sinful. Stating that a woman breast-feeding a male colleague at least five times would create a symbolic mother-son relationship between them and sanction their meeting in the relative privacy of their offices,[227] the *fatwa* was rescinded by the Head of the Hadith Department of the Azhar University, but then confirmed by a prominent Saudi religious authority[228]

Expressing contradictory views on an issue does not appear to be problematic. One of the new wealthy media stars, Sheikh Qaradawi, an Egyptian Azharite who lives in Qatar, seems to be attempting to rise above the competition by simultaneously portraying himself as the face of moderation in a field of extremists while attempting to compete with them by trying to justify some acts of terrorism. For example, he condemns the killing of hostages in vague terms by declaring that the *shari'a* does not sanction these acts,[229] then goes on to provide a justification for the murders by citing the killing of two prisoners several centuries ago because they were "war criminals."[230]

In recent decades, religion has become a profitable business through television appearances, audiotapes, lectures, seminars, subsidized books, etc. The field has attracted individuals who have no religious education (physicians and pharmacists, for example)[231] but who are astute enough to see the profit potential in this new line of work. Obviously not all the aspirants fulfill their dreams of stardom, but the success of some, such as Amr Khalid,[232] a business school graduate whose income from the religious trade runs into millions, generates envy and provides a powerful incentive for others to compete for media recognition. And there is no shortage of those able to recognize the potential of this new market and ready to cater to it. When a Saudi businessman realized that the market for preachers addressing the urban segment of Egyptian society had become saturated, he sought new faces to address the rural population. The new stars-in-the-making sought to demonstrate their extremist credential to their benefactors by demanding the firing of all female presenters from the station in compliance with their view that it is a sin for women to work outside the house.[233] The demand certainly posed no hardship for the media entrepreneur who complied with it immediately.

The role of tacit official approval in promoting some of the more successful religious "authorities" and proponents of the imported values should not be underestimated. Nor should their influence. One such "authority" is the well-financed and well-connected geologist Zaghloul el-Naggar. His sojourn in the oil countries during the 1960s appears to have provided him with the prerequisites for becoming a media star and an influential opinion leader upon his return. He also appears to have a stamp of official approval and clearly benefits from frequently being granted whole pages in major national newspapers for his articles and from being a permanent guest on several Egyptian and Arab television channels. He is invited regularly to scientific research institutions where "scientists sit before him [listening] in amazement to his scientific discoveries."[234] In a glowing profile in the semi official newspaper *Al Ahram Weekly*, el-Naggar is described as having had "a brilliant academic career in the Gulf Arab countries."[235] He is credited with having inspired "millions of readers and viewers with his wit and wonderful revelations about natural science and the Quran."[236] El-Naggar is also described as being "open-minded and free in thinking."[237] He has "impeccable academic credentials as a scientist," claims the profusive profiler, and "is perhaps the leading Islamic authority on scientific facts as revealed in the Holy Quran."[238] El-Naggar regularly reminds his gullible audience of his scientific credentials and that he is utilizing scientific research and findings to explain the world in everyday language. Perhaps one or two examples of these "scientific" explanations might throw more light on both his message and his methodology. When asked to explain natural disasters such as hurricanes, floods and earthquakes, his reply was:

> I cannot find a better description of an earthquake than that mentioned in the Quran. The Quranic explanation is scientific. The word Earth is mentioned 461 times in the Holy Quran to describe the planet, its outer rocky cover or the soil section on top of that cover. There are 110 verses of geological interest.[239]

He explains the hidden significance of the proliferation of high-rise buildings by telling his readers in *Al Ahram* that the spread of such buildings around the world "is offensive to the earth and is a display of arrogance and reflects attempts to show off."[240] This, the professor goes on to explain, is a very significant development that portends a momentous event foretold by the archangel Gabriel, who stated that the signs of the approach of Judgment Day were that "the unclothed, barefooted, parasitic, sheep herders would reach up in their buildings."[241]

Another of el-Naggar's "scientific" discoveries is two short religious verses that apparently contain a complete explanation of the geological development of the planet earth from the day it was created, including explanations of: the continental drift, the nature of the earth's crust, the ice age, the development of mountains, and other geological areas of research.[242] Such explanations might sound amusing to the rational segment of the population, but the notion that the development of the planet earth from the Big Bang till today can be understood by reading two short verses has a great deal of appeal to many people.

There is nothing new or unusual about laypersons shying away from complicated scientific explanations of natural phenomenon and being attracted to simpler explanations. This occurs in every society. However, bizarre claims and theories tend to be found on the fringes of society and in publications that cater to the less scientifically inclined segment of the public. Those who wish to discover the scientific benefits of snake oil, for example, do not look for them in *The New York Times*, *The Washington Post*, the French *Le Monde*, or the British *Times*, *The Independent*, or *The Guardian*. Those who understand the beneficial properties of snake oil are also unlikely to be invited to explain them to the faculty of bona fide scientific research institutions. What makes the contemporary sellers of snake oil a real and imminent danger to Egyptian society is that they are so well financed that they are not selling the snake oil but giving it away free, are granted space in national publications, are invited to exhibit their wares at scientific institutions, and are provided with almost unlimited television exposure.

The rational minority finds itself swimming against a powerful tide that is perhaps better described as a tsunami, and television preachers, as one researcher has observed, have now replaced religious scholars as arbiters of religion.[243] For the majority of television viewers obsessed with trivia, myths, and downright fairytales, evening television shows or telephone calls to one of the numerous new oil-financed telepreachers hosting the shows are easier routes to the guidance they seek than reading the works of learned religious scholars. Consequently, the Bedouin owned or Wahabi inspired satellite channels have become very profitable enterprises that, through advertising income and telephone charges billed to viewers, quickly recoup their initial investment and turn a profit. In addition to being robbed of their culture and identity, Egyptian viewers with limited incomes are, therefore, also financing the already wealthy robbers in their task.

The Second Bedouin Invasion

Egypt is being subjected to a second invasion from the Arabian Peninsula that is no less serious or less determined than the 641 *"fath."* The troops of the second Arab invasion are very different from the troops of the first invasion. They are neither hungry, emaciated, or barefooted, nor dressed in tattered rags. Many arrive in Egypt carrying wads of cash, wearing their best quality, spotless white *thobes,* with their wives following in expensive, imported, designer fashions under their black head-to-toe *niqabs*. The culture that they bring with them, however, is much the same culture that they brought to the newly conquered country in the seventh century. They are not in a position to impose that culture on the Egyptians by force of arms as they did after the first invasion, but their determination to impose it has not abated. Cash is their new weapon and the substantial numbers of Egyptians who have been won to the Bedouin cause by various means aid them in the task of penetrating all levels of society and opening numerous fronts in their assault on Egyptian culture. The seemingly limitless funds available to these twenty-first century conquerors has allowed them to co-opt some decision makers or public figures, to either buy or take control of many Egyptian business enterprises, and to use their financial power to re-impose their Bedouin values on Egypt through a variety of other channels.

Many sidewalks in Egyptian cities are now littered with stands distributing books that are given either free of charge or sold for next to nothing. Some expensively produced hardback books sell for little more than the price of a packet of cigarettes. These books, without exception, contain bizarre and illogical myths and carry messages of ignorance, hate, and intolerance presented as religious principals. One example of these books was cited by Sayyid el-Qemany, a moderate Islamic scholar, as an example of the absurdity and hatred that these publications promote. The book is authored by two of the most influential Saudi sheikhs and is distributed free of charge in Egypt.[244] The religious *fatwas* offered in the book include the advice that passing the book to others would earn the reader a reward from God. The book then goes on to warn against any *bed'a* (the term means innovation, heresy, novelty, unorthodoxy) and tells the reader which direction to face, what to say, and how to breathe when drinking water from Zamzam (a water spring in Mecca).[245] The book also warns the readers against befriending non-believers or residing in their countries.[246]

When two journalists decided to investigate some of the bookshops distributing these imported books, they discovered that these establishments were well organized and integrated into an extensive distribution network.[247] The reporters also concluded that the aim of these publications is more ambitious than merely spreading the extremist Wahabi interpretation of religion. The aim, one of the journalists suggests, is to change Egyptian identity, heritage, and dress code, and replace them with the Bedouin culture and moral code.[248] The scale of the assault on Egyptian culture might be better put in perspective if we consider the recent press report that two million copies of these books in circulation are authored by only two of the numerous prominent Saudi preachers.[249] The books, as a small minority of Egyptian intellectuals have long suspected, are another component of an insidious campaign to change the very core of Egyptian society.

Another important medium that the invaders use very effectively to spread their cultural practices is audiotapes. Songs that extol violence and urge war against nonbelievers[250] and the lectures and sermons of established as well as aspiring telepreachers are recorded and the cassettes then sold at a price far below the cost of their production (about 0.19 U.S dollars).[251] Public transportation in the country appears to be a major target market for the producers of these tapes because passengers are captive audiences. They are forced to either listen to the tapes for the duration of their journey, or risk being branded as infidels or apostates if they complain to the driver. Although the Public Transportation Authority prohibits its drivers from playing these tapes on its buses, the ban, as the drivers freely admitted to a journalist, is not enforced. Some of these tapes appear to have been specially produced for the public transportation drivers and include appeals to them to spread the extremist message, advise them on the best strategies for doing so, and urge them to play the tapes to their passengers throughout their shifts. The "expression of disgust on some passengers' faces," that one driver admitted having noticed at times, does not deter him from playing the tapes.[252]

The invaders' determination to spread not just the Word but also their practices is reflected in the vast amounts of money they are willing to pour into the Nile, as one Saudi, the new owner of the Grand Hyatt Hotel in Cairo, demonstrated. The moment he took possession he declared his new acquisition alcohol-free and had eight million Egyptian Pounds worth of alcoholic drinks poured down the drain.[253]

More far-reaching than making the Nile fish drunk, or financing telepreachers and frauds such as el-Naggar to promote Wahabi ideology,[254] the natives of the Arabian Peninsula have extended their weapon of choice for indoctrination and coercion, the mass media, to stations based in Egypt. One Saudi owned satellite television station, for example, employs women presenters (mainly Egyptian) only if they agree to wear the *hegab*.[255] Pressure, mainly through financial inducements, is applied to the stations that may not adhere to Wahabi values and conventions to force them to fall in line.[256] One satellite television station that broadcasts from Egypt has decided to take the covering up of women one-step further by banning the *hegab*. Instead, the station requires all of its announcers to wear the *niqab*.[257]

Coercion has also severely affected the field of artistic production, with dire consequences for freedom of artistic expression, and the President of the Union of Artistic Syndicates has publicly admitted that representatives of Gulf companies and television channels already control artistic planning in Egypt.[258] Emissaries from the Arabian Peninsula arrive in Egypt with large bundles of cash[259] to bribe some performers to retire from acting, to purchase "stolen manuscripts and original copies of rare recordings of [classic] Egyptian movies, or to finance media attacks on democracy, secularism, and human rights."[260] Their interest in classic Egyptian movies is still unclear. Perhaps the intention is to take them out of circulation due to what is viewed as their immodest or liberal content. More likely, it is to use them as a marketing ploy to attract subscribers to their satellite television stations since throughout the Arabic speaking world these movies are very popular. With exclusive rights to these movies, the new owners can also edit them as they see fit, depriving the public, especially in Egypt, of their film heritage, and censoring the viewing of the adult audience.[261]

The Internet has become yet another effective tool for spreading the extremist ideology and changing Egyptian culture. Countless web sites propagating different aspects of the Bedouin Wahabi message have sprung up on the Internet. Some sites advertise books carrying their extremist message that are free or sold at a nominal cost; others give their visitors the option of downloading these books. Most sites have chat rooms and encourage dialogue between their members. Some have news sections in which they publish and comment on the news items that are of interest to them. Artwork and photographs, though generally viewed as sinful, are used at times to ensure that their visitors clearly understand their message. For example, one site has photographs of Egyptians singing religious songs and dancing in celebration of birthdays of holy men, and the visitors are urged to eradicate all these "un-Islamic customs."[262] Ironically this is a very different role for the Internet than the one played in the 2011 Egyptian revolution.

Beyond buying control of the means of mass communication and of artistic production in Egypt, the influence of petrodollars is evident in the financial and organizational strength of Egypt's extremist religious groups. These organizations now form an extensive web of offices, information and social service centers, distribution networks, and business enterprises that extend to every corner of the country, and virtually all of them receive funding and support in one form or another from the oil countries. Exposés of these entangled webs that some journalists have published and the government's anti money-laundering act have had little impact on these organizations. They appear to have become too entrenched in society to feel any negative effects from ineffectively enforced legislation or lone journalistic voices attempting to call attention to the outside sources that fund these determined campaigns and to the threat they pose to society.²⁶³

Successive Egyptian governments have been oblivious to the seriousness of the threat and of the significance of their decision, despite popular opposition, to cede two small islands in the Gulf of Aqaba,²⁶⁴ currently designated as a nature reserve, to Saudi Arabia. The Saudis are eager to build a bridge to link the islands to both Sinai and the Saudi and Egyptian coasts,²⁶⁵ which does not bode well for any future efforts to confront the further peril that ease of movement would pose to society.

Egypt is often described as the cradle of civilization, the "mother of the world" who in her gentle embrace casts a strange spell on those born there, and those who have adopted her as their home. With the complexity of such emotions mixed with the social, economic and political issues of today's reality, it is perhaps not surprising that it is a poet like Ahmad Abdel Mo'ti Hegazi who is able to express what is happening in contemporary Egyptian society simply and succinctly. Hegazi likens the current struggle for the soul of Egypt to the struggle between good and evil in the myth of the ancient gods Isis and Osiris and Seth²⁶⁶ in which Osiris and Isis represented goodness and fertility and his brother Seth represented evil and barrenness. The god and goddess of goodness and fertility won the battle in ancient Egypt, but in the twenty-first century, it is Seth who appears to be winning.²⁶⁷ Hegazi sees Egyptian parliamentary elections as symbolizing that struggle, with some candidates fighting hard for the privilege of being assigned one of the desert symbols (the camel or the palm tree) as their campaign logo. He contends that the desert has declared war against Egypt and that Egyptians have to take a position in that war.²⁶⁸ They have to decide whether to fight with the forces of the past, or of the future, the valley, or the desert. They should decide whether they are on the side of democracy, enlightenment, and human rights or despotism and enslavement. They should either stand with "the emissaries of enlightenment and creators of life, or with the terrorists and merchants of death. They should choose the banner either of Seth or of Osiris."²⁶⁹

The threat to Egypt's culture and wellbeing is real, but Hegazi's brave and persistent attempts at ringing the danger bell do not appear likely to stem the advance of the forces of darkness to which he refers. Those who might contemplate joining him in ringing the alarm bell risk retribution that could, and has at times, gone as far as murder. Dialogue with people who have the funds to buy media outlets, to turn their messengers into media stars that dominate the networks that they own, to co-opt intellectuals, to buy decision makers and who could murder those who persist in opposing them, is unrealistic. It also appears unlikely that decision makers will comprehend the seriousness of the threat in the near future. They understand the threat of terrorism but view it as purely a security problem. They do not seem to realize that the battle cannot be won as long as those who preach the ideologies promoting terrorism and nurturing terrorists, however indirectly or clandestinely, are allowed to spread their message and continue to breed future terrorists. A small ray of hope lies in the growing global recognition of the direct link between terrorism and organizations purporting to be educational or charitable but whose mission is to spread the culture of hatred and intolerance and inspire and finance terrorist acts.[270] Ignoring the overwhelming evidence of either implicit or explicit financing and support by private individuals and official bodies from the Arabian Peninsula for terrorist organizations around the world appears to be ending.[271] If that proves to be the beginning of a move to curtail the efforts of those who nurture and propagate the hate ideologies, Egypt would be a major beneficiary and would eventually be able to climb out of the despair now engulfing the country.

Afterword

Egypt once spawned a unique and magnificent civilization that prospered, despite some ups and downs, for four millennia until the death of the last Pharaoh. Cleopatra's death signaled the end of independence and the beginning of two thousands years of occupation by mostly unenlightened and despotic foreign rulers who systematically stripped the country of its resources, including scholars and craftsmen at one time, and shipped them to far away shores. The occupation eventually brought about the loss of the indigenous language, religion, culture, and social system that produced the ancient civilization.

Although the pharaonic civilization has long been dead, the ancients bequeathed their descendants an inheritance, not merely a heritage, in the impressive monuments that still, even today, provide millions of Egyptians with a living through tourism. While the ancient Egyptian genetic pool has been diluted over the centuries through intermarriage with the immigrant invaders, modern Egyptians must carry within them *some* trace of their ancient ancestors in their genes or their collective conscience. Would if be too fanciful to imagine that the spark that inspired the ancients to build their impressive edifices is still alive and hidden somewhere in the collective psyche? Perhaps. Perhaps for Egypt to emerge from the swamp it has been, and still is, struggling within, a conscious and concerted movement to draw on characteristics contained within the genetic code passed down through the ages is needed. Would it be unrealistic to hope that genes could effect this change at some future point in time? Or will Egypt continue to be swallowed up by the swamp?

Traces of ancient beliefs and social values are observable in contemporary Egypt, so perhaps there is something to build upon. The fear of chaos and willingness to relinquish a large measure of personal freedom to guarantee stability and social order, which has always played into the hands of despotic rulers, is probably one of the most easily observed social characteristics. Characteristics central to the Egyptian personality that survived through centuries of invasion: a *joi de vivre*, a live and let live attitude, an easygoing and relaxed approach to religion despite the enduring centrality of belief in personal lives, and a dislike of violence and tendency to opt for the more peaceful means of settling disputes, are cultural traits that are easily observable, making their decline today all the more obvious. Gone is the lightness of heart, the sense of humor and the jokes, and what has replaced them is a smoldering anger expressed in rampant sexual harassment, a greater rigidity in belief (discussed in detail earlier), and altercations leading to actual physical violence rather than merely the exchange of loud insults and oaths. Have these traits become so embedded in the culture as to make it impossible to discard them, or are they little more than passing responses to current problems?

The ancients' influence endures even in the Arabic language imposed by the seventh century conquerors and still used in modern Egypt. Some aspects of Egyptian Arabic: its grammar, vocabulary and phonology, reflect the influence of the Coptic language, the language of the ancients that has developed into the language of the Coptic Church

The pharaonic heritage is also easily observed in many of the rituals connected with celebrating happy or commemorating sad occasions. For example, *el-sebou'* (the seventh) which is the naming *ceremony* that takes place a week after the birth of a baby, which only began to die out in recent decades, was celebrated in much the same way that it was in ancient times. The family gathered together after the baby was bathed and dressed in new clothes, then salt was scattered on the mother and around the house to keep the evil eye away and the baby was carried around the house by the family carrying candles and singing. Then it was the grand parents' turn to make loud noises, usually by banging a mortar and pestle while bidding the baby to obey its father and mother, after which sweets were distributed to everyone.

Even religious celebrations have retained some elements of the ancient culture. Celebrations commemorating the *mouled* (birthday) of Abul Haggag in Luxor in Upper Egypt take place where his shrine was built on the site of an earlier Christian church, which in turn had been erected on top of a pharaonic temple. The event is celebrated in a manner almost identical to the Apet (also spelt Opet) festival that reenacts the god Amon's journey from Luxor temple down the Nile to meet with his consort the goddess Mut. Other customs such as visiting graves and distributing specially baked bread on feast days, and burying the dead in underground rooms rather than straight in the earth or sand are all pharaonic customs.

While these vestiges of the ancient culture that have survived through the millennia seem today to be fading at a precipitous rate under the external influences the country faces, could a concerted, multi-faceted effort to reverse this trend offer hope? Does today's population still have the ability to build a society that their distant forefathers might have viewed as an achievement to be proud of? The pessimists among contemporary Egyptians believe that this is beyond the abilities of today's population. They maintain that the builders of the pharaonic civilization are long dead and gone and the sense of continuity, common identity, culture and social values that made past achievements possible have been replaced by the imported, inward-looking, exclusionist, misogynist, Bedouin culture and social values which now, to a large extent, define the Egyptians' worldview. That, they assert, is *the* major reason for the country's seeming inability to join the modern world or to construct a society that might have been able to provide better opportunities for its youth, a more meaningful and satisfying life, and better living standards for all its members. This viewpoint contends that Egypt's fate was sealed long ago. The vagaries of fate, an accident of geography, gifted Egypt with the Nile but located it in a bad neighborhood whose poverty-stricken and unhappy inhabitants had always, understandably, envied Egypt's people and coveted its riches. Thus its destiny was sealed centuries ago and has precluded the possibility of a renaissance any time in the foreseeable future. This viewpoint cannot be dismissed out of hand. Culture and social values are the main determinants of social development, and cultural change is a prerequisite for modernity. While possible, that change, widely researched and reported upon by social scientists, is extremely difficult both to achieve and to influence.

This seems to be especially true of the Bedouin culture. What is perhaps unique in this case is the culture's continuing ability to resist outside influences despite the loss of the remoteness and isolation that protected it in the past from the outside world. The veneration of some of its adherents for some millennium-old practices, such as the tradition of pillage, illustrates this unique imperviousness to outside influences and is illustrated in, for example, the continuous regard for and use of the term itself. Obviously one of the secrets of the culture's consistency in preserving much of its core values unchanged is the severe punishment imposed on violators of a variety of its norms.

These traits would not be as critical to study if it were not for the fact that oil wealth has given its adherents an immense ability not only to preserve the status quo where it originated but to influence the outside world way beyond its own neighborhood. This book, even though it frequently refers to Bedouin culture, does not, however, attempt to analyze or explain such resistance but leaves it to future researchers.

In contrast to this lack of any substantial cultural evolution, the common creative experience of building a civilization in the distant past is embedded in the Egyptian national psyche. If this is preserved in what Wilhelm Reich and Carl Jung termed the collective unconscious, with the right approach perhaps it could be recaptured and relied upon to aid in the construction of a society that is able to provide its members with better and more fulfilling lives.

An impartial and objective examination of the historical developments that gave rise to contemporary society and to the current problems is, however, a fundamental prerequisite for achieving that goal. Only then might it be possible for Egyptians to feel a sense of purpose and enough national confidence to resist the tenacious attempts to foist upon them the mode of dress, customs, and social practices of a preliterate nomadic tribal group. Only then might it be possible to begin the process of regaining a native identity that has been overwhelmed by specious imported identities, by the imported exclusionist social values that promote stasis, inertia, and fear of the other, all of which are inimical to modern life.

Appendix

Gamal Abdel Nasser

Nasser cast such a giant and lasting shadow over the country that studying the dramatic changes in Egypt during the 1950s and 60s is, as some authors have observed,[1] almost synonymous with studying Nasser himself. The task is somewhat complicated by the paucity of biographical material on him, especially during the early formative years of his childhood and youth.[2] The most reliable means of gaining insight into his character are his public utterances, actions, and policies. The mountain of books and articles written about the adult Nasser by academics, journalists, and those who worked with him, or were influenced by him or his policies, constitute another resource providing the material is treated with caution. Much of what has been written is polemical, and portrays him either as the image of perfection or the incarnation of evil. Some works are no more than attempts to settle old scores,[3] which makes them too subjective to be reliable; others are too full of praise to be wholly believable.[4] Nevertheless, careful analysis of some of the works about Nasser and examination of his policies, conduct, and patterns of behavior do provide us with enough material to draw a reasonably accurate portrait of the man.

Vatikiotis identifies three stages of Nasser's personal and political development. The first stage was his unhappy early life when the main stimuli behind his actions were his feelings of alienation, isolation, and despondency.[5] The second stage provided a measure of stability when he found refuge in the military for his instinctive traditionalism and his inborn tendency to be domineering.[6] The third stage was his experience in the 1948 Palestine war, when his main stimuli were feelings of dishonor and disgrace at the loss on the battlefield and the loathing for the political régime that was responsible for it.[7] Several sources have suggested that Nasser's interest in acquiring power seems to have developed during the latter part of the second stage and during the third stage, between 1946 and 1949. It was during that period that his juvenile yearning for fame as a novelist, reflected in an unfinished novel, seems to have been sublimated and replaced by a craving for political control of the country.[8]

Upper Egyptian Roots

Nasser was born on January 15, 1918 in cosmopolitan Alexandria, the son of a barely literate[9] minor clerk in the Egyptian postal service. His father had moved there from Bani Murr, a village in Upper Egypt where some Arab tribes, from one of which his grandfather claimed descent, had settled after the Arab invasion. Contemporary *sa'idis* tend to be more socially conservative than *bahari's* (those who come from Lower Egypt), and the area traditionally suffered from regular outbreaks of violence, insurgency, and lawlessness,[10] suggesting that the area's relative remoteness enabled the Arab settlers to retain some of their Bedouin social values.[11] Even today, there are periodic media reports that suggest that Bedouin social values and a propensity to disregard the law are still widespread in some of these isolated pockets of the country.[12] A socio-cultural background rooted in tribal nomadic traditions, combined with his father's humble rank in society would, in all likelihood, have provided the foundation for several of Nasser's character traits. Nasser apparently felt pride in his Arab roots and seems to have shared the durable emotional attachment that some contemporary *sa'idis* have to their Arab ancestors who migrated to Egypt after the seventh century invasion.

He also seems to have shared the attitude, sometimes held by earlier immigrants to a country, that those who arrive later than them do not quite belong. His ancestors had come to Egypt, perhaps centuries earlier, as part of the occupation forces and had been partially assimilated with the passage of time. Nevertheless, their attachment to their Arab roots remained strong, and Nasser appears to have retained the original Arab conquerors' view that ethnic Arabs are the only people entitled to make Egypt their home and become Egyptians. He seems to have denied that possibility to later non-Arab immigrants and, often used the term "Egyptianized"[13] disparagingly in his speeches to refer to descendants of later non-Arab arrivals such as the royal family whose founder, Mohammed Ali, had arrived in Egypt only a century and a half before the coup. He seems to imply that the only 'real' Egyptians are the Arab immigrants. In this sense, his attitude appears to echo the attitude of his Bedouin Arab ancestors who nursed a deep grievance against the Mamluks. The Bedouin Arabs, especially those who settled in Upper Egypt constantly rebelled against the Mamluks, who were not ethnically Arab,[14] because they believed that being Arab gave them more right to rule the country.[15] The Arabs' feelings towards the country they conquered and lived in also appear to have been those of possession rather than of belonging. Ironically, Mohammed Ali, the Albanian great grandfather of the man that Nasser exiled, who was born in the Macedonian town of Kavala[16] and whom most historians refer to as the founder of modern Egypt, appears to have felt a stronger emotional commitment to Egypt and its potential than Nasser, who was born in Egypt.

Social conservatism that is often expressed in restrictive attitudes towards women and their position in society, in xenophobic tendencies, and in an exaggerated sense of personal dignity and pride are among the most prominent characteristics of this *sa'idi* cultural background, and Nasser took great pride in identifying with that background.[17] These classic *sa'idi* traits that Anwar el-Sadat observed in Nasser[18] can be seen then as the normal outcome of his childhood experiences and of the socialization practices of the Upper Egyptian families that came from lower middle-class segment of society. Great concern with honor and appearances, wariness in all interpersonal relationships, suspicion of outsiders, and social conservatism are all traits that are nurtured in this environment.

Such social conservatism continued to be a prominent feature of Nasser's personality throughout his rule and a major influence on his policies as well as on his personal conduct. His wife, for example, always stayed in the background and her photograph was rarely seen in the media. She was never featured on the national scene even in connection with what are termed women's issues, often a first lady's favorite public relations role. His *sa'idi* attitudes were too deeply entrenched to allow for the possibility of making a superficial concession to appearances, or even to the demands of the role of head of state.[19]

Nasser's conservative ideas about women [20] extended beyond his own family and clearly created something of a conflict since they often jarred with those of other leaders he admired and wished to emulate. After Nasser attended the Bandung Conference of Non-Aligned Nations in 1955, he began to see himself as a world leader of the caliber of Nehru of India and Tito of Yugoslavia, and their opinions of him apparently mattered to him. When Tito was on one of his frequent visits to Cairo, his wife commented to Nasser on the absence of women in leadership positions on the Egyptian national stage. The comment evidently had an impact on Nasser because as soon as his guests left he announced, to everyone's surprise, that he had decided to appoint a woman minister for the first time in Egypt. When Amer, another socially conservative *sa'idi*, heard of this development, he vowed that he would not serve in a Cabinet with a female colleague. Being mindful of Amer's feelings, Nasser waited until Amer left the Cabinet to become vice-president and went ahead and appointed Dr. Hekmat Abu Zaid to the ministry of social affairs.[21] Researchers acquainted with Egyptian cultural practices, however, were aware that the act reflected his concern with appearance rather than the progressive and modernizing attitudes still prevalent in Egypt until the sixties,[22] and the selection process provides ample evidence of the hollowness of the gesture. Nasser, to the surprise of his staff, asked for photographs of prospective candidates despite the fact that he knew most of them. It became apparent after the appointment that Nasser had been staring at these photographs in search of the least attractive candidate to avoid the possibility that anyone might think that the new minister was selected because she had an inappropriate personal relationship with him. Apparently, the strategy was successful because Amer often mocked the unfortunate appointee afterwards, telling his colleagues that Nasser tricked them all into believing that they had a woman with them in the Cabinet.[23]

Early Life

Nasser, under the dictates of an unaffectionate father, was shunted back and forth during his early life between relatives and friends and separated from the mother to whom he was very attached, which can only have been unsettling to the young boy. The loss of his mother at the age of eight would have been a major traumatic event for Nasser and was compounded by the humiliation of learning of her death and of his father's hasty remarriage only when he returned home for the summer break.[24] That hasty remarriage and the life-long gulf between father and son[25] were probably among the causes of Nasser's insecurity, caution, secretiveness, and lack of concern for others, as well as his feeling of humiliation and exaggerated concern with pride.[26] These inherent *sa'idi* traits, exacerbated by his difficult relationship with his father, seem to have combined into a need for total control. Although soft-spoken, he was single-minded, and had, in Jean Lacouture's terms, an "almost native taste for deviousness."[27] He was cunning and suspicious[28] of everyone, a zealous schemer,[29] and a bitter, manipulative, and street savvy individual.

Teenage Influences

Other aspects of Nasser's character are likely to have been rooted in his high school and military experiences (1933 to 1937, and 1937 to 1952). That period is, as Vatikiotis points out, key to understanding Nasser's web of complex passions, sentiments, and urges that were often in conflict with one another. His inflated sense of his own dignity went hand in hand with humiliating others. He publicly promoted modernization, while at heart he was a conservative adherent to traditional *baladi* values who carefully guarded the privacy of his family life. His belief in epic romantic ideals and of himself as the romantic hero meting out justice went hand in hand with indecisiveness, cynical and callous egotism, self-protectiveness, a proclivity for scheming, and a propensity for the limelight.[30]

Nasser's high school readings of Mahmoud Abbas el-Aqqad and Tawfiq el Hakim appear to have left a lasting impression on him.[31] The former wrote at length about heroic personalities in

Muslim history, and the latter explored the theme of Egypt's rejuvenation and rebirth at the hands of a leader endowed with extraordinary talent and a strong personality.[32] These writings were probably the most likely sources of his dreamy and idealistic notions of gallantry and valor,[33] and the turbulent political debates of the 1930s and 1940s were bound to have left their mark on him.[34]

Sharing the same uncertainties and anxieties of his generation, and coping with his tense family relationship and insecurity about his future made him ripe for recruitment to the Young Egypt Society. Its fiery and impassioned utterances and proclamations would have been too enticing for him to resist, and the most discernible influence on Nasser's political formation was his reading of the Society's fervently anti-British articles in their newspaper, *el-Sarkha*, in addition to the tenets espoused by the Muslim Brothers and el-Wafd's blue shirts.[35]

The Young Egypt Society's espousal of a program that was a mix of religion, quasi-fascism, anti-colonialism, and xenophobia, and that called for land reform, social justice, and the violent overthrow of the government[36] appealed to Nasser's inborn tendencies and internalized social values,[37] and he joined the group two or three years after it was formed.[38] These were the same sentiments that drew him to the Muslim Brothers[39] and to developing a close personal friendship with one of its major theoreticians Sayyid Qotb, whom he trusted and appointed as his cultural advisor after the coup.[40] For Nasser, the ardent and stirring mix of patriotism, religion, and politics fused his personal apprehensions and dilemmas with the national turmoil.[41] The society's rhetoric offered Nasser simple, or in the view of some observers, simplistic, answers to both levels of his concerns.[42]

The influence of the Young Egypt Society on Nasser's political development is clearly reflected in the similarity between the writings of Ahmad Hussein, the group's founder, and Nasser's clandestine activities and early policies.[43] Nasser's social and political profile placed him squarely in the socio-economic class that one researcher termed "the new *effendiyya*," who divided the world into east and west and placed Egypt into the "eastern"[44] sphere as opposed to the Mediterranean or "western" where European educated intellectuals such as Taha Hussein placed it.[45] Many of the members of this society came from a similar background to Nasser, and the parallels between that group's ideas and the Free Officers' goals, as well as the fact that some of its members were appointed to senior positions after Nasser took power, also seem to support the claim of the groups' influence on Nasser's political views.[46] Fathi Radwan, one of the society's founders who knew both Nasser and Ahmed Hussein well, maintains that Nasser was a great admirer of Ahmed Hussein, looked up to him as a role model, and imitated his style of public speech.[47]

Although he was heavily influenced by the ideas of the Young Egypt Society and the tenets of the Muslim Brothers, there is little concrete evidence that Nasser involved himself much in either of the two groups' political activities. The state controlled media during Nasser's reign and some of Nasser's biographers have tended to magnify his participation in student demonstrations against corrupt governments and the British occupation. These political events, however, as Vatikiotis points out, were unlikely to have been major influences on his character formation.[48] Accounts of Nasser's earlier political struggles on behalf of patriotic causes and of his being injured (in fact slightly) in one of the demonstrations could probably be more accurately viewed through the lens of the hero building, myth making, and sycophancy that were integral ingredients of the Nasser era.

College Experience

One of the other factors that played a role in shaping Nasser's personality was his military college experience. The Egyptian military, unlike the European, was not an institution that was shaped and molded by an elite segment of society and characterized by a well-developed subculture of distinctive social values and ethics.[49] Furthermore, the 1936 agreement with Britain had allowed Egypt more freedom of action in the area of defense, which Britain had previously been solely responsible for. This in turn necessitated an increase in the size of the army. As a result the government relaxed the entrance requirements to the military college, and the number of the newly admitted cadets were Muslims who hailed from socioeconomic backgrounds that were closer to the bottom than the top of the social scale.⁵⁰ Nasser's admission to the military college in March 1937, therefore, did not signal an entrée into a well-defined subculture or an exclusive club. He was not joining an elite officer corps and beginning a process of being socialized into its long established rites, ceremonies and distinctive military ethics and traditions. Instead, he was joining a group of young men many of whom came from similar socio-economic backgrounds to his and had similar social and political experiences and views.⁵¹ He was, as would be expected of a serious young man who saw life in a military barracks as the only escape from an unhappy home life,⁵² a single-minded student throughout his one and a half years at the college. A military uniform must have been a powerful incentive for him, holding out as it did the prospect of the authority, personal respect, social esteem, economic security, and opportunity for a role in politics that he craved.⁵³

He had no public political involvement, however, until 1945,⁵⁴ and seems to have jealously guarded his privacy and anonymity.⁵⁵ His excessive concern with pride and dignity, which was an integral part of his personal makeup from early in his life, does not appear to have been ameliorated by donning the military uniform. The uniform may in fact have intensified it since dignity became a recurring theme in his speeches after he came to power.⁵⁶ President Sadat's first impression of Nasser when he met him in 1939 soon after his graduation from the military college was that he was serious, touchy, and humorless.⁵⁷ Although he listened attentively to his colleagues' political discussions, he kept himself apart from them and did not like his colleagues to joke with him lest they insulted his dignity. As a result, they all avoided him.⁵⁸

Political Education

Although a man of very limited formal education, who may in fact have never read an entire book other than those required in the Military College,⁵⁹ and *The Prince* by Machiavelli, which he claimed to have read seventeen times,⁶⁰ he was a fervent reader of the print news media.⁶¹ That passion for news must have served him well when he was assessing the possible implications of the coup he was contemplating prior to 1952. Attuned to the Young Egypt Society and the Muslim Brothers through his own involvement with these groups, the knowledge of local and international political developments that he gleaned from these publications would have been useful in assessing both the foreign and other local players on the Egyptian political scene before the coup. Nasser had also been introduced to the prominent journalist Ahmad Abul Fath six years before the coup.[62] He visited him on a regular basis to engage in political discussions, and must have benefited from his considerable knowledge, insight, and experience. During that period and through the first few months after the coup Nasser was apparently a good listener,[63] and he appeared to have been drawn to the company of journalists.

Nasser's shallow view of the world could, therefore, probably be directly attributed to his almost total reliance on oral discussions, newspapers, and magazines as sources of information, rather than books in which the topics addressed could be examined in more depth. His offer of the premiership to Ahmad Lutfi el-Sayyid shortly after the coup[64] is indicative of his sketchy knowledge of the intellectual currents in the country. He was obviously unfamiliar with el-Sayyid's writings and did not know that his views on national identity were radically different from those Nasser himself had formulated from the newspapers that he had been reading. Unlike Nasser, who eventually expunged the word Egypt from the map and replaced it with the word Arab, el-Sayyid's long held view was that denying one's Egyptian identity amounted to treachery and self-hatred.[65]

He never formulated a clear ideology that informed his policies and tended to see the world in simplistic terms where everything was either black or white with no shades of grey. *The Philosophy of the Revolution*,[66] published soon after he assumed power, provides clear evidence of this lack of ideological focus. Nasser may have claimed to be a socialist, and many of the policies that he implemented were indeed socialist. The motives that drove these socialist policies, however, were anything but socialist. Nasser used socialist terminology, but there is much anecdotal evidence to suggest that his sentiments were neither ideological nor idealistic. Many of those around Nasser have readily admitted to his lack of political focus. Khalid Mohi el-Din maintains in his memoirs that Nasser was not a socialist but that he did edge towards socialism and implemented socialist policies to appease the workers and peasants.[67] This is evident in his hackneyed, clichéd, and tangled public statements about his version of socialism.[68] He certainly did not tolerate committed socialists, whom he hounded, jailed, and tortured or murdered, as happened with Professor Shohdi Attia in 1960.[69] The triteness of Nasser's socialist policies is illustrated in a statement that he made to Hassan Abbas Zaki, one-time Minister of the Treasury, of Economics, and of External Trade, as well as Deputy Prime Minister. Zaki once asked Nasser why he wanted to implement socialism.[70] Nasser's surprising answer was that he was convinced that people wanted him to implement socialism because whenever he went to an Om Kalthoum[71] performance people clapped whenever she sang, "you [Nasser] are at the forefront of all the socialists."[72]

His early associations with the right wing MB, the Young Egypt Society, and left leaning officers such as Mohi el-Din show that he was searching for an ideology, but his actions and statements also show that he never fully committed himself to one. His decision to publish a left leaning newspaper showed that his concern with appearance remained a stronger motivation than any socialist notions. The reason that he gave Mohi el-Din for wanting the newspaper was that he felt a sense of dishonor at not having a leftist newspaper like other Arab countries and that he wanted an evening paper because it would have smaller readership.[73]

There were other decisions that might, mistakenly, have appeared to be motivated by a socialist impulse but were nothing more than a reflection of personality issues such as a family or childhood issue,[74] or negative feelings towards land owners and the financial and social elite,[75] or fear that the wealthy could pose a danger to his régime and should be stripped of their resources.[76] Whatever the motivation behind Nasser's pursuit of socialist policies, it certainly was not his belief in socialist principles. It was not ideology but animosity towards the socio-economic elite, self-protection, and/or his pedestrian and simplistic views of complex issues that were most likely at the root of Nasser's socialist policies. These same characteristics also appear to be at the root of his impulsive behavior, and examples of spur of the moment decisions in a variety of situations are not difficult to find. Cabinet ministers,[77] military commanders, and government employees were often hired and fired on a whim.[78]

More serious was the impact of this impetuosity on foreign relations. Unsubstantiated reports led him once to make a speech attacking and insulting the United States and on another occasion to sever diplomatic relations with Iran.[79] Decisions affecting the nation were, it seems, frequently nothing more than reflections of Nasser's moods.[80] Nasser never managed to develop a political insightfulness or acuity that matched his stature as the leader of the Arab World. His simplistic and shallow worldview contrasted sharply with the high level of respect that he commanded as an influential Third World player on the world stage. In spite of his near absolute power, and his unprecedented popular appeal, Nasser remained no more than an able conspirator whose defeat in the 1967 war was precipitated by a mundane and simplistic view of the world and an absence of meaningful political insight into what happened during the Suez crisis of 1956.[81] Even those who knew Nasser well never ceased to be taken aback by his one-dimensional approach to matters of vital importance.

His shallow grasp of state affairs was reflected in his statement to a colleague that he had "discovered" Israel's war objectives by reading a British newspaper.[82] This simplistic approach extended even to technical military details that were presumably his forte, his field of special expertise that his media touted by reminding the public on occasion that he used to teach in the Staff College. Yet the questions he asked General Kamal Hassan Ali[83] after the 1967 Israeli invasion surprised him by their simplicity and the lack of knowledge they reflected.

In Nasser's Egypt, every aspect of life became a reflection of one aspect or another of his personality quirks and idiosyncrasies. His social conservatism, his impulsiveness, and his simplistic worldview all influenced life in Egypt during that period. Nasser's burning, almost monomaniacal need for power and total control, coupled with his equally unhealthy obsession with secrecy, meant that virtually all major, as well as countless minor and inconsequential decisions, were made solely by him. These personal traits, combined with Nasser's impetuousness and dreams of being Egypt's savior, noted by Vatikiotis,[84] his *sa'idi* background, and the fact that he never seemed to outgrow his role as a secret conspirator, are probably the most logical explanations for many of his actions.

Governing Style

The promulgation of a new constitution on January 16, 1956 and the dissolution of the RCC removed the last vestige of collective leadership and signaled that Nasser was well on the road to absolute power. That power was soon demonstrated in June of that year when a plebiscite was held and Nasser was elected president of Egypt by 99.8 percent of the voters.[85] Thereafter, holding a plebiscite became a favorite practice, and several were held during Nasser's reign, always with the same impressive results, and Nasser himself began to believe these results[86] despite having rigged them himself.[87]

Nasser had a need to strive for total control of what takes place in the country, and that was reflected in his choices for top positions such as vice-president and ministerial posts. He was convinced that he had all answers to all problems and eventually cast out all independent thinkers from his inner circle. Khalid Mohi el-Din, for example was exiled, tamed, and given editorship of a low circulation evening newspaper shortly after the military coup. Zakaria Mohi el-Din and Abdel Latif el-Boghdadi were sidelined and resigned eventually. That Anwar Sadat and Hussein el-Shafei were the only members of the original conspiracy who remained with him until he died was no accident. The former was smart enough to give the impression of being unambitious, vacuous, and compliant throughout his association with Nasser. Hussein el-Shafei on the other hand was apparently the ideal candidate for high position. Nasser described him as the best member of the RCC, as a God-fearing nonviolent man who was useless and neither did any good nor caused any harm because all he cared about was his moustache, the way he put on his beret, and being photographed at an angle that showed his good looks.[88]

Mustafa Amin, the journalist and onetime Nasser informer[89] reports that Nasser told him on one occasion that he planned to appoint some intellectuals to ministerial positions and asked Amin to compile for him a list of possible candidates. When Amin complied with the request, Nasser rejected all the nominations saying, he was looking for ministers that he could manage not ones who would manage him.[90] Sadat's statement that Ali Sabry's fear of taking responsibility for making any decisions had been the reason that Nasser selected him for the premiership adds creditability to Amin's anecdote.[91] Mahmoud Fawzi was another of Nasser's favorite appointees who never fell afoul of Nasser and served for years as minister of foreign affairs. He was another member of Nasser's team who was referred to as a Man of the Hour/Clock[92] behind his back.[93]

Nasser never wavered in his belief that he knew best, in his determination to keep a tight hold on the reins of power, or in his refusal to entrust the Cabinet with any major decisions. This was true even in the aftermath of the 1967 disaster when he was announcing to the public that he was in the process of making radical changes in the way that he ran the country by allowing voices other than his to be heard. His statement to his intelligence chief, Salah Nasr, provides a clear indication of his intended policy. He told Nasr that he did not want anyone to "philosophize and state his opinion,"[94] and that simply listening to him and carrying out his orders are what he expected of everyone around him.[95] This leaves no doubt whatsoever that contrary to his public statements; it was business as usual as far as Nasser was concerned. The Cabinet would continue to be merely a stage for him and a forum where the ministers were no more than passive participants.[96] They were expected simply to be attentive, write down his directives, and not attempt to discuss the merits of any of these instructions, and he was liable to explode in anger if any of them broached a topic that displeased him.[97] Nasser ran the country as a private fiefdom, or as a powerful Bedouin chief ran his tribe. He appeared to view social and political institutions and processes as either part of the décor or as mere personal sources of information or tools of control. Hassan Sabry el-Kholi, who was his personal representative reported that in his ten years in the post, he met with Nasser alone twice, and both times were at his (el-Kholi's) own request.[98] Hussein Zolfiqar Sabry, his foreign affairs advisor confided to a friend that the only question that Nasser ever asked him was after he had been his advisor for nine months. They had both been at the wedding of a senior officer and as Nasser passed Sabry's table, he asked him how he was.[99]

Means of Political Control

The extensive security apparatus, which formed a significant mainstay of Nasser's régime and kept tight control of every segment of society, was a reflection of his belief in secrecy and need for total control. By the mid-fifties, Nasser had established the Military Investigations Office, the Military Intelligence Organization, the General Intelligence Organization, and the General Investigations Organization.[100] Secret cells were formed within the military and among the students at the Military College.[101] Another security organization attached to the office of the president was assigned the task of spying on government departments and high-ranking officials,[102] and eventually tens of thousands of ordinary citizens were recruited to these organizations[103] which gave him control of almost every aspect of life in Egypt.[104] He encouraged competition between all the security organizations,[105] and promoted fear to sustain this competition[106] by assigning the same task to individuals who were known to mistrust each other[107] while he himself never fully trusted any of them.[108]

His long-time aide, Sami Sharaf, provides a glimpse of the minute details[109] that Nasser was interested in. Sharaf recounts with pride in his memoirs that Nasser knew the smallest details of everything that took place in the country and that if an inconsequential chat between any two individuals meeting in a club touched upon political subjects or certain activities, he would hear about it and submit a report about the conversation to Nasser.[110] If a group of people sat together, somewhere like the Gezira Sporting Club for example,[111] and criticized him, Nasser was told about it. Even jokes were reported to him and analyzed. Another example recounted by Sharaf is of an obscure schoolteacher who once made a joke using inappropriate language (sexual innuendo) and it was reported to Nasser who was offended by it.[112]

Social psychologists researching small group dynamics have shown that as a group size begins to increase, so does the number of possible combinations of alliances within the group. Nasser seems to have been instinctively aware of that and to have relied upon inter-personal rivalries, differences of opinion, and shifting alliances to keep abreast of all currents within his original small group of conspirators and to keep a firm grip on it. There was always someone willing to tell him who said or did what, and his knowledge of what might have been no more than petty quarrels, casual conversations or inconsequential tidbits of gossip were useful tools that helped him to manipulate the group.

He sincerely believed that he could manage the whole society in the same manner as he did the original group, that the resources of the state and the vast number of spies would enable him to continue using the same tactics to run the country that had been effective in controlling his original group. He took the time to listen to reports about taped casual conversations and mete out punishments[113] for the type of minor indiscretions or inconsequential infractions that many people, let alone heads of state, would have had neither the time nor the inclination to listen to.[114]

While eavesdropping and acting upon casual conversations might have satisfied an apparent streak of pettiness in Nasser's character, they also gave him a sense of control over the people that he dealt with. The taped conversations gave him something to threaten others with, and he seemed to enjoy delivering the threat personally at times. For example, he once made a prominent journalist listen to recordings of a tryst with his mistress[115] and did the same to one of his Cabinet members.[116] Ironically, Nasser's passion for total control and his inability to accept the physical impossibility of one man listening in on every conversation in the country allowed those around him to have some control over him by being selective in terms of what tidbits of gossip they passed on and convincing him to fire[117] or jail[118] their rivals or enemies.

Both the Muslim and Christian religious establishments were brought under control. For example, Abdel Hakim Amer was given direct control of the Sufi organization. The Grand Sheikh of el-Azhar was no longer elected by senior religious scholars but appointed by Nasser, and similar mechanisms were utilized to control the Christian organizations' appointments to leadership positions.[119]

The press fell under Nasser's control even before it was nationalized. Censorship, opportunism, fear, and sycophancy were his weapons of choice in that field. Forty-two newspapers were closed down soon after the coup[120] and new ones such as *el-Gomhuriyya* were established. Cooperative journalists, such as the former king's press secretary, Karim Thabet, who published his memoirs demonizing the king that he once praised, were in abundance. Even prominent journalists were not immune to sycophancy,[121] but Mohammed Hassanein Heikal who came from a more humble social stratum, was pushier, and better motivated, managed to push them all out of the way and soon became Nasser's confidant.[122]

Those who did not fall in line immediately were fired,[123] often for obscure,[124] insignificant,[125] or even unspecified missteps,[126] or publicly accused of receiving secret allowances from previous governments to sully their reputation, and others were jailed after being convicted of various offences by kangaroo courts.[127] Even the renowned literary figure, Taha Hussein, who had once defended the revolution's right to protect itself from some writers through censorship,[128] suffered similar indignities.[129]

Nasser never hid the fact that he sought control of the press. He summoned Ehsan Abdel Qoddous to his house after releasing him from jail for writing an offensive article and told him that he subjected him to psychological therapy by throwing him in jail.[130] Evidently, the therapy was successful since it was Abdel Qoddous who later called for nationalization of the press.[131] Nasser wanted nothing less than complete control of everything that was written or published anywhere in the country which is what the Journalism Organization Law enacted on May 24, 1960 guaranteed.[132]

In spite of all the measures that Nasser took to ensure his control of every aspect of life in the country, his overly suspicious nature, and conspiracy orientation, seem to have denied him the luxury of ever feeling fully secure in his position. When former King Farouk, who was as ineffectual in exile as he was while on the throne, collapsed and died in a Rome restaurant on March 18, 1965, the rumor in Egypt was that Nasser had poisoned him. The rumor was never substantiated, but the secrecy surrounding the king's burial supports the contention that Nasser persisted in the belief that the king, even after his death and contrary to all evidence, was a threat to his own position in the country.[133] Nasser denied Farouk's wish to be buried in the Rifa'i Mosque in Cairo next to his father, but Ismail Shireen, the king's brother-in-law, managed to convince him to grant Farouk's wish to be buried in Egypt.[134] The body was secretly flown into Cairo after midnight on March 30, and the king was buried without fanfare in a secret location away from his father's grave with only his sisters and their husbands in attendance. The public was informed only after the fact.[135]

Eloquence, Charisma, and Consequences

One of Nasser's unique characteristics was his overpowering charisma and his superb eloquence, articulateness, and oratory talent. He had charm and a powerful presence that often overwhelmed those who met him in person, and he presented himself well and hid his innate suspicion of foreigners in their company.[136] But his public statements and speeches presented a different side of him. They were replete with chauvinistic and intolerant pronouncements and constituted an important component of the public image that he projected to the masses that shared these feelings. These sentiments were sincere and the masses came to view him as one of them.[137]

However, charismatic leadership does have one major drawback. A charismatic leader's popularity is dependent upon his ability to provide his flock with one accomplishment after another,[138] and Nasser, true to type, presented Egyptians with a constant stream of 'victories', most of which were either no more than mere slogans or later turned out to have had disastrous effects on Egypt's national interests. These purported victories were usually presented at huge, well-choreographed events, attended by large carefully selected crowds of mostly uneducated workers and peasants, where he would dramatically reveal a new 'triumph' to his audience.[139]

The first 'victory' was the evacuation agreement with the British in 1954 that solidified his position in the power struggle with Naguib by raising his popularity. Nasser's success in presenting the agreement as a victory in spite of its well-known flaws and widespread opposition to it must have been a powerful indicator to him of the utility of that tactic. The Egyptian media, under his control, touted that first 'victory' and began to promote him as a national super hero and recite his praises in popular songs.[140] Apparently seduced by his own fabrications, he too began to believe that these were real victories.

In 1955 developments on the international stage contributed to solidifying Nasser's own belief in his role as Egypt's savior and to increasing his popularity among the masses. The conference of Non-Aligned Nations in Bandung, Indonesia was a watershed event. Summit conferences are great ego boosters. For politicians in general and dictators in particular, they provide them with the opportunity to appear alongside world leaders and make what are often meaningless announcements on the important matters they discussed, at no political cost to them. The thirty-seven-year-old ex-army officer who came from a modest background and had little education, now found himself sitting with, and being taken seriously by, such world leaders as Chou En Lai of China, Nehru of India, and Tito of Yugoslavia. He conducted himself well at the conference, charmed these leaders, and began to develop a personal relationship with them.[141] He was enthralled by his success,[142] which must have confirmed in his own mind his sense of mission and the notion that he was a hero, as well as setting off his lifelong love affair with summit conferences.[143]

Another watershed event was the Soviet arms deal concluded later that same year, which was announced with much fanfare and presented to the public as a great victory for the nation. An Israeli raid on the Egyptian administered Gaza strip a few months before the arms deal was concluded had served to highlight the need for finding a solution to the West's reluctance to sell defensive arms to the Nasser régime.[144] Nasser's popular appeal both at home and in the Arab world soared after that deal, which was probably the moment when he began to see himself not only as an Arab leader, but also as a world leader.

Basking in the glory of these 1955 successes, Nasser appears to have lost all sense of proportion and decided to take on the British and the French. The Suez crisis of 1956 that ensued is both an illustration of how momentous decisions affecting a whole nation became dominated by the impetuous caprices of one man and of that man's ability to delude both himself and the public contrary to the glaring evidence in front of them. In his speech in Alexandria on July 26, 1956, Nasser provided the audience with the usual litany of victories against imperialism, the agents of imperialism, and the reactionaries who were all plotting against the country. Then he dramatically announced that he was nationalizing the Suez Canal Company, that his orders to take it over were being implemented as that very moment, and that the revenue from the Canal would help build the High Dam.[145]

The buildup to the crisis was also classic Nasser. He had taken a fancy to the old project to build another dam on the Nile in the southernmost part of Egypt, which had been proposed by a Greek-Egyptian engineer and rejected by previous governments. Dr. Abdel Aziz Ahmad, a leading authority on the Nile at the time, and chairman of both the Nile Water Control Board and the Hydroelectric Power Commission, also strongly opposed the project on both technical and ecological grounds.[146] Initially the World Bank, with support from the United States and Britain, had offered to finance the dam, but the British and American offer was withdrawn in 1956[147] because of Nasser's increasingly hostile attitude and violent tirades against the West. The deteriorating relationship with the West had started after Bandung when Nasser began to see himself as an anti-imperialist world leader. Nasser, ever sensitive to real or imagined insults to his dignity, which he confused with Egypt's dignity, took the West's reneging on its offer to finance the dam as a personal insult and decided to retaliate by nationalizing the Suez Canal Company.

The decision, like most of his other decisions was impetuous, not well thought out, and taken without advice from those who were more knowledgeable and levelheaded and who might have counseled against it. Although most of the Canal company's shareholders were either British or French, the company was legally Egyptian, and its concession to manage the Canal was due to run out in 1966 or 1968[148] when control of the waterway would, legally and peacefully, revert to the Egyptian Government. Nasser was either too impatient or in need of another 'victory' for the masses to wait till then. Any rational political analysis would have shown that the nationalization, combined with Cairo's constant stream of anti-Western rhetoric that had created an atmosphere of hostility towards Nasser's régime in Europe, would lead to serious consequences. In Egypt, the proverbial man-on-the-street predicted that a serious retaliatory response by France and Britain would be an almost certain consequence of nationalization.[149]

Nasser apparently did not share that assessment and had kept his intentions secret from most of his lieutenants. According to el-Boghdadi, Nasser informed him of the decision to nationalize the Canal during a trip back from Yugoslavia on July 18, 1956.[150] His closest friend and commander of the armed forces, Amer, was, according to Salah Nasr, the intelligence chief, not informed of the decision until they were both on the train to Alexandria where Nasser was planning to make the nationalization speech. Amer, naturally, was offended at not being consulted about such an important decision.[151]

The decision-making process in this case provides several clues to Nasser's character and management style. It shows that he never outgrew the suspicious, conspiratorial aspect of his character, or the need to play one person against another by confiding the decision to some colleagues and not others. It also speaks to his growing belief in his own infallibility. He expressed this fantasy in clear terms to his intelligence chief once when he declared to him that there was not a single person in the country (of thirty million people) who could "grasp" everything except him.[152] These thirty million unfortunate Egyptians had, of course, to suffer the consequences of such an ill-considered decision. They believed Nasser's declaration that he was nationalizing the Canal so that he could use the revenue to build the High Dam. Instead, acting as if Egypt was a private estate whose income he was free to spend as he pleased, Nasser apparently donated the entire revenue of the Canal to a favourite personal charity and kept his magnanimous gesture secret from the public. Algeria's former president, Ahmad Ben Bella, who greatly admired Nasser, stated in a 2001 interview that one of the reasons for his continuing idealization of Nasser was that he handed over *all* of the Suez Canal's revenue to the National Liberation Front's (FLN)[153] leaders after it was nationalized.[154]

The decision to nationalize the Canal also reflects the degree to which Nasser's impetuosity allowed him to ignore or, perhaps, compartmentalize the realities staring him in the face. It could also be argued that arrogance had also set in and that he believed himself to be infallible. The reality was, however, that by 1956 the British had concluded that Nasser was not the best alternative to King Farouk after all. He was meddling in the affairs of other Arab countries[155] and threatening Britain's interests in the region. The French were alarmed at the intensifying war in Algeria where Nasser was arming,[156] training,[157] and financing[158] the FLN, which was fighting an increasingly bloody war to expel them from the country. The two powers convinced the Israelis, who were always amenable to an opportunity to grab their neighbor's land, to join them in an invasion of Egypt. The Suez Canal nationalization was the excuse they needed for their move. The plan called for Israel to launch a land attack on Sinai, then for Britain and France to issue a joint ultimatum to Israel to withdraw to a distance of ten miles east of the Canal, and for Egypt to withdraw to a distance of ten miles west of the Canal. The two European powers would then land their forces in the Canal Zone, ostensibly, to separate the combatants and protect the Canal.[159] Preparations for the attack had been underway for weeks and troops were being stationed in Cyprus, but the Egyptian intelligence apparatus was either too busy spying on Egyptians or too incompetent to notice the buildup.

When the invasion began the Egyptian army's chain of command promptly collapsed. The 'infallible' Nasser panicked and, according to Sadat, went to the command center on October 29, 1956 and issued an order to the whole army to withdraw from Sinai immediately.[160] The hasty and chaotic withdrawal of the army resulted in the loss of hundreds, perhaps thousands of lives; however, a reliable official estimate of the actual number was never disclosed to the public. The much-touted Soviet arms that cost Egypt dearly were destroyed, and Sinai was occupied. The Suez Canal was closed to navigation and its revenue, which would have been enough to buy the Suez Canal Company's shares on the open market, was lost.[161] Disastrous as the outcome was, it would have been worse if world opinion had not been outraged at the naked aggression, and the United Nations, lead by the United States, had not demanded a cease-fire and withdrawal of the three armies from Egyptian soil.

The régime, primarily because of America's condemnation of the attack, survived, although the offensive was, by any standards, a resounding defeat for Egypt. The Israelis occupied Sinai and the British and French occupied the Canal Zone, but in a demonstration of Nasser's talented demagoguery and ability to both manipulate the masses and believe his own fantasies, he turned into a miracle maker who reached into a bag of unequivocal failures and reversals and produced a shining triumph for his spectators.[162] He began to refer to the event as a resounding victory over imperialism, while Israel embarked on an analysis of the events in preparation for the next round.[163]

The 'victory' required Nasser to make two major concessions that were kept secret from the public. The first was that Egypt would drop its claim that international maritime agreements put the Tiran Straits, at the mouth of the Gulf of Aqaba, within Egypt's territorial waters and agree to allow Israeli shipping through it.[164] The second was that, despite the fact that it was Israel that attacked Egypt not visa-versa, Egypt, not Israel, would now be obligated to keep its army ten kilometers away from the border and to station United Nations observers on its soil along its border with Israel. What was widely disseminated in the media instead were naïve and childish accounts about the heroic exploits of the Egyptian air force and the army's shrewd and well-planned retreat to the west side of the Suez Canal.[165] Some of these accounts serve to illustrate both Nasser's increasingly firm grip on both the media and the opinion-makers in the country as well as to support Tawfiq el Hakim's assertion that Nasser had an extraordinary ability to induce a mass loss of consciousness that prevented his audience from seeing the lack of logic in his pronouncements. For example, the media at the time praised the leadership's foresight in having seen through 'the plot' as soon as the attack on Egypt began, and sending all Egypt's military planes to neighboring countries to protect them from the invading forces. It occurred to no one, or perhaps no one dared, to ask the logical question: why spend so much on building and equipping an air force only to send it all abroad to save it from destruction when the country was attacked?

The 1956 'victory' proved to be a bad omen and a harbinger of more future 'victories'. The military junta had only been in power for four years, and it had already brought a major disaster upon the country, yet Nasser's popularity with the masses in both Egypt and the Arab World soared, and he, as Sadat recounts, became preoccupied with the legend that he began to be turned into. The myth grew in both Egypt and the Arab world, which started to view him as the hero who had achieved a great victory over two formidable powers, Britain and France.¹⁶⁶ Mohsen Abdel Khaleq, one of the original group of Free Officers concurs with Sadat's view. He recounted a conversation with Nasser in 1956 after his newly acquired status as the nation's savior that left him with the definite impression that Egypt was embarking on an era of adventures.[167]

The building of a personality cult now began in earnest and appears to have both reinforced and magnified fundamental and deep-seated aspects of Nasser's personality. The society as a whole began to be gradually molded in Nasser's image. Self-delusion, vindictiveness,[168] xenophobia, suspicion,[169] and paranoia, seeing plots everywhere, and viewing the world in simplistic terms, were no longer confined to a small segment of the population. In Nasser's Egypt, these traits became part of the mainstream culture and the generally accepted norm in society. To be sure these characteristics had always lurked below the surface among certain segments of the Egyptian population, but they were always less widespread among the intellectuals, the Western-educated social and political elite. The dangers inherent in such a personality cult and the total control it allowed Nasser became glaringly evident in Nasser's reaction to Israel's other stunningly successful attack on Egypt a decade later and in the public's wholesale acceptance of his self-serving version of events.

Nasser moved from one blunder to another after 1956. He rushed into a hasty, financially costly, and ill-considered union with Syria in February 1958 only to see it collapse in September 1961. Rather than being the outcome of careful planning[170] and consideration, the union was meant to be a strike against Iraq and Jordan,[171] whose leaders he was feuding with and whom he denounced as traitors.[172] Nasser was riled by the loss of face and the perceived insult to his dignity when the union collapsed. He blamed King Saud of Saudi Arabia for the failure of the venture, which, according to his confidant, Heikal, was the reason that he readily agreed to support the 1962 rebellion against the Imam of Yemen. King Saud sided with the Imam in the civil war that ensued and Nasser did not want to give Saud an opportunity to score another victory against him.[173] The result was that the Egyptian army was mired for years in a tribal war in a country where Egypt had no vital or fundamental interests.[174] Everyone, as General Kamal Hassan Ali maintains, was against Egypt's intervention in Yemen: the USA, the USSR, Saudi Arabia, France, Jordan, Iran, and Pakistan. Nasser was finally forced to withdraw his forces from Yemen after the June 1967 disaster. That October, as the last Egyptian troops massed in the port of Hodeida to board the ships that would take them home, young Yemenis held a violent anti-Egyptian demonstration.[175] One hundred Egyptians were killed by the very same people that they had been sent there to save before the demonstration was controlled.[176] This "unnecessary war," as General Mortagi, who commanded the Egyptian army in Yemen called it, cost the army between ten and fifteen thousand casualties.[177] The financial cost of that entanglement ran into billions of pounds and was never disclosed to the people who paid the price in blood and treasure.

By 1966, the fallout from Nasser's 'victories' and from his governing by whim and caprice was beginning show on every front. His squandering of Egypt's wealth on supporting any opportunist around the world who set up a group and called it a liberation movement began to be felt. Inflation was rising and food shortages were becoming endemic,[178] but those in power never had to go short.[179] Factories were idle due to shortages of spare parts,[180] and the country lost a large number of professionals who left the country when Nasser, anxious to relieve some of the pressure, decided to allow emigration.[181] On the political front, there was a wave of arrests: MBs charged with plotting a coup, communists on various charges, others labeled reactionaries and feudalists.[182] The net was cast so wide and the régime's paranoia was so deep that the security services were once sent to arrest a member of the ancien régime who had died ten years earlier.[183] On another occasion, they arrested a prominent Christian as a member of the Muslim Brothers.[184]

The Committee to Liquidate Feudalism, formed in 1966,[185] lifted the country towards another level of fear, subjugation, and degradation.[186] It had been formed after a simple brawl in a rural railway station escalated, a man was killed, and his wife informed Nasser's brother that the "feudalists" killed her husband. Upon hearing the story, Nasser ordered the formation of the committee,[187] which quickly expanded its mission to cover the whole country and began an extensive campaign of interrogations and intimidation by the Military Intelligence.[188] Agricultural land, houses, cattle, thoroughbred horses, and agricultural machinery were confiscated,[189] and an atmosphere of terror permeated the countryside.

The armed forces were in no better shape than the rest of society. Keeping seventy thousand troops fighting in Yemen[190] had drained on the military budget and forced Nasser to reduce allocations to other areas of the military.[191] Thus the reserve units, according to General Mohammed Fawzi, the former Commander-in-Chief, were discharged three months before the end of their service in order to save funds.[192] In addition, a plan to reduce the size of the armed forces by a third was launched on May 1, 1967.[193] The army suffered shortages in every area: 40 percent in personnel, 30 percent in small weapons, 24 percent in artillery pieces, 45 percent in tanks, and 70 percent in trucks.[194] The air force was in an equally deplorable state. Trained pilots and equipment to repair runways and provide land services were all in short supply, and some airports had no air defense at all.[195] The shortage of trained pilots was so acute that a whole squadron of Sokhoy planes was stored in the crates in which they were imported,[196] and no one dared to question the decision to purchase such expensive equipment just to keep it in storage. General Kamal Hassan Ali, who led an armored division in 1967, claimed that the relationship between the political and military leaderships was so tense in May 1967 that Amer, the Commander-in-Chief of the Armed Forces, rarely went to his office in the command center and left everything to his office manager, the inexperienced, Shams Badran, who lacked intelligence, imagination and foresight.[197] Confusion, Ali added, reigned on both the political and military levels.[198] General Anwar el-Kadi, who was the Chief of Operations in 1967, also claimed in his memoirs that senior military personnel would sometimes spend months attempting to see Amer or contact him without success.[199] Yet no orders could be carried out unless they were signed by Amer, and the chief of staff had no authority other than conveying Amer's orders.[200] During the five-year period between 1962 and 1967, Amer carried out only three inspection tours of the forces in Sinai.[201] Training was often cancelled for what was termed "security reasons,"[202] or because it would be too "tiring" for the officers who had served for a long time in Yemen.[203] Those in charge of the country's defenses viewed training so cavalierly that in 1965/66 the infantry tank support units did not fire one shot in maneuvers.[204]

On the international level, Egypt's relations with many countries were either severed or strained, and Nasser, to his great chagrin, was being depicted in the Saudi and Jordanian media as a coward who was unable to defend his borders and hid behind the UN force in Sinai.[205] True to form, Nasser, whose purported victory in 1956 had gained him a reputation as the savior of the Arab World, is reported by his intelligence chief to have been irked by the accusation and eager to expel this force[206] in spite of the appalling state of his armed forces. When the Syrians and the Soviets brought fabricated[207] news of Israel massing its troops on its border with Syria[208] he walked into the trap and decided to be a hero again and take the pressure off Syria.

In May 1967, he expelled the UN force that had been stationed at the border with Israel since his last 'victory' in 1956,[209] ordered the Egyptian troops to Sinai and provoked Israel further by belligerent and fiery rhetoric and by blockading the Tiran Straits to Israeli shipping,[210] thus vastly increasing the probability of an Israeli attack. This brinkmanship, in view of the dire economic and political conditions in the country[211] and the deplorable lack of preparedness of the armed forces, was a classic illustration of Nasser's shortsightedness. It demonstrated once more his pedestrian understanding of world affairs. His shallow grasp of the situation was exemplified by his astounding claim to Kamal el-Din Hussein that there was no risk of an Israeli attack before six or seven months and that Russia was prepared to start WW III if the West intervened.

That statement was made on May 29, 1967, when Hussein warned him, in the presence of Hassan Ibrahim and Abdel Latif el-Boghdadi that closing the Tiran Straits would bring about a swift Israeli attack.[212] It was a tragic replay of his 1956 blunder. Even the proverbial man-in-the-street, if Mrs. Mortagi can be taken as an example, understood the implications of Nasser's actions and challenged her husband, General Mortagi. She asked how they could send the army into Sinai, assume an offensive posture and threaten to start a war when it was clear to the ordinary person that Israel would take advantage of the fact that most of the army was in Yemen and attack Egypt.[213] Nasser apparently did not understand that simple fact until three years later when he met with the Arab heads of state in Cairo on September 25, 1970, by which time the Israelis were well dug in on the east bank of the Suez Canal. The Arab leaders, true to their tradition of generosity with Egypt's blood and treasure appear to have been urging some risky venture upon Nasser because he retorted by informing them that he was not willing to antagonize Israel and give it an excuse for another attack.[214]

In the event, Israel's surprise attack on Egypt on June 5, 1967 showed that Mrs. Mortagi's understanding of the situation was better than Nasser's. The attack destroyed the Egyptian air force, and Nasser's incompetent commander-in-chief, Abdel Hakim Amer, promptly panicked and ordered a chaotic and disastrous complete withdrawal of the army from the Sinai Peninsula. After six days of a one-sided war, the Egyptians were left with no army or air force to defend them. Only seven tanks were left in Cairo,[215] and Nasser decided to offer his resignation. The Nasser magic effectively ended after that event, and although he remained in office for another three years, his era was deemed by some historians to have ended then.

Final Note

Nasser appeared on the Egyptian political scene at a point in history when the country was ripe for a major political change and a significant transformation was bound to take place. He, as both his defenders and his detractors are apt to admit, possessed unique qualities. The forces arrayed against this young adventurer and his group of unremarkable junior officers as he made his bid for power were numerous and powerful, but none proved to be a match for the charismatic and able conspirator.

He eventually won to his side all those who might have blocked his path to power. He had the ability to make those he talked to believe that he agreed with them[216] and that he was candid and trustworthy.[217] Nasser did not limit his contacts to those who shared his views and won his opponents' support by leading them to believe that he shared their views.[218] This enabled him to play on the differences between the political forces that might have opposed him, fan the flames between them, then stand back and watch as they fought and weakened each other. The Wafd, for example, was used against the MB, and the different factions within the MB against each other.[219] He was a skillful manipulator who played a different tune to each one of his potential opponents, and when the time was ripe, he eliminated those he saw as real or potential nuisances or as still standing in his way. To the Americans he was an anti-communist socio-political reformer. To the leftist parties and activists he was either a sympathizer with the leftist HADETU, or if the rumor was true, a secret member whose code-name was Maurice.[220] Either way, he appeared as a democratic campaigner for equality and social justice. To the Muslim Brothers he was a fellow believer in their cause and onetime member who had stood in the customary darkened room and sworn an oath of allegiance and obedience to their Supreme Guide. To the masses, once he began his public career, he was the orator and demagogue par excellence.

The masses were one of his main pillars of support. To them he was the liberator and master spellbinder who was adept at utilizing the Bedouin rooted fascination with words, slogans, and grandstanding rhetoric to keep them mesmerized and under his spell in spite of the often glaringly obvious contradictions between what he said and what they saw with their own eyes. Dignity, for example, was a favorite theme in Nasser's speeches,[221] and he enthralled his audience by his constant use of a set of code words that evoked pride and a sense of self-worth in them.[222] Repeated references to the thwarted plots by the usual coterie of bogymen, enemies of the revolution, reactionaries, Zionists, imperialists, and their representatives and spies, exhilarated the crowds. Talk of his resounding victories against these powerful enemies electrified the masses. His claims of successes in settling scores and paying them back for their perceived misdeeds and evil machinations were spellbinding. He offered his audience the comfort of beautifully strung words while corrosion gnawed away at society.[223] National resources were squandered on foreign adventures while every aspect of life in society deteriorated. One of his favorite slogans "raise your head brother, the era of enslavement is over" was often quoted by the media. And the crowds appeared to be oblivious to reality, to the point of being delusional, when they accepted his rather arrogant claim in 1954, only a few short months after grabbing power, that he, a young officer with limited education and experience, was the one who "taught them pride and dignity."[224] These same crowds failed to grasp the contradiction between the man's words and actions. He, as Vatikiotis correctly points out, "perhaps unwittingly, imposed the greatest and widest servility on the country in its modern history,"[225] and drove it to the brink of bankruptcy and ruin. As Louis Awad notes, he talked so much about freedom that the public began to believe that Egypt was the protector of all oppressed peoples around the globe, and that it was endeavoring to liberate everyone, break everyone's chains, and banish everyone's fears.[226] Yet the Egyptians themselves became ever more fearful and their chains grew ever more restrictive.[227] The terms "freedom" and the "era of freedom" were endlessly bandied about in speeches, songs, and slogans, yet anything even whispered without Nasser's explicit approval led to jail.[228]

It is a sad irony that Nasser's personal strengths were also his, and Egypt's, undoing. His strength of personality, superb gift for plots, intrigue and manipulation of others, and overwhelming charisma, enabled him to become a near absolute ruler of a country that had great potential and whose problems could have been manageable. These same qualities were what led that country to bankruptcy and set the seeds of the litany of problems that the country suffers from till today. It would certainly be difficult for a neutral observer to deny the negative impact of abolishing democracy, squandering Egypt's resources on foreign ventures, destabilizing the currency, destroying the old middle class, vilifying the entrepreneurial segment of society, devaluing the rule of law, and turning the army into a giant and enormously influential institution in society. That was Nasser's lasting legacy.

Notes

Chapter 1

1. E.A. Wallis Budge, trans., *The Egyptian Book of the Dead* (University of Pennsylvania African Studies Center) http://www.africa.upenn.edu/Books/Papyrus_Ani.html/ (accessed June 19, 2008).
2. Joyce Tyldesley, *Daughters of Isis: Women of Ancient Egypt* (London, Penguin Books, 1995), 8.
3. Joyce Tyldesley, *Judgment of the Pharaoh: Crime and Punishment in Ancient Egypt* (London, Weidenfeld and Nicolson, 2000), 16.
4. Ibid, 18.
5. The Egyptians' deeply ingrained fear of chaos and preoccupation with order were used very effectively by modern governments to avoid instituting genuine democracy.
6. Phiroze Vasunia, *The Gift of the Nile*, (Berkeley: University of California Press, 2001), 128.
7. Tyldesley, *Judgment of the Pharaoh*, 22.
8. For a concise review of the Egyptian myths of creation and the links between the realm of the gods and the realm of humans, see http://re-shafim.org.il/ad/egypt/texts/shabaka_stone.htm (accessed September 14, 2005).
9. For a brief overview of the interplay between religion and science in ancient Egypt, see Blake L. White, "Ancient Egypt Provides an Early Example of How A Society's Worldview Drives Engineering and the Development of Science," The Strategic Technology Institute, 2003, http://www.strategic-tech.org/images/Egyptian_Engineering_and_Culture.pdf. (accessed October 30, 2005).
10. Tyldesley, *Daughters of Isis*, 208.
11. Tyldesley, *Judgment of the Pharaoh*, 5.
12. Emile Durkheim, *The Elementary Forms of Religious Life* (New York: Free Press, 1965).

13. Robert A. Armour, *Gods and Myths of Ancient Egypt* (Cairo, The American University in Cairo Press, 2001), 152–155.
14. Ibid, 153-154.
15. Ibid, 154.
16. Ibid.
17. Ibid.
18. Ibid.
19. Victoria Ions, *Egyptian Mythology* (London: Hamlyn, 1982), 21; 33.
20. Philip K Hitti, *History of the Arabs* (London: Macmillan St. Martin's Press, 1970), 33.
21. Ibid.
22. Ahmad 'Adel Kamal, *el-Fath el-Islami li Misr* (Cairo: el-Sharika el-dawliyya lil tiba'a, 2003), 14.
23. Nicolas Grimal, *A History of Ancient Egypt* (Blackwell Publishing: Malden, Mass: 1994), 186.
24. This is not to suggest that ancient Egyptian society was impervious to external social forces, or that local culture was so rigid that it was never impacted by cultural diffusion from outside its borders. Numerous cultural practices were imported over the years but the process was generally selective, gradual, and limited. Consequently, the imports were Egyptianized and integrated into the existing culture without replacing it. One obvious example of this is the importation of several Canaanite goddesses during the New Kingdom that the religious system was flexible enough "to find a niche [for] in the official pantheon without any undue fuss." Tyldesley: *Daughters of Isis*, 254.
25. Ibid, 261.
26. Tyldesley, *Daughters of Isis*, 264.
27. See for example, Taqi el-Din Ahmad bin Ali el-Maqrizi, *el-Mawa'iz wal i'tibar fi dhikr el-khitat wal aathar* vol. 1 (Cairo: Maktabat Madbouli, 1998), 75; 84.
28. The lack of attachment to the soil among the inhabitants of the Arabian Peninsula appears to have survived, at least to some extent, until today. One of the anecdotes related by an Egyptian academic who was teaching in Saudi Arabia in 1990 was that whenever he asked the Kuwaitis who fled there after the Iraqi invasion of their country what their plans were, now that their country was occupied, the answer, invariably was "Sabbah [Kuwait's ruler] will find us a home." Ibrahim el-Zaini, *Misr bayna el-'aql wal 'eqal* (n.p., n.d.), 60-61.

Chapter 2

1. For a brief review of Alexander's campaign in Egypt, see: Robin Lane Fox, *Alexander the Great* (London: Penguin, 1986).
2. Vasunia, 272.
3. Aziz Khanki, *el-Iskandar el-akbar* (Cairo: el-Matba'a el-'asriyya, n.d.), 150
4. The truth or falsehood of this or any other legend is of no concern in this instance. W.I. Thomas's assertion that "If men define situations as real, they are real in their consequences," suggests that what should be of concern here is what is what people believed to be true.
5. Vasunia, 266.
6. Ibid, 267.
7. Ibid.
8. Ibid, 268.
9. For a brief historical review of Ptolemaic and Byzantine Egypt see H. Idris Bell, *Egypt From Alexander The Great To The Arab Conquest* (London: Oxford University Press), 1966.
10. For an historical review of Egyptian society during Cleopatra's reign, see Michel Chauveau, *Egypt in the Age of Cleopatra: History and Society under the Ptolemies*, trans. David Lorton (Ithaca, N.Y.: Cornell University press, 2000).
11. Department of Egyptian Art. "Roman Egypt," in *Timeline of Art History*. New York: The Metropolitan Museum of Art, http://www.metmuseum.org/toah/hd/regy/hd_regy.htm (October 2000) (accessed June 17, 2008.)
12. Carlo Maria Franzero, *The Life and Times of Cleopatra*, (London: Alvin Redman Limited, 1957), 18.
13. Ibid, 30.
14. *Encyclopaedia Romana*, "Temple of Serapis," http://penelope.uchicago.edu/~grout/encyclopaedia_romana/greece/paganism/serapeum.html (accessed June 16, 2011).
15. Jack Lindsay, *Cleopatra*, (New York: Coward McCann and Geoghegan, 1941), 15.
16. Franzero, 63.
17. Ibid, 17; see also, Julia Samson, *Nefertiti and Cleopatra*, (London: The Rubicon Press, 1990), 105.
18. Franzero, 21.
19. Lindsay, 61.
20. Ibid, 18.
21. Franzero, 61
22. Ibid; see also, Samson, 108.
23. Lindsay, 59.

24. Ibid; see also, Franzero, 61.
25. Bell, 67
26. Samson, 117–118; Lindsay, 72–73.
27. Plutarch, *Lives of the noble Grecians and Romans*, ed. A.H. Clough (The Project Gutenberg, 1996), http://www.gutenberg.org/etext/674 (accessed February 10, 2009).
28. Bell, 75.
29. Ibid, 75–76.
30. Ibid.
31. Livia Capponi, *Augustan Egypt* (New York: Routledge, 2005), 176.
32. Ibid.
33. Ibid, 29.
34. Jason Thompson, *A History of Egypt: From Earliest Times to the Present* (Cairo: American University in Cairo Press, 2008), 135.
35. Michael Grant, *Cleopatra* (New York: Barnes and Noble, 1992), 89-90.
36. Mustafa el-Abbady, *Misr min el-Iskandar el-akbar ila el-fath el-Araby*, (Cairo: Anglo-Egyptian Bookshop, 1999), 161.
37. Bell, 67
38. Abbady, 217.
39. Simon P. Ellis, *Greco-Roman Egypt* (Princes Risborough, U.K.: Shire Publications, 1992), 41.
40. Capponi, 170.
41. For an introduction to history of Christianity in Egypt, see *The Encyclopedia Coptica*, http://www.coptic.net/EncyclopediaCoptica/ (accessed December 16, 2006).
42. In 286, CE Diocletian divided the empire into two halves, east, and west and Egypt became part of the eastern half.
43. Bell, 104
44. Ellis, 13.
45. Bayyoumi Qandil, *Hadir el-thaqafa fi Misr* (Alexandria: Dar el-wafaa lidonya el-tiba'a wal nashr wal tawzee', 1999).
46. Ibid, 218.
47. Ibid, 30.
48. Ibid, 13.
49. Some historians put the date at 430 CE.
50. For a brief account of Hypatia's life and the Library of Alexandria, see Carl Sagan, *Cosmos* (New York: Random House 2002). A more detailed account is provided in: Maria Dzielska, trans. F. Lyra. Hypatia of Alexandria (Cambridge, Mass.: Harvard University Press, 1995).
51. Bell, 115.
52. Robert Drews, "Medinet Habu: Oxcarts, Ships, and Migration Theories," *Journal of Near Eastern Studies*, 59, No. 3 (Jul., 2000), 161-190.

Chapter 3

1. Hitti, 7.
2. For an interesting review of some of these travel accounts and writings see Tim Fulford, and Peter J. Kitson eds., *Romanticism and Colonialism: Writing and Empire ,1780-1830* (Cambridge: Cambridge University Press, 1998); or Kathryn Tidrick, *Heart-Beguiling Araby*, (London: Tauris, 1989).
3. Sayyida Ismail Kashef, *Misr fi 'asr el-wolah min el-fath el-Araby ila el dawlah el-tuluniyyah*, (Cairo: el-Hai'a el-Misriyya el-'amma lil ketab, 1988), 51.
4. Hitti, 23.
5. Ibid, 20.
6. Ahmad Amin, *Fagr el Islam* (Cairo: Maktabat el-nahda el-Misriyya, 1965), 140–141.
7. Ahmad bin Yehia bin Gaber el Baladhuri, *Ketab futuh el buldan*, Maktabat al turath al Islami, http://www.aleman.com/islamlib/viewchp.asp?BID=235&CID=29 (accessed April 2, 2007).
8. Ibid.
9. Ahmad Amin, *Zahr el-Islam*, vol. 2, (Cairo: Maktabat el-nahda el-Misriyya, 1961, 1962), 235.
10. Ibid.
11. Hitti, 50.
12. Ibid.
13. Ibid, 11.
14. ibn Khaldun, vol. 4, 418-419.
15. Ibid.
16. Amin, *Fagr el-Islam* 48.
17. Ibid.
18. Ibid.
19. *Ghelman* is the plural form of *gholam*, which means boy but is usually used to refer to the particularly effeminate or good-looking boys who were kept as sex toys. For examples of these poems, see Ahmed Amin, *Zahr el-Islam*, vol. 2 (Cairo: Maktabat el-nahda el-Misriyya, 1961-1962), 130-158.
20. Galal el-Din Abdel Rahman bin Mohammed bin Osman el-Suyuti, *Tarikh el kholafa* (Cairo: el-maktaba el-tegariyya el-kobra, 1969), 221.
21. Ibid, 128.
22. Abul Hassan Ali bin Abi Alkaram Mohammed bin Mohammed bin Abdel Karim el-Shaibani, *el-Kamel fil tarikh* (Beirut: Dar el-kotob el-'lmiyya, 1987), vol. 8, 182.

23. The first four caliphs, Abu Bakr, Omar, Osman, and Ali were all members of the sahaba (companions of the Prophet) and later became revered as *el-Kholafa' el-Rashedeen* (the Guided Caliphs).
24. Hitti, 45.
25. A very small number of contemporary Islamic scholars have attempted to discard the rose-colored glasses and conduct a more critical examination of Abu Bakr's motives and policies. Sheikh Dr. Ahmad Subhy Mansour, a former assistant professor at the prestigious el-Azhar University in Egypt, and currently living in exile in the United States, suggests an unorthodox view of these events in Ahmad Subhy Mansour, "Abu Bakr el-Seddik: Madha tabaqqa minu fil fiqh el-Sunni?," *Arab Times*, http://www.arabtimes.com/writer/ahmad/doc5.hhtml/ (accessed October 3, 2005).
26. Abu Jafar Mohammed el-Tabari, *The History of al-Tabari, vol. 11, The Challenge to the Empires*, trans. Khalid Yahya Blankinship (Albany: State University of New York Press, 1993), 178.
27. The term is also spelled Khalif in some sources.
28. Hitti, 54.
29. Ibid.
30. El-Maqrizi, vol. 1, 69.
31. Ibid, 74. He was probably talking about some form of early indoor plumbing, which would have been something that he had never seen before visiting Egypt.
32. Ibid, 75.
33. Ibid, 88. The fact that we have no evidence of what Adam or Noah may or may not have said is immaterial. What is important is what the Arabs believed them to have said, since our behavior is influenced by what we believe to be true regardless of whether it actually is or not.
34. El-Maqrizi, vol. 1, 149.
35. Ibid, 152; see also Abil Hassan Ali bin el-Hussein bin Ali el-Mas'udi, *Murug el-dhahab wa ma'adin el gawaher* (Cairo: el-maktaba el-tegariyya el-kobra, Sa'adah 1958), vol. 1, 340.
36. Omar bin Mohammed bin Yousef el-Kindi, *Fada'l Misr el-Mahrousa*, (Cairo: Maktabat el-Khangi, 1997), 7-21.
37. Ibid, 39–53.
38. Ibid, 28.
39. *Christian Apostolic Church of Egypt*, http://www.coptic.net/articles/EgyptInTheBible.txt. (accessed May 25, 2009).
40. There is some doubt as to Amr's age when he died. See Alfred J. Butler, *The Arab Conquest of Egypt and the Last Thirty Years of the Roman Dominion* (Oxford: Clarendon Press, 1978), appendix E, 546.

41. El-Kindi, *Fada'l*, 32.
42. There is some disagreement as to whether he actually visited Egypt or only heard about it from people that he met while traveling.
43. El-Kindi, *Fada'l*, 28.
44. This section relies heavily on Butler.
45. Hitti, 175.
46. Butler, 248–274.
47. The Babylon referred to here was a fort outside old Cairo not the ancient city in Iraq, which was the home of the Hanging Gardens.
48. Amr and subsequent Arab historians thought that this was part of George's name, but the Mukaukas is a form of address for a Prefect. Consequently, there is some disagreement among modern historians as to the true identity of this person. See Butler, 508-509.
49. Butler, 252–253.
50. Ibid, 336.
51. Ibid, 331.
52. Ibid, 331
53. Ibid, 332
54. Ibid, 367–370.
55. Galal el-Din Abdel Rahman bin Mohammed bin Osman el-Suyuti, *Husn el-mohadara fi akhbar Misr wal Qahera* (Beirut: Dar el-kotob el-'ilmiyya, 1997), 74-75
56. El-Maqrizi, vol. 1, 466.
57. Ibid, 447 - 466
58. Elias Ayyoubi, *Tarikh Misr el-Islamiyya min el-fath el-Araby sanat 640 ila el-fath el-Othmani sanat 1517*, (Cairo: Matba'at el raghayib, n.d.), 90.
59. El-Maqrizi, vol. 1, 84.
60. Butler, 277.
61. Subhi Wahida, *Fi usul el-mas'alah el-Misriyya* (Cairo: Maktabat Madbouli, n.d.) 62; Kashef, *Misr fi 'asr el-wolah*, 115.
62. Abdel Rahman ibn Khaldun, *The Muqqadema: an Introduction to History*, trans. Franz Rosenthal, (New York: Pantheon Books, 1958), vol. 3, 314.
63. See for example: Muna Fadhil, "Isis Destroys Thousands of Books and Manuscripts in Mosul Libraries," *The Guardian*, February 26, 2015, https://www.theguardian.com/books/2015/feb/26/isis-destroys-thousands-books-libraries (accessed August 12, 2016); Robert Corn-Revere, "Bonfires of Insanity: A History of Book Burnings From Nazis to ISIS," *The Daily Beast*, February 2, 2015, http://www.thedailybeast.com/articles/2015/02/28/bonfires-of-insanity-a-history-of-book-burnings-from-nazis-to-isis.html (accessed December 13, 2016); Rose Troup Buchanan and Heather Saul, "Isis Burns Thousands Of Books And Rare Manuscripts From Mosul's Libraries," *The Independent*,

February 28, 2015, http://www.independent.co.uk/news/world/middle-east/isis-burns-thousands-of-rare-books-and-manuscripts-from-mosuls-libraries-10068408.html (accessed December 13, 2016).
64. For a short discussion of the origin or the term, see Butler, 339–340.
65. Suyuti, *Husn*, 74-75.
66. Butler, 442-443
67. Ayyoubi, 110–111.
68. Ibrahim Ahmad el-Adawi, *Misr el-Islamiyya* (Cairo: Anglo-Egyptian Bookshop, 1976), 82.
69. Kashef, *Misr fi 'asr el-wolah*, 54.
70. Ibid, 137
71. Ibid, 140.
72. Ayyoubi, 180; see also Adawi, 196.
73. El-Maqrizi, vol.3, 141
74. Kashef, *Misr fi 'asr el-wolah*, 140
75. Ibn Khaldun, vol. 1, 302-303.
76. Hitti, 26.
77. El-Maqrizi, vol.3, 141.
78. Kashef, *Misr fi 'asr el-wolah*, 143
79. Butler, 450.
80. This estimate is based on The World Islamic Trading Organisation's standard weight of 4.25 grams of gold per dinar, which, they assert, was the standard set by Omar ibn el-Khattab. *The World Islamic Trading Organisation*, http://www.321gold.com/info/gold_dinar.html/ (accessed June 17, 2008.). See also, Warren C. Schultz, "The Monetary History of Egypt (642-1517)," in *The Cambridge history of Egypt* vol. 1, ed. Carl F. Petry (New York: Cambridge University Press, 1998), 331
81. El-Maqrizi, vol. 1, 809; Ahmad bin Yehia bin Gaber el-Baladhuri, *Ketab futuh el-buldan*, Maktabat al turath al-Islami, http://www.al-eman.com/islamlib/viewchp.asp?BID=235&CID=1 (accessed April 9, 2006).
82. Ahmad bin Yehia bin Gaber el-Baladhuri, *Ketab futuh el-buldan*, Maktabat a turath al-Islami, http: //www.al-eman.com/islamlib/viewchp.asp?BID=235&CID=1 (accessed April 9, 2006).
83. Ibn Abdel Hakam, *Futuh Misr wa akhbaruha* (Cairo, Dar el-ta'awon, 1974), 105.
84. Butler, 166.
85. Ibid.
86. The exalted status of Amr ibn el-Aas was illustrated by the media's storm of criticism of Usama Anwar Okasha's comments on Amr. The Egyptian playwright and leading writer of television serials was asked in 2005 if he would ever consider writing a script for a television dramatization of Amr's life. Okasha said he would not because he

would be expected to portray him as a perfect human being, whereas Amr was a man not a saint and that, just like any other mortal, he had weaknesses as well as strengths.
87. Butler, 457.
88. Ibn Abdel Hakam, 113. The very fact of mentioning these items in particular is in itself an indication of the caliph's limited knowledge of the huge variety of food available outside the impoverished environment of the Arabian Peninsula where palm dates and camel meat were the main staples and camel milk was a delicacy.
89. Ibid, 112.
90. El-Maqrizi, vol. 1, 284.
91. This estimate is based on the standard weight of 4.25 grams of gold per dinar, Schultz, 331.
92. Ibn Abdel Hakam, 113
93. Abu Ga'far Mohammed ibn Garir el-Tabari, *Tarikh el-rusul wal muluk*, vol.4, (Cairo: Dar el-ma'aref, vol.4 1960), 100.
94. Ibid.
95. El-Maqrizi, vol. 1, 830.
96. Afaf Al-Sayyid Marsot, *A Short History of Modern Egypt* (Cambridge: Cambridge University Press, 2002), 5.
97. Lane-Poole, Stanley, *A history of Egypt in the Middle Ages* (London: Methuen, 1901), 24.
98. See for example the findings of the Islamic scholar Sheikh Dr. Ahmad Subhy Mansour in, "el-Maskout 'annoh fi sirat Omar ibn el-Khattab fil fikr el-Sunni," *Arab Times*, http://www.arabtimes.com/writer/ahmad/doc3.hhtml/ (accessed October10, 2005).
99. El-Maqrizi, vol. 1, 813.
100. El-Mas'udi, *Murug el-dhahab*, vol.2, 341–342.
101. Ibid, 343.
102. Ibid, 341–342.
103. Ibid.
104. Butler, 460–461.
105. Ibn Abdel Hakam, 65.
106. Butler, 458.
107. Ibid.
108. Ibn Abdel Hakam, 153-154; el-Maqrizi, 225.
109. Butler, 223.
110. In fact, a cursory review of contemporary news media would reveal that even today, many similar or worse atrocities are committed by peoples and governments who like to refer to themselves as civilized.
111. Butler, 456.
112. El-Maqrizi, vol.1, 228.

113. Abi Omar Mohammed bin Yousef el-Kindi, *Wolat Misr* (Beirut: Dar sader, n.d.), 29; see also Ayyoubi, 298–302. Disagreements among historians about which month a certain event occurred results in some slight discrepancies when these dates are converted from the Higri to the Gregorian calendar.
114. El-Kindi, *Wolat*, 29; 54.
115. Ayyoubi, 170–180.
116. Butler, 465–466.
117. El-Maqrizi, vol. 1, 474.
118. Butler, 459.
119. Ibid, 459–460.
120. *Wali* is the term generally used to refer to a caliph's representative in Egypt from the seventh to the nineteenth century.
121. Butler, 489
122. Ibid.
123. Ibn Khaldun, vol.1, 302
124. Kashef, *Misr fi 'asr el-wolah*, 202.
125. Ibid.
126. El-Maqrizi, vol.1, 218–219.
127. One of their favorite metaphors was to compare Egypt to a cow or a camel.
128. "ihleb el-dorr hatta yanqate' wahleb el-dumm hatta yansarem"el-Kindi, *Fada'l*, 37.
129. Butler, 489.
130. Zubayda Ata, *el-Fallah el-Misri fil qarnayn el-sadis wal sabi' el-miladiyayn*, (Cairo: el-Hai'a el-Misriyya el-'amma lil ketab, 1991), 7.
131. Ibid, 6.
132. Ibid, 86–87.
133. Adawi, 194.
134. Ata, 65.
135. El-Maqrizi, vol. 1, 78.
136. Ibid, 75.
137. Ibid, 73.
138. Ibid; see also, 231-232.
139. Lane-Poole, 25.
140. El-Maqrizi, vol. 1, 284.
141. Marsot, *A Short History*, 6.
142. Ibid, 8–9.
143. Ibid; see also el-Maqrizi, vol.1, 868–879.
144. Mas'udi, *The Meadows Of Gold By Mas'udi*, trans. Paul Lunde and Caroline Stone, (London; New York: Kegan Paul International, 1989), 331.
145. Lane-Poole, 111.

146. Ibid, 121.
147. Ibid.
148. The dinar weighed 4.25 grams of gold but this weight fluctuated a little during the Fatimid period. See Schultz, 331.
149. One ardab equals 150 kilograms of wheat.
150. Ata, 90.
151. El-Maqrizi, vol. 1, 327–328
152. Ibid, 328.
153. Ibid.
154. Ibid, 319.
155. Ibid, 330.
156. Ibid.
157. Ibid, 337.
158. Ibid, 339–337.
159. Mas'udi, *Meadows*, vol. 1, 376.
160. El-Maqrizi, vol. 1, 437–438.
161. Mas'udi, *Meadows*, vol. 1, 376; el-Maqrizi, vol. 1, 437–438.
162. John, Bishop of Nikiu, *Chronicle*, http://www.tertullian.org/fathers/nikiu2_chronicle.htm#201 (accessed April 12, 2009).
163. Butler, 277.
164. Ibid, 277.
165. El-Tabari, *Tarikh el-rusul wal muluk*, vol. 4, 110.
166. Abul Hassan Ali bin Mohammed bin Abdel Karim bin Abdel Wahed el-Shaibani ibn el-Athir, *el-Kamel fil Tarikh*, vol.2 (Beirut: Dar el-kotob el-'lmiyya, 1987), 407.
167. El-Tabari, *Tarikh el-rusul wal muluk*, vol. 4, 110.
168. For details of the ayyam el Arab wars, see Abd Awn el-Rawdan, *Mawsu'at tarikh el-Arab*, vol.1 (Amman, Jordan: el-Ahliyya, 2004), 195–229.
169. Hitti, 87.
170. Ibid, 89–90.
171. Ibid.
172. Kashef, *Misr fi 'asr el-wolah*, 72.
173. Ibid, 87.
174. Ibn Khaldun, vol. 1, 304.
175. Ayyoubi, 114-134.
176. Taqi el-Din Ahmad bin Ali el-Maqrizi, *el-Mawa'iz wal i'tibar bi dhikr el-khitat wal aathar*, vol. 1, (Cairo: Maktabat Madbouli, 1998); 150; Mas'udi, *Murug el-dhahab*, 363.
177. Ibid, 420; Ibn el-Athir, *el-Kamel fil Tarikh*, vol.3, 229-231.
178. Marsot, *A Short History*, 5.
179. Ibrahim Ahmad el-Adawi, *Misr el-Islamiyya* (Cairo: Anglo-Egyptian Bookshop, 1976), 66.

180. Ibid.
181. Gamal Hamdan, *Shakhsiyyat Misr*, vol.2 (Cairo: 'Alam el-kotob, 1980–1984), 299.
182. Ibid, vol.2, 208.
183. Kashef, *Misr fi 'asr el-wolah*, 70.
184. Ibid, 142.
185. The source of the dates of tenure listed here is Hamdy Osman, *Haula' hakamu Misr* (Cairo: el-Hai'a el-Misriyya el-'amma lil ketab, 2000), 200–202.
186. For a short review of that period and a short analysis of the decline of the Umayyads, see Hitti, 81-93; 279-287.
187. Ibid, 81.
188. Kashef, *Misr fi 'asr el-wolah*, 31.
189. Osman, 200–202.
190. Walter N. Burks, *A short history of Islamic Egypt from the Arab conquest to Mohammed Ali* (Cairo: Société Orientale De Publicite, 1951), 32.
191. Amin Ma'louf, *The Crusades Through Arab Eyes*, trans. Jon Rothschild (Schocken Books: New York, 1984), 159-160.
192. El-Maqrizi, vol. 1, 789. The Fatimids did not have a monopoly on acts of barbarism. When Amalric, the Frankish king of Jerusalem, led crusade to Egypt and captured the city of Bilbeys on November 3, 1168 he massacred its Muslim and Christian inhabitants regardless of their age or sex. Ma'louf, 168-169; Stanley Lane-Poole, *A history of Egypt in the Middle Ages* (Methuen, London, 1901), 183-184.
193. Burks, 32.
194. El-Maqrizi, vol. 1,151.
195. Some Arab writers claim that the Prophet has advised them to partake from Egypt's bounty but warned of the dangers of making it their home. Among these dangers are prevalent adultery, deadening of the heart and eliminating jealously. See, Abi Abdullah Ahmad bin Mohammed bin Ishaq el-Hamadhani (ibn el-Faqih), *Ketab el-Buldan*, (Beirut: 'Alam el-kotob, 1996), 128-129.
196. Kashef, *Misr fi 'asr el-wolah*, 29.
197. Ibid.
198. Butler, 462.
199. Ibid.
200. Ibid.
201. Hitti, 57.
202. A more detailed analysis of the roots and religious connotation of the title caliph is provided in Patricia Crone and Michael Hinds, *God's Caliph* (Cambridge: Cambridge University Press, 2003).
203. Suyuti, *Tarikh*, 263.

204. Ibid, 105.
205. Kashef, *Misr fi 'asr el-wolah*, 217.
206. Tyldesley, *Judgment of the Pharaoh*, 16.
207. Ibid, 18.
208. Ibid, 15.
209. Crone and Hinds, 2.
210. Ibid, 11.
211. Ibid, 106–107.
212. Albert Hourani, *Arabic Thought in the Liberal Age: 1798–1939* (Cambridge: Cambridge University Press, 2003), 6.
213. Ibid.
214. Ibid, 10.
215. Ibid, 14–15.
216. Nabil Hilal Hilal, *el-Estebdad* (Damascus: Dar el-ketab el-Araby, 2005), 119–120; see also, Hitti, 82.
217. Ibn Abdel Hakam, 106.
218. Ibid, 67; el-Maqrizi, vol. 1, 814.
219. Hilal, 20; 87.
220. The term can be taken to mean: appeal, attraction, glamour, spell, temptation, seduction, disorder, or trial, but it has religious overtones that imply sinfulness.
221. Nabil Hilal Hilal, *E'tiqal el-'aql el-Muslim* (Damascus: Dar el-ketab el-Araby, 2005), 163.
222. Severus (Sawiros) ibn al-Muqaffa', *History of The Patriarchs of The Coptic Church Of Alexandria*, http://www.tertullian.org/fathers/severus_hermopolis_hist_alex_patr_04_part4.htm#JOSEPH, (accessed April 30, 2006).
223. Ibid.
224. Ibid.
225. Ibid.
226. El-Maqrizi, vol. 1, 230–232.
227. Ibn el-Muqaffa'.
228. Suyuti, *Tarikh*, 218-219.
229. Hilal, *el-Estebdad*, 113.
230. Ibid, 117.
231. A green leafy plant of the mustard family.
232. For an entertaining account of el-Hakem bi Amr ellah, see Bensalem Himmich, *The Theocrat*, trans. Roger Allen (Cairo: The American University in Cairo Press, 2005).
233. El-Maqrizi, vol.3, 244–249.
234. Hitti, 621.
235. Afaf Lutfi Al-Sayyid Marsot, *Women and Men in Late Eighteenth-Century Egypt* (Austin: University of Texas Press, 1995), 132–133.

236. Suyuti, *Tarikh*, 5; Marsot, *A Short History*, 14.
237. Marsot, *A Short History*, 12-13.
238. Ibid, 19.
239. Quraish was "divided into ten clans, Hashem, Umayya, Nawfal, Zohra, Asad, Taim, 'Adi, Makhzum, Gomah, and Sahm.", De Lacy O'Leary, *Arabia Before Mohammed* (London: Kegan Paul, Trench, Trubner & Co.), 192.183.
240. Ibid, 211.
241. Said Abdel Fattah, *el-'Asr el-mamaliki fi Misr wal sham* (Cairo: Dar el-nahda el-Arabiyya, 1965), 1–2.
242. Marsot, *Women and Men*, 20.
243. Ali Ibrahim Hassan, *Derasat fi tarikh el-mamalik el-bahariyya wa fi 'asr el-Nasser Mohammed bewaghon khas* (Cairo: Maktabat el-nahda el-Misriyya, 1944), 31–43.
244. Ibid.
245. Sayyida Ismail Kashef, *Ahmad ibn Tulun* (Cairo: el-Dar el-Misriyya lil ta'lif wal targama, 1965), 17.
246. Ibid, 59
247. Ibid, 49.
248. See: The World Islamic Trading Organisation, http://www.321gold.com/info/gold_dinar.html/ (accessed September 27, 2014.); *Gold Price*, http://goldprice.org/ (accessed September 27, 2014).
249. El-Maqrizi, vol. 1 868.
250. Ibid, 71.
251. Sayyida Ismail Kashef, *Misr fi 'ahd el-Ikhseedeyyeen* (Cairo: Fuad el-awwal University Press, 1950), 17.
252. Ibid.
253. Ibid, 20–21.
254. Ibid.
255. Ibid.
256. Osman, 200.
257. Kashef, *Misr fi 'ahd el-Ikhseedeyyeen*, 23.
258. Ibid, 34.
259. Marsot, *Women and Men*, 24.
260. Ibid, 127.
261. Ibid.
262. Marsot, A Short History, 12–13.
263. The exact dates of several of the events referred to in this section are subject to debate between historians, but the discrepancies are minor and are not relevant to the present discussion, which has, for the purpose of consistency, relied on the dates in Osman.
264. Ashur, *el-'Asr el-mamaliki*, 3.

265. Said Abdel Fattah Ashur, *el-Ayyoubeyyeen wal mamalik fi Misr wal sham* (Cairo: Dar el-nahda el-Arabiyya, 1976), 197.
266. Hassan, 29.
267. Ibid.
268. Ashur, Said Abdel Fattah Ashur, *el-Ayyoubeyyeen*, 134–145.
269. Ibid.
270. Ibid.
271. Ibid.
272. Ibid.
273. For a more detailed review of the Mamluk era, see Ibid, and Ashur, *el-'Asr el-mamaliki*.
274. Ashur, *el-Ayyoubeyyeen*, 134–145.
275. Edward William Lane, *An Account of The Manners and Customs of the Modern Egyptians* (Cairo; New York: The American University in Cairo Press, 2003), 338.
276. Ibid, 440.
277. Ashur, Said Abdel Fattah, *el-'Asr el-mamaliki*, 12.
278. Ibid, 206.
279. Ibid, 323–325.
280. Wahida, 98.
281. Ashur, Said Abdel Fattah, *el-'Asr el-mamaliki*, 314.
282. Ibid.
283. Ibid.
284. Ibid, 314–318.
285. Ibid.
286. Ibid.
287. Ibid.
288. Ibid.
289. Ibid, 326.
290. Mohammed ibn Ahmad ibn Iyas, *Badi' el-zuhur fi waqai' el-duhur* (Cairo: Franz Steiner Verlag GMBH, Wiesbaden, 1961), vol. 5, 155.
291. Ibid.
292. Ibid, 156.
293. Ibid, 178-179.
294. Ibid, 182-189
295. Ibid, 186
296. Ibid, 186-188.
297. Ibid, 207.
298. Ibid, 162.
299. Ibid, 169.
300. Ibid, 163.
301. Ibid, 207.

302. Ibid, 147-148.
303. Ibid, 167.
304. Ibid, 183.
305. Marsot, *A Short History*, 43.
306. Ibid.
307. Osman, 340-342; see also Hitti, 719.
308. Ahmed Galabi Abdel Ghani, *Awdah el-esharat fiman tawalla Misr el-qahera min el-wozara' wal bashawat*, ed. Fuad Mohammed el-Maui (Cairo: Dar el-ansar, 1977), 146.
309. Ibid, 146-147.
310. Examples of such short tenures include governors who sat for: six months, Ibid, 144-145; seven months, Ibid, 145-146; nine months, Ibid, 151-152; four months, Ibid, 161-162; seven months, Ibid, 162, 167; and two months, Ibid, 169.
311. Wahida, 91.
312. Abdel Rahman el-Gabarti, *'Aga'b el-aathar fil taragem wal akhbar*, vol. 5 (Cairo: el-Hai'a el-Misriyya el-'amma lil ketab, 1988), vol.5, 389.
313. El-Gabarti, vol. 3, 150.
314. Sayyid Uways, *Qirra'at fi mawsu'at el-mogtama' el-Misri*, (Cairo: Rose Al Yossef 1988), 26. See also "Frustrated Masses Head to Cemeteries to Lodge Complaints," *Egyptian Gazette*, November 7, 2001, 2.
315. Tyldesley, *Judgment of the Pharaoh*, 12-13.
316. Galal el-Din Abdel Rahman bin Abi Bakr el-Suyuti, *Tarikh el-kholafa* (Cairo: el-Maktaba el-tegariyya el-kobra, 1969), 263.

Chapter 4

1. Bedouins had no word for theater as the concept was outside their cultural experience.
2. El-Maqrizi, vol. 1, 466.
3. El-Mas'udi, *Murug el-dhahab*, vol.1, 374.
4. Louis Antoine Fauvelet de Bourrienne, *The Memoirs of Napoleon - Complete*, (The Project Gutenberg, 2004, e-text 3567), vol.2, 2, http://www.gutenberg.org/dirs/etext02/nb02v11.txt. (accessed September 11, 2006).
5. Ibid, 84.
6. Louis Antoine Fauvelet de Bourrienne, *The Memoirs of Napoleon - Complete*, (The Project Gutenberg, 2004, e-text 3567), vol.3, 3, http://www.gutenberg.org/dirs/etext02/nb03v11.txt. (accessed September 11, 2006).
7. Marsot, *A Short History*, 4.
8. Hamdan, vol.4, 16–21; see also Marsot, *A Short History*, 4.
9. El-Maqrizi, vol. 1, 151.
10. Hamdan, vol. 4, 525.

11. Ibid.
12. Helen Anne B. Rivlin, *The Agricultural Policy of Mohammed Ali in Egypt*, (Cambridge, Mass: Harvard University Press, 1961), 6.
13. Marsot, *A Short History*, vii.
14. Hamdan, vol. 4, 575.
15. Ibid, vol. 4, 575-576.
16. Hamdan, vol.3, 575 - 579.
17. Ibid.
18. Kashef, *Misr fi 'asr el-wolah*, 217.
19. Mohammed ibn Ahmad ibn Iyas, *An Account of the Ottoman Conquest of Egypt in the Year A.H. 922 (A.D. 1516)*, trans. W. H. Salmon (London: The Royal Asiatic Society, 1921), 59.
20. Ibid.
21. El-Gabarti, vol.4, 388.
22. El-Maqrizi, vol. 1, 236.
23. Kamal, *el-Fath el-Islami*, 74.
24. Traces of the ancient Egyptian language can be found in Egypt today. See for example, Wilson B. Bishai, "Coptic Lexical Influence on Egyptian Arabic," *Journal of Near Eastern Studies* 23, no. 1 (1964): 39-47; or Youssef, From Pharaoh's Lips.
25. For a more detailed description of the ancient Egyptian calendar, see Armour, 186–187; Ahmad Abdel-Hamid Youssef, *From Pharaoh's Lips*, (Cairo: The American University Press, 2003), 66-69.
26. Tyldesley, *Judgment of the Pharaoh*, 7.
27. El-Maqrizi, vol1, 747 - 757.
28. Nabil Hilal, *E'itiqal*, 110.
29. El-Mas'udi, *Murug el-dhahab*, vol.2, 204–205.
30. Ibid.
31. Ibid.
32. El-Maqrizi, vol. 1, 786.
33. Ibid.
34. Ibid.
35. Ibid.
36. Ibid.
37. El-Gabarti, vol. 1, 2; el-Maqrizi, vol. 1, 744–788.
38. Adawi, 86.
39. El-Maqrizi, vol. 1, 744-746.
40. It can also mean dissoluteness, profligacy, wantonness, dissipation, immorality, bawdry, license, or whoredom.
41. El-Maqrizi, vol. 1, 744-746.
42. Ibid. Some ancient traditions did survive through being incorporated into the newly imported religion and launched under more acceptable

labels. Perhaps the best example of that is the annual birthday celebration of Abul Haggag, a thirteenth century Arab immigrant who is revered as a Muslim holy man. Abul Haggag's *mouled* (birthday) is celebrated in Luxor in Upper Egypt where his shrine was built on the site of an earlier Christian church, which in turn had been erected on top of a pharaonic temple. The event is celebrated in a manner almost identical to the Apet (also spelt Opet) festival that reenacts the god Amon's journey from Luxor temple down the Nile to meet with his consort the goddess Mut.

43. The Feddan is a unit of land measurement equaling 1.038 acres.
44. Ibn Abdel Hakam, 97.
45. Ibid, 111.
46. Kashef, *Abdel Aziz bin Marawan*, 78.
47. Wahida, 60.
48. In addition to the high birth rate among the Arabs, there is also the fact that, as Wahida points out, "indigenous people rebelled continually and were killed or taken slaves or became Muslims until they became an almost negligible minority" in their country. Ibid, 60.
49. Osman was the caliph who succeeded Omar ibn el-Khattab and fired Amr for his alleged leniency with the Egyptians and his claim that they would be unable to carry a heavier burden of taxation
50. Mohammed bin Habib bin Omayya bin Amr el-Boghdadi, *el-Mohammed min akhbar Quraish*, http://www.al-eman.com/Islamlib/viewchp.asp?BID=170&CID=38&SW=%C8%E6%D2%E4%E5%C7#SR1(accessed April 19, 2010).
51. Ibn Abdel Hakam, 69.
52. Ibn Khaldun, vol.1, 299.
53. Kashef, *Misr fi 'asr el-wolah*, 112.
54. Abi Omar Mohammed bin Yousef el-Kindi el-Misri, *Ketab el-wolah wa ketab el-qodah* (Beirut: Matba'at el-aaba el-yasou'yyin, 1908), 397–405.
55. For the poems, see Ibid, 399–403.
56. Herodotus, *An Account of Egypt*, trans. George Campbell Macaulay (The Project Gutenberg, 2000, e-text 2131), http://www.gutenberg.org/files/2131/2131/-h/2131-h.htm, (accessed February 13, 2008).
57. Amin, *Fagr el-Islam*, 164.
58. Hitti, 26.
59. Ibid.
60. Kashef, *Misr fi 'asr el-wolah*,140
61. One of the factors that gives the areas of attitudes towards women, the law, and work particular significance today is that research in the field of modernization suggests that they play a key role in the development process.

62. Mahmoud Salam Zanati, *el-Mosawah bayna el-gensain fi Misr el-fara'oniyyah wa min ashkal el-tamyeez did el-nisa' 'ind el-Arab*, (Cairo: el-Nisr el-dhahabi, 2000).
63. Ibid, 47.
64. Ibid.
65. Ibn Abdel Hakam, 30–31.
66. El-Maqrizi, vol. 1, 149; 401.
67. Ibn Abdel Hakam, 30–31.
68. Ibid, 180; Tyldesley, *Judgment of the Pharaoh*, 78.
69. Tyldesley, *Daughters of Isis*, 46.
70. Ibid, 47.
71. Ibid, 52.
72. Ibid, 53.
73. Ibid, 54.
74. Ibid, 43.
75. Ibid, 40.
76. Ibid, 44.
77. The British Museum. "*Tomb-painting*," http://britishmuseum.org/research/collection_online/collection_object_details.aspx?assetId=244310001&objectId=112658&partId=1. (accessed August 25, 2017).
78. An example of an author who uses the term harem throughout the book is Mohammed Ali Sa'd Allah, *el-Dawr el-siyasi lil malikat fi Misr el-qadimah*, (Alexandria: Mu'assasat shabab el-gami'a, 1988).
79. See, for example, ibn Khaldun, vol. 1, 303–304.
80. Hamdan, vol.4, 575.
81. Less surprising, perhaps, is the fact that pharaohs are not treated any better by the English language where tyrant, despot, usurper, oppressor, and slave driver are all listed as synonyms of the term. *Roget's International Thesaurus*, 4th ed., s.v. "pharaoh."
82. E. Wallis Budge, *The Dwellers on the Nile*, (New York: Dover Publications, 1977), 81.
83. El-Maqrizi, vol.3, 244 - 249
84. Sa'd Allah, 54.
85. Ibid, 155.
86. For a more detailed account of the workers' rights in ancient Egypt see, Morris Bierbrier, *The Tomb-Builders of the Pharaohs*, (Cairo: The American University in Cairo Press, 1989); or John Romer, *Ancient Lives : Daily Life In Egypt of the Pharaohs* (New York: Holt, Rinehart and Winston, 1984); see also Anne Austin, "Paid Sick Days And Physicians At Work: Ancient Egyptians Had State-Supportedhealth **Care**," *The Conversation*, February 16, 2015, http://theconversation.com/paid-sick-days-and-physicians-at-work-ancient-egyptians-had-state-supported-health-care-3632 (accessed August 23, 2017).

87. Tyldesley, *Judgment of the Pharaoh*, 8.
88. Ibid, 8.
89. For a concise review of pharaonic law, see A. Theodorides, "The Concept of Law in Ancient Egypt," in *The Legacy of Egypt*, ed. J. R. Harris (Oxford: Clarendon Press, 1971), 291-322
90. Tyldesley, *Judgment of the Pharaoh*, 11.
91. Ibid, 55–56.
92. Severus (Sawiros) ibn al-Muqaffa', *History of The Patriarchs of The Coptic Church Of Alexandria*, http://www.tertullian.org/fathers/severus_hermopolis_hist_alex_patr_04_part4.htm#JOSEPH, (accessed April 30, 2006).
93. Ibid, 12–13.
94. Youssef, *From Pharaoh's Lips*, 22.
95. Hitti, 170.
96. Qandil, 50.
97. Hitti, 170.
98. Abil Farag Abdel Rahman ibn Ali ibn Mohammed ibn el-Gozi, *manaqeb amir el-mo'meneen Omar ibn el-Khattab*, (Alexandria: Dar ibn Khaldun, 1996), 208.
99. Hitti, 170.
100. Ayyoubi, 170–180.
101. Hafez Wahaba, *Geziret el-Arab filqarn el-'eshreen* (Cairo: Lagnat el-talef wal targama wal nashr, 1935), 152.
102. Ibn Khaldun, vol.1, 303.
103. Ibid, 303–305.
104. Nabil Hilal, *el-Estebdad*, 17-18.
105. El-Maqrizi, vol. 1, 298; 303; 304; 306; 309.
106. Ahmad Taymour Basha, *El-amthal el-'ammiyya* (Cairo: Markaz el-Ahram lil tiba'a wal nashr, 1986), 298.
107. Hitti, 90; see also Amin, *Fagr el-Islam*, 164.
108. Ibid. The affinity for exaggeration was expressed in the verse: a'dhab el-she'r akdhaboh (the sweetest of poetry is the most false).
109. Hitti, 21
110. Some contemporary sheiks suggest that this probably stems from an early misunderstanding of a hadith that advised early Muslims to rely on sighting the moon with the naked eye rather than on astronomical calculations to determine the start and end of their lunar calendar. See, for example, el-Qaradawi, "Fatawi Ramadan," http://www.qaradawi.net/site/topics/article.asp?cu_no=2&item_no=3978&version=1&template_id=215&parent_id=196 (accessed June 21, 2008).
111. Hilal, *E'tiqal*, 57.

112. Ibrahim el-Zaini, *Misr Bayna el-'aql wal 'eqal* (Cairo: n.p.: n.d.).
113. Ibid, 43.
114. Ibid.
115. Quoted in Zaini, 43.
116. Sa'd ibn Abi Waqqas.
117. Ibn Khaldun, vol.3, 114. Some historians have suggested that when The Temple of Serapis in Alexandria was destroyed by a Christian mob in 391 C.E. but the library attached to it survived and its book collection was found by Amr ibn el-Aas who burned them. See el-Maqrizi, vol. 1, 447, for example. Other historians, however, maintain that the historical evidence does not support that assertion. See, Butler, 402-427.

Chapter 5

1. Louis Antoine Fauvelet de Bourrienne, *The Memoirs of Napoleon - Complete*, (The Project Gutenberg, 2004, e-text 3567), vol.2, 2, http://www.gutenberg.org/dirs/etext02/nb02v11.txt. (accessed September 11, 2006).
2. Ibid, vol.2, 2.
3. de Bourrienne, vol.3, 3, http://www.gutenberg.org/dirs/etext02/nb03v11.txt. (accessed September 11, 2006).
4. Ibid.
5. Ibid.
6. El-Gabarti, vol. 5, 262.
7. Ibid, 263.
8. Ibid.
9. Marsot, *Women and Men*, 90.
10. Louis Awad, *Tarikh el-fikr el-Misri el-hadith*, vol.2 (Cairo: Dar el-Hilal, 1969), 38.
11. Nicola Turk, *Dhikr tamaalok gomhoor el-faransawiyya lil aqtar el-Misriyya wal belad el-shamiyya aw el-hamla el-frensiyya 'ala Misr wal Sham* (Beirut: Dar el-Farabi, 1990), 62.
12. Turk's account is neither as extensive nor as reliable as el-Gabarti's is. He was a Christian from the mountains of Lebanon who was sent by Prince Bashir el-Shehabi (Turk, 6-7) of the Shouf Mountains to observe and report to him on the situation in Egypt. His main sources appear to have been limited to the ruling elite and the resident Shami (Syrian and Lebanese) Christians. He appears to have been unable to distinguish between the other nationalities that lived in Egypt and lumps the rest of the population together as simply Muslims. The only distinction that Turk appears to make is when he refers to Arabs in the provinces. He does, for example, specify that it was the Arabs in the

Behaira province who looted and pillaged the town of Damanhour, Turk, 88. The incident took place in May 1799 and is also recorded by el-Gabarti, vol. 5, 97.
13. Turk, 63.
14. Ibid.
15. Awad, *Tarikh el-fikr el-Misri el-hadith*, vol.2, 35
16. Ibid.
17. Ibid, 52–53.
18. Ibid, 36.
19. Ibid, 37.
20. Ibid, 39.
21. Ibid, 32.
22. The father, most likely in fear for his own life, was forced to disown her and repudiate her behavior.
23. El-Gabarti, vol.5, 306-307.
24. Awad, *Tarikh el-fikr el-Misri el-hadith*, vol.2, 42.
25. Ibid.
26. Some historians maintain that Bonaparte was sincere in his plans to reform every aspect of society in Egypt. See for example Shafiq Ghorbal, *Mohammed Ali el-Kabir* (Cairo: Dar ehyaa el-kotob el-Arabiyya, 1944), 17-25.
27. Awad, *Tarikh*, 71.
28. El-Gabarti, vol.5, 154.
29. Awad, *Tarikh el-fikr el-Misri el-hadith*, vol.2, 73-74.
30. El-Gabarti, vol.5, 154.
31. Ibid, 158.
32. Ibid, 182.
33. Ibid.
34. Ibid, 98.
35. Ibid, 157.
36. Ibid, 155.
37. Ibid, 153.
38. Ibid, 153.
39. Ibid, 157.
40. Ibid, 192.
41. See for example Ibid, 153-154.
42. Awad, *Tarikh el-fikr el-Misri el-hadith*, vol.2, 71-78.
43. El-Gabarti, vol.5, 164.
44. Ibid, 165.
45. Ibid, 166. My emphasis.
46. Ibid, 169.
47. Ibid, 318.

48. Ibid, 306-307.
49. Ibid, 134.
50. Ibid, 191.
51. Ibid.
52. Almost all contemporary Arab historians interpret el-Gabarti's account differently. El-Halabi is viewed as a hero of the Arab/Islamic cause rather than a hired killer; the riots are viewed as a nationalist revolt and the foreign (Maghribi, Hegazi, Turkish) participants in the riots as fellow comrades in the fight against foreign domination. The return to subjugation by the Ottoman Empire is viewed by these historians as a victory for Egypt.
53. El-Gabarti, vol.5, 182.
54. Ibid, 182-183.
55. Valentine Chirol, *The Egyptian Problem* (London: Macmillan, 1920), 19.
56. Ibid.
57. Marsot, *A Short History*, 51-53.
58. Ibid.
59. Ibid, 52.
60. El-Gabarti, vol.6, 521; Marsot, *A Short History*, 153.
61. El-Gabarti, vol.6, 521.
62. Marsot, *A Short History*, 51-53.
63. Antoine Barthelemy Clot-Bey, *Lamha 'ama ila Misr*, trans. Mohammed Mas'oud (Cairo: Matba'at Abil Hawl, n.d. Originally published in 1840), 129; Ghorbal, 65.
64. Hourani, 51-52.
65. Abdel Malek, 49–50. There were constant minor skirmishes between Mohammed Ali's and the Mamluks' forces, but he refused to be provoked into an open war with them even when one of the Mamluk princes, Ahmed bey, attempted to kill him after being taken prisoner and brought to Mohammed Ali's house with a fellow Mamluk prince, Hassan bey Shabka. El-Gabarti, vol. 6, 541-544.
66. Marsot, *A Short History*, 54.
67. Ibid, 65.
68. Kashef, *Misr fi 'asr el-wolah*, 53; 203.
69. Marsot, *A Short History*, 59.
70. Ibid, 56.
71. Ibid, 60.
72. Ibid, 57.
73. Ibid, 58.
74. Ibid, 54-63.
75. Said Ismail Ali, *Tarikh el-tarbiya wal ta'alim fi Misr* (Cairo: 'Alam el-Kotob 1985), 311–318. For a more detailed review of Mohammed Ali's

educational reforms see Ahmad Ezzat Abdel Karim, *Tarikh el-ta'lim fi 'asr Mohammed Ali* (Cairo: Maktabat el-nahda el Misriyya, 1938).
76. Mona Russell, "Competing, Overlapping, and Contradictory Agendas: Egyptian Education under British Occupation, 1882-1922," *Comparative Studies of South Asia, Africa and the Middle East*, 21.1 &2 (2001), 50 - 51.
77. Ali, *Tarikh*, 305.
78. Hitti, 723–724.
79. Louis Awad, *Aqne'at el-Naseriyya el-sab'a* (Beirut: Dar el-qadaya, 1975), 161.
80. Hourani, 68-69.
81. Ibid, 73.
82. Marsot, *A Short History*, 64.
83. Ali, *Tarikh*, 361–363.
84. Abdel Karim, *el-Ta`lim*, 68.
85. Marsot, *A Short History*, 65.
86. Ibid, 66.
87. Ibid.
88. Ibid.
89. Afaf Lutfi Al-Sayyid-Marsot, *Egypt and Cromer: a Study in Anglo-Egyptian Relations* (London: Murray, 1968) 4.
90. Marsot, *A Short History*, 97.
91. For more details see Robert F. Hunter, *Egypt under the Khedives 1805-1879*, (Cairo: The American University Press, 1999), 179 - 226.
92. Ibid, 181.
93. Ibid, 182.
94. Ibid, 183.
95. Marsot, *Egypt and Cromer*, 1.
96. Marsot, *A Short History*, 69.
97. See, for example, Pierre Crabités, *Ismail the Maligned Khedive* (London: George Routledge and Sons, Ltd., 1933), or James C. McCoan, Egypt (New York: Peter Fenelon Collier, 1898), 217-218. Cited in Russell, 50.
98. Marsot, A Short History, 68. For a history of the development of the Egyptian parliament see, Yunan Labib Rizq, *Qissat el-barlaman el-Misri* (Cairo: Dar el Hilal, 1991).
99. Marsot, *Egypt and Cromer*, 8-9.
100. Ahmad Shfiq who worked for Tawfik for many years paints an extremely positive picture of him in his memoirs: Shafiq, Ahmad, *Modharkkarati fi nisf qarn*, vol I, (Cairo: Matba't Misr, 1934).
101. Ibid, 21.
102. Ibid, 26.
103. Marsot, *Egypt and Cromer*, 32.

104. Ibid, 54.
105. Marsot, *A Short History*, 75-76.
106. Lawrence John Lumley Dundas, Marquis of Zetland, *Lord Cromer: Being the Authorized Life of Evelyn Baring, First Earl of Cromer*, (London: Hodder and Stoughton, 1932), 164–165.
107. Marsot, *A Short History*, 75–76.
108. Zetland, 164–165.
109. Baron Selig de Kusel, *An Englishman's Recollections of Egypt, 1863 To 1887: With an Epilogue Dealing with the Present Time 1914* (London: John Lane, 1915), 19-20.
110. Marsot, *Egypt and Cromer*, 196.
111. Abdel Malek, 261.
112. Russell, 54.
113. Ibid, 51.
114. Marsot, *Egypt and Cromer*, 176.
115. Russell, 53.
116. Ibid, 51.
117. Ibid, 53.
118. Zetland, 89.
119. Marsot, *A Short History*, 78.
120. Ibid, 86.
121. Anne Alexander, *Nasser: His Life and Times* (Cairo: The American University in Cairo Press, 2005), 5.
122. Peter Mansfield, *The British in Egypt* (London: Cox & Wyman Ltd., 1971), 139-141. Cited in Russell, 58.
123. The Earl of Cromer, *Modern Egypt* (New York: Macmillan, 1908), vol.2, 538-539.
124. Marsot, *Egypt and Cromer*, 105.
125. Marsot *A Short History*, 78.
126. For details of this incident, see Mohammad Gamal el-Din Ali el-Masaddi, *Dinshway* (Cairo: el-Hai'a el-Misriyya el-'amma lil ketab, 1974).
127. The following provide more detailed accounts of British policies that contributed to turning the tide of British public opinion against the occupation of Egypt: Wilfrid Scawen Blunt, *Atrocities of Justice under British Rule in Egypt* (London: Unwin, 1906); Wilfrid Scawen Blunt, *Secret History of the English Occupation of Egypt: Being a Personal Narrative of Events* (New York: H. Fertig, 1967, c1922).
128. Marsot, *Egypt and Cromer*, 169-171.
129. Ibid, 179.
130. His memoirs provide interesting glimpses of the period of his rule. See, *Abbas Hilmi II, The last Khedive of Egypt: Memoirs of Abbas Hilmi II*, trans. Amira Sonbol (Reading, UK: Ithaca Press, 1998).

131. Zetland, 200.
132. Ibid, 195–196.
133. Marsot, *A Short History*, 79.
134. Lawrence R. Murphy, *The American University in Cairo*, 1919-1987 (Cairo: American University in Cairo Press, 1987), 2-3.
135. Ibid, 6.
136. Ibid, 11-12.
137. Ibid.
138. For a brief general account of a number of persons who played a role in the struggle for independence during the first half of the twentieth century, see Mohammed Naguib, *Shakhsiyat wa dhikrayat fil siyasa el-Misriyya* (Cairo: Ketab el-gomhoriyya), 1972.
139. Marsot, *A Short History*, 81.
140. Marsot, *Egypt and Cromer*, 151 - 154.
141. Ahmad Abdel Rehim Mustafa, *Tatawwor el-fkir el-seyasi fi Misr el haditha* (Cairo: Ma'had el-bohouth wal derasat el-Arabiyya, 1973), 43.
142. Ibid, 44.
143. Ibid, 46.
144. Ibid, 44.
145. Ibid, 53-54.
146. Ibid, 58-59.
147. Ibid, 56-57.
148. The poem may be found on: http://en.wikipedia.org/wiki/Hafez_ Ibrahim (accessed August 28, 2010).
149. Ahmad Lutfi al Sayyid and Salama Musa were two of the proponents of modernizing Arabic's written form, see, Esmat Nassar, *Fikrat el-tanwir bayna Ahmad Lutfi al-Sayyid wa-Salama Musa* (Alexandria: Dar el-wafa' li donya el-teba'a wal nashr, 2000), 97-98.
150. Abdel Aziz Fahmy presented the proposal to the Arabic Language Academy in January 1944. Abdel Aziz Fahmy, *el-Horouf el-latiniyya li ketabat el-arabiyya* (Cairo: Dar el-Arab lil Bustani, 1993).
151. Louis Awad, *Mudhakkarat taleb be'tha* (Cairo: Mu'assasat *Rose al Youssef*, 1965). Mustafa Musharrafa, *Qantarat elladhi kafar* (Cairo: Megallat el-dab wal naqd, 1991), is another example of experimentation with colloquial Egyptian is a novel written during the nineteen forties but not published until the early nineteen sixties. A very small number of authors have attempted during the following decades to repeat Awad's experiment and write in colloquial Egyptian Arabic. See, for example Mahmoud Bayram el-Tunsi, *el-Sayyid we meratoh fi Paris* (Alexandria: el-Markaz el-Araby lil nashr wal twazi', 1982) Originally published twenty years earlier. Or Yousef el-Qu'aid, *Laban el-'asfour* (Cairo: Dar el-Hilal, 1994).

152. P. J. Vatikiotis, *Nasser and His Generation* (London: Croom Helm,1978), 57; 59.
153. Marsot, *A Short History*, 82.
154. Selma Botman, *Egypt from Independence to Revolution, 1919–1952*, (Syracuse, N.Y: Syracuse University Press, 1991), 67.
155. Ibid, 59.
156. Ibid, 32, 59, 68–69.
157. Marsot, *A Short History*, 90.
158. For a discussion of the development of Egyptian nationalism during the last decades of the nineteenth and early decades of the twentieth centuries, see Hourani, 193-221.
159. Israel Gershoni and James P. Jankowski, *Egypt, Islam, and the Arabs: The Search for Egyptian Nationhood: 1900-1930*, (Oxford: Oxford University Press, 1995), 20.
160. Ibid, 6-8; Hourani, 200
161. Gershoni and Jankowski, *Egypt*, 6-8; Jamal Mohammed Ahmed, *The Intellectual Origins of Egyptian Nationalism* (London: Oxford University Press, 1960), 105-108.
162. Ibid, 15.
163. For a more detailed review of the attitude of Egypt's intellectuals towards the Arabs, see Ibid, 96-129. Ralph M. Coury maintains that support for Arabism was more widespread among Egypt's educated elite than reported by some researchers. See Ralph M. Coury, "Who 'Invented' Egyptian Arab Nationalism? Part 2," *International Journal of Middle East Studies*, 14, No. 4, (November 1982), 459-479.
164. For an example of Hakim's view of the Bedouin Arabs expressed in his fictional work, see Tawfiq el-Hakim, *'Awdat el-roah* (Cairo: Maktabat el-aadab, 1933), vol.2, 24-28; Tawfiq el-Hakim, *Tahta shams el-fikr* (Cairo: Maktabat Misr, 1932), 48-51.
165. For an example of Heikal's view of the Arabs see the article originally published June 3, 1925 in Mohammed Hussein Heikal, *Fi awqat el-faragh* (Cairo: Maktabat el-nahda el-Misriyya, n.d), 368-371.
166. Abu Khaldun Sati el-Hosary, *Abhath mukhtara fil qawmiyya el-Arabiyya* (Beirut: Markaz derasat el-wehda el-Arabiyya, 1985), 125.
167. Hourani, 196; see also Jamal Mohammed Ahmed, *The Intellectual Origins of Egyptian Nationalism* (Oxford University Press: London, 1960), 82.
168. Ahmed, 82. When contemporary writers acknowledge the Syrians' collaboration with the forces of occupation and the Egyptians' negative feelings towards them they tend to either avoid the use of such strong language or skim over the topic, or they attempt to justify

these acts. See, for example, Abdulla Mohammed Ezbawi, *el-shawam fi Misr fil qarnayn el-thamen wal tase' 'ashar* (Cairo: el-Hai'a el-Misriyya el-'amma lil ketab, 1986), 132.
169. Ahmad Lutfi el-Sayyid, *Qissat hayati* (Cairo: Dar el-Hilal, n.d.), 137-138.
170. Ibid.
171. Ibid. Sayyid has repeated this advice on more than one occasion. See, for example, Ahmad Lutfi el-Sayyid, *Ta'ammulat fil siyasa wal adab* (Cairo: Dar el-ma'aref, 1946), 64.
172. Ibid.
173. Nassar, 281-282.
174. Israel Gershoni and James P. Jankowski, *Redefining the Egyptian Nation, 1930-1945* (Cambridge: Cambridge University Press), 1995, 37.
175. Ibid, 37.
176. Ibid, 216.
177. Ibid, 54.
178. Ibid, 82.
179. Ibid, 88.
180. Ibid, 22, 224. For a review of Syrian migration to Egypt, see Thomas Philipp, *The Syrians in Egypt, 1725-1975* (Stuttgart: Steiner, 1985).
181. C. Ernest Dawn, "The Rise of Arabism in Syria," *Middle East Journal*, 16, No. 2 (1962), 153.
182. Ibid, 149. For a record of the daily conference proceedings see, *el-Mo'tamar el-Araby el-awwal*, (Cairo: Matba'at el-bosfor, 1923).
183. Gershoni and Jankowski, *Egypt*, 17.
184. Sayyid, *Qissat*, 137-138.
185. Hosary, 124-126.
186. Ibid, 124-125.
187. Coury, 459-479; 461.
188. The amusing claim is one of the popular topics of discussion on Arab blogging sites. See, for example, http://www.aljazeeratalk.net/forum/showthread.php?t=166303; http://vb.altareekh.com/t39539/ http://www.jeddahnews.net/vb/t78986.html; http://www.islamicdawa.org/ (accessed August 28, 2010).
189. Gershoni and Jankowski, *Redefining*, 51.
190. Ibid, 28.
191. Ibid, 29.
192. Yahia al Shaer, *The Other Side of the Coin, Suez War 1956* (Cairo: Akhbar el-Yom, 2006), http://www.geocities.com/yahia_al_shaer//YS-King-Farouk.htm/ (accessed October 7, 2006).
193. 'Adel Sabet, *Farouk el-awwal* (Cairo: Akhbar el-Yom, 1989), 66.
194. Al Shaer.

195. Sabet, *Farouk el-awwal*, 66.
196. Ibid.
197. Mohsen Mohammed, *Saqata el-nizam fi arba'at ayyam* (Cairo: Dar el-shorouq, 1992), 75.
198. 'Adel Abdel Sabour, *Farouk* (Cairo: el-Dar el-'alamiyya lil wal nashr, 2000), vol.1, 148–151.
199. Karim Thabet, *el-Malek Farouk* (Cairo: Matba'at el-ma'aref wa Maktabatoha, 1944).
200. Thabet, who called his earlier book *el-Malek Farouk* (King Farouk), did not bother with the formality of using the term king in a second book (Farouk As I Knew Him), published after the coup, in which Farouk is depicted as the embodiment of evil. See *Farouk kama 'ariftuhu* (Beirut: Dar el-shorouq, 2000). The memoirs were published with Nasser's help; see Ahmad Abul Fath, *Gamal Abdel Nasser* (Cairo: el-Maktab el-Misri el-hadith, 1991), 207.
201. 'Adel Sabet, *Farouk el-awwal* (Cairo: Akhbar el-Yom, 1989), 67.
202. Mortada el-Maraghi, who was the undersecretary of in the ministry of interior, relates in his memoirs an incident that took place in May 1949 when he was summoned by the king to discuss a report about communist activities in Egypt. On his way out after his meeting, the king's Italian pedicurist stopped him and asked him what he thought of the report and proudly informed him that he was the one who wrote it. El-Maraghi, 169.
203. Salah el-Shahed, *Dhekriati fi 'ahdayn* (Cairo: Dar el-ma'aref, 1974), 67-68.
204. El-Mahrousa (the protected one), built in 1865, was the first ship to enter the Suez Canal after it was opened, and even though its name was a term that refers to Egypt, it was changed after the coup to el-Horriyya (Liberty); see *Galal Alluba, el-Malek wa amir el-bahr: mudhakkarat amir el-bahr hadrat saheb el-ezza Galal Bek Alluba qa'id el-yokhout el-malakiyya wa yawer galalet el-malek* (Cairo: Max Group, 1998), 97.
205. Alluba, 108.
206. Ibid, 61-63
207. Ibid, 89.
208. Ibid, 93.
209. Ibid, 89-93.
210. Ibid, 31-35.
211. Ibid, 66-67.
212. Botman, 45.
213. Ibid. 35-45.
214. Marsot, *A Short History*, 102–103.

215. Ibid.
216. Mustafa Abdel Ghani, *el-Muthaqqafoun wa Abdel Nasser* (Kuwait: Dar Su'ad el-Sabbah, 1993), 120–121; See also Mohammed, *Saqata el-nizam*, 77; Tariq Habib, *Milaffat thawrat Yulyu: shahadat 122 min sinna'iha wa mu'asiriha* (Cairo: Markaz Al Ahram, 1997), 69–71; See also Sayyid Mar'i, *Awraq siyasiyya* (Cairo: el-maktab el-Misri el-hadith: 1978/1979), vol.1, 176.
217. The last Minister of Interior, Mortada el-Maraghi, states in his memoirs that Princess Fayza, the king's sister told him on one occasion that Farouk "will lead us all to ruination," and urged him to do what he could to stop him because the other members of the family were too cowardly to face him. Mortada el-Maraghi, *Shahed 'ala hokm Farouk* (Cairo: Dar el-ma'aref, 2007).
218. Kirk J. Beattie, *Egypt During the Nasser Years: Ideology, Politics, and Civil Society*, (Boulder: Westview Press, 1994), 61.
219. Botman, 111–135.
220. Marsot, *A Short History*, 104.
221. Abdel Malek, 78-79.
222. Mortada el-Maraghi, who was appointed minister of interior on the day following the Cairo fire (January 27, 1952) launched an immediate investigation. A leaflet distributed by the Free Officers (FO) inciting the setting of fire to certain places in Cairo to create unrest in the country came to light and led him to believe that the FO played an active role in inciting the fire. El-Maraghi, 54–57. His suspicions were strengthened when the fire was not among the many old issues that the military junta investigated after the success of the July 1952 coup. Ibid, 57-58. He also claims that the king either had prior knowledge of the event, or abetted the perpetrators in the hope of using the unrest to justify dismissing the popular Wafd government's. Ibid, 54–57. He bases that assertion on a set of suspicious circumstances surrounding a banquet for army and police officers that the king held on the day of the fire, which seemed to have been hastily arranged on a day that had no special significance. The invitees were informed of the event by phone less than twenty-four hours earlier and neither the minister of interior nor minister of war invited. Ibid, 22-24. In addition, the Army did not seriously move to quell the disturbances till 11:00 PM. Ibid, 26-30. Moreover, Hafez Afifi, head of the royal court visited el-Maraghi soon after the fire and advised him to wind down his investigation of the fire and put it all behind him. Ibid, 54–57.

Chapter 6

1. Mohammed Tawfiq el-Azhari, *el-Bikbashi Youssef Seddik: monqidh thawrat Yulyu* (Cairo: Maktabat Madbouli, 1999), 55.
2. Ibid.
3. Abdel Azim Ramadan, ed., *Awraq Youssef Seddik*, (Cairo: el-Hai'a el-Misriyya el-'amma lil ketab, 1999), 102.
4. Seddik denied a persistent rumor that Nasser an Amer had bought two tickets for el-Falouga Movie Theater as an alibi in case the coup failed and were escaping when they bumped into him. See Abdel Azim Ramadan, ed., *Awraq*, 130.
5. Hamdy Lutfi, *Thuwwar Yulyu: el-wagh elaakhar*, (Cairo: Dar el-Hilal, 1977), 112–113; see also, Abdel Menem Abdel Raouf, *Arghamtu Farouk 'ala el-tanazol 'an el-'arsh*, (Cairo: el-Zahra' lil e'lam el-Araby, 1988), 73-78; Ramadan, ed., *Awraq*, 19, 100–112; el-Azhari, 55
6. Ramadan, ed., *Awraq*, 19, 102.
5. Khaled Mohi El Din, *Walaan atakallam*, (Cairo: Markaz Al Ahram lil targama wal nashr, 1992), 150.
8. Ramadan ed., *Awraq*, 100–112; Ahmed Hamroush, *Qessat thawrat 23 Yulyu* (Cairo: Maktabat Madbouli, 1983-1984), vol.1, 199.
9. Hamroush, vol.1, 200.
10. Raouf, 73-78; see also, Habib, 86-87.
11. Mohammed Naguib, *Kalimati lil tarikh* (Cairo: Dar el-ketab el-game'i, 1981),188; Hassanein Heikal also puts the number of Free Officers at 90, see, Fuad Matar, *Bisaraha 'an Abdel Nasser: hewar ma'a Mohammed Hassanein Heikal* (Beirut: Dar el-qadaya, 1975), 36. FO member Hussein Mohammed Ahmad Hammouda puts the number at ninety-nine. Hussein Mohammed Ahmad Hammouda, *Asrar harakat el-dhobbat el-ahral wal ikhwam el-muslimoun* (Cairo: el-zahra' lil e'lam el-Araby, 1985), 193
12. Mahmoud Fawzi, *el-Zobbat el-ahrar yatahaddathoun* (Cairo: Maktabat Madbouli, 1990), 31.
13. Hamroush, vol.1, 215.
14. Abdel Malek, 271.
15. Ibid; see also Hamroush, vol.1, 215.
16. Hamroush, vol.1, 217.
17. Hamroush, vol.1, 183.
18. Vatikiotis, 116
19. For details of the secret contacts between the Free Officers and the CIA, see, Miles Copeland, *The Game of Nations: the Amorality of Power Politics*, (London: Weidenfeld & Nicolson, 1969).
20. Azhari, 79; Fawzi, *el-Zobbat el-ahrar*, 71; Lutfi, *Thuwwar*, 135–136.
21. Vatikiotis, 122.

22. McNamara, 29.
23. Khalid Mohi el-Din, *Memories of a Revolution: Egypt, 1952* (Cairo: American University in Cairo Press, 1995), 79; Hamroush, vol.1, 187.
24. Ibid.
25. McNamara, pvi.
26. Mohammed, *Saqata el-nizam*, 75.
27. Habib, 41.
28. Hamroush, vol.1, 222; 196–197.
29. 'Adel Hammouda, *Ahmed Fuad el-thani*, (Cairo: Sphinx lil tiba'a wal nashr, 1991), 131.
30. Alluba, 102-103.
31. Ibid.
32. Hamroush, vol.1, 226.
33. The incident took place on July 26. Raouf, 73-78.
34. The claim of cowardice is supported by Salah el-Shahed, who was with the protocol department of the premier's office. He recalls in his memoirs that he was summoned by Asila Hanem (Queen Nariman's mother and el-Shahed's relative) on the evening of July 22. He found the king with her and she informed el-Shahed of a possible coup in progress and asked his opinion as to what should be done. He suggested to the king that he should put on his military uniform and go to the command center in Cairo to talk to the officers but Farouk refused and stated that the rebels might arrest or assassinate him. An RCC member later informed el-Shahed after the coup that if the king had come to them they would have returned to the barracks. El-Shahed, 228.
35. Habib, 86–87.
36. Ibid.
37. Hamroush, vol.1, 206-207.
38. Ibid, vol.1, 220.
39. Anwar el-Sadat, *el-Bahth 'an el-dhat* (Cairo: el-maktab el-Araby el-hadith, 1978), 145.
40. Hamroush, vol.1, 220
41. Alluba, 100-103; The Minister of the Interior confirms that the yacht was under orders to be ready to sail at dawn, el-Maraghi, 273.
42. Ibid.
43. Ibid.
44. Ibid.
45. Ibid.
46. Ibid.
47. Hamroush, vol.1, 222
48. Ibid, 180.
49. Ibid, 170.
50. Louis Awad, *Aqne'at el-naseriyyah el-sab'a* (Beirut: Dar el-qadaya, 1975), 162.

51. Habib, 88–89; Hamroush, vol.1, 229-230.
52. Admiral Alluba, the Captain of the yacht lists those who arrived with Naguib as Gamal Salem, Ahmed Shawki, Hussein el-Shafei, and Ismail Farid. Alluba, 111.
53. Military traditions were not deeply rooted among the junior officers and military discipline began to collapse immediately after the coup. Admiral Alluba recounts in his memoirs that when he was summoned to the Navy Command Center only three days after the coup to receive the orders to take the king into exile, the junior officers did not bother to salute him. Alluba, 108.
54. Habib, 88–89; Hamroush, vol.1, 229-230.
55. Hamroush, vol. 4, 227.
56. Alluba, 112-113
57. Ibid.
58. Belief in the concept of the just dictator was deeply embedded in the culture and the public tended to have contradictory attitudes towards democracy. On the one level, many were influenced by the widespread support for democracy among the Western-oriented elite and their advocacy of the parliamentary system of government and yet on another level their sentiments were often in the direction of the just dictators who could right all wrongs.
59. For a brief review of the swift collapse of the political parties after the coup, see Mar'i, vol.1, 212-225.
60. Mohi el-Din, *Memories*, 142.
61. Ibid, 245.
62. Revolutionary Command Council members preferred to use the term coup in their public speeches as well as their private conversations. Nasser also used that term in the beginning, see, Salah Nasr, *Modhakkarat Salah Nasr* (Abu Dhabi: Mu'assasat el-ettihad lil sahafa wal nashr, 1986), vol.1, 108.
63. Abdel Ghani, *el-Muthaqqafoun*, 200-202
64. Ibid, 210-211.
65. Naguib, *Kalimati lil tarikh*, 101.
66. Naguib, *Masir Misr*, (Cairo: Dar diwan lil tiba'a wal nashr, 1995), 39.
67. Ibid, 100.
68. Ibid, 114.
69. Ibid, 88.
70. The original nine members were: Colonel Gamal Abdel Nasser, Major Abdel Hakim Amer, Major Salah Salem, Colonel Anwar el-Sadat, Wing Commander Gamal Salem, Wing Commander Abdel Latif el-Boghdadi, Squadron Leader Hassan Ibrahim, Major Khalid Mohi el-Din, Major Kamal el-Din Hussein. The five new members that were added at Nasser's urging were: General Naguib, Colonel Youssef Seddik, Colonel Zakaria Mohi el-Din, Colonel Hussein el-Shafei, and Colonel Abdel Menem Amin, see, Hamroush, vol.1, 235.

71. Hamroush, vol.1, 246.
72. Naguib, *Kalimati lil tarikh*, 81.
73. Sequestration was a process that was ostensibly intended to rein in, constrain, or weaken wealthy members of the ancien régime who were regarded as corrupt and a threat to the military junta. Reactionaries, exploitive capitalists, and agents of imperialism were all terms that were used to justify the imposition of sequestration. The process consisted of taking inventory of all the assets owned by a certain individual and his family, including personal jewelry, cars, home furnishings, and anything else of value. Everything would then be impounded and the individual would be granted a monthly living allowance that was taken out of his impounded assets and charged an administration fee for the service. The sequestrators had complete control of these assets and could dispose of them as they saw fit.
74. The author was one of the eyewitnesses to these events.
75. Abul Fath, 15.
76. 'Adel Hammouda, el-Malek, 107.
77. Ibid, 10. For more examples see, Hussein el-Ramli, *Mugawharat usrat Mohammed Ali wal arbi'in harami: balagh ila el-mudda'i el-'am el-eshtiraki* (Cairo: el-maktab el-Misri, 1983).
78. Fawzi, *el-Zobbat el-ahrar*, 102.
79. Mohammed, *Saqata el-nizam*, 281-282.
80. Fawzi, *el-Zobbat el-ahrar*, 1990), 304
81. Ibid.
82. Ibid, 304-305.
83. That was a desert reclamation project, which was announced with much fanfare and was touted in the media as one of the new régime's great achievements but was a failure. Hassanein was in charge of the project.
84. Fawzi, *el-Zobbat el-ahrar*, 304-305.
85. Naguib, *Kalimati lil tarikh*, 100; see also Hamroush, vol.1, 322-323.
86. Waheed Ra'fat, *Fusul min thawrat 23 Yulyu* (Cairo: Dar el-shorouq, 1987), 121.
87. Fathi, 13–20; 446.
88. Khalid Mohi el-Din, *Memories,* 114.
89. Ra'fat, *Fusul*, 122-123.
90. An extremist Islamist group, Hamroush, vol.1, 311.
91. Ibid, 234-235.
92. Ra'fat, *Fusul*, 127.
93. Hamroush, vol.1, 312.
94. In February 1953 members of the Revolutionary Command Council were: General Naguib; Colonel Gamal Abdel Nasser; Colonel Anwar Sadat; Colonel Hussein el-Shafei; Colonel Abdel Menem Amin; Colonel Youssef Sed-

dik; Colonel Zakaria Mohi el-Din; Major Salah Salem; Major Abdel Hakim Amer; Major Khalid Mohi el-Din; Major Kamal el-Din Hussein; Wing Commander Abdel Latif el-Boghdadi; Wing Commander Gamal Salem; Squadron Leader Hassan Ibrahim. Abdel Azim Ramadan, *Awraq*, 21.
95. Mohi el-Din, *Memories*, 142.
96. Ibid; see also Abdel Ghani, *el-Muthaqqafoun*, 220-222.
97. Habib, 109.
98. Lutfi, *Thuwwar*, 139; Fawzi, *el-Zobbat el-ahrar*, 137; Hamroush, vol.1, 289.
99. Abdel Ghani, *el-Muthaqqafoun*, 273.
100. Hamroush, vol.1, 242.
101. The mere creation of the new ministry as well as the appointment of Radwan, one of the founders of a quasi-fascist group, *Misr el-Fatat* (Young Egypt), to run it might in itself have been an adequate answer to the question.
102. Abdel Malek, 260.
103. For a short review of the swift collapse of the political parties after the coup see Mar'i, vol.1, 212-225
104. Fawzi, *el-Zobbat el-Ahrar*, 13
105. The term was coined by Gershoni and Jankowski, *Redefining*, 37.
106. Hamroush, vol.1, 214.
107. Ibid.
108. Abdel Malek, 271.
109. Ibid.
110. Salah Isa, *el Brgowaziya el-Misriyya wa le'bat el tard khareg el halaba* (Beirut: Dar el-tanwir, 1982), 214.
111. The term means local, native, or Egyptian, and is a slightly snobbish or patronizing term that is used to refer condescendingly to urban lower class tastes and practices.
112. Vatikiotis, 341.

Chapter 7

1. Vatikiotis, 110.
2. Nasser's ruthless pursuit of power became clearly evident as he began to systematically to remove all obstacles that stood in his path to absolute control of Egypt. Not surprisingly, the Free Officers were the first group that had to be eliminated after the 1952 coup. Nasser, according to both Khalid Mohi el-Din and Abul Fadl el-Gizawi, was suspicious of the FO because of the experience that they had gained from participation in the original conspiracy and wanted to get rid of all who participated in the coup because they gave him a sense of insecurity. Mohi el-Din, *Memories*, 104–105. Once they had served their purpose, first by making the coup possible, then by preparing a list of over five hun-

dred officers who were cashiered from the army within the first three months after the coup, they became, for various reasons, dispensable. Some were appointed to diplomatic posts as ambassadors and military attachés, some were given civilian posts in one of the ministries or public organizations, and others were simply jailed. Hamroush, vol.1, 309-325. This discriminatory handling of possible threats illustrates an important aspect of Nasser's character. He had the ability to recognize that one-size-fits-all solutions to security problems are impractical, and that co-option, intimidation, or jail, are all effective strategies depending on the situation, and he took personal charge of making the majority of these decisions. Nasser's relationship with Abdel Hakim Amer is also a possible indication of his passion for power. Amr, his right hand man, although a fellow socially conservative *sa'idi*, seems to have been Nasser's opposite in many ways. Amer's family was well connected, and his uncle, a Pasha, had been the minister of war, which certainly placed Amer in the social group that Nasser despised. Amer's personality also contrasted sharply with Nasser's. Amer was an open, generous, easygoing man, who was jocular, fun loving and fiercely loyal to his friends. He became Nasser's closest friend from the time they met in military college, and after their graduation they shared a flat. According to Abdel Mohsen Kamel Mortagi, who had been a fellow cadet at the military college, Amer covered more than his share of their expenses and often paid for Nasser's food and clothing. Habib, 378 As a loner who always preferred the company of one or two people, Nasser had very few friends and was socially dependent upon the more sociable Amer who had a large circle of friends. Mohammed Abdel Samad, *el-'Esha' el-akheer lil mushir*, (Cairo: Dar el-ta'awon, 1979), 129. Amer's many contacts had an important practical value too, in that such a wide circle facilitated the recruitment of new officers to the secret organization once it was formed. These two personal characteristics, loyalty and sociability, must have made him the perfect candidate for the role of the right hand man in Nasser's view. Nasser appeared to trust Amer implicitly, and their friendship was described as exemplary. Amer called his eldest son Gamal, Nasser called his youngest son Abdel Hakim, and Nasser's brother, married Amer's eldest daughter. Lutfi, *Ma'sat*, 24; Nasr, vol.1, 118-119. None of this, however, counted, when Nasser found it convenient to throw Amr to the wolves after 1967.
3. Salah Shadi, *Safahat min el-tarikh: hesad el-'omr* (Kuwait: sharikat el-sho'a', 1981), 211–213.
4. Beattie, 83; Shadi, *Safahat*, 211-214. Salah Shadi was arrested and sentenced to death during the 1954 crack on the MB by Nasser. Obviously this fact alone makes his book a far from an objective recounting of

events and should be viewed with caution, which is a consideration that Beattie was evidently aware of because he confirmed the statement with two other sources. In addition, the fact that so many individuals were present at that meeting tends to weigh in favor of the accuracy of this particular reference.

5. 'Adel Hammouda, "Tahreeb selah fi bakherat el-ra'is," *Al Ahram*, February 15, 2003, http://www.ahram.org.eg/archive/Index.asp?CurFN=WRIT0.HTM&DID=-30000 (accessed February 15, 2003). It is also worth noting that the ship referred to in the article's title as "the president's ship" (bakherat el-ra'is) was the royal yacht el-Mahrousa, a term used often to refer to Egypt. Nasser kept the vessel for his own use after the coup and changed its name to el-Horiyya (liberty).
6. A remark made by Nasser to Kamal el-Din Hussein while in Abdel Menem Amin's luxurious apartment on July 18, 1952 suggests that he saw personal gain as the main reason for aspiring to change the régime. Amin reports having heard him whisper to Hussein "Why does he want a revolution when he has everything." Hamroush, vol.4, 245.
7. Robert St. John, *The Boss* (New York: McGraw Hill, 1960), 135.
8. Hamroush, vol.1, 319.
9. Ibid, 235.
10. Ibid, vol.1, 235. The added members were Mohammed Naguib, Youssef Seddik, Zakaria Mohi el-Din, Hussein el-Shafei, and Abdel Menem Amin.
11. Ramadan, *Awraq*, 148. See also Naguib, *Kalimati*, 158.
12. Hamroush, vol.1, 320.
13. Abdel Latif el-Boghdadi, *Modhakkarat Abdel Latif el-Boghdadi* (Cairo: el-Maktab el-Misri el-hadith, 1977), vol.1, 144.
14. Hamroush, vol.1, 312
15. Ibid.
16. Mohi el-Din, *Memories*, 263-264.
17. Abdel Ghani, *el-Muthaqqafoun*, 227-229.
18. Ibid.
19. Ibid.
20. Mohi el-Din, *Memories*, 265.
21. R. Hrair Dekmejian, *Egypt Under Nasir: A Study in Political Dynamics* (Albany: State University of New York Press, 1971), 25.
22. Hamroush, vol.1, 273-280; Abul Fath, 168.
23. Hamroush, vol.1, 319.
24. See also Habib, 149.
25. Ibid, 316.
26. Abul Fath, 218-219.

27. Abul Fath, 255.
28. Ibid, 220.
29. Hamroush, vol.1, 235.
30. Sarwat Okasha, *Modhakkarati fil siyasa wal thaqafa* (Cairo: Maktabat Madbouli, 1987), vol.1, 126.
31. Okasha, vol.1, 126. See also Hamroush, vol.1, 353-354.
32. El-Azhari, 152. See also Ramadan, *Awraq*, 26; Hamroush, vol. 4, 176.
33. Seddik was arrested on April 1, 1954 and his wife, Aleyya, on May 1, 1954. Aleyya Tawfik, *Yousef Seddik wa Gamal Abdel Nasser wa ana* (Cairo: Markaz el-Ahram lil targama wal nashr, 2000), 121-124. Several of their nephews, including a thirteen-year-old boy, were also arrested at the same time. Ibid, 127.
34. Hamroush, vol. 4, 176; Okasha, vol.1, 126.
35. Azhari, 152.
36. Hamroush, vol. 4, 44.
37. Lutfi, *Thuwwar*, 142; Habib, 128.
38. Lutfi, *Thuwwar*, 178, 209; see also Ra'fat, *Fusul*, 127.
39. Fawzi, *el-Zobbat el-ahrar*, 65–66; Lutfi, *Thuwwar*, 178.
40. Habib, 126.
41. Hamroush, vol. 4, 126.
42. Abdel Ghani, *el-Muthaqqafoun*, 200.
43. Hamroush, vol.4, 54.
44. Lutfi, *Thuwwar*, 224.
45. Abdel Ghani, *el-Muthaqqafoun*, 261.
46. Ibid, 170.
47. Abul Fath, 210-214.
48. Ibid, 208-209.
49. Ibid.
50. Ibid.
51. Ibid, 212-214.
52. Ibid.
53. Ibid, 328; Hamroush, vol.1, 273-280; Abul Fath, 168.
54. Abul Fath, 210-211.
55. Naguib, *Masir*, 118.
56. Ibid, 114–115; Mamdouh Anis Fathi, *Misr min el-thawra ila el-naksa* (Abu Dhabi: Emirates Center for Studies and Strategic Research, 2003), 69.
57. 'Adel Hammouda, *el-Watha'q el-khassah bil ra'is Naguib* (Cairo: Rose al Youssef, 1985), 89.
58. Vatikiotis, 142.
59. Hamroush, vol.1, 328-329.
60. Hamroush, vol.4, 16.
61. Kirk J. Beattie, *Egypt during the Nasser Years: Ideology, Politics, and Civil Society* (Boulder: Westview Press, 1994), 90-91.

62. Abul Fath, 182.
63. Ibid.
64. Sami Gohar, *el-Sametoun yatakallamoun* (Cairo: el-Maktab el-Araby el-hadith, 1997), 12.
65. Ibid, 220.
66. Riad Sami, *Shahed 'ala 'asr el-ra'is Naguib* (Cairo: el-Maktab el-Araby el-hadith, 2002), 37.
67. Abdel Ghani, *el-Muthaqqafoun*, 326; Hamroush, vol.1, 235.
68. Abul Fath, 176-177.
69. El-Hadidi, Mohamed el-Hadidi, *Isterdad Misr: hal min makhrag memma nahnu feeh* (Cairo: Markaz el-hadara el-Arabiyya, 2001), 17.
70. Ra'fat, *Fusul*, 159.
71. Hamroush, vol.1, 335.
72. Ibid, vol.1, 275.
73. Ibid, 334–335.
74. Abdel Ghani, *el-Muthaqqafoun*, 279-280.
75. Ibid.
76. El-Boghdadi, vol.1, 172.
77. Habib, 116.
78. Hamroush, vol.1, 336–337.
79. Abul Fath, 393-398.
80. Ibid; see also Vatikiotis, 306-307.
81. Hamroush, 335–336; see also Fawzi, *el-Zobbat el-ahrar*, 296–297
82. Sami Sharaf and Abdullah Imam, *Abdel Nasser hakadha kana yahkum Misr* (Cairo: Madbouli el-saghir, 1996), 454
83. Hamroush, vol.1, 333.
84. Ibid, 333-334.
85. Ibid.
86. Hamroush, vol.1, 332.
87. Ibid, vol. 1, 339; Vatikiotis, 142.
88. Hamroush, vol.1, 342.
89. Abdel Ghani, *el-Muthaqqafoun*, 275-276.
90. The Muslim Brothers had never been at the forefront of the supporters of democracy. Therefore, the most likely explanation for their participation in the coalition is that they were searching for a political role because they were beginning to suspect that the FO might renege on their promise to grant them a major role in government.
91. El-Azhari, 106-111.
92. Abdel Ghani, *el-Muthaqqafoun*, 275-276.
93. Ibid.
94. Ibid.
95. Hamroush, vol.4, 17.

96. Ramadan, *Awraq*, 22. See also Lutfi, *Thuwwar*, 204.
97. El-Boghdadi, vol. 1, 172.
98. Ibid, 172-173.
99. Hamroush, vol.1, 342.
100. El-Boghdadi, vol.1, 171.
101. Ibid, 144.
102. Mohi el-Din, *Memories*, 230; see also Hamdi Lutfi, *Thuwwar*, 139.
103. Ra'fat, *Fusul*, 186; also Habib, 157–160; Abdel Ghani, *el-Muthaqqafoun*, 288.
104. *Akhbar el-Yom* was founded and owned the prominent journalists Ali and Mustafa Amin. Both brothers were opportunists who tried to curry favor with Nasser after the coup. A few years later, however, Nasser imprisoned Ali on a transparently false charge of spying, and Mustafa, who was abroad at the time, wisely remained in exile until Nasser died.
105. Ra'fat, *Fusul*, 186; see also Habib, 157-160; el-Azhari, 107.
106. Ra'fat, *Fusul*, 186.
107. Abdel Ghani, *el-Muthaqqafoun*, 289.
108. Ibid, 289.
109. Ibid, 292.
110. Ibid, 294.
111. Abdel Ghani, *el-Muthaqqafoun*, 294-296; Nasser's exaggerated sense of personal dignity bordered on the irrational and led him to prohibit el-Sanhouri from holding any public office for causing him loss of face by making his public accusation. Sallam, Ana, 71.
112. Sa'd el-Issawi, *Madhbahat el-'adala* (Alexandria: el-Maktab el-game'i el-hadith, n.d.), 29; Habib, 286.
113. Abdel Ghani, *el-Muthaqqafoun*, 206-207.
114. Naguib, *Kalimati*, 224.
115. Hamroush, vol.1, 350.
116. El-Boghdadi, vol.1, 164.
117. Ibid, 146.
118. Ibid, 181; see also Ramadan, *Awraq*, 107, el-Azhari, 107; Habib, 159-160.
119. Hamroush, vol.1, 349; Beattie, 97.
120. Hamroush, vol.1, 349
121. Ibid; Hamroush, vol. 4 135-136.
122. Hamroush, 349–350.
123. Ibid, 350.
124. Ibid, 351; Beattie, 137.
125. Hamroush, vol.1, 352.
126. Gohar, 16.

127. Mohi el-Din, *Memories*, 142.
128. Abul Fath, 245.
129. Abdel Ghani, *el-Muthaqqafoun*, 210.
130. Hamroush, vol. 4, 287.
131. Abdel Ghani, *el-Muthaqqafoun*, 176.
132. Ibid, 284.
133. Ibid, 297–298.
134. Ibid, 303-307.
135. Anthony Nutting, *Nasser* (London: Constable, 1972), p. 66.
136. Abul Fath, 245-250.
137. Ibid, 260.
138. Mohi el-Din, *Memories*, 142. The rest of the slogan was "the age of despotism has ended."
139. El-Hakim, *'Awdat el-wa'i*, 50. See also Badawi, 247.
140. Vatikiotis, 234.
141. Hamroush, vol.1, 356.
142. Robert McNamara, Britain, *Nasser and the Balance of Power in the Middle East 1952-1967* (London: Frank Cass, 2003), 34.
143. Nasr, vol. 4, 199-201.
144. Naguib, *Kalimati*, 161.
145. Habib, 161.
146. Abul Fath, 245.
147. Nasser had succeeded in getting the MB to turn their back on Naguib and support him instead by promising to release their imprisoned members, returning the Society's funds which, had been confiscated after the March 1954 crisis, and allowing them to operate freely. Nasr, vol.1, 171.
148. Hamroush, vol.1, 299.
149. Ibid, 300–301.
150. Hammouda, 69.
151. Ibid.
152. Nasser had met and befriended el-Sanadi before the coup. El-Baqoury, 72; Hammouda, 34-35.
153. Hamroush, vol.1, 303; Hamroush, vol. 4, 310.
154. Hamroush, vol.1, 303.
155. Omayma Abdel Latif, "Nasser and the Brotherhood," *Al Ahram Weekly*, June 27 to July 3, 2002, http://weekly.ahram.org.eg/2002/592/special.htm (accessed April 22, 2007).
156. Hamroush, vol.1, 305-306
157. Beattie, 81
158. Ibid.
159. Hamroush, vol.1, 307; Beattie, 84.

160. Many people including the prominent historian Abdel Azim Ramadan maintain that the assassination attempt was real. See for example, Habib, 174–176.
161. Nasser's daughter claims that Naguib had been in contact with the Muslim Brothers and implies that he knew of the attempt on her father's life. Hoda Gamal Abdel Nasser, "Sira tarikhiyya lil ra'is Gamal Abdel Nasser," Bibliotica Alexandrina, *Mawqi' el-ra'is Gamal Abdel Nasser*, http://nasser.bibalex.org/Common/pictures01-%20sira.htm#6 (accessed July 9, 2009).
162. Abul Fath, 331-332.
163. Mohammed Abdu, "Ennama yanhad bil shark mostabeddon 'adel," in Mohammed 'Emara, ed., *el-A'mal el-kamela lil sheikh el-imam Mohammed Abdu*, vol. 1 (Cairo: Dar el-shorouq, 1993), 845-846.
164. The Muslim Brothers still call their leader el-Morshed el-'am (the term means the general/supreme guide and implies reason, rationality, or maturity), and no one appears to see anything unusual in the implication that adults of sound mind need a guardian to do their thinking for them.
165. Tawfiq el Hakim, *Shagaret el-hokm* (Cairo: Maktabat el-aadab wa matba'ateha, 1938).
166. Isa, 34.
167. A few years after he got what he wished for, Fikry Abaza, had cause to regret his call for a dictator. When he wrote ten lines in his weekly column about freedom and democracy, he was fired and was only reinstated several months later after he was allowed to write a humiliating apology on the front page of *Al Ahram* newspaper. Musa Sabry, *el-Sadat: el-haqiqa wal ostoura* (Cairo: el-maktab el-Misri el-hadith, 1985), 523.
168. Abdel Malek, 155.
169. Ahmed Amin, *Fagr el-Islam*, 164.
170. Khalid Dawoud, "The Red Major" *Al Ahram Weekly*, July 18-24, 2002, http://weekly.ahram.org.eg/2002/595/sc81.htm (accessed October, 17 2006)
171. Salah Montaser, "When the People Chose Dictatorship." *Akhbar el-Yom*, October 23, 2004, 28.
172. Abdel Ghani, *el-Muthaqqafoun*, 236-238; see also Montaser.
173. Ibid
174. Ibid
175. Abdel Ghani, *el-Muthaqqafoun*, 236-238.
176. Okasha, vol.1, 127.
177. Sami, 48.
178. Hilmi Sallam, *Ana wa thuwwar Yulyu* (Cairo: Dar Sabet, 1986), 43.

179. Ibid.
180. Ibid.
181. Habib, 169.
182. 'Adel Hammouda, *el-Watha'q*, 32–36.
183. Ibid.
184. Ibid, 39.
185. Ibid, 91.
186. Ibid, 40.
187. Ibid, 43.
188. Ibid, 39–40.
189. Lacouture, 198.
190. Mansour, 208.
191. Okasha, vol.1, 127.
192. Ibid.
193. The term used by Gershoni and Jankowski in *Redefining* to refer to those who began to dominate public debate in Egypt in the 1940s. They differed from the earlier intellectuals in their lower-middle class origins, their Arab and/or Islamist rather than European orientation.
194. Magdi Abdelhadi, "Egyptians Look to Military 'Savior,'" *BBC*, http://news.bbc.co.uk/2/hi/middle_east/8113349.stm (accessed July 5, 2009).
195. Vatikiotis, 330.
196. El-Sayyid, *Ta'ammulat*, 402.
197. Ibid.
198. Ibid; Mohi el-Din, *Memories*, 127.
199. Beattie, 102.
200. Abdel Ghani, *el-Muthaqqafoun*, 273.
201. Beattie, 99.
202. Hamroush, vol.1, 292.
203. McNamara, 34.
204. Nasser began to build the extensive web of secret networks that was the hallmark of his régime as soon as the military junta succeeded in grabbing power. In early 1953, he set up an office called the special/private section that was part of military intelligence and was run by Zakaria Mohi el-Din who was ordered to report to him personally, and this extensive web was fully developed soon afterwards. Fathi, 29; Sharaf, and Imam, 69
205. Abdel Rahman Badawi, who served as Cultural Attach in Switzerland states that even Egyptians who were living abroad were spied upon, Badawi, 231
206. Dekmejian, 307.
207. Vatikiotis, 292.

208. When the journalist asked Nasser whether he was a leftist or rightist his reply was "I'm a conspirator. Beattie, 68.
209. El-Sadat, *el-Bahth*, 78; 105-107.
210. Abdel Ghani, *el-Muthaqqafoun*, 366-367.
211. Abdel Malek, 230; Vatikiotis, 294.
212. Abdel Ghani, *el-Muthaqqafoun*, 405; see also Abul Fath, 416.
213. Abul Fath, 416.
214. Louis Awad and Tawfiq el Hakim, both influential writers, have attempted to explain the role of demagoguery during that era and came to differing conclusions. El-Hakim contends that Nasser's considerable personal charisma and talented demagoguery induced a loss of consciousness in Egypt that lasted throughout the nearly two decades of his rule. He admits that it might have been understandable that the public would applaud and believe Nasser's alarming, patently naïve, and one-dimensional public declarations, but wonders how intellectuals, himself included, were taken in. El-Hakim, *'Awdat*, 37-38. Awad disputes the loss of consciousness thesis, and argues that everyone knew exactly what Nasser was saying and approved wholeheartedly. Nasser's talent, Awad stressed, lay in his instinctive intimate understanding of the culture, which enabled him to tell the people what they most wanted to hear and his rhetoric gave pride to both the Egyptian and the Arab masses. Awad, *Aqne'at*, 53.
215. Vatikiotis, 322.
216. Heikal has long since ceased to be a mere journalist. He became an institution and a controversial figure about whom many books were written. There is no doubt that an objective reviewer of Heikal's career would find some aspects of his life or his views to be legitimately critical of, but a substantial number of these books are nothing more than personal attacks motivated by envy of his exalted rank in the Arab media.
217. Several researchers have recognized the similarity between Nasser's era and the Mamluks'. See, for example, Mo'nes.
218. Nasser himself acknowledged these spheres of influence in a conversation with Sadat in his house in February 1967 when he told him, "The country is governed by a gang, Anwar." el-Sadat, *el-Bahth*, 220. In public, however, Nasser and his spokesman, Mohammed Hassanein Heikal, avoided using the term gang and referred to the twentieth century Mamluk fiefdoms as the "centers of power.
219. Herodotus.
220. The 1956 'victory' against the attempted invasion by Britain, France, and Israel, appears to have both exposed and reinforced Nasser's xenophobia, and gave him an opportunity to act upon his deep suspi-

cion of foreigners. He declared to a friend during a private conversation shortly afterwards that it would be a serious mistake not to use the attack as an excuse to purge the country of all foreign influence. St. John, 268-270. He wasted no time in putting his plan into action. All syndicates (professional and trade associations) were ordered to Egyptianize their membership rolls, and expel their non-Egyptian members. Ibid. The foreign educational institutions' association with the ancien régime's Western-oriented elite, many of whose children attended these schools, must have made them twice as abhorrent to Nasser. Over four-dozen British and French schools were taken over immediately and turned into Egyptian schools staffed by local teachers and British and French movies were boycotted. St. John, 268-270.

221. Egypt had dozens of private foreign language schools that were originally established by the various resident foreign communities to educate their own children. However, the high standards of instruction provided by these schools attracted an increasingly larger number of Egyptian parents who were willing to pay the relatively high fees that were charged to guarantee a good education for their children. Several of these schools were established as early as the nineteenth century, e.g. the Armenian school (1828), the Greek school (1847), and the Italian school (1860). Abdel Karim, 669-674. For a review of the development of these schools, see, Mohammed Seliman, *el-Aganeb fi Misr: derasa fi tarikh Misr el-egtima'i* (Cairo: 'ain lil derasat wal bohouth el-insaniyya wal igtima'iyya, 1996) 205-250.

222. Awad, *Aqne'at*, 74.

223. The "purification" campaign that was carried out in 1953 ousted many of the senior government bureaucrats and labeled them as corrupt. All those who held public office prior to 1952 were deprived of their civil rights and barred them from holding any public office and the new breed of "revolutionary" public officials proved to be vey different from those of the ancien régime. The caliber of public officials in Egypt was exemplified by a Minister of Agriculture who once announced a novel method of budget cutting. The Minister announced that he was planning to retire all the animals in the Cairo Zoo and replace each of them with a colored plaster replica of the same size and color. Audiotapes of the sounds made by each of the animals that these statues represented would be played continuously to add to the Zoo visitor's pleasure. The minister's plan met with complete silence in the media until a caricaturist had the courage to poke fun at it by drawing a man standing before a large desk and asking the person sitting behind it whether he really was a Cabinet minister or just a plaster statue. More recently, the Governor of Giza announced

a plan to dig up all the palm trees planted along the streets of that Cairo suburb and replace them with the more expensive but prettier (in his opinion) and more durable plastic trees. The plan was not enthusiastically received, and fortunately, it was quietly shelved. Samir Mokhtar, "el-Tamatheel el-molawwana wa mo'atheratiha el-sawtiyya," *Al Ahram*, March 10, 2004, http://www.ahram.org.eg/archive/Index.asp?CurFN=opin11.htm&DID=8056 (accessed May 19, 2008). The caliber of the revolutionary era's public officials was also illustrated by their conduct when the government proposed amending the constitution in 2005. The Speaker of the Parliament asked members to submit their proposals for amendments as answers to a list of nine questions on a form that he distributed to them. The questions revolved around topics such as the role of the ministerial Cabinet, the extent of the president's authority, and the most desirable type of electoral system. Only two out of four hundred and forty-three members responded to the questionnaire during the following two months. The speaker extended the deadline for submitting the proposals for a further two months and a total of twenty-five responses were submitted. Although none of the members claimed that the dog ate the form, their answers to a journalist who asked them about the reasons their poor response to such an important issue would have been familiar to any schoolteacher. The answers ranged from the simple "I am sorry," to "I am waiting to find out what others say," to one who said that he forgot because he was so busy, and another who said that he only had just remembered the task. One member admitted having received the questions some time ago but claimed that he did not respond because he did not know the deadline set for the responses. Another claimed to have been sick, and yet another member found the questions "very difficult." Sawsan el-Gayyar, "el-Nowwab fashalou fil egaba 'ala waraqat ta'deel el-dostour," *Rose al Yossef*, June 10, 2005, 24-25. The same individuals who found amending the constitution not worth their attention devoted a great deal of time and energy to discussing a four-minute performance by an oriental dancer in a private function. It had become a fad recently for students attending private high schools to hold their proms at the end of an academic year in five star hotels. The events are private functions and quintessential examples of conspicuous consumption with students in different schools competing to outdo each other by hiring famous media personalities to provide entertainment for the evening. They are usually organized by the students and paid for by their parents with the school administration taking no responsibility for them, as they are not held on the school grounds. A famous orien-

tal dancer put in an appearance in one of these events and was asked to dance and she agreed to give a short performance in her street clothes, as she had not brought her dance outfit with her. When some members of parliament heard about the performance later, they were so offended by the "sexually stimulating" dance that they found it worthy of debating the issue in the parliament. The parliamentary Education and Scientific Research Committee met and called on "all the concerned authorities to take every deterrent measure possible against the De La Salle School in Daher following the great moral scandal caused by the school by inviting the dancer Dina to dance in a private function in a Cairo hotel." They recommended the "school be subjected to unprecedented penalties" to make an example of it and to "be a warning to anyone who contemplates holding such perverted functions," and they demanded the ministers of the interior, culture, and education to come to parliament and participate in the continuing discussions. See, Tarek Mustafa, "Dina: el-ladheena hagamouni yad'ouni fi afrah abna'hem," *Rose al Yossef*, May 24, 2008, 96; "el-Hafl balaghat taklefatoh 103 aalaf genaih, el-barlaman yotaleb el-hokouma bi 'oqoubat radi'a did madras at De La Salle Frères ba'd da'wat Dina lil raqs amam el-tollab, *el-Masryoon*, May 24, 2008, http://www.almesryoon.com/ShowDetails.asp?NewID=49058&Page=1 (accessed May 25, 2008).
224. Dekmejian, 171.
225. The officer who headed the Tourism Organization, which managed all the big hotels in Egypt, for example, spoke no foreign languages. Se'da, 112-120.
226. Ibid.
227. Abdel Mohsen Mortagi, *el-fariq Mortagi yarwi el-haqa'q*, (n.c.: el-watan el-Araby, n.d.), 31.
228. Mohammed Fawzi, *Harb*, 50.
229. El-Hadidi, *Shahed*, 64.
230. Mohammed Fawzi, *Harb*, 10.
231. Ali, *Mashaweer*, 193, 219, 256.
232. Mortagi, 82.
233. Afifi, 40.
234. Ibid, 37-38.
235. Mortagi, 58-60.
236. Ali, *Mashaweer*, 216.
237. El-Gamasy, *Modhakkarat*, 71.
238. Mohammed Fawzi, *Harb*, 128.
239. Ibid, 133.
240. El-Hadidi, *Shahed*, 179-180.

241. Ramadan, *Harb October*, 18.
242. Ibid, 19.
243. Ibid.
244. El-Sadat, el-*Bahth*, 228.
245. Mohammed Fawzi, *Harb*, 151-154.
246. Ibid.
247. Mortagi, 163.
248. Ibid, 58-60.
249. Ali, *Mashaweer*, 236.
250. Ibid, 239.
251. Mortagi, 153.
252. Mohammed Fawzi, *Harb*, 219-220.
253. Mortagi, 159.
254. Ibid, 166.
255. Raymond Aron, *De Gaulle, Israel and the Jews*, trans. John Sturrock (New Brunswick, New Jersey: Transaction Publishers, 2004), 10.
256. True to form, the only thing that occupied Nasser's thoughts was how to preserve his position as head of state. Vatikiotis, 246. Protecting himself from any possible conspiracies and planning counter conspiracies were Nasser's first order of business. Both Nasser and his lieutenants deemed it more important to protect him than to protect the Suez Canal cities. Major General Abdel Mohsen Kamel Mortagi was the Commander of the Land Forces then. He reports in his memoirs that Nasser informed him that he had summoned the commander of the Republican Guard on June 11, to enquire about the strength of his force. When the Commander reported that all he had were his 350 troops because his tanks had been sent to protect the Suez Canal cities, Nasser's instructions to him defied logic. He ordered the force to leave its defensive positions on the Canal front and return to Cairo, justifying his order by telling the Commander "it does not matter what Israel does, we will show them what war is like." Mortagi, 201. See also, Ramadan, *Harb October*, 20. Again, when the Russians sent seventy tanks to Egypt as an emergency measure immediately after the destruction of the army in Sinai, they were assigned to the Republican Guard to protect Nasser because, according to Shams Badran, who was the Minister of War at the time, that was the top priority. Habib, 358. Another incident that took place only four days after the catastrophe also indicates that conspiracies and possible threats to his position of power and not the defense of Egypt were uppermost in Nasser's mind at the time. At 4 PM on June 9, Mortagi, one of the very few capable and uncorrupt senior officers, was ordered to Cairo for an urgent meeting with the Commander-in-

Chief, Abdel Hakim Amer. Upon his arrival at 6 P.M., Amer informed him that the reason for this urgent recall from the war front was to listen to Nasser's speech scheduled to be broadcast from Cairo Radio at 7 P.M. When Mortagi, seeing through the transparently illogical statement, protested that he was needed more at the war front, he was told that his presence in Cairo was "desired" at the moment, and that he would not be going back to the front. Mortagi, 193-195. Mortagi understood the reason for the patently irresponsible recall only later when he learned that an article in a British newspaper had speculated that, as he was a popular commander, the army might back him if he chose to make a bid for the presidency. Nasser's concern with the speculation, Mortagi goes on to add, casts doubt on the sincerity of his (Nasser's) purported resignation that same evening. Mortagi, 193-195.

257. Fawzi, *Mo'amarat*, 101.
258. Habib, 357-358.
259. For an account of the ten hours that Heikal spent with Nasser on June 9, 1967 before the speech see, *Mohammed Hassanein Heikal, Kalam fil siyasa: 'aman min el-azamat*, (Cairo: el-Misriyya lil nashr el-Araby wal dawli, 2001).
260. Ibid, 221.
261. Ibid, 205-234.
262. See the appendix for an overview of the speech and the events of the following day.
263. Vatikiotis, 281.
264. For the full text of the speech see, Bibliotica Alexandrina, *Mawqi' el-ra'is Gamal Abdel Nasser*, "Bayan el-ra'is Gamal Abdel Nasser ila el-sha'b wal omma bi i'lan el-tanahhi 'an re'asat el-gomhuriyya min mabna el-edha'a wal tevision," http://nasser.bibalex.org/Speeches/browser.aspx?SID=1221 (accessed August 1, 2007).
265. Vatikiotis, 284.
266. Bibliotica Alexandrina, *Mawqi' el-ra'is Gamal Abdel Nasser*, Bayan."
267. Gohar, 168.
268. Ibid.
269. El-Boghdadi, 2, 301.
270. Nasr, vol. 3, 285.
271. Ibid. 280.
272. Ibid.
273. Ibid, 280- 281. Nasr does not admit that he had been taping Nasser's telephone calls, but inclusion of the script implies exactly that.
274. Nutting, 425.
275. Gohar, 42.

276. Nutting, 426.
277. Lacouture, 311.
278. Habib, 437.
279. Ibid.
280. Ibid.
281. For the text of the speech, see, Bibliotica Alexandrina, *Mawqi' el-ra'is Gamal Abdel Nasser* "Khitab el-ra'is Gamal Abdel Nasser fi el-ehtifal bil 'eed el-khames 'ashar lil thawra, http://nasser.bibalex.org/Speeches/browser.aspx?SID=1223 (accessed June 1, 2009).
282. Ibid.
283. Ibid.
284. Wagih Abu Zekry, *Madhbahat el-abriya'*, (Cairo: el-maktab el-Misri el-hadith, 1988), 419.
285. Sidky and el-Ghoul were among the military commanders that Nasser pinned the humiliating defeat on.
286. Vatikiotis, 186.
287. Ibid, 196.
288. Ibid, 185; see also Dekmejian, 258.
289. Vatikiotis, 186.
290. Ibid, 187.
291. Ibid, 186.
292. Dekmejian, 258.
293. Mohammed el-Gawwadi, *el-Nokhba el-Misriyya el-hakema* 1952-2000 (Cairo: Maktabat Madbouli, 2002), 125
294. Dekmejian, 258.
295. Vatikiotis, 177-178.
296. Ibid, 187.
297. Ibid, 188.
298. Dekmejian, 261-262.
299. Ibid, 266-268.
300. Ibid.
301. Ibid.
302. Ibid, 266.
303. Ibid, 267.
304. Ibid.
305. Dekmejian, 270.
306. Okasha, 502.
307. El-Gawwadi, *Derasa*, 92.
308. Ibid.
309. Vatikiotis, 179.
310. Okasha, vol. 2, 501.
311. Ibid.

312. Ibid, 497.
313. Ibid, 503.
314. Ibid, 504.
315. Abdel Meguid Farid, *Nasser: The Final Years* (Reading: UK: Ithaca Press, 1994), 42.
316. Ibid.
317. Ibid, 41.
318. Vatikiotis, 246.
319. Mansour, 235. The resolution called on Israel to end its occupation of Sinai in return for certain concessions by Egypt.
320. Tawfiq el Hakim, *'Awdat el-wa'i* (Beirut: Dar el-shorouq, 1974), 75.
321. Vatikiotis, 16.
322. Ibid.
323. Ibid.
324. An incident that occurred in 1949 provides an example of Nasser's exaggerated sense of dignity and his tendency to harbor a grudge for years after an imagined affront to his dignity. The police had discovered an army-training manual in the possession of one of the Muslim Brothers (MB) secret cells. The manual on the use of hand grenades was restricted to the army and had Nasser's name on it. The government was alarmed by the discovery and its implications, namely that the MB had succeeded in infiltrating the army. The Prime Minister, Ibrahim Pasha Abdel Hadi, summoned Nasser to his office to along with the Chief of Staff, General Osman el-Mahdi to question him. Nasser claimed that he had lent the manual to a fellow officer who had been killed in Palestine. Abdel Hadi, although furious, assumed Nasser to be an honorable man whose assurance could be trusted and accepted his word after warning him to stay away from such groups. Nasser related the incident more than twelve years later and claimed that he did not take revenge on Abdel Hadi for the imagined offense, after he came to power. Mohammed, *Saqata el-nizam*, 93; Mohi el-Din, *Memories*, 32. Sallam, 76-77. Nasser was not only guilty of the offense but also participated in weapon training for the MB. See el-Baqoury, 71.
325. Ali, *Khamsoun*, 442.
326. Hussein is praised by some coup supporters for bringing a revolutionary spirit to education. This 'revolutionary spirit' was apparently illustrated by an incident that took place when he was visiting Misr el-Gadida Secondary school for boys and noticed that its courtyard was small. When he looked around and noticed a vacant lot next door to the school, he simply told the school administration to take it over. Ali, *Khamsoun*, 443. That incident certainly demonstrated Hus-

sein's concern for the size of the schoolyard in that one school, but new classrooms continued to be built in other schoolyards. More significantly, that incident demonstrated the arbitrary power that Hussein enjoyed, and his ability to make changes as he saw fit even when these changes required the immediate taking possession of private property without the need to clear his decision with other members of the Cabinet or the law courts.

327. Ali, *Khamsoun*, 468-469.
328. Ibid, 445.
329. Ibid.
330. The date is significant because it came only nine days after Nasser's resignation speech and was obviously part of his strategy to project a new image.
331. Seliman, *el-Aganeb*, 307.
332. Ibid.
333. Ibid.
334. The author is a member of the faculty at a provincial university, see, Faculty of Arts, History Department, *Zagazig University*, http://www.arts.zu.edu.eg/ (accessed May 5, 2009).
335. See for example, the author's comments in Seliman, 209.
336. Mahmoud el-Qi'i, "el-Loghat el-agnabiyya toshawweh 'oqool atfal Misr," *Al Ahram*, October 6, 2010, http://www.ahram.org.eg/311/2010/10/06/25/42245.aspx (accessed October 6, 2010).
337. For a brief review of the changes in the legal standing of foreign schools in Egypt after the coup see, Sahar Hamouda and Colin Clement eds., *Victoria College: A History Revealed* (Cairo: American University in Cairo Press, 2002., 187-243.
338. Ahmed, 175.
339. Fatemah Farag, "Egypt's Eton Recalled," *Al Ahram Weekly*, October 31 to November 6, 2002, http://weekly.ahram.org.eg/2002/610/fe1.htm (accessed May 29, 2008).
340. Hamouda and Clement eds., 208.
341. Ibid.
342. Ibid, 199.
343. Ibid, 206; 229; 230; 224; 233.
344. Farag.
345. Abdel Azim el-Basel, "fi Bandar Kafr el-Dawwar: ommiyoun fi madares e'dadiyya," *Al Ahram*, October 29, 2003, http://www.ahram.org.eg/Index.asp?CurFN=INVE2.HTM&DID=7923 (accessed October 23, 2003).
346. Karima Swaidan, "Settat 'ashara milliar fi goyoub el-embratoar wal za'im wal ostaz," *Rose al Yossef*, June 18-24, 2005, 44.
347. "15 Milliard genaih doroosan khososiyya sanawiyya wa mostawa

el-kharrigeen da'eef," *Al Ahram*, November 16, 2005, http://www.ahram.org.eg/Index.asp?CurFN=fron8.htm&DID=8672 (November 16 2005).

348. Amir el-Sarraf, "Mahlza fi imtahanat el-e'dadiyya bi Qena: awliya' el-omour addo el-imtahanat badalan min abna'him," *Alwafd*, January 23, 2006, http://www.*Alwafd*.org/front/detail.php?id=11093&cat=smal&PHPSESSID=bdbae28556a63d559b1f597dd9a006 (accessed February 11, 2007).

349. *Al Ahram*, June 3, 2006, 24.

350. Ali, *Khamsoun*, 446-447.

351. Wafaa Sha'ira, "Abhath kashf haqa'q wa abhath mamnou'a min el-nashr," *Rose al Yossef*, May 28 to June 3, 2005, 51-55.

352. Daniel Del Castillo, "The Arab World's Scientific Desert," *The Chronicle of Higher Education*," March 5, 2004, http://chronicle.com/cgi2-bin/printable.cgi?article=http://chronicle.com/free/v50/i26/26a03601.htm (accessed May 30, 2008).

353. Mabro, 156.

354. Egypt 2008 Yearbook (Cairo, State Information Service, 2008), 323, http://www.sis.gov.eg (accessed August 26, 2008).

355. Ministry of Higher Education, http://www.egy-mhe.gov.eg/chart1_data.asp#e1 (accessed August 26, 2008).

356. Atef el-Kilani, "el-Talib ya'taberaha rashwa moqadda wal ostaz yara annaha haq moktasab: loqmat 'aish el-ketab el-game'i," *Rose al Yossef*, February 17, 2007, 44.

357. Ibid.

358. See, for example, Ayman el-Mahdi, "Wazir el-tarbiya wal ta'lim: el-thanawiyya el-'amma kharrabet el-ta'lim," *Al Ahram*, March 27, 2006, 25; Saleh Shalabi, "Hilal ya'taref: la yougad fi Misr ta'lim gayyid," *Nahdat Misr*, December 12, 2006, 3; "Fasad ma'a martabat el-sharaf," *Rose al Yossef*, February 17, 2007, 35-60; Ali Khaled, "el-Misriyya lil nohood bil tofola tarsod enheyar el-ta'leem," *Albedaiah*, July 19, 2016, http://albedaiah.com/news/2016/07/19/117007 (accessed August 24, 2016); "wazeer el-ta'leem: tadahwor el-ta'leem fi Misr yarga' limirath thaqeel min el-fasad," *Youm 7*, February 21, 2013, http://www.youm7.com/953717 (accessed August 24, 2016).

359. This is not to suggest that they eschew degrees or diplomas. On the contrary, they place a great deal of importance on acquiring academic qualifications, but it is only the piece of paper that they value, not the knowledge that is implied by it. The general public knows full well that when influential persons enroll in graduate programs they are handed a worthless piece of paper at the end of their 'studies' because no one would dare fail them. No one would seriously sug-

gest, for example, that when Salah Nasr, the much feared intelligence chief enrolled in a graduate program he did any academic work. Yet that piece of paper was still sought after. Such an attitude is not as contradictory, as it might seem as first glance given the Arab culture's emphasis on form rather than content.

360. History Department, Faculty of Arts, *Tanta University*, http://www.tanta.edu.eg/ar/Tanta/art/history.html (accessed May 22, 2009).
361. Fuad el-Morsy Khater, *Hawla el-fikra el-Arabiyya fi Misr* (Cairo: el-Hai'a el-Misriyya el-'amma lil ketab, 1985), 26-27.
362. Qandil, 145.
363. Those who believe that they are Arab descendants of the Prophet.
364. This fuzziness was noted and commented upon by some writers in the media. See for example, Ahmed Abdel Mo'ti Hegazi, "Ma'a man anta," *Al Ahram*, November 16, 2005, http://www.ahram.org.eg/Index.asp?CurFN=writ1.htm&DID=8672 (accessed November 16, 2005).
365. Bibliotica Alexandrina, *Mawqi' el-ra'is Gamal Abdel Nasser*, "Khitab el-ra'is Gamal Abdel Nasser fi wafd Libnan min qasr el-dhiyafa bi Dimashq," http://nasser.bibalex.org/Speeches/browser.aspx?SID=609 (accessed June 11, 2008).
366. Abul Fath, 325.
367. Ibid, 405.
368. For an example of these sentiments, see, el-Maqrizi, vol.1, 137-138; 150.
369. Bibliotica Alexandrina, *Mawqi' el-ra'is Gamal Abdel Nasser*, "Khitab el-ra'is Gamal Abdel Nasser fil mo'tamar el-sha'bi lil ehtifal 'al'a morour sab' sanawat 'ala el-thawra," http://nasser.bibalex.org/Speeches/browser.aspx?SID=763 (accessed June 11, 2008).
370. Anis Mansour, *Abdel Nasser el-moftara 'laih wal moftari 'lina* (Cairo: Nahdat Misr, 2002), 159.
371. Ibid. The visit might have been intended as an expression public support for el-Mallakh who had been having problems with his boss at the time.
372. Ibid.
373. "La'eb remaya Misri yotheer ghadab mawaqe' el-tawasol ba'dama rafa' 'alam el-Se'oudiyya," *Sout el-Omma*, August 6, 2016, https://www.soutalomma.com/316966 (accessed August 6, 2016).
374. The fate of the once elegant winter resort of Helwan is an example of the urban deterioration caused by policy blinders.
375. S.E. Smith and A. Abdel Dader, "Coastal erosion along the Egyptian Delta." *Journal of Coastal Research*, 4, no. 2 (1988): 245-255.
376. Lori Pottinger, "Environmental Impacts of Large Dams: African

examples," *International Rivers' Mission* (1996) http://www.internationalrivers.org/en/africa/environmental-impacts-large-dams-african-examples (accessed May 31, 2008).

377. C. Geerling, C. A. Drijver and ir.W.T.de Groot, "Ecological Guidelines for River Basin Development," *Dutch Commission on Ecology and Development Cooperation* (1986) https://openaccess.leidenuniv.nl/dspace/bitstream/1887/8055/1/11_512_075.pdf. (accessed June 4, 2008).

378. Mabro, 94-95.

379. Ibid.

380. Mostafa K. Tolba and Najib W. Saab, eds., *2009 Report Of The Arab Forum For Environment and Development: Impact of Climate Change on Arab Countries*, (Beirut: Arab Forum For Environment and Development, 2009), 61-63. http://www.afedonline.org/afedreport09/default.asp (accessed May 15, 2011).

381. Katherine Weist, "Development Refugees: Africans, Indians and the Big Dams," *Journal of Refugee Studies*, 8 (1995): 163-18. I

382. For details of their demands, see, "el-Hegra el-khamesa ila belad el-dhahab," *Rose al Youssef*, April 11, 2009, 37-49; or Ragab el-Morshedi, "Mu'amara ba'da montasaf el-lail li tahweel moshkelat el-Nouba ila qadiyya dawliyya," *Rose al Youssef*, April 25, 2009, 18-21.

383. Trevor Mostyn, *Egypt's Belle Époque* (London: Tauris Parke, 2006), 3.

384. For more details see, Cynthia Myntti, *Paris along the Nile: Architecture in Cairo from the Belle Époque* (Cairo; New York: American University in Cairo Press, 2003); Suhayr Zaki Hawwas, *el-Qaherah el-khediwiyya: Rasad wa tawthiq 'imarat wa 'umran mintaqat wasat el-madina* (Cairo: Markaz el-tasmimat el-me'mariyya, 2002); also Nevine el-Aref, "Clearing the rubble of urban chaos," *Al Ahram Weekly*, August 19-25, 2004, http://weekly.ahram.org.eg/2004/704/fe1.htm (accessed May 14, 2008).

385. For some examples of villas that have been turned into schools see, Atef el-Kilani, "Bi hokm el-mahkama enha ehtilal el madares lil qosour el-nadera," *Rose al Youssef*, June 19-25, 2004, 45-47.

386. For some examples see, Samir Raafat, *Cairo, the Glory Years: Who Built What, When, Why and for whom* (Alexandria: Harpocrates, 2003).

387. Esam Abdel Aziz, "Helwan wadda'at zaman el-qosour wal bashawat, *Rose al Youssef*, July 6, 2007, 59-63.

388. "Min qiblat el-sina's ilal martaba el-thalitha fi qa'imat el-akthar talawwothan: Helwan ard el-'ashwa'iyyat," *Rose al Youssef*, May 2, 2008, 40.

389. The city has twenty-nine large factories and fifteen hundred small and medium size factories, and the area has turned into slums that lack many basic services. "Min qiblat el-sina's ilal martaba el-thalitha

fi qa'imat el-akthar talawwothan: Helwan ard el-'ashwa'iyyat," *Rose al Youssef*, May 2, 2008, 40. But Helwan's fate was no accident. The tragedy, as one writer termed the deterioration in Cairo's environment, began soon after the military coup in 1952. Said Abdel Khaleq, Tafrigh el-Qahera daroura qabla fawat el-awan," *Al Ahram*, December 22, 2001. http://www.ahram.org.eg/archive/Index.asp?CurFN=OPIN3.HTM&DID=7247 (accessed May 16, 2008). The writer goes on to point out that "security expert" was charged with devising a plan to protect the revolution from those described as reactionary enemies of the people and of socialism. The "expert" advised concentrating all factories in and around Cairo so that "the proletariat" could be brought out to protect the revolution if the need arose. This was done in violation of basic economic principles. An iron and steel factory, for example, was built in Helwan even though, according to the same article, each ten tons of iron ore needed to produce one ton of steel have to be transported one thousand kilometers from Aswan in Upper Egypt, and from an oasis in the Western Desert. The cost of this lack of economic logic was inadvertently pointed out recently by the president of the mining sector in the Bahari Oasis, 'Adnan Nada, who was discussing the increased costs of transportation due to the deterioration of the railway line. According to Nada, while the cost of mining a ton of iron ore is seventeen pounds, the cost of transporting that ton from the oasis is twenty-five pounds by rail and forty pounds by road. Mahmoud Samaha, "Qal'at el-hadid wal solb fi 'ard qitar khorda," *Rose al Youssef*, December 9, 2006, 85-89. Before production, therefore, the cost of the final product, steel, has been increased significantly due to the cost of transportation. This increase must be even more pronounced for the iron ore transported from Aswan.

390. The urban decline in all of Cairo's neighborhoods has led to the loss of its rich architectural heritage, despite valiant efforts by lone individuals such as Samir Ra'fat to document and preserve it. For some examples see, Samir Ra'fat, *Cairo, the Glory Years: Who Built What, When, Why and for Whom* (Alexandria: Harpocrates, 2003). One example of an historic building that is left to decay and rot is Count Patrice de Zoghed's former residence in Alexandria. The mansion, according to Art professor Zeinab Nour, is one of the best examples of French neo-Renaissance architecture left in the city and contained many wall and ceiling frescos that have decayed and peeled off. Zeinab Nour, "Azizu Fannen dholla," *Rose al Youssef*, June 9, 2007, 52-53. Many villas were pulled down. 'Enayat Morgan, el-Qahera bayna el-tahdith wa ehteram el-qeyam el-torathiyya: hat tatahawwal el-Qa-

hera ila mahmiyya torathiyya," *Al Ahram*, June 23, 2002. See also Ragab el-Mordshedi, Alaa el-Din Daher, and Marwa Emara, "Harrero el-mabani el-athariyya min ehtelal el-masaleh el-hokumiyya," *Rose al Yossef*, September 5, 2008, 27-29. Most were replaced by unattractive concrete structures, and since the new elite did not appreciate the value of public parks and green areas, the gardens of some historic residences were built upon. The Cairo Zoo, for example, and several other public parks lost parts of their green areas to housing, colleges, government offices, theaters, youth centers, sewage facilities, and bus stations. The result is that green areas in Cairo, according to press reports, are now about seventy-five centimeters per resident as opposed to eighteen meters in New York or sixteen meters in London. Ne'mat Ahmed Fuad, "el-hada'q fi tarikh Misr, *Al Ahram*, October 30, 2002, http://www.ahram.org.eg/archive/Index.asp?CurFN=WRIT2.HTM&DID=7559. (accessed May 12, 2008).

391. Several writers from very different professional backgrounds have commented on the prevailing ugliness. Okasha, Nasser's onetime Minister of Culture, states in his memoirs that when he returned to Cairo in 1957 after a three-year absence he was struck by the depressing prevalence of ugliness and the general deterioration of the urban environment. Okasha, vol.1, 249. He saw the rapid decline as a consequence of the change in social values and attributed it to the emergence of a new elite that appeared to be "detached from civilization, but controlled everything and impose[d] its taste" on society. Okasha, vol.1, 249. Other writers have echoed the same sentiments. Samir Sarhan, for example complains of the ubiquitous grime of Egyptian cities that people now appear to enjoy. Samir Sarhan, *Harb el-thaqafa* (Cairo: Dar Akhbar el-Yom, 2000), 85-86. Ahmad Abdel Mo'ti Hegazi notes that the ugliness of contemporary Egyptian villages and cities is unprecedented. Ahmed Abdel Mo'ti Hegazi, "Na'am aana el-awan," *Al Ahram*, September 29, 2004, http://www.ahram.org.eg/archive/Index.asp?CurFN=writ0.htm&DID=8259 (accessed May 12, 2008). The noise pollution produced by the proliferation of scores of loudspeakers on every street corner reflects another aspect of the deterioration of Egyptian cities and villages. Ahmed Abdel Mo'ti Hegazi, Hal aana lana an norage' hadha kolloh," *Al Ahram*, January 2, 2002, http://www.ahram.org.eg/archive/Index.asp?CurFN=WRIT0.HTM&DID=7258 (accessed May 12, 2008); Ahmed Abdel Mo'ti Hegazi, "Microphone likol mowaten," *Al Ahram*, September 15, 2004, http://www.ahram.org.eg/archive/Index.asp?CurFN=writ0.htm&DID=8245 (accessed May 12, 2008). Anis Mansour complains about the trend of building on areas of private gardens and public parks, of felling the street

trees, and of building on arable land instead of the desert outskirts of Cairo. Ahmed Abdel Mo'ti Hegazi, Hal aana lana an norage' hadha kolloh," *Al Ahram*, January 2, 2002, http://www.ahram.org.eg/archive/Index.asp?CurFN=WRIT0.HTM&DID=7258 (accessed May 12, 2008); Ahmed Abdel Mo'ti Hegazi, "Microphone likol mowaten," *Al Ahram*, September 15, 2004, http://www.ahram.org.eg/archive/Index.asp?CurFN=writ0.htm&DID=8245 (accessed May 12, 2008). Abdulla 'Enan also notes a marked general deterioration in every aspect of society from taste, to architecture, to the arts, Mohammed el-Gawwadi, *Takween el-'aql el-Araby: modhakkarat el-tarbawiyyeen wal mofakkereen* (Cairo; Dar el-khayyal, 2003), 235-245. All four prominent thinkers and educators whose memoirs were reviewed by Mohammed el-Gawwadi have attributed the deterioration of all aspects of culture in Egypt to the military rule and Raga'i Atiyya expresses puzzlement at Egyptians' seeming inability to recognize ugliness. Raga'i Atiyya, "Limadha da'a el-ehsas bil qobh," *Algomhuria*, http://www.gom.com.eg/algomhuria/2002/12/16/colums/detail03.shtml (accessed August 2, 2009).
392. Nevine el-Aref, "Clearing the rubble of urban chaos," *Al Ahram Weekly*, August 19-25, 2004, http://weekly.ahram.org.eg/2004/704/fe1.htm, (accessed May 14, 2008).
393. St. John, 268–270.
394. El-Aref.
395. Vatikiotis, 361.
396. "Zeyadat el-nasl moshkela yowagehoha ra'is el-wozara'," *Akhbar el-Yom*, June 29, 2002, 11.
397. Ibid.
398. Naguib, *Masir*, 94.
399. Huwaidy, *Ma'a*, 222.
400. Sa'd Eddin Ibrahim, "State, Women, And Civil Society: An Evaluation of Egypt's Population Policy," in *Arab Society*, eds. Nicholas S. Hopkins and Sa'd Eddin Ibrahim, 85-104 (Cairo: The American University In Cairo Press, 1997), 87.
401. Matar, 105.
402. Hamroush, vol. 4, 89
403. Matar, 105.
404. Ibid.
405. Ra'fat, *Fusul*, 251.
406. Nasser, as would be expected, was still claiming success in achieving these goals twelve years after the coup on March 26, 1964, see, Bibliotica Alexandrina, *Mawqi' el-ra'is Gamal Abdel Nasser*, "Khitab el-ra'is Gamal Abdel Nasser fi eftitah magles el-omma," http://nasser.bibal-

ex.org/Speeches/browser.aspx?SID=1071 (accessed June 15, 2008).
407. Hamroush, vol.1, 178; Lacouture, 118-119.
408. A recent study by the National Research Center was reported in the news media to have found only fourteen cases of bribery among the 8400 crimes reported in 1950. Yet, the new military régime embarked in 1952 upon what it referred to as the purification program. Although the purification program was ostensibly intended to eradicate corruption, in reality Nasser had no interest in eliminating it among his new appointees because it kept them happy, beholden to him, and vulnerable to blackmail by him. The study also reported that the substantial increase in corruption after the coup led to the formation of several new bureaucracies aimed at investigating and disciplining corrupt officials, and yet the Ministry of Interior's statistics show a decline in corruption in spite of the fact that all other indicators suggest that it is on the increase. See: Asma' Rashed, "Hewar ma'a sahebat derasa mohemma: 50 'aman fil fasad," *Rose al Yossef*, November 18, 2006, 42-43; The UNDP's Arab Human Development Report 2004 has also confirmed that corruption was "pervasive" throughout the Arab World, United Nations Development Programme, *Human Development Reports*, http://hdr.undp.org/en/reports/regionalreports/arabstates/name,3278,en.html (accessed May 19, 2008). Corruption reflected in rampant building code violations in all of Egypt's cities is one of the factors that have contributed to the degradation of the urban environment. The mass media is replete with reports of these violations and building collapses but they rarely lead to any action by the authorities. A seventeen-story apartment building erected in a narrow side street barely two and a half meters wide is not an uncommon violation. Nor is ignoring the requirement to provide parking spaces for all new buildings. See, for example, "Corruption blamed for Alexandria building collapse," *New Civil Engineer*, January 2, 2008, http://www.nce.co.uk/corruption-blamed-for-alexandria-building-collapse/411747.article (accessed November 9, 2011); "No injuries in Alexandria building collapse," Wonders Of Arabia, October 19, 2011, http://www.wondersofarabia.com/index.php/middle-east-news-channels/middle-east-news-headlines/egypt-news/item/137282-html (accessed November 9, 2011); "Corrupt work blamed in Egypt building collapse," *Associated Press*, December 29, 2007, http://www.msnbc.msn.com/id/22432355/ns/world_news-mideast_n_africa/t/corrupt-work-blamed-egypt-building-collapse/#.TromDnGYWUY (accessed November 9, 2011); Hanan el-Misri, "el-iskandariyya aayela lil soqoot," *Al Ahram*, November 4, 2011, http://www.ahram.org.eg/Provinces/News/110835.aspx (accessed November 4, 2011); Mus-

tafa el-Kholy, Qoul ya baset," *Rose al Yossef*, April 15, 2005, 79. These and other violations have contributed to the creation of serious traffic problems in Cairo and other cities. An estimated seventy percent of building owners in Cairo have, in collusion with corrupt local officials, turned garages under their buildings into shops and storage facilities which are more profitable, in spite of the fact that according to the Cairo Traffic department, the number of vehicles in the city is already five times the capacity of its streets. The former military men who occupy most senior positions in the bureaucracy appear unwilling or incapable of coping with these problems. They either issue a constant stream of press releases to sing their own praises, or blame someone else for the problems. For example, the deputy Governor of Cairo (a retired General) found it sufficient to promise the media in 2004 that all the unused garages would be reopened. When asked to comment on the problem, the Secretary General of the Cairo Governorate (another retired General) avoided making any promises and shirked his responsibility for the traffic issue altogether by stating that the cause of the problem is lack of respect for the law. Karim Sobhy, Wafa' Sha'ira, and Omayma Sadek, "Takhtaneq el-Qahera," *Rose al Yossef*, October 16, 2004, 38-40. Meanwhile seventy-five thousand shops in Giza (part of greater Cairo) are operating without a license because they happen to be located in buildings that are in violation of the building code, and the Governorate has not acted because it is busy examining the means of "legalizing" these shops. *Rose al Yossef*, December 30, 2006, 73. Corruption has become a permanent topic of press reports and the government is impervious to these reports and appears to view them as merely a harmless means of letting off steam by the public.
409. Matar, 108–109.
410. Abul Fath, 500.
411. Ibid.
412. Vatikiotis, 269.
413. El-Sadat, *el-Bahth*, 217.
414. "El-Hai'a el-'amma li mahw el-ommiya fashalat fi mohemmateha ba'd 16 sana min ensha'ha wal ra'is yatahaffaz howwa mafeesh 'eqab tayyeb?," *el-Dostour*, September 13, 2007, 4.
415. Seventeen intellectuals offer their reasons for the decline in Mo'awwad, Ezzat, *Thawrat Yulyu wa azmat el-thaqafa*, (Cairo: el-Hai'a el-Misriyya el-'amma lil ketab, 1991).
416. Ahmed Abdel Mo'ti Hegazi, a prominent intellectual has written several articles dealing with that topic. See, for example, Ahmed Abdel Mo'ti Hegazi, "Dameer." The decline has also been noted by some

454   Notes

Arab intellectuals. See, for example, the series of articles by Iraqi historian Sayyar Al-Jamil. Sayyar Al-Jamil, "Thawrat 1917 lil mosiqa wal ghena' fi Misr," *Rose al Yossef*, May 16, 2009, 82-84; Sayyar Al-Jamil, "Hawas el-she'arat la yongeb el-'amaleqa," *Rose al Yossef*, May 9, 2009, 22-23; Sayyar Al-Jamil, "60 'aman min el-naksa el-thaqafiyya fil thaqafa," *Rose al Yossef*, April 11, 2009, 80-81; Sayyar Al-Jamil, "el-Thaqafa el-Arabiyya tahtag ila ghorfat in'ash," *Rose al Yossef*, April 18, 2009, 86-87

417. P.J. Vatikiotis also cites the military junta's control of all aspects of cultural life as a major contributor to the poor quality of cultural endeavors, see, Vatikiotis, 219.

Chapter 8

1. The impact of the elite socio-economic stratum on the rest of society was identified more than six centuries ago by ibn Khaldun in his Muqaddema. He obviously did not use modern sociological terminology, but his analysis, referred to earlier, was insightful and is still valid today. The essence of his thesis was that the slave would always imitate his master in everything he does in the subconscious belief that it is the master's mannerisms, style of dress, and personal habits that constitute his hidden strength and that have made him a master and not a slave. Ibn Khaldun, vol. 1, 299-300.
2. Much of the deterioration in the urban environment can be attributed either directly or indirectly to the spreading values of the new middle class. For example, rent control, which deprived landlords of both the financial means and incentive to maintain their buildings stemmed from hostility to the old elite and the view that landlords were exploiting the tenants. For examples of the deterioration see Nevine el-Aref, "Clearing the rubble of urban chaos," *Al Ahram Weekly*, August 19-25, 2004, http://weekly.ahram.org.eg/2004/704/fe1.htm, (accessed May 14, 2008); Iman Matar, "'asemat elgamal fi sallat el-mohmelat," *Rose al Yossef*, July 31-August 6, 2004, 53-57.
3. Hamroush, vol. 1, 137; see also Vatikiotis, 136.
4. Hamroush, vol.1, 309.
5. Ali, *Mashaweer*, 117.
6. The principle of ignoring expertise in public appointments eventually became enshrined in law. The 160/1962 act prohibited all personnel departments in government agencies, ministries, public and many private organizations from appointing any employee or laborer prior to informing the Commander-in-Chief's office and waiting for a month while the army determined if a military person could be found to oc-

cupy the vacant position. Fathi, 278–279. Moreover, the 25/1966 act formalized the creation of a privileged class by making all crimes committed by members of the military the sole concern of the military judicial apparatus unless civilians were involved in the crime. Ibid. Inevitably, the devaluation of technical competence, knowledge, and expertise began to filter down and affect the society's culture and system of social values. The new social value that began to take root and to form an integral part of the Egyptian value system was that acquiring expertise was not the best means of self-advancement. The specter of unqualified people of trust occupying the positions of power and prestige in the new Egypt served as living examples of the validity of the new precept.
7. Mohi el-Din, *Memories*, 158.
8. There was widespread dissatisfaction with this decree among the officer corps because it meant that the military rank had become meaningless. Mohi el-Din, *Memories*, 158. The promotion signaled the end of discipline dictated by seniority, and ranking officers began to feel subservient to any junior officers who had contacts with the new commander-in-chief or members of his entourage. Hamroush, vol.1, 322. The traditional army chain of command collapsed and was replaced by cliques and clandestine personal connections. Ibid. Amer possessed a sociable, outgoing personality that made him popular and well liked, but his fellow officers had never considered him a good soldier or a serious military man or disciplinarian. Vatikiotis, 161. His colleagues always saw him as more like an 'umda (village headman) than as a professional soldier. He enjoyed socializing, partying until the early hours of the morning, and having many people around him. Mohi el-Din, *Memories*, 242-243. Amer's appointment was a significant landmark that exemplified the values and new style of leadership whereby someone like Hafez Ismail who graduated at the top of his 1937 class in the military college was now working as the office manager for Amer who graduated at the bottom of his 1939 class. Mohammed el-Gawwadi, *Modhakkarat qadat el-mokhabarat wal mabaheth: el-amn elqawmy li Misr* (Cairo: Dar el-Khayyal, 1999), 36-37.
9. He worked on Amer's staff in a similar capacity to Hafez Ismail but was far more influential. He was then a mere Captain, but was put in charge of all the armed forces personnel affairs. He controlled officers' postings and the composition of training missions abroad. More important still, he supervised the overall work of military intelligence. Vatikiotis, 163, el-Hadidi, *Shahed*, 28. Since military rank had become meaningless as an indication of qualifications, experience, and expertise after the coup, Badran's promotion to the rank of brigadier without requiring any further professional credentials Vatikiotis, 163; el-Hadidi, Shahed,

26, was not viewed as an unusual occurrence. His appointment to the ministry of war in 1966 came on the heels of an extensive wave of reassignments within the higher echelons of the army structure that he had complete charge of. The principle that governed all these reassignments was not expertise but trust and loyalty. Vatikiotis, 163.

10. Graduation from the military college became the sole requirement for appointment to positions ranging from factory manager to director of desert reclamation programs. Humor, as is often the case in Egypt, articulated the national feelings. It was said that a young man no longer had to decide early in life what career he wanted to follow or commit himself to a specific field of specialization by applying to a university. Instead he should apply to the military college because once he graduated he would be qualified to follow whatever career he wanted, doctor, lawyer, accountant, etc. Army officers were no longer committed to a military career to the exclusion of all other options. It would be impossible to list the names of all those whose military training was the sole qualification for other careers, but a few short examples would provide a glimpse of the extensive opportunities that had become available to army officers. Ahmad Hamroush, Kamal Ref'at, Kamal el-Din el-Hennawi, Abdel Aziz Sadek, Mustafa el-Mestikawi all became writers. Se'da, 183 Yousef el-Seba'i became an author, journalist, Secretary General of the Higher Council for Arts, Secretary of the Novelists Club, as well as occupying various other positions in the "culture" field. For an example of his writings see el-Seba'i, Youssef el-Seba'i, *Ayyam Abdel Nasser* (Cairo: Maktabat el-Khangi, 1971). Ezz el-Din Zolfaqar became a movie director, Hamroush, vol. 4, 359; Gamal Hammad a writer and a historian, Habib, 286; and Ahmad Mazhar a movie actor. "Some officers became literary giants by presidential decree." *Se'da*, 112-120. *Mandoub el-qiyada* was the new term that was coined to describe the large number of trusted members of the military who were appointed to all branches of the bureaucracy, Vatikiotis, 130, to be the eyes and ears of the junta. Junior officers who had no qualifications or expertise in business or financial transactions were given the top positions in large banks and insurance companies. St. John, 268–270. Officers became presidents of sports clubs, Mansour, 261. and headed sports organizations such as the Wrestling Union and the Soccer Union. Imam, *Ali Sabry Yatadhakkar*, 83. This is not to suggest, however, that every officer who changed careers was incompetent. Several of those who ventured into civilian life were talented, proved themselves capable, and became very successful in their new careers. The military's control of society became so extensive that it extended to obscure tasks such as the assignment

of vacant apartments. Anwar el-Sadat, *el-Bahth*, 209–210. The Minister of Religious Foundations Ahmad Hassan el-Baqoury, found himself in a Cabinet composed of military officers who always wrote the letters AH (*arkan harb*) after their signatures to denote their graduation from the staff college. El-Baqoury, who seems to have had a sense of humor, began to sign his name as AH el-Baqoury and when his puzzled colleagues queried him, he answered that these were simply his initials. El-Gawwadi, *Derasa*, 239.

11. Awad, *Aqne'at*, 283.
12. Fathi, 543.
13. Ibid; Fawzi, *Mu'amarat*, 93.
14. El-Gawwadi, *Derasa*, 2003, 239.
15. Gamal Hammad, *el-Hokuma el-khafiya fi 'ahd Abdel Nasser* (Cairo, el-zahraa lil i'lam el-Araby, 1986), 134-140.
16. A Free Officer turned writer and historian.
17. Habib, 445.
18. Habib, 120-122.
19. Sharaf spent decades out of the limelight but has now been rehabilitated and occasionally writes a column in *Al Ahram*.
20. Lutfi, *Thuwwar*, 26–27.
21. This is not to suggest that undesirable traits such as opportunism, sycophancy, and willingness to abandon basic integrity did not exist in Egypt prior to 1952 or that other societies are free of them. The claim made here is merely that they were less widespread, less widely accepted, and more commonly and publicly disapproved of and frowned upon.
22. The author did not provide any names but the country referred to was most probably Spain.
23. Mo'nes, 129-130.
24. Ibid, 136.
25. Ibid, 128-137.
26. Sharaf and Imam, 5–6.
27. Ibid, 441-444.
28. Ibid, 465.
29. Ibid, 252
30. Ibid.
31. Sharaf and Imam, 399.
32. Abul Fath, 524.
33. Sharaf and Imam, 475.
34. Hussein el-Shafei and Salah el-Imam, *Hussein el-Shafei wa asrar thawrat Yulyu wa hukm el-Sadat* (Cairo: matba'at Osiris, 1993, 69.
35. Ibid, 75.

36. Ibid, 36.
37. Ibid, 132.
38. The level of thinking and muddled logic of Hussein el-Shafei was evident in a court case that he brought against the owners of a villa in the choicest private beach in Alexandria, which he was renting for 300 pounds per annum (the cost of a few packets of cigarettes). The villa was built on the grounds of the Montaza Royal Palace where King Farouk used to spend his summer vacation. After ownership of the villa was given to a government owned company, the management notified him that it was raising the annual rent to its true market value of to 30,000 pounds per annum El-Shafei's lawyer contended before the court that since the lease was a civil contract unconnected to el-Shafei's position as vice president, raising the rent would be in violation of the property law. At the same time el-Shafei maintained that, he was given the villa because he was Nasser's vice president. He told the press that when Nasser learned that both he and his fellow vice president Zakaria Mohi el-Din had no vacation houses, he called them and asked them to select a location inside the palace. Nasser sent Ali el-Sayyid (later minister of housing) with a map, they chose the location, and "this rest house has become part of my life." He added that he also had a right to the low rent because he "commanded the force composed of infantry, artillery, and armored vehicles that surrounded the palace" on the morning of the coup (the palace was empty at the time, the king having moved out with his family, but el-Shafei did not know that till the following day). Furthermore, el-Shafei added, "I gained nothing from the revolution but participated in it because we empathized when we were officers with the poor people and wanted to take care of them socially." Wafa' Sha'ira, "Hussein el-Shafei yanqol neza'aho ma'a wezaret el-seyaha ila el-mahkama el-dostoriyya," *Rose al Yossef*, November 5, 2004, 22.
39. Ibid, 115-119.
40. Ibid, 91.
41. Ibid, 86-93.
42. Ibid, 163-164.
43. Ibid, 103.
44. Ibid, 157.
45. Abdullah Imam, *Ali Sabry Yatadhakkar*, 83.
46. Ibid.
47. Ibid, 59.
48. Sharaf and Imam, 439.
49. Ibid, 458.
50. Amin Huwaidy, *Ma'a Abdel Nasser*, (Cairo, Dar el-mostaqbal el-Araby,

1985, 48.
51. Ibid.
52. Ibid.
53. Abdel Samad, 29; el-Hadidi, *Isterdad*, 2001), 43.

Chapter 9

1. El-Seba'i, *Ayyam*, 55.
2. Lacouture, 347.
3. The 1948/49 national budget, merely three years before the 1952 coup makes interesting reading, *Al Masry Al Youm*, July 11, 2016, Mizneyyet Misr fi 'ahd Farouk, http://lite.almasryalyoum.com/extra/102671/ (accessed July 11, 2016).
4. Vatikiotis, 201.
5. Anwar el-Sadat, *el-Bahth*, 294-295.
6. Ibid.
7. Dekmejian, 156, 228.
8. Ibrahim Dasuqi Abaza, *el-Khatya el-'ashr min Abdel Nasser ila el-Sadat* (Cairo: Dar Misr lil tiba'a, 1983), 45.
9. Mortagi, 39-40.
10. Most needles sold in the country today are imported from China.
11. Awad, *Aqne'at*, 81.
12. The Egyptian media reported the visit long after Nasser died.
13. Rose al Youssef, "'ailat Abu Regaila totaleb bi hai'at el-naql el-'am," January 31, 2003, 86-87.
14. Even the claim of having introduced free education was not accurate. The Wafd governments of 1942-1944 and 1950 abolished all school fees up to university level, and what Nasser abolished in 1962 was only university fees. Said Ismail Ali, "el-Ta'leem fi thawrat Yulyu 1952," in Mohammed Saber Arab and Ra'ouf Abbas Hamed, eds. *Khamsoun 'aman 'ala thawrat Yulyu 1952: Abhath el-lagna el-dawliyya allati 'oqimat fil fatra min 20-22 Yulyu 2002, 431-484* (Cairo: Matba'at Dar el-kotob wal watha'q el-qawmiyya, 2002), 467.
15. Vatikiotis, 109.
16. Ali, *Khamsoun*, 468-469.
17. Ibid, 446-44.
18. Habib, 313.
19. Issawi, 49.
20. El-Sadat, *el-Bahth*, 112.
21. Habib, 116-117.
22. Matar, 95-96.
23. Ra'fat, *Fusul*, 196.

24. El-Sadat, *el-Bahth*, 259
25. Ibid.
26. Ra'fat, *Fusul*, 196; Vatikiotis, 295.
27. Vatikiotis, 311.
28. For examples, see, Mo'nes, 73-80.
29. Abaza, 43-44.
30. Abul Fath, 518.
31. Vatikiotis, 222.
32. El-Hadidi, *Shahed*, 48; Vatikiotis, 162.
33. Vatikiotis, 310.
34. Ibid, 258.
35. El-Sadat, *el-Bahth*, 257.
36. Ibid, 376.
37. Abul Fath, 393.
38. Ibid, 524.
39. Mahmoud Riad, *Modhakkarat Mahmoud Riad* (Cairo: Dar el-mustaqbal el-Araby, 1985-1986), vol. 3, 91-92.
40. Sami, 59.
41. El-Sadat, *el-Bahth*, 174–176.
42. Ibid, 209-210.
43. Musa Sabry, *el-Sadat*, 248.
44. Ibid, 249.
45. Ibid.
46. Sabry, *el-Sadat*, 196.
47. El-Sadat, *el-Bahth*, 38-94; 63; 67; 86.
48. For Weber's classic statements on power see, Max Weber, *Economy and Society: An Outline of Interpretive Sociology*, eds. Guenther Roth and Claus Wittoch, trans. Ephraim Fischoff et. al., (Berkeley: University of California Press, 1978).
49. El -Sadat, *el-Bahth*, 29.
50. Lacouture, 40.
51. Ibid, 40.
52. Nutting, 14.
53. Ibid.
54. Hoda Abdel Nasser, "Sira dhatiyya lil ra'is Gamal Abdel Nasser," Bibliotica Alexandrina, *Mawqi' el-ra'is Gamal Abdel Nasser*, http://nasser.bibalex.org/Common/pictures01-%20sira.htm. (accessed February 4, 2008).
55. Anwar el-Sadat, *In Search of Identity: An Autobiography* (London: Collins, 1978), 141.
56. Lutfi, *Ma'sat*, 37.
57. Ibid, 37.

58. El-Sadat, *el-Bahth*, 27.
59. Lutfi, *Ma'sat*, 37-39
60. Ibid.
61. As the platform was being towed from the Mediterranean to southern Africa on its way for Suez, the Egyptian intelligence managed to destroy it when it stopped to refuel in Abidjan. Amin Hamed Huwaidy, *el-Foras el-da''ah: el-qararat el-hasema fi harbbai el-istenzaf wa October* (Beirut: Sharikat el-matbu'at lil tawzi' wal nashr, 1992), 155-161.
62. El-Hadidi, *Isterdad*, 37.
63. Sabry, *Watha'q 15 Mayo*, 242-242.
64. Vatikiotis, 218.
65. Ibid, 216.
66. Mabro, 133.
67. Anwar el-Sadat, *el-Bahth*, 288.
68. Ibid, 288.
69. Ibid, 294-295.
70. Abdel Ghani, *el-Muthaqqafoun*, 364-365.
71. Dekmejian, 63.
72. Abdel *el-Muthaqqafoun*, 218.
73. Abdel Malek, 20-21.
74. Ibid.
75. Awad, *Aqne'at*, 81.
76. Abdel Ghani, *el-Muthaqqafoun*, 368.
77. Abdel Rahman Badawi found that the officers turned diplomats that he served with in the Egyptian embassy in Switzerland lacked knowledge of their country's affairs, history, world politics, and maintains, "ignorance, superficiality, and sycophancy were their distinguishing characteristics." Badawi, vol. 1, 251-252.
78. Abdel Malek, 32-33.
79. Abaza, 45.
80. Ibid, 290-291.
81. Sabry, *el-Sadat*, 626.
82. Another joke was that Sadat asserts that he "would follow Nasser's line closely . . . with an eraser." el-Hadidi, *Isterdad*, 130.
83. When the military junta nationalized a substantial part of the economy and instituted a policy of appointing all university graduates in the government and public sector, the ranks of these employees began to swell very rapidly. The Egyptian bureaucracy has become so bloated that even the government owned media admits that it has become an impediment to the normal operation of the various government bodies. See: Olfat Sa'd, "Koll el-mowazzafoun yahtagoun tadriban 'sriyyan min asghar el-daragat ila el-edara el-'olya," *Rose al Youssef*,

March 19-25, 2005, 31-32. One clear example of this is the reported one hundred and eighteen approvals that an investor intending to set up a new business is required to obtain. "El-Bureaucratiyya," *el-Akhbar*, April 8, 2002, 12. The Minister of Administrative Development has admitted to the media that the 7.5 million bureaucrats employed by the government include about half a million *farrash* (office boys), most of whom do not have any work to do, and that virtually all these bureaucrats are in need of retraining. These figures, he states, indicate that twenty-nine percent of the total workforce in the country are bureaucrats, whereas international standards suggest between six and eight percent. Sa'd, "Koll el-mowazzafoun. A former finance minister who served in Nasser's administration has admitted to the press that the explosive growth in the bureaucracy was the direct result of Nasser's orders to offer a government job to every university graduate despite the fact that they had no work to do. Amira Khawasek, "Abdel Aziz Hegazi: Khas'rna fi harb Yunyu balaghat 'asharat miliarat genaih," *October Magazine*, December 3, 2004, http://www.octobermag.com/Issues/1466/artDetail.asp (accessed December 3, 2004); One example of the bureaucracy's inefficiency was reflected in its mismanagement of the new suburbs that were built outside Cairo to relieve some of the pressures on its infrastructure. A recent report has suggested that some of these new developments are in danger of turning into "ghost cites" as a result of the bureaucracy's apparent inability to deal effectively with land speculators who are keeping thousands of building plots vacant and off the market to await possible future increases in land prices. Saber Shawkat and Hesham Atiyya, Hatta la tatahawwal ila modon lil ashbah: wizarat el-eskan tarfa' el-kart el-ahmar fi wagh toggar el-aradi," *Akhbar el-Yom*, October 23, 2004, 14.

84. Sabry, *Watha'q 15 Mayo*, 166.
85. Raymond William Baker, *Sadat and After: Struggles for Egypt's Political Soul* (Cambridge, Mass.: Harvard University Press, 1990), 83-84.
86. Dekmejian, 230.
87. Sabry, *Watha'q 15 Mayo*, 140-144.
88. The committee's members were Ali Sabry, Labib Shoqair, Dia' el-Din Dawood, Abdel Mohsen Abul Nour, and Sha'rawi Gom'a. Ibid, 179. Abdel Mohsen Abul Nour, Secretary General of the ASU discusses these events in his memoirs. Abdel Mohsen Abul Nour, *el-haqiqa 'an thawrat 23 Yulyu* (Cairo: el-Hai'a el-Misriyya el-'amma lil ketab, 2001), 307-338. However, his account is transparently self serving and unreliable
89. Ibid, 83.
90. El-Sadat, *el-Bahth*, 55-58.

91. Sabry, *Watha'q 15 Mayo*, 63-64.
92. Sabry, *Watha'q harb*, 216.
93. Ibid, 155-156
94. Ibid, 69.
95. Ibid, 70.
96. Ibid, 75-76.
97. For partial transcripts of the plotters interrogation, and their recorded conversations see, Ibid, 169-182; 184-201; 235-236, 242-243.
98. Abdel Azim Ramadan, *el-haqiqa el-tarikhiyyah hawla harb October* (Cairo; el-Hai'a el-Misriyya el-'amma lil ketab, 2002), 87; Ramadan, *Harb October*, 43; el-Gamasy, 213. Sadat met with editors of the national newspapers after these demonstrations and attempted to win their cooperation in calming the situation. For details see, Sabry, *Watha'q harb*, 275-299.
99. The meddling had became a source of constant friction with Arab countries, and the expulsion of Egypt's military attachés from countries in the region had long become a regular occurrence. In Lebanon, for example, explosives were found in the attaché's home and car and he was expelled. Attachés were also expelled from Libya and Ethiopia for inciting public disturbances and from Tunisia, Saudi Arabia, and Jordan for being involved in assassination plots. Ra'fat, *Fusul*, 196; St. John, 274
100. Habib, 236-238.
101. Ramadan, *el-haqiqa*, 104.
102. For a personal review of the state of Nasser's army by one of its officers, see, el-Hadidi, *Isterdad*; or Mohammed Hussein Younis, *khatawat 'al el-ard el-mahboosa* (Cairo: Dar el-Mostaqbal el-Araby, 1983).
103. Vatikiotis, 160.
104. Ibid; see also Lutfi, *Ma'sat*, 178-180.
105. Lacouture, 362.
106. Fathi, 261.
107. Ibid, 280.
108. Habib, 271.
109. El-Sadat, *el-Bahth*, 209-210.
110. El-Hadidi, *Shahed*, 48.
111. Louis Awad, *Aqne'at*, 168.
112. Mazhar, 17.
113. Ibid, 44
114. Ibid.
115. Okasha, vol. 2, 489-499.
116. Ibid.
117. Mohammed Fawzi, *Harb el-thalath sanawat: 1967-1970*, (Cairo: Dar

el-mostaqbal el-Araby, 1984), 248.
118. Ibid, 9.
119. El-Sadat, *el-Bahth*, 242-243.
120. Ali, *Mashaweer*, 245-246.
121. Ibid, 262-263.
122. Mohammed Fawzi, *Harb*, 238.
123. Ibid.
124. Ibid, 62-63.
125. Ibid. There is no doubt that as a Commander-in-Chief, Fawzi was a major improvement on the Amer and Badran team. Nevertheless, he, as memoirs show, was a man of the past who did not share Sadat's views and vision of the new army. For example, he did not have the confidence in himself to be able to resist putting a photograph of Nasser with him in the background on the cover of his memoirs, in addition to the other twelve photographs of the two of them that the book contained (there was a single photograph that did not include Nasser in the book). He consistently uses the singular pronoun, "I," when discussing successes and the plural "they," or "the leadership" when discussing anything negative. He also tends to rely on either classic Nasserist rhetoric or rather naïve and simplistic reasoning to support his arguments. For example, he lists as a victory the fact that a few soldiers managed to cross the Canal and blow up an Egyptian ammunition storage depot that was left intact after the withdrawal. Ibid, 221. He states that Egypt's involvement in Yemen was one of the causes of the 1967 defeat. Ibid, 9. Then goes on to state that the Yemen venture was a strategic success because it "opened the Yemenis eyes to the outside world;" began the liberation of Southern Yemen; initiated the awareness of the importance of a national strategic presence in the Arab area; changed "the exploitive policies of the US and British oil companies in the area;" and opened the way for north and south Yemen for independence and receiving arms from the soviet Union, Ibid, 25-26. He absolves himself from responsibility for the 1967 events by claiming that he, as Chief of Staff was powerless because Amer, Badran, and the land forces command had complete authority over the armed forces, Ibid, 38 and as a result, he had nothing to do. Yet he does not offer any explanations for the fact that he did not resign. Instead, he states that he spent his time traveling to India, Yugoslavia, and Arab countries "to kill time." Ibid, 56. At the same time, he cannot resist attempting to lessen the enormity of the defeat by providing what might charitably termed unconvincing arguments. He states, for example, that Sinai was difficult for the Israelis to control because of the scarcity of both paved roads and water,

which impacted their "production and development plans and lowered their morale," Ibid, 213-215. He adds that they "exploited Sinai in only small ways limited to tourism and the oil wells" and built tourist facilities and roads to Sharm el-Sheikh and to St. Catharine's Monastery. Ibid, 217.
126. El-Gamasy *Modhakkarat*, 20.
127. Air vice Marshal Abdel-Hamid el-Dighidi, who once commanded the air force and the air defense, made that point in an interview when he stated "The intelligence service in my command station, however, were spying on me, not for me." "A Lesson we should have learned," *Al Ahram Weekly*, June 5-11, 1997, http://weekly.ahram.org.eg/archives/67-97/sup10.htm (accessed 23 September. 2007).
128. El-Sadat, *el-Bahth*, 356.
129. Sabry, *el-Sadat*, 294; see also Ramadan, *Harb October*, 53-56.
130. Sabry, *Watha'q harb* October, 15-19.
131. For minutes of meeting see, Ibid, 35-90.
132. Ramadan, *el-haqiqa*h, 9.
133. Musa Sabry, *Watha'q harb*, 35-90.
134. Ramadan, *el-haqiqa*h, 9; see also Ramadan, *Harb October*, 56.
135. Ramadan, *Harb October*, 56.
136. Ibid, 81.
137. Ibid, 82-83.
138. See el-Sadat, *el-Bahth*, 321.
139. Alexander, 144.
140. Mansour, 162.
141. 'Adel Yousry, *Reheat el-saq el-mo'allaqa min ras el-'ish ila ras el-kobry* (Cairo: Dar el-ma'aref, 1974), 36.
142. Ibid.
143. Dekmejian, 288.
144. General Abu Ghazala has attempted, rather unconvincingly, to present the war of attrition in a more positive light. See, *Mohammed Abdel Halim Abu Ghazala, Wa intalaqat el-madafi' end el-zohr*, (Cairo: Dar el-sha'b, 1975), 59-71.
145. Baker, 95; see also Fawzi, Harb, 225.
146. Ramadan, *Harb October*, 30.
147. Dekmejian, 288, Ramadan, *Harb October*, 28-30.
148. Mohammed Fawzi, *Harb* (Cairo: Dar el-mostaqbal el-Araby, 1984), 224.
149. Baker, 95.
150. El-Gamasy, *Modhakkarat*, 174.
151. Ramadan, *Harb October*, 35.
152. Ibid, 36.

153. Yousry, 74.
154. Ibid.
155. Ramadan, *el-haqiqa*, 50-52.
156. Ibid.
157. El-Sadat, *el-Bahth*, 329.
158. Ibid, 327.
159. Ibid, 326-327.
160. Saad el-Shazly, *The Crossing of the Suez Canal* (San Francisco: American Research Center, 2003), 75.
161. Ibid.
162. Ibid, 75; Ramadan, *Harb October*, 91-93; Hassan el-Badry, *el-Gawla el-Arabiyya el-Israeliyya el-rabi'a, October 1973* (Cairo: el-Sharika el-mottahida lil nashr wal tawazi', 1974, 64; Ramadan, *el-haqiqa*, 212-213.
163. Ramadan, *el-haqiqa*, 212-213.
164. Ibid.
165. El-Gamasy, 285.
166. Ibid.
167. Ibid.
168. Ibid, 287.
169. Ramadan, *el-haqiqa*, 212-213.
170. El-Gamasy, 301; Ramadan, *el-haqiqa*, 212-213.
171. Yousry, 71; el-Sadat, *el-Bahth*, 337.
172. Sabry, *Watha'q 15 Mayo*, 106.
173. Baker, 95.
174. Ramadan, *el-haqiqa*, 248.
175. Yousef Afifi, *Abtal el-ferqa 19: moqateloun fawqqa el-'ada* (Hurghada: Dar el-safwa lil tiba'a wal nashr, 1990), 117.
176. For an eyewitness description of the Bar Lev line, see, el-Badry 39-63. See, also, Abu Ghazala, 73-82.
177. El-Gamasy, 329-330.
178. Ibid.
179. Afifi, 112.
180. Ibid.
181. El-Shazly, 8.
182. El-Badry, 42.
183. Afifi, 112.
184. El-Shazly, 8.
185. El-Gamasy *Modhakkarat*, 329-330.
186. El-Shazly, 56-57.
187. El-Badry, 48.
188. Sabry, *Watha'q harb*, 389-391.
189. The Israeli engineer who designed them happened to be on an in-

spection visit at the front on October 6, 1973 and was taken prisoner, Ibid.
190. El-Gamasy, *Modhakkarat*, 329-330.
191. El-Badry, 43.
192. See el-Sadat, *el-Bahth*, 310.
193. See Ibid, 334-357 for Sadat's account of these events.
194. El-Badry, 64; Ramadan, *el-haqiqa*, 87.
195. El-Sadat, *el-Bahth*, 382-383.
196. Ibid, 384.
197. Yousry, *Rehlat*, 115.
198. El-Gamasy *Modhakkarat*, 288.
199. Afifi, 49; el-Badry, 92; Ramadan, *Harb October*, 97-98.
200. El-Gamasy, *Modhakkarat*, 304.
201. Afifi, 100; el-Sadat, *el-Bahth*, 335.
202. Afifi, 101.
203. El-Gamasy, *Modhakkarat*, 305; see also el-Badry, 92; el-Shazly, 222; Yousry, 117; Ali, *Mashaweer*, 292-307. Ali commanded the artillery during the operation.
204. El-Gamasy, *Modhakkarat*, 310.
205. El-Badry, 86.
206. El-Gamasy, *Modhakkarat*, 305-306; 299-305 for further details.
207. Ibid, 307; see also el-Badry, 99-108.
208. El-Gamasy, *Modhakkarat*, 307-308.
209. Ibid.
210. El-Badry, 106-107.
211. Sabry, *Watha'q harb*, 389-390.
212. Ramadan, *Harb October*, 99.
213. El-Badry, 64; Ramadan, *el-haqiqa*, 106-107.
214. The young Coptic engineer was later promoted to the rank of General and awarded the Medal of the Republic First Class for his role in liberating Sinai.
215. Ramadan, *el-haqiqa*, 290-298.
216. El-Sadat, *el-Bahth*, 337.
217. Ibid, 345.
218. Ramadan, *el-haqiqa*, 395.
219. El-Badry, 106-107.
220. Ibid, 108.
221. Ali, *Mashaweer*, 307-311; see also el-Gamasy, *Modhakkarat*, 359; el-Sadat, *el-Bahth*, 347.
222. El-Gamasy, *Modhakkarat*, 397; Ali, *Mashaweer*, 311.
223. Ramadan, *Harb October*, 107-108.
224. Ibid, 131-133.

225. El-Gamasy, 312-13.
226. Ali, *Mashaweer*, 331.
227. Ibid, 332.
228. Sabry, el-Sadat, 358.
229. Sabry, *Watha'q harb*, 612-613.
230. Ibid, 611.
231. Ibid; el-Gamasy, *Modhakkarat*, 412; Ramadan, *Harb October*, 141.
232. Sabry, *Watha'q harb*, 612-613.
233. El-Gamasy, *Modhakkarat*, 412.
234. Ibid, 415.
235. El-Sadat, *el-Bahth*, 348.
236. Ibid, 248.
237. Ibid.
238. Ibid, 249.
239. General Shazly took the demotion badly, never admitted his error of judgment, and seems to have decided to devote the rest of his life attempting to even the score with Sadat by attacking him in the media.
240. El-Sadat, *el-Bahth*.
241. For details, see ibid, 348-355.
242. Ibid, 350.
243. Ibid, 385.
244. Ramadan, *Harb October*, 159.
245. Ali, *Mashaweer*, 314; see also el-Gamasy, *Modhakkarat*, 426-429.
246. El-Sadat *el-Bahth*, 353.
247. El-Gamasy, *Modhakkarat*, 431.
248. Ibid, 435.
249. Ibid,
250. Afifi, 163-165.
251. El-Gamasy, *Modhakkarat*, 433.
252. El-Sadat, *el-Bahth*. 355.
253. Ibid, 355.
254. Ibid, 356.
255. Baker, 81.
256. The national newspaper referred to here is *el-Gomhuriyya*, Sabry, *el-Sadat*, 521.
257. Ibid.
258. Sabry, el-Sadat, 539-578.
259. Ibid, 137-138.
260. Ibid, 539-578.
261. Ibid, 137-138.
262. Ibid, 154.
263. Ibid, 574.

264. Ibid, 521.
265. Ibid, 296-297.
266. Declan Walsh, "Wikileaks Cables Portray Saudi Arabia as a Cash Machine for Terrorists," *The Guardian*, December 5, 2010, http://www.guardian.co.uk/world/2010/dec/05/wikileaks-cables-saudi-terrorist-funding?INTCMP=SRCH (accessed January 11, 2011).
267. See, e.g., "el-Nadalah el-ikhwaniyya ma' el-harakat el-'ommaliyya" *Rose al Yossef*, December 23, 2006; Karam Gabr, "Limadha hiya mahzoura," *Rose al Yossef*, February 22, 2008.
268. See, for example, Mahmoud Samaha, "Aswaq el-salafiyyeen tagneed wa tatarrof wa arbah," *Rose al Yossef*, June 7, 2008, 48-50.
269. Ibid.
270. Sabry, *el-Sadat*, 131.
271. Ibid, 122.
272. Ibid, 718.
273. Ibid.
274. Ibid.
275. Ibid, 721.
276. Ibid, 719.
277. See Abaza for a critical, but largely objective review of Sadat's régime.
278. Baker, 98.

Chapter 10

1. Salama Ahmed Salama, "Min qareeb," *Al Ahram*, February 10, 2003, http://www.ahram.org.eg/archive/Index.asp?CurFN=AMOD4.HTM&DID=-30000 (accessed, April 7, 2009).
2. Galal Amin, *Wasf Misr fi nehayat el-qarn el-'eshreen* (Cairo: Dar el-shorouq, 2000), 94-101.
3. Ibid, 96.
4. Ibid.
5. Ibid, 98.
6. Mustafa el-Feki, "Intellectuals and the modern state," *Al Ahram* Weekly, June 1–25, 2003, http://weekly.ahram.org.eg/2003/643/op11.htm (accessed June 19, 2003).
7. Khalid Dawoud, "Mobilising for Sa'dawi," *Al Ahram* Weekly, June 14-20, 2001, http://weekly.ahram.org.eg/2001/538/eg7.htm (accessed May 18, 2008).
8. Diya' Abu Wakila, "Roll el-mahakem: Nawal el-Sa'dawi," *Akhbar el-Yom*, May 10, 2008, 31.
9. The argument for marriage annulment is based on the religious prohi-

bition of marriage between a Muslim and someone condemned as an apostate.
10. "A short guide to 20th-century Egypt: 1990-1999," *Al Ahram* Weekly, December 30,1999- January 5, 2000, http://weekly.ahram.org.eg/1999/462/1990.htm, (Accessed May 6, 2008).
11. Ibid, http://weekly.ahram.org.eg/1999/462/1990.htm (accessed May 6, 2008).
12. Khalid Dawoud "The landmarks," *Al Ahram Weekly*, September 23-29, 1999, http://weekly.ahram.org.eg/1999/462/1990.htm, (Accessed May 6, 2008).
13. Rania Khallaf "The plot thickens," *Al Ahram* Weekly, July 21-27, 2005, http://weekly.ahram.org.eg/2005/752/eg3.htm, (accessed May 6, 2008). See also Wael Lutfi, "Sayyid el-Qemany: Lan a'tadher 'amma katabt," *Rose al Yossef*, July 4-10, 2009, 77-79
14. Sayyid el-Qemany, Laysa fil Islam mashyakha, *Newsweek. Alwatan*, http://newsweek.alwatan.com.kw/Default.aspx?MgDid=781232&pageId=127 (accessed August 5, 2009).
15. In spite of Sabra's long association with Mubarak he supported the January 25 revolution and had been in Tahrir Square with his daughter.
16. Mohammed Ghoneim, "Video: asrar khateera fi hayat Mubarak," *Al Wafd,* Marsh 1, 2011, http://www.Alwafd.org/index.php?view=article&catid=1%3Alatest-news&id=19647%3A2010-08-30-09-37-57&tmpl=component&print=1&layout=default&page=&option=com_content&Itemid=69 (accessed March 3, 2011).
17. Reem Leila, "Now History: What Happened to Mrs. Suzanne Mubarak and her Foundations," *Al Ahram Weekly*, February 17 – 23, 2011 http://weekly.ahram.org.eg/2011/1035/sc72.htm (accessed March 3, 2011).
18. Paul Adams, "Mubarak's Rejected Roots," *BBC*, February 14, 2011, http://www.bbc.co.uk/news/world-middle-east-12460834 (accessed February 14, 2011).
19. Mohammed Donya, Ismael Gom'a, and Sameh Lasheen, "Rigal 'ashoo fi zell Mubarak," *Al Ahram*, March 1, 2011, http://www.ahram.org.eg/archive/Al-Ahram-Files/News/65068.aspx (accessed December 19, 2016)
20. Mubarak was an avid backgammon enthusiast, see, Hana Qandil, "Ostadh el-game'a alladhi saytara 'ala Mubarak bi 'ashara tawla," *elfagr*, http://www.elfagr.org/Detail.aspx?nwsId=46548&secid=25&vid=2 (accessed October 29, 2011).
21. See, for example Jim Sciutto, "Classified 9/11 Documents Detail Link to Saudi Arabia," *CNN*, July 14, 2016, http://edition.cnn.com/videos/us/2016/05/12/9-11-saudi-role-lead-sciutto-dnt.cnn/video/playlists/9-11-terror-attacks/ (accessed May 9, 201).

22. See, for example, Ahmed Abdel Hafez, "Ettiham Ibrahim Kamel bil esteelaa ala 28 million mitr fil Ghardaqa," *el-Shorouq*, February 24, 2011, 3.
23. See, for example, Mahmoud el-Dab', "Ezz wa Abul 'ainain wa Rasekh wa Heikal wa Thabet wal Gammal, wa Omar Tantawi eqtaradoo miaat el-malayeen min bank el-eskindiriyya bidoun damanat," *Sout el-Omma*, March 12, 2011, http://www.soutelomma.org/NewsDetails.aspx?NID=8429 (accessed March 16, 2011).
24. January 25 is marked on the calendar as police day.
25. See http://www.youtube.com/watch?v=zcWDg03R0aU (accessed July 28, 2016), for an example of one of these very small gatherings.
26. Facebook, http://www.facebook.com/pages/Khaled-Said/100792786638349 (accessed February 16, 2011).
27. "Meet Asmaa Mahfouz and the blog that Helped Spark the Revolution," *YouTube*, http://www.youtube.com/watch?v=SgjIgMdsEuk (accessed April 26, 2011).
28. For examples of this corruption see, Hamdy Hassan, "Mofagaat gadida fi ard el-sharika el-Kuwaitiyya," *AlShaab*, March 8, 2011, http://www.alshaab.com/news.php?i=27161 (accessed March 8, 2011); Ahmed Abul Khair, "Rigal el-a'mal alladhina nahabu Misr, *Sout el-Omma*, February 8, 2011, http://www.soutelomma.org/NewsDetails.aspx?NID=8175 (accessed February 8,2011); Mohammed Sabry, Ettiham, Kharboush wa Abul Fotouh bi ehrad malayeen el-gonayhat," *Al Ahram*, March 1, 2011, http://www.ahram.org.eg/458/2011/03/01/12/65161.aspx (accessed March 1, 2011); Ahmed Abdel Hafez, "Ettiham Ibrahim Kamel bil esteelaa ala 28 million mitr fil Ghardaqa," el-Shorouq, February 24, 2011, 3; Emad el-Fiqi, Mohammed Ghanem, and Mustafa Tammam, Egraat hokoumiyya limulahaqat el-fasad," *Al Ahram*, March 15, 2011, http://www.ahram.org.eg/The-First/News/67389.aspx (accessed March 15, 2011); Mohammed Donya, Ismail Gom'a, and Sameh Lasheen, Mounir Thabet tawalla samsarat bai' 71 sharika qita' 'am," *Al Ahram*, March 1, 2011 http://www.ahram.org.eg/ (accessed March 15, 2011); Mohammed Donya, Ismail Gom'a, and Sameh Lasheen, Mounir Thabet tawalla samsarat bai' 71 sharika qita' 'am," *Al Ahram*, March 1, 2011 http://www.ahram.org.eg/ (accessed March 15, 2011); Abdel Khalek Khalifa, "Mounir Thabet shaqiq el-hanem wa shareek nahb Misr," *Alwafd*, February 17, 2011, 13; Ahmed Abul khair, "Rigal el-a'mal alladhina nahabu Misr, *Sout el-Omma*, February 8, 2011, http://www.soutelomma.org/NewsDetails.aspx?NID=8175 (accessed February 8, 2011); "Interpol yatlob el-qabd 'ala saheb Damak el-emaratiyya," *Rosadaily*, 1, June 14, 2011.
29. See, for example, *el-Shorouq*, January 25, 2011, 5; *Alwafd*, January 24, 2011, 1.

30. http://www.islammemo.cc/vedio-images/vedio/2011/02/13/117108.html (accessed February 18, 2011).
31. Mamdouh Hassan, Khaled Abdel Rasoul, Rania Rabi, and Riham Seoud, Donia salem, Abdel Rahman Yousef, and Ahmed Badrawi, "Kotat el-hogoum wal defa' fi youm el-ghadab," *el-Shorouq*, January 25, 2011, 5.
32. Amira Howeidy, "Worried About the Future," *Al Ahram Weekly*, September 21 to 27, 2006, http://weekly.ahram.org.eg/2006/813/eg5.htm (accessed November 22, 2009).
33. Mohammed Farag and Sa'd Hussein, "'Asharat el-aalaf yowaseloun masirat el-taayeed li Mubarak," *Rose Al Youssef*, February 4, 2011, http://www.rosaonline.net/Daily/News.asp?id=102517 (accessed February 4, 2011).
34. Examples of these chants and placards include: You're 83. Get some rest now [Mubarak]; Enough, Egypt is tired; Go [Mubarak], my arm is getting tired [carrying the placard]; He is [Mubarak] fed up and wants to leave but can't because of the curfew; [Obama to Mubarak] Say goodbye to the Egyptians. [Mubarak's response] Why where are they going? [Young girl's banner] Go quickly. This is history and I'll have to memorize it all at school. (This joke refers to the so-called educational system that relies solely on memorization); Mubarak, Mubarak, Ben Ali awaits you (a reference to the Tunisian ruler ousted a month earlier); One young woman carried a banner that said "Forgive me Egypt for being so late in coming for you;"
35. "Asrar enhiyar dawlat el-ro'b el- bolisiyya," *elfagr*, February 12, 2011, http://www.elfagr.org/Portal_NewsDetails.aspx?nwsId=5666&secid =51 (accessed February 12, 2011).
36. There is conclusive evidence that Hamas, Hezbollah, and Palestinian extremists were smuggled into Egypt during the chaos to storm the maximum-security prison in wadi el-natrun and were responsible for the release of several members of the Muslim Brothers who were incarcerated there. See: Daniel Greenfield, "How Hamas Helped Morsi Break Out of Prison," *FrontPage Mag*, August 26, 2013, http://www.frontpagemag.com/2013/dgreenfield/how-hamas-helped-morsi-break-out-of-prison/ (accessed November 29, 2014), Hamza Hendawi, "Egypt Court: Muslim Brotherhood, Hamas, and Hezbollah Broke President Morsi Out Of Jail In 2011," *Business Insider*, June 23, 2013 http://www.businessinsider.com/how-president-morsi-got-out-of-jail-in-2011-2013-6 (accessed November 29, 2014).
37. Mohammed Hesham 'Abeeh, "Bil video: qafashat el-rais Mubarak min "khallehom yetsallo ila ehna kollena konna foqara," *el-Dostor*, December 10, 2010, http://dostor.org/politics/egypt/10/december/19/33565 (accessed December 10, 2010).

38. The Saudis and Emaratis have, according to some reports later, threatened to freeze their relations with Egypt and to withdraw their investments from the country if the Mubarak family is tried for corruption. "Doghout khaligiyya (Se'oudiyya-Emaratiyya) 'ala el-Qahera liman' mohakamat Mubarak,) *elfagr*, March 17, 2011, http://elfagr.org/DailyPortal_NewsDetails.aspx?nwsId=152&secid=1 (accessed March 17, 2011).
39. "Gamal Mubarak eqtaraha fath hadiqat el-hayawanat wa etlaq el-hayawanat el-moftarisa 'ala el-motazahereen," *elfagr*, March 18, 2011, http://www.*elfagr*.org/DailyPortal_NewsDetails.aspx?nwsId=203&secid=1 (accessed March 19, 2011).
40. Daniel Williams and Michael Ross, "Most of Disputed Taba Awarded to Egypt: Israel Left With Slim Hope of Keeping Its Sinai Beach Resort," *Los Angeles Times*, September 30, 1988, http://articles.latimes.com/1988-09-30/news/mn-3185_1_beach-resort (accessed August 29, 2016).
41. Harriet Sherwood, "Inside The Tunnels Hamas Built: Israel's Struggle Against New Tactic In Gaza War," *The Guardian*, August 2, 2014 https://www.theguardian.com/world/2014/aug/02/tunnels- (accessed August 29, 2016).
42. Nadia Radi, "gesr el-malek Salman yarbot bayna Mist wal seou'diyya abraz ettifaqiyyat el-malek wal Sisi," *Almrsal*, April, 8, 2016, http://www.almrsal.com/post/329075 (accessed August 29, 2016); "el-malek Fahd wal ra'is Mubarak ettafaqa qabl 14 'aman 'ala tashyeedoh 'abr madayeq Tiran," *Alriyadh*, February 8, 2006, http://www.alriyadh.com/129136 (accessed August 29, 2016); "Saudi Arabia and Egypt Announce Red Sea bridge," *BBC*, April 8, 2016, http://www.bbc.co.uk/news/world-middle-east-35999557 (accessed August 29, 2016).
43. Mubarak's interview was with Markam Mohammed Ahmed in *Al Musawwar* on September 24, 1993, see, Yasser Barakat, "el-'esaba," *elmogaz*, http://elmogaz.com/?q=node/5705 (accessed August 23, 2011)
44. Mohamed Hassanein Heikal, "Mubarak and his time: from the Podium to the Square," *el-Shorouq*, February 19, 2012, 8-9.
45. Herodotus.
46. Amr el-Ansari, "el-Rais el-sabeq li ahad el-'ameleen fil qasr: Misr betetsereq min ayyam fara'oan, *Rose Al Youssef*, June 11, 2011, 58-61.
47. Farouk Goweda, "Man saraqa el-qosour el-malakiyya?," *Al Ahram*, June 11, 2011, 7.
48. The Saudi government's bulldozing of historic sites they became venerated was another manifestation of these same values. A palace for the king has replaced the Prophet's grandson's house and public lavatories have replaced the Prophet's wife's house. See, Daniel Howden,

"Shame of the House of Saud: Shadows over Mecca," *The Independent*, April 19, 2006, http://www.independent.co.uk/news/world/middle-east/shame-of-the-house-of-saud-shadows-over-mecca-474736.html (accessed October 29, 2011).
49. Wael el-Ebrashi, "Burundi towaqqi'," *Elkamis*, March 10, 2011, 14.
50. Ibid.

Chapter 11

1. "Tashkeel lagnat ta'deel el-dostoor bire'asat Tareq el-Bishri," *Al Ahram*, February 16, 2011, http://www.ahram.org.eg/archive/The-First/News/62983.aspx (accessed August 24, 2016).
2. 'Adel Hammouda, "el-Thawra laysat 'awra linoghattiha bi roq'a min el-ta'deelat el-dostouriyya allati la tastor shai'a," *elfagr*, March 21, 2011, http://elfagr.org/Portal_NewsDetails.aspx?nwsId=7013&secid=48 (accessed March 21, 2011).
3. Amira Howeidy, "Between Two Constitutions, *Al Ahram Weekly*, March 10-16, 2011, http://weekly.ahram.org.eg/2011/1038/eg501.htm (accessed March 19, 2011).
4. Mamdouh Sha'ban, So'ad Tantawi, and Ali Mohammed Ali, "el-nataeg el-nehaeyya limagles el-sha'b," *Al Ahram*, January 22, 2012, https://web.archive.org/web/20130115174853/http://www.ahram.org.eg/The-First/News/126247.aspx (accessed August 24, 2016).
5. Heba Saleh, "Egypt's Constitutional Court Halts Work, *Financial Times*, December 2, 2012, https://www.ft.com/content/f08f7e-fc-3c75-11e2-86a4-00144feabdc0 (accessed August 24, 2016).
6. Bill Gertz, "Egypt's Muslim Brotherhood filling pro-Western military's ranks with Islamists," *Washington Post*, March 29, 2013, http://www.washingtontimes.com/news/2013/mar/29/egypts-muslim-brotherhood-filling-pro-western-mili/ (accessed December 8, 2014).
7. Amer Mahmoud and Amr Amer, "el-genaralat wal ekhwan: el-sedam el-moaagal," *Vito*, March 12, 2013/ (accessed December 8, 2014).
8. Ahmed Eleiba, "Those missing and the uninvited," *Al Ahram weekly*, October 11 – 17, 2012, http://weekly.ahram.org.eg/2012/1118/eg6.htm (accessed December 8, 2014).
9. Harriet Sherwood, "Egypt-Israel Border Attack Leaves Over A Dozen Dead," *The Guardian*, https://www.theguardian.com/world/2012/aug/05/attack-across-egypt-israel-border (accessed August 24, 2016).

Chapter 12

1. It would be incorrect to imagine that the 1952 coup was the only cause

of the social change that has taken place in Egypt. This is not what is claimed here. Undoubtedly many other variables helped to initiate as well as give momentum to the development of the attitudes and values discussed in this section. What is claimed here is that the coup was an important factor and that it helped create the conditions that facilitated change and helped to determine its nature and direction.
2. M. Ali Ibrahim, "Tell me More About Obscenities and Bad Words That Dominate Our Daily Language," *The Egyptian Gazette*, http://www.eltahrir.net.eg/gazette/1/5.asp (accessed March 31, 2004); Farouk Gowaida, "el-share' el-Misri waloghat el-hewar el-habet," *Al Ahram*, September 16, 2016, http://www.ahram.org.eg/NewsQ/551213.aspx (accessed September 16, 2016).
3. Ahmed Abdel Mo'ti Hegazi, "el-farq shase' baynana wa baynahom," *Al Ahram*, January 8, 2003, http://www.ahram.org.eg/ARCHIVE/Index.asp?CurFN=WRIT1.HTM&DID=7629 (accessed May 30, 2008).
4. Magdy Arafa, "Madha hadatha lil ibda' fi Misr," *Al Ahram*, November 11, 2002, http://www.ahram.org.eg/archive/Index.asp?CurFN=OPIN8.HTM&DID=7571 (accessed May 19, 2008); Ahmed Abdel Mo'ti Hegazi, "Aana lana an nas'al," *Al Ahram*, December 11, 2002, http://www.ahram.org.eg/archive/Index.asp?CurFN=WRIT1.HTM&DID=7601 (accessed December 11, 2002).
5. Ahmed Abdel Mo'ti Hegazi, "Dameer la yakdhib wala yunafeq," *Al Ahram*, December 18, 2002, http://www.ahram.org.eg/archive/Index.asp?CurFN=WRIT0.HTM&DID=7608 (accessed December 18, 2002).
6. Ibid.
7. Ahmed Abdel Mo'ti Hegazi, "Hawla 'ilaqat el-dawla bil thaqafa," *Al Ahram*, January 29, 2003.
8. The pace of the decline was somewhat slower during the 1960s largely due to the enlightened leadership of Sarwat Okasha, who was the most capable and most effective minister of culture since the 1952 coup.
9. Abdel Salam Nour el-Din, *el-'aql wal hadhara*, (Beirut, Dar el-tanweer lil tiba'a wal nashr, 1987), 116.
10. Ibid, 110.
11. Ibid, 124.
12. Mona Abu Senna, "Waqai' takfeer Edward Said wa Arthur Miller wa Wael Sonica fi game'at 'Ain Shams," *Rose al Youssef*, 78-79, February 3, 2007 (accessed February 3, 2007).
13. One of the faculty members claimed that the terms used are atheistic because they imply creation, which is the sole province of God, and that the term globalism should only be used in reference to Islam and not to human thought. Mona Abu Senna, "Waqai' takfeer Edward Said wa Arthur Miller wa Wael Sonica fi game'at 'Ain Shams," *Rose al Youssef*, 78-79, February 3, 2007 (accessed February 3, 2007).

14. A committee investigated the conference exonerated it conference of the charge of atheism but recommended canceling it anyway.
15. Sara Elkamel, A Harsh Prison Sentence for a Novel Writer Has Egypt's Arts Community Worried, *Huffington Post*, February 23, 2016, http://www.huffingtonpost.com/entry/ahmed-naji-egypt-writer-prison_us_56cc8357e4b0928f5a6d3fe8 (accessed August 26, 2016).
16. Lara Rebello, "Egyptian writer Fatima Naoot gets 3-year sentence for insulting Islam," *International Business Times*, January 28, 2016, http://www.ibtimes.co.uk/egyptian-writer-fatima-naoot-gets-3-year-sentence-insulting-islam-1540503 (accessed August 26, 2016); Mahmoud Mourad, "Egyptian Poet Goes On Trial Accused Of Contempt Of Islam," Reuters, January 28, 2015, http://www.reuters.com/article/us-egypt-courts-poet-idUSKBN0L121M20150128 (accessed August 26, 2016).
17. The sentence was reduced in appeal. See: Amira El-Fekki, "Naoot Receives A Reduced Suspended Sentence Of Six Months," *Daily News*, November 24, 2016 http://www.dailynewsegypt.com/2016/11/24/court-upholds-charges-insulting-islam-writer-fatima-naoot/ (accessed January 1, 2017).
18. Ahramonline, "Egyptian Court Sends TV Host Islam Behery To Jail For One Year Over Blasphemy," December 29, 2015, http://english.ahram.org.eg/News/177654.aspx (accessed December 1, 2016); Sarah El-Sheikh, "El-Behairy To Resume Work After Presidential Pardon Release," November 29, 2016, http://www.dailynewsegypt.com/2016/11/20/599527/ (accessed December 1, 2016).
19. Ahmed Abdel Mo'ti Hegazi, "Aana lana an nas'al," *Al Ahram*, (accessed December 11, 2002).
20. Ibid.
21. Hegazi, "Ma'a man anta"
22. See, Ahmed Sobhy Mansour, "Godhour el-haraka el-seyasiyya el-salafiyya el-rahena," http://www.rezgar.com/debat/show.art.asp?t=2&aid=42552 (accessed May 31, 2008), for a brief review of the roots of activist salafiyya.
23. Hegazi, "Ma'a man anta"
24. Ibid.
25. Hegazi, "Ma'a man anta."
26. Ibid.
27. Arabs like to point with pride to the scientific achievements of the Islamic civilization but the greatest majority of these scientists are non-ethnic Arabs who originated from the societies that were heirs to ancient civilizations. Many were either Egyptian or Iranian.
28. "Magholoun wazza'o fatwa qadima lil sheikh el-rahel Atiyya Saqr,"

Alarabiya, http://www.alarabiya.net/articles/2008/04/28/49010.html (accessed April 26, 2009).
29. Ahmed el-Shoki, "Ulama wa mashayekh ettafaqou ala tahreem el-feseekh," *Alwafd,* April 30, 2009, http://www.Alwafd.org/details.aspx?nid=18491 (accessed May 15, 2009).
30. http://www.google.com.eg/search?hl=en&safe=off&q=%22%D8%B4%D9%85+%D8%A7%D9%84%D9%86%D8%B3%D9%8A%D9%85%22+%22%D8%AA%D8%AD%D8%B1%D9%8A%D9%85+++%22&btnG=Search&meta=&aq=f&aqi=&aql=&oq=&gs_rfai= (accessed July 28, 2016).
31. http://www.google.com.eg/search?client=firefox-a&rls=org.mozilla%3Aen-US%3Aofficial&channel=s&hl=en&source=hp&q=%D8%AA%D8%AD%D8%B1%D9%8A%D9%85+%D8%A7%D9%84%D9%81%D8%B3%D9%8A%D8%AE&meta=&btnG=Google+Search (accessed July 28, 2016).
32. See, for example, "Tanbeeh el-Muslimeen ila hokm el-ehtifal bi Sham el-Nessim," http://tr.youtube.com/watch?v=6wIwGrfR1_I; or, "hokm el-ehtifal bi Sham el-Nessim," http://tr.youtube.com/watch?v=B0596r77-Jc&feature=related (accessed May 15, 2009).
33. Sheikh R. Ali, *Oil, Turmoil, and Islam in the Middle East* (New York: Praeger, 1986), 33.
34. Saudi nationals are also vulnerable to these punishment. For example seven juveniles convicted of robbery were sentenced to execution and crucifixion. "Saudi Arabia Delays Execution Of Seven Facing Crucifixion And Firing Squad," The Guardian, March 5, 2013, https://www.theguardian.com/world/2013/mar/05/saudi-arabia-delays-execution (accessed September 3, 2016).
35. Even minor offences such as a barber cutting off a customer's moustache by mistake could lead to jail. Salman el-Salmi, "el-mahkama tanzor qadiyyat qas shanab mowaten," *Okaz,* February 29, 2012, http://www.okaz.com.sa/new/Issues/20120229/Con20120229482148.htm (accessed September, 3, 2016).
36. For example, two Egyptian doctors who prescribed morphine to Saudi princess in pain were convicted of turning her into an addict. The same drug had apparently been prescribed to the woman when she went for treatment in the United States. Nevertheless, one of the doctors was sentenced to 1500 lashes to be administered on a weekly basis during the fifteen-year jail term that was part of his sentence, and the second was sentenced to fewer lashes and a shorter sentence. See, "Egypt doctor's Saudi Lashing Worse Than Death," *Arab Times,* http://www.arabtimesonline.com/kuwaitnews/pagesdetails.asp?nid=24166&ccid=11 (accessed October 31, 2008); "Egyptian Doctor Severely Punished

for treatment of Saudi Princess," *darkgovernment.com*, http://www.darkgovernment.com/news/egyptian-doctor-severely-punished-for-treatment-of-saudi-princess/ (accessed October 31, 2008); Manar Ammar, "Egyptian doctor lashed in Saudi for 'inducing addiction,'" *Egypt Daily News*, http://www.thedailynewsegypt.com/article.aspx?ArticleID=17416 (accessed November 13, 2008); Gom'a Hamad Allah, "el-qonsol el-Misri fi Jeddah: qaddamna eltimasan lil malek Abdulla bi takhfeef 'oqoubat el-gald 'an el-tabeebayn wa lam nattalw' ala mantooq el-hokm," *Al Masry Al Youm*, October 30, 2008, http://www.almasry-alyoum.com/printerfriendly.aspx?ArticleID=184414 (accessed October 30, 2008). Although the princess apparently denied the charges that were levied against the doctor the authorities proceeded with the first set of lashings after which he collapsed and was taken to the intensive care unit. "El-Amira el-Se'odiyya tanfi el-ettiham el-mollafaq lil tabib el-Misri wal doctor Ra'ouf enhar ba'da awwal wagbat gald w noqel ila ghorfat el-enyaa el-morakkaza," *Arab Times*, http://www.arabtimes.com/portal/news_display.cfm?Action=&Preview=No&nid=2480&a=1 (accessed November 18, 2008). Another recent example is that of a tailor was also sentenced to sixty lashes after being convicted of having "deliberately touched sensitive areas" in a girl's body while taking her measurements. Abdulla el-Qorani "60 sawtan li khayyat Misri taharrash bi fatah," *el eqtisadiyya el-elektroniyya*, October 1, 2009, http://www.aleqt.com/2009/10/01/article_281953.html (accessed October 2, 2009). There is a constant stream of media reports on severe punishment for seemingly minor violations of the laws on segregation of the sexes. For example, two writers were arrested after attempting to get their copies of a book signed by its female author. "Tawqeef rewaiyyin hawala tawqee' ketab min zamilatihima bil Se'oudiyya," *CNN*, March 29, 2009, http://arabic.cnn.com/2009/entertainment/3/7/saudi.detention/index.html (accessed February 10, 2010). Another example is the punishment meted out to a seventy-five year old Syrian woman who violated the sex segregation laws by allowing two young men into her house to deliver bread. She was sentenced to forty lashes, four months in jail followed by deportation. "40 galda li 'agouz Souriyya mottahama bi kholwa ghair shar'iyya bil Se'oudiyya," *CNN*, April 8, 2009, http://arabic.cnn.com/2009/entertainment/3/9/syrian.elderly_lashes/index.html (accessed February 10, 2010). More serious offenses are treated far more harshly. See for example, "Saudi Arabia: Witchcraft and Sorcery Cases on the Rise: Cancel Death Sentences for 'Witchcraft'," *Human Rights Watch*,), http://www.hrw.org/en/news/2009/11/24/saudi-arabia-witchcraft-and-sorcery-cases-rise (accessed December 1, 2009;

or Souhail Karam, Inal Ersan, ed., "Saudi Court Upholds Child Rapist Crucifixion Ruling," *Reuters*, November 3, 2009, http://in.reuters.com/articlePrint? articleId=INIndia-43639120091103 (accessed December 8, 2009).
37. "Saudi Arabia: 'sorcery' execution condemned as 'appalling'," *amnesty.org*, http://www.amnesty.org.uk/news_details.asp?NewsID=19702 (accessed September 20, 2011); Oliver Pickup, "The Moment Man Was Publicly Beheaded In A Saudi Arabian Car Park For Being A 'Sorcerer'," *The Mail On line*, October 31, 2011, http://www.dailymail.co.uk/news/article-2055636/Sudanese-man-beheaded-Saudi-Arabia-car-park-sorcerer.html (accessed November 1, 2011).
38. "E'dam Misri bil Se'oudiyya limomarasitih 'el-sehr wal sha'watha'," *Al Masry Al Youm*, November 14, 2011, http://today.almasryalyoum.com/article2.aspx?ArticleID=81823 (accessed May 15 2017).
39. Sebastian Usher, "Death 'Looms for Saudi Sorcerer'," *BBC News*, April 1, 2010, http://news.bbc.co.uk/2/hi/middle_east/8598134.stm.
40. Arab workers generally fare somewhat better than workers from South-eastern Asia who are "treated as less than human" according to Human Rights Watch. "UAE: Address Abuse of Migrant Workers," *Human Rights Watch*, http://www.hrw.org/en/news/2006/03/28/uae-address-abuse-migrant-workers (accessed December 1, 2009). See also Hadi Ghaemi, Building Towers, Cheating Workers Exploitation of Migrant Construction Workers in the United Arab Emirates, *Human Rights Watch*, Volume 18, No. 8 (E), http://www.hrw.org/reports/2006/uae1106/uae1106web.pdf (accessed December 1, 2009).
41. Anh Nga Longva, "Keeping Migrant Workers in Check: The Kafala System in the Gulf," *Middle East Report*, no. 211 (Summer, 1999), 20-22.
42. "Misri yoharreb ostadha gami'iyya wa teflayha fi sandouq sayyaratehi min al Se'odiyya ila Misr," *Donia Alwatan*, September 18, 2007, http://www.alwatanvoice.com/arabic/content-104223.html (accessed May 5, 2009).
43. Ibid.
44. See for example, the article entitled "Because They Dared To Ask Him For Their Rights, a Kuwaiti Sponsor Detains Seventy Egyptian Workers In a Warehouse, Shaves Their Moustaches, and Abuses Them Sexually," Nada Mohammed Ali, "liannahom tagarra'ou wa talabu minnoh hoqouqihim kafeel Kuwaiti yahtagez 70 'amelan Misriyyan fi makhzan yahlaq shawaribahom wa yantakek a'radehim," *elfagr*, May 26, 2008, 18; or the article entitled "An Egyptian Citizen Threatens to Blow himself Up in Front of the Saudi Embassy After his Sponsor Swindled Him", Mohammed el-Sawi, "Mowaten Misri yohadded be tafgeer nafsahu amam el-sefara el-Se'odiyya ba'ada an nasaba 'alay-

hi kafeeloh," elfagr, September 22, 2008, 19; or the article entitled "A Saudi Sponsor Detains Six Egyptian Doctors and Their Salaries and Refuses Their Return to Egypt": Gom'a Hamad Allah, "Kafeel Se'oudi yahtagez 6 atebba' Misriyyin wa rawatebahom wa yarfod 'awdatehem li Misr," *Al Masry Al Youm,* October 12, 2009, http://www.almasry-alyoum.com/article2.aspx?ArticleID=229002&IssueID=1556 (accessed October 12, 2009); or the article entitled "He refused to give him his dues or transfer his sponsorship or terminate his contract: an Egyptian physician trapped in Saudi because of the sponsor." Nahed Nasr, "Eafada manhoh hoqouqoh aw naql kafalatoh aw enha' 'aqdoh: tabeeb Misri mohasar fil Se'odiyya bisabab el-kafeel," *youm7*, December 7, 2009, http://www.youm7.com/News.asp?NewsID=163580 (accessed December 7, 2009).

45. "Min haq el-kafeel el-Se'oudi ehtigaz gothman el-' amel el-masri fil thallaga ila an yatanazal el-waratha 'an hoqoqehim," *Arab Times,* http://www.arabtimes.com/portal/news_display.cfm?Action=&Preview=No&nid=21183 (accessed March 28, 216).

46. A humorous incident that was witnessed by the author in the United States illustrates the way in which the term wafed and mowaten are viewed as ascribed traits that are not linked to a particular geographic location. An Arab from the Gulf was irate at being denied a certain request and reminded the American who turned him down that his request should be granted because he was a *mowaten* (citizen), then proceeded to admonish him for his firm refusal to comply with the request. When the American, who understood the connotations of these terms, was not swayed by the implied threat, and told the *mowaten* that it was he (the American) who is a mowaten (citizen), the complainant seemed utterly puzzled and at a loss for words.

47. Ibn Khaldun vol.1, 299-300.

48. The behaviorist thesis, applied somewhat loosely here, is derived from B. F. Skinner, *Beyond Freedom and Dignity* (New York: Knopf, 1972), and John B, Watson, *Behaviorism* (New York: The People's Institute, 1930).

49. The niqab is a loose garment that covers the woman from head to toe with two slits for the eyes and is usually black or dark brown and complimented by wearing matching color gloves.

50. Hoda el-Misri, "el-Niqab ahamm min el-Araby wal hesab," *Rose al Yossef,* 13 September 2008, 42-45.

51. The hegab covers the hair and neck, which is believed by many to be mandated by religion. Slave women were exempted from the requirement to wear the hegab. See, for example: Taqi el-din ibn Taymiah, "magmoo' fatawi ibn Taymiah," *Islam Web,* http://www.islamweb.net/

newlibrary/display_book.php?flag=1&bk_no=22&ID=1599 (accessed August, 26, 2016).
52. The incident took place in the author's presence.
53. El-Hakim, *'Awdat*, 75.
54. Vatikiotis, 352.
55. For a review of Sayyid Qotb's views of his foreign experience of living abroad (in America) see, Salah Abdel Fattah el-Khalidy, *America minal dakhel bi minzar Sayyid Qotb* (el-Mansoura, Egypt: Dar el-wafa', 1986).
56. The reality, of course, is that simplicity and virtue had never been traits that were associated with Bedouin life. Before they began raiding their rich neighbors in Iran, the Fertile Crescent, and Egypt, life was both harsh and fraught with life-threatening perils for the Bedouins. Until Amr ibn el-Aas conquered Egypt, excavated the ancient Amir el-Mo'meneen Canal, and began to send huge food shipments from Egypt to the Arabian Peninsula on a regular basis, famine occurred with such frequency that it became a simple fact of daily living. Bedouin history is merely the record of their incessant tribal raids in quest of meager rewards, and it was not unusual in that desolate and unforgiving desert environment for the inhabitants to kill each other over a handful of dates, which along camel meat occasionally, constituted their main diet. It was not surprising therefore; that the two Christian tribes referred to earlier fought the forty-year war (*harb el-Basus*) with each other over an injury to a camel. However, it would be misleading to suggest the twenty-first century Wahabis are the only group of people who romanticize the past and cling to the myth of a lost paradise. That concept appears to be a culture universal although some groups try harder than others to return to that mythical lost paradise.
57. For example a young blogger convicted of insulting Islam was sentenced to ten years in jail and one thousand lashes to be administered in public at the rate of twenty per week over a period of twenty weeks and a fine of about a quarter million dollars. "khamsat ashya' qad lata'rifoha 'an gald el-modawwen el-Se'oudi Raif Badawi, *BBC*, January 16, 2015, http://www.bbc.com/arabic/middleeast/2015/01/150116_saudi_blogger_facts (accessed August 29, 2016); "Saudi Blogger Receives First 50 Lashes Of Sentence For 'Insulting Islam'," *The Guardian*, January 10, 2015, https://www.theguardian.com/world/2015/jan/09/saudi-blogger-first-lashes-raif-badawi (accessed August 29, 2016); Ali Sa'd el-Mousa, "qessat Raif Badai: limatha reddat el-fe'l," *Al-watan*, January 22, 2015, http://www.alwatan.com.sa/Articles/Detail.aspx?ArticleID=24804 (accessed August 29, 2016); Elham Mane', "ma alladhi qalahu Raif Badawi," *Civic Egypt*, January 30, 2014 http://

www.civicegypt.org/?p=46683 (accessed September, 6, 2016); "qadiyyat Raif Badawi: el-mahkama el-'olya to'ayyed el-hokm," *AlHurra*, June 7, 2015, http://www.alhurra.com/a/saudi-supreme-court-raaf-badawi/272662.html (accessed August 27, 2016); Ian Black, "A Look At The Writings Of Saudi Blogger Raif Badawi – Sentenced To 1,000 Lashes," *The Guardian*, January 14, 2015, https://www.theguardian.com/world/2015/jan/14/-sp-saudi-blogger-extracts-raif-badawi (accessed August 27, 2016); Abdulla el-Barqawi, "tanfeeth hokm el-gald 'ala Raif Badawi bisabab 'ebarat kafriyya wa 'oqooq waledoh," *Sabq*, January 9, 2015, https://sabq.org/srvgde (accessed August 27, 2016); "hokm fi Misr bisegn Islam el-Behairy moqadden el-barameg el-deeniyya 'aman," *BBC*, December 29, 2015, http://www.bbc.com/arabic/middleeast/2015/12/151229_egypt_programme_presenter_sentence (accessed August 27, 2016).

58. Women are regularly beheaded if convicted of sorcery, see, for example: "e'dam Se'oudiyya limomarasitiha 'el-sehr wal sha'watha'," *Arabian Business*, September, 12, 2011, http://arabic.arabianbusiness.com/politics-economics/society/2011/dec/12/66247/ (accessed August 29, 2016).
59. "sahifa Se'oudiyya taqool anna hai'at el-ma'roof amsakat mash'ootha 'ariya taheer," *AlArabiya*, May 22, 2006, https://www.alarabiya.net/articles/2006/05/29/24177.html / (accessed August 29, 2016).
60. Galal Amin, *The Modernization of Poverty* (Leiden: E. J. Brill. 1974), 2.
61. Ibid.
62. "Saudi Issues 'Fatwa' Against Pokémon," *ABC News*, March 26, 2016, http://abcnews.go.com/International/story?id=81345&page=1 (accessed August 5, 2016).
63. "Saudi scholar issues TV death fatwa," *Aljazeera*, http://english.aljazeera.net/news/middleeast/2008/09/2008913181844832341.html. (accessed November 28, 2009); "Saudi cleric says 'depraved' TV moguls may be killed," *Middle East Times*, September 12, 2008, http://www.metimes.com/Politics/2008/09/24/egypt_cleric_says_mickey_mouse_is_not_agent_of_satan/afp/ (accessed September 25, 2008).
64. "Saudi cleric says 'depraved' TV moguls may be killed," *Middle East Times*, September 12, 2008, http://www.metimes.com/Politics/2008/09/24/egypt_cleric_says_mickey_mouse_is_not_agent_of_satan/afp/ (accessed September 25, 2008).
65. "One Fatwa too Far," *Middle East Times*, September 22, 2008, http://www.metimes.com/Editorial/2008/09/22/one_fatwa_too_far/7727/ (accessed September 25, 2008); Bill Wallace, "Saudi Arabian Cleric: Mickey Mouse Must Die," *Cultural Marxism*, January 29, 2015, http://culturalmarxism.net/saudi-arabian-cleric-mickey-mouse-must-die/

(accessed August 26, 2016); Mohammed Sadeq Diab, "fatwa qatl micky mouse," *Aharq Al-Awsat*, September 23, 2016, http://archive.aawsat.com/leader.asp?article=487961&issueno=10892#.V7v5L47AT-Gw (accessed August 23, 2016).

66. Hafr News, March 26, 2009, http://hfrnews.com/news.php?action=show&id=729 (accessed March 26, 2009).
67. "One Fatwa too Far," *Middle East Times*.
68. "Ragol deen Se'oudi: momarasat el-banat lil riyada haram shar'an," *al-Quds al-Araby*, http://www.alquds.co.uk/ (accessed May 24, 2010).
69. "Saudi Cleric Backs Gender Segregation With Fatwa," *Reuters*, February 23, 2010, http://in.reuters.com/article/worldNews/idINIndia-46408620100223 (accessed March 4, 2010).
70. "Election is Banned in Islam: Saudi Scholar," *Emirates 24/7*, January 17, 2013, http://www.emirates247.com/news/region/election-is-banned-in-islam-saudi-scholar-2013-01-17-1.491522 (accessed September 8, 2016); "Cleric Issues 48-Page Fatwa Against Democracy," *Gulf News*, April 16, 2011, http://gulfnews.com/news/gulf/saudi-arabia/cleric-issues-48-page-fatwa-against-democracy-1.777772Staff (accessed September 8, 2016); Benjamin Wurtzel, "Saudi Mufti on Democracy and Twitter, *Institute for Gulf Affairs*, November 13, 2016, http://www.gulfinstitute.org/saudi-mufti-on-democracy-and-twitter/ (accessed September 8, 2016).
71. Atef Helmi, "el-sayyida allati totaleb bi 'awdat el-gawari tahaddathat lana," *Rose Al Youssef* , June 11, 2011, 36-37.
72. Alexandra Sims, "Escaped Isis Sex Slave Nadia Murad Calls On Britain To Help Yazidis Tortured By Terror Group," *The Independent*, July 9, 2016, http://www.independent.co.uk/news/world/middle-east/escaped-isis-sex-slave-nadia-murad-calls-on-britain-to-help-yazidis-tortured-by-terror-group-a7128656.html (accessed August 26, 2016).
73. "Qeta' el-edha'a el-Se'oudiyya," Ministry of Culture and Information, http://www.info.gov.sa/SectDetails.aspx?id=19 (accessed August 29, 2016)
74. Anup Kaphle, "13 Times U.S. Presidents And Saudi Kings Have Met," *The Washington Post*, January 27, 2015, https://www.washingtonpost.com/news/worldviews/wp/2015/01/27/13-times-u-s-presidents-and-saudi-kings-have-met/?utm_term=.fd2a58996872 (accessed January 2, 2017).
75. Amin, *The Modernization*, 2. However, some influential religious scholars maintain that the king's action does not imply that slavery was abolished as only an infidel would make such a claim. See for example: Alarabiyya-news, "Hai'at ulama' el-nikah fil Se'oudiyya: saby el-nisaa elazediyyat halal," August 8, 2014, http://alarabiya-news.

com/view.3538/ (accessed January 2, 2017); Al-Islam so'al wa gawab, "hal milk el-yameen mawgood ila el-yoam?,"January 2, 2017, https://islamqa.info/ar/222559 (accessed January 2, 2017); Daniel Pipes, "Islamist Calls for Slavery's Legalization," danielpipes.org, October 15, 2014, http://www.danielpipes.org/blog/2003/11/saudi-religious-leader-calls-for-slaverys#lates (accessed December 30, 2016).

76. "qeta'el- television el-Se'oudi," Ministry of Culture and Information, http://www.info.gov.sa/SectDetails.aspx?id=3 (accessed August 29, 2016).

77. See. For example, "Kuwaiti," http://www.kuwaity.net/vb/caaaeeii-caociae/7351-cayeaei-cauiiee-aaoii-cauacae-ceae-eco.html (accessed August, 28, 2009); Lizzie Dearden, "Saudi Muslim Cleric Claims The Earth Is 'Stationary' And The Sun Rotates Around It," *The Independent*, February 18, 2015, http://www.independent.co.uk/news/world/middle-east/saudi-muslim-cleric-claims-the-earth-is-stationary-and-the-sun-rotates-around-it-10053516.html (accessed August 26, 2016).

78. "King Fahd ibn Abdul Aziz Patronizes the Inaugural Ceremony of the Third Shoura (Consultative) Council for the Third Session," *Ain Al Yaqeen*, May 23, 2003. http://www.ainalyaqeen.com/issues/20030523/feat2en.htm (accessed May 20, 2005).

79. *Rose al Yossef*, March 26 to April 1, 2005, 104.

80. Ibid.

81. Ibid.

80. See: Saudi women's small steps on path to progress," *BBC*, April 13, 2015, http://www.bbc.co.uk/news/world-middle-east-32282856 (accessed August 29, 2016).

83. "El-samah lil mar'ah el-Se'oudiyya bi emtilak noskha min aqd el-zawag," *Alwafd*, May 3, 2016, http://alwafd.org/printing/1159289 (accessed August 4, 2016).

84. "12-Year-Old Saudi Girl in Divorce Battle With 80-Year-Old Husband," *The Times*, February 9, 2010, http://www.timesonline.co.uk/tol/news/world/middle_east/article7019754.ece (accessed February 9, 2010).

85. "el-Se'oudiyya yadkholna el-maktabat li awwal marra," *Al Ahram*, March 27, 2006, 2.

86. There has been a recent resurgence in interest in the medicinal value of drinking camel urine. It believed to be a cure for many ailments ranging from cancer, to baldness, liver, ringworm, tinea and abscesses, hepatitis, cuts, toothache, eye diseases, blood clots, asthma, dandruff, baldness, and intestinal diseases. See the following web sites for the medical benefits of drinking camel milk, especially the milk of young she camels, http://www.lebnights.net/vb/t57578.html (accessed April 29, 2010); *Islam Questions and Answers*, http://www.islam-

qa.com/en/ref/83423 (accessed April 29, 2010); http://www.youtube.com/watch?v=rJutiynUW8g (accessed April 29, 2010).

87. Farah Mustafa Wadi, "Nano-particles in Camels' urine may help treat cancer, *Saudi Gazette*, August 23, 2009, http://www.saudigazette.com.sa/index.cfm?method=home.regcon&contentID=2009071143333 (accessed August 24, 2009).

88. Caroline Davies, "Saudi Arabia Plans New City For Women Workers Only," *The Guardian*, August 12, 2012, https://www.theguardian.com/world/2012/aug/12/saudi-arabia-city-women-workers (accessed September, 3, 2016).

89. Deema Almashabi and Vivian Nereim, "Prince Says Saudi Arabia Not Yet Ready to Allow Women to Drive," *Bloomberg*, April 26 2016, http://www.bloomberg.com/news/articles/2016-04-26/prince-says-saudi-arabia-not-yet-ready-to-allow-women-to-drive (accessed August 29, 2016).

90. "Saudi Arabia's Top Cleric Defends Female Driving Ban Saying Women Would Be 'Exposed To Evil'," *The Telegraph*, April 2, 2016, http://www.telegraph.co.uk/news/2016/04/11/saudi-arabias-top-cleric-defends-female-driving-ban-saying-women/ (accessed August 29, 2016) ; "Saudi Women drivers 'Freed from Jail'," BBC, February 13, 2015, http://www.bbc.co.uk/news/world-middle-east-31449972.

91. Ben Hubbard, "Saudi Arabia Agrees to Let Women Drive," NY Times, September, 26, 2017, https://www.nytimes.com/2017/09/26/world/middleeast/saudi-arabia-women-drive.html (accessed January 13, 2018).

92. Sobhy Shabana, "Noura el-Fayewz: Awwal na'bat wazir Se'odiyya: mohemmatiu el-sa'ba tawheed el-manaheg bayna el-banin wal banat, kafana tafreqa 'ala asas el-gens," *Rose al Yossef*, February 27, 2009, 80-81. Other recent significant changes in that society were granting women the right to vote and stand for municipal elections (see, Caryle Murphy, "First Step for Saudi Women's Rights," *BBC*, September 25, 2011, http://www.bbc.co.uk/news/world-middle-east-15055066 (accessed September 29, 2011); and overturning the court ruling sentencing a woman to ten lashes for driving a car (see, "Saudi Woman Driver's Lashing 'Overturned By King,'" *BBC*, September 29, 2011, http://www.bbc.co.uk/news/world-middle-east-15102190 (accessed September 29, 2011).

93. "Shariah court approves SMS divorce," *Arab News*, April 9, 2009, http://www.arabnews.com/?page=24&section=0&article=121367&d=9&m=4&y=2009 (accessed November 29, 2009.)

94. AlArabiya News, November 1, 2010,"Saudi Wants Divorce After Husband Lifts Her Veil," https://www.alarabiya.net/articles/2007/10/08/40103.html (accessed December 22, 2016).

95. The father was an academic living in Britain where the daughter was raised. The father told her that he was taking her on holiday to Morocco and took her to Saudi Arabia instead. Alice Ross, "Father of Woman 'Locked Up' in Saudi Arabia Must Allow Her to Return to UK," *The Independent*, August 3, 2016, https://www.theguardian.com/law/2016/aug/03/saudi-academic-told-to-return-imprisoned-daughter-to-uk (accessed August 26, 2016).
96. "Mahkama Se'oudiyya tarfod talaq tefla fil thamena, *egynews.net*, http://www.egynews.net/wps/portal/news?params=56829 (accessed September 27, 2009).
97. Hanan el-Zir, "Sageenat entahat moddat 'oqoubatehin was yarfodna el-ahl khorougahin," *AlArabiya*, November 19, 2006, http://www.alarabiya.net/Articles/2006/11/19/29214.htm (accessed November 19, 2006).
98. Ibid.
99. Ibid.
100. Ibid.
101. Ibid.
102. Ibid.
103. Ibid.
104. Ibid.
105. Ibid.
106. Ibid.
107. For one Egyptian woman's view of the causes of these attitudes, see, for example, Mona Eltahawy, "Why Do They Hate Us?," *Foreign Policy*, April 23, 2013 http://foreignpolicy.com/2012/04/23/why-do-they-hate-us/ (accessed April 23, 2013).
108. "Woman Drowns in Dubai after Father Blocks Rescue to Save Her from 'Dishonour'," *France 24*, Latest update August 12, 2015, http://www.france24.com/en/20150810-dubai-father-stops-rescue-drowning-daughter-dishonour (accessed August 5, 2016).
109. The Somalis took this obsession a step further by decreeing that brassieres are sinful and whipping any woman caught wearing one. Abdi Sheikh, "Somali Islamists Whip Women for Wearing Bras," *Reuters*, October 16, 2009, http://af.reuters.com/article/oddlyEnoughNews/idAFTRE59F1K420091016 (accessed October 29, 2009). Alaa Al-Aswany, "When Women are Sinners in the Eyes of Extremists: Somalia is in the Grip of Famine and Chaos but Officials there are Inspecting Bras," *The Independent*, October 28, 2009, http://www.independent.co.uk/opinion/commentators/alaa-alaswany-when-women-are-sinners-in-the-eyes-of-extremists-1810447.html (accessed October 28, 2009).

110. Mahmoud Samaha and Asma; Nassar, "Mosta'mara gadida lil salafiyya fi 'Ain Shams," *Rose al Yossef*, May 17, 2008, 30-33.
111. Asma Nassar, "Da'iyat tahqeer el-nisaa," *Rose al Yossef*, June 7, 2008, 44-47.
112. Ahmed Abdel Mo'ti Hegazi, "Dameer."
113. See, for example, "50 Mokhlafa taqa' fiha el-nisaa," Megallat el-ebtisama, http://www.ibtesama.com/vb/showthread-t_16839.html (accessed May 3, 2008); "50 Mokhlafa taqa' fiha el-nisaa," Mexat, http://www.mexat.com/vb/showthread.php?t=2359 (accessed May 3, 2008); "50 Mokhlafa taqa' fiha el-nisaa," ***Multaqa el-mohandeseen el-Arab***, http://www.arab-eng.org/vb/t12605.html (accessed May 3, 2008); "50 Mokhlafa taqa' fiha el-nisaa," ***Montadayat Samira'***, http://www.samera1.com/vb/showthread.php?t=1966 (accessed May 3, 2008); "50 Mokhlafa taqa' fiha el-nisaa," Islami, http://www.islami.i8.com/50wrong.htm. (accessed May 3, 2008).
114. "50 Mokhlafa taqa' fiha el-nisaa," http://www.elakhbar.org.eg/net/islam/islam.asp?action=view&id=28 (accessed May 3, 2008).
115. Ibid.
116. Iman el-Ashraf, "Aisha Abdel Hadi fil Iskandariyya: la na'ref hagm el-'amala el-Misriyya fil khareg wal rawateb fi Misr mateftahsh bait," *el-Dostor*, August 15, 2009, http://dostor.org/ar/index.php?option=com_content&task=view&id=29848&Itemid=1 (accessed August 16, 2009).
117. Eqbal el-Seba'i, "Misriyyoun yuqallidoun el-khleegiyyeen fi ketabat asma'him," *Rose al Yossef*, February 26, 2005, 68-69.
118. Sarhan, 71. For examples of the more tradional modes of dress as depicted of the 1950s and 1960s movies, see "bil sowar fannanat el-zaman el-gameel bil burka wal melaya el-laff: Taheyya Carioka tartadeeh bi mahragan Caan wa Faten Hamama fil haram," *Sada el-balad*, October 12, 2015, http://www.elbalad.news/1742282 (accessed May 14, 2017).
119. Some tribal leaders masquerading as modern presidents of republics actively encourage tribalism. See, for example the analysis of what was billed as "a historic speech" by Colonel Gaddafi of Libya's to the Bedouin tribes in Sinai. El-Sayyid Yasin, "Ehya' lil qabila am tafkik lil dawla el-qawmiyya," *Al Ahram*, August 24, 2008.
120. The word means son of, and a name such as Mohammed Ali Hassan, for example, would instead become Mohammed bin Ali bin Hassan.
121. El-Seba'i, "Misriyyoun."
122. Ahmed Abdel Mo'ti Hegazi, "Dameer."
123. See, for example the column by a member of the Higher Council for Islamic Affairs in a major national newspaper that specifies what phrases should be used depending on whether the person is walking,

sitting, or riding, and whether it should be in the singular or the plural tense, Mohammed Abdel Sami' Shabana, "Taheyyat el-muslimeen ba'dihim li ba'd," *Al Ahram*, January 9, 2002; see also Ahmed Abdel Mo'ti Hegazi, "Salam badalan min hello" *Al Ahram*, November 2001, 21, http://www.ahram.org.eg/ARCHIVE/Index.asp?CurFN=WRIT0.HTM&DID=7202 (accessed June 30, 2008).

124. Hoda el-Misri and Asma' Nassar, "Momarredat yartadeen el-niqab bishakl gama'i," *Rose al Yossef*, November 10, 2007, 16-17.
125. "Fadiha tebbiyya was hadariyya: el-mala'ka ertadat el-niqab fi mostashfayat wezaret el-sehha," *Rose al Yossef*, November 10, 2007, 18-25.
126. Yasmine Saleh, "Saudi Sheikhs' fatwas in the spotlight," *Daily News Egypt*, http://www.thedailynewsegypt.com/article.aspx?ArticleID=16833 (Accessed October 9, 2008).
127. Angelique Chrisafis, "French Mayors Refuse To Lift Burkini Ban Despite Court Ruling," *The Guardian*, August 28, 2016, https://www.theguardian.com/world/2016/aug/28/french-mayors-burkini-ban-court-ruling (accessed September 9, 2016); "France Burkini: Corsica Court Upholds Local Ban," *BBC*, September 7, 2016, http://www.bbc.co.uk/news/world-europe-37293201 (accessed September 9, 2016).
128. Asmaa Nassar and Hani el-Waziri, "Gama'at el-amr bi ma'rouf wal nahy 'an el-ta'leem fi Dar el-'oloum," *Rose al Yossef*, March 28, 2008, 46-48.
129. Yasmine Saleh, "Egypt Teacher Fired For Cutting Girls' Uncovered Hair," *Reuters*, October 17, 2012, http://www.reuters.com/article/us-egypt-headscarf-idUSBRE89G1KI20121017 (accessed August 30, 2017).
130. Shawqy Esam, "el-tadrees bidoun hegab batel: waqai' edtihad modaressa shabba," *Rose al Yossef*, February 23-29, 2008, 24-25.
131. A religious ruling that she had committed a sin and should be executed.
132. So'ad Saleh, "wagh el-mar'a laysa 'awra wal niqab laysa fardan," *Rose al Yossef*, October 14, 2006, 80-83.
133. Abayas are the loose long black cloak type garments that are worn over the clothes.
134. Human Rights Watch, "Saudi Arabia: Religious Police Role in School Fire Criticized," *Human Rights News*, http://www.hrw.org/press/2002/03/saudischool.htm (accessed April 26, 2008).
135. "200 lashes for Saudi gang rape victim," *The Telegraph*, November 17, 2007, http://www.telegraph.co.uk/news/main.jhtml?xml=/news/2007/11/17/wsaudi117.xml (accessed April 26, 2007).
136. Ibid.
137. Ibid.

138. Sawsan el-Gayyar, "Gara'm magmou'at el-88," *Rose al Yossef*, December 16-22, 2006, 27-29.
139. Katie Sola, "Breaking With Iran Could Cost Saudi Arabia Billions In Revenue From Pilgrims, *Forbes*, January 5, 2016, https://www.forbes.com/sites/katiesola/2016/01/05/saudi-arabia-iran/#4c359bd64c35 (accessed May 17 2017).
140. Hosam Abdel Hadi, "E'lan siahi mottaham bil'sa'a li som'at Misr," *Rose al Yossef*, 98-99, June 26, to July1, 2005.
141. Ibid.
142. George Mikhail, "What's behind Egyptian Campaign To Delay Saudi Pilgrimages?," *Almonitor*, December 16, 2016, http://www.al-monitor.com/pulse/en/originals/2016/12/campaign-delay-umrah-pilgrimage-boost-egypt-economy.html (accessed May 17, 2017).
143. "Egypt Tourism Revenue Down 66 Pct In Q1 2016, *Reuters*, April 25, 2016, http://www.reuters.com/article/egypt-tourism-idUSL3N17S-3DT (accessed May 17 2017).
144. Hegazi, "Dameer."
145. Ibid.
146. "Tollab yo'menouna anna ma yadresoonahu haram," *Rose al Yossef*, April 15-21, 2006, 88-90.
147. "Dafn el-ro'ous fil remal laysa howa el-hall," *Rose al Yossef*, April 22-28, 2006, 90-91.
148. "Waqai' estiqalat ostaz game'a besabab el-tatarrof wal fahlawa," *Rose al Yossef*, April 29, 2006, 58-60.
149. Ibid.
150. Riad Abu Awad, "Fatwa against Statues Triggers Uproar in Egypt," *Middle East Online*, April 3, 2006, 2006-04-03 http://www.middle-east-online.com/english/?id=16142 (accessed May 11, 2009).
151. Amr Bayyoumi, "el-Baba yamna' el-rohban min esteghdam el-mobile wa yoshabbeh sane' el-tamatheel bil morabi wal zania," *Al Masry Al Youm*, April 30, 2009, http://www.almasry-alyoum.com/article2.aspx?ArticleID=205457 (accessed May 12, 2009).
152. "Monaqqaba hattamat a'amal Hassan Heshmat wa heya tahtef haram ya kafara" *Rose al Yossef*, April 29 to May 5, 2006, 58-60.
153. Ahmed Rashid, "After 1,700 years, Buddhas Fall to Taliban Dynamite," *The Telegraph*, http://www.telegraph.co.uk/news/worldnews/asia/afghanistan/1326063/After-1700-years-Buddhas-fall-to-Taliban-dynamite.html (accessed May 8, 2009).
154. "Under The Vandals' Hammer: The Willful Destruction Of Historic Monuments Does Not Belong To A Barbaric, Bygone Era. In Saudi Arabia, Historic Sites Are Being Deliberately Razed By Religious Fundamentalists," *Apollo Magazine*, October, 2005, BNET, http://

findarticles.com/p/articles/mi_m0PAL/is_524_162/ai_n15947643 (accessed 7 June 2008).

155. See for example: Aslam Abdullah, "Demolition of Islam's Historical Sites, *Islamic City*, July 19, 2005, http://www.islamicity.org/2672/demolition-of-islams-historical-sites/ (accessed May 14 2017); Oliver Wainwright, "City in the sky: world's biggest hotel to open in Mecca," *The Guardian*, May 22, 2015, https://www.theguardian.com/artanddesign/architecture-design-blog/2015/may/22/worlds-biggest-hotel-to-open-in-mecca (accessed May 14 2017); Oliver Smith,, "The world's largest hotel - another step towards 'Mecca-hattan' ," *The Telegraph*, August 10, 2016, http://www.telegraph.co.uk/travel/destinations/middle-east/saudi-arabia/articles/mecca-largest-hotel-in-world/ (accessed May 14 2017); Mimi Kirk, "Has Mecca Become a Disneyland for the Rich?," *City Lab*, September 13, 2016, http://www.citylab.com/politics/2016/09/has-mecca-become-a-disneyland-for-the-rich/499766/ (accessed May 15 2017).

156. See for example: Ismat Salah Mangla, "Hajj 2014: For Saudi Arabia, The Muslim Pilgrimage Is Big Business, *International Business Times*, July 10, 2014, http://www.ibtimes.com/hajj-2014-saudi-arabia-muslim-pilgrimage-big-business-1700108 (accessed May 19 2017); Riazat Butt, "Mecca makeover: how the hajj has become big business for Saudi Arabia," *The Guardian*, November 14, 2010, https://www.theguardian.com/world/2010/nov/14/mecca-hajj-saudi-arabia (accessed May 17 2017).

157. Daniel Howden, "The Destruction of Mecca: Saudi Hardliners are Wiping Out Their Own Heritage," *The Independent*, August 6, 2005,http://www.independent.co.uk/news/world/middle-east/the-destruction-of-mecca-saudi-hardliners-are-wiping-out-their-own-heritage-501647.html (accessed May 11, 2009); Jerome Taylor, "The Photos Saudi Arabia Doesn't Want Seen – And Proof Islam's Most Holy Relics Are Being Demolished In Mecca," *The Independent*, March 15, 2013, http://www.independent.co.uk/news/world/middle-east/the-photos-saudi-arabia-doesnt-want-seen--and-proof-islams-most-holy-relics-are-being-demolished-in-mecca-8536968.html (accessed March 15, 2013).

158. Almontada, http://www.montada.com/showthread.php?t=496869 (accessed July 16, 2009).

159. Ibid.

160. Sarah Almukhtar, "The Strategy Behind The Islamic State's Destruction Of Ancient Sites," *New York Times*, Updated March 28, 2016, http://www.nytimes.com/interactive/2015/06/29/world/middleeast/isis-historic-sites-control.html?_r=0 (accessed August 4, 2016).

161. Sawsan el-Gayyar, "Gara'm magmou'at el-88," *Rose al Yossef*, December 16-22, 2006, 27-29.
162. Basing its judgment "on the ancient code of an 'eye-for-an-eye'," a Saudi court sentenced a man to having his spinal cords severed in punishment for having paralyzed another during a physical altercation. Ashish Kumar Sen, "Saudi Court Rules: Paralyze Man Who Crippled Another," *The Washington Times*, August 23, 2010, http://www.washingtontimes.com/news/2010/aug/23/saudi-court-rules-paralyze-man-crippled-another/ (accessed December 22, 2016).
163. Shawqi Esam, "Nowwab el-ikhwan yotalibouna bi qat' yadd el-sareq wa ragm el qatel," *Rose al Yossef*, March 27, 2010, 20-22.
164. See, for example: Rod Nordland, "ISIS Militants Stone an Iraqi Couple Accused of Adultery," *New York Times*, March 24, 2015, http://www.nytimes.com/2015/03/25/world/middleeast/isis-stones-couple-accused-of-adultery-in-mosul-iraq.html (accessed August 4, 2016); Kamel Daoudnov. 20, 2015, Saudi Arabia, an ISIS That Has Made It," *New York Times*, November 20,, 2015, http://www.nytimes.com/2015/11/21/opinion/saudi-arabia-an-isis-that-has-made-it.html (accessed August 4, 2016); Priya Joshi, "Isis militants in Syria stone two teenage girls to death for committing adultery," International Business Times, February 26, 2016, http://www.ibtimes.co.uk/isis-militants-syria-stone-two-teenage-girls-death-committing-adultery-1546089 (accessed August 4, 2016).
165. "el-Sign wal gald lil mo'tadi fil mal'ab," *Al Ahram*, April 4, 2005, 1.
166. Asma Nassar, Man' ekhtelat el-talaba wal talebat fi ebb el-menoufiyya batel," *Rose al Yossef*, September 27, 2008, 32- 34.
167. Mona Helmy, "Mish 'ayza aqra' garayed," *Rose al Yossef*, October 2, 2004, 100.
168. Mona Helmy, "el-Sheteema hiya ga'zati el-kobra," *Rose al Yossef*, May 13, 2006, 70.
169. Ibid.
170. Matt Payton, "Women Must Undergo Female Genital Mutilation To Curb Male 'Sexual Weakness', Egyptian MP Says, *"The Independent,"* September 6, 2016, http://www.independent.co.uk/news/world/africa/women-must-undergo-female-genital-mutilation-fgm-egyp-curb-male-sexual-weakness-mp-elhamy-agina-a7227841.html (accessed March 25, 2016); "Naib bil barlaman el-Masri yotheer el-ghadab bisabab tasreehatoh 'an el-daaf el-gensi lil regal, *BBC*, September 7, 2016, http://www.bbc.com/arabic/middleeast/2016/09/160907_egypt_impotence (accessed March 25, 2016).
171. Sawsan el-Gayyar, "Gara'm magmou'at el-88," *Rose al Yossef*, December 16, 2006, 27-29.

172. Ibid. See also Sawsan el-Gayyar, "el-Dawafi' el-gensiyya lil estigwabat el-siyasiyya," *Rose al Yossef*, February 23-29, 2008, 19-21.
173. See for example Sahar Tal'at, "Maglis el dawla yarfod bil aghlabiyya ta'yeen el-enath qadiyat," *youm7*," February 15, 2010, http://www.youm7.com/News.asp?NewsID=189972 (accessed February 15, 2010). The deputy head of the State Council informed the press that a committee has been formed to determine women's suitability for the position of judge and that sociologists and psychologists would advise its members on the physical and biological nature of women. Wafa Sha'ira, Farghaly: mostasharo khas magles el-dawla yasta'noona bi 'olama 'elm el-egtema' wal nafs li kashf tabi'at el-maraa el-Misriyya," *Rose al Yossef*, March 27, 2010, 33.
174. This is not intended as a veiled criticism of those who do not speak up. The threat to their lives is very real, and the probability of success in resisting the insidious imported culture is very small.
175. Mona Helmy, "Tahakkom el-mawta fi masir el-ahya'," *Rose al Yossef*, September 10, 2004, 70.
176. Abdel Wahab Hamed, "el-Mafhoum el-oroppi lil tanweer la yasloh lil mogtama'at el-Arabiyya wal Islamiyya," *Al Ahram*, December 12, 2001, 22.
177. See for example, Amr Ismail, "el-erhab el-fikry kateb: mota'slem namoudhagan," *Elaf*, http://www.elaph.com/AsdaElaph/2005/2/42286.htm (accessed May 8, 2008).
178. Hilal, *el-Estebdad*, 30.
179. Ibid 21.
180. Ibid.
181. See for example Ragab el-Banna, "Ya Arab limadha takhallafna?," *October Magazine*, December 3, 2004, http://www.octobermag.com/Issues/1466/artDetail.asp (accessed December 3, 2004).
182. "Egyptian Court Sends TV Host Islam Behery to Jail for One Year Over Blasphemy," *Ahram Online*, December 29, 2015, http://english.ahram.org.eg/NewsContent/1/64/177654/Egypt/Politics-/Egyptian-court-sends-TV-host-Islam-Behery-to-jail-.aspx (accessed August 4, 2016); "hokm fi Misr bisegn Islam el-Behairy moqadden el-barameg el-deeniyya 'aman," *BBC*, December 29, 2015, http://www.bbc.com/arabic/middleeast/2015/12/151229_egypt_programme_presenter_sentence (accessed August 27, 2016).
183. Hamdan is the author of the widely and deservedly acclaimed *Shakhsiyyat Misr: derasa fi 'abqariyyat el-makan*, (Egypt's Personality: A Study of the Genius of Location).
184. Hamdan, vol. 295.
185. Ibid, 298-608.

186. Ibid, 626.
187. Ibid, 664.
188. Ibid, 667.
189. Ibid, 672-673.
190. Some Egyptians, for example commemorated the passing of five hundred years of Ottoman opening (conquest) of Egypt. See *Al Ahram*, "Akhbar el-sabah,", July 28, 2016, http://www.ahram.org.eg/NewsQ/539983.aspx (accessed August 4, 2016).
191. Ashur, *el-'Asr el-mamaliki*, 314.
192. The eighteenth century historian Abdel Rahman el-Gabarti for example uses the two terms interchangeably.
193. Wael Lutfi, "Gara'm el-mashaykh fil hikma wal rahma wal nas mostamerra wala yougad mas'oul wahed yohasebohom," *Rose al Yossef*, May 30, 2008, 58-61.
194. Ibid.
195. Patrick Clawson, "Arab Human Development Report 2004: Towards Freedom in the Arab World," *The Middle East Quarterly*, 13, no. 1 (2006), http://www.meforum.org/article/900 (accessed June 4, 2008.).
196. Ibid.
197. UNDP, Human Development Report 2004: Towards Freedom in the Arab World, http://www.undp.org/arabstates/PDF2004/AHDR_2004_Executive_Summary.pdf (accessed June 4, 2008).
198. Ibid.
199. UNDP, *Human Development Report 2004: Towards Freedom in the Arab World*, http://www.undp.org/arabstates/PDF2004/9PR_AHDR04_E.pdf (accessed June 4, 2008).
200. Mona Helmy, "Tahakkom el-mawta fi masir el-ahya'," *Rose al Yossef*, 10 September 2004, 70.
201. Ibid.
202. Nadine el-Hadi, "1001 Nights' Faces Legal Ban Again," *Al Masry Al Youm*, http://www.almasryalyoum.com/en/news/1001-nights-faces-legal-banagain (accessed May 20, 2010).
203. See, for example, Sayyar Al-Jamil, "el-Tarikh el-Araby yamshi 'ala okkaz," *Rose al Yossef*, July 25-31, 2009, 82-83.
204. Ibrahim Badran, Hawla el-Tarikh wal taqaddom fil 'Alam el-Araby, (Beirut: el-mu'assa el-Arabiyya lil derasat wal nashr, 1991), 133.
205. Ibid, 164-165.
206. Ibid, 162.
207. Ibid, 138.
208. Karam Gabr, "Khotorat el-doar el-siasyi li regal el-din," *Rose al Yossef*, December 24, 2004, 34-35.
209. See, for example, "Bil video: hewar bayna modhe' wa 'jini' 'ala

el-hawaa," *elfagr*, August 19, 2011, http://www.elfagr.org/Detail. aspx?nwsId=41991&secid=5&vid=2 (accessed August 19, 2011).
210. Dawood el-Sharyan, "Jinn 'ala al hawaa fi bernameg el-thamena wa mofti 'am el-Se'oudiyya: aghlab el-roqah la togeedoona qeraat el-fateha," *Arabic CNN*, November 29, 2016, http://arabic.cnn.com/entertainment/2016/11/29/saudi-althamena-roqia-charia (accessed December 3, 2016); Aziz el-Selimani, "Haqiqat Jinn yastakhdemoona whatsapp wa kayfiyyat hodooth dhalek wa hal howa haqiqah am khayal," *newsaraby*, November 29, 2016, http://news-araby.com/?p=13026 (accessed December 3, 2016).
211. The answer was yes some Jinn were Muslims and some are not, "el-Jinn," *Al Ahram*, January 13, 2002, 33. The Jinn in the Arab tradition are creatures that are somewhat similar to the elves at the bottom of the garden, some of which are good, some are naughty and mischievous, and some are evil. Only people possessing special powers are able to communicate with them.
212. The answer was marriage during that period between the two main Islamic feasts was allowed, "Fatwa: 'aqd el-qaran fi bain el-'idain?," *Al Ahram*, January 13, 2002, 33.
213. The answer was it is not allowed, "Fatwa: Hal naha el-Islam 'an mohawalat ma'rifat el-ghaib?," *Al Ahram*, March 19, 2002, 33.
214. The answer was no, it is not a sin for women to vote in an election, "Fatwa: el-shar' hal yamna' el-mar'a min el-edla' bi sawtiha fil intikhab?," *Al Ahram*, March 19, 2002, 29.
215. The answer was no to both questions. Ibid.
216. Other examples include one reader who wanted to know if divulging marital secrets was prohibited, and Dr. Ahmad Youssef Seliman of Dar el-'Uloum informed him that it was. "Fatwa: ifsha' el-asrar el-zawgiyya," *Al Ahram*, December 25, 2001, 27. Another asked if playing chess was a sin and, therefore, prohibited. Dr. Seliman's answer was that playing chess was allowed providing that it was not: a) played for money, b) used as a means of wasting time, c) did not distract from remembering God, prayers, or any religious or social duties, and d) did not lead disputes and discord. Seliman concluded the advice by noting that since playing chess is "suspicious," it is best to avoid it altogether. "Fatwa: Hal hadha sahih," *Al Ahram*, January 9, 2002, 29. One reader wanted to know if the heirs of a deceased person whose illness had forced him to miss a few days of fasting during the month of Ramadan were required to make amends by fasting for the same number of days missed by the deceased, and the reader was told that that was indeed what they had to do. "Fatwa: Hokm man mat wa alayhi siam ayyam min shahr Ramadan," *Al Ahram*, 22 2001, 29.

217. Sheikh Abdel Monsef Mahmoud.
218. "Fatwa: Hal ya'lam el-mawta bi ahwal el-ahya'?," *Al Ahram*, March 9, 2002, 33.
219. Ibid. The newspaper also published a contribution by another scholar (presumably unsolicited) on the same page, entitled "The Common denominator in the Science of Islamic Statistics" by Dr. Samir Mahmoud, Professor of Statistics at Zagazig University. The professor informed the readers that the date 2/2/2002 was subject of study, discussion and analysis by numerous scientists because of the repeated occurrence of the number two which would never happen again. He went on to add that the number two is mentioned many times in the Holy Book and is the foundation of many theories of probabilities in statistics. Samir Mahmoud, "el-Qasem el-moshtarak el-a'zam fi 'lm el-ehsaa el-Islami," *Al Ahram*, March 9, 2002, 33. The professor provided no further details on the analysis that was carried out by all these scientists.
220. See for example, Ragab el-Morshedy, "Ostadh bi kolliat osoul el-din yattahem el-'ameed bil sareqa el-'elmiyya," *Rose al Yossef*, December 9, 2006, 35-36; Atef el-Kilany, "Ahmed Abdel Mo'ti Hegazi Kha'f 'ala e; balad min salbiyyat el-Azhar wal barlaman," *Rose al Yossef*, December 9, 2006, 35-36; Mahmoud el-Dab', "Game'at el-Azhar tatasattar 'ala fadiha 'ilmiyya mogamala li doctora qaddamat 3 abhath masrouqa min bahetheen aganeb," *Sout el-Omma*, 22 September 2008, 2.
221. Sayyid el-Qemany, "Horriyet el-fawda wa ma'na el-mowatana," *Rose al Yossef*, April 15, 2005, 21-23.
222. This new breed of sheikhs has at one time or another declared it sinful for a woman to take a cab unaccompanied, to sit on a chair, or to surf the internet unsupervised by a mehrem (father, son, uncle or another close relative that she would not be eligible to marry). Other prohibitions include giving flowers to friends, playing soccer unless the teams are eleven players playing either one or three halftimes with no referee or lines painted on the field, wearing high heals, giving military salutes, claiming that the earth is rotating, studying chemistry because that is magic. See, Nahed Ezzat, "Aaakher ma antagatho mikinat el-takhallof wal tatarrof," *Rose al Yossef*, April 6, 2007, 40-42. One Egyptian sheikh issued a fatwa that those who do not pray should be executed, see Hasan Yaqout Hassan, "Fatwa bi qatl tarek el-salah," *Rose al Yossef*, June 21-21, 2003.
223. Bilal Ramadan, "Khotba qadina lil Hawini 'an nizan el-riq wal gawari totheer gadalan 'ala Facebook," *youm7*, May 22, 2011, http://www.youm7.com/News.asp?NewsID=418494 (accessed My 22, 2011). To be fair the sheikh did protest that his statements, while accurately re-

ported, were "taken out of context." Mohammed Ismail, "el- Hawini yogaded hadithoh 'an el-raqiq," *youm7*, May 23, 2011, http://www.youm7.com/News.asp?NewsID=418971 (accessed My 23, 2011).
224. Kamel Kamel, "da'eya salafi yotaleb bitatbiq hadd el-haraba 'ala el-fannanin," *youm7*, June 26, 2016, http://www.youm7.com/news/newsprint?newid=2776705 (accessed August 12, 2016).
225. "Modtarroun li monaqashat fatwa el-mufti allati totheer el-'awasef: el-mar'a allati tongib ba'da arba' sanawat min wafat zawgiha laisat zaniya!!," *Rose al Yossef*, September 22, 2006, 44-45.
226. Ibid. Other examples are cited in, Fathi Hussein, "Fatawi harq el-dam," *youm7*, September 24, 2010, http://www.youm7.com/News.asp?NewsID=2821551 (accessed September 23, 2010).
227. Gamal Nkrumah and Mohamed el-Sayed, "Tragedy and Farce: A Scandalous Religious Edict Had the Papers Howling," *Al Ahram Weekly*, May 31- June 6, 2007, http://weekly.ahram.org.eg/2007/847/pr1.htm (accessed May 11, 2009); Wafaa Sha'ira, "el-Edariyya el-'olya taktafee bi lawm sahib fatwa erda' el-kabir liannahu egtahad fi hodoud fahmo," *Rose al Yossef*, May 29, 2009, 62-64.
228. Ghada Mohammed. "el-'Obaikn yo'eed fatwa erda' el-maraa lil ragol el-agnabi," *elaf*, http://www.elaph.com/Web/news/2010/5/563334.html (accessed May 22, 2010).
229. Sayyid el-Qemany, "Hai'at 'olama' el-erhab," *Rose al Yossef*, October 2, 200416-17.
230. Ibid.
231. See for example, Asma Nassar and Mahmoud Samaha, "Kharitat el-tanzimat el-salafiyya fi Misr," *Rose al Yossef*, May 30, 2008, 62-65.
232. Amr Khalid, an unsuccessful accountant, is a pioneer of the new breed of preachers in the tradition of the successful and popular televangelists who are amassing fortunes by catering to the lowest common denominator. His income in 2007 was reported to be 2.5 million dollars. alarabiya.net, "Amr Khaled Richest Islamic Preacher: Forbes," http://www.alarabiya.net/articles/2008/02/28/46255.html (accessed March 31, 2010). See also, Wael Lutfi, "Masader tharawat Amr Khaled wal do'ah el godod," *Rose al Yossef*, May 30, 2008, 58-61. The method that they use is the same tried and true formula. They offer the innocently credulous a shallow and simplistic view of religion, play on their audience's emotions, fears and insecurities, either scare them with a message of hell and damnation, or if the situation demands it, offer them hope by showing them an easy to follow road to salvation. Some of these new stars may well be sincere despite their limited and superficial understanding of religious doctrine. Some are unscrupulous and merely use religion as an easy route to

stardom and previously undreamt of riches. Both groups, however, reinforce the values of fatalism, contempt for the intellect, underdevelopment, and economic, intellectual, and cultural stagnation. That turns a segment of society into easy prey for extremist and terrorist movements.

233. Wael Lutfi, "Gara'm el-mashaykh fil hikma wal rahma wal nas mostamerra wala yougad mas'oul wahed yohasebohom," *Rose al Yossef*, May 30, 2008, 58-61.
234. Sayyid el-Qemany, "E'qru el-Gamal," *Mawqi' a'mal el-doctor Sayyid el*-Qemany, comment posted March 6, 2006, http://quemny.blog.com/1268746/ (accessed May 20, 2008).
235. Gamal Nkrumah, "Zaghloul el-Naggar: Scientific Being," *Al Ahram Weekly*, November 17-23, 2005, http://weekly.ahram.org.eg/Archive/2005/769/profile.htm. (accessed September 9, 2016).
236. Ibid.
237. Ibid.
238. Ibid.
239. Ibid
240. Zaghloul el-Naggar, "min el-e'gaz el-elmi fil sonna el-nabawiyya: el-tatawol fil bonyan min 'alamat el-sa's," *Al Ahram*, November 2, 2003, 20.
241. Ibid.
242. Zaghloul el-Naggar, "Min asrar el-Quran," *Al Ahram*, December 31, 2001, http://www.ahram.org.eg/ARCHIVE/Index.asp?CurFN=OPIN6.HTM&DID=7256 (accessed May 19, 2008; see also Zaghloul el-Naggar, "Min asrar el-Quran," *Al Ahram*, October 20, 2008, http://www.ahram.org.eg/Index.asp?CurFN=opin1.htm&DID=9741 (accessed October 20, 2008).
243. Galal Amin, *'Asr el-Gamaheer el-Ghafeera* (Cairo: Dar el-shorouq, 2003), 30.
244. Sayyid el-Qemany, "el-karahiya wall ghamm: moqtatafat mohemma min fatawi foqha' el-karahiya," *Rose al Yossef*, September 24, 2004, 73-.75.
245. Ibid.
246. Ibid.
247. Mahmoud Samaha and Asma; Nassar, "Mosta'mara gadida lil salafiyya fi 'ain shams," *Rose al Yossef*, 17 May 2008, 30-33.
248. Ibid.
249. Sayyid Ghannam, "Tafaseel 'amaliyyat el-tamweel el-seriyya lil gama'at el-Islamiyya," *Rose al Yossef*, May 24, 2008, 87-88.
250. The cost of one of these tapes at one location was approximately 0.47 U.S dollars and that price included a free book, see, Ahmed el-Rou-

mi, "Taraga'a el-erhab wa lam tataraga' aghaneeh," *Rose al Yossef*, 16 May 2009, 58-61.
251. Esam Abdel Gawwad, Micorbasat el-tatarrof el-'am," *Rose al Yossef*, December 30, 2006, 43-44.
252. Ibid.
253. Alex Dziadosz, "At Cairo's Grand Hyatt, alcohol ban met with cheer and uncertainty," *The daily Star*, May 5, 2008, http://www.dailystaregypt.com/article.aspx?ArticleID=13456 (accessed May 5, 2008).
254. The efforts to spread the Wahabi message are not limited to Egypt. Press interviews with some former British members of extremist movements indicate that the Saudis also appear determined to influence the Muslim communities in Europe and elsewhere. See, for example, Johann Hari," Renouncing Islamism: To the Brink and Back Again," *The Independent*, http://www.independent.co.uk/opinion/commentators/johann-hari/renouncing-islamism-to-the-brink-and-back-again-1821215.html (accessed November 28, 2009); "Saudi Teacher on Trial in Jakarta," *BBC*, February 24, 2010, http://news.bbc.co.uk/2/hi/asia-pacific/8533720.stm (accessed February 24, 2010).
255. Mohammed Fattouh, "Shorout wa thawabet el-Islam el-khaligi wa atharahu 'ala el-sho'oub," *Rose al Yossef*, August 20-26, 2005, 80.
256. See, for example, Hoda el-Misri, "Khamsat 'ashar sayyida Se'odiyya yoqarrerna egbar el-fada'iyyat 'ala el-tamassok bil fadila," *Rose al Yossef*, October 4, 2008, 96-98.
257. Shahinaz Azzam, "Modhi'a fi qanah fada'iyya lil monaqqabat faqat: hayati modern geddan," *Rose al Yossef*, August 1-7, 2009.
258. Tariq Mustafa, "Mamdouh el-Laithi: el-wasat el-fanni nesfoh mohaggabat!," *Rose al Yossef*, May 30-June 5, 2009, 94-95.
259. Ahmed Abdel Mo'ti Hegazi, "laisat el-thaqafa wahdaha innahu el-watan kolloh," *Al Ahram*, January 15, 2003.
260. Ibid.
261. The Saudi billionaire who bought a substantial part of Egypt's cinematic heritage does appear to have a plan that was termed "moral and religious." He recently expressed his disapproval of some television stations that he labeled as nothing more than "prostitution on the airwaves" and stated that he feels pride and self-exaltation to be the owner of television stations that "practices strict and rigorous censorship of the movies that it shows." Tariq Mustafa, "Wasaya el-sheikh Saleh fil e'lam 'el-saleh' wal taleh," *Rose al Yossef*, April 17-23, 2010, 90. See also Hosam Abdel Hadi, el-Walid bin Tallal yashtari tholth torath el-cenima el-Misriyya li yoteq qanat aflamoh el-gadida," *Rose al Yossef*, March 13-19, 2004, 24-25.
262. Montadayat Amal el-Islam, http://www.amalislam.com/ib/lofiversion/index.php?t3042.html (accessed April 22, 2007).

263. Sayyid Ghannam, "Tafaseel 'amaliyyat el-tamweel el-seriyya lil gama'at el-Islamiyya," *Rose al Yossef*, May 24, 2008, 87-88.
264. "ghadab fi Misr b'ad e'laniha taba'iyyat gaziratay tiran wa sanafir lil Se'oudiyya," *BBC*, April 11, 2016, http://www.bbc.com/arabic/middleeast/2016/04/160410_rage_egypt_saudi_islands (accessed September, 1, 2016).
265. "ettifaq 'ala ensha gesr yarbot bayn el-Se'oudiyya wa Misr," *BBC*, April 8, 2016, http://www.bbc.com/arabic/middleeast/2016/04/160408_egypt_saudi_bridge (accessed September, 1, 2016).
266. Hegazi, "Ma'a man anta." See also Tarek Haggi, "Tatarrof Islam am tatarrof bashar," *Akhbar el-Yom*, November 33, 2001, 9.
267. Ibid.
268. Ibid.
269. Ibid.
270. See, for example: Lori Plotkin Boghardt, "Saudi Funding of ISIS, *Washington Institute*, June 23, 2014, http://www.washingtoninstitute.org/policy-analysis/view/saudi-funding-of-isis / (accessed August 5, 2016); Josh Rogin, "America's Allies Are Funding ISIS," *The Daily Beast*, June 14, 2014, http://www.thedailybeast.com/articles/2014/06/14/america-s-allies-are-funding-isis.html (accessed August 5, 2016); Kamel Daoud, "Saudi Arabia, an ISIS That Has Made It, *New York Times*, November 20, 2015, http://www.nytimes.com/2015/11/21/opinion/saudi-arabia-an-isis-that-has-made-it.html (accessed August 5, 2016); "Is Saudi Arabia to Blame for Islamic State?," *BBC*, December 19, 2015, http://www.bbc.co.uk/news/world-middle-east-35101612 (accessed August 5, 2016); Roy Greenslade, "Saudi Arabia (white Daesh) is the Father of Isis, Says Writer," *The Guardian*, November 25, 2015, https://www.theguardian.com/media/greenslade/2015/nov/25/saudi-arabia-white-daesh-is-the-father-of-isis-says-writer (accessed August 5, 2016); "Chomsky: Saudi Arabia is the "Center of Radical Islamic Extremism" Now Spreading Among Sunni Muslims," *Democracy Now*, May 17, 2016, http://www.democracynow.org/2016/5/17/chomsky_saudi_arabia_is_the_center (accessed September 8, 2016); Mohammad Javad Zarif, "Let Us Rid the World of Wahhabism," *New York Times*, September 13, 2016, http://www.nytimes.com/2016/09/14/opinion/mohammad-javad-zarif-let-us-rid-the-world-of-wahhabism.html?_r=0 (accessed September 17, 2016); Zalmay Khalilzad, "'We Misled You': How the Saudis Are Coming Clean on Funding Terrorism, *Politico*, September 14, 2016, "http://www.politico.com/magazine/story/2016/09/saudi-arabia-terrorism-funding-214241 (accessed September 17, 2016); Christina Pazzanese, "All Politics is Personal; VP Biden Delivers Address at Ken-

nedy School Forum," October 3, 2014, *Harvard Gazette*, https://www.hks.harvard.edu/news-events/news/articles/joe-biden-forum-event (accessed October 19, 2016).

271. Jim Sciutto, Ryan Browne, Deirdre Walsh," Congress Releases Secret '28 Pages' On Alleged Saudi 9/11 Ties;" *CNN*, July 16, 2016, http://edition.cnn.com/2016/07/15/politics/congress-releases-28-pages-saudis-9-11/ (accessed September 17, 2016); David Smith, Spencer Ackerman, "9/11 Report's Classified '28 Pages' About Potential Saudi Arabia Ties Released," *The Guardian*, July 15, 2016, https://www.theguardian.com/us-news/2016/jul/15/911-report-saudi-arabia-28-pages-released (accessed September 17, 2016); Jennifer Rizzo, "Prince and the '28 pages': Indirect 9/11 Link to Saudi Royal Revealed," *CNN*, August 5, 2016, http://edition.cnn.com/2016/08/05/politics/28-pages-saudi-prince-bandar-9-11/index.html?utm_source=feedburner&utm_medium=feed&utm_campaign=Feed%3A+rss%2Fcnn_latest+%28RSS%3A+CNN+-+Most+Recent%29 (accessed August 8, 2016); Robert Fisk, "Don't be Fooled by the News that Al-Qaeda and Nusra Have Split for the Good of the Syrian-People," *The Independent*, July 29, 2016, http://www.independent.co.uk/voices/dont-be-fooled-by-the-news-that-al-qaeda-and-nusra-have-split-for-the-good-of-the-syrian-people-a7161776.html (accessed May 21 2017); Robert Fisk, "After Splitting With Al-Qaeda, Al-Nusra is Being Presented to the West as a Moderate Force. It's Nothing of the Sort," *The Independent*, May 10, 2016 http://www.independent.co.uk/voices/after-splitting-with-al-qaeda-al-nusra-is-being-presented-to-the-west-as-a-moderate-force-it-s-a7022271.html (accessed May 21 2017).

Appendix: Gamal Abdel Nasser

1. This section relies heavily on Vatikiotis.
2. Vatikiotis, 18.
3. See, for example, Abdel Halim Khafagi, *Endama ghabat el-shams* (Mansoura: Dar el-wafa', 1987) or Shafiq Ahmed Ali, *el-mar'a allati ahabbaha Abdel Nasser: asrar wa khetabat bint el-basha allati lam yatazawwagaha*, Cairo: Dar Nubar lil tiba'a, 1989).
4. See, for example, Samir Abdu, *el-Tahlil el-nafsi li shakhsiyyat Gamal Abdel Nasser* (Cairo: Dar el-ketab el-Araby, 1992), or Youssef el-Seba'i, *Ayyam Abdel Nasser* (Cairo: Maktabat el-Khangi, 1971).
5. Vatikiotis, 42.
6. Ibid.
7. Ibid.

8. Ibid.
9. Nasser's father did not complete the primary school education, see, Lutfi, *Ma'sat Abdel Hakim Amer* (Cairo: Dar el-Hilal, 1980) 37.
10. Vatikiotis. 23.
11. Even the Arabs who did not settle in remote areas have tended to preserve their Bedouin attitudes, traditions, and social values. The Arab residents of Cairo during the nineteenth century, for example, were viewed as being different from the rest of the population and were always referred to as Bedouins in historical documents. They retained their proclivity for pillaging and feuding among themselves. They remained separate, unassimilated, and neither intermarried nor mixed with non-Arabs. Abdel Rehim Abdel Rahman Abdel Rehim, *Fusul min tarikh Misr el-eqtisadi wal egtima'i fil 'asr el-Othmani* (Cairo: el-Hai'a el-Misriyya el-'amma lil ketab, 1990), 306-307.
12. See, for example, Nermeen Qotb, "Etawat el-Erban tohadded mashrou' ebni baitak," *Al Ahram*, September 30, 2010, http://www.ahram.org.eg/305/2010/09/30/25/41263.aspx, (accessed September 30, 2010); or Mahmoud Samaha, "Bil bokhour wal dinameet Magharba yabhathoun 'an el-zaibaq el-ahmar fi sahara' el-Minya," *Rose al Yossef*, May 29, 2009, 38-45; or Antar Abdel Latif, "el-Badw yahkomouna Misr waya'taberounaha dawla dakhel el-dawla," *Sout el-Omma*, June 16, 2008, 9; or Osama Khaled and Saleh el-Bek, "Al Masry Al Youm taqdi 48 sa'a fil 'alam el-serri li matareed Sina, "*Al Masry Al Youm*, http://www.almasry-alyoum.com/printerfriendly.aspx?ArticleID=255004 (accessed May 16, 2010); or "Battles Between Bedouins and Shop Owners in Sharm el-Sheikh," *Ahram Online*, June 24, 2011, http://english.ahram.org.eg/~/NewsContent/1/64/14927/Egypt/Politics-/Battles-between-Bedouins-and-shop-owners-in-Sharm-.aspx (accessed June 24, 2011); or "Egypt Government Seeks Help of Sinai Tribes to Protect Gas Pipeline," *Ahram Online*, June 23, 2011, http://english.ahram.org.eg/NewsContent/1/64/14883/Egypt/Politics-/Egypt-government-seeks-help-of-Sinai-tribes-to-pro.aspx (accessed June 24, 2011); "aghezat el-amn tangah fi tahrir aakher thalathat mokhtatifeen qabilat el-ashraf min qabdat Arab el-samta bi Qena," *elfagr*, November, 12, 2011, http://www.elfagr.org/Detail.aspx?nwsId=81318&secid=8&vid=2 (accessed November 12, 2011).); "ta'leem taht rosas el-tha'r: talameedh fi qena yowagehoon el-moat bisabab neza'at el-Arab wal hawwara," *Al Masry Al Youm*, http://sharek.almasryalyoum.com/cities/qena/490110/ (accessed August 19, 2016); Fatima el-Desouki, "fi waqi'at maqtal wakeel neyabet el-daher," *Al Ahram*, August 19, 2016, http://www.ahram.org.eg/NewsQ/544631.aspx (accessed Augustt19, 2016).
13. See for example his speech in Port Said on December 23, 1962; Bibli-

otica Alexandrina, *Mawqi' el-ra'is Gamal Abdel Nasser*, "Khitab el-ra'is Gamal Abdel Nasser fi el-ehtifal bi'eed el-nasr el-sades bi Port Said," http://nasser.bibalex.org/NasserSpeeches/browser.aspx?SID=1035 (accessed January 14, 2007); or his speech in Cairo on May 2, 1967, Bibliotica Alexandrina, *Mawqi' el-ra'is Gamal Abdel Nasser*, "Khitab el-ra'is Gamal Abdel Nasser fi el-ehtifal bi 'eed el-'ommal bi Shobra el-Khaima," http://nasser.bibalex.org/Speeches/browser.aspx?SID=1214 (accessed August 24, 2009).

14. Said Abdel Fattah Ashur, *el-'Asr el-mamaliki fi Misr wal sham* (Cairo: Dar el-nahda el-Arabiyya, 1965), 315.
15. As Egypt was a conquered nation, the native Egyptians, the Copts, were not viewed as a threat to the power play and were excluded from that struggle.
16. Marsot, *Short History*, 55.
17. See for example his remarks in, Mustafa Badr, *Abdel Nasser ba'idan' 'an el-siyasa* (Cairo: Madbouli el-saghir, 2001), 118-119.
18. Vatikiotis, 25.
19. For example, there was an awkward protocol incident when Nasser visited Greece in 1960. As the king and Queen of Greece went to accompany President and Mrs. Nasser to the formal dinner that they were holding in their honor, the king attempted to link arms with Mrs. Nasser, while the Queen attempted to do the same with Nasser. To the surprise and embarrassment of the royal hosts, both Mr. and Mrs. Nasser pulled away. Referring to the incident later, Nasser explained it by saying "I am a *sa'idi* and cannot abide seeing my wife linking arms with another man even if he was a king." el-Shahed, 328-329; Badr, 118-119.
20. Another incident occurred when Mrs. Nasser decided to spend an evening at the Cairo Opera. The director of the opera house kept news of the impending visit to himself to avoid possible competition for the first lady's attention, but the deputy director, who was in charge of the keys to the royal box, learned of the planned visit and showed up for the occasion. He later related the incident to a friend during a telephone conversation and complained about his boss's pettiness. Apparently, someone listened in to the phone conversation and related details of the grumbling session to the boss. The boss, as was the case with all of Nasser's appointees, was one of were *ahl el-theqa* the "people of trust," and had special privileges and access to people in high positions. He complained about his deputy to Nasser's' aide, Ali Sabry. Soon afterwards, Fathi Radwan, the Minister of Culture, who had not heard of the squabble, was surprised to receive a presidential decree ordering the immediate retirement of the opera house's depu-

ty director. Sabry then telephoned Radwan to follow-up on the execution of the presidential decree. When Radwan expressed surprise at the order, Sabry informed him that Nasser had issued the decree because he was displeased by the use of his wife's name in the telephone conversation. Fathi Radwan, *72 Shahran ma'a Abdel Nasser* (Cairo: Dar el-horriya, 1986), 168.
21. Mahmoud Fawzi, *Mo'amarat ightiyal el-mushir Amer* (Cairo: Dar el-nashr hatiyeh, 1992), 17-18.
22. It might be worth noting that Nasser's restrictive view of women during the 1960s would be viewed as liberal by the attitudes that began to spread in Egypt after the mid 1970s.
23. Mohammed el-Gawwadi, *Derasa fi sina'at el-qarar el-seyasi: kayfa asbaho wozaraa* (Cairo: Dar el-khayyal, 2003), 89-90. The implication was that the unfortunate lady's appearance was more masculine than feminine.
24. Vatikiotis, 24.
25. Ibid.
26. Ibid, 25.
27. Jean Lacouture, *Nasser*, trans. Daniel Hofstadter (New York: Alfred A. Knopf, 1973), 112.
28. Vatikiotis, 267.
29. St. John, 19.
30. Vatikiotis, 16-17. His fellow MB member Hussein Mohammed Ahmad Hammouda also claims that Nasser was searching for a heroic role to play. Hammouda, *Asrar*, 161. The theatrically dramatic nature of the initiation ceremony that Nasser went through before being admitted to MB membership must also have appealed to Nasser's view of himself as the romantic hero. The ritual involved secret knocks on doors, darkened rooms, and swearing an oath in the dark on a gun and the Holy Book before a man completely covered by a sheet. For details see, Hammouda, *Asrar*, 33-3.5.
31. Vatikiotis, 28.
32. Ibid.
33. Ibid.
34. For a brief review of the political, social turmoil in Egypt prior to coup, which may have influenced Nasser's intellectual, see, Awad, *Aqne'at*, 45-55.
35. The blue shirts were the semi militarized youth wing of the party. Vatikiotis, 29.
36. For details see, Ibid, 67-88.
37. Ibid, 33.
38. Ibid, 50.
39. Nasser's fellow FO Kamal el-Din Hussein recalled that they both

joined the group together after graduation from the military college. Hussein Mo'nes, *Bashawat wa super bashawat*, (Cairo: el-zahra' lil e'lam el-Araby, 1988), 328-329. A former deputy of the MB Supreme leader has also confirmed Nasser's membership in the group, that his codename was Zagloul Abdel Qader, and adds that he trained their members in the use of weapons. Ahmad Hassan el-Baqoury, *Baqaya dhekrayat*, (Cairo, Markaz el-Ahram lil targama wal nashr, 1988), 77.

40. Abdel Ghani, *el-Muthaqqafoun*, 206-207.
41. Vatikiotis, 57.
42. Ibid.
43. Ibid, 62.
44. Gershoni and Jankowski, *Egypt*, 37.
45. Hourani, 330.
46. Gershoni and Jankowski, *Egypt*, 37.
47. Mustafa Abdel-Ghani "Of Generals and People," *Al Ahram Weekly*, July 18-24, 2002, http://weekly.ahram.org.eg/2002/595/sc101.htm (accessed 22 May 2009).
48. Vatikiotis, 26.
49. Ibid, 47.
50. Ibid, 110.
51. Ibid.
52. St. John, 33.
53. Vatikiotis, 58.
54. Ibid, 37.
55. Ibid, 58.
56. Ibid, 288.
57. El-Sadat, *el-Bahth*, 32.
58. Ibid.
59. El-Hadidi, *Isterdad*, 23; His confidant, Mohammed Hassanein Heikal, disputes that assertion and maintains that Nasser did read a great deal, had a private library with hundreds of books and a staff supervised by a university professor who "summarized" books for him, and that he even read "some of these books." Matar, 180.
60. Hammouda, *Asrar*, 161.
61. Vatikiotis, 29; Lacouture, 358.
62. Abul Fath, 349.
61. Ibid, 393.
64. Abdel Ghani, *el-Muthaqqafoun*, 303-307.
65. El-Sayyid, *Ta'ammulat*, 66.
66. Gamal Abdel Nasser, *Falsafet el-thawra* (Cairo, Information department, n.d).
67. Mohi el-Din, *Memories*, 240.

68. Vatikiotis, 265-266.
69. Lacouture, 229.
70. Habib, 256-257.
71. Om Kalthoum was a popular singer whose monthly public performance was eagerly awaited throughout the Arab world.
72. Habib, 256-257.
73. Ibid, 259
74. Nasser gave his uncle as an example to justify his intention to nationalize modest establishments such as a car mechanic's workshop whose only employee could be a young apprentice. He told his colleagues in the RCC that the uncle owned three trucks, and earned six hundred pounds per month by exploiting the labor of his hired drivers. El-Boghdadi, 2, 229.
75. The recollections of Mohammed Farghaly, published after Nasser's death, lend some weight to this argument. Farghaly, a wealthy pre-coup businessman who had initially supported the coup and whose cotton trading business was nationalized, expresses puzzlement in his recollections about the manner in which the nationalization policy was carried out. He states that non-Egyptians whose businesses were nationalized were compensated fairly and were not put under sequestration but the Egyptian owners businesses were rarely compensated, and the sequestrators appeared intent on taking revenge on the business owners rather than simply implementing a policy. Furthermore, changing the names of Egyptian owned companies after they were taken over while retaining the names of non-Egyptian businesses tends to lend weight to the animosity thesis. Mohamed Ahmed Farghaly, 'Eshtu hayati bayna ha'ola' (Cairo: Matab'et Al Ahram el-tegariyya, 1984), 173-177.
76. Habib, 258.
77. Sarwat Okasha, one of the original Free Officers who had been exiled to Europe, was serving in the Egyptian embassy in Rome in 1958 and was, as he recounts in his memoirs, perfectly contented in his new role as a diplomat when a sudden decision by Nasser took him in another direction. It happened one night when he went home with his wife after an evening at the opera and turned on the radio to listen to the news bulletin from Cairo and heard an official announcement that he had been appointed Minister of Culture. Nasser had neither asked him if he was interested in the position, nor informed him of the proposed appointment before it was publicly announced. Okasha, vol.1, 466.
78. Another incident that the under secretary for the ministry of education, recounts illustrates this impulsiveness. Nehru, the Prime Minis-

ter of India was visiting an old mosque with Nasser when he asked for a book about the historic mosques of Cairo. Nasser's ordered the Minister of Education, Kamal el-Din Hussein, to find one and Hussein called Abdel Menem and instructed him to find one and deliver it to Nasser immediately. Abdel Menem found a book in the Department of Tourism's library, called Rashad Morad, the department's director who rushed to the library, broke down the door, smashed the bookcase containing the book, and rushed with it to Nasser. Morad was told that nothing else was required of him, and he went home. When Nasser moved on to his next stop, which was the Cairo Citadel, he turned around to ask Morad something and when he discovered that he had gone home, he ordered him fired immediately. Hassan Abdel Menem, *Layilat zifaf bint el-ra'is* (Cairo: el-Hai'a el-Misriyya el-'amma lil ketab, 1987), 122.

79. Nasser was due to give a speech in Port Said. The then Prime Minister, Ali Sabry, went to see him five minutes before he began his speech. He informed Nasser that the minister of Supplies had asked the American Ambassador about the expected date of arrival of the wheat shipment the US was providing as aid to Egypt and that the Ambassador answered in a manner that insulted Egypt. The U.S. Ambassador contacted Nasser's press secretary after the offending speech and denied the story and the minister of Supplies confirmed the Ambassador's version. Nasser then calmed down and asked Sadat and Abdel Hakim Amer to mend fences with the U.S., whereupon they invited the U.S. ambassador to dinner at the home of Nasser's press secretary to try to make amends and contain the situation. El-Sadat, *el-Bahth*, 32, 70, 217, 290-291.

80. The impulsive behavior was often commented upon. See, for example Lacouture, 155; Badawi, 240, 264; . El-Hakim, *'Awdat el-wa'i*, 39.

81. Vatikiotis, 353-354.

82. El-Boghdadi, vol. 2, 295.

83. After Ali's service with the fourth armored division, he served as Chief of Intelligence (75/79), Minister of Defense, Commander of the Armed Forces (8-84), and Prime Minister (84-85).

84. Vatikiotis, 16-17.

85. Lacouture, 150.

86. One incident that supports the contention that he did sincerely believe his own fabrications was related by el-Boghdadi. Presidential elections had been held on March 15, 1965 and when the results were announced the next day, Nasser had, as usual, won 99.999 percent of the vote with only sixty-five people in the whole country casting a vote against him. Three days later, on March 18, Nasser, inexplicably,

issued a presidential decree lifting the sequestration order that had been placed on el-Baghdadi's brother in retaliation for his (el-Baghdadi's) resignation the previous year. El-Boghdadi was baffled and tried to find an explanation for the sudden return of his brother's property. The reason, as it turned out later, was that Nasser had checked the results of the polling center where el-Boghdadi had voted and concluded that he must have voted for him because there was not a single vote against him cast in that center. El-Boghdadi, *Modhakkarat*, vol. 2, 249-250.

87. One example of this rigging was witnessed firsthand by Ibrahim Abdu who had not bothered to cast his vote in one of Nasser's plebiscites. He went later to pay the fine stipulated by law for those who had not voted only to discover that he was not liable for the fine because the records showed that he had voted. Ibrahim Abdu, *Tarikh bela watha'q* (Cairo: Mu'assasat segel el-Arab, 1975), 77.
88. Abul Fath, 397–398.
89. Abdel Ghani, *el-Muthaqqafoun*, 238–239.
90. Ibid, 343.
91. El-Sadat, *el-Bahth*, 213
92. El-Gawwadi, *Derasa*, 2003, 239.
93. Abdel Rahman Badawi who worked with him found him vacuous and ignorant of the essence of diplomacy and, Badawi, 242.
94. Nasr, vol. 3, 303.
95. Ibid.
96. Vatikiotis, 185, quoting Fathi Radwan in *Rose al Yossef*, September, 1, 1975.
97. Ibid.
98. Radwan, 124.
99. Ibid.
100. Fathi, 43.
101. Ibid, 285.
102. Ibid.
103. Ibid.
104. He personally led one of his secret organizations, *el-tanzim el-tali'i* (the Vanguard Organization). It was comprised of cells of ten persons each that were selected by a leader who then submitted their names to be vetted by the intelligence organization. By 1970, the membership had reached an estimated one hundred to one hundred and fifty thousand but neither the Parliament Speaker, Sadat, nor the Armed Forces Commander Amer, were among them. The group's motto was "Liberty, socialism, and unity." Sharaf and Imam, 191-199; Abdulla Imam, *Ali Sabry Yatadhakkar* (Cairo: Mu'assasat Rose al Yossef, 1987), 30; 120-121; Hamroush, vol. 4, 55.

105. Ibid, 39; 43; 285.
106. Nasr, vol. 4, 299; Abul Fath, 400.
107. Vatikiotis, 294.
108. Habib, 285.
109. Even the pettiest of rumors seemed to warrant the head of state's attention and action. Apparently, Sharaf, a married man, was rumored to be involved with another woman but Nasser, who disapproved of such liaisons, thought the rumor false. He called Sharaf one day and ordered him to arrest Mrs. Hussein el-Shafei for passing the rumor to Nasser's wife. Habib, 381.
110. Sharaf and Imam, 211-212.
111. Sharaf contradicts himself only a couple of pages later when he tries to defend his boss by saying that people were free to talk and that no punishment was meted out to people for merely chatting in coffee shops.
112. Sharaf and Imam, 211-212; Nasser kept a telephone tapping system in his home which he operated personally at first, then later entrusted to his secretary Sami Sharaf. He tapped the conversations of colleagues, ministers, and journalists to learn about their private lives and kept the tapes in a safe in his office. Nasr, vol. 3, 23.
113. A case in point is the treatment Abdel Latif el-Boghdadi received when he resigned on March 16, 1964 in protest over the lack of collective leadership. Nasser wanted to keep the resignation secret, but a friend of el-Boghdadi, Abdel Raouf Nafie, managing director of the government owned Dar el-Hilal Publishing House, apparently discussed this resignation with another friend, the journalist Ali Amin. When Nasser, inevitably, was informed of the conversation, he fired Nafie. In another show of pettiness, el-Baghdadi's brother was put under sequestration in retaliation for his brother's resignation. When the police were instructed to put the brother's office under seal on March 25, 1964, they found themselves in a quandary because the sequestration department had been abolished on March 21, 1964 and the order had been issued on March 24 1964. The problem was solved the same evening when they were instructed to consider that the order was issued on March 13, 1964. El-Boghdadi, vol. 2, 247-248.
114. Other petty harassments included sending Salah Nasr, the intelligence chief, to advise el-Boghdadi not to receive any visitors on the pretext that they had information that Israel was planning to assassinate him. When el-Baghdadi's son-in-law, Mohammed Nosseir, who was in graduate school in London, returned to Egypt with his wife for a vacation he was denied an exit visa to return to his studies. El-Boghdadi was also prohibited in 1965 from going on the pilgrim-

age to Mecca, and his son Tariq was prevented from registering for classes at the American University in Cairo (under sequestration at that time) when he took a semester off to get some work experience. Habib, 463-464; Gohar, 56-59
115. Lutfi, *Ma'sat*, 26-27.
116. Nasr, vol. 2, 324-325.
117. An anecdote related by Abdel Latif el-Boghdadi illustrates how Nasser's minions induced him to take action against some rivals by the information they passed on to him. A friend of el-Baghdadi's, Dr. Rashwan Fahmi, made an innocuous observation at a dinner of physicians at the Gezira Sporting Club. He stated that if Kasr el-Aini, a free public hospital, received the same financial support as the Suez Canal Authority, its administration would be just as successful. Of those present, only Dr. Osman Wahabi clapped. The incident was reported to Nasser and on August 21, 1966, both physicians were fired from their faculty positions at the university by presidential decree and placed, along with their families, under sequestration. Rashwan was also fired from the Arab Socialist Union (ASU) and relieved of his position as head of the Medical Syndicate because its bylaws stipulated that its head had to be an ASU member. When the official carrying out the sequestration order arrived at his one-bedroom flat, he asked him for a list of his and his wife's property. Dr. Fahmi replied that he was single, had no property and his bank account had a one hundred pound overdraft which he had borrowed after pledging his salary as security. The official, who had obviously believed Nasser' rhetoric that the purpose of sequestration was to take from the rich to give to the poor, was puzzled. Gohar, 182-190; Habib, 273. The incident was also recounted by Abdel Rahman Badawi, a personal friend of Rashwan. He states that the dinner ended at midnight and the sequestration order was issued at 4:00 P.M. Badawi, 362-364.
118. For example, Ehsan Abdel Qoddous was jailed for three months for writing an offensive article in 1954. That Nasser told him after his release that he had not read the article, Anne Alexander, *Nasser: His Life and Times* (Cairo: The American University in Cairo Press, 2005), 146.
119. Fathi, 296.
120. Abdel Ghani, *el-Muthaqqafoun*, 408.
121. When Mohammed el-Tabei was replaced by an officer (Amin Shaker) in the Akhbar el-Yom daily, he announced that that he was a greatly honored by the act. Galal el-Din el-Hamamsi and the Amin brothers also competed to curry favor with him. Ibid, 422–423; 234–235; 238-239; 241.
122. Beattie, 136.

123. Fikry Abaza was fired for writing ten lines about freedom and democracy. Sabry, *Watha'q 15 Mayo*, 373.
124. For example, Anis Mansour was fired for an article about a Sufi historical figure because it was interpreted as a veiled criticism of the régime. Sharaf and Imam, 236.
125. Musa Sabry was fired for making an unflattering remark about the voice of a well-connected radio announcer. Musa Sabry, *Watha'q 15 Mayo* (Cairo: el-Maktab el-Misri el-hadith, 1977), 359-361
126. Mustafa Mahmoud was fired because no one, according to Nasser's aide, had been able to make out what his true political views were and whether he was an atheist, a communist, or a Muslim Brother. Sharaf and Imam, 236.
127. Ali Abul Khair, for example, was sentenced to fifteen years with hard labor. The two Abul Fath brothers received suspended sentences of ten and fifteen years respectively. Their newspaper *el-Misri* was closed on May 5, 1954 and all their and their family's property, including their home furniture, was confiscated. Abdel Ghani, *el-Muthaqqafoun*, 300-301; see also Abul Fath, 19; 20; ; Ibrahim Se'da, *Sanawat el-hawan*, (Cairo: el-maktab el-Misri el-hadith, 1975), 120-131.
128. Abdel Ghani, *el-Muthaqqafoun*, 414.
129. Ibid, 422–423,
130. Abdel Ghani, *el-Muthaqqafoun*, 431. For Abdel Ghani's interview with Abdel Qoddous see, "A shifting relationship," *Al Ahram Weekly*, July 18-24, 2002, http://weekly.ahram.org.eg/2002/595/sc111.htm (accessed 22 May 2009).
131. Abdel Ghani, *el-Muthaqqafoun*, 420.
132. Ibid, 416-422.
133. The rumor was kept alive by Ibrahim Boghdadi, an intelligence officer who had a long personal association with Nasser, and whose manner during television numerous interviews left the viewer with the impression that he was an unstable character. He maintained that he had been in Rome recovering from a medical operation that he had had in England, came across the restaurant where Farouk dined frequently chance, and took a job tending tables there because he was bored and coincidently witnessed the king's death. No one has corroborated Baghdadi's claims or admitted first-hand knowledge of any plots to murder the king. The only indisputable facts are that he never fell out of favor with Nasser, who appointed him to positions that ranged from Presidential Aide, to diplomat, to college dean, to Governor of Cairo. He even served on the notorious Committee to Liquidate Feudalism that was chaired by Amer during the period between 1965 and 1967. Boghdadi may well be a nothing more than a

mere publicity seeker who makes up stories to stay in the limelight. His claims are more useful as an example of the caliber of the type of persons that Nasser trusted, and as evidence of Nasser's continued feelings of insecurity. For details, see Habib, 96-98; Mahmoud Fawzi, *Ibrahim Boghdadi Kayfa Qatalt el-Malek Farouk?!!*, (Cairo: Dar el-nashr hatiyeh, 1992), 68-74, 23.

134. After Nasser's death, Sadat agreed to carry out the king's wish and his remains were moved to the Rifa'i Mosque where he was reinterred next to his father, Mohammed, *Saqata el-nizam*, 283.

135. Even after almost two decades of total power, Nasser it seems, could not escape that ubiquitous sense of insecurity, which is probably the most charitable explanation for his inexplicable reaction to receiving a letter from Tawfiq el Hakim, whom he greatly admired. el-Hakim recounts the chain of events set in motion by a respectful, innocuous two-page letter that he had sent to Nasser merely to suggest that Heikal, whom Nasser had just appointed minister of information, could serve Nasser's and the nation's goals better by retaining his position as Al Ahram's editor. While the tone and content of the letter were mild and utterly inoffensive, el-Hakim, reflecting the atmosphere of fear in the country, decided to have it vetted by Heikal before handing it to Hatem Sadek, Nasser's son in law, in April 1970, to pass on to Nasser. The bizarre outcome of this simple act was the interrogation and arrest of Heikal's secretary, her husband, as well as two of their friends, on the charge that the secretary had seen the letter and discussed it with the other three during an evening that the two couples had spent together. They were all kept in jail for over six months without trial until Nasser died in September 1970. The Kafkaesque tone of their interrogation (the book included excerpts from the official records) clearly conveys the atmosphere of fear that was the hallmark of the Nasser years and seems to reflect the insecurity on Nasser's part that led to the actions that often produced such fear. El-Hakim relates the incident in Tawfiq el Hakim, *Watha'q fi tariq 'awdat el-wa'i* (Cairo: Dar el-shorouq 1975), to counter the accusation of hypocrisy that Nasserists leveled at him for waiting till Nasser died to be critical of him in *'Awdat el-wa'i* (the Return of Consciousness).

136. Lacouture, 360.
137. Vatikiotis, 266.
138. Dekmejian, 44.
139. McNamara, 28.
140. Nasser's official web site lists 1217 "patriotic songs" about the revolution and 138 poems about Nasser, Bibliotica Alexandrina, *Mawqi' el-ra'is Gamal Abdel Nasser*, "Abdel Nasser wal thaqafa," http://nasser.

bibalex.org/NasserCulture/NasserCulture.aspx (accessed August 8, 2008).
141. Beattie, 120.
142. Ibid.
143. Dekmejian, 43.
144. Vatikiotis, 190.
145. For the text of the speech, see, Bibliotica Alexandrina, *Mawqi' el-ra'is Gamal Abdel Nasser*, "Khitab el-ra'is Gamal Abdel Nasser fi el-ehtifal bil 'eed el-khames 'ashar lil thawra," http://nasser.bibalex.org/Speeches/browser.aspx?SID=1223 (accessed June 1, 2009).
146. Leila Ahmed, *A Border Passage*, (Penguin Books, New York, 2000), 17-18. The project was also opposed by other specialists in the Ministry of Public Works, see, Robert Mabro, *The Egyptian Economy, 1952-1972* (Oxford: Clarendon Press, 1974), 88.
147. Dekmejian, 45.
148. The date discrepancy is due to different legal interpretations of the date of the concession. See Nikshoy C. Chatterji, *Muddle of the Middle East* (New Delhi, India: Abhinav Publications, 1973), 99.
149. There was widespread expectation of retaliation by Britain and France within the author's family and circle of acquaintants.
150. Hamroush, vol. 4, 225.
151. Ibid, 188.
152. The term he used was "yastaw'ib," Nasr, vol. 2, 318.
153. The FLN was the organization that fought for Algeria's independence from France.
154. Nkrumah, Gamal, "Ahmed Ben Bella: Plus ça change," *Al Ahram Weekly*, May 10-16, 2001 http://weekly.ahram.org.eg/2001/533/profile.htm (accessed April 12, 2006) ; see also Alexander, 82.
155. McNamara, 159-206.
156. Hamroush, vol. 4, 193; Hammouda, Tahreeb, *Al Ahram*, February 15, 2003, http://www.ahram.org.eg/archive/Index.asp?CurFN=WRIT0.>HTM&DID=-30000 (accessed October 17, 2006
157. Hamroush, vol. 4:89.
158. Nkrumah.
159. Alexander, 94-95; Sharaf and Imam, 155.
160. El-Sadat, *el-Bahth*, 190; see also Hamroush, vol. 4, 235.
161. Abul Fath, 533.
162. Vatikiotis, 276.
163. Fathi, 139-143.
164. The public only heard of the concession on May 19, 1967. See Gohar, 117.
165. Vatikiotis, 275.

166. El-Sadat, *el-Bahth*, 194.
167. Habib, 210.
168. Lacouture, 112.
169. Ibid, 361.
170. According to Kamal el-Din Hussein, Nasser told Gamal Salem that he accepted unity with Syria to help it solve its multitude of problems. Gohar, 50.
171. Vatikiotis, 235.
172. See for example Nasser's speech in Damascus on February 27, 1958, Bibliotica Alexandrina, *Mawqi' el-ra'is Gamal Abdel Nasser*, "Kalimat el-ra'is Gamal Abdel Nasser min qasr el-diyafa bi Dimashq fi wofood el-mohannieen bil wehda," http://nasser.bibalex.org/Speeches/browser.aspx?SID=594 (accessed April 4, 2008)
173. Matar, 158.
174. Ali, *Mashaweer*, 180.
175. Ibid, 188.
176. Ibid.
177. Habib, 243.
178. Vatikiotis, 182-183.
179. Alexander, 130.
180. Abdel Mohsen Mortagi, *el-fariq Mortagi yarwi el-haqa'q*, (n.c.: el-watan el-Araby, n.d.), 40.
181. Vatikiotis, 182-183.
182. Ibid, 183.
183. Marsot, *A Short History*, 123.
184. Ibid.
185. Fathi, 260.
186. El-Sadat, *el-Bahth*, 216.
187. Habib, 269-271.
188. Ibid.
189. Fathi, 543.
190. El-Sadat, *el-Bahth*, 211.
191. Salah el-Din el-Hadidi, *Shahed 'la harb 67* (Cairo: Dar el-shorouq 1975), 31.
192. Fawzi, Harb, 65.
193. Mortagi, 40.
194. Fawzi, Harb, 65.
195. Mortagi, 122.
196. Fawzi, Harb, 65; see also Seliman Mazhar, *E'terafat qadat harb Yunyu: nosous shahadatehim amam lagnat tasgeel tarikh el-thawra* (Cairo: Dar el-horiyya: 1990), 194.
197. Ali, *Mashaweer*, 206.

198. Ibid.
199. Mohammed el-Gawwadi, *Qadat el-'askareyya el-Misriyya 1967* (Cairo: Dar el-khayyal, 2000), 270.
200. Fawzi, Harb, 54-55.
201. Abdel Ghani el-Gamasy, *Modhakkarat el-Gamasy: harb October 1973* (Paris; el-manshurat el-sharqiyya, 1990), 61; Mohammed Fawzi, Harb, 61.
202. Ibid, 39.
203. Mortagi, 31.
204. Ibid, 61.
205. Hamroush, vol. 4, 194; Ali, *Mashaweer*, 196-19; Mortagi, 13.
206. Hamroush, vol. 4, 194.
207. Abdel Azim Ramadan, *Harb October fi mahkamat el-tarikh*, (Cairo: Maktabat el-osra, 1995), 12.
208. Ali, *Mashaweer*, 206-207.
209. Ali maintains that Nasser assigned the task of examining the feasibility of expelling the UN force from Sinai to a panel that he selected. They recommended against taking that step, but Nasser ignored the recommendation and the force was withdrawn on May 21, 1967. Salah Nasr, the intelligence chief maintains that he was among a delegation that visited Pakistan during the fall of 1966 and that Nasser instructed Amer in his presence before they left to send him a coded cable from the Egyptian embassy in Pakistan demanding the removal of the UN force. His motive was to test the Americans' reaction, as they, in all likelihood, would intercept the message and decode it, and Nasser made the decision to expel the force later without consulting anyone, Ali, *Mashaweer*, 197 and 209; see also Hamroush vol. 4,194
210. Amer's reaction to the report of the study group assigned to analyze possible consequences of blockading the Tiran Straits had advised against it was to order the early retirement of all the officers who served on it, Ali, *Mashaweer*, 196-197.
211. Vatikiotis, 184.
212. Gohar, 114-120.
213. Mortagi, 210.
214. Musa Sabry, *Watha'q harb October* (Alexandria: el-Maktab el-Misri el-hadith, 1974), 193.
215. El-Gamasy, *Modhakkarat*, 115.
216. Abul Fath, 389.
217. Ibid, 391
218. Ibid, 524.
219. Ibid,

220. Ibid, 385-387; see also el-Baqoury, 106. Khalid Mohi el Din maintains that Nasser was not a member of HADETU but merely supported goals and that Maurice was simply a code name given to Nasser. Mohi el-Din, *walaan*, 99, 204.
221. Vatikiotis, 288.
222. Ibid, 296.
223. Vatikiotis, 295.
224. For the text of the speech, see, Bibliotica Alexandrina, *Mawqi' el-ra'is Gamal Abdel Nasser* "Khitab el-ra'is Gamal Abdel Nasser fi midan el-manshiyya bil iskandariyya bimonasabat 'id el-gala'," http://nasser.bibalex.org/Speeches/browser.aspx?SID=263 (accessed June 7, 2008).
225. Vatikiotis, 268.
226. Awad, *Aqne'at*, 71.
227. Ibid.
228. El-Hakim, *'Awdat*, 75.

Glossary Terms

Amon	One of the gods of ancient Egypt.
Abbasids	The caliphate which ruled from Baghdad (750-935 CE).
AH	Anno Hegirae of the Islamic calendar.
Ahl el-Diwan	A listing of the Arabs who migrated to Egypt after the conquest. All were entitled to a monthly living allowance.
Amir el-Momneen	Title adopted by some Muslim rulers, literally prince of the believers.
Amon	An important deity and head of the Egyptian pantheon.
Baladi	A slightly snobbish or patronizing term that is used to refer condescendingly to Egyptian urban lower class tastes and practices.
BCE	Before Common Era.
CE	Common Era.
Caliph	Title used by rulers of the state after the advent of Islam, literally successor.
Chora	Province or district.
Da'esh	An Acronym for *el-dawla el-islamiyya fil 'iraq wal sham* (the Islamic State in Iraq and Syria).
El-Kholafaa el-Rashedeen	The Guided Caliphs.
El-Mahrousa	A term which means the protected one and is used often to refer to Egypt.
Fath	The term used to describe Arab conquests, literally opening.
Fatwa	Religious ruling.
Feddan	Unit of land measurement that equals 1.038 acres.

Glossary

Gaheliyya	Pre-Islamic age in the Arabian Peninsula.
Gizya	Tax imposed by Arabs on non-Muslims.
Higra	The Prophet's migration from Mecca to Medina.
Hegab	A piece of clothing worn by some women to cover their hair and neck.
Hadith	Sayings of the Prophet.
Horus	The sky god, son of Isis and Osiris.
Kemet or Kemi	What the ancient Egyptians called their country.
Khedive	Ottoman title of Egypt's viceroy.
Khnum	The ram god who created life on a potter's wheel and who controlled the gates of Nile's annual inundation.
Maat	The goddess of order, law, justice and truth who protects against chaos.
Mawali	Clients or subject peoples of Arab conquests.
Mukaukas	Byzantine term of respect used in reference to the governor of Egypt.
Murtadda	Apostates.
Naqeeb el-Ashraf	Doyen of the descendants of the Prophet.
Niqab	A loose garment that covers the woman from head to toe with two slits for the eyes. Usually black or dark brown and complimented by wearing matching color gloves.
El-'oloog	Derogatory term used to refer to non-Arabs
Pagarch	Provincial Roman official in Egypt.
Pasha	Turkish title given to the Ottoman sultans local representative.
Quraish	The Prophet's tribe.
Satrap	Byzantine term meaning governor.
Shari'a	Religious doctrine.
Tarboush	Fez. Head covering used by men in Egypt until 1952.
Ulama	Religious scholars.
Umayyads	The caliphate which ruled from Damascus (661-750 CE).
Upper Egypt	Southern Egypt.

Wa'd el-banat	The pre-Islamic practice burying newly born baby girls in the sand and leaving them to die.
Wali	Viceroy, governor, representative of the caliph.
Wezir or (Wazir)	Minister or high official.
Zakat	Annual tithe.

Select Bibliography

Abaza, Ibrahim Desouqi. *el-Khataya el 'shr min Abdel Nasser ila el Sadat.* Cairo: Dar Misr lil tiba'a, 1983.
Abbady, Mostafa el. *Misr min el-Iskandar el akbar ila el-fath el-Arabi.* Cairo: Anglo-Egyptian Bookshop, 1999.
Abdel Ghani, Mustafa. *el-Muthaqqafun wa Abdel Nasser.* Kuwait: dar Su'ad el Sabbah, 1993.
Abdel Malek, Anouar. *el-Mogtama' el-Misri wal gaish 1952 – 1957.* Cairo: Markaz el-mahrousa lil bohuth wal tadrib wal nashr, 1998.
Abdel Menem, Hassan. *Layilat zafaf bint el-Ra'is.* Cairo: el-Hai'a el Misriyya el-'amma lil ketab, 1987.
Abdel Moti, Abdel Baset. *el-Tabaqat el-egtimaeyya wa mostaqbal Misr: ettigahat el-tagayyor wal tafa'olat.* Cairo: Merit, 2002.
Abdel Nasser, Gamal. *Falsafet el-thawra.* Cairo: Information department, n.d.
Abdel Sabour, 'Adel. *Farouk malek Misr wal Sudan 1936-1952.* Cairo: el Dar el 'alamiyya lilkotob wal nashr, 2000.
Abdel Samad, Mohammed. *el-'Esha' el-akheer lil Mushir.* Cairo: Dar el-ta'awon, 1979.
Abu Ghazala, Mohammed Abdel Halim. *Wa intalaqat el-madafi' end el-zohr.* Cairo: Dar el-sha'b, 1975.
Abu Zekry, Wagih. *Madhbahat el-abriyaa.* Cairo: el-Maktab el-Misri el hadith, 1988.
Abul Fath, Ahmd. *Gamal Abdel Nasser.* Cairo: el maktab el Misri el hadith, 1991.
Abul Magd, Sabry. *Sanawat ma qabla el-thawrah : 1930-1952.* Cairo: el-Hai'a el Misriyya el-'amma lil ketab, 1987-1991.
Adawi, Ibrahim Ahmed el-. *Misr el-Islamiyya.* Cairo: Anglo-Egyptian Bookshop, 1976.
Ahmed, Jamal Mohammed. *The Intellectual Origins of Egyptian Nationalism.* London: Oxford University Press, 1960.
Ahmed, Leila. *A Border Passage.* New York: Penguin Books, 2000.
Akoush, Mahmoud. *Misr fi 'ahd el -slam.* Cairo: dar el-kotob el-Misriyya, 1941.

Alexander, Anne. *Nasser: His Life And Times*. Cairo: The American University in Cairo Press, 2005.
Ali, Kamal Hassan. *Mashaweer el-'omr*. Cairo: dar el-Shorooq, 1995.
Ali, Said Ismail. *Tarikh el tarbiya wal ta'lim fi Misr*. Cairo: 'alem el-kotob, 1985.
Ali, Sheikh R. *Oil, Turmoil, and Islam in the Middle East*. New York: Praeger, 1986.
Amin, Ahmed. *Fagr el-Islam*. Cairo: Maktabet el-nahda el-Misriyya, 1965.
Amin, Galal. *The Modernization of Poverty*. Leiden: E.J.Brill, 1974.
—. *Wasf Misr fi nehayat el-qarn el-'eshreen*. Cairo: Dar el-shorooq, 2000.
Armour, Robert A. *Gods and Myths of Ancient Egypt*. Cairo: The American University in Cairo Press, 2001.
Aron, Raymond. *De Gaulle, Israel and the Jews*. Translated by John Sturrock. New Brunswick, New Jersey: Transaction Publishers, 2004.
Ashur, Said Abdel Fattah. *el-Ayyoubeyyeen wal mamalik fi Msir wal sham*. Cairo: Dar el-nahda el-Arabiyya, 1976.
—. *el-'Asr el mamaliki fi Misr wal sham*. Cairo: Dar el-nahda el-Arabiyya, 1965.
Ata, Zubaydah. *el-Fallah el-Misri fil qarnayn el-sadis wal sabi' el-miladiyayn*. Cairo: el-Hai'a el-Misriyya el-'amma lil ketab, 1991.
Awad, Louis. *Aqne'at el-naseriyyah el-sab'a*. Beirut: Dar el-qadaya, 1975.
—. *el-Horriyya wa naqd el-horriyya*. Cairo: el-Hai'a el-Misriyya el-'amma lil taalif wal nashr, 1971.
—. *Tarikh el-fikr el-Misri el-hadith*. Vol. 2. 2 vols. Cairo: Dar el-helal, 1969.
Ayyoubi, Elias el-. *Tarikh Misr el-Islamiyya min el-fath el-Arabi sanat 640 ila el-fath el Othmani sanat 1517*. Cairo: Matba'at el-raghayib, n.d.
Azhari, Mohammed Tawfik el. *el-Bikbashi Yousef Seddik: monqiz thawrat yulyu*. Cairo: Madbouli bookshop, 1999.
Badawi, Abdel Rahman. *Sirat hayati*. Beirut: el-Mu'assa el-Arabiyya lil dirasat wal nashr, 2000.
Badr, Mustafa. *Abdel Nasser ba'idan 'an el-seyasa*. Cairo: Madbouli el-saghir, 2001.
Baker, Raymond William. *Sadat and After : Struggles for Egypt's Political Soul*. Cambridge, Mass. : Harvard University Press, 1990.
Basha, Amhed Taymour. *el-Amthal el-'ammiyya*. Cairo: Markaz el-Ahram lil tiba'a wal nashr, 1986.
Beattie, Kirk J. *Egypt During The Nasser Years : Ideology, Politics, And Civil Society*. Boulder : Westview Press, 1994.
Bell, Idris H. *Egypt From Alexander The Great To The Arab Conquest*. Oxford: Clarendon Press, 1966.
BiblioticaAlexandrina. *Mawqi' el-Ra's Gamal Abdel Nasser*. http://nasser.bibalex.org/Common/pictures01-%20sira.htm (accessed 2 4, 2008).

Botman, Selma. *Egypt from Independence to Revolution, 1919 – 1952.* Syracuse, N.Y: Syracuse University Press, 1991.
Burks, Walter N. *Islamic Egypt.* Cairo: S.O.P. Press, 1951.
Butler, Alfred J. *The Arab Conquest Of Egypt And The Last Thirty Years Of The Roman Dominion.* Oxford : Clarendon Press, 1978.
Capponi, Livia. *Augustan Egypt.* New York: Routledge, 2005.
Chatterji, Nikshoy C. *Muddle of the Middle East.* New Delhi, India: Abhinav Publications, 1973.
Chirol, Sir Valentine. *The Egyptian Problem .* London : Macmillan, 1920 .
Clot, Antoine B. *Lamha Aama ila Misr.* 2 vols. Cairo: Matbaat Abil Hawl, n.d. Originally published in 1840.
Coury, Ralph M. "Who 'Invented' Egyptian Arab Nationalism." *International Journal of Middle East Studies,* November 1982: 459-479.
Cromer, Earl Of. *Modern Egypt.* 2 vols. London: Macmillan, 1908.
Crone, Patricia, and Michael Hinds. *God's Caliph.* Cambridge: Cambridge University Press, 2003.
Dahlan, Ahmad bin Zaini. *el-Futuhat el-Islamiyya.* Cairo: Mu'assasat el-Halabi, 1968.
Dawn, C. Ernest. "The Rise of Arabism in Syria." *Middle East Journal,* 1962: 145-168.
de Bourrienne, Louis Antoine Fauvelet. "The Memoirs of Napoleon--1798." The Project Gutenberg Etext. <http://www.gutenberg.org/dirs/etext02/nb02v11.txt (accessed September 11, 2006).
Dekmejian, R. Hrair. *Egypt under Nasir : A Study In Political Dynamics.* Albany: State University of New York Press, 1971.
'Alluba, Galal. *el-Malek wa amir el bahr: mudhakkarat amir el-bahr hadrat saheb el-ezza Galal Bek 'Alluba qa'id el yokhout el malakiyya wa yawer galalet el malek.* Cairo: Max Group, 1998.
el-Badry, Hassan. *el-Gawla el-Arabiyya el-Israeliyya el-Rabi'a, October 1973.* Cairo: el-Sharika el-Mottahida Lil Nashr Wal Twazi, 1974.
el-Baladhuri, Ahmad Ibn Jabir. "Kitab Futuh el-Buldhan." *Nedaa al-eman.* <http://www.al-eman.com/islamlib/viewchp.asp?BID=235&CID=1> (accessed April 9, 2006).
el-Baqoury, Ahmad Hassan. *Baqaya dhekrayat.* Cairo: Markaz el-Ahram lil tergama wal nashr, 1988.
el-Boghdadi, Abdel Latif. *Mudhakkirat Abdel Latif el-Boghdadi.* Vol. 1. 2 vols. Cairo: el-maktab el-Misri el hadith, 1977.
el-Faqih, Abi Abdullah Ahmad bin Mohammed bin Ishaq el-Hamadhani ibn. *Ketab el-Buldan.* Beirut: 'Alam el-kotob, 1996.
el-Gabarti, Abdel Rahman. *'Agaib el-aathar fil taragem wal akhbar.* 6 vols. Cairo: el-Hai'a el-Misriyya lil ketab, 2003.
el-Gamasy, Abdel Ghani. *Mudharrat el-Gamasy: harb October 1973.* Paris: el-Manshurat el-sharqiyya, 1990.

el-Gawwadi, Mohammed. *Derasa fi sina'at el qarar el-seyasi: kayfa asbaho wozara'*. Cairo: Dar el-khayyal, 2003.

—. *el-Nokhba el-Misriyya el-hakema 1952-2000*. Cairo: Maktabat Madbouli, 2002.

—. *Modhakkarat qadat el-mokhabarat wal mabaheth*. Cairo: Dar el-khayyal, 1999.

—. *Modhakkarat wuzara' el-thawra*. Vol. 1. Cairo: Dar el-shorouq, 1995.

—. *Qadat el-Askareyya el-Misriyya 1967*. Cairo: Dar el-Khayyal, 2000.

—. *Takween el-'aql el-Arabi: modhakkarat el-mofakkereen wal tarbawiyyeen*. Cairo: Dar el-khayyal, 2003.

el-Geretli, Ali. *Khamsah wa ishroonna aaman : dirasah tahliliyah lilsiyasat el-iqtisadiyyah fi Misr, 1952-1977*. Cairo: el-Haiaa el-'Aamah lil kitab, 1977.

el-Hakim, Tawfik. *Awdat el-wai*. Beirut: Dar el-horooq, 1974.

—. *Shagaret el-hokm*. Cairo: Maktabat el aadab wa matba'ateha, 1938.

el-Hosary, Abu Khaldun Sati. *Abhath mukhtara fil qawmiyya el-Arabiyya*. Beirut: Markaz derasat el wehda el-Arabiyya, 1985.

el-Husseiny, el-Gharib. *Sanawat fil balat el malaki: mudhakkarat el-Gharib el-Husseiny el-hares el khas lil malek Farouk*. Cairo: Akhbar el-Yoam, 1998.

el-Issawi, Saad. *Mathbahat el-'adala*. Alexandria: el-Maktab el-gamei el-hadith, n.d.

el-Kindi, Omar Bin Mohammed Bin Yousef. *Fadael Misr el-Mahrousa*. Cairo: Maktabat el-Khangi, 1997.

el-Kindi, Yousef. *Wolat Misr*. Beirut: Dar Sader, n.d.

Ellis, Simon P. *Graeco-Roman Egypt*. Princes Risborough, U.K: Shire Publications, 1992.

el-Maqrizi, Taqi el Din Ahmed bin Ali. *el-Mawaiz wal i'tibar fi dhikr el khitat wal aathar*. 3 vols. Cairo: Matba'at Madbouli, 1998.

el-Maraghi, Mortada. *Shahed 'ala hokm Farouk*. Cairo: Dar el-ma'aref, 2007, 2007.

el-Masri, Sanaa. *Hawamish el-fath el-Arabi li Misr: hikayatel-dukhul*. Cairo: Sina lil nashr, 1996.

el-Rawdan, Abd Awn. *Mawsu'at tarikh el-Arab*. 2 vols. Amman, Jordan: el-Ahliyya, 2004.

el-Sadat, Anwar. *el-Bahth 'an el-dhat*. Cairo: el-Maktab el-Misri el-hadith, 1978.

—. *In Search of Identity: An Autobiography*. London: Collins, 1978.

el-Sayyid, Ahmad Lutfi. *Qissat hayati*. Cairo: Dar el-helal, n.d.

—. *Ta'ammulat fil siyasa wal adab*. Cairo: Dar el-ma'aref, 1946.

el-Sebai, Yousef. *Ayyam Abdel Nasser*. Cairo: Maktabet el-khangi, 1971.

el-Suyuti, Galal el-Din Abdel Rahman bin Mohammed bin Osman. *Tarikh el kholafa*. Cairo: el-maktaba el-tegariyya el-kobra, 1969.

—. *Husn el-mohadara fi akhbar Misr wal Qahera*. Beirut: Dar el-kotob el-'ilmiyya, 1997.

el-Tabari, Abu Gaafar Muhammad Ibn Garir. *Tarikh el-rusul wal muluk.* 10 vols. Cairo: Dar el-Ma'aref, 1960.
Ezbawi, Abdulla Mohammed. *el-Shawam fi Misr fil qarnayn el-thamen wal tase' 'ashar.* Cairo: el-Hay'a el-Misriyya el-'amma lil ketab, 1986.
Farghaly, Mohamed Ahmed. *'Eshtu hayati bayna ha'ola'.* Cairo: matabe' Al Ahram el tegariyya, 1984.
Farid, Abdel Magid. *Nasser: The Final Years.* Reading, UK: Ithaca Press, 1994.
Fathi, Mamdouh Anis. *Misr minal thawra ila el-Naksa.* Abu Dhabi: Emirates Center for Studies and Strategic Research, 2003.
Fawzi, Mahmoud. *el-Dhobbat el-Ahrar Yatahaddathoun.* Cairo: Matba'et Madbouli, 1992.
—. *Ibrahim Boghdadi kayfa qatalt el-malek Farouk.* n.c.: Dar el-Nashr Hatieh, 1992.
—. *Muamarat Ightiyal el-Mushir Amer.* Cairo: Dar el-Nashr Hatiyih, 1992.
Fawzi, Mohammed. *Harb el thalath sanawat 1967 - 1970.* Cairo: Dar el mostaqbal el Arabi, 1984.
Franzero, Carlo Maria. *The Life And Times Of Cleopatra.* Londin: Alvin Redman Limited, 1957.
Fulford, Tim, and Peter J. Kitson. *Romanticism And Colonialism: Writing And Empire, 1780-1830.* Edited by Tim Fulford and Peter J. Kitson. Cambridge: Cambridge University Press, 1998.
Ghorbal, Shafiq. *Mohammed Ali el-Kabir.* Cairo: Dar ehyaa el-kotob el-Arabiyya, 1944.
Gohar, Sami. *Al-Sametoon yatakallamoon.* Cairo: el-Maktab el-Arabi el-hadith, 1997.
Grant, Michael. *Cleopatra.* New York: Barnes and Noble, 1992.
Grimal, Nicolas. *A History of Ancient Egypt.* Malden, Mass: Blackwell Publishing, 1994.
Habib, Tariq. *Milaffat Thawrat Yulyu: Shahadat 122 Min Sinna'iha Wa Mu'siriha.* Cairo: Markaz Al Ahram, 1997.
Hadidi, Mohammed. *Isterdad Misr: hal min makhrag memma nahnu feeh.* Cairo: Markaz el-hadara el-Arabiyya, 2001.
Hadidi, Salah el-Din. *Shahed 'ala Harb 67.* Cairo: Dar el-Shorouq, 1974.
Hamdan, Gamal. *Shakhsiyyat Misr 1981.* 4 vols. Cairo: Aalamel--otob, 1980-1984.
Hammad, Gamal. *el-Hokuma el-khafiya fi 'ahd Abdel Nasser.* Cairo: el-Zahraa lil i'lam el-Arabi, 1986.
Hammouda, 'Adel. *el Malek Ahmed Fouad el thani.* Cairo: Sphinx lil tiba'a wal nashr, 1991.
—. *el-Wathaiq el-khassah bil rais Naguib.* Cairo: Rose Al Youssef, 1985.
Hammouda, Hussein Mohammed Ahmad. *Asrar harakat el-dhobbat el-ahrar wal ikhwam el-muslimoun.* Cairo: el-Zahra' lil e'lam el-Araby, 1985.

Hamroush, Ahmed. *Qessat Thawrat 23 Yulyu*. 4 vols. Cairo: Matba'at Madbouli, 1983.
Hassan, Ali Ibrahim. *Dirasat fi tarikh el--amalik el-bahariyya wa fi 'asr el-Nasser Mohammed Bewaghon Khas*. Cairo: Maktabat el-nahdah el-Misriyya, 1944.
Hawwas, Suhayr Zaki. *el-Qaherah el-khediwiyya : Rasad wa tawthiq 'imarat wa 'umran mintaqat wasat el-madina*. Cairo: Markaz el-tasmimat el-me'mariyya, 2002.
Heikal, Mohammed Hussein. *Fi awqat el faragh*. Cairo: Maktabat el nahda el Misriyya, n.d.
Helal, Nabil Helal. *Eitiqal el-'aql el-Arabi*. Damascus: Dar el-Ketab el-Arabi, 2005.
—. *el-Estebdad*. Damascus: Dar el-ketab el-Arabi, 2005.
Herodotus. *An Account of Egypt, by Herodotus*. Edited by G. C. Macaulay. Vers. agypt10a.txt. Project Gutenberg Etexts. ftp://ftp.archive.org/pub/etext/etext00/agypt10.txt (accessed June 20, 2007).
Hitti, Philip K. *The Arabs*. London: Macmillan, 1950.
Hosny, Hussein. *Sanawat Maa el-malek Farouk*. Cairo: Dar el-shorouq, 2001.
Hourani, Albert. *Arabic Thought in the liberal age 1798 – 1939*. Cambridge: Cambridge University Press, 1983.
Hunter, Robert F. *Egypt Under the Khedives 1805 - 1879*. Cairo: The American University Press,, 1999.
Hussein, Ahmad. *Mo'allafat Ahmad Hussein*. Cairo: Dar el-shorouq, 1981.
Huwaidy, Amin Hamed. *el-Foras el-da''ah: el-qararat el-hasema fi harbbai el istenzaf wa October*. Beirut: Sharikat el-matbu'at lil tawzi; wal nashr, 1992.
Huwaidy, Amin. *Maa Abdel Nasser*. Cairo: Dar el-mustaqbal el-Arabi, 1985.
Ibn Abdel Hakam, Abil Qasim Abdel Rahman Ibn Abdallah. *Futuh Misr Wa Akhbaruha*. Edited by Muhammad Subayh. Cairo: Dar el-taawon, 1974.
Ibn el-Athir, Abul Hasan Ali bin Mohammed bin Abdel Karim bin Abdel Wahed El Shaibani. "el-Kamel fil tarikh. accessed 28 April, 2006." http://www.al-hakawati.net/arabic/Civilizations/book8vol2x.asp (accessed 4 28, 2006).
Ibn Iyas, Muhammed Ibn Ahmed. *An Account of the Ottoman Conquest of Egypt in the Year A.H. 922*. Translated by W.H.Salmon. London: The Royal Asiatic Society, 1921.
—. *Badi el-zuhur fi waqai el-duhur*. Vol. 5. 5 vols. Wiesbaden: Franz Steiner Verlag GMBH, 1961.
Ibn Khaldun, Abdel Rahman. *The Muqqadema: An Introduction to History*. Bollingen Series XLIII . Translated by Franz Rosenthal. 3 vols. New York: Pantheon Books, 1958.

Ibn Qotaiba, Abi Mohammed Abdulla bin Muslim. *Ketab el-Imama wal siyasa*. Cairo: Matba'at el Nil, 1904.
Ibrahim, M. Al. "Tell Me More About the Obscenities and Other Bad Words Dominate Our Daily Language." *The Egyptian Gazett*, March 31, 2004.
Ibrahim, Saad Eddin. "State, Women, and Civil Society: An Evaluation of Egypt's Population Policy." In *Arab Society ed*, edited by Nicholas S. Hopkins and Saad Eddin Ibrahim, 85 - 104. Cairo: The American University In Cairo Press, 1997.
Imam, Abdalla. *Ali Sabry yatathakar*. Cairo: Mu'assasat Rose Al Youssef, 1987.
Ions, Victoria. *Egyptian Mythology*. London: Hamlyn, 1982.
Isa, Salah. *el-Borgowaziya el-Misreya wa leebat el-tard khareg el-halaba*. Beirut: Dar el-tanwir, 1982.
James, T.G.H. *Egypt: The Living Past*. London: British Museum Press, 1992.
Jankowsk, Israel Gershoni and James P. *Israel Gershoni and James P. Jankowski, Egypt, Islam, and the Arabs: The Search for Egyptian Nationhood: 1900-1930*. Oxford: Israel Gershoni and James P. Jankowski, Egypt, Islam, and theOxford University Press, 1995.
Jankowski, Israel Gershoni and James P. *Redefining the Egyptian Nation, 1930-1945*. Cambridge: Cambridge University Press, 1995.
Kamal, Ahmed 'Adel. *el-Fath el-Islami Li Misr*. Cairo: el-Sharika el-Dawleyya lil tiba'a, 2003.
Karim, Ahmad Ezzat Abdel. *Tarikh el-ta'lim fi 'asr Mohammed Ali*. Cairo: Maktabat el-nahda el Misriyya, 1938.
Kashef, Sayyida Ismail. *Abdel Aziz Ben Marawan*. Cairo: Dar el-ketab el-Arabi, 1967.
—. *Ahmed Ibn Toloun*. Cairo: el-Dar el-Misriyya lil taalif wal targama, 1965.
—. *Misr Fi Ahd el-Ikhseedeyyeen*. Cairo: Fuad el-awwal University Press, 1950.
—. *Misr fi 'asr el-wolah min el-fath el-Arabi ila el-dawlah el-tuluniyyah*. Cairo: el-Haiaa el-Misriyya el-'amma lil ketab, 1988.
Khanki, Aziz. *el-Iskandar el-akbar*. Cairo: el-Matba'a el-'asriyya, n.d.
Lacouture, Jean. *Nasser*. Translated by Daniel Hofstadter. New York: Alfred A. Knopf, 1973.
Lane-Poole, Stanley. *A history of Egypt in the Middle Ages*. London: Methuen , 1901.
—. *A History of Egypt in the Middle Ages* . London: Methuen, 1901.
Lewis, Bernard. *Islam in History*. Chicago, Illinois: Open Court, 2001.
Lindsay, Jack. *Cleopatra*. New York: Coward McCann and Geoghegan,, 1941.
Lutfy, Hamdy. *Ma'sat Abdel Hakim Amer*. Cairo: Dar el-helal, 1980.

—. *Thuwwar Yulyu: el-wagh el-aakhar*. Cairo: Dar el-helal, 1977.
Maalouf, Amin. *The crusades Through Arab Eyes*. Translated by Jon Rothschild. New York: Schocken Books, 1984.
Mabro, Robert. *The Egyptian Economy*. Oxford : Clarendon Press, 1974.
Mansour, Anis. *Abdel Nasser el-Moftara 'alaih wal moftari 'alina*. Cairo: Nahdat Misr, 2002.
Marei, Sayed. *Awraq Seyaseyya*. Vol. 1. 3 vols. Cairo: el-Maktab el-Misri el-adith, 1978/1979.
Marfleet, Rabab El-Mahdi & Philip. *Egypt : the Moment of Change*. Edited by Rabab El-Mahdi & Philip Marfleet. London: Zed Books, 2009.
Marsot, Afaf Al-Sayyid. *A Short History of Modern Egypt*. Cambridge: Cambridge University Press, 2002.
—. *Egypt And Cromer: A Study In Anglo-Egyptian Relations*. London: Murray, 1968.
—. *Women and Men in Late Eighteenth-Century Egypt*. Austin: University of Texas Press, 1995.
Masudi, Abil Hassan Ali Bin El Hussein Bin Ali. *Masudi, The meadows of Gold by Masudi*. Edited by Paul Lunde and Caroline Stone. Translated by Paul Lunde and Caroline Stone. London; New York, NY: Kegan Paul International. Routledge, Chapman and Hall, 1989.
Masudi, Abil Hassan Ali Bin el-Hussein Bin Ali. *Murug el-dahab wa ma'adin el-gawaher*. Cairo: el-Maktaba el-tegariyya el-kobra, Saadah, 1958.
Matar, Fuad. *Bisaraha 'an Abdel Nasser*. Beirut: Dar el-qadaya,, 1975.
Mazhar, Seliman. *E'terafat qadat harb yunyu: nosous shahadatehim amam lagnat tasgeel tarikh el-thawra*. Cairo: Dar el-horiyya, 1990.
McNamara, Robert. *Britain, Nasser and the Balance of Power in the Middle East 1952 – 1967*. London: Frank Cass, 2003.
Mohammed, Mohsen. *Saqata el-Nizam fi arbaat ayyam*. Cairo: Dar el-shorook, 1992.
Mohi El Din, Khaled. *Memories of a Revolution : Egypt 1952*. Cairo: The American University in Cairo Press, 1995.
Mo'nes, Hussein. *Bashawat wa super bashawat*. Cairo: el-Zahra' lil e'lam el Arabi, 1988.
Mortagi, Abdel Mohsen. *el-Fariq Mortagi yarwi elhaqaiq*. n.c.: el-Watan el-Arabi, n.d.
Mostyn, Trevor. *Egypt's Belle Epoque*. London: Tauris Parke, 2006.
Murphy, Lawrence R. *The American University in Cairo, 1919-1987*. Cairo: American University in Cairo Press, 1987.
Musharrafa, Mustafa. *Qantarat elladhi kafar*. Cairo: Megallat dab wa naqd, 1991.
Mustafa, Ahmad Abdel Rehim. *Tatawwor el-fir el-seyasi fi Misr el haditha*. Ahmad Abdel Rehim Mustafa, TataCairo: Ma'had el-bohouth wal derasat el-Arabiyya, 1973.

Myntti, Cynthia. *Paris along the Nile : Architecture in Cairo from the Belle Epoque.* Cairo ; New York: American University in Cairo Press, 2003.
Naguib, Mohammed. *Kalimati lil tarikh.* Dar el-Kitab el-Gamei, 1981.
—. *Masir Misr.* Cairo: Dar Diwan, 1995.
—. *Shakhsiyat wa dhikrayat fil seiyasa el-Missriya.* Cairo: Ketab el-gomhoriyya, 1972.
Nasr, Salah. *Muthakirat Salah Nasr.* 3 vols. Cairo: Dar el-khayal, 1999.
Nassar, Esmat. *Fikrat el tanwir bayna Ahmad Luttfi al-Sayyid wa-Salama Musa.* Alexandria: Dar el-wafa' li donya el-teba'a wal nashr, 2000.
Nasser, Gamal Abdel. *Falsafet el-Thawra.* Cairo: Maslahet el-estelamat, n.d.
Nieuwenhuijze, van C. A. O. *Social Stratification and the Middle East: An Interpretation.* Leiden: E. J. Brill, , 1971.
Nkrumah, Gamal. "Ahmed Ben Bella: Plus ça change." *Al-Ahram Weekly On-line.* May 1o-16, 2001. http://weekly.ahram.org.eg/2001/533/profile.htm (accessed 12 4, 2006).
Nour, Abdel Mohsen Abul. *el-Haqiqa 'an thawrat 23 Yulyu.* Cairo: el-Hai'a el Misriyya el 'amma lil kitab, 2001.
Nutting, Anthony. *Nasser.* London: Constable, 1972.
O'Leary, De Lacy. *Arabia Before Muhammad.* London: Kegan Paul, Trench, Trubner & Co, 1927.
Okasha, Sarwat. *Mudhakkarati fil seyasa wal thaqafa.* 2 vols. Cairo: Matba'at Madbouli, 1987.
Osman, Hamdy. *Haulaa hakamu Misr.* Cairo: el-Hai'a el-Misriyya el-'amma lil ketab, 2000.
Philipp, Thomas. *The Syrians in Egypt, 1725-1975.* Stuttgart: Steiner, 1985.
Qandil, Bayyoumi. *Hadir el-haqafa fi Misr.* Alexandria: Dar el-wafaa lidonya el-tibaa wal nashr wal tawzee, 1999.
Qu'aid, Yousef el-. *Laban el 'asfour.* Cairo: Dar el-helal, 1994.
Qutb, Seyyid. *Milestones.* Damascus, Syria: Dar al-ilm, n.d.
Raafat, Samir. *Cairo, the Glory Years : Who Built What, When, Why and for Whom.* Alexandria: Harpocrates, 2003.
Raafat, Waheed. *Fusul min thawrat 23 Yulyu.* Cairo: Dar el-shorooq, 1987.
Radwan, Fathi. *72 Shahran ma'a Abdel Nasser.* Cairo: Dar el-horriya, 1986.
Ramadan, Abdel Azim. *Awraq Yousef Seddik.* Cairo: el-Hai'a el-Misriyya el-'amma lil ketab, 1999.
—. *el-Haqiqa el-tarikhiyya hawla harb October.* Cairo: el-Hai'a el-Misriyya el-'amma lil ketab, 2002.
—. *el-Haqiqah el-tarikhiyyah hawla qarartaamim sharikat qanat el-suways.* Cairo: el-Hai'a el-Misriyya el-'amma lil ketab, 2000.
—. *Harb October fi mahkamat el-tarikh.* Cairo: Maktabat el-osra, 1995.
—. *Heikal wal kahf el-Nasseri.* Cairo: el-Hai'a el-Misriyya el-'amma lil ketab, 1995.

Raouf, Abdel Menem. *Arghamtu Farouk ala el-tanazol aan el-'arsh.* Cairo: el-Zahraa lil e'lam el-Arabi, 1988.
Reader, John. *Man on Earth.* Austin: University of Texas Press, 1988.
Riad, Mahmoud. *Mudhakkarat Mahmoud Riad.* Vol. 3. 3 vols. Cairo: Dar el-Mustaqbal el-Araby, 1985-1986.
Rivlin, Helen Anne B. *The Agricultural Policy of Muhammad Ali in Egypt.* Cambridge, Mass: Harvard University Press, 1961.
Rizq, Yunan Labib. *Qissat el-barlaman el-Misri.* Cairo: Dar el helal, 1991.
Russell, Mona. "Competing, Overlapping, and Contradictory Agendas: Egyptian Education Under British Occupation, 1882-1922." *Comparative Studies of South Asia, Africa and the Middle East* 21 , no. 1 and 2 (2001): 50 - 60.
Saad Allah, Mohammed Ali. *el-Dawr el-Siyasi lil malikat fi misr el-qadimah.* Alexandria: Muassasat Shabab el-gami'a, 1988.
—. *Tatawwor el-mothol el-olya fi Misr el-qadima.* Alexandria: Muassasat Shabab el-gami'a, 1989.
Sabry, Musa. *Wath'q harb October.* Alexandria: el-Maktab el Misri el-hadith, 1974.
Sabry, Musa. *el-Sadat: el haqiqa wal ostoora.* Cairo: el-Maktab el Misri el-hadith, 1985.
—. *Watha'q 15 Mayo.* Cairo: Maktab el-Misri el-hadith, 1977.
Sagan, Carl. *Cosmos.* New York: Random House,, 2002.
Salem, Latifa Mohammed. *Farouk wa soqout el-malakiyya fi Misr: 1936-1952.* 1996: Maktabat Madbouli, Cairo.
Sallam, Hilmi. *Ana Wa Thuwar Yuliyu.* Cairo: Dar Thabet, 1986.
Samad, Mohammed Abdel. *el-Eshaai el-akheer lil mushir.* Cairo: Dar el-ta'awon, 1979.
Sami, Riad. *Shahed ala 'asr el-rais Mohammed Naguib.* Cairo: el-Maktab el-Arabi el-hadith, 2002.
Samson, Julia. *Nefertiti and Cleopatra: Queen-Monarchs of Ancient Egypt.* London: The Rubicon Press, 1990.
Sarhan, Samir. *Harb el-thaqafa.* Cairo: Dar Akhbar el-Yom, 2000.
Seda, Ibrahim. *Sanawat el-hawan.* Cairo: el-Maktab el-Misri el-hadith, 1975.
Selim, Gamal. *el-Tanzeemat el-siriyya li thawrat 23 Yulu.* Cairo: Maktabat Madbouli, 1982.
Selim, Sabry Abul Khair. *Tarikh Misr fil 'ahd el-bezanti.* Cairo: Ein For Human And Social Studies, 1997.
Seliman, Mahmoud Mohammed. *el-Aganeb fi Misr: derasa fi tarikh Misr el egtima'i.* Cairo: Ein for human and social studies, 1996.
Shadi, Salah. *Safahat min tarikh.* Kuwait: el-Shoaa lil nash, 1981.
Shaer, Yahia Al. *The Other Side of the Coin, Suez War 1956.* Cairo: Akhbar El Yom, 2006.

Shafie, Hussein el- and Salah el-Imam. *Hussein el-Shafie wa asrar thawrat Yulu wa hukm el-Sadat.* Cairo: Matabaat Osiris, 1993.
Shahed, Salah el-. *Dhekriati fi 'ahdayn.* Cairo: Dar el-ma'aref, 1974.
Shalata, Ahmed Zaghloul. *el-Hala el-Salafeya el-Moasera fi Misr.* Cairo: Maktabat Madbouli, 2010.
—. *el-Hala el-Salafeya el-Moasera fi Misr.* Cairo: Madbouli , 2010.
Sharaf, Sami and Abdulla Imam. *Abdel Nasser hakatha kan yahkum Misr.* Cairo: Madbouli el-saghir, 1996.
Sharqawi, Abdullah el-. *Tohfat el-nazereen fi man walla Misr min el-molouk wal salateen.* Edited by Rehab Abdel Hamid el Qary. Cairo: Maktabat Madbouli, 1996.
Shazly, Saad el-. *The Crossing of the Suez Canal.* San Francisco: American Research Center, 2003.
St. John, Robert. *The Boss.* New York: McGraw Hill, 1960.
Tabari, Abu Gaafar Muhammad Ibn Garir el-. *Tarikh el-rusul wal muluk.* 10 vols. Cairo: Dar el-Ma'aref, 1960.
Tabari, Abu Jafar Muhammad Al. *The History of al-Tabari Volume XI: The Challenge to the Empires.* Translated by Khalid Yahya Blankinship. Vol. XI. Albany, N.Y.: State University of New York Press, 1993.
"Tarikh el-Nadalah el-Ikhwaniyya Ma' el-Harakat el- 'ommaliyya"." *Rose El Youssef,* no. 4098 (December 2006): 52-54.
Tawfik, Aleyya. *Yousef Seddik wa Gamal Abdel Nassr wa ana.* Cairo: Markaz Al Ahram lil tergama wal nashr, 2000.
Thabet, Adel. *Farouk el-awwal.* Cairo: Akhbar el-Yom, 1989.
Thabet, Karim. *el-Malek Farouk.* Cairo: Dar el-Ma'aref, 1944.
—. *Farouk kama afiftahu.* Beirut: Dar el-shoroouq, 2000.
—. *Galalet el-malek bayna Misr wa oroppa : rehlat galaletihi fi almanya wa Chechoslovakia Wa Swesra.* Cairo: Dar el-Helal, 1931.
Tidrick, Kathryn. *Heart-Beguiling Araby.* London : Tauris, 1989.
Tunsi, Mahmoud Bayram el-. *el-Sayyid we meratoh fi Paris.* Alexandria: el-Markaz el-Arabi lil nashr wal twazi', 1982.
Tyldesley, Joyce. *Daughters of Isis: Women of Ancient Egypt.* London: Penguin Books, 1995.
—. *Judgement of the Pharaoh : Crime and Punishment in Ancient Egypt.* London: Weidenfeld and Nicolson, 2000.
Uways, Sayyid. *Qirraat fi mawsu'at el-mugtam' el-Misri.* Cairo: Rose Al Yossef, 1988.
Vasunia, Phiroze. *The Gift Of the Nile.* Berkely: University of Californis Press, 2001.
Vatikiotis, P. J. *Nasser And His Generation.* London: Croom Helm, 1978.
Wahidah, Subhi. *Fi usul el-mas'alah el-Misriyya.* Cairo: Maktabat Madbouli, n.d.

White, Blake L. "Ancient Egypt Provides an Early Example of How A Society's Worldview Drives Engineering and the Development of Science." *The Strategic Technology Institute*. The Strategic Technology Institute. 2003. http://www.strategic-tech.org/images/Egyptian_Engineering_and_Culture.pd (accessed 10 30, 2005).

Zaini, Ibrahim el-. *Misr bayna el-'aql wal 'iqal*. n.p, n.d.

Zanati, Mahmoud Salam. *el-Mosawah bayna el-gensain fi Misr el fara'oniyyah wa min ashkal el-tamyeez did el-nisa' 'ind el-Arab*. Cairo: el-Nisr el-dhahabi, 2000.

Zetland, Lawrence John Lumley Dundas, Marquis of. *Lord Cromer : Being the Authorized Life of Evelyn Baring, First Earl of Cromer*. London: Hodder and Stoughton, 1932.

Index

A
Abu Khaldun Sati el-Hosary, 132
Adel Hammouda, 163
'Awdat el-roah. See The Liberal Period
'umra ploy, 165
1840 treaty of London. See Mohammed Ali
1913 Arab Congress held in Paris, 132
1919 revolution, 125, 137, 131
1954 crisis. See down with liberty
1956 invasion, 210
Abbas Pasha. See Mohammed Ali
Abbasid, 67
Abdel Aziz el-Shal, 167
Abdel Fattah el-Sisi, 316
Abdel Hakim Amer, 143, 188, 193, 194, 196, 198, 2015, 228, 243, 255, 256, 257, 258
Abdel Latif Abu Regaila, 239
Abdel el-Latif el-Boghdadi, 164, 171, 173, 176, 188, 199, 206, 276, 384, 390
Abdel Razzaq el-Sanhouri. See State Council
Abdication, 137, 149, 155
Abdullah el-Nadim, 131
Abdullah Ibn Sa'd, see famine
Adly Mansour, 315
Admiral Galal Alluba, 148, 149
Admission to the military college. See Sadat

Adulthood and women, 331
Afterlife, ancient view of, 6; nomads view of, 7
Ahl el-diwan, 37, 97
Ahmad Abul Fath, 165, 167, 171, 1791, 214, 332, 373
Ahmad Lutfi el-Sayyid. 126 , 130 , 179 , 373
Ahmad Orabi rebellion, 119, 183
Ahmed Maher. See Revolution
Alaa Mubarak, 287
Alexander the Great, 9
Alexandria Library, 11, 21, 34
Alexandria Lighthouse, 51, 68
Algeria, 108, 219, 220, 384
Ali Sabry, 145, 234, 250, 252, 337
Alliance with the Mamluks, 110; Caisse de la Dette Publique, 118; Bombardment of Alexandria, 120; Dinshway, 123, 124; 1807 invasion, 112; financing the Cairo rebellion, 109; siege to a police station, 140; Sir Evelyn Baring, 118, 120; white man's burden, 108
American University in Cairo, Charles R. Watson, 125
Amir el-Momneen Canal, 38
Ammianus Marcellinus, 11
Amon, 9, 10, 16
Amr Ibn el-Aas, 30, 32, 33, 37, 47
Anthony Nutting, 179, 245
April 6 Youth Movement, 295, 296

Arabian Peninsula, 5, 22, 25, 26, 27, 28, 29, 35, 37, 38, 42, 60, 62, 55, 56, 79, 80, 85, 87, 90, 94, 104, 112, 115, 276, 279, 319, 322, 328, 329, 334, 354, 356, 359

Arabs, 26; feuding, 38; hunger, 27; migration to Egypt, 37, 87, 101; poverty, 26; reciting poetry, 38, 45, 89, 97, 98, 99; taxation, 48; view of Egypt, 30, 81

Ashraf, 66, 214

Asmaa Mahfouz, 295

Assassin of Egyptian education. See Douglas Dunlop

Assassination, 128, 181, 183, 203, 280, 286, 314

Attitudes towards the French, 106, 107, 110

Authoritarianism, 98, 99

B

Babylon, surrender of, 32

Bar Lev line, 254, 255, 259, 260, 263, 264, 266, 267, 569; Water pumps, 268

Battle of Abu Kir, 110

Bedouins, 5, 27; attire, 27; attitudes toward inability to be unjust, 98; birth rate, 88; contacst with native Egyptians, 38; dates, 27; famine, 27; language, 15; literacy, 27; literature, 15; plunder, 16, 18, 26, 24, 34, 43, 51, 52, 73, 97, 344; values, 88, 101, 106, 308, 319, 340, 341, 342, 354; women's seclusion, 92, 93

black land, 214

blasphemy, 289

blockade of the Tiran Straits, 193

British, occupation, 120, 125; Sir Miles Lampson, 137, 138;

C

Caesar, 11, 12, 13, 16

Cairo fire, 140, 142

Cairo rebellion, 108, 109;

calendar, 13, 26, 35, 80, 83; Coptic, 18, 84; higra, 85; Iranian, 85; lunar, 7; use today, 86

Caliph, 29, 61; Ahl el-diwan, 37; Abu Bakr el-Seddik, 2; Alexandria lighthouse, 51; Baghdad, 38; communiqués to Amr, 41, 44, 45; el-Kholafa' el-Rashedeen, 57; el-Mo'tasem, 37; famine, 47; Fatimid, 49, 58, 67; Haroun el-Rashid, 58; Mu'awiya, 37; Omar ibn el-Khattab, 31; in Madina, 35; Mu'awiya ibn Abi Sufyan, 82; Osman, 45, 56; Patriarch Sophronius, 40; poll tax, 42, 48; pseudo-people, 82; right to rule, 62; Seliman ibn Abdel Malek, 47; tax rebellions, 64, 65; tax revenue, 47; treasuries, 48, 49; whimsical actions, 65, 66

Caliphate, 29, 31; Abbasid, 57, 67, 69, 184; Fatimid, 58, 66, 70; governorship of Egypt, 31; Mu'awiya, 37; office of, 60, 61, 62, 63, 83; Ottoman, 127

canal, Amir el-Momneen Canal, 38, 42

Charles R. Watson. See the American University in Cairo

chemical fertilizers, 216

Christians, ancient monuments, 19; Byzantines, 22; Cyrus Bishop of Phasis, 31; Mohammed Ali, 114; monogamy, 88; Byzantine persecution of, 17; view of themselves, 18;

Cleopatra, 11, 12, 13, 14, 16, 20, 52, 74, 362

colloquial Egyptian Arabic, 128
collective consciousness, 86
Committee for the Prevention of Vice and propagation of Virtue, 328
Committee to Liquidate Feudalism, 192, 255, 388
concubines, 28, 37, 38, 43, 50, 88, 98, 105, 113, 329, 350,
consultative assembly, 114, 119
corruption, 49, 73, 129, 135, 139, 145, 152, 153, 158, 221, 223, 238, 241, 248, 278, 282, 286, 289, 291, 292, 295, 296, 307
corvée labor, 117
councils of Ephesus and Chalcedon, 21, 36
Cromer, Lord, 121, access to primary education, 122; position of women, 123; retirement, 124, education; 126, free press, 127
Cyrus, Bishop of Phasis, see Christians

D
Damascus, 49, 56, 57, 62, 62, 67, 80, 194, 214, 269
despotism, 52, 65, 73, 74, 76, 77, 79, 81, 82, 94, 98, 99, 123, 322, 343,. 345, 346, 361, 358,
Diodorus of Sicily, 11
Douglas Dunlop, 122
down with liberty, 173, 174
dramatic acts, Sadat, 244

E
ecumenical councils of Ephesus and Chalcedon, 21
educational system, 105, 114, 115, 122, 126, 208, 209, 213, 237, 250, 326
Edward Said, 211

effendiyya, the new, divided the world into east and west and placed Egypt in the east, 131; open to both the Arab and the Islamist orientations, 133; and the Free Officers; the lower middle class; Nasser, 370
Egyptian Communist Party, 157
Egyptianization, Ptolemies, 15 Romans, 15. Mohammed Ali, 113; Nasser, 367
Egyptians, fear of chaos, 1; conservatism, 90; joi de vivre, 6; Kemet, 214; relations between the sexes, 91; stability, 1
Ehsan Abdel Qoddous, 173, 183, 380
el-Fustat, 35, 37, 38, 39, 43, 51, 58, 68, 88
el-Hizb el-Watani, 127
el-Kholafa' el-Rashedeen, 47
el-Mahmal, 72
el-mostabedd el-'adel, 183
el-Sawi Ahmad el-Sawi, 176
el-Wafd, 129, 370
el-Waqai' el-Misriyya, 114, 155
el-Zawya el-Hamra, 279
Emperor Diocletian, 17, 18
Emperor Heraclius, 31
Emperor Theodosius, 20
Esraa Abdel Fattah, 295
expatriates, 325, 338
extortionate taxation, 49, 81, 118

F
famine, 27, 28, 42, 47, 49, 70,
fatalism, 323, 347
fatwa, 64, 321, 329, 350, 351
Fellah, fellahin, 47, 110
Ferdinand de Lesseps, 117
feseekh, 321
fifty violations. See women

First Arab Congress, 132
first city of the civilized world, 11
first modern university, 124
flash mobs, 293, 295
France, 148, 195, 388; attack on Egypt in 1956, 192, 210, 218, 219, 233, 385, 387; ban on the burkini, 337; battle of Abu Kir, 110; control of communications and trade, 103; Egypt's debt, 117, 118; Louis IX, 71; military tradition, 226; Mohammed Ali's educations missions to, 114, 122; Orabi rebellion, 119, Suez Canal nationalization, 383
Free Officers, 142, 144, 146, 149, 152, 153, 154, 157, 158, 180, 187, 229, 242, 308, 317, 371, 387
French ahkam, el-Gabarti 110; freedoms, 105; liberties, 106; veils, 106

G
Galal Alluba, 136, 146, 148, 149
gallabiyyas, 335
Gamal Mubarak, 297; president-in-waiting 301; putting down demonstrations, 306; Egypt's national debt, 307; future elections 311; SCAT, 313
General Jean-Baptiste Kléber, 110
General Mohammed Naguib, 142, 144, 147, 149, 151, 152, 155, 156, 159, 163, 164, 165, 166, 168, 169, 170, 171, 173, 174, 175, 176. 177, 179.181, 185, 186, 187, 188, 219, 289, 381
ghelman, 28
gold, 13, 26, 34, 40, 41, 42, 43, 46, 47, 50, 51, 59, 66, 69, 73, 74, 75, 85, 88, 96, 154, 184, 192, 238, 333
Gulf, Arab, Persian, building projects, 322; cultural trends, 329, 330, 333; Egyptian workers in, 325, 334, 335, 339; extremists exile in, 274, 277; interpersonal altercations, 321, 322; Media, 350, 352, 356; Mohamed Morsi, 313; Mubarak visits, 291; oil bonanza, 276; slogans, 220; war, 288

H
Hafez Ibrahim, 132
Hassan Abbas Zaki, 238, 274
Hassan el-Banna, 133, 181
Hassan el-Tohami, 228, 234
hegab, 93, 208, 326, 335, 336, 356
Hegaz, Hegazis, Eastern Arabian Peninsula, 26; migration to Egypt after the Arab conquest, 56; pillage during the Cairo rebellion, 108; armed gangs, 109hosary
Helwan, 218, 262
Henry Kissinger, 258, 266, 267, 269, 271
Herodotus, 89, 191, 307
High Dam, 199, 215, 216, 217, 224, 233, 234, 383, 384
Hizb el-Umma, 127
Hosni Mubarak, 255, 285, 287, 289, 290, 291, 292, 293, 295, 296, 297, 299, 301, 303, 304, 305, 306, 307
Hussein Fawzi, 133, 178
Hyksos, 5
Hypatia, 21; ambushed, 21

I
ibn Abdel Hakam, 34, 40, 43, 91
ibn Khaldun, 34, 38, 46, 56, 60, 61, 88, 94, 97, 100, 112, 326
ibn Tulun, 39, 49, 52, 68, 70
Ides of March, 13
illiteracy, 40, 45, 99, 101, 112, 219, 223

inability to be unjust, 98
infrastructure, , 53, 68, 81, 98, 116, 119, 192, 218, 239, 262, 288, 307
Isis, 12, 15, 17, 118, 358
Ismail Pasha (Khedive), 117

J
Jefferson Caffery, 145, 188
just dictator. See Mohammed Abdu

K
kafeel, 324
Kafr el-Dawwar textile factory strike, 157, 166, 178
Kamal el-Din Hussein, 171, 177, 181, 201, 206, 208
Kamal Hassan Ali, 227, 256, 375, 387, 389
Karim Thabet, 134, 380
Kemet, Kemi, ancient Egypt,
Khaled Said, 294, 295
Khalid Mohi el-Din, 145, 156, 164, 166, 172, 174, 179, 180, 184, 188, 373, 376
Khan el-Khalili, 109
Khedive Abbas Helmy II, 124
Khedive Tawfik, 119, 120, 124
Khnum, Nile god, 4
Khumarawaih, 49
King Hussein of Jordan, 211
King Farouk, childhood, 133, 134, Antonio Pulli; confidants, 135, 136; abuses, 141; politically untutored, 145, 146, 148; 149, 153, 223, 246, 305, 380, 384
King Fuad, 128, 129, 133, 134, 246
King Simon of Bulgaria, 211
Kuttab, 122; promoting as a cost cutting measure, see Douglas Dunlop

L
Land Reform Law, 158
last Pharaoh, 10, 11
Lawyers Syndicate, 174, 175
The Liberal Period, vibrant intellectual pursuits, 126, 128
Liberation Rally, 168, 169, 170, 175, 177, 182
lower middle class, see the new effendiyya
Louis Awad, 128
Louis IX, the king of France, 71

M
Maat, 1, 2, 82
Mahmoud Fahmi el-Nuqrashy Pasha, murdered, 138
Mahmoud Mokhtar, 128
Mamdouh Salem, 252
Mamluk massacre, 113
Mamluks, 67, 68, 70, 71, 72, 73, 74, 75, 76, 82, 86, 108, 109, 110, 111, 112, 113, 191, 223, 282, 367
Mark Anthony, 13, 14
mawali, 82, 96, 97
Mecca, 27, 72, 85, 112, 355
Medina, 27, 35, 41, 42, 43, 47, 56, 57, 85, 112
military occupation. See British
Misr, 77, 128, 129, 132, 213, 214
Misr el-Fatat, 129, 139, 140, 144, 275
mobilization. 193, 263, 271
modern infrastructure. See Ismail Pasha
modernization program. See Ismail Pasha
Mohamed Morsi, 313
Mohammed Abdu, 126, 183
Mohammed Ali, 72, 111, 112, 113, 114, 115, 116, 120, 122, 135, 222, 223, 247, 367
Mohammed Bouazizi, 294

Mohammed Fawzi, 255, 256, 257, 389
Mohammed Hassanein Heikal, 130, 169, 184, 190, 196, 197, 200, 202, 203, 204, 205, 219, 221, 240, 243, 251, 252, 275, 275, 380, 287
Moharram, 84
mokhabarat, Amin Huwaidy, chief of, 219, el-Tohami's odd behavior 235
Monophysites, 21
Montaza Palace, 148
Moses, 91
mosque, 38, 39, 65, 72, 77, 90, 169, 297, 316, 340, 380
Mrs. Mubarak, Suzanne, 287, 290, 291
murtadda, 29, 36
Muslim Brothers Society (MB), 130, 137, 138, 139, 140, 144, 158, 161, 162, 167, 173, 180, 181, 202, 203, 277, 288, 297, 298, 299, 311, 312, 315, 370, 371, 373, 388, 392
Mussolini, 129
Mustafa Amin, 169, 184, 185, 275, 376
Mustafa Kamel, 126, 130, 131
myths, 17, 18, 19, 52, 339, 353, 354

N
Nagdis, 26
Nahdat Misr, 128
Napoleon, 81, 104; barbarism, 104 Description de l'Egypte, 105; just government and reform, 105; Liberté, Egalité, Fraternité, 105, 108, 123; L'Institute d'Egypte, 105
Nasr Hamed Abu Zeid, 289
Nasserists, 220, 253, 259, 272, 276, 278
national identity, 130, 203, 204, 213, 214, 215, 226, 231, 236, 281, 320, 326, 373
Nawal el-Sa'dawi, 289
New Year celebration, 86
Nile, annual inundation, 1, 2, 3; god, 4
niqab, 208, 325, 335, 336, 337, 339, 354, 356
Noah, 30
non-people, 82

O
Oasis of Siwa, 9, 10
Octavian, 13, 14
Oil, 199, 205, 234, 247, 261, 276, 319, 321, 322, 323, 325, 326, 327, 330, 335, 349, 352, 353, 357, 364
old middle class, 318, 325, 393
Om Kalthoum, 129, 231, 374
Omar Makram, 109
Omar Sharif, 211
one party system, 184, 185, 206, 272, 281
OPEC members, 322
Opera House, 119, 318
Oracle of Siwa, 9
Oracle of Delphi,
Ottomans, 70, 74, 75, 76, 86, 108, 110, 111, 113, 114, 116, 118, 124, 127, 130, 222, 226

P
Palestine, 5, 29, 56, 138, 262, 366
parliament, parliamentary, 118, 120, 137, 155, 156, 158, 162, 163, 164, 165, 166, 172, 173, 174, 1725, 178, 187, 192, 201, 203, 233, 235, 236, 237, 238, 243, 288, 295, 304, 305, 313, 330, 338, 341, 358,
Patriarch Benjamin, 31, 36
Peasants, 3, 18, 47, 48, 49, 63, 66, 70, 87, 97, 110, 111, 113, 117, 124,

159, 176, 190, 220, 226, 257, 374, 381
people of trust, 213, 227, 228.250, 256, 257, 282, 318
Pharaoh, 1, 2, 3, 4, 5, 10, 11, 15, 16, 17, 18, 19, 20, 21, 22, 37, 53, 79, 81, 83, 94, 95, 208, 214, 224, 264, 308, 309, 361
pharaonism, 214
Philosophy of the Revolution, 373
plebiscites, 221, 507
Plutarch, 13
Pokémon, 329
Police Day, 293, 295, 297
political parties were dissolved, 125, 129, 139, 147, 150, 162, 164, 165, 172, 174, 175, 178, 180, 181, 203, 295, 297
Pope Shenouda III, 279
position of women. See Bedouin values
president-in-waiting. See Gamal Mubarak
press censorship, Sadat abolished, 253
Prime Minister Menahem Begin, 264
Princess Fayza, 153
private schools, 210, 211
Proconsul-general, See Lord Cromer
Pulli, Antonio, see King Farouk
pyramids, 98; building 3; destruction, 50, 51, Khufu, 224

Q
Queen Nariman, 135, 146
Queen Nazli, 134
Queen, Farida, 136, 138, 153
Queen Philopator and Pharaoh. 11
Quraish, 26, 29, 55, 56, 57, 62, 67

R
reforms, Mohammed Ali, 112, 113; Abbas, 116; Ismail, 117; Tawfik, 119; Lord Cromer, 124; 1952 coup, 158; Nasser, 201
Regency Council, 155, 156, 165, 166
revolution, accidental, 150, 151; aid to Algeria, 220; arm shipments, 254; Ba'thist régime, 194; Committee to Record the History, 255; end of Egypt's budding industrial revolution, 116; enemies of, 392; free education, 239, 240; French, 105, 121; Illiteracy, 223; the internet, 357; January 2011, 290, 293, 294, 299, 301, 311; jokes, 172; makes its own legal precedents, 156; Nasser, 373; neglect of pre 1952 history, 326; rote memorization, 209; Salah Salem, 173; Sami Sharaf, 232, 233; six goals of the revolution, 148, 167, 202, 221; social values, 229; State Council meeting, 175
Revolutionary Command Council (RCC), 152, 156, 280
Rifa'a el-Tahtawi, 115, 122, 126, 349
Royal Yacht el-Mahrousa, 135, 148, 149

S
Sa'd Zaghloul, 122, 125, 126, 131
Sa'd Zayed Governor of Cairo, 240
sacks of gold, Amr Ibn -el-Aas, 42
Sadat, 187, 200, 204, 231, 232, 233, 234, 237, 238, 240, 241, 242, 243, 244, 245, 2146, 247, 249, 250, 251, 260. 263, 264, 266, 267, 268, 269, 270, 271, 272, 273, 274, 277, 279
Saddam Hussein, 2376, 277, 280
Said Pasha, 116
Saint Mark, 18

salafiyya, 321
Salama Musa, 130
sardine fishing, 216
Sarwat Okasha, 166, 187, 205, 204, 206, 229, 256
Sayyid Qotb, 176, 298, 327, 370
Seal of the Martyrs, 17
Séance, 228
Secret Apparatus, 182
security apparatus, 189, 253, 288, 289, 294, 301, 308, 378
Seliman el-Halabi, 110
Seliman Hafez, 156, 164
Severus Ibn el-Muqaffa', 17, 65
Shabab Mohammed, 140, 156
Shagaret el-Dorr, 72
Sham el-Nessim, 321
Shams Badran, 196, 205, 228, 257, 389
silt, 2, 3, 16, 17
Sir Evelyn Baring. See Lord Cromer
six goals of the revolution, 148, 167
social contract, 83
social values, 1, impact of Christianity, 18; Bedouin, 25, 26, 27, 28; change in Egypt, 33, 35, 79, 87, 88, 89, 90, 92, 93, 94, 98, 99, 100; French, 104, 107; influence of the 1952 coup, 142, 159, 161, 162, 163, 176, 191, 208, 209, 213, 216, 218, 225, 227, 229; sharp contrast between Nasser and Sadat's, 258, 274, 282; 308, 320, 322, 325, 327, 331, 334, 335, 362, 363, 364, 366, 370, 371
soil erosion, 216
Soviet military advisors, 264
Soviets, 192, 194, 198, 206, 228, 241, 242, 254, 258, 259, 260, 264, 268, 269, 271, 286, 382, 385, 390
splendor, 33, 80
St. Cyril, 21

St. Mark, 17
Star of the East diamond, 153
State Council, 156, 164; Abdel Razzaq el-Sanhouri injured, 175
Sublime Port, 109, 117
Sudan, 67, 116, 180, 238, 246, 276, 280, 323,
Suez Canal, concession, 117; shares sold, 118; British bases, 137; British military personnel attacked, 139; British lay siege to a police station, 140; evacuation agreement, 145, 179; nationalized, 192, 199, 220, 232; Israelis occupy east bank, 235, 241, 258, 263, 264; crossing, 266; reopened, 272; financial backing for Muslim Brothers Society, 277; nationalization, 383; closed to navigation 385, 386
Sultan Salah el-Din Yousef bin Ayyoub, see pyramid destruction
Sultan, el-Aziz Osman Salah el-Din bin Yousef, see pyramid destruction
Supreme Constitutional Court, 313, 315, 198
Supreme Council of the Armed Forces, 312
Supreme Guide, 181, 182, 298, 313, 392
Syria, attitudes towards, 130, 131; Bedouin incursions, 29, 56; migration to Egypt, 127; proposing a ceasefire in 1973, 260; provocations to Israel, 192; role in 1967 war, 194, 390; support for Arab nationalism, 132; Toran Shah arrives from, 71; union with Egypt, 192, 193, 387

T

Taha Hussein, 130, 133, 178, 349, 370, 380
Tahani el-Gebali, 312
Tahrir Square, 293, 299, 301, 302, 305, 312, 315
Tale of the Eloquent Peasant, 77, 96
tamarrod, 315
tattoo, 48
Tawfik (also Tawfiq) el-Hakim, 128, 197, 202, 206, 114, 207
taxation, high 47, extortionate, 49, 81
telepreachers, 347, 350, 353, 355, 356
Temple of Serapis Alexandria, 11, 15, 20
temporary constitution, 165
terrorist cells, 279
Thugs, 52, 77, 108, 109, 110, 299, 300, 302, 303
trappings of power, Mubarak, 287, 290
tribal chiefs, 30, 32, 43, 63, 67
tribal raids, 28, 29, 55
tribal Structure, 27
Turkish, 68, 76, 84, 108, 127, 151, 344

U

Ulama, 63, 64, 66, 67, 111, 121
Umayyads, 49, 57, 62, 67
UN Sinai force withdrawal, 193
Union with Syria, 192
United Arab Republic, 213
Upper Egypt, 4, 31, 32, 36, 43, 48, 50, 73, 74, 77, 84, 112, 200, 207, 236, 363, 366, 367

V

Vanguard Organization, 205, 243, 252, 253
Vatikiotis, 159, 162, 187, 207, 326, 366, 369, 371, 238, 375, 393

Viceroy, 111, 112, 113, 116

W

wa'd el-banat, 27, 28, 90
wafed, 325, 327
Wahabi, 77, 112, 293, 328, 332, 333, 336, 342, 347, 349, 354, 355, 356, 359
Waheed Ra'fat, 156
walis, 39, 45, 46, 47, 48, 51, 57, 58, 59, 60, 65, 67, 68, 69, 70, 75, 82, 96, 97, 98, 111, 112, 121, 191, 247, 308, 309
war of attrition, 261, 262
wezir, 49
women, 34, 35, Bedouin, 28, concubines, 28; Egyptian, 65, 36, 43, 49, 51,52; fifty violations, 333; freedom, 90; Greek, 92; harem revolt, 107; immoral movies, 333; moral crimes, 332; rights, 90, 91, 92
Workers Vanguard Movement, 151

Y

Yemen, 192, 201, 234, 241, 255, 277, 287, 288, 289, 290
Yousef el-Seba'i, 237
Yousef Seddik, 142; his troops arrest Nasser and Amer, 143; opposes recalling of parliament, 164; resigns, 166, 188

Z

Zainab el-Bakriyya, 107
Zakaria Mohi el-Din, 171, 188, 199, 200, 229, 376
zakat, 29
Zamalek, 153
Zeus, 9, 10

www.ingramcontent.com/pod-product-compliance
Lightning Source LLC
Chambersburg PA
CBHW021131230426
43667CB00005B/79